ALSO BY HAROLD BLOOM

Omens of Millennium: The Gnosis of Angels, Dreams, and Resurrection

The Western Canon: The Books and School of the Ages

The American Religion: The Emergence of the Post-Christian Nation

Ruin the Sacred Truths: Poetry and Belief from the Bible to the Present

The Poetics of Influence: New and Selected Criticism

The Breaking of the Vessels

Agon: Towards a Theory of Revisionism

The Flight to Lucifer: Gnostic Fantasy

Deconstruction and Criticism

Wallace Stevens: The Poems of Our Climate

Figures of Capable Imagination

Poetry and Repression: Revisionism from Blake to Stevens

Kabbalah and Criticism

A Map of Misreading

The Anxiety of Influence: A Theory of Poetry

The Ringers in the Tower: Studies in Romantic Tradition

Yeats

Romanticism and Consciousness

Selected Writings of Walter Pater

The Literary Criticism of John Ruskin

Blake's Apocalypse: A Study in Poetic Argument

The Visionary Company: A Reading of English Romantic Poetry

Shelley's Mythmaking

The Bright Book of Life

The Bright Book of Life

NOVELS TO READ AND REREAD

Harold Bloom

 ALFRED A. KNOPF · NEW YORK · 2020

THIS IS A BORZOI BOOK
PUBLISHED BY ALFRED A. KNOPF

www.aaknopf.com

Knopf, Borzoi Books, and the colophon
are registered trademarks of Penguin Random House, LLC.

Library of Congress Cataloging-in-Publication Data

Names: Bloom, Harold, author.
Title: The bright book of life : novels to read and reread / Harold Bloom.
Description: First edition. | New York : Alfred A. Knopf, 2020. |
"This is a Borzoi Book published by Alfred A. Knopf"—Title page verso. |
Identifiers: LCCN 2020014640 (print) | LCCN 2020014641 (ebook) |
ISBN 9780525657262 (hardcover) | ISBN 9780525657279 (ebook)
Subjects: LCSH: Fiction—History and criticism. | Best books. |
Books and reading—United States.
Classification: LCC PN3491 .B56 2020 (print) | LCC PN3491 (ebook) |
DDC 809.3—dc23
LC record available at https://lccn.loc.gov/2020014640
LC ebook record available at https://lccn.loc.gov/2020014641

Jacket design by Chip Kidd

Manufactured in the United States of America

First Edition

For Ursula Le Guin

Contents

The Lost Traveller's Dream

H E SAID THAT THE STORY WAS NOT HIS. Whose was it, then? I never could ask, because he spoke it like a torrent. After a time I lost the words and heard only their sound and tumult.

It seemed like a dream narrative, spasmodic and flickering, yet a miracle of coloring, as though erotic beckoning were its only substance. I knew him well enough to find no relevance to his personality as it rocketed along. His was a dry soul, a limp leaf waiting for combustion.

He dreamed of a Western gate with vine leaves crimson on the wall. They whispered to him, and some seemed flying words that meant to strike him.

I gave up listening and walked away. Directions have always been preternaturally hard for me. Rarely can I tell east from west. When I was younger, hiking was a burden, as I always got lost.

Hopelessly I wandered on. And then I tripped and fell downward into what seemed a darkening hall. Landing on my feet was painful but not disabling. A lover of Cervantes, like everyone else, retrospectively I realized I was imitating Don Quixote's descent into the Cave of Montesinos (Part 2, Chapters XXII–XXIII). Cervantes was parodying the epic journeys to Hades by Odysseus and Aeneas, though the Sorrowful Countenance is let down by a rope that is tied around him and then is hauled back up after rather less than an hour. He returns in what seems deep sleep and with his usual passionate conviction says that he has been below for several days. The Knight describes a crystal palace created by Merlin the wicked enchanter:

"With no less pleasure do I recount it," responded Don Quixote. "And so I say that the venerable Montesinos led me into the crystalline palace, where, in a downstairs chamber that was exceptionally cool and made all of alabaster, there was a marble sepulcher crafted with great skill, and on it I saw a knight stretched out to his full length, and made not of bronze, or marble, or jasper, as is usual on other sepulchers, but of pure flesh and pure bone. His right hand, which seemed somewhat hairy and sinewy to me, a sign that its owner was very strong, lay over his heart, and before I could ask anything of Montesinos, who saw me looking with wonder at the figure on the sepulcher, he said:

"'This is my friend Durandarte, the flower and model of enamored and valiant knights of his time; here he lies, enchanted, as I and many others are enchanted, by Merlin, the French enchanter who was, people say, the son of the devil; and what I believe is that he was not the son of the devil but knew, as they say, a point or two more than the devil. How and why he enchanted us no one knows, but that will be revealed with the passage of time, and is not too far off now, I imagine. What astonishes me is that I know, as well as I know that it is day, that Durandarte ended the days of his life in my arms, and that when he was dead I removed his heart with my own hands; and the truth is that it must have weighed two pounds, because according to naturalists, the man who has a larger heart has greater courage than the man whose heart is small. If this is the case, and if this knight really died, why does he now moan and sigh from time to time, as if he were alive?'"

(trans. Edith Grossman)

This being Cervantes, the delight of absurdity is mixed with the Hispanic sublime. Durandarte is both dead and noisily alive. Belerma, his true love, keeps marching by, holding his heart in her hands. A young peasant girl, a friend of the immortal Dulcinea of Toboso, approaches Don Quixote with a new cotton underskirt as security for a loan of a half-dozen reales that Dulcinea desperately requires. The noble Knight declines the security and empties his pockets to find no more than four reales, which he swiftly gives.

I cannot say that I found Durandarte, let alone Dulcinea, but my dream returned to one of Ursula K. Le Guin's realms. Surrounded by shadowy forms, I strained to hear the voice of a woman chanting:

"The money burned to ashes, the gold thrown away. Footsteps on the air."

In the dream I could not recollect the source. I see now that I quoted the end of *The Telling* (2000). Sutty, Le Guin's surrogate, sums up the complex experience of a journey to the planet Aka in search of its lost spirituality.

In her *The Word for World Is Forest* (1972), Le Guin cites a report that a Malaysian community, the Senoi, constructed their culture as a dream world founded on the formula: "Where did you fall to, and what did you discover?" Le Guin's supple prose intimates a charming skepticism, yet the formula is helpful.

In last night's bad dream, my late and beloved friend John Hollander and I had arranged to meet for lunch somewhere in lower Manhattan. Again I got lost, and fell down an open grate. Where did I fall to, and what did I discover?

I have had a great deal of trouble getting up to my study recently. My friend and trainer of the last thirteen years is away in Florida, and it might be a little dangerous to attempt it without her. In the dream I fell into my own study, onto a pile of novels strewn about. One was by my friend Cormac McCarthy, but when I picked it up I did not recognize it. I assumed that it was his work in progress. He phoned me this morning, when I was still iced over from a dreadfully early excursion to pick up my new hearing aids. In our conversation he talked about his almost completed new novel. Only later did I realize that my dream had been proleptic.

Today, in mid-afternoon I suddenly remembered two quatrains of William Blake and realized that I had seen them engraved over a gateway in a dream several nights ago:

Verses from "The Gates of Paradise"
[Epilogue]. To the Accuser who is The God of this World

Truly, my Satan, thou art but a dunce,
And dost not know the garment from the man;
Every harlot was a virgin once,
Nor canst thou ever change Kate into Nan.
Tho' thou art worship'd by the names divine
Of Jesus and Jehovah, thou art still
The Son of Morn in weary Night's decline,
The lost traveller's dream under the hill.

In my nightmare, the gate was flanked by fearsome Cherubim waving flaming swords and frowning fiercely. Only now do I recall John Milton's expulsion of Adam and Eve from Eden:

They looking back all th' Eastern side beheld
Of Paradise, so late thir happie seat,
Wav'd over by that flaming Brand, the Gate
With dreadful Faces throng'd and fierie Armes:
Som natural tears they drop'd, but wip'd them soon;
The World was all before them, where to choose
Thir place of rest, and Providence thir guide:
They hand in hand with wandring steps and slow,
Through *Eden* took thir solitarie way.

I try to puzzle it out. Is my lost traveller's dream only another attempt to restore the Satanic-Promethean figure of Lucifer, son of the morning? My heart is with Blake and not with Milton, though the shadow of Milton all but eclipsed Blake's vision of "the human form divine." What is the dream of reading your own way into secular revelation, the enterprise of my long life, if at last you must founder on the reef of intersubjectivity? Are we purely social beings, or have we experiences so inward that great poets, novelists, dramatists, storytellers can at once achieve adequate outward forms for them while retaining a sense of solipsistic glory, or is that only another delusion?

I was myself the compass of that sea:
I was the world in which I walked, and what I saw

Or heard or felt came not but from myself;
And there I found myself more truly and more strange.

(Wallace Stevens, "Tea at the Palaz of Hoon")

That ecstasy is not social. I live, day to day, reciting these lines among many others.

I have always understood that my imagination requires a Covering Cherub or blocking agent in order to raise itself for mental fight and not collapse into solipsism. This has never been a question of my will but of my character or fate. A strong critic, like a strong poet, has no choice. To defend the aesthetic is to defend poetry, but this is a defense that initially may seem an attack upon poetry.

Today is Sunday, February 4, 2018, and it is thawing outside. I am still not ready to leave the house or to climb up to my study. I reread *Pride and Prejudice* this morning and necessarily enjoyed it. I then decided rather sadly to replace *Persuasion* by it, because I have never published anything on the most popular of Jane Austen's novels.

When I finished the book, I read my late acquaintance Tony Tanner's 1972 introduction to *Pride and Prejudice,* reprinted at the back of the Penguin Classics edition of 2003. It retains freshness, and the insights are still helpful. Tanner defends Jane Austen from the strictures Charlotte Brontë expressed in a letter to G. H. Lewes, George Eliot's partner. Brontë opined that she would not like to live with Jane Austen's people in their confined lives.

Though Jane Austen was a contemporary of the English High Romantics, she was a throwback to the age of Dr. Samuel Johnson and Samuel Richardson, her authentic precursor. Ralph Waldo Emerson, in his journal for the summer of 1861, expressed an ultimate dismissal of Jane Austen:

Never was life so pinched & narrow. The one problem in the mind of the writer in both the stories I have read, "Persuasion", and "Pride & Prejudice", is marriageableness; all that interests in any character introduced is still this one, Has he or she money to marry with, & conditions conforming? 'Tis "the nympholepsy of a fond despair", say rather, of an English boarding-house. Suicide is more respectable.

Emerson, no great lover of Lord Byron, nevertheless quotes from Childe Harold's *Pilgrimage,* Canto iv, Stanza 115:

EGERIA! sweet creation of some heart
Which found no mortal resting-place so fair
As thine ideal breast; whate'er thou art
Or wert,—a young Aurora of the air,
The nympholepsy of some fond despair;
Or, it might be, a beauty of the earth,
Who found a more than common votary there
Too much adoring; whatsoe'er thy birth,
Thou wert a beautiful thought, and softly bodied forth.

Emerson can be forgiven. He did not like novels anyway, and even dismissed those by his Concord walking companion Nathaniel Hawthorne. The summer of 1861 was hardly a good time for a Northern abolitionist, and the romance of Elizabeth and Darcy, though timeless, did not appeal to the Sage of Concord.

Jane Austen will have multitudes of readers until the end of time and beyond. Stendhal famously defined love as a blend of lust and vanity. For Jane Austen, love is affection, a mutual esteem that remains within the compass of a narrow social class. Her precursors—Shakespeare, Dr. Johnson, Samuel Richardson—taught her how to represent change in her more complex characters. Darcy and Elizabeth change by listening to one another and sometimes overhearing what they say in their most affectionate moments.

If you are questing for the transcendental and extraordinary, you need not read Jane Austen, but who can quest day after day throughout a lifetime? Elizabeth Bennet has little in common with Clarissa Harlowe. Jane Austen does not present us with Protestant saints. Shakespeare's Rosalind is a closer forerunner, though even Elizabeth cannot compare to that superb vision of a woman.

Intersubjectivity is enough of a problem for me without sliding over into the occult. Many years ago, I wrote a commentary on Henry Corbin's *Alone with the Alone: Creative Imagination in the Sufism of Ibn 'Arabi;* the book was published in French in 1958. My preface dates from 1997, and I have not reread it since then. I recall that the preface was very substantial and devoted mostly to what the Sufis call Hurqalya, the imaginal realm:

> Between the world of pure spiritual Lights (*Luces victoriales, the world of the "Mothers" in the terminology of Ishraq*) and the sensory universe, at the boundary of the ninth Sphere (the Sphere of Spheres) there opens a *mundus imaginalis* which is a concrete spiritual world of archetype-Figures, apparitional Forms, Angeles of species and individuals; by philosophical dialects its necessity is deduced and its plane situated; vision of it in actuality is vouchsafed to the visionary apperception of the Active Imagination. The essential connection in Sohravardi which leads from philosophical speculation to a metaphysics of ecstasy also establishes the connection between the angelology of this neo-Zoroastrian Platonism and the idea of the *mundus imaginalis*. This, Sohravardi declares, is the world to which the ancient Sages alluded when they affirmed that beyond the sensory world there exists another universe with a contour and dimensions and extension in a space, although these are not comparable with the shape and spatiality as we perceive them in the world of physical bodies. It is the "eighth" keshvar, the mystical Earth of Hurqalya with emerald cities; it is situated on the summit of the cosmic mountain, which the traditions handed down in Islam call the mountain of Qaf.
>
> (*The Man of Light in Iranian Sufism*)

Ibn 'Arabi calls Hurqalya "Creative Imagination." Corbin translates from 'Arabi's major work, *The Book of the Spiritual Conquests of Mecca:*

> Know that when God had created Adam who was the first human organism to be constituted, and when he had established him as the origin and archetype of all human bodies, there remained a surplus of the leaven of the clay. From this surplus God created the palm tree, so that this plant (*nakhla,* palm tree, being feminine) is Adam's *sister;* for us, therefore, it is like an aunt on our father's side. In theology it is so described

and is compared to the faithful believer. No other plant bears within it such extraordinary secrets as are hidden in this one. Now, after the creation of the palm tree, there remained hidden a portion of the clay from which the plant had been made: what was left was the equivalent of a sesame seed. And it was in this remainder that God laid out an immense Earth. Since he arranged in it the Throne and what it contains, the Firmament, the Heavens and the Earths, the worlds underground, all the paradises and hells, this means that the whole of our universe is to be found there in that Earth in its entirety, and yet the whole of it together is like a ring lost in one of our deserts in comparison with the immensity of that Earth. And that same Earth has hidden in it so many marvels and strange things that their number cannot be counted and our intelligence remains dazed by them.

(Spiritual Body and Celestial Earth [1977])

To me it is the loveliest of creation myths. From the remnant of the clay left over after Adam's creation, God made the palm tree, Adam's sister. That highly original making still left another tiny remainder, and from that God created the immensity of the heavens and the earths, the paradises and hells.

My dreams were commonplace. I sat at the dining-room table surrounded only by the ghosts of dead friends. I tried talking to them, but there were no answers. Baffled, I started to recite poems: Yeats, E. A. Robinson, Eliot, Stevens, Hart Crane, Shelley, and many others. It all went into the void, and my throat became sore. I left the table to find water and as usual got lost.

When I reached a river, it was too far below me, and my thirst was unabated.

The Bright Book of Life

CHAPTER 1

Don Quixote (1615)

MIGUEL DE CERVANTES

C ERVANTES, in relation to the Spanish language, stands with the titans of European and American literature. He is what Shakespeare is to English, Dante to Italian, Goethe to German, Pushkin to Russian: the glory of the vernacular. There may be no single eminence in French: Rabelais, Racine, Molière, Montaigne, Victor Hugo, Baudelaire, Stendhal, Balzac, Flaubert, Proust, Paul Valéry are among writers of the first order. In Russian, Tolstoy alone challenges Pushkin.

The Desert Island Question ("If just one book, which?") has no universal answer, but many readers would choose among three: the King James Bible, the complete Shakespeare, and *Don Quixote* by Miguel de Cervantes. Is it an oddity that the three competitors were almost simultaneous? The King James Bible appeared in 1611, six years after the publication of the first part of *Don Quixote,* in 1605 (the second part came a decade later, in 1615). In 1605, Shakespeare matched the greatness of Cervantes's masterwork with *King Lear,* and then went on rapidly to *Macbeth* and *Antony and Cleopatra.*

It could be argued that *Don Quixote* is the central work of the last half-millennium, since the greater novelists tend to be as much Cervantes's children as they are Shakespeare's. Shakespeare teaches us how to talk to ourselves, whereas Cervantes instructs us how to talk to one another. Hamlet scarcely listens to what anyone else says (except it be the Ghost); Falstaff so delights himself that Prince Hal can seem merely the best of resentful students and half-voluntary audiences. But Don Quixote and Sancho Panza change and mature by listening to each other, and their friendship is the most persuasive in all of literature.

Sancho Panza or Falstaff? Don Quixote or Hamlet? Hamlet has only Horatio. Falstaff dies almost solitary. But Don Quixote dies in the loving presence of Sancho, who proposes new quests to his heroic Knight. I have frequently argued that Shakespeare invented the ever-growing inward self, condemned to be its own adventure, as Emily Dickinson affirmed.

Cervantes, whose life was arduous and darkly solitary, either had endless bad luck or had to battle against the stigma of being a "New Christian," a *converso* of Jewish descent. He insisted he was of "untainted blood" and allows Sancho Panza to denounce "the Jews." Yet he had to go into exile to Italy, for legal reasons, and then enlisted in the Spanish military. He fought with exemplary courage at the naval Battle of Lepanto in 1571, under the command of Don John of Austria, and sustained three serious bullet wounds. He underwent half a year of rehabilitation, and permanently lost the use of his left arm. When he enlisted again, he was captured by Barbary pirates, and endured five years of captivity in Algiers. Finally, he was ransomed by a monk of the Trinitarian Order and by his parents.

His vicissitudes were far from finished. He was imprisoned for several months when he served as a purchasing agent for the Spanish navy, and had later difficulties as a tax collector. Despite the instant success of *Don Quixote, Part I* (1605), he received no royalties and had to bring out the second part in 1615, when a plagiarist published a dubious sequel to Part I. He could not find sufficient patronage from noblemen, but finally received enough of a stipend so he could devote himself to writing in his final years.

Cervantes (1547–1616) died the day before Shakespeare (1564–1616) and doubtless never heard of the English dramatist. Shakespeare had so uneventful and colorless a life that no biography of him can be at all persuasive. The significant facts can be stated in a few paragraphs. Cervantes, however, experienced a difficult and violent existence, though no account of his life worthy of the subject exists as yet in English.

Reading *Don Quixote*, I am not at all convinced that scholars who believe book and writer devout are at all accurate, if only because they miss his irony. But, then, many scholars tell us that Shakespeare was Catholic, and again I am not persuaded, since his major allusions are to the Geneva Bible, a very Protestant version. *Don Quixote*, like the later Shakespeare, seems to me more nihilistic than Christian, and both of these greatest Western imaginers hint that annihilation is the final fate of the soul.

What is it that makes *Don Quixote* Shakespeare's only rival for the highest aesthetic glory? Cervantes is superbly comic, as is Shakespeare, but *Don Quixote* is no more to be characterized as comedy than is *Hamlet*. Philip II, who exhausted the resources of the Spanish Empire on behalf of the Counter-Reformation, died in 1598, a decade after the fiasco of the Spanish Armada, destroyed by the gales and English seamen. The Spain depicted in *Don Quixote* is post-1598: impoverished, demoralized, clergy-ridden, with the underlying sadness of having wrecked itself a century before by exiling or driving underground its large and productive Jewish and Muslim communities. Much of *Don Quixote*, as of Shakespeare, needs to be read between the lines. When the amiable Sancho Panza shouts that he himself is an Old Christian and hates the Jews, does the subtle Cervantes intend us to receive this without irony? The context of *Don Quixote* is squalor, except for the noble houses, which are bastions of mockery and racism, subjecting the wonderful Don Quixote to horrible practical jokes.

As masters of representation, Shakespeare and Cervantes alike are vitalists, which is why Falstaff and Sancho Panza bear the Blessing. But these two foremost of modern writers are also skeptics, so that Hamlet and Don Quixote are ironists, even when they behave like madmen. Gusto, a primal exuberance, is the shared genius of the Castilian father of the novel and the English poet-dramatist beyond all others, before or since, in any language.

Freedom, for Quixote and for Sancho, is a function of the order of play, which is disinterested and precarious. The play of the world, for Quixote, is a purified view of chivalry, the game of knights-errant, virtuously beautiful and distressed damozels, nasty and powerful enchanters, as well as giants, ogres, and idealized quests. Don Quixote is courageously mad and obsessively courageous, but he is not self-deceived. He knows who he is, but also who he may be, if he chooses. When a moralizing priest accuses the Knight of an absence in reality, and orders him to go home and cease wandering, Quixote replies realistically that as knight-errant he has righted wrongs, chastised arrogance, and crushed assorted monsters.

Why did the invention of the novel have to wait for Cervantes? Now, in the twenty-first century, the novel seems to be experiencing a long day's dying. Our contemporary masters—Pynchon, the late Philip Roth, and others—seem forced to retreat back to picaresque and the romance form, pre-Cervantine. Shakespeare and Cervantes created much of human personality as we know it, or at least the ways in which personality could be represented: Joyce's Poldy, his Irish Jewish Ulysses, is both Quixotic and Shakespearean, but Joyce died in 1941, before Hitler's Shoah could be fully known. In our Age of Information and of ongoing Terror, the Cervantine novel may be as obsolete as the Shakespearean drama. I speak of the genres, and not of their supreme masters, who never will become outmoded. The Knight and Sancho, between them, know all that there is to know. They know at least exactly who they are, which is what, finally, they will teach the rest of us.

WHICH DESCRIBES THE CONDITION AND PROFESSION OF THE FAMOUS GENTLEMAN DON QUIXOTE OF LA MANCHA

Somewhere in La Mancha, in a place whose name I do not care to remember, a gentleman lived not long ago, one of those who has a lance and ancient shield on a shelf and keeps a skinny nag and a greyhound for racing. An occasional stew, beef more often than lamb, hash most nights, eggs and abstinence on Saturdays, lentils on Fridays, sometimes squab as a treat on Sundays— these consumed three-fourths of his income. The rest went for a light woolen tunic and velvet breeches and hose of the same material for feast days, while weekdays were honored with dun-colored coarse cloth. He had a housekeeper past forty, a niece not yet twenty, and a man-of-all-work who did everything from saddling the horse to pruning the trees. Our gentleman was approximately fifty years old; his complexion was weathered, his flesh scrawny, his face gaunt, and he was a very early riser and a great lover of the hunt. Some claim that his family name was Quixada, or Quexada, for there is a certain amount of disagreement among the authors who write of this matter, although reliable conjecture seems to indicate that his name was Quexana. But this does not matter very much to our story; in its telling there is absolutely no deviation from the truth.

(trans. Edith Grossman)

The opening of Part I of *The Ingenious Gentleman Don Quixote of La Mancha* by Miguel de Cervantes more than sets the tone of this first and greatest of all Western novels. I quote it here and throughout from the skilled translation by Edith Grossman (2003).

Cervantes stations Don Quixote in a Spain just before his own, a country declining from the glory of the naval victory of Lepanto over the Ottoman Empire on October 7, 1571. In 1588, the Spanish Armada failed against the English fire ships and then was scattered by fierce storms. The Dutch, allies of the English, blockaded the Spanish army in the Netherlands, employing flyboats to splendid effect.

Throughout the seventeenth century, Spain declined from its earlier Golden Age, of which Cervantes was the great ornament, and instead lost its financial, military, and political dominance. *Don Quixote* is poised at the turning point between the culture's glory and its fading away into a harsh land of the Inquisition, the torture and burning of Jewish and Muslim converts suspected of backsliding.

I enjoy the exuberant comic elements, but the Knight of the Sorrowful Countenance and poor Sancho suffer every kind of violence and ridicule as they continue questing. At the close, the Knight suffers shattering defeat, and goes home to die.

Let us begin with Don Quixote in his early glory. His mind crazed by chivalric romances, he determines to become a knight-errant and rather outrageously sets about the labor of finding the proper equipment:

The truth is that when his mind was completely gone, he had the strangest thought any lunatic in the world ever had, which was that it seemed reasonable and necessary to him, both for the sake of his honor and as a service to the nation, to become a knight errant and travel the world with his armor and his horse to seek adventures and engage in everything he had read that knights errant engaged in, righting all manner of wrongs and, by seizing the opportunity and placing himself in danger and ending those wrongs, winning eternal renown and everlasting fame. The poor man imagined himself already wearing the crown, won by the valor of his arm, of the empire of Trebizond at the very least; and so it was that with these exceedingly agreeable thoughts, and carried away by the extraordinary pleasure he took in them, he hastened to put into effect what he so fervently desired. And the first thing he did was to attempt to clean some armor that had belonged to his great-grandfathers and, stained with rust and covered with mildew, had spent many long years stored and forgotten in a corner. He did the best he could to clean and repair it, but he saw that it had a great defect, which was that instead of a full sallet helmet with an attached neckguard, there was only a simple headpiece; but he compensated for this with his industry, and out of pasteboard he fashioned a kind of half-helmet that, when attached to the headpiece, took on the appearance of a full sallet. It is true that in order to test if it was strong and could withstand a blow, he took out his sword and struck it twice, and with the first blow he undid in a moment what it had taken him a week to create; he could not help being disappointed at the ease with which he had hacked it to pieces, and to protect against that danger, he made another one, placing strips of iron on the inside so that he was satisfied with its strength; and not wanting to put it to the test again, he designated and accepted it as an extremely fine sallet.

If there is irony here it is washed away by surpassing tenderness. Cervantes loves his Knight and so do we. It would have been more than enough had Cervantes given us only Don Quixote and Cervantes himself. Genius triumphant presents us with the Squire of Squires, Sancho Panza:

During this time, Don Quixote approached a farmer who was a neighbor of his, a good man—if that title can be given to someone who is poor—but without much in the way of brains. In short, he told him so much, and persuaded and promised him so much, that the poor peasant resolved to go off with him and serve as his squire. Among other things, Don Quixote said that he should prepare to go with him gladly, because it might happen that one day he would have an adventure that would gain him, in the blink of an eye, an ínsula, and he would make him its governor. With these promises and others like them, Sancho Panza, for that was the farmer's name, left his wife and children and agreed to be his neighbor's squire.

It is an irony to call Sancho brainless. He is shrewd, sly, awake to reality, and his greatness justifies Franz Kafka's parable in which Don Quixote is only Sancho's daemon:

Without making any boast of it Sancho Panza succeeded in the course of years, by feeding him a great number of romances of chivalry and adventure in the evening and night hours, in so diverting from himself his demon, whom he later called Don Quixote, that this demon thereupon set out, uninhibited, on the maddest exploits, which, however, for the lack of a preordained object, which should have been Sancho Panza himself, harmed nobody. A free man, Sancho Panza philosophically followed Don Quixote on his crusades, perhaps out of a sense of responsibility, and had of them a great and edifying entertainment to the end of his days.

("The Truth about Sancho Panza," trans. Edwin and Willa Muir)

Kafka manifests critical acuity by placing Sancho at the center. Sancho dreams, and his daemon or genius rides out into the ultimate elegance, the imagined land. That realm is and is not Castile. If we set aside Kafka's lovely joke about the Squire's sense of responsibility, what we witness is the birth of the loving friendship between Sancho Panza and Don Quixote, which will become the unextinguished hearth of the book. The impetuous Knight is both rash and violently forceful. Sancho, prudent and passively peaceful, will be carried along from catastrophe to virtual immolation, and yet, like his Knight, somehow he attains survival.

As they were talking, they saw thirty or forty of the windmills found in that countryside, and as soon as Don Quixote caught sight of them, he said to his squire:

"Good fortune is guiding our affairs better than we could have desired, for there you see, friend Sancho Panza, thirty or more enormous giants with whom I intend to do battle and whose lives I intend to take, and with the spoils we shall begin to grow rich, for this is righteous warfare, and it is a great service to God to remove so evil a breed from the face of the earth."

"What giants?" said Sancho Panza.

"Those you see over there," replied his master, "with the long arms; sometimes they are almost two leagues long."

"Look, your grace," Sancho responded, "those things that appear over there aren't giants but windmills, and what looks like their arms are the sails that are turned by the wind and make the grindstone move."

"It seems clear to me," replied Don Quixote, "that thou art not well-versed in the matter of adventures: these are giants; and if thou art afraid, move aside and start to pray whilst I enter with them in fierce and unequal combat."

And having said this, he spurred his horse, Rocinante, paying no attention to the shouts of his squire, Sancho, who warned him that, beyond any doubt, those things he was about to attack were windmills and not giants. But he was so convinced they were giants that he did not hear the shouts of his squire, Sancho, and could not see, though he was very close, what they really were; instead, he charged and called out:

"Flee not, cowards and base creatures, for it is a single knight who attacks you."

Just then a gust of wind began to blow, and the great sails began to move, and, seeing this, Don Quixote said:

"Even if you move more arms than the giant Briareus, you will answer to me."

And saying this, and commending himself with all his heart to his lady Dulcinea, asking that she come to his aid at this critical moment, and well-protected by his shield, with his lance in its socket, he charged at Rocinante's full gallop and attacked the first mill he came to; and as he thrust his lance into the sail, the wind moved it with so much force that it broke the lance into pieces and picked up the horse and the knight, who then dropped to the ground and were very badly battered. Sancho Panza hurried to help as fast as his donkey could carry him, and when he reached them he discovered that Don Quixote could not move because he had taken so hard a fall with Rocinante.

"God save me!" said Sancho. "Didn't I tell your grace to watch what you were doing, that these were nothing but windmills, and only somebody whose head was full of them wouldn't know that?"

Sometimes I regret that tilting at windmills has become the key signature of Cervantes's masterpiece. Yet Cervantes and the Knight know exactly what they are doing. Extravagance, going beyond limits, and exuberant disregard for safety or comfort are necessities if the order of play is to triumph over the commonplace.

The Knight is neither madman nor fool. He plays at knight-errantry. We love Don Quixote because he trusts in his own freedom, and also in its seclusion and disinterestedness, and, finally, in its limits. When he is defeated, he gives up the game, goes back to sanity, "and dies." I second the remark of Miguel de Unamuno (1864–1936), that the Knight quests for his authentic country and finds it only in exile.

So varied are the exploits of Don Quixote that more summary quickly becomes useless. I move on to one of the more magnificent achievements of Cervantes, the first of the two appearances of the master illusionist Ginés de Pasamonte, a grand confidence man:

Behind all of them came a man of about thirty who was very good-looking except that one eye tended to veer slightly toward the other. He was shackled differently from the rest, because around his foot was a chain so large it encircled his entire body, and there were two fetters around his neck, one attached to the chain and the other, the kind called a keeper or a brace, from which there hung two irons that reached to his waist, and on these were two manacles holding his hands and locked with a heavy padlock, so that he could not raise his hands to his mouth or lower his head to his hands. Don Quixote asked why that man wore so many more shackles than the others. The guard responded that it was because he alone had committed more crimes than all the rest combined, and was so daring and such a great villain that even though he was bound in this way, they still did not feel secure about him and were afraid he would escape.

"What crimes can they be," said Don Quixote, "if they have deserved no greater punishment than his being sent to the galleys?"

"He's going for ten years," replied the guard, "which is like a civil death. All you need to know is that this is the famous Ginés de Pasamonte, also known as Ginesillo de Parapilla."

"Señor Commissary," the galley slave said, "just take it easy and let's not go around dropping all kinds of names and surnames. My name is Ginés, not Ginesillo, and my family is from Pasamonte, not Parapilla, as you've said; and if each man looks to his own affairs, he'll have plenty to tend to."

"Keep a civil tongue," replied the commissary, "you great thief, unless you want me to shut you up in a way you won't like."

"It certainly seems," responded the galley slave, "that man proposes and God disposes, but one day somebody will know whether or not my name is Ginesillo de Parapilla."

"Well, don't they call you that, you liar?" said the guard.

"They do," responded Ginés, "but I'll make sure they don't, or I'll tear out their hair and they know where. Señor, if you have anything to give us, give it and go with God; your wanting to know so much about other people's lives is becoming irritating, but if you want to know more about mine, know that I'm Ginés...even for two hundred *ducados*."

"Is it that good?" said Don Quixote.

"It's so good," responded Ginés, "that it's too bad for *Lazarillo de Tormes* and all the other books of that genre that have been or will be written. What I can tell your grace is that it deals with truths, and they are truths so appealing and entertaining that no lies can equal them."

"And what is the title of the book?" asked Don Quixote.

"The Life of Ginés de Pasamonte," Ginés replied.

Ginés will reappear in Part II as the trickster Master Pedro, whose puppet show is destroyed by Don Quixote. Lope de Vega (1562–

1635), described by Cervantes as "the Monster of Literature," was the insanely prolific and successful rival of our beloved creator of Quixote and Sancho. There are about three thousand sonnets, nine epics, seven novellas and novels, and perhaps five hundred plays accepted as being by Lope. He must have written from morning to night on a daily basis. Cervantes attempted to write dramas but had no chance against Lope and Calderón. Whatever distress that gave the greater writer, we can appreciate his two depictions of Lope as a picaroon and as an illusionist:

"And is it finished?" asked Don Quixote.

"How can it be finished," he responded, "if my life isn't finished yet? What I've written goes from my birth to the moment when they sentenced me to the galleys this last time."

"Then you have been there before?" said Don Quixote.

"To serve God and the king, I've already spent four years on the galleys, and I know the taste of the hardtack and the overseer's whip," responded Ginés. "And I'm not too sorry to go there, because I'll have time to finish my book, for I still have lots of things to say, and on the galleys of Spain there's more leisure than I'll need, though I don't need much for what I have to write because I know it by heart."

"You seem clever," said Don Quixote.

"And unfortunate," responded Ginés, "because misfortunes always pursue the talented."

"They pursue villains," said the commissary.

"I've already told you, Señor Commissary," responded Pasamonte, "to take it easy; those gentlemen didn't give you that staff of office for you to abuse us poor wretches but to lead and guide us to wherever His Majesty commands. If not, by the life of . . . Enough! One day those dark stains at the inn may come to light, so let's all hold our tongues, and live well, and speak better, and keep walking; the joke's gone on too long."

The commissary raised his staff to strike Pasamonte in response to his threats, but Don Quixote placed himself between them and asked that he not abuse the prisoner, for it was not surprising that a man whose hands were so tightly bound would have a rather loose tongue. And turning to all those on the chain, he said:

"From everything you have said to me, dear brothers, I deduce that although you are being punished for your faults, the penalties you are about to suffer are not to your liking, and you go to them unwillingly and involuntarily; it might be that the lack of courage this one showed under torture, that one's need of money, another's lack of favor, and finally, the twisted judgment of the judge, have been the reason for your ruination, and for not having justice on your side. All of which is pictured in my mind, and is telling, persuading, and even compelling me to show to all of you the reason that heaven put me in the world and made me profess the order of chivalry, which I do profess, and take the vow I took to favor those in need and those oppressed by the powerful. But, because I know that one of the rules of prudence is that what can be done by good means should not be done by bad, I want to ask these gentlemen, the guards and the commissary, to be so good as to unchain you and let you go in peace; there will be no lack of other men to serve the king under better circumstances, for to me it seems harsh to make slaves of those whom God and nature made free. Furthermore, these poor wretches have done nothing against you gentlemen. Each man must bear his own sin; there is a God in heaven who does not fail to punish the wicked or reward the good, and it is not right for honorable men to persecute other men who have not harmed them. I ask this quietly and calmly because if you comply, I shall have reason to thank you, and if you do not comply willingly, this lance and this sword, and the valor of this my arm, will force you to comply against your will."

This superbly mad oration soars beyond any question as to who is guilty or innocent. We love the Knight because his politics are anarchist. The "order of play" must overturn every social order and every constraint. We need not ask whether Cervantes endorses the stance of Don Quixote. Both of them know what they know, and they do not always know the same things:

"A fine piece of nonsense!" responded the commissary. "He's finally come out with it! He wants us to let the king's prisoners go, as if we had the authority to free them or he had the authority to order us to do so! Your grace, Señor, be on your way, and straighten that basin you're wearing on your head, and don't go around looking for a three-legged cat."

"You're the cat, the rat, and the scoundrel!" responded Don Quixote.

Speaking and acting were all one, and he charged so quickly that he did not give the commissary time to defend himself and knocked him to the ground, wounding him with a thrust of his lance, and it was fortunate for Don Quixote that he did, for this was the man holding the flintlock. The other guards were stunned, overwhelmed by this unexpected turn of events, but they came to their senses, and those on horseback put their hands on their swords, and those on foot grasped their javelins, and they charged Don Quixote, who very calmly waited for them; matters undoubtedly would have gone badly for him if the galley slaves, seeing the opportunity presented to them to obtain their freedom, had not attempted to achieve it by breaking the chain to which they were fettered. So great was the confusion that the guards, turning now to the galley slaves, who were breaking free, and now to Don Quixote, who was attacking them, did nothing of any use.

Sancho, for his part, helped to free Ginés de Pasamonte, who was the first to leap into the battle free and unencumbered, and, rushing at the fallen commissary, he took his sword and flintlock, and by pointing it at one and aiming it at another, without ever firing he cleared the field of guards because they all fled from Pasamonte's flintlock and from the shower of stones that the galley slaves, who were free by now, were hurling at them.

This made Sancho very sad, because it seemed to him that those who were fleeing would inform the Holy Brotherhood, who would then come looking for the lawbreakers, sounding the alarm, and he told this to his master and begged that they leave immediately and hide in the mountains, which were not far away.

"That is all very well and good," said Don Quixote, "but I know what must be done now."

And calling to all the galley slaves, who were in a state of frenzy and had stripped the commissary down to his skin, they gathered round to see what he wanted of them, and he said:

"It is customary for wellborn people to give thanks for the benefits they receive, and one of the sins that most offends God is ingratitude. I say this, Señores, because you have already seen and had manifest proof of what you have received from me, and in payment it is my wish and desire that, bearing the chain which I removed from your necks, you immediately set out for the city of Toboso, and there appear before the lady Dulcinea of Toboso, and say that her knight, he of the Sorrowful Face, commends himself to her, and you will tell her, point by point, every detail of this famous adventure, up to the moment when you achieved your desired freedom; having done this, you may go wherever you wish, and may good fortune go with you."

Ginés de Pasamonte responded for all of them, and he said:

"What your grace, our lord and liberator, orders us to do, is absolutely impossible for us to carry out, because we cannot travel the roads together but must go our separate ways, each man on his own, trying to burrow into the bowels of the earth so as not be found by the Holy Brotherhood, who, beyond any doubt, will come looking for us. What your grace can do, and it is right and proper that you do so, is to change this service and tribute to the lady Dulcinea of Toboso into a certain number of Ave Marías and Credos, which we will say on your grace's behalf, and this is something that can be done night or day, fleeing or at rest, at peace or at war; but to think that we will go back to our miseries in Egypt, I mean to say, that we will take up our chain and set out for Toboso, is to think that night has fallen now when it is not yet ten in the morning; asking that of us is like asking pears of an elm tree."

Ginés is totally justified; does the reader agree with him or not? The aesthetic strength wielded by Cervantes must slash even the most attentive into hearers wounded by wonder:

"Well, then, I do swear," said Don Quixote, his wrath rising, "Don Whoreson, Don Ginesillo de Paropillo, or whatever your name is, that you will go alone, your tail between your legs, and the entire chain on your back!"

Pasamonte was not a man of great forbearance; already aware that Don Quixote was not very sane, for he had done something so foolish as wanting to give them their freedom, and seeing himself spoken to in this way, he winked at his companions, and, moving a short distance away, they began to throw so many stones at Don Quixote that he could not even manage to protect himself with his shield, and poor Rocinante paid no more attention to his master's spurs than if he had been made of bronze. Sancho hid behind his donkey, protecting himself in this way from the hailstorm of rocks pouring down on them. Don Quixote could not shield himself as well as Sancho, for so many stones found their mark on his body, and with so much force, that they knocked him to the ground; as soon as he had fallen, the student attacked him and took the basin from his head and struck him three or four blows with it on his shoulders and smashed it an equal number of times on the ground until he had shattered it. They took a doublet he wore over his armor and would have taken his horse if the greaves of his leg armor had not prevented them from doing so. From Sancho they took his coat, leaving him in shirtsleeves; then, after dividing among themselves the other spoils of battle, each went his separate way, more concerned with escaping the Brotherhood, which they feared, than with picking up the chain and carrying it to the lady Dulcinea of Toboso.

The donkey and Rocinante, Sancho and Don Quixote, were left alone; the donkey, pensive, with bowed head, twitching his ears from time to time, thinking that the tempest of stones had not yet ended and was still falling around his ears; Rocinante, lying beside his master, for he too had fallen to the ground in the shower of stones; Sancho, in his shirtsleeves and afraid of the Holy Brotherhood; Don Quixote, grief-stricken at seeing himself so injured by the very people for whom he had done so much good.

Miguel de Unamuno could be as sublimely mad as his lord Don Quixote: "All of which should teach us to liberate galley slaves precisely because they will not be grateful to us for it." The battered Knight Quixote probably would not have accepted Unamuno, a numinous Basque exegete, since he pledges to Sancho that he has learned his lesson, but the wary Sancho ripostes: "Your grace will learn the lesson the same way I'm a Turk." It was Cervantes who took warning, because of his affection for his minor but superb creation Ginés de Pasamonte, "the lying crook." Ginés, confidence man and shamanistic imp of the perverse, is what might be called one of the canonical criminal characters in literature, like Shakespeare's Barnardine in *Measure for Measure* or Balzac's superb Vautrin. If Vautrin can reappear as Abbé Carlos Herrera, then Ginés can manifest himself as Master Pedro, the puppet master.

Critics argue that the difference between Ginés and the Don, picaroon trickster and chivalric visionary, is partly an opposition of two literary genres, the picaresque and the novel, which Cervantes essentially invented, in much the same way that Shakespeare (who did not know Greek tragedy, only its crippled remnant in the Roman Seneca) invented modern tragedy and modern tragicomedy as well. As in the Shakespearean protagonists, authentic inwardness incarnates itself in Don Quixote, whereas the scamp Pasamonte is all outwardness, despite his deep talents at duplicity. Ginés is a shapeshifter; he cannot change except in externals. The Knight, like the great Shakespearean characters, cannot stop changing: that is the purpose of his frequently irascible but always finally loving conversations with the faithful Sancho. Bound together by the order of play, they are also united by the endless love they induce in one another. Their quarrels are frequent; how could they not be, in the realm of the Quixotic? Sancho hesitates sometimes on the verge of abandoning the relationship, yet he cannot; partly he is fascinated, but in the end he is held by love, and so is the Don. The love cannot perhaps be distinguished from the order of play, but that is as it should be. Certainly one reason for Ginés de Pasamonte's return in Part II is that he never participates in play, even as puppet master.

Every reader recognizes that the difference between the two parts of *Don Quixote* is that everyone who matters most in Part II is either explicitly credited with having read Part I or knows that he was a character in it. That provides a different frame for the reappearance of the picaroon Ginés when we reach the moment in Part II,

Chapter XXV, when we encounter a man clad in chamois skin, hose, breeches, and a doublet, and with a patch of green taffeta over one eye and that whole side of his face. This is Master Pedro, come, as he says, with the divining ape and the spectacle of the freeing of Melisendra by her husband, the famous knight-errant Don Gaiferos, she being the daughter of Charlemagne held captive by the Moors, and he being a principal vassal of Charlemagne.

The landlord at the inn where Master Pedro joins Don Quixote and Sancho Panza says of the puppet master, "He talks more than six men and drinks more than twelve." After he identifies the Don and Sancho, at the advice of his divining ape (whose divination goes only backward, from present to past), Ginés-Pedro stages the puppet show, certainly one of the metaphorical splendors of Cervantes's masterpiece. The classic exegesis here is from Ortega y Gasset, in his *Meditations on Quixote;* he compares Master Pedro's puppet show to the Velázquez *Maids of Honor,* where the artist, in painting the king and queen, simultaneously places his studio in the picture. It is not a painting upon which Don Quixote could safely have gazed, and he is certainly the worst possible audience for the puppet show:

> And Don Quixote, seeing and hearing so many Moors and so much clamor, thought it would be a good idea to assist those who were fleeing; and rising to his feet, in a loud voice he said:
>
> "I shall not consent, in my lifetime and in my presence, to any such offense against an enamored knight so famous and bold as Don Gaiferos. Halt, you lowborn rabble; do not follow and do not pursue him unless you wish to do battle with me!"
>
> And speaking and taking action, he unsheathed his sword, leaped next to the stage, and with swift and never before seen fury began to rain down blows on the crowd of Moorish puppets, knocking down some, beheading others, ruining this one, destroying that one, and among many other blows, delivered so powerful a downstroke that if Master Pedro had not stooped, crouched down, and hunched over, he would have cut off his head more easily than if it had been so much marzipan.

That downward stroke, by no means unintended, may be the heart of this delightful intervention. Master Pedro has intruded in the order of play, where he has no place, and it moves to avenge itself upon the picaroon. A while before, Don Quixote has said to Sancho that the puppet master must have made a bargain with the devil, because "the monkey replies only to past or present things, which is as far as the devil's knowledge can go." The Knight's suspicion of the trickster continues when he criticizes Master Pedro's mistakes in ascribing church bells to the Moorish mosques. Ginés-Pedro's defensive reply further prepares us for the Don's shattering of the show:

> "Your grace should not concern yourself with trifles, Señor Don Quixote, or try to carry things so far that you never reach the end of them. Aren't a thousand plays performed almost every day that are full of a thousand errors and pieces of nonsense, and yet are successful productions that are greeted not only with applause but with admiration? Go on, boy, and let them say what they will, for as long as I fill my purse, there can be more errors than atoms in the sun."

Don Quixote's reply is dark: "That is true." Master Pedro has become Cervantes's great literary rival, the monstrously productive and successful poet-playwright Lope de Vega. The Knight's subsequent assault upon pasteboard illusions is at once a critique of public taste and a metaphysical manifestation of Quixotic or visionary will, making ghostlier the demarcations between art and nature. The humor of disjunction is salted by literary satire, hardly mitigated by the aftermath in which the chastened Knight makes financial amends for his generous error and blames the usual wicked enchanters for having deceived him.

It would hurt me too much to rehearse again the final defeat, surrender of identity, and virtuous death of Alonso Quijano the Good, who had been Don Quixote. Sancho Panza urges his friend to rise up and go on fresh adventures, but the good Alonso declines. All is redeemed by the final entry of Miguel de Cervantes:

> For me alone was Don Quixote born, and I for him; he knew how to act, and I to write; the two of us alone are one, despite and regardless of the false Tordesillan writer who dared, or will dare, to write with a coarse and badly designed ostrich feather

about the exploits of my valorous knight, for it is not a burden for his shoulders or a subject for his cold creativity; and you will warn him, if you ever happen to meet him, to let the weary and crumbling bones of Don Quixote rest in the grave, and not attempt, contrary to all the statutes of death, to carry them off to Castilla la Vieja, removing him from the tomb where he really and truly lies, incapable of undertaking a third journey or a new sally; for to mock the many undertaken by so many knights errant, the two he made were enough, and they have brought delight and pleasure to everyone who knows of them, in these kingdoms as well as those abroad. And with these you will fulfill your Christian duty, by giving good counsel to those who do not wish you well, and I shall be pleased and proud to have been the first who completely enjoyed the fruits of his writing, just as he wished, for my only desire has been to have people reject and despise the false and nonsensical histories of the books of chivalry, which are already stumbling over the history of my true Don Quixote, and will undoubtedly fall to the ground. *Vale.*

I experience the same sadness here that afflicts me when Sir John Falstaff departs forever. For just this once in my life, I will quote Ezra Pound at his elegiac best:

And sorrow, sorrow like rain.
              ("Lament of the Frontier Guard," in *Cathay* [1915])

CHAPTER 2

Clarissa (1748)

SAMUEL RICHARDSON

W HEN I WAS YOUNG, I devoted most of my days to reading
poetry. Otherwise I read mythology, history, religious texts,
novels, and stories. I omit the reading of Shakespeare, which was
constant. Reaching back into time, I remember an early obsession
with the novels of Thomas Hardy. He led me on to D. H. Lawrence
and then to Virginia Woolf and E. M. Forster.

As a Cornell undergraduate of seventeen, I had the good fortune to
participate in a seminar on the novel taught by Professor William M.
Sale, Jr. Sale was a lean, rangy Kentuckian who spoke with a slow
drawl and demonstrated a fierce reluctance to deal with fools. At
seventeen I was afraid of him, but by the time I graduated I had
spent many afternoons in his house with him, his gracious wife,
Helen Stearns, and with his oldest son, William, who became a distinguished classicist and a lifelong friend until his death in Saint
Louis in 2017.

In a yearlong seminar with Professor Sale, we began with Samuel
Richardson's *Clarissa*. We devoted a month to that extraordinary
novel, reading it uncut. I regard *Clarissa* and *In Search of Lost Time*
as the two most eminent of all novels, surpassing even Tolstoy and
Dickens. I realize that again I will always be Sale's student. I am
assuming that *Don Quixote, Moby-Dick*, Joyce's *Ulysses*, and Victor
Hugo's *Les Misérables* are closer to epics than to novels.

Sale's seminar was eclectic, and included *Wuthering Heights, Middlemarch, Vanity Fair, Nostromo, Absalom, Absalom!*, and *Howards End*. Not everything was on that level. Sale's personal taste gave us John P. Marquand's *H. M. Pulham, Esquire*, and Robert Penn Warren's *All the King's Men*. Several years ago I tried to reread *Pulham* but failed, and though Warren's best novel holds up, it remains less impressive than his later poetry.

Sale's impact on me remains largest when I reread *Clarissa*, which I do every other year or so, as I do also with *In Search of Lost Time*. Richardson's art converts an epistolary novel into a narrative frequently tumultuous and just as often given to a kind of unearthly stasis. Clarissa Harlowe dies majestically but with an excruciating slowness. Dr. Samuel Johnson, who admired the novel with absolute conviction, famously remarked to Boswell, "Why, sir, if you were to read Richardson for the story... you would hang yourself.... You must read him for the sentiment."

Shakespearean inwardness can be said to have been absorbed by Richardson more fully than by any other novelist except for Proust. Clarissa Harlowe remains the ultimate Protestant heroine. I say this warily, because for the last quarter-century I have been beaten up by Christian critics for my heretical views on what I have come to call the American Religion and its relation to the spiritual history of the Protestant will. In my exhausted old age, I do not know whether the School of Resentment or the orthodox oxen are more unmannerly. Perhaps being gored by a Christian is more salubrious than being speared by a Franco-Heideggerian, but I will not know that until I get to the place of rest.

I do not know of a more ambivalent erotic relationship between a woman and a man than the mutually destructive passion of Clarissa Harlowe and Robert Lovelace. The only rival might be Shakespeare's Cleopatra and Antony. It is very difficult to compare the strife of empires to a domestic trauma, though the tragic grandeur of Clarissa Harlowe is not lessened by juxtaposition with the Egyptian queen.

How could a marriage between Clarissa and Lovelace have worked? Lovelace is the Restoration rake resurrected, while Clarissa is a Protestant martyr. Her slow death becomes for her a mounting glory, for him an annihilation of the will.

It is only a step from that to his dying words after he has lost his duel with Colonel Morden, Clarissa's kinsman:

Blessed—said he, addressing himself no doubt to Heaven; for his dying eyes were lifted up—a strong convulsion prevented him for a few moments saying more—But recovering, he again with great fervour (lifting up eyes, and his spread hands) pronounced the word *Blessed*—Then, in a seeming ejaculation, he spoke inwardly so as not to be understood: at last, he distinctly pronounced these three words,

LET THIS EXPIATE!

And then, his head sinking on his pillow, he expired; at about half an hour after ten.

Lovelace dies invoking a goddess, the transfigured Clarissa Harlowe. It is hardly a Christian death. Clarissa dies a Protestant death but one very much transmembered by the force of her will:

I beseech ye, my good friends, proceeded she, mourn not for one who mourns not, nor has cause to mourn, for herself. On the contrary, rejoice with me that all my worldly troubles are so near their end. Believe me, sirs, that I would not, if I might, choose to live, although the pleasantest part of my life were to come over again: and yet eighteen years of it, out of nineteen, have been very pleasant. To be so much exposed to temptation, and to be so liable to fail in the trial, who would not rejoice that all her dangers are over!—All I wished was pardon and blessing from my dear parents. Easy as my departure seems to promise to be, it would have been still easier had I had that pleasure. BUT GOD ALMIGHTY WOULD NOT LET ME DEPEND FOR COMFORT UPON ANY BUT HIMSELF.

Richardson wishes us to remember that the sublime Clarissa is only nineteen. To say that God withdraws all comfort except Himself is not exactly a humble sentiment. She dies on her own terms and accepts God's esteem in a mutual exchange of overwhelming wills. Poor Lovelace is quite accurate at the close. His final view of Clarissa is not so very different from her own self-estimate.

I have always been impatient with critics who ascribe flaws to Clarissa Harlowe. Far more than Richard Lovelace, who cannot quite bridge the gap between Restoration libertine and Herculean hero in the mode of John Dryden's dramas, Clarissa has the wholeness of the great Shakespearean personalities. Richardson appropriates from Shakespeare the representation of inwardness, and Clarissa is as persuasive as Rosalind or Portia, though she stems from Shakespearean tragedy and not from comedy.

In 1987, I edited a volume of critical essays on Samuel Richardson, including work by Ian Watt, Martin Price, and Mark Kinkead-Weekes. Rereading it now, in 2018, I am captivated by the final essay, "Reading the Fire Scene in *Clarissa*," by Rosemary Bechler. It seems to me the most enlightening discussion I have encountered on this Protestant masterpiece of internal struggle to achieve the original bareness of the soul confronting the divine.

Bechler returns me to William Law (1686–1761), who has always been a spiritual preceptor to me since my early years as a scholar of William Blake, when I wrote a long study, *Blake's Apocalypse* (1963), and also composed an immense commentary for my friend David V. Erdman's edition of *The Complete Poetry and Prose of William Blake* (1965). William Law was the center of a circle around Samuel Richardson, who was a printer and publisher as well as a novelist. The group included two physicians, George Cheyne and John Freke, as well as the poet John Byrom, disciple of William Law and author of the poem *Enthusiasm* (1752). William Law's most famous work remains *A Serious Call to a Devout and Holy Life* (1729), which inspired a marvelous response from the magnificent Dr. Samuel Johnson:

> When at Oxford, I took up Law's *Serious Call to a Holy Life*, expecting to find it a dull book…and perhaps to laugh at it. But I found Law quite an overmatch for me; and this was the first occasion of my thinking in earnest of religion, after I became capable of rational inquiry.

Law's later work was in the hermetic tradition that had been revived by Jacob Boehme (1575–1624). Boehme, a shoemaker, had mystical visions that identified God the Father as fire, and the Son as light. To be saved, we have to go through hell in this life, and learn to read *The Signature of All Things*. William Blake read Boehme with some sympathy, as he initially did with Swedenborg, but then decided that a poet like John Milton contained the larger truths that the mystics could only touch.

Samuel Richardson and his group were conscious of reviving the seventeenth-century tradition of the English Inner Light Puritans: at one point Lovelace remarks that the light of the Bible "is too glaring to be borne." Against it, he sets on fire the house of assignation in which he has confined Clarissa:

Meantime Dorcas, after she had directed me upstairs, not knowing the worst was over, and expecting every minute the house would be in a blaze, out of tender regard for her lady (I shall for ever love the wench for it) ran to her door, and rapping loudly at it, in a recovered voice, cried out with a shrillness equal to her love, Fire! Fire!—The house is on fire!—Rise, madam!—This instant rise—if you would not be burnt in your bed!

No sooner had she made this dreadful outcry, but I heard her lady's door with hasty violence unbar, unbolt, unlock, and open, and my charmer's voice sounding like that of one going into a fit.

You may believe how much I was affected. I trembled with concern for her, and hastened down faster than the alarm of fire had made me run up, in order to satisfy her that all the danger was over.

When I had *flown down* to her chamber door, there I beheld the charmingest creature in the world, supporting herself on the arm of the gasping Dorcas, sighing, trembling, and ready to faint, with nothing on but an under-petticoat, her lovely bosom half-open, and her feet just slipped into her shoes. As soon as she saw me, she panted, and struggled to speak; but could only say, oh, Mr Lovelace! and down was ready to sink.

I clasped her in my arms with an ardour she never felt before: My dearest life! fear nothing: I have been up—the danger is over—the fire is got under—And how (foolish devil! to Dorcas) could you thus, by your hideous yell, alarm and frighten my angel!

Oh Jack! how her sweet bosom, as I clasped her to mine, heaved and panted! I could even distinguish her dear heart flutter, flutter, flutter, against mine; and for a few minutes, I feared she would go into fits.

Lest the half-lifeless charmer should catch cold in this undress, I lifted her to her bed, and sat down by her upon the side of it, endeavouring with the utmost tenderness, as well of action as expression, to dissipate her terrors.

But what did I get by this my generous care of her, and by my *successful* endeavour to bring her to herself?—Nothing, ungrateful as she was! but the most passionate exclamations: for we had both already forgot the occasion, dreadful as it was, which had thrown her into my arms; I, from the joy of encircling the almost disrobed body of the loveliest of her sex; she, from the greater terrors that arose from finding herself in my arms, and both seated on the bed from which she had been so lately frighted.

The sadistic element in Lovelace's lust for Clarissa cannot be overstated. There is a schizophrenic trace in his alternations as rake and as Dryden's Herculean hero, more in the mode of Marlowe than of Shakespeare. As sadistic rake he rapes Clarissa Harlowe, in the actual presence of procuress and whores, and with the aid of drugged alcohol. The rape will destroy them both. With her will and integrity violated, Clarissa's possible love for him vanishes forever. The tragedy, because of her spiritual eminence, is greater for her, yet for Lovelace it is tragic also, because the heroic strain in him authentically loves her.

I had no suspicion yet that these women were not indeed the ladies they personated; and I blamed myself for my weak fears—It cannot *be*, thought I, that *such* ladies will abet treachery against a poor creature they are so fond of. They must undoubtedly *be* the persons they *appear* to be—what folly to doubt it! The air, the dress, the dignity, of women of quality— How unworthy of them, and of my charity, concluded I, is this ungenerous shadow of suspicion!

So, recovering my stupefied spirits as well as they could be recovered (for I was heavier and heavier; and wondered to Dorcas what ailed me; rubbing my eyes, and taking some of her snuff, pinch after pinch, to very little purpose), I pursued my employment: but when that was over, all packed up that I designed to be packed up; and I had nothing to do but to *think;* and found them tarry so long; I thought I should have gone distracted. I shut myself into the chamber that had been mine; I kneeled, I prayed; yet knew not what I prayed for: then ran out again. It was almost dark night, I said: where, where, was Mr Lovelace?

He came to me, taking no notice at first of my consternation and wildness (what they had given me made me incoherent and wild): All goes well, said he, my dear!—A line from Captain Tomlinson!

All indeed did go well for the villainous project of the most cruel and most villainous of men!

I *demanded* his aunt!—I *demanded* his cousin!—The evening, I said, was closing!—My head was very, *very* bad, I remember, I said—And it grew worse and worse.

Terror, however, as yet kept up my spirits; and I insisted upon his going himself to hasten them.

He called his servant. He raved at the *sex* for *their* delay: 'twas well that business of consequence seldom depended upon such parading, unpunctual triflers!

His servant came.

He ordered him to fly to his cousin Leeson's; and to let his aunt and cousins know how uneasy we both were at their delay: adding, of his own accord, Desire them, if they don't come instantly, to send their coach and we will go without them. Tell them I wonder they'll serve me so!

I thought this was considerately and fairly put. But now, indifferent as my head was, I had a little time to consider the man and his behaviour. He terrified me with his looks, and with his violent emotions as he gazed upon me. Evident *joy-suppressed* emotions, as I have since recollected. His sentences short, and pronounced as if his breath were touched. Never saw I his abominable eyes look, as then they looked—triumph in them!—fierce and wild; and more disagreeable than the women's at the vile house appeared to me when I first saw them: and at times, such a leering, mischief-boding cast!—I would have given the world to have been an hundred miles from him. Yet his behaviour was decent—a decency, however, that I might have seen to be struggled for—for he snatched my hand two or three times with a vehemence in his grasp that hurt me; speaking words of tenderness through his shut teeth, as it seemed; and let it go with a beggar-voiced humble accent, like the vile woman's just before; half-inward; yet his words and manner carrying the appearance of strong and almost convulsed passion!—Oh my dear! What mischief was he not then meditating!

I complained once or twice of thirst. My mouth seemed parched. At the time, I supposed that it was my terror (gasping often as I did for breath) that parched up the roof of my mouth. I called for water: some table-beer was brought me. Beer, I suppose, was a better vehicle (if I were not dosed enough before) for their potions. I told the maid that she knew I seldom tasted malt-liquor: yet, suspecting nothing of this nature, being extremely thirsty I drank it, as what came next: and instantly, as it were, found myself much worse than before; as if inebriated, I should fancy: I know not how.

His servant was gone twice as long as he needed: and, just before his return, came one of the pretended Lady Betty's, with a letter for Mr Lovelace.

He sent it up to me. I read it: and then it was that I thought myself a lost creature; it being to put off her going to Hampstead that night, on account of violent fits which Miss Montague was pretended to be seized with: for then immediately came into my head his vile attempt upon me in this house; the revenge that my flight might too probably inspire him with on that occasion, and because of the difficulty I made to forgive him and to be reconciled to him; his very looks wild and dreadful to me; and the women of the house such as I had more reason than ever, even from the pretended Lady Betty's hints, to be afraid of: all these crowding together in my apprehensive mind, I fell into a kind of frenzy.

I have not remembrance how I was for the time it lasted: but I know that in my first agitations I pulled off my head-dress, and tore my ruffles in twenty tatters; and ran to find him out.

When a little recovered, I insisted upon the hint he had given of their coach. But the messenger, he said, had told him that it was sent to fetch a physician, lest his chariot should be put up, or not ready.

I then insisted upon going directly to Lady Betty's lodgings.

Mrs Leeson's was now a crowded house, he said: and as my earnestness could be owing to nothing but groundless apprehension (and oh what vows, what protestations of his honour did he then make!), he hoped I would not add to their present concern. Charlotte, indeed, was used to fits, he said, upon any great surprises, whether of joy or grief; and they would hold her for a week together if not got off in a few hours.

You are an *observer of eyes,* my dear, said the villain; perhaps in secret insult: saw you not in Miss Montague's now and then, at Hampstead, something wildish?—I was afraid for her then—Silence and quiet only do her good: your concern for *her,* and her love for *you,* will but augment the poor girl's disorder, if you should go.

All impatient with grief and apprehension, I still declared myself resolved not to stay in that house till morning. All I had in the world, my rings, my watch, my little money, for a coach! or, if one were not to be got, I would go on foot to Hampstead that night, though I walked it by myself.

A coach was hereupon sent for, or pretended to be sent for. Any price, he said, he would give to oblige me, late as it was; and he would attend me with all his soul—But no coach was to be got.

Let me cut short the rest. I grew worse and worse in my head; now stupid, now raving, now senseless. The vilest of vile women was brought to frighten me. Never was there so horrible a creature as she appeared to me at the time.

I remember, I pleaded for mercy—I remember that I said *I would be his—indeed I would be his—*to obtain his mercy—But no mercy found I!—My strength, my intellects, failed me!—And then such scenes followed—Oh my dear, such dreadful scenes!—fits upon fits (faintly indeed, and imperfectly remembered) procuring me no compassion—but death was withheld from me. That would have been too great a mercy!

Lovelace will come to understand that his rape of Clarissa was an apocalyptic defeat for him.

His realization is slow: it comes when Lovelace suddenly apprehends the dialectical entrapment Clarissa has been for him:

A horrid dear creature!—By my soul, she made me shudder! She had need, indeed, to talk of *her* unhappiness, in falling into the hands of the only *man* in the world who could have used her as I have used her! She is the only *woman* in the world who could have shocked and disturbed me as she has done—So we are upon a foot in that respect. And I think I have the *worst* of it by much. Since very little has been my joy; very much my trouble: and *her* punishment, as she calls it, is *over:* but when *mine* will, or what it may be, who can tell?

Here, only recapitulating (think, then, how I must be affected at the time), I was forced to leave off, and sing a song to myself. I aimed at a lively air; but I croaked rather than sung: and fell into the old dismal thirtieth of January strain. I hemmed up for a sprightlier note; but it would not do: and at last I ended, like a malefactor, in a dead psalm melody.

High-ho!—I gape like an unfledged kite in its nest, wanting to swallow a chicken, bobbed at its mouth by its marauding dam!—

What a devil ails me!—I can neither think nor write!—

Lie down, pen, for a moment!—

(Letter 226)

The devil that ails him is the beginning of his own end, his falling outward and downward from his last shreds of a libertine ideology into the dreadful inner space of his defeat by Clarissa, his enforced realization that self-willing and self-assertion are permanently over for him. Clarissa, a great Puritan withholder of esteem, will not accept him at his own evaluation, and he begins to know that pragmatically they have destroyed one another. His actual death is a release from the death-in-life he has suffered since Clarissa's death.

Clarissa Harlowe is a larger form than all the heroines of the Protestant will descended from her: Jane Austen's Elizabeth Bennet, Emma Woodhouse, Anne Elliot; Hawthorne's Hester Prynne;

George Eliot's Dorothea Brooke; Thomas Hardy's Sue Bridehead; Henry James's Isabel Archer, Milly Theale; D. H. Lawrence's Ursula Brangwen; E. M. Forster's Margaret Schlegel; and Virginia Woolf's Lily Briscoe. The largeness is Samuel Richardson's Shakespearean triumph. The fire of divine wrath is mitigated by Clarissa's inward light. If there could be a Protestant version of Dante's Beatrice, it would be Clarissa Harlowe.

CHAPTER 3

Tom Jones (1749)

HENRY FIELDING

WILLIAM EMPSON increasingly seems to me the most useful literary critic of the twentieth century. I owe a lot more to the great Canadian magus Northrop Frye, whose writings formed me for twenty years, from 1947 to 1967, when I reacted against them after a night of bad dreams concerning the figure that Ezekiel and William Blake called the Covering Cherub:

> Thou art the anointed cherub that covereth; and I have set thee so: thou wast upon the holy mountain of God; thou hast walked up and down in the midst of the stones of fire.
> Thou wast perfect in thy ways from the day that thou wast created, till iniquity was found in thee.
> By the multitude of thy merchandise they have filled the midst of thee with violence, and thou hast sinned: therefore I will cast thee as profane out of the mountain of God: and I will destroy thee, O covering cherub, from the midst of the stones of fire.
>
> (Ezekiel 28:14–16, KJV)

My distinguished former student Leopold Damrosch, Jr., in his book *God's Plot and Man's Stories* (1985), begins with the judgment that the most eminent literary work of the eighteenth century is

Fielding's *Tom Jones*. I am more attached to Samuel Richardson's *Clarissa* than to *Tom Jones,* and wonder why Damrosch prefers Fielding to Jonathan Swift, Alexander Pope, Samuel Johnson, and William Blake. Still, Damrosch argues a considerable case. For him *Tom Jones,* though a farewell to providential fiction, nevertheless affirms the presence of a benign God:

> The marvel of *Tom Jones* is that it balances so perfectly between determinism of plot and freedom of character. Within the large patterns of causality that God ordains, human beings remain free to improvise and change. Like Bunyan and Richardson, Fielding is a Christian, and like them he therefore asserts a providential universe, but fallen life looks altogether different to him, and his mode of fiction stands in permanent opposition to theirs.

I am not sure what Empson would make of that. He did not much care for the neo-Christianity of T. S. Eliot and his critical disciples. Fallen life to Fielding, indeed, is very different from the visions of Bunyan and Richardson. Pragmatically, it seems at its best Edenic. The marriage of Sophia Western and Tom Jones at the close of the book is that of an unfallen Eve and a regenerate Adam.

My late friend and colleague Martin Price observed, "Fielding can reward his heroes because they do not seek a reward." Another friend and former teacher, the late Frederick W. Hilles, enjoyed comparing *Tom Jones* to Joyce's *Ulysses,* though he acknowledged that Fielding as narrator was neither indifferent nor invisible. *Tom Jones* is a comic *Odyssey,* and so the ancestor of both Charles Dickens and James Joyce.

I have idolized Dr. Samuel Johnson all my life but am somewhat baffled that he strongly disliked all of Fielding's work. I myself share Johnson's preference for Samuel Richardson over Fielding, though I love *Tom Jones,* but, then, *Clarissa* always seems to me much the strongest novel in the English language, surpassing even the works of Jane Austen, George Eliot, Henry James, and all their descendants. There is the alternative tradition that includes Dickens and Joyce, and it finds its great precursor in *Tom Jones,* and yet certainly they surpass Fielding even at his best.

For Johnson, Fielding was simplistic, but the greatest of our critics misread how shrewd a moralist the comic Fielding could be. I recall venturing that Fielding and Richardson in effect split up Shakespeare between them. Shakespeare's unique gift for representing inwardness was partly absorbed by Richardson, whereas Fielding chose to emphasize the Shakespearean power that could depict the world of romance so deftly that it seemed to become more real than reality.

Readers of *Tom Jones* sometimes identify with the rambunctious hero, whose exuberance renders him always ready for rapid activity, whether it be fighting, whoring, hunting, or exercising his good-heartedness at every moment that comes along. He falls truly and permanently in love with Sophia Western, yet follows a labyrinthine path until, at last, they are united, at the very close of the book.

You do not go to Fielding to trace the progress of the soul. His mode excludes inwardness, and his skepticism even toward his own created self, the "Fielding" who as narrator is always with us, absolves him from the burden of self-consciousness. Johnson, pushing away Boswell's protests, insisted, "There is more knowledge of the heart in one letter of Richardson's, than in all '*Tom Jones*.'" This excessive judgment depends upon Johnson's conviction that Richardson gave us "characters of nature" whereas Fielding could only give us "characters of manners." Richardson, an extraordinary psychologist, insisted that he would not read *Tom Jones*. I suspect that he did read it, since he comments that Fielding neglected Probability. *Tom Jones* was published only some weeks after the yearlong appearance of the seven volumes of *Clarissa*. Both evidently sold quite well, and Fielding, a much more genial person than the dour Richardson, consumed all of *Clarissa* and then wrote a generous letter of praise to Richardson. The two novelists were as antithetical as Henry James and James Joyce, or as Flaubert and Victor Hugo.

For me, and I would believe for most readers, the glory of *Tom Jones* has to be the quite Shakespearean Squire Western, Sophia's improbable father, magnificently played by Hugh Griffith in the 1963 film version directed by Tony Richardson from the screenplay of John Osborne. Charming as Albert Finney was as the bastard Tom Jones, Griffith steals the movie with his absolutely mindless energy, violence, and daemonic force. He seems to be the Freudian bodily ego run rampant. Squire Western is hardly Shakespeare's Falstaff or Chaucer's Wife of Bath. They have dangerous wit and indisputably heroic vitalism. They give us life. Western parodies vitalism, and yet he touches the limits of representation and can live outside the novel in that world beyond mimesis that only Shakespeare, Cervantes, Chaucer, and Dante can give us. Here is an instance of the Squire run wild:

Western had been long impatient for the event of this conference, and was just now arrived at the door to listen; when, having heard the last sentiments of his daughter's heart, he lost all temper, and, bursting open the door in a rage, cried out— 'It is a lie! It is a d—n'd lie! It is all owing to that d—n'd rascal Jones; and if she could get at un, she'd ha' un any hour of the day.' Here Allworthy interposed, and addressing himself to the squire with some anger in his look, he said, 'Mr Western, you have not kept your word with me. You promised to abstain from all violence.'—'Why, so I did,' cries Western, 'as long as it was possible; but to hear a wench telling such confounded lies—Zounds! doth she think, if she can make vools of other volk, she can make one of me?—No, no, I know her better than thee dost.'—'I am sorry to tell you, sir,' answered Allworthy, 'it doth not appear, by your behaviour to this young lady, that you know her at all. I ask pardon for what I say; but I think our intimacy, your own desires, and the occasion justify me. She is your daughter, Mr Western, and I think she doth honour to your name. If I was capable of envy, I should sooner envy you on this account than any other man whatever.'—'Odrabbit it!' cries the squire, 'I wish she was thine, with all my heart—wouldst soon be glad to be rid of the trouble o' her.'—'Indeed, my good friend,' answered Allworthy, 'you yourself are the cause of all the trouble you complain of. Place that confidence in the young lady which she so well deserves, and I am certain you will be the happiest father on earth.'—'I confidence in her?' cries the squire. ''Sblood! what confidence can I place in her, when she won't do as I would ha' her? Let her gi' but her consent to marry as I would ha' her, and I'll place as much confidence in her as wouldst ha' me.'—'You have no right, neighbour,' answered Allworthy, 'to insist on any such consent. A negative voice your daughter allows you, and God and nature have thought proper to allow you no more.'—'A negative voice!' cries the squire—

'Ay! ay! I'll show you what a negative voice I ha.—Go along, go into your chamber, go, you stubborn—.' 'Indeed, Mr Western,' said Allworthy, 'indeed you use her cruelly—I cannot bear to see this—you shall, you must behave to her in a kinder manner. She deserves the best of treatment.'—'Yes, yes,' said the squire, 'I know what she deserves: now she's gone, I'll show you what she deserves. See here, sir, here is a letter from my cousin, my Lady Bellaston, in which she is so kind to gi' me to understand that the fellow is got out of prison again; and here she advises me to take all the care I can o' the wench. Odzookers! neighbour Allworthy, you don't know what it is to govern a daughter.'

Lady Bellaston, a bower of lust, had taken Tom Jones for her lover and attempted to dispose of Sophia Western by having her raped by a kinsman and thus forced into an unhappy marriage. Tom, condemned to death for having slain a man who survives quite boisterously, is released, to the discomfort of Squire Western, who himself seeks to marry Sophia to the dreadful pill Blifil, in the expectation that Blifil will be Squire Allworthy's heir. When all this is reversed, Squire Western jubilantly swings to the other extreme. Eavesdropping, he hears Sophia resolutely rejecting both Tom and the horrible Blifil. He bursts in like a tempest:

At this instant Western, who had stood some time listening, burst into the room, and, with his hunting voice and phrase, cried out, 'To her, boy, to her, go to her.—That's it, little honeys, O that's it! Well! what, is it all over? Hath she appointed the day, boy? What, shall it be to-morrow or next day? It shan't be put off a minute longer than next day, I am resolved.' 'Let me beseech you, sir,' says Jones, "don't let me be the occasion'— 'Beseech mine a—,' cries Western. 'I thought thou hadst been a lad of higher mettle than to give way to a parcel of maidenish tricks.—I tell thee 'tis all flimflam. Zoodikers! she'd have the wedding to-night with all her heart. Would'st not, Sophy? Come, confess, and be an honest girl for once. What, art dumb? Why dost not speak?' 'Why should I confess, sir,' says Sophia, 'since it seems you are so well acquainted with my thoughts?'— 'That's a good girl,' cries he, 'and dost consent then?' 'No, indeed, sir,' says Sophia, 'I have given no such consent.'—'And

wunt not ha un then to-morrow, nor next day?' says Western.—
'Indeed, sir,' says she, 'I have no such intention.' 'But I can tell
thee,' replied he, 'why hast nut; only because thou dost love to
be disobedient, and to plague and vex thy father.' 'Pray, sir,' said
Jones, interfering—'I tell thee thou art a puppy,' cries he. 'When
I vorbid her, then it was all nothing but sighing and whining,
and languishing and writhing; now I am vor thee, she is against
thee. All the spirit of contrary, that's all. She is above being
guided and governed by her father, that is the whole truth on't.
It is only to disoblige and contradict me.' 'What would my papa
have me do?' cries Sophia. 'What would I ha thee do?' says he,
'why, gi' un thy hand this moment.'—'Well, sir,' says Sophia, 'I
will obey you.—There is my hand, Mr Jones.' 'Well, and will you
consent to ha un to-morrow morning?' says Western.—'I will
be obedient to you, sir,' cries she.—'Why then to-morrow morning be the day,' cries he. 'Why then to-morrow morning shall
be the day, papa, since you will have it so,' says Sophia. Jones
then fell upon his knees, and kissed her hand in an agony of joy,
while Western began to caper and dance about the room, presently crying out—'Where the devil is Allworthy? He is without
now, a talking with that d—d lawyer Dowling, when he should
be minding other matters.' He then sallied out in quest of him,
and very opportunely left the lovers to enjoy a few tender minutes alone.

I wonder why Johnson, who was willing to call *Tom Jones* "the
Comedy of Romance," made no comment upon the whirligig of
Squire Western. Johnson memorably extolled Sir John Falstaff,
brushing away his own moral qualms. Afflicted by a vile melancholy,
Johnson depended upon good company to keep him going. He found
in Falstaff what is truly there: the joy of existence. Squire Western is
deliciously funny as he reverses himself without the slightest realiza-
tion of inconsistency. Perhaps it was the absence of mind that caused
Johnson to turn from the mad Squire. Johnson found true wit in
Falstaff and was nourished by it. A latecomer disciple of the Grand
Cham, I have been vitalized by Falstaff for the last seven decades,
and Squire Western, alas, is no Falstaff. But I take what I can get, and
Squire Western gratifies me.

CHAPTER 4

Pride and Prejudice (1813)

JANE AUSTEN

A T DIFFERENT TIMES in my life I have preferred *Persuasion* and *Emma* to *Pride and Prejudice,* but in my advanced old age the three seem equally grand. The same holds for *Mansfield Park,* but I will neglect it in this book.

Probably *Pride and Prejudice* is the most popular Austen. It is frequently hilarious, always amiable, and with a curious profundity that is difficult to assess. Why did Mr. Bennet marry the absurd Mrs. Bennet? The question is unanswerable since the mismatch is preposterous:

> Mr. Bennet was so odd a mixture of quick parts, sarcastic humour, reserve, and caprice, that the experience of three-and-twenty years had been insufficient to make his wife understand his character. Her mind was less difficult to develop. She was a woman of mean understanding, little information, and uncertain temper. When she was discontented, she fancied herself nervous. The business of her life was to get her daughters married; its solace was visiting and news.

Mr. Bennet's favorite necessarily is Elizabeth, whose quickness of mind, spirit, and sensibility, and an amiable reserve are beyond even her father's apprehension. Jane Austen herself, in a letter to her sister Cassandra, January 29, 1813, gives Elizabeth the ultimate guerdon:

> I must confess that I think her as delightful a character as ever appeared in print, and how I shall be able to tolerate those who do not like her at least, I do not know.

I might vote for Don Quixote and Sancho Panza as rivals, but who else is there? The answer has to be Sir John Falstaff, and Rosalind, and Cleopatra, and Feste, and who you will in Shakespeare. Of course, Cleopatra is something other than delightful, and in another way so is Panurge. Delight goes back to the Latin *delicere*, "to allure." Elizabeth Bennet allures Fitzwilliam Darcy, and the reader, by her lightness and quickening power, ultimately the power both of her mind and of her sexuality.

If the authentic test for a great novel is rereading, and the joys of yet further rereadings, then *Pride and Prejudice* can rival any novel ever written. Though Jane Austen, unlike Shakespeare, practices an art of rigorous exclusion, she seems to me finally the most Shakespearean novelist in the language. When Shakespeare wishes to, he can make all his personages, major and minor, speak in voices entirely their own, self-consistent and utterly different from one another. Austen, with the similar illusion of ease, does the same. Since voice in both writers is an image of personality and also of character, the reader of Austen encounters an astonishing variety of selves in her socially confined world. Though that world is essentially a secularized culture, the moral vision dominating it remains that of the Protestant sensibility. Austen's heroines waver in one judgment or another, but they hold fast to the right of private judgment as the self's fortress. What they call "affection" we term "love," of the enduring rather than the Romantic variety, and when they judge a man to be "amiable," it is akin to whatever superlative each of us may favor for an admirable, humane person. Where they may differ from us, but more in degree than in kind, is in their profound reliance upon the soul's exchanges of mutual esteem with other souls. In *Pride and Prejudice* and *Emma* in particular, your accuracy in estimating the nature and value of another soul is intimately allied to the legitimacy of your self-esteem, your valid pride.

The moral comedy of the misunderstandings between Elizabeth Bennet and Darcy has been compared, by several critics, to the combat of wit between Beatrice and Benedick in Shakespeare's *Much Ado About Nothing*. As a comparison, this has limited usefulness: Elizabeth is not primarily a wit or a social ironist. Her true Shakespearean precursor is Rosalind in *As You Like It*. Rosalind resorts to furious wit in properly squelching Jaques and Touchstone, but her fundamental strength is a sure sense of self, with the wisdom that only an accurate self-estimate can bring. Such wisdom transcends detachment and welcomes a generous concern with other selves. It leads to a pride that is also playful, which is an intense contrast to Darcy's implacable pride. His sense of self relies upon an immense conviction of personal as well as societal eminence. We cannot dispute his conviction; he is socially formidable, morally fairminded, and a better judge of character than Elizabeth sometimes proves to be. But his aggressiveness is excessive, despite Elizabeth's final, justified verdict: "He is frequently amiable." There is a touch of the quixotic in Elizabeth, whereas Darcy stands outside what could be termed the order of play. Tact without playfulness can yield too readily to moral zeal; but the quixotic not only can be tactless, it can decay into misguided exuberance.

Such reflections, though germane to *Pride and Prejudice*, are sadly abstract when applied to the lively comedy of the novel. Surprise keeps breaking in, and nothing turns out as anyone in the book expects. We are indeed in a Shakespearean world, as random in its way as Rosalind's Forest of Arden. Only the level firmness of Austen's narrative voice holds together a social world that borders oddly upon the bizarre, for everyone in it is rather more idiosyncratic than at first they appear to be. *Pride and Prejudice* has an authentic monster in Mr. Collins, a poseur in Wickham, a tyrant of pride in the odious Lady Catherine, and a master of destructive satire in Mr. Bennet. There is a marvelous comic tension between Austen's seemingly normative tone and the eccentric personages who perpetually render the story more vivid and more strange.

Irony, which essentially is saying one thing while meaning another, is Austen's characteristic mode. Austen's irony, though endlessly genial, unsettles all her meanings. Where we seem most assured of the happiness or perfection attained by her heroines, we learn to look more closely and to surmise the implied reservations of this ironic vision. A great master of metaphor, Austen is also a genius of the unsaid: she expects the astute reader to say it for her. Not that Austen, in the manner of her Darcy, is a triumph of tact; she is more in the mode of her Elizabeth Bennet, and is a triumph of playfulness. In some ways, Austen is more like Shakespeare's Rosalind than Elizabeth ever could be, and so Austen's largest triumph is in the sheer psychic and spiritual health of her magnificent wit and invention.

The grandest comic moment in *Pride and Prejudice* is the outrageous proposal made by Mr. Collins to Elizabeth Bennet. One remembers Melville Cooper, perfect in the role of Mr. Collins in the 1940 motion picture of the novel:

> My reasons for marrying are, first, that I think it a right thing for every clergyman in easy circumstances (like myself) to set the example of matrimony in his parish; secondly, that I am convinced that it will add very greatly to my happiness; and thirdly—which perhaps I ought to have mentioned earlier, that it is the particular advice and recommendation of the very noble lady whom I have the honour of calling patroness. Twice has she condescended to give me her opinion (unasked too!) on this subject; and it was but the very Saturday night before I left Hunsford—between our pools at quadrille, while Mrs. Jenkinson was arranging Miss de Bourgh's footstool, that she said, 'Mr. Collins, you must marry. A clergyman like you must marry. Choose properly, choose a gentlewoman for my sake; and for your own, let her be an active, useful sort of person, not brought up high, but able to make a small income go a good way. This is my advice. Find such a woman as soon as you can, bring her to Hunsford, and I will visit her.' Allow me, by the way, to observe, my fair cousin, that I do not reckon the notice and kindness of Lady Catherine de Bourgh as among the least of the advantages in my power to offer. You will find her manners beyond anything I can describe; and your wit and vivacity, I think, must be acceptable to her, especially when tempered with the silence and respect which her rank will inevitably excite. Thus much for my general intention in favour of matrimony; it remains to be told why my views were directed to Longbourn instead of my own neighbourhood, where I assure you there are many

amiable young women. But the fact is, that being, as I am, to inherit this estate after the death of your honoured father (who, however, may live many years longer), I could not satisfy myself without resolving to choose a wife from among his daughters, that the loss to them might be as little as possible, when the melancholy event takes place—which, however, as I have already said, may not be for several years. This has been my motive, my fair cousin, and I flatter myself it will not sink me in your esteem. And now nothing remains for me but to assure you in the most animated language of the violence of my affection. To fortune I am perfectly indifferent, and shall make no demand of that nature on your father, since I am well aware that it could not be complied with; and that one thousand pounds in the 4 per cents, which will not be yours till after your mother's decease, is all that you may ever be entitled to. On that head, therefore, I shall be uniformly silent; and you may assure yourself that no ungenerous reproach shall ever pass my lips when we are married.

This has to be the funniest marriage proposal in Western literature. Its apex is the ultimate outrage:

And now nothing remains for me but to assure you in the most animated language of the violence of my affection.

Jane Austen is so accomplished a novelist that one does her wrong to wish she had also written stage dramas. I have never been carried out of the legitimate theater because I became helpless with laughter, but on two occasions I became so borne away by frightening hilarity that I had to leave two cinemas, the first when Melville Cooper concluded his proposal, and the second after viewing *The Fatal Glass of Beer*, the brief masterpiece of W. C. Fields (1933).

Setting aside the undoubted good looks of Laurence Olivier as Fitzwilliam Darcy, are we to share Elizabeth Bennet's final estimate of him? I met the late Tony Tanner only once, in Rome, introduced to him by his wife, Nadia Fusini, a critic and translator. We talked about recognition in literature and argued my friend Angus Fletcher's surmise that all imaginative literature depends upon *partial* recognition, since total recognition is a kind of death. Tanner found in Jane Austen a kind of total recognition that enhanced life and could help banish melancholy. I realized later that Tanner had to struggle with a more dangerous melancholy than I tended to experience, except in my own midlife crisis in 1965.

The question is: are we to agree with Jane Austen that Darcy is the all-but-perfect husband for Elizabeth Bennet? Tanner followed Marvin Mudrick in observing Jane Austen's deprecation of any merely sexual attraction. I am not certain that I find that altogether convincing. She died at forty-one, in considerable pain, and we have no reason to believe that she did not die a virgin. And yet, though she made light of it, she does seem to have experienced an authentic and mutual falling in love with Tom Lefroy, a young Irishman, when both of them were twenty in 1796. That was the year she began what was to become *Pride and Prejudice.* In his biographical study, *Becoming Jane Austen* (2003), Jon Spence shrewdly suggested that Lefroy was a model for Darcy, but that Austen transposed her qualities to Darcy, and Lefroy's to Elizabeth Bennet. Jane Austen's pride in her aesthetic autonomy evades her ironical sense, and is transmuted into Fitzwilliam Darcy's pride of social and personal integrity. The evidently charming Tom Lefroy bestows upon Elizabeth Bennet a quickness of wit and spirit that also reaches beyond irony.

Though the quality of criticism devoted to *Pride and Prejudice* is unusually high, it does not often go deep enough. Austen's own somewhat ironic critique of the book gently laments what we would call its refusal of the abyss. Negative reflection, in a somewhat Hegelian mode, yields knowledge of a kind that allows Elizabeth Bennet a partial but firm recognition both of Fitzwilliam Darcy and of herself. Their mutual affection does not lack sexual passion yet nevertheless is compounded of two legitimate prides that exchange esteems. Pride is thus redeemed, and prejudice becomes judicious in that it grants otherness its place in knowledge.

It may be too easy to love Austen's *Pride and Prejudice.* It is the work of a very young woman of astonishing genius whose hopes have been kindled, set aside, but not yet extinguished. Tom Lefroy and Jane Austen gave each other up because neither had any money. It is more than two centuries since *Pride and Prejudice* was first published, and all social contexts have evaporated. We now might say that Lefroy and Austen ought to have married and enjoyed, despite financial vicissitudes, two decades together. But how can that be said? Austen evidently turned down two later suitors, perhaps because she still longed for Lefroy. We cannot know completely. Four years after *Pride and Prejudice* was published, Jane Austen died at forty-one. Six great novels and some remarkable fragments survive her. A day after my eighty-eighth birthday, I am more sentimental than ever. Grateful for the books, one wishes she could have had a more prolonged and fulfilled life. Still, she revered Dr. Samuel Johnson, who in his *Idler* remarked:

Philosophy may infuse stubbornness, but Religion only can give patience.

No one would think of Jane Austen as a religious writer, but there is something stubborn in her spirit, as there is in Elizabeth and Darcy. She teaches patience inflected by wit and the joy of being.

CHAPTER 5

Emma (1815)

JANE AUSTEN

JANE AUSTEN'S least accurate prophecy as to the fate of her fictions concerned *Emma*, whose heroine, she thought, "no one but myself will much like." Aside from much else, Emma is immensely likable, because she is so extraordinarily imaginative, dangerous and misguided as her imagination frequently must appear to others and finally to herself. On the scale of being, Emma constitutes an answer to the immemorial questions of the sublime: More? Equal to? Or less than? Like Clarissa Harlowe before her and the strongest heroines of George Eliot and Henry James after her, Emma Woodhouse has a heroic will and, like them, she risks identifying her will with her imagination. Socially considered, such identification is catastrophic, since the Protestant will has a tendency to bestow a ranking on other selves, and such ranking may turn out to be a personal phantasmagoria. G. Armour Craig rather finely remarked: "Society in *Emma* is not a ladder. It is a web of imputations that link feelings and conduct." Yet Emma herself, expansionist rather than reductionist in temperament, imputes more fiercely and freely than the web can sustain, and she threatens always, until she is enlightened, to dissolve the societal links, in and for others, that might allow some stability between feelings and conduct.

Armour Craig usefully added, "*Emma* does not justify its heroine nor does it deride her." Rather, it treats her with ironic love (not loving irony). Emma Woodhouse is dear to Jane Austen, because her errors are profoundly imaginative and rise from the will's passion for autonomy of vision. The splendid Jane Fairfax is easier to admire, but I cannot agree with Wayne Booth's awarding the honors to her over Emma, though I admire the subtle balance of his formulation:

> Jane is superior to Emma in most respects except the stroke of good fortune that made Emma the heroine of the book. In matters of taste and ability, of head and of heart, she is Emma's superior....
>
> (Wayne C. Booth, "Point of View and the Control of Distance in *Emma*," *Nineteenth-Century Fiction*, vol. 16, no. 2 [Sept. 1961])

Taste, ability, head, and heart are a formidable fourfold; the imagination and the will, working together, are an even more formidable twofold and clearly may have their energies diverted to error and to mischief. Jane Fairfax is certainly more *amiable* even than Emma Woodhouse, but she is considerably less interesting. It is Emma who is meant to charm us and who does charm us. Austen is not writing a tragedy of the will, like *Paradise Lost,* but a great comedy of the will, and her heroine must incarnate the full potential of the will, however misused for a time. Having rather too much her own way is certainly one of Emma's powers, and she does have a disposition to think a little too well of herself. When Austen says that these were "the real evils indeed of Emma's situation," we read "evils" as lightly as the author will let us, which is lightly enough.

Can we account for the qualities in Emma Woodhouse that make her worthy of comparison to George Eliot's Gwendolen Harleth and Henry James's Isabel Archer? The pure comedy of her context seems world enough for her; she evidently is not the heiress of all the ages. We are persuaded, by Austen's superb craft, that marriage to Mr. Knightley will more than suffice to fulfill totally the now perfectly amiable Emma. Or are we? It is James's genius to suggest that, although Osmond's "beautiful mind" was a prison of the spirit for Isabel, no proper husband could exist anyway, since neither Touchett nor Goodwood is exactly a true match for her. Do we, presumably against Austen's promptings, not find Mr. Knightley something of a confinement also, benign and wise though he be?

I suspect that the heroine of the Protestant will, from Richardson's Clarissa Harlowe through to Virginia Woolf's Clarissa Dalloway, can never find a fit match, because wills do not marry. The allegory or tragic irony of this dilemma is written large in *Clarissa*, since Lovelace, in strength of will and splendor of being, actually would have been the true husband for Clarissa (as he well knows) had he not been a moral squalor. His death cry ("Let this expiate!") expiates nothing and helps establish the long tradition of the Anglo-American novel in which the heroines of the will are fated to suffer either overt calamities or else happy unions with such good if unexciting men as Mr. Knightley or Will Ladislaw in *Middlemarch*. When George Eliot is reduced to having the fascinating Gwendolen Harleth fall hopelessly in love with the prince of prigs, Daniel Deronda, we sigh and resign ourselves to the sorrows of fictive overdetermination. Lovelace or Daniel Deronda? I myself do not know a high-spirited woman who would not prefer the first, though not for a husband!

Emma is replete with grand comic epiphanies, of which my favorite comes in Volume 3, Chapter XI, when Emma receives the grave shock of Harriet's disclosure that Mr. Knightley is the object of Harriet's hopeful affections:

> When Harriet had closed her evidence, she appealed to her dear Miss Woodhouse, to say whether she had not good ground for hope.
>
> "I never should have presumed to think of it at first," said she, "but for you. You told me to observe him carefully, and let his behaviour be the rule of mine—and so I have. But now I seem to feel that I may deserve him; and that if he does choose me, it will not be any thing so very wonderful."
>
> The bitter feelings occasioned by this speech, the many bitter feelings, made the utmost exertion necessary on Emma's side to enable her to say in reply,
>
> "Harriet, I will only venture to declare, that Mr. Knightley is the last man in the world, who would intentionally give any woman the idea of his feeling for her more than he really does."
>
> Harriet seemed ready to worship her friend for a sentence so satisfactory; and Emma was only saved from raptures and fondness, which at that moment would have been dreadful

penance, by the sound of her father's footsteps. He was coming through the hall. Harriet was too much agitated to encounter him. "She could not compose herself—Mr. Woodhouse would be alarmed—she had better go;"—with most ready encouragement from her friend, therefore, she passed off through another door—and the moment she was gone, this was the spontaneous burst of Emma's feelings: "Oh God! that I had never seen her!"

The rest of the day, the following night, were hardly enough for her thoughts.—She was bewildered amidst the confusion of all that had rushed on her within the last few hours. Every moment had brought a fresh surprise; and every surprise must be matter of humiliation to her.—How to understand it all! How to understand the deceptions she had been thus practising on herself, and living under!—The blunders, the blindness of her own head and heart!—she sat still, she walked about, she tried her own room, she tried the shrubbery—in every place, every posture, she perceived that she had acted most weakly; that she had been imposed on by others in a most mortifying degree; that she had been imposing on herself in a degree yet more mortifying; that she was wretched, and should probably find this day but the beginning of wretchedness.

The acute aesthetic pleasure of this turns on the counterpoint between Emma's spontaneous cry, "Oh God! that I had never seen her!" and the exquisite comic touch of "she sat still, she walked about, she tried her own room, she tried the shrubbery—in every place, every posture, she perceived that she had acted most weakly." The acute humiliation of the will could not be better conveyed than by "she tried the shrubbery" and "every posture." Endlessly imaginative, Emma must now be compelled to endure the mortification of reducing herself to the postures and places of those driven into corners by the collapse of visions that have been exposed as delusions. Jane Austen, who seems to have identified herself with Emma, wisely chose to make this moment of ironic reversal a temporary purgatory, rather than an infernal discomfiture.

Paul H. Fry, like the late Geoffrey Hartman, an astonishingly erudite scholar of the transition from the Age of Sensibility, commencing with the death of Alexander Pope, on to the High Romanticism that ended with the early deaths of John Keats, Percy Bysshe Shelley, and Lord Byron, wrote a brilliant essay on *Emma* in regard to the influence of Romance on Jane Austen's most rugged personage:

> Emma is not, then, a victim of bad reading. Rather her tendency not to read is a facet of her more subtle sort of quixotism. Like Quixote, and in this regard like Charlotte Lennox's *Female Quixote* (1752), she lives in isolation, estranged partly by circumstance and partly by preference from suitable company. This is one of the many conditions she shares unwittingly with Mrs. Elton: "all her notions were drawn from one set of people, and one style of living" (IV:272). As is the case with Lennox's Arabella, Emma's mother is dead and her father cannot discipline her. Her regal bearing at Hartfield, where she favors frightened girls with her notice, suggests the tempting self-isolation of royalty, and her frustration at Mrs. Elton's usurping her function as "'queen of the evening'" (IV:329) at the Crown is much too pronounced.
>
> (Paul H. Fry, "Georgic Comedy: The Fictive Territory of Jane Austen's
> *Emma*," *Studies in the Novel*, vol. 11, no. 2 [summer 1979])

One can agree with the learned Paul Fry and still enjoy his own ambivalence in that judgment. Like the rest of us, Fry very nearly falls in love with Emma:

> "If you were as much guided by nature in your estimate of men and women," says Mr. Knightley to Emma, "and as little under the power of fancy and whim in your dealings with them, as you are where these children are concerned, we might always think alike" (IV:98–99). Emma thinks, again, like a very bright and autocratic child. Readers have puzzled over Jane Austen's fondness for a heroine "whom no one but myself will very much like." But if we see that even Emma's most disagreeable blunders stem from a single remediable flaw—imaginism in an empty space not wholly self-created, mind without object—then we can see that the remedy awaiting Emma, her discovery of clear-sightedness through the embrace of Experience in the person of Mr. Knightley, is not at all an arbitrary or miraculous conversion.

That admirable observation yields to Jane Austen's own redemption of the charming Emma. Still more subtle is Fry's apprehension of Austen's own ambivalence:

Like her ethics and her politics, Jane Austen's territory is determinate and fixed. Being quite aware that it is potentially stultifying, she is ambivalent about any comic dance that remains disagreeably "'a crowd in a little room'" (IV:249). Without the fresh air and "grown-up health" (IV:39; re Emma) of the "home-farm of Donwell," and without "the beauty of truth and sincerity" made available to Emma as an acceptably open vista, the absence of Prospect, of the invigorating scope even of mystery and exile, is a depressing condition which the passage of time, in the land of nonfiction, could only worsen. Georgic marriage, with its "perfect happiness," is a generic solution, an artifice, but unlike the topographically and morally displaced unions of Romance, it finds near at hand, in "English culture," a familiar and attractive mirror of itself. The unsituated "Garden of England" is transformed by Jane Austen to a *rus conclusus,* an enclosed farmland ample enough in range to unite adjoining parishes, but firmly immured against outlying fictions.

To be "firmly immured against outlying fictions" is part of Austen's triumph and yet remains a touch disquieting. It was not until she composed *Persuasion* that she fully met the challenge of the Age of Wordsworth, and of its intricate dialectics of memory, resolution, and a reopening to Romance. *Persuasion,* like the greatest Wordsworth, is almost a renaissance of the Renaissance, a return to Shakespearean capaciousness, sorrow, and the ending of sorrow.

CHAPTER 6

Persuasion (1817)

JANE AUSTEN

P ERSUASION" IS A WORD derived from the Latin for "advising" or "urging," for recommending that it is good to perform or not perform a particular action. The word goes back to a root meaning "sweet" or "pleasant," so that the good of performance or nonperformance has a tang of taste rather than of moral judgment about it. Jane Austen chose it as the title for her last completed novel. As a title, it recalls *Sense and Sensibility* or *Pride and Prejudice* rather than *Emma* or *Mansfield Park.* We are given not the name of a person or house and estate, but of an abstraction, a single one in this case. The title's primary reference is to the persuasion of its heroine, Anne Elliot, at the age of nineteen, by her godmother, Lady Russell, not to marry Captain Frederick Wentworth, a young naval officer. This was, as it turns out, very bad advice, and, after eight years, it is mended by Anne and Captain Wentworth. As with all of Austen's ironic comedies, matters end happily for the heroine. And yet each time I finish a rereading of this perfect novel, I feel very sad.

This does not appear to be my personal vagary; when I ask my friends and students about their experience of the book, they frequently mention a sadness which they also associate with *Persuasion,* more even than with *Mansfield Park.* Anne Elliot, a quietly eloquent being, is a self-reliant character, in no way forlorn, and her sense of self never falters. It is not *her* sadness we feel as we conclude the book: it is the novel's somberness that impresses us. The sadness enriches what I would call the novel's canonical persuasiveness, its way of showing us its aesthetic distinction.

Persuasion is among novels what Anne Elliot is among novelistic characters—a strong but subdued outrider. The book and the character are not colorful or vivacious; Elizabeth Bennet of *Pride and Prejudice* and Emma Woodhouse of *Emma* have a verve to them that initially seems lacking in Anne Elliot, which may be what Austen meant when she said that Anne was "almost too good for me." Anne is really almost too subtle for us, though not for Wentworth, who has something of an occult wavelength to her. Juliet McMaster notes "the kind of oblique communication that constantly goes on between Anne Elliot and Captain Wentworth, where, though they seldom speak to each other, each constantly understands the full import of the other's speech better than their interlocutors do."

That kind of communication in *Persuasion* depends upon deep "affection," a word that Austen values over "love." "Affection" between woman and man, in Austen, is the more profound and lasting emotion. I think it is not too much to say that Anne Elliot, though subdued, is the creation for whom Austen herself must have felt the most affection, because she lavished her own gifts upon Anne. Henry James insisted that the novelist must possess a sensibility upon which absolutely nothing is lost; by that test (clearly a limited one), only Austen, George Eliot, and James himself, among all those writing in English, would join Stendhal, Flaubert, and Tolstoy in a rather restricted pantheon. Anne Elliot may well be the one character in all of prose fiction upon whom nothing is lost, though she is in no danger of turning into a novelist.

The aesthetic dangers attendant upon such a paragon are palpable: how does a novelist make such a character persuasive? Poldy, in Joyce's *Ulysses,* is overwhelmingly persuasive because he is so complete a person, which was the largest of Joyce's intentions. Austen's ironic mode does not sanction the representation of completeness: we do not accompany her characters to the bedroom, the kitchen, the privy. What Austen parodies in *Sense and Sensibility* she raises to an apotheosis in *Persuasion:* the sublimity of a particular, inwardly isolated sensibility. Anne Elliot is hardly the only figure in Austen who has an understanding heart. Her difference is in her almost preternatural acuteness of perception of others and of the self, which are surely the qualities that most distinguish Austen as a novelist. Anne Elliot is to Austen's work what Rosalind of *As You Like It* is to Shakespeare's: the character who almost reaches the mastery of perspective that can be available to the novelist or playwright, lest all dramatic quality be lost from the novel or play.

More even than Hamlet or Falstaff, or than Elizabeth Bennet, or than Fanny Price in *Mansfield Park*, Rosalind and Anne Elliot are almost completely poised, nearly able to see all around the play and the novel. Their poise cannot transcend perspectivizing completely, but Rosalind's wit and Anne's sensibility, both balanced and free of either excessive aggressivity or defensiveness, enable them to share more of their creators' poise than we ever come to do.

Austen never loses dramatic intensity; we share Anne's anxiety concerning Wentworth's renewed intentions until the novel's conclusion. But we rely upon Anne as we should rely upon Rosalind; critics would see the rancidity of Touchstone as clearly as they see the vanity of Jaques if they placed more confidence in Rosalind's reactions to everyone else in the play, as well as to herself. Anne Elliot's reactions have the same winning authority; we must try to give the weight to her words that is not extended by the other persons in the novel, except for Wentworth.

Even the reader must fall into the initial error of undervaluing Anne Elliot. The wit of Elizabeth Bennet or of Rosalind is easier to appreciate than Anne Elliot's accurate sensibility. The secret of her character combines Austenian irony with a Wordsworthian sense of deferred hope. Austen has a good measure of Shakespeare's unmatched ability to give us persons, both major and minor, who are all utterly consistent in their separate modes of speech, and yet completely different from one another. Anne Elliot is the last of Austen's heroines of what I think we must call the Protestant will, but in her the will is modified, perhaps perfected, by its descendant, the Romantic sympathetic imagination, of which Wordsworth was the prophet. That is what helps to make Anne so complex and sensitive a character.

Jane Austen's earlier heroines, of whom Elizabeth Bennet is the exemplar, manifested the Protestant will as direct descendants of

Samuel Richardson's Clarissa Harlowe, with Samuel Johnson hovering nearby as moral authority. Marxist criticism inevitably views the Protestant will, even in its literary manifestations, as a mercantile matter, and it has become fashionable to talk about the socioeconomic realities that Jane Austen excludes, such as the West Indian slavery that is part of the ultimate basis for the financial security most of her characters enjoy. But all achieved literary works are founded upon exclusions, and no one has demonstrated that increased consciousness of the relation between culture and imperialism is of the slightest benefit whatsoever in learning to read *Mansfield Park*. *Persuasion* ends with a tribute to the British navy, and with Wentworth on land, gently appreciating the joys of affection with Anne Elliot. But once again, Austen's is a great art founded upon exclusions, and the sordid realities of British sea power are no more relevant to *Persuasion* than West Indian bondage is to *Mansfield Park*. Austen was, however, immensely interested in the pragmatic and secular consequences of the Protestant will, and they seem to me a crucial element in helping us appreciate the heroines of her novels.

Austen's Shakespearean inwardness, culminating in Anne Elliot, revises the moral intensities of Clarissa Harlowe's secularized Protestant martyrdom, her slow dying after being raped by Lovelace. What removes Clarissa's will to live is her stronger will to maintain the integrity of her being. To yield to the repentant Lovelace by marrying him would compromise the essence of her being, the exaltation of her violated will. What is tragedy in *Clarissa* is converted by Austen into ironic comedy, but the will's drive to maintain itself scarcely alters in this conversion. In *Persuasion* the emphasis is on a willed exchange of esteems, where both the woman and the man estimate the value of the other to be high. Obviously, outward considerations of wealth, property, and social standing are crucial elements here, but so are the inward considerations of common sense, amiability, culture, wit, and affection.

Austen's major heroines—Elizabeth, Emma, Fanny, and Anne—possess such inward freedom that their individualities cannot be repressed. Austen's art as a novelist is not to worry much about the socioeconomic genesis of that inner freedom, though the anxiety level does rise in *Mansfield Park* and *Persuasion*. In Austen, irony becomes the instrument for invention, which Dr. Johnson defined as the essence of poetry. A conception of inward freedom that centers upon a refusal to accept esteem except from one upon whom one has conferred esteem, is a conception of the highest degree of irony. The supreme comic scene in all of Austen might be Elizabeth's rejection of Darcy's first marriage proposal, where the ironies of the dialectic of will and esteem become very nearly outrageous. That high comedy, which continued in *Emma,* is somewhat chastened in *Mansfield Park,* and then becomes something else, unmistakable but difficult to name, in *Persuasion,* where Austen has become so conscious a master that she seems to have changed the nature of willing, as though it, too, could be persuaded to become a rarer, more disinterested act of the self.

No one has suggested that Jane Austen becomes a High Romantic in *Persuasion;* her poet remained William Cowper, not Wordsworth, and her favorite prose writer was always Dr. Johnson. But her severe distrust of imagination and of "romantic love," so prevalent in the earlier novels, is not a factor in *Persuasion.* Anne and Wentworth maintain their affection for each other throughout eight years of hopeless separation, and each has the power of imagination to conceive of a triumphant reconciliation. This is the material for a romance, not for an ironical novel. The ironies of *Persuasion* are frequently pungent, but they are almost never directed at Anne Elliot and only rarely at Captain Wentworth.

There is a difficult relation between Austen's repression of her characteristic irony about her protagonists and a certain previously unheard plangency that hovers throughout *Persuasion.* Despite Anne's faith in herself, she is very vulnerable to the anxiety, which she never allows herself to express, of an unlived life, in which the potential loss transcends yet includes sexual unfulfillment. I can recall only one critic, the Australian Ann Molan, who emphasizes what Austen strongly implies: "Anne...is a passionate woman. And against her will, her heart keeps asserting its demand for fulfillment." Since Anne had refused Wentworth her esteem eight years before, she feels a necessity to withhold her will, and thus becomes the first Austen heroine whose will and imagination are antithetical.

There is no civil war within Anne Elliot's psyche, or within Austen's; but there is the emergent sadness of a schism in the self, with memory taking the side of imagination in an alliance against the will. The almost Wordsworthian power of memory in both Anne and Wentworth has been noted by Gene Ruoff. Since Austen was anything but an accidental novelist, we might ask why she chose to found *Persuasion* upon a mutual nostalgia. After all, the rejected Wentworth is even less inclined to will a renewed affection than Anne is, and yet the fusion of memory and imagination triumphs over his will also. Was this a relaxation of the will in Jane Austen herself? Since she returns to her earlier mode in *Sanditon*, her unfinished novel begun after *Persuasion* was completed, it may be that the story of Anne Elliot was an excursion or indulgence for the novelist. The parallels between Wordsworth and *Persuasion* are limited but real. High Romantic novels in England, whether of a Byronic kind like *Jane Eyre* and *Wuthering Heights* or of a Wordsworthian sort like *Adam Bede*, are a distinctly later development. The ethos of the Austen heroine does not change in *Persuasion*, but she is certainly a more problematic being, tinged with a new sadness concerning life's limits. It may be that the elegant pathos *Persuasion* sometimes courts has a connection to Jane Austen's own ill health, her intimations of her early death.

Stuart Tave, comparing Wordsworth and Austen, shrewdly noted that both were "poets of marriage" and both also possessed "a sense of duty understood and deeply felt by those who see the integrity and peace of their own lives as essentially bound to the lives of others and see their lives of all in a more than merely social order." Expanding Tave's insight, Susan Morgan pointed to the particular affinity between Austen's *Emma* and Wordsworth's great "Ode: Intimations of Immortality from Recollections of Early Childhood." The growth of the individual consciousness, involving both gain and loss for Wordsworth but only gain for Austen, is the shared subject. Emma's consciousness certainly does develop, and she undergoes a quasi-Wordsworthian transformation from the pleasure of near solipsism to the more difficult pleasures of sympathy for others. Anne Elliot, far more mature from the beginning, scarcely needs to grow in consciousness. Her long-lamented rejection of Wentworth insulates her against the destructiveness of hope. Instead of hope, there is a complex of emotions, expressed by Austen with her customary skill:

> How eloquent could Anne Elliot have been,—how eloquent, at least, were her wishes on the side of early warm attachment, and a cheerful confidence in futurity, against that over-

anxious caution which seems to insult exertion and distrust Providence!—She had been forced into prudence in her youth, she learned romance as she grew older—the natural sequel of an unnatural beginning.

Here learning romance is wholly retrospective; Anne no longer regards it as being available to her. And, indeed, Wentworth returns, still resentful after eight years, and reflects that Anne's power with him is gone forever. The qualities of decision and confidence that make him a superb naval commander are precisely what he condemns her for lacking. With almost too meticulous a craft, Austen traces his gradual retreat from this position, as the power of memory increases its dominance over him and as he learns that his jilted sense of her as being unable to act is quite mistaken. It is a beautiful irony that he needs to undergo a process of self-persuasion while Anne waits, without even knowing that she is waiting or that there is anything that could rekindle her hope. The comedy of this is gently sad, as the reader waits also, reflecting upon how large a part contingency plays in the matter.

While the pre-Socratics and Freud agree that there are no accidents, Austen thinks differently. Character is fate for her also, but fate, once activated, tends to evade character in so overdetermined a social context as Austen's world. In rereading *Persuasion,* though I remember the happy conclusion, I nevertheless feel anxiety as Wentworth and Anne circle away from each other in spite of themselves. The reader is not totally persuaded of a satisfactory interview until Anne reads Wentworth's quite agonized letter to her:

"I can listen no longer in silence. I must speak to you by such means as are within my reach. You pierce my soul. I am half agony, half hope. Tell me not that I am too late, that such precious feelings are gone for ever. I offer myself to you again with a heart even more your own, than when you almost broke it eight years and a half ago. Dare not say that man forgets sooner than woman, that his love has an earlier death. I have loved none but you. Unjust I may have been, weak and resentful I have been, but never inconstant. You alone have brought me to Bath. For you alone I think and plan.—Have you not seen this? Can you fail to have understood my wishes?—I had not waited even these ten days, could I have read your feelings, as I think you must have penetrated mine. I can hardly write. I am every instant hearing something which overpowers me. You sink your voice, but I can distinguish the tones of that voice, when they would be lost on others.—Too good, too excellent creature! You do us justice indeed. You do believe that there is true attachment and constancy among men. Believe it to be most fervent, most undeviating, in F.W.

"I must go, uncertain of my fate; but I shall return hither, or follow your party, as soon as possible. A word, a look will be enough to decide whether I enter your father's house this evening, or never."

I cannot imagine such a letter in *Pride and Prejudice,* or even in *Emma* or *Mansfield Park.* The perceptive reader might have realized how passionate Anne was, almost from the start of the novel, but until this there was no indication of equal passion in Wentworth. His letter, as befits a naval commander, is badly written and not exactly Austenian, but is all the more effective thereby. We come to realize that we have believed in him until now only because Anne's love for him provokes our interest. Austen wisely has declined to make him interesting enough on his own. Yet part of the book's effect is to persuade the reader of the reader's own powers of discernment and self-persuasion; Anne Elliot is almost too good for the reader, as she is for Austen herself, but the attentive reader gains the confidence to perceive Anne as she should be perceived. The subtlest element in this subtlest of novels is the call upon the reader's own power of memory to match the persistence and intensity of the yearning that Anne Elliot is too stoical to express directly.

The yearning hovers throughout the book, coloring Anne's perceptions and our own. Our sense of Anne's existence becomes identified with our own consciousness of lost love, however fictive or idealized that may be. There is an improbability in the successful renewal of a relationship devastated eight years before which ought to work against the texture of this most "realistic" of Austen's novels, but she is very careful to see that it does not. Like the author, the reader becomes persuaded to wish for Anne what she still wishes for herself. Ann Molan has the fine observation that Austen "is most satisfied with Anne when Anne is most dissatisfied with herself." The reader is carried along with Austen, and gradually Anne is also persuaded and catches up with the reader, allowing her yearning a fuller expression.

Dr. Johnson, in *The Rambler,* Number 29, on "The Folly of Anticipating Misfortunes," warned against anxious expectations of any kind, whether fearful or hopeful:

> because the objects both of fear and hope are yet uncertain, so we ought not to trust the representations of one more than the other, because they are both equally fallacious; as hope enlarges happiness, fear aggravates calamity. It is generally allowed, that no man ever found the happiness of possession proportionate to that expectation which incited his desire, and invigorated his pursuit; nor has any man found the evils of life so formidable in reality, as they were described to him by his own imagination.

This is one of a series of Johnsonian pronouncements against the dangerous prevalence of the imagination, some of which his disciple Austen had certainly read. If you excluded such representations, on the great critic's advice, then Wordsworth could not have written at all, and Austen could not have written *Persuasion.* Yet it was a very strange book for her to write, this master of the highest art of exclusion that we have known in the Western novel. Any novel by Jane Austen could be called an achieved ellipsis, with everything omitted that could disturb her ironic though happy conclusions. *Persuasion* remains the least popular of her four canonical novels because it is the strangest. Poised as she is at the final border of the Age of Sensibility, she shares with Wordsworth an art dependent upon a split between a waning Protestant will and a newly active sympathetic imagination, with memory assigned the labor of healing the divide.

CHAPTER 7

I Promessi Sposi (The Betrothed) (1827, 1840)

ALESSANDRO MANZONI

A NYONE WHO HAS LIVED in Italy for protracted stays will encounter the aura of Alessandro Manzoni. Though he wrote only a single novel, *The Betrothed: A Tale of XVII Century Milan,* and a few memorable poems, he is for literate Italians a cultural titan akin to Dante, Verdi, Leopardi, Ungaretti.

When Alessandro Manzoni died at the age of eighty-eight on May 22, 1873, Italy observed a day of mourning. In the United States, it is inconceivable that there should have been a day of mourning for Walt Whitman or Herman Melville, to this moment our most enduring writers. Manzoni is hardly of Dante's eminence, but, then, who is, except for Shakespeare, Cervantes, and Montaigne? Yet in Italy, where alas so few now read Dante, Manzoni still finds an audience.

Though he sets *The Betrothed* in the seventeenth century, Manzoni writes for his own era of romanticized Christianity and for what he hoped would be the future. He found his desired precursors in Virgil and in Dante, but actually he could not have composed his novel without the example and procedures of Sir Walter Scott. His essay *On the Historical Novel,* on which Manzoni labored from 1828 to 1850, was an apologia for his novel, which he kept revising until 1840. He never mentions *The Betrothed* but relies implicitly on his readers to know his hidden theme: can the historical novel survive?

A great poet and a great historian may be found in the same man without creating confusion, but not in the same work. In fact, the two opposite criticisms that furnished the lines of argument for the trial of the historical novel had already showed up in the first moments of the genre and at the height of its popularity, like germs of an eventually mortal illness in a healthy-looking baby.

And is the historical novel still popular? Is there the same desire to write historical novels and the same desire to read those that are already written? I don't know, but I can not help imagining that, if this essay had come out some thirty years ago, when the world was eagerly awaiting and avidly devouring the novels of Walter Scott, it would have seemed eccentric and brash in its treatment of the historical novel. Nor can I help imagining that, if anyone now were willing to trouble himself enough to call it these names, it would be for an altogether different reason. And thirty years ought to be no time at all for a genre of art that was destined to live on.

(trans. Sandra Bermann)

I remember pondering this matter in 1984, when I reviewed Gore Vidal's *Lincoln* and judged it to be something close to a legitimate revival of the historical novel. Years later, I visited Vidal and his partner near Rome and enjoyed his reaction to Manzoni and to Calvino. It seems likely that Manzoni was an accurate prophet; even the most talented historical novels now seem tainted by a lack of freshness whenever they appear.

Manzoni's *The Betrothed*, as I reread it, does not seem like a historical novel. The man is the book. What comes through on every page is the warmth, Christian compassion, wry humor, and gentle yet surprising strength to deal vividly with horrors like the plague, famine, riots, random violence, and the painful separation of the young peasant lovers Lucia and Renzo, who are menaced by the dreadful Don Rodrigo, a Spanish nobleman who lusts after Lucia and who has frightened the parish priest Don Abbondio into refusing to perform the marriage of the betrothed couple.

Don Abbondio is a comic weakling, unique in this novel because all the rest of the clergy are wise, benign, and even heroic. Sometimes I think that the most surprising achievement of Manzoni is to overcome my skepticism in this regard. The Capuchin monk Fra Cristoforo is superbly heroic as he confronts Don Rodrigo:

'Well, advise her to come and put herself under my protection. She'll have everything she wants, and no one'll dare molest her, or I'm no gentleman.'

At this suggestion the friar's indignation, which he had held in check with difficulty till then, burst out. All his resolutions of prudence and patience went to the winds; his old self joined up with the new: in such cases, in fact, Fra Cristoforo really had the energy of two men.

'Your protection!' exclaimed he, recoiling a couple of paces, leaning proudly on his right foot, putting his right hand to his hip, pointing the other with outstretched forefinger towards Don Rodrigo, and fixing on him a pair of blazing eyes—'your protection! It's a good thing you said that; it's a good thing you made such a suggestion. You've gone over the limit: and I'm not afraid of you any more.'

'How dare you talk to me like that, friar!'

'I'm talking as one talks to one abandoned by God, who cannot frighten any longer. Your protection! I well knew that innocent girl was under God's protection; but you—you've filled me with such a certainty of it now that I no longer need to take care what I say to you. Lucia, I say—see how I pronounce her name with head high and steady eyes.'

'What! In this house...!'

'I pity this house. A curse hangs over it. You will see if the justice of God can be kept out by a few stones, or frightened off by a pair of sentries. You think God made a creature in His own image in order to give you the pleasure of tormenting her! You think God won't be able to defend her! You've spurned His warning. You are judged for it! Pharaoh's heart was as hard as yours, and God found a way to crush it. Lucia is safe from you; I—a poor friar—I tell you that; and as for yourself, listen to what I foretell for you. A day will come...'

Up to now Don Rodrigo had been standing rooted there, speechless with rage and amazement; but when he heard this beginning of a prophecy being intoned, a vague, mysterious dread was added to his rage.

Quickly he seized that lifted, threatening hand, and, raising his voice to drown that of this prophet of ill-omen, shouted: 'Get out of my sight, you impudent peasant, you lout in a cowl.'

Don Rodrigo, though more than nasty enough, is dwarfed by the book's grand villain, known only as the Unnamed. He is based upon an actual historical monster, Francesco Bernardino Visconti, a scion of the Dukes of Milan, famous for being converted from iniquity to goodness by the benevolent Cardinal Federigo Borromeo, Manzoni's authentic hero. Until that transformation, the Unnamed is all but hilariously wicked:

The fame of our tyrant, however, had long been diffused throughout the whole of the Milanese provinces. Everywhere his life was a subject for popular tales, and his name bore with it the idea of something compelling, strange, and fabulous. The suspicion that he had his agents and hired assassins everywhere also contributed to keeping his memory alive everywhere. These were only suspicions—for who would openly avow such a dependence? —but every petty tyrant might be his colleague, every little malefactor one of his men. And this very uncertainty made the conception of it vaster, and the fear of it deeper. Whenever a set of unknown and unusually savage-looking bravoes put in an appearance anywhere, whenever some appalling crime was committed whose author could not be pointed out or guessed at once, people muttered the name of the man whom, thanks to that blessed circumspection of our authorities, we shall be constrained to call the Unnamed.

Any plot summary of *The Betrothed* can sound quite silly, since the melodramatic elements can make one wince a bit. Still, menace and the horror of the plague work to redeem the *Perils of Pauline* aspects of the novel. Poor Lucia suffers intensely mental and moral anguish, to the point where she promises the Virgin Mary that she will renounce marriage to Renzo or anyone else if the divine powers rescue her from the well-known fate worse than death, rape by Don

Rodrigo. It will take Fra Cristoforo to persuade her that God and the Virgin Mother want her to marry Renzo.

Rereading *The Betrothed,* I enjoy myself greatly despite my lack of interest in Catholic piety. Manzoni is able to touch the universal because of the primordial strength of his character and personality, and his considerable ability to play with an assortment of narrative voices throughout his masterwork. Though everything ends as it should, with Lucia and Renzo happily married with many children, Don Rodrigo miserably dead from the plague, the Unnamed a patron of the poor, Fra Cristoforo a living martyr to the victims of the plague, and Manzoni a voice that comforts and elevates the reader, something is still lacking. Perhaps the Italian original, a language experiment in the Tuscan vernacular, loses too much even in the eloquent translation of Archibald Colquhoun, who also wrote a very useful study, *Manzoni and His Times* (1954).

I find that my reservations sadden me, since Manzoni has given me so much pleasure. One cannot ask every novel to be *Don Quixote* or *Clarissa* or *In Search of Lost Time. The Betrothed* finds its place in a group that includes the best of Sir Walter Scott, such as *The Heart of Midlothian,* Joseph Conrad's *Nostromo,* and Fielding's *Tom Jones.* That is an illustrious galaxy but not quite *Les Misérables* or *War and Peace.*

CHAPTER 8

The Red and the Black (1830)

STENDHAL

S TENDHAL, a pseudonym for Marie-Henri Beyle, died in Paris in
1842 at the age of fifty-nine. His death was caused by the absurd
treatments for syphilis, a disease he had suffered for some time. Few
major novelists have had a personality so winsome as Stendhal's. His
vision of life is rather like a masked ball or a carnival performance.
His torrent of letters are playful, wistful, and frequently a study in
erotic nostalgia.

Paul Valéry, the major French poet and person-of-letters of the
twentieth century, praised Stendhal for his gift of liveliness. That
seems to me the first accomplishment of Stendhal, whose wit was
endless and infectious, a gift given to "the happy few," as he characterized his ideal readers.

I love Valéry's observation that Stendhal makes the reader proud
to be his reader. The heart of Stendhal is in Valéry's reflection that
his favorite novelist felt the spur of literary vanity but more deeply
an absolute pride that knew it had to depend on nothing but itself.

Valéry's final judgment is that Stendhal was so radically himself
that he could not be reduced to a writer.

Still, I know Stendhal primarily as a novelist. His strongest work
to me is the unfinished *Lucien Leuwen,* yet it is too fragmentary
for the common reader. The perpetual popularity of *The Red and*

the Black and *The Charterhouse of Parma* is more than deserved. I myself vacillate between the two, since Julien Sorel is a richer character than anyone in *The Charterhouse* yet the liveliness of Stendhal's Italy is a relief after his occluded France.

Despite all ironies, I find it difficult not to see Julien Sorel as Stendhal's surrogate. Julien's imagination is Stendhal's, which is to say that it is Napoleonic and Byronic. Whether Stendhal is a Shakespearean writer is open to dispute. Julien is hardly a Shakespearean protagonist, yet the narrator is. Stendhal gives Julien the uncanny ability to turn his erotic preferences on or off by acts of will. At the novel's close, a transfigured Julien is again fiercely in love with Madame De Rênal and all but indifferent to Mathilde de La Mole, except insofar as she carries what he trusts will be their son. We never will find out the gender of the baby or whether Mathilde will or will not marry again. What we confront at the end is a suicidal Julien. You can regard his attitude as resignation, but there is a troubling element of pathology. Even an attractive craziness remains madness, a sad fate for the energetic, vital, and ambitious Julien Sorel.

Like Cervantes, Stendhal is most himself as *Homo Ludens,* to cite the great book of 1938 by Johan Huizinga, a profound study of the play element in the arts and in history. Reading Huizinga, I arrive at the formula: all is play except in games. How much of the quixotic element remains in Julien Sorel?

Stendhal's own erotic career was rather vexed. His mother died when he was seven. His relations with his father were hostile. At twenty-one, he lived in Marseilles with the actress Mélanie Guilbert, but by 1806 he had taken up a post as a Napoleonic *intendant* in Brunswick. When in the army in 1800 in Milan, he had fallen in love with Angelina Pietragrua, who became his mistress eleven years later, on his return to Milan. Yet the major attachment of his life began in 1818, when he fell in love with Matilde Viscontini Dembowska, who totally rejected him. He never married, and went from debacle to debacle. In 1824, there was a love affair with Comtesse Clémentine Curial, but she broke with him three years later. In 1829, he tried again, this time with Alberthe de Rubempre, but it proved ephemeral. Finally, he proposed marriage to Giulia Rinieri. Though he was refused by her guardian, eight years later he became involved with her, but the relationship waned. By 1841, he was sustained mostly by his two dogs and perhaps had another failed affair. Weakened by syphilis and the peculiar remedies then used for it, he died in 1842.

As a theorist of Eros, Stendhal was a master, though clearly not very pragmatic in his quest for it. His transcendent wit and sense of delight kept him going in life as in art. I have been rereading *The Red and the Black,* first in the original and also in the useful translation by Roger Gard, for some weeks now and cannot seem to get weary of it. Sometimes I put it down and come back to it a few days later. I find myself wondering why I am so held by it.

The novel began as a tale called "Julien," based on one Antoine Berthet, who shot a Madame Michoud de la Tour and was guillotined. I recall reprinting a strong essay by Carol A. Mossman in a volume I edited on *The Red and the Black* in 1988. Ms. Mossman articulates the various strands that come together in what could be called Julien's novel and also Mathilde's novel. When he triumphs over Mathilde, Julien prematurely says that his novel is completed. Mathilde models herself upon Marguerite de Valois, heroine of a Dumas novel, and historically the daughter of Catherine de' Medici, who ruled France through her sons until the line came to an end. Henry of Navarre, first of the Bourbon kings as Henry IV, married Marguerite de Valois, a political match marked by friendship but little passion. Queen Marguerite had many lovers, among them Joseph Boniface Hyacinth, Lord La Mole. A Huguenot, the audacious La Mole was beheaded after he joined in a plot to free Henry of Navarre. The legend is that Marguerite caused La Mole's head to be embalmed and kept afterward in a casket bedecked by jewels. Mathilde's novel, and Stendhal's, concludes:

—I want to see him, she said.

Fouqué had the resolution neither to speak nor to rise. He pointed with his finger at a large blue cloak on the floorboards; in that was wrapped what remained of Julien.

She threw herself on her knees. The memory of Boniface de La Mole and Marguerite de Navarre inspired her, no doubt, with superhuman resolve. Her trembling hands opened the cloak. Fouqué turned away his eyes.

He heard Mathilde walking about rapidly in the room. She

lit a large number of candles. When Fouqué summoned up the strength to look at her, she had placed Julien's head on a little marble table in front of her, and was kissing its brow…

Mathilde followed her lover to the tomb he had chosen. A large band of priests escorted the bier and, unknown to all, alone in her veiled carriage, she carried on her knees the head of the man she had so dearly loved.

Coming in this way almost to the summit of one of the highest mountains in the Jura, in the depths of the night, and in that little cave now magnificently lit up by innumerable tapers, twenty priests celebrated the service for the dead. All the inhabitants of the little mountain villages that the convoy had crossed followed it, attracted by the singularity of this strange rite.

Mathilde appeared in the midst of them in long mourning robes and, at the end of the service, had many thousand five-franc pieces scattered in the crowd.

Left alone with Fouqué, she insisted on burying her lover's head with her own hands. Fouqué narrowly avoided losing his mind with grief.

By Mathilde's agency this wild cavern was decorated with marble carvings sculpted in Italy at great expense.

Mme de Rênal was faithful to her promise. In no way did she seek to take her own life; but three days after Julien, she died, her children in her arms.

The End

To The Happy Few

Stendhal takes a throwaway attitude toward endings. Madame de Rênal is too pious for suicide. We are not told what kills her after three days. Unless she had expected a resurrected Julien, it is rather difficult to see anyone dying of grief alone. Mathilde, crazier even than Julien, perhaps finds comfort in acting the part of Queen Marguerite of Navarre. Carol Mossman shrewdly retraces Stendhal's web that weaves together the Roman Emperor Julian the Apostate, Saint John the Baptist, Napoleon, and the dancer Salome, who kisses and lustfully caresses the severed head of John after it has been brought to her on a silver platter.

And what of Julien Sorel? How is he when Stendhal takes him away from us? He is and he is not admirable. Toward Mathilde he is dreadful. Having gone through so much for him, she is made to feel like an intruder. He scarcely bothers to pretend any love for her. But toward Madame de Rênal, whose murder he has attempted, he mounts to an ecstasy of love beyond anything he has ever known, and in which she fully shares. Except for dramatic irony, Stendhal's stance eschews sardonicism.

Why does Julien choose death? He passes judgment on himself, on society, on Christianity, and on Stendhal's novel that denies him any other exit. A book that has been comedy cannot accommodate a tragic conclusion. It is impossible not to like Stendhal. It is very difficult to have any affection for Julien, or indeed for anyone else in the novel. Perhaps it is simply that the myth of Napoleon, still so potent for Stendhal, Balzac, Victor Hugo, has worn itself out. Without Napoleon, no Julien Sorel.

Surmise is rather baffled by Stendhal's aversion to completion. I am persuaded that he loves Julien Sorel almost as much as Cervantes loved Don Quixote. The Sorrowful Knight graciously ends because he accepts defeat. I do not think that Julien Sorel has been defeated, though he chooses to end graciously anyway. Consider how far Julien has come in the course of the novel. He has achieved the love of two remarkable women, whatever their limitations or his. He has come within a notch of triumphing over his origins, in a society that despises peasants who seek to rise into the world of aristocrats.

Stendhal endows Julien with almost all that nature can give. He is very handsome, courageous, capable of intellectual brilliance, a leader, not a follower, yet motherless, pragmatically unfathered. Even at the close he has only sporadic moments of dark inertia. He eddies between lucidity and passion, as does his creator, Stendhal.

Julien is saved (in a purely secular way) by his capacity for deep feeling. Despite all the hypocrisies forced upon him by his situation, his quest is for love and for the spirit's freedom.

CHAPTER 9

The Charterhouse of Parma (1839)

STENDHAL

T HOUGH STENDHAL CALLED this a short novel, it is quite substantial, in length as in design. And yet he wrote it in less than two months, in late 1838. It is set in the north of Italy, his favorite region, in the aftermath of Napoleon, his sometime hero. Stendhal had a fantasy that he was half Italian and hints that Fabrizio del Dongo, the delightful male protagonist and nephew-by-marriage of the marvelous Duchess Gina Sanseverina, who is in love with him, was the illegitimate son of Lieutenant Robert, who turns up later in the novel on the battlefield of Waterloo. When he reappears, he is General Count d'A*** Robert, whom Fabrizio has no way of recognizing, yet, as Stendhal remarks, "How happy he would have been to find Fabrizio del Dongo!" With Stendhalian irony, the father steals the son's horse.

Fabrizio's experience of Waterloo is a famous set-piece. He fights on the side of the French, sees and hears cannon fire and gunfire and even, at a distance, the Emperor Napoleon, though by then the young Italian nobleman is so high on brandy he cannot be sure what he sees. The French army breaks up, and the victorious Prussian cavalry causes such hysteria in the ranks that poor Fabrizio, obeying orders, is severely wounded by French deserters. The noble scamp finds his way back home eventually, and Stendhal charges on.

Stendhal, a lover of Shakespeare, composes his own version of *Romeo and Juliet* in *The Charterhouse of Parma*. Fabrizio is an improvement upon Romeo, but no one could improve upon Juliet, who is one of Shakespeare's triumphs. The Juliet of Fabrizio is the pious Clelia, whom I find rather colorless and hardly worthy of the Stendhalian gusto. However, like all readers, I am fascinated by the magnificent Gina del Dongo, who is a young widow, fifteen years older than Fabrizio, and is known under the name of Gina Pietranera, the Duchess Sanseverina. Gina is totally in love with her nephew by marriage, and so there is no incest barrier, but Fabrizio, who will become a high dignitary of the Church, is very wary of any actual consummation with his aunt, though they come close. He is not in love with her, though he regards her more highly than anyone else alive.

Count Mosca, who is in his later middle age, is fiercely in love with Gina, but her motto is: If Fabrizio is not happy, then I cannot be happy. An amiable Machiavel, Mosca shuttles in and out as first minister to the Princes of Parma, initially to the despotic father and then to the twenty-two-year-old son, when he comes into power. The older Prince of Parma lusts after Gina, to no effect, and the younger one lusts even more fiercely and at last, to the great detriment of his court, which is lifeless without the Sanseverina, enjoys her very briefly. Chagrined, the high-minded Duchess sacrifices herself to save Fabrizio's life, and then departs Parma for good.

The plot of *The Charterhouse of Parma* is a labyrinth of escapades, intrigues, sudden outbursts of violence, unexpected kindnesses, above all the passionate *sprezzatura,* the art of throwaway high-mindedness exemplified by the Sanseverina, Fabrizio, and the outlaw poet Ferrante Palla. If *The Charterhouse* has a fault, aside from Stendhal's slapdash weakness at endings, it would be the profusion of plot. Fabrizio is so impulsive that he cannot stop moving from place to place, woman to woman, duel to duel, scrape to scrape, wound to wound. Stendhal being Stendhal, Fabrizio will end as the pious, revered, and eloquent Archbishop of Parma.

The model for Fabrizio is the sixteenth-century Alessandro Farnese, the grandson of Pope Paul III and himself a cardinal and famous collector of the arts. His aunt Gina also seems to be more sixteenth than nineteenth century in her recklessness, lavish gener-

osity, and high sense of love and life. The sixteenth-century throw-
backs include the poet, bandit, and self-styled tribune of the people
Ferrante Palla, who is a medical doctor but has been outlawed and
forbidden to practice his profession since he is a radical rebel against
the regime that governs Parma, and is under sentence of death. Like
almost every other male in the novel, he is passionately in love with
Gina, though he has five children by a woman he has reft away from
her husband:

'But how do you survive?' asked the duchess, much moved.

'The children's mother spins. The oldest girl gets her board
at the farm of some liberal or other, where she watches over
the sheep. As for me, I hold people up along the road from
Piacenza to Genoa.'

'How do you reconcile robbery with your liberal principles?'

'I keep a note of the people I rob, and if ever I have anything,
I shall give them back the sums I've stolen. I adjudge that a
tribune of the people such as myself is performing a task which,
on account of the danger, is worth a good hundred francs a
month. So I'm very careful not to take more than twelve hundred francs a year. Actually, that's wrong, I steal a small amount
over and above that, because that way I can meet the costs of
getting my works printed.'

'What works?'

'...*will she ever have a room and a budget?*'

'What,' said the duchess, in astonishment, 'that's you, signore,
one of the greatest poets of the century, the famous Ferrante
Palla?'

'Famous perhaps, but very unfortunate, that's for sure.'

'And a man with your talent, signore, is obliged to steal in
order to live!'

'It's for that reason that I have some talent perhaps. Up until
now, all our authors who have become known were people
paid by the government or by the religion they were trying to
undermine. I, *primo*, risk my life; *secundo*, signora, imagine
the disturbing thoughts I have when I go out stealing! Am I in
the right? I ask myself. Does the position of tribune perform
a service truly worth a hundred francs a month? I have two

shirts, the coat that you see, a few poor weapons and I'm sure to finish by the rope. I dare to think I'm disinterested. I would be happy were it not for the fatal love which lets me find only unhappiness with the mother of my children. Poverty weighs on me, it's ugly. I love fine clothes, white hands...'

(trans. John Sturrock)

Before the novel concludes, Ferrante Palla has led an insurrection against the young Prince of Parma, after the death of the tyrannical father. The rebellion is financed by the Sanseverina, an act unknown to Count Mosca, who quells the uprising quite firmly with some necessary bloodshed. Ferrante Palla escapes and remarks later to the duchess that you cannot have a republic without republicans and that it will take a century to change Parma.

The whirligig goes on spinning for five hundred pages, one delight after another, only to end in sadness. Fabrizio, now the Archbishop of Parma and hopelessly in love with Clelia, who is married to someone else, insists that his son by her, the young child Sandrino, be abducted so as to unite him with his actual father. Everything goes wrong, as could be expected:

This abduction, very neatly carried out, had a most unhappy outcome. Having been installed secretly in a large and beautiful house where the marchesa came to see him almost every day, Sandrino died at the end of a few months. Clelia imagined that she had been struck by a just punishment for having been unfaithful to her vow to the Madonna. She had seen Fabrizio so often in the light, twice even in broad daylight, and with such transports of tenderness, during Sandrino's illness. She survived this beloved son for only a few months, but she had the comfort of dying in the arms of her lover.

Fabrizio was too much in love and too much of a believer to resort to suicide. He hoped to find Clelia again in a better world, but he was too intelligent not to feel that he had much to atone for.

Stendhal must have realized he did not know how to end anything. What kills Clelia? We are not told. Fabrizio, a totally sincere Christian, may believe in an afterlife, but few readers will agree that he needs to atone. Once Stendhal starts to end, he cannot stop himself:

> Countess Mosca had strongly approved, with time, that her husband should resume the ministry, but she had never been willing to return to the States of Ernest V. She held court in Vignano, a quarter league from Casal-Maggiore, on the left bank of the Po and consequently within the States of Austria. In the magnificent palazzo of Vignano, which the count had had built for her, she received the whole of Parma's high society every Thursday, and her numerous friends every day. Fabrizio would not fail to come to Vignano one day. In a word, the countess had conjoined all the appearances of happiness, but she survived Fabrizio for only a very short time, the Fabrizio whom she had adored and who spent only one year in his charterhouse.
>
> The prisons of Parma were empty, the count was immensely rich and Ernest V was adored by his subjects, who compared his government to that of the grand dukes of Tuscany.
>
> TO THE HAPPY FEW

The usual questions return. What kills Fabrizio? In turn, why does Gina, now married to Mosca, also depart so abruptly? Stendhal doesn't know, nor do we. We are not moved to rejoicing that Mosca is so wealthy; how does he feel about losing Gina? I am grateful to Stendhal but find myself wishing he had lived long enough to revise, following the suggestions of Balzac, who was intoxicated by *The Charterhouse of Parma*.

CHAPTER 10

The Vautrin Saga:

Old Goriot (1835), *Lost Illusions* (1837), The Splendor and Misery of the Courtesans (1838)

HONORÉ DE BALZAC

*T*HE HUMAN COMEDY OF BALZAC overflows with fabulous persons, all of them fiercely energetic and many of them daemonic, guided by a highly individual genius. I am not fully immersed in the maelstrom of Balzac, since I have read only twelve of the full-length novels and a handful of the stories. I am not therefore in a position to judge who in this storm of genius stands on an eminence far above the others. Still, I am obsessed by Vautrin, the master of the criminal world who at last changes into the head of the Paris police. His real name is Jacques Collin, and he also appears as Abbé Carlos Herrera, a supposed Spanish cleric. To the underworld and to the authorities, he is known as Dodge-Death, called the Dab by his underlings.

Vautrin is physically powerful and intellectually overwhelming. He wars against society not so much in the name of the insulted and injured, as Victor Hugo's heroic young men fight in *Les Misérables*, as in his own various names, particularly in that of Dodge-Death. In a subtle way he battles the overt heterosexual basis of nineteenth-century French society. Balzac makes clear that Vautrin is homo-erotic and scorns all womankind. To that degree he is scarcely a surrogate for Balzac, who may have had repressed desires, but was a fierce womanizer even after he fell in love with and eventually married Ewelina Hańska, a Polish noblewoman, who survived him by almost a third of a century and took many lovers.

I have always been puzzled by the criticism composed by Henry James, master of the art of fiction. At its worst, it can be astonishingly bad. I would be unfair if I cited his review of Walt Whitman's *Drum-Taps* (1865), which did not have to confront "When Lilacs Last in the Dooryard Bloom'd," the great elegy for Abraham Lincoln that the mature James came to love, since that was printed in an edition six months later that also contained "The Sequel to Drum-Taps." In any case, James, who was only twenty-two when he wrote the review, later referred to it with a shudder as that "little atrocity."

The really peculiar criticism written by Henry James is in his ambivalent accounts of Hawthorne, Dickens, and George Eliot. He owed too much to Hawthorne and could not acknowledge it. On Dickens he is just dreadful.

After all this, I am happy to grant Henry James his extraordinary distinction as a critic of Shakespeare, particularly of *The Tempest*, of Turgenev, and most of all of Balzac:

> The lesson of Balzac, under this comparison, is extremely various, and I should prepare myself much too large a task were I to attempt a list of the separate truths he brings home. I have to choose among them, and I choose the most important; the three or four that more or less include the others. In reading him over, in opening him almost anywhere to-day, what immediately strikes us is the part assigned by him, in any picture, to the *conditions* of the creatures with whom he is concerned. Contrasted with him other prose painters of life scarce seem to see the conditions at all. He clearly held pretended portrayal as nothing, as less than nothing, as a most vain thing, unless it should be, in spirit and intention, the art of complete representation.
>
> ("The Lesson of Balzac," in *The Question of Our Speech*)

That is certainly a major insight, but does it apply to Vautrin? Like Iago and Milton's Satan, Vautrin seems able to create *conditions* all his own. You could say that Vautrin is not altogether representative of *The Human Comedy,* and yet Balzac's close friends habitually called him Vautrin. Many of Balzac's people may try to change their condition of life, but who succeeds fully except Vautrin? There is

Rastignac, endless social climber though redeemed by some warmth of heart, but he happily accepts the condition to which he has risen.

We are introduced to Vautrin in *Old Goriot* (1835), where one of the climaxes is his arrest by the Paris police:

Silence fell on the room. The lodgers made way for three of the men, who had each a hand on a cocked pistol in a side pocket. Two policemen, who followed the detectives, kept the entrance to the sitting-room, and two more men appeared in the doorway that gave access to the staircase. A sound of footsteps came from the garden, and again the rifles of several soldiers rang on the cobblestones under the window. All chance of salvation by flight was cut off for Trompe-la-Mort, to whom all eyes instinctively turned. The chief walked straight up to him, and commenced operations by giving him a sharp blow on the head, so that the wig fell off, and Collin's face was revealed in all its ugliness. There was a terrible suggestion of strength mingled with cunning in the short, brick-red crop of hair, the whole head was in harmony with his powerful frame, and at that moment the fires of hell seemed to gleam from his eyes. In that flash the real Vautrin shone forth, revealed at once before them all; they understood his past, his present, and future, his pitiless doctrines, his actions, the religion of his own good pleasure, the majesty with which his cynicism and contempt for mankind invested him, the physical strength of an organization proof against all trials. The blood flew to his face, and his eyes glared like the eyes of a wild cat. He started back with savage energy and a fierce growl that drew exclamations of alarm from the lodgers. At that leonine start the police caught at their pistols under cover of the general clamor. Collin saw the gleaming muzzles of the weapons, saw his danger, and instantly gave proof of a power of the highest order. There was something horrible and majestic in the spectacle of the sudden transformation in his face; he could only be compared to a cauldron full of the steam that can send mountains flying, a terrific force dispelled in a moment by a drop of cold water. The drop of water that cooled his wrathful fury was a reflection that flashed across his brain like lightning. He began to smile, and looked down at his wig.

"You are not in the politest of humors to-day," he remarked to the chief, and he held out his hands to the policemen with a jerk of his head.

"Gentlemen," he said, "put on the bracelets or the handcuffs. I call on those present to witness that I make no resistance."

(trans. Marriage)

This is Vautrin in his moment of Satanic magnificence. He saves his life by an astonishing act of self-control that prevents the police from shooting him down. Again he dodges death.

"These folks will amuse themselves by dragging out this business till the end of time to keep me idle. If they were to send me straight to jail, I should soon be back at my old tricks in spite of the duffers at the Quai des Orfèvres. Down yonder they will all turn themselves inside out to help their general— their good Trompe-la-Mort—to get clear away. Is there a single one among you that can say, as I can, that he has ten thousand brothers ready to do anything for him?" he asked proudly. "There is some good there," he said tapping his heart; "I have never betrayed any one!—Look you here, you slut," he said to the old maid, "they are all afraid of me, do you see? but the sight of you turns them sick. Rake in your gains."

He was silent for a moment, and looked round at the lodgers' faces.

"What dolts you are, all of you! Have you never seen a convict before? A convict of Collin's stamp, whom you see before you, is a man less weak-kneed than others; he lifts up his voice against the colossal fraud of the Social Contract, as Jean Jacques did, whose pupil he is proud to declare himself. In short, I stand here single-handed against a Government and a whole subsidized machinery of tribunals and police, and I am a match for them all."

It is very difficult to resist Vautrin at this moment. Indeed, he has never betrayed anyone and can assert that he is an authentic disciple of Rousseau. Something in Balzac both defies the Social Contract and affirms it. Vautrin is not so ambivalent, but since he is Balzac's creation, we will see him undergo an astonishing transformation in Part IV of *The Splendor and Misery of the Courtesans,* shrewdly titled "The Last Incarnation of Vautrin."

We need to start further back, with the handsome young Lucien Chardon, protagonist of Balzac's novel *Lost Illusions* (1837). Lucien is descended on the maternal side from the old family de Rubempré, and aspires to join the nobility. More important, this strangely beautiful young man regards himself as a poet (the evidence given us by Balzac shows Lucien to be a very weak poet indeed) and departs the provinces for Paris seeking glory and fortune. Though we come to like him well enough, his weakness extends to more than his verses, and his illusions are devastated. At the novel's close he is about to commit suicide when he is taken up by Vautrin in his disguise as the Abbé Carlos Herrera. They make a pact by which Vautrin will assume the role of financing and guiding Lucien so that this second time he will conquer Paris. Precisely what Vautrin is to secure is left rather ambiguous by Balzac. Though Vautrin has homosexual experience in prison, and is in love with Lucien, it seems doubtful that their relationship is overtly sexual. Rather, Vautrin desires to revenge himself upon society and sees Lucien as his instrument in that enterprise.

In *Splendeurs et misères des courtisanes,* published in four parts from 1838 to 1847, and titled *A Harlot High and Low* in the splendid translation of Rayner Heppenstall (1970), a newly resplendent Lucien is triumphant at a masked revelry where Vautrin also appears masked. Only Rastignac, whom Vautrin failed to seduce in *Old Goriot,* is allowed by Dodge-Death to recognize him.

The expenses of creating the new Lucien compel Vautrin to a scheme in which his protégé is to woo and marry an enormously wealthy and sadly rather ugly young woman. When Lucien and Esther, a remarkable whore known as the Torpedo, fall in love with one another, the undaunted Vautrin employs Lucien to persuade the unfortunate Esther to give herself to the horrible Baron Nucingen. He is an immensely rich financier who lusts after her. Esther yields just once, after a long delay. She is disgusted and commits suicide.

Balzac is so adroit that he makes this outrageous plot work, though any summary would seem to find it tiresome. The Paris police, suspicious of Lucien and Vautrin, arrest them on the possibility that they were complicit. Lucien breaks under testimony and reveals Vautrin's true identity. In remorse, he hangs himself in his cell. Vautrin, true Dodge-Death, momentarily persuades the police that he is the Abbé Carlos Herrera. Though ravaged by grief for Lucien, he has the wit to exploit his unique advantage. In his possession are the profuse love letters sent to Lucien by Clotilde de Grandlieu, who had hoped to marry him, and by the Comtesse de Sérisy and the Duchesse de Maufrigneuse, who had been Lucien's mistresses. Three great houses closely aligned with the king and the government will be victimized by scandal, and the regime could well be compromised.

A remarkable duel takes place between Vautrin and the Comte de Granville, who is the attorney general of France. Balzac is at his most sublime as this duel works itself through. Vautrin is overwhelmed by the generosity and high moral nature of Granville. The attorney general in turn recognizes the negative greatness of his adversary.

With Granville's permission, Vautrin attends the burial of Lucien, where the extraordinary Dodge-Death faints in his grief. When he comes out of it, he is in a cab between two police agents. They bring him to Granville, who urges him to save the Comtesse de Sérisy from madness, since she, too, has collapsed in grief. Vautrin, who possesses a final love letter that Lucien had addressed to the Comtesse de Sérisy but never sent, becomes a doctor of the soul and, with the letter and the false assurances that Lucien had loved only her, restores her to composure.

In a final Balzacian coup, Granville reprieves a former lover of Vautrin, and appoints Jacques Collin to the position of deputy head of the Paris police, to become the head of that august body after another half year. The conclusion is wry and direct: Jacques Collin directs the Paris police force for fifteen years and then retires.

I confess to considerable sadness that I wish Balzac had ended the saga of Vautrin in a very different way. Aesthetically, this is akin to Milton's Satan yielding and rejoining the angelic chorus. Another dark analogue would be Iago repenting and taking pleasure in the survival of Desdemona and Othello and their ongoing union. Balzac is an amazing novelist, but he is neither Shakespeare nor Milton. Vautrin deserved more from him.

CHAPTER 11

The Captain's Daughter (1836)

ALEXANDER PUSHKIN

A READER LIKE MYSELF who has no Russian has to take the greatness of Pushkin's poetry on faith, since it seems untranslatable, even by the chess master V. Nabokov. But the prose fiction has been translated by Richard Pevear and Larissa Volokhonsky in one large volume, *Novels, Tales, Journeys: The Complete Prose of Alexander Pushkin* (2016). The wonder of the book is the novella *The Captain's Daughter* (1836), a historical fiction founded on the Pugachev Rebellion (1773–74). Pushkin had access to the tsarist archives and initially wrote *The History of Pugachev*, which gave him the *materia poetica* for *The Captain's Daughter*. Yemelyan Pugachev, executed in 1775 at the age of thirty-three, was a Don Cossack who became a pretender to the throne occupied by Catherine the Great. Claiming he was the murdered Emperor Peter III, he manifested considerable skill and appropriate viciousness while gathering a large force of Cossacks and peasants. He captured Kazan but then was defeated by the Russian army and delivered by his followers in a cage, where he was kept until his public execution, in which he was drawn and quartered after decapitation.

It is difficult for me to describe Pushkin's unassuming and apparently straightforward style of narration. Russian critics speak of its return to folktales. Tolstoy owed as much to Pushkin as the major

Russian poet seems, to me at least, to quarry Shakespeare for modes of characterization. Pugachev in Pushkin's novella has a complicated nature. I do not know whether to call his a humorous savagery or a savage humor:

Pugachev was sitting in an armchair on the porch of the commandant's house. He was wearing a red Cossack kaftan trimmed with galoons. A tall sable hat with gold tassels was pulled down to his flashing eyes. His face seemed familiar to me. Cossack chiefs surrounded him. Father Gerasim, pale and trembling, stood by the porch with a cross in his hands and seemed to be silently pleading with him for the soon-to-be victims. A gallows was being hastily set up on the square. When we came closer, the Bashkirs drove the people aside, and we were introduced to Pugachev. The bells stopped ringing; a deep silence ensued.

"Which is the commandant?" asked the impostor. Our sergeant stepped out of the crowd and pointed to Ivan Kuzmich. Pugachev looked menacingly at the old man and said to him:

"How was it you dared oppose me, your sovereign?"

The commandant, growing faint from his wound, gathered his last strength and replied in a firm voice:

"You are not my sovereign, you are a thief and an impostor, see here!"

Pugachev frowned darkly and waved a white handkerchief. Several Cossacks picked up the old captain and dragged him to the gallows. The mutilated Bashkir whom we had questioned the day before turned up sitting astride the crossbar. He held a rope in his hand, and a moment later I saw poor Ivan Kuzmich hoisted into the air. Then Ivan Ignatyich was brought before Pugachev.

"Swear allegiance," Pugachev said to him, "to the sovereign Pyotr Feodorovich!"

"You're not our sovereign," Ivan Ignatyich answered, repeating his captain's words. "You, uncle, are a thief and an impostor!"

Pugachev waved his handkerchief again, and the good lieutenant hung beside his old superior.

It was my turn. I looked boldly at Pugachev, preparing to repeat the response of my noble-hearted comrades. Then, to my indescribable amazement, I saw Shvabrin among the rebel chiefs, his hair in a bowl cut and wearing a Cossack kaftan. He went up to Pugachev and said a few words in his ear.

"Hang him!" said Pugachev, without even glancing at me.

They threw the noose around my neck. I began to recite a prayer to myself, offering God sincere repentance for all my transgressions and asking for the salvation of all who were near to my heart. They dragged me under the gallows.

"Don't be afraid, don't be afraid," repeated my undoers, perhaps truly wishing to hearten me. Suddenly I heard a shout:

"Stop, you fiends, wait! ..."

The executioners stopped. I looked: Savelyich was lying at Pugachev's feet.

"Dear father!" my poor tutor was saying. "What is the death of my master's child to you? Let him go; you'll get a ransom for him; and as an example and so as to put fear into people, have them hang my old self instead."

Pugachev gave a sign, and they unbound me at once and let me go.

"Our father pardons you," they said to me.

I cannot say that I was glad at that moment of my deliverance, though I also cannot say I regretted it. My feelings were too blurred. They brought me to the impostor again and made me go on my knees before him. Pugachev offered me his sinewy hand.

"Kiss his hand, kiss his hand!" said those around me. But I would have preferred the most cruel punishment to such base humiliation.

"Dearest Pyotr Andreich!" Savelyich whispered, standing behind me and prodding me. "Don't be stubborn! What is it to you? Spit on it and kiss the vill—...pfui!...kiss his hand."

I did not stir. Pugachev lowered his hand, saying with a little smirk:

"Seems his honor's stupefied with joy. Stand him up!"

They stood me up and set me free. I started watching the continuation of the gruesome comedy.

The narrator, Pyotr Andreevich Grinyov, is very likable yet strangely dispassionate or fatalistic, though he is courageous and loving. He is seventeen and the only child of his military father to survive past infancy. Following family tradition, he enters the army and is sent to Orenburg. Pyotr gets lost, hardly able to see in a blizzard, yet finds his way out with an unknown guide. Thankful, he gives his warm coat to the stranger, who will turn out to be Pugachev. The curious perplexities both of Grinyov and of Pugachev are illuminated for me by the leading Pushkin scholar David M. Bethea:

In writing *The Captain's Daughter* Pushkin was clearly trying to return to an older set of precepts and values, ones determined in the harsh, often wartime conditions of the eighteenth century, that (as he perceived it) didn't allow space for nuance and interpretation. In his compromised situation in the last years of his life it was this old-fashioned clarity, especially when defending the honor of one's family and name, for which he yearned. The essence of this clarity is the ability of a gesture to be beautiful in its own right, to possess both a moral and aesthetic dimension, to stand alone, as something proving nobility of character at a moment when that character is most severely challenged. In *The History of Pugachev* the most impressive example of such a gesture is when the Muslim Bikbai, preparing to be executed by Pugachev's forces, crosses himself and puts his own head into the noose. By giving the fictional Pugachev the ability to recognize the beauty in a deed and to show generosity, that is, to repay beauty with more beauty, Pushkin was improving on the reality of the uprising in two ways. First, he was showing that, despite the ancient class distrust and the factors that led to the uprising in the first place, both peasant and nobleman could share a sense of honor. Second, he was showing that this "paying it forward" has a way of breaking through class enmity and establishing relations in more human terms, which is Iurii Lotman's point in his celebrated piece on the "ideational structure" of *The Captain's Daughter*. When Pugachev learns that Shvabrin is holding an orphan hostage and possibly abusing her, he is moved to act. The weak should not be taken advantage of by the strong. Likewise, when it becomes clear that Masha is the daughter of his sworn enemy and Pugachev still decides to continue in his role as matchmaker/surrogate father and to release the young couple, the result is similar:

the moral and the aesthetic come together in an extravagantly beautiful gesture of being big enough as a person (lichnost') not to keep score.

(Alyssa Dinega Gillespie, ed., *Taboo Pushkin*)

A strange thought occurred to me: it seemed to me that Providence, which had brought me to Pugachev a second time, was giving me the chance to carry out my intention. I decided to take advantage of it and, having no time to think over what I decided, I answered Pugachev's question:

"I was going to the Belogorsk fortress to rescue an orphan who is being mistreated there."

Pugachev's eyes flashed.

"Who of my people dares to mistreat an orphan?" he cried. "Though he be sly as a fox, he won't escape my justice. Speak: Who is the guilty one?"

"Shvabrin," I replied. "He's holding captive the girl you saw sick at the priest's wife's and wants to force her to marry him."

"I'll teach Shvabrin," Pugachev said menacingly. "He'll learn from me what it means to do as he likes and mistreat people. I'll hang him."

"Allow me to put in a word," said Khlopusha in a hoarse voice. "You were in a hurry to appoint Shvabrin commandant of the fortress, and now you're in a hurry to hang him. You've already offended the Cossacks by setting up a nobleman as their superior; don't frighten the nobility now by executing them at the first bit of slander."

"There's no cause to pity them or approve of them," said the little old man with the blue ribbon. "Nothing's wrong with executing Shvabrin; but it wouldn't be bad to give Mister Officer here a proper questioning as to why he was pleased to come calling. If he doesn't recognize you as the sovereign, he needn't look to you for your justice, and if he does, why has he sat there in Orenburg with your enemies up to now? Why don't you order him taken to the guardhouse and have them start a little fire there: something tells me his honor's been sent to us by the Orenburg commanders."

I found the old villain's logic quite persuasive. Chills came over me at the thought of whose hands I was in. Pugachev noticed my confusion.

"Eh, Your Honor?" he said, winking at me. "My field marshal seems to be talking sense. What do you think?"

Pugachev's mockery restored my courage. I replied calmly that I was in his power and he was free to do whatever he liked with me.

The interplay between Grinyov and Pugachev is one of Pushkin's grand inventions. Something that moves beneath the world of slaughter and human conscience binds the two together in a covenant more cavernous than was the murderous intrigue that destroyed Pushkin, according to Lermontov (who never met Pushkin) and others.

Grinyov sounds the perfect chord to maintain his bond with Pugachev:

"Ah! I almost forgot to thank you for the horse and the coat. Without you I wouldn't have made it to the town and would have frozen on the way."

My ruse worked. Pugachev cheered up.

"One good turn deserves another," he said, winking and narrowing his eyes. "Tell me now, what have you got to do with the girl Shvabrin's mistreating? Not the darling of a young lad's heart, is she?"

"She's my bride-to-be," I replied to Pugachev, seeing the weather change for the better and finding no need to conceal the truth.

"Your bride-to-be!" cried Pugachev. "Why didn't you say so before? We'll get you married and feast at your wedding!" Then, turning to Beloborodov: "Listen, Field Marshal! His honor and I are old friends; let's sit down and have supper; morning's wiser than evening. Tomorrow we'll see what we'll do with him."

I would have been glad to decline the proposed honor, but there was no help for it. Two young Cossack women, the daughters of the cottage's owner, covered the table with a white tablecloth, brought some bread, fish soup, and several bottles of vodka and beer, and for the second time I found myself sharing a meal with Pugachev and his frightful comrades.

Released with Masha, Grinyov finds precarious refuge with his old parents, only to find them besieged by their own serfs under the leadership of Shvabrin and a few other Pugachev varlets. Shvabrin, authentic villain of *The Captain's Daughter*, has been compared to Iago, but on the scale of *Othello*'s malignant Ancient, Shvabrin is no more than a water bug. A dreadful creature, he is moved by lust for Grinyov's beloved Masha, the captain's daughter. Rebuffed by her, he fights a duel with Grinyov and wounds the noble protagonist. Joining Pugachev's thugs, he preserves himself and hopes to ravish Masha. In time, Pushkin keeps score on him:

Just then we heard several voices outside the door. I silently made a sign to my mother and Marya Ivanovna to retreat into a corner, drew my sword, and leaned against the wall right next to the door. My father took the pistols, cocked them both, and stood beside me. The padlock clacked, the door opened, and the bailiff's head appeared. I struck it with my sword and he fell, blocking the entrance. At the same moment my father fired a pistol through the doorway. The crowd besieging us ran off cursing. I dragged the wounded man across the threshold and bolted the door from inside. The yard was full of armed men. Among them I recognized Shvabrin.

"Don't be afraid," I said to the women. "There's hope. And you, father, don't shoot again. Let's save the last shot."

Mother silently prayed to God; Marya Ivanovna stood beside her, waiting with angelic calm for our fate to be decided. Outside the door we heard threats, abuse, and curses. I stood in my place, ready to cut down the first daredevil to come in. Suddenly the villains fell silent. I heard the voice of Shvabrin calling me by name.

"I'm here. What do you want?"

"Surrender, Grinyov, it's useless to resist. Have pity on your old ones. Obstinacy won't save you. I'm going to get you all!"

"Just try it, traitor!"

"I won't risk my neck for nothing, or waste my people's lives.

I'll order them to set the granary on fire, and then we'll see what you do, Don Quixote of Belogorsk. It's dinnertime now. Sit there for a while and think things over at your leisure. Goodbye, Marya Ivanovna, I won't apologize to you: you're probably not bored there in the dark with your knight."

Shvabrin went away and left a guard by the granary. We were silent. Each of us was thinking to himself, not daring to share his thoughts with the others. I imagined all that the resentful Shvabrin was capable of inflicting on us. I cared little about myself. Shall I confess it? Even my parents' lot did not horrify me so much as the fate of Marya Ivanovna. I knew that my mother was adored by the peasants and the house serfs; that my father, for all his strictness, was also loved, for he was a fair man and knew the true needs of the people subject to him. Their rebellion was a delusion, a momentary drunkenness, not the expression of their indignation. Here mercy was likely. But Marya Ivanovna? What lot had the depraved and shameless man prepared for her? I did not dare to dwell on that horrible thought, and prepared myself, God forgive me, sooner to kill her than to see her a second time in the hands of the cruel enemy.

About another hour went by. There was drunken singing in the village. Our guards were envious and, vexed with us, swore and taunted us with torture and death. We awaited the sequel to Shvabrin's threats. Finally there came a big commotion in the yard, and again we heard Shvabrin's voice:

"So, have you made up your mind? Do you voluntarily surrender to me?"

No one answered him. Having waited a little, Shvabrin ordered straw brought. After a few minutes, a burst of fire lit up the dark granary, and smoke began to make its way through the chink under the door. Then Marya Ivanovna came to me and, taking me by the hand, said softly:

"Enough, Pyotr Andreich! Don't destroy yourself and your parents on account of me. Let me out. Shvabrin will listen to me."

"Not for anything," I cried hotly. "Do you know what awaits you?"

"I won't survive dishonor," she replied calmly. "But maybe

I'll save my deliverer and the family that so magnanimously sheltered a poor orphan. Farewell, Andrei Petrovich. Farewell, Avdotya Vasilyevna. You were more than benefactors to me. Give me your blessing. Farewell and forgive me, Pyotr Andreevich. Be assured that...that..." Here she burst into tears and buried her face in her hands...I was like a madman. My mother wept.

"Enough nonsense, Marya Ivanovna," said my father. "Who is going to let you go to these brigands alone? Sit here and be quiet. If we're going to die, we'll die together. Listen, what are they saying now?"

"Do you surrender?" Shvabrin shouted. "See? In five minutes you'll be roasted."

"We don't surrender, villain!" my father answered him in a firm voice.

His face, covered with wrinkles, was animated by astonishing courage, his eyes flashed menacingly under his gray eyebrows. And, turning to me, he said:

"Now's the time!"

He opened the door. Flames burst in and shot up the beams caulked with dry moss. My father fired his pistol and stepped across the blazing threshold, shouting: "Everyone, follow me!" I seized my mother and Marya Ivanovna by the hands and quickly led them outside. By the threshold lay Shvabrin, shot down by my father's decrepit hand; the crowd of brigands, who fled before our unexpected sortie, at once took courage and began to surround us. I still managed to deal several blows, but a well-thrown brick struck me full in the chest. I fell down and lost consciousness for a moment. On coming to, I saw Shvabrin sitting on the bloody grass, and before him our whole family. I was supported under the arms. The crowd of peasants, Cossacks, and Bashkirs stood around us. Shvabrin was terribly pale. He pressed one hand to his wounded side. His face expressed suffering and spite. He slowly raised his head, looked at me, and pronounced in a weak and indistinct voice:

"Hang him...hang all of them...except her..."

The crowd of villains surrounded us at once and, shouting, dragged us to the gates. But suddenly they abandoned us and scattered; through the gates rode Zurin and behind him his entire squadron with drawn swords.

All's well that ends well except that the recuperated Shvabrin testifies to Grinyov's apparent collaboration with Pugachev. To protect Masha from any recrimination, quixotic Grinyov refuses to defend himself. All's well then ends well, because Pushkin shrewdly borrows from Sir Walter Scott's *The Heart of Midlothian* (1818), where Jeanie Deans travels, frequently by foot, from Edinburgh to London, in order to prevail upon the Duke of Argyle to persuade Queen Caroline to pardon her sister Effie. Falsely accused of infanticide, Effie would have been executed, but Jeanie Deans is successful.

On that model, Pushkin suddenly allows Masha's personality to flower. On her own initiative, she moves to save Grinyov by requesting an audience with Catherine the Great. That complex monarch, pretending to be only a court lady, rather plainly dressed, is persuaded by Masha and reprieves Grinyov. She does much more. Masha has lost her father and mother to Pugachev's ruffians, and the Empress Catherine is lavish in financial compensation.

Pushkin has to have the final words:

The notes of Pyotr Andreevich Grinyov end here. From family tradition it is known that he was released from prison at the end of 1774, by imperial order; that he was present at the execution of Pugachev, who recognized him in the crowd and nodded to him with his head, which a moment later was shown, dead and bloodied, to the people. Soon afterwards Pyotr Andreevich married Marya Ivanovna. Their descendants still prosper in Simbirsk province. Twenty miles from *** there is a village belonging to ten landowners. In one wing of the manor house a letter in the hand of Catherine II is displayed under glass and in a frame. It was written to Pyotr Andreevich's father and contains the vindication of his son and praise of the mind and heart of Captain Mironov's daughter. Pyotr Andreevich Grinyov's manuscript was furnished us by one of his grandsons, who learned that we were occupied with a work related to the time described by his grandfather. We have decided, with the family's permission, to publish it separately, having found a suitable epigraph for each chapter and allowed ourselves to change some proper names.

(The Publisher, 19 Oct. 1836)

The last words are those of Pushkin's paladin:

The equilibrium in Russia's family romance has been restored (momentarily) through fiction, if not through history. In the final analysis, the forbidden knowledge about Pugachev and his uprising that Pushkin's novel imparts to the reader is not simply that they existed (if Catherine had had her way, all evidence of this tragic episode would have been expunged from historical memory) but that their existence at some level, despite the horrific carnage, is understandable. They were the return of the repressed on a mass level, the haunting of Russian history by memories impossible to forget.

CHAPTER 12

Wuthering Heights (1847)

EMILY BRONTË

I F THERE IS A NOVEL IN *Wuthering Heights,* it centers upon Catherine Earnshaw, caught between the social reality of Edgar Linton and the daemonic Byronism of Heathcliff. Once Catherine Earnshaw and the Lintons are dead, the book is entirely romance. *Wuthering Heights* is almost uniquely the story of early marriage and early death. Catherine Earnshaw dies at eighteen, Heathcliff's son, Linton, at seventeen, Hindley at twenty-seven, Edgar at thirty-nine, poor Isabella at thirty-one, and Heathcliff at about thirty-eight (if my arithmetic is right). Edgar Linton is twenty-one and Catherine Earnshaw seventeen when they marry. Hindley marries Frances at twenty, and the marriage made in hell between Heathcliff and Isabella starts when he is nineteen and she is eighteen. The survivors, Hareton Earnshaw and Catherine Linton, make the only happy marriage, at twenty-four and eighteen, respectively. Everyone marries very young because they intuit they will not live long. Unless Hareton and the second Catherine can defy their lineage, no protagonist in Emily Brontë's cosmos reaches forty, unhappily prophesying that even the stalwart Charlotte did not attain thirty-nine. Emily died at thirty of the family malady, tuberculosis.

I first wrote about *Wuthering Heights* as a Cornell undergraduate in 1947. Whatever that was like, I cannot know, since time's siftings have stilled it. Since then I have written three essays on Emily

Brontë's one romance, all we have of her except for her mixed yet frequently magnificent body of poems. Rereading her at eighty-eight, I find, more strongly than before, that what fascinates me most is the abyss at the center of the book. Nearly all Heathcliff is in that void and perhaps more than half of the first Catherine. I mean "abyss" in the sense of Genesis 1:2, the Hebrew *tehom*, for a turbulent bottomless sea. In the Gnostic heresy the Pleroma or Divine Fullness is equated with that abyss, which precedes Elohim, the normative godhead.

Though Emily Brontë's father, an Irishman who became an Anglican priest, was devout, Christianity had little effect upon the visionary of *Wuthering Heights*. Her poetry celebrates the "God within my breast":

No coward soul is mine
No trembler in the world's storm-troubled sphere
I see Heaven's glories shine
And Faith shines equal arming me from Fear

O God within my breast
Almighty ever-present Deity
Life, that in me hast rest,
As I Undying Life, have power in Thee

Vain are the thousand creeds
That move men's hearts, unutterably vain,
Worthless as withered weeds
Or idlest froth amid the boundless main

To waken doubt in one
Holding so fast by thy infinity,
So surely anchored on
The steadfast rock of Immortality.

With wide-embracing love
Thy spirit animates eternal years
Pervades and broods above,
Changes, sustains, dissolves, creates and rears

Though earth and moon were gone
And suns and universes ceased to be
And Thou wert left alone
Every Existence would exist in thee

There is not room for Death
Nor atom that his might could render void
Since thou art Being and Breath
And what thou art may never be destroyed.

In "Self-Reliance," the sacred Emerson gave me my guiding spur: "As men's prayers are a disease of the will, so are their creeds a disease of the intellect." How far is that from Emily Brontë?

Vain are the thousand creeds
That move men's hearts, unutterably vain,
Worthless as withered weeds
Or idlest froth amid the boundless main

Though some scholars believe that Charlotte wrote this astonishing poem, to anyone with an inner ear this must be Emily Brontë at her greatest:

Often rebuked, yet always back returning
To those first feelings that were born with me,
And leaving busy chase of wealth and learning
For idle dreams of things which cannot be:

To-day, I will seek not the shadowy region;
Its unsustaining vastness waxes drear;
And visions rising, legion after legion,
Bring the unreal world too strangely near.

I'll walk, but not in old heroic traces,
And not in paths of high morality,
And not among the half-distinguished faces,
The clouded forms of long-past history.

I'll walk where my own nature would be leading:
It vexes me to choose another guide:
Where the gray flocks in ferny glens are feeding;
Where the wild wind blows on the mountain side.

What have those lonely mountains worth revealing?
More glory and more grief than I can tell:
The earth that wakes *one* human heart to feeling
Can centre both the worlds of Heaven and Hell.

I find this difficult and revelatory. John Keats—rather than Byron, Wordsworth, Shelley—might have admired the final, contemplative stanza.

William Blake, one of the poets I loved most in my childhood, would have dismissed this as Natural Religion. I do not think that would have been accurate; this transcends nature and tosses away religion.

Moral judgments, whether of her own day or of ours, become rapidly irrelevant in the world of Emily Brontë's one novel. Though the book portrays both social and natural energies, these are dwarfed by the preternatural energies of Heathcliff and of the antithetical side of the first Catherine. Where daemonic energy so far exceeds ours, then daemonic suffering will also be present, perhaps also in excess of our own. But such suffering is foreign to us; Emily Brontë accepts the aesthetic risk of endowing Heathcliff with very little pathos recognizable by us. We wonder at his terrible sufferings, as he slowly dies from lack of sleep and lack of food, but we do not *feel* his agony, because he has become even more distant from us. We are partly moved by the first Catherine's death, since both society and nature are involved in her decline, but partly we stand away from participation, because Catherine is also very much of the realm she shares with Heathcliff. For the last half-year of his life, she is a ghostly presence, but one not much different from what she has been for him before.

I cannot think of a relationship in prose romance more extreme than that of Heathcliff and Catherine Earnshaw. It is grotesque to think of Heathcliff and the first Catherine coupling. They might go up in smoke. In essence they are one.

Emily Brontë is so much an original that in a sense she had

no precursors. She knew the classics, the King James Bible, all of Shakespeare, and perhaps most immediately Sir Walter Scott. And yet her language, stance, vision, even mode of romance are her own. Her descendants in her kind of Northern romance include Thomas Hardy, D. H. Lawrence, and the now neglected John Cowper Powys.

I can locate the spirit of Emily Brontë in one living poet, the Canadian Anne Carson, particularly in her fierce and rending poem "The Glass Essay" (1994):

> and I was downstairs reading the part in *Wuthering Heights*
> where Heathcliff clings at the lattice in the storm sobbing
> Come in! Come in! to the ghost of his heart's darling,
>
> Pitiless too are the Heights, which Emily called Wuthering
> because of their "bracing ventilation"
> and "a north wind over the edge."
>
> Whaching a north wind grind the moor
> that surrounded her father's house on every side,
> formed of a kind of rock called millstone grit,
>
> taught Emily all she knew about love and its necessities—
> an angry education that shapes the way her characters
> use one another. "My love for Heathcliff," says Catherine,
>
> "resembles the eternal rocks beneath
> a source of little visible delight, but necessary."
> Necessary? I notice the sun has dimmed
>
> and the afternoon air sharpening.
> I turn and start to recross the moor towards home.
> What are the imperatives
>
> that hold people like Catherine and Heathcliff
> together and apart, like pores blown into hot rock
> and then stranded out of reach
>
> of one another when it hardens? What kind of necessity is that?

"Whaching" was Emily Brontë's spelling for "watching" and is adopted by Carson. "Necessity" must mean the ancient Greek *ananke,* compulsive force, Anne Carson being a scholar of the classics. "People like Catherine and Heathcliff": I have never met any, except Anne Carson herself, whom I met only once, but with whom many years ago I carried on an extensive correspondence.

Heathcliff is both a person and a daemon. A foundling of uncertain origin, perhaps lascar or Gypsy, picked up on the streets of Liverpool by the elder Earnshaw, he is raised with Catherine Earnshaw as a quasi-brother. They become so close that they *are* one another, which is neither possible nor sane. But, then, the crucial element in the first Catherine is also daemonic. She and Heathcliff share a cosmos that is not ours, or indeed that of anyone else in *Wuthering Heights.* The most profound discussion I have found of Heathcliff is that of Henry Staten in his *Spirit Becomes Matter* (2014):

> There is in Heathcliff no despair at the finality of the death of the body; no nostalgia for the heaven that once was; no turn to Christian morality as a replacement for Christian belief; no stance of bitter, or resigned, or heroic defiance of religious metaphysics. . . . Like an authentic pagan, Heathcliff merely despairs in the wake of Catherine's death, with no thought of any kind regarding transcendence.

Staten compares mourning in Emily Brontë to lamentation, not in the Biblical mode, but in Homer's *Iliad.* He also strongly defends Heathcliff from accusations of sadism, noting both the endless violence of the book, and Heathcliff's reluctance to return physical injury. The initial reaction to Emily Brontë's startling narrative brutality was that of the poet-painter Dante Gabriel Rossetti, in an 1854 letter to the Irish poet William Allingham:

> I've been greatly interested in Wuthering Heights, the first novel I've read for an age, and the best (as regards power and sound style) for two ages, except Sidonia. But it is a fiend of a book—an incredible monster, combining all the stronger female tendencies from Mrs. Browning to Mrs. Brownrigg.

The action is laid in hell,—only it seems places and people have English names there. Did you ever read it?

Sidonia the Sorceress by Wilhelm Meinhold (1848) was rendered into English by Lady Jane Wilde (the divine Oscar's mother) the next year. The nastiness toward Elizabeth Barrett Browning is typical of Dante Gabriel Rossetti; Mrs. Brownrigg was hanged in 1767 for whipping her young female servants so viciously that one died of the infected wounds.

Sheila Smith, in a useful 1992 essay on Emily Brontë and traditional ballads, "'At Once Strong and Eerie,'" illuminates aspects of the preternatural in this Northern romance:

In *Wuthering Heights* Emily Brontë revitalizes the literary form of the novel by use of structural devices, motifs, and subjects which properly belong to the oral tradition with which all the Brontë children were familiar, particularly through the agency of Tabitha Aykroyd, the Yorkshire woman who for thirty years was a servant in the Brontë household. Elizabeth Gaskell, in her biography of Charlotte, says of Tabby that 'she had known the "bottom", or valley, in those primitive days when the fairies frequented the margin of the "beck" on moonlight nights, and had known folk who had seen them.'

Smith continues her discussion with a passage from *Wuthering Heights:*

The country folks, if you asked them, would swear on their Bible that he *walks*. There are those who speak to having met him near the church, and on the moor, and even within this house—Idle tales, you'll say, and so say I. Yet that old man by the kitchen fire affirms he has seen two on 'em, looking out of his chamber window, on every rainy night, since his death. I was going to the Grange one evening—a dark evening threatening thunder—and, just at the turn of the Heights, I encountered a little boy with a sheep and two lambs before him, he was crying terribly, and I supposed the lambs were skittish, and would not be guided.

'What is the matter, my little man?' I asked.

'They's Heathcliff and a woman, yonder, under t' Nab,' he blubbered, 'un' Aw darnut pass 'em.'

Heathcliff and Catherine Earnshaw are revenants, quite visible ghosts returned from the apparently dead. But were they not in some sense always revenants from the very beginning? Emily Brontë sometimes seems to me a kind of revenant herself, a being totally uncanny.

CHAPTER 13

Vanity Fair (1848)

WILLIAM MAKEPEACE THACKERAY

I FIRST READ *Vanity Fair* in 1947, just before going up to my freshman year at Cornell. With each successive reading I am more and more delighted by Becky Sharp and even more puzzled by William Makepeace Thackeray. The voice speaking the book is frequently intolerable to me. Charlotte Brontë, who venerated Thackeray, drives me away by her brutality toward her male readers. I do not like to be thumped over the head as I read. Poor Rochester, a surrogate for George Gordon Lord Byron, is progressively mutilated by Charlotte Brontë and her surrogate Jane Eyre. Approaching eighty-eight, I do not want either to be cudgeled or sneered at by a novelist. Back in the days when I spent some time in the company of Philip Roth, he would cheer me by saying: "Harold, we are here to be insulted." Perhaps.

I have read most of Thackeray's fiction and admire, in addition to *Vanity Fair, The History of Henry Esmond* (1852). For reading about Thackeray, I recommend Juliet McMaster and John Sutherland. There are also Gordon Ray's admirable biographical studies of Thackeray. But the more I read about Thackeray as a person, the sillier he becomes. *Vanity Fair* for me *is* Becky Sharp, a superb antiheroine who does what she has to do in a society that gives her lack of an income no options whatsoever.

In a rather dreadful introduction to the Penguin Classics *Vanity Fair*, the egregious John Carey asserts that *Vanity Fair* has strong claims to be the greatest novel in the English language and is superior to Tolstoy's *War and Peace*. Poor Thackeray; he does not deserve that. But, then, Thackeray could not stop moralizing:

> It is only when their naughty names are called out that your modesty has any occasion to show alarm or sense of outrage, and it has been the wish of the present writer, all through this story, deferentially to submit to the fashion at present prevailing, and only to hint at the existence of wickedness in a light, easy, and agreeable manner, so that nobody's fine feelings may be offended. I defy any one to say that our Becky, who has certainly some vices, has not been presented to the public in a perfectly genteel and inoffensive manner. In describing this siren, singing and smiling, coaxing and cajoling, the author, with modest pride, asks his readers all round, has he once forgotten the laws of politeness, and showed the monster's hideous tail above water? No! Those who like may peep down under waves that are pretty transparent, and see it writhing and twirling, diabolically hideous and slimy, flapping amongst bones, or curling round corpses; but above the water-line, I ask, has not everything been proper, agreeable, and decorous, and has any the most squeamish immoralist in Vanity Fair a right to cry fie? When, however, the siren disappears and dives below, down among the dead men, the water of course grows turbid over her, and it is labour lost to look into it ever so curiously. They look pretty enough when they sit upon a rock, twangling their harps and combing their hair, and sing, and beckon to you to come and hold the looking-glass; but when they sink into their native element, depend on it those mermaids are about no good, and we had best not examine the fiendish marine cannibals, revelling and feasting on their wretched pickled victims. And so, when Becky is out of the way, be sure that she is not particularly well employed, and that the less that is said about her doings is in fact the better.

There is a disturbing flavor to that paragraph. Thackeray was unfortunate in his own erotic life. As a young man in London, he frequently visited bordellos and made an unfortunate marriage when he was twenty-five to a nineteen-year-old Irish girl of no particular abilities. Three daughters were born to them, but the third brought on a postnatal melancholia that became incurable. Thackeray put his wife away into private care and centered his life upon his daughters. Yet, in 1842, he fell in love with a woman married to a college friend. Although the passion was useless and agonizing, it continued for several years, during which he composed *Vanity Fair*. The novel was enormously successful and established Thackeray as a supposed rival to Dickens, not at all an agon that Thackeray could win.

Dead at fifty-two, Thackeray could be judged as not having fulfilled his indubitable gifts, except for *Vanity Fair* and *Henry Esmond*. Dickens loved Shakespeare; Thackeray considered *King Lear* to be a "bore" and regarded *Hamlet* as being trivial. I suppose you could defend Thackeray by saying he was averse to tragedy, but that does not give him very much. I now cease all dispraise by embracing Becky Sharp. I have no idea who would want to embrace William Makepeace Thackeray, yet I grant how greatly he was admired by George Eliot and Anthony Trollope as well as by Charlotte Brontë.

Among recent scholar-critics, Thackeray enjoys the esteem of Wolfgang Iser, the heretofore mentioned Juliet McMaster, John Sutherland, Gordon Ray and also Maria DiBattista and J. Hillis Miller. A touch reluctantly, I would join that company by fantasizing that Thackeray loved Becky Sharp more than he would acknowledge. If Flaubert was Madame Bovary, is not Thackeray Becky Sharp?

This is perhaps clearest in Chapter 64, entitled "A Vagabond Chapter." It does begin with the unfortunate mermaid paragraph I have quoted already. It then goes on to Becky making a bohemian life for herself in the French port of Boulogne:

> She was, in fact, no better than a vagabond upon this earth. When she got her money, she gambled; when she had gambled it, she was put to shifts to live; who knows how or by what means she succeeded? It is said that she was once seen at St Petersburg, but was summarily dismissed from that capital by the police, so that there cannot be any possibility of truth in the report that she was a Russian spy at Töplitz and Vienna afterwards. I have even been informed, that at Paris she discovered a relation of her own, no less a person than her maternal

grandmother, who was not by any means a Montmorenci, but a hideous old box-opener at a theatre on the Boulevards. The meeting between them of which other persons, as it is hinted elsewhere, seem to have been acquainted, must have been a very affecting interview. The present historian can give no certain details regarding the event.

Thackeray is enjoying himself while keeping Becky at a judicious distance. That distance is always in danger of vanishing as Thackeray yields to her gusto:

So Becky, who had arrived in the diligence from Florence, and was lodged at an inn in a very modest way, got a card for Prince Polonia's entertainment, and her maid dressed her with unusual care, and she went to this fine ball leaning on the arm of Major Loder, with whom she happened to be travelling at the time— (the same man who shot Prince Ravoli at Naples the next year, and was caned by Sir John Buckskin for carrying four kings in his hat besides those which he used in playing at *écarté*)—and this pair went into the rooms together, and Becky saw a number of old faces which she remembered in happier days, when she was not innocent, but not found out. Major Loder knew a great number of foreigners, keen-looking whiskered men with dirty striped ribbons in their button-holes, and a very small display of linen; but his own countrymen, it might be remarked, eschewed the Major. Becky, too, knew some ladies here and there—French widows, dubious Italian countesses, whose husbands had treated them ill—faugh—what shall we say, we who have moved among some of the finest company of Vanity Fair, of this refuse and sediments of rascals? If we play, let it be with clean cards, and not with this dirty pack. But every man who has formed one of the innumerable army of travellers has seen these marauding irregulars hanging on, like Nym and Pistol, to the main force; wearing the king's colours, and boasting of his commission, but pillaging for themselves, and occasionally gibbeted by the roadside.

Well, she was hanging on the arm of Major Loder, and they went through the rooms together, and drank a great quantity of champagne at the buffet, where the people, and especially the Major's irregular corps, struggled furiously for refreshments, of which when the pair had had enough, they pushed on until they reached the Duchess's own pink velvet saloon, at the end of the suite of apartments (where the statue of Venus is, and the great Venice looking-glasses, framed in silver), and where the princely family were entertaining their most distinguished guests at a round table at supper. It was just such a little select banquet as that of which Becky recollected that she had partaken at Lord Steyne's—and there he sat at Polonia's table, and she saw him.

Evidently, Thackeray liked *King Henry V* more than he cared for *King Lear* and *Hamlet,* and his employment of Nym and Pistol is adroit. Becky would like to get at Lord Steyne but she cannot, since the company she keeps is rock bottom. In time, she and the lustful Steyne will have their adulterous moment, and it will help end Becky's marriage to Rawdon Crawley. Rawdon is a younger son, a cardsharp, a good soldier, and infatuated with Becky until, at last, he comes to understand how manipulative, immoral, cold, and dangerous she truly is.

Thackeray distances himself from his story and characters by presenting himself as the showman of a booth at Vanity Fair. Crucial to the novel from the title onward is John Bunyan's vision of the Pilgrims at Vanity Fair in his great work *The Pilgrim's Progress: From This World to That Which Is to Come* (1678). Here is the crucial passage from Bunyan:

Then I saw in my dream, that when they were got out of the wilderness, they presently saw a town before them, and the name of that town is Vanity, and at the town there is a fair kept, called Vanity Fair. It is kept all the year long; it beareth the name of Vanity Fair, because the town where it is kept is lighter than vanity, and also because all that is there sold, or that cometh thither, is vanity. As is the saying of the wise, "all that cometh is vanity."

This fair is no new-erected business, but a thing of ancient standing; I will show you the original of it.

Almost five thousand years agone there were pilgrims walking to the Celestial City, as these two honest persons are, and Beelzebub, Apollyon, and Legion, with their companions, perceiving by the path that the pilgrims made that their way to the city lay through this town of Vanity, they contrived here to set up a fair; a fair wherein should be sold all sorts of vanity, and that it should last all the year long. Therefore at this fair are all such merchandise sold, as houses, lands, trades, places, honours, preferments, titles, countries, kingdoms, lusts, pleasures, and delights of all sorts, as whores, bawds, wives, husbands, children, masters, servants, lives, blood, bodies, souls, silver, gold, pearls, precious stones, and what not.

And, moreover, at this fair there is at all times to be seen jugglings, cheats, games, plays, fools, apes, knaves, and rogues, and that of every kind.

Here are to be seen, too, and that for nothing, thefts, murders, adulteries, false swearers, and that of a blood-red colour.

And as in other fairs of less moment there are the several rows and streets under their proper names, where such and such wares are vended; so here likewise you have the proper places, rows, streets, (viz. countries and kingdoms), where the wares of this fair are soonest to be found. Here is the Britain Row, the French Row, the Italian Row, the Spanish Row, the German Row, where several sorts of vanities are to be sold. But as in other fairs some one commodity is as the chief of all the fair, so the ware of Rome and her merchandise is greatly promoted in this fair; only our English nation, with some others, have taken a dislike thereat.

Now, as I said, the way to the Celestial City lies just through this town where this lusty fair is kept; and he that will go to the City, and yet not go through this town, must needs 'go out of the world.' The Prince of princes himself, when here, went through this town to his own country, and that upon a fair day too; yea, and as I think, it was Beelzebub, the chief lord of this fair, that invited him to buy of his vanities, yea, would have made him lord of the fair, would he but have done him reverence as he went through the town. Yea, because he was such a person of honour, Beelzebub had him from street to street, and showed him all the kingdoms of the world in a little time, that he might, if possible, allure that Blessed One to cheapen and buy some of his vanities; but he had no mind to the merchandise, and therefore left the town without laying out so much as one farthing upon these vanities. This fair therefore is an ancient thing, of long standing, and a very great fair.

Beelzebub, Lord of the Flies, is replaced by Thackeray, who on the title page calls his story "A Novel without a Hero." It has two heroes, Thackeray the Showman and his shadow self, Becky Sharp. Some readers suggest that William Dobbin is heroic, but he seems to me a dry stick, amiable enough yet easily forgettable. Thackeray as a personality and character defies my understanding. He is inconstant in tone and in stance, ambivalent in regard to all his characters, yet somehow his real presence pervades the novel. His tone is insinuating, condescending, knowingly snobbish, and edgy, as if he despises his own moralism. A wicked intelligence must be granted him.

Thackeray intends Becky Sharp to be an anti-heroine. You can heap up all her demerits: she is not motherly toward her only son, she is incapable of loving anyone except herself, and she sells herself when she has nothing else to sell. It seems likely that she murders one unfortunate character in order to reap his insurance. She will not bail her husband out of a debtor's confinement, even when Lord Steyne has showered her with banknotes and valuable jewelry. She lives defiantly for all the pleasure she can gain. One could extend the catalogue, but take her out of the novel and who would ever read it? It is her sexuality that sustains the book as much as Cleopatra's triumphant ecstasies provide Shakespeare's great play with fire and air.

The joys of *Vanity Fair* can be encapsulated in a cunning paragraph playing point-counterpoint between Becky and her impresario:

'It isn't difficult to be a country gentleman's wife,' Rebecca thought. 'I think I could be a good woman if I had five thousand a year. I could dawdle about in the nursery, and count the apricots on the wall. I could water plants in a greenhouse and pick off dead leaves from the geraniums. I could ask old women about their rheumatisms, and order half-a-crown's worth of soup for the poor. I shouldn't miss it much out of five thousand a year. I could even drive out ten miles to dine at a neighbour's, and dress in the fashions of the year before last. I could go to church and keep awake in the great family pew, or go to sleep behind the curtains, with my veil down, if I only had practice. I could pay everybody, if I had but the money. This is what the conjurors here pride themselves upon doing. They look down with pity upon us miserable sinners who have none. They think themselves generous if they give our children a five-pound note, and us contemptible if we are without one.' And who knows but Rebecca was right in her speculations—and that it was only a question of money and fortune which made the difference between her and an honest woman? If you take temptations into account, who is to say that he is better than his neighbour? A comfortable career of prosperity, if it does not make people honest, at least keeps them so. An alderman coming from a turtle feast will not step out of his carriage to steal a leg of mutton; but put him to starve, and see if he will not purloin a loaf. Becky consoled herself by so balancing the chances and equalizing the distribution of good and evil in the world.

"I think I could be a good woman if I had five thousand a year." Becky's motto would do very well for a refrain in a poem by Kipling or Bert Brecht. It may as well be Thackeray's motto. Is it not ours? Who would not be Jean Valjean if he or she were starving?

The puzzle of Thackeray makes me wonder if my own excess of affect is at fault in my ambivalence toward him. Erotic disappointment was almost the law of his life. That could be an element in the sadomasochistic narcissism of George Osborne contemplating his bride-to-be Amelia:

This prostration and sweet unrepining obedience exquisitely touched and flattered George Osborne. He saw a slave before him in that simple yielding faithful creature, and his soul within him thrilled secretly somehow at the knowledge of his power. He would be generous-minded, Sultan as he was, and raise up this kneeling Esther and make a queen of her: besides, her sadness and beauty touched him as much as her submission, and so he cheered her, and raised her up and forgave her, so to speak. All her hopes and feelings, which were dying and withering, this her sun having been removed from her, bloomed again and at once, its light being restored. You would scarcely have recognized the beaming little face upon Amelia's pillow that night as the one that was laid there the night before, so wan, so lifeless, so careless of all round about. The honest Irish maid-servant, delighted with the change, asked leave to kiss her face that had grown all of a sudden so rosy. Amelia put her arms round the girl's neck and kissed her with all her heart, like a child. She was little more. She had that night a sweet refreshing sleep, like one—and what a spring of inexpressible happiness as she woke in the morning sunshine!

It is merely outrageous that the odious young Osborne *forgave* poor Amelia. We do not like Osborne any better after he dies heroically at Waterloo. Do I go on being delighted by Becky as she performs Clytemnestra in a charade?

The second part of the charade takes place. It is still an Eastern scene. Hassan, in another dress, is in an attitude by Zuleikah, who is perfectly reconciled to him. The Kislar Aga has become a peaceful black slave. It is sunrise on the desert, and the Turks turn their heads eastwards and bow to the sand. As there are no dromedaries at hand, the band facetiously plays "The Camels are coming." An enormous Egyptian head figures in the scene. It is a musical one—and to the surprise of the oriental travellers, sings a comic song, composed by Mr Wagg. The Eastern voyagers go off dancing, like Papageno and the Moorish King in the "Magic Flute." "Last two syllables," roars the head.

The last act opens. It is a Grecian tent this time. A tall and stalwart man reposes on a couch there. Above him hang his helmet and shield. There is no need for them now. Ilium is down. Iphigenia is slain. Cassandra is a prisoner in his outer halls. The king of men (it is Colonel Crawley, who, indeed, has no notion about the sack of Ilium or the conquest of Cassandra), the *anax andrôn* is asleep in his chamber at Argos. A lamp casts the broad shadow of the sleeping warrior flickering on the wall—the sword and shield of Troy glitter in its light. The band plays the awful music of 'Don Juan', before the statue enters.

Ægisthus steals in pale and on tiptoe. What is that ghastly

face looking out balefully after him from behind the arras? He raises his dagger to strike the sleeper, who turns in his bed, and opens his broad chest as if for the blow. He cannot strike the noble slumbering chieftain. Clytemnestra glides swiftly into the room like an apparition—her arms are bare and white—her tawny hair floats down her shoulder—her face is deadly pale— and her eyes are lighted up with a smile so ghastly, that people quake as they look at her.

A tremor ran through the room. 'Good God!' somebody said, 'it's Mrs Rawdon Crawley.'

Scornfully she snatches the dagger out of Ægisthus's hand and advances to the bed. You see it shining over her head in the glimmer of the lamp, and—and the lamp goes out, with a groan, and all is dark.

In one sense the role of Clytemnestra scarcely suits Becky, because she could not have cared less had she borne Iphigenia and had that splendid young lady been sacrificed so the Greek ships could sail. Otherwise it is a splendid part for Becky, as she has much to revenge against the male world of power, authority, wealth, and the denial of a grand woman's sexuality. Becky Sharp lacks Clytemnestra's grandeur but does very well as a Victorian reduction.

One could say of Becky Sharp that of course she gets up each morning determined both to enjoy her existence and to fight off the male world of wealth, power, hypocrisy. She accepts the price of her own duplicity:

She never was Lady Crawley, though she continued so to call herself. His Excellency Colonel Rawdon Crawley died of yellow fever at Coventry Island, most deeply beloved and deplored, and six weeks before the demise of his brother, Sir Pitt. The estate consequently devolved upon the present Sir Rawdon Crawley, Bart.

He, too, has declined to see his mother, to whom he makes a liberal allowance, and who, besides, appears to be very wealthy. The Baronet lives entirely at Queen's Crawley, with Lady Jane and her daughter; whilst Rebecca, Lady Crawley, chiefly hangs about Bath and Cheltenham, where a very strong party of excellent people consider her to be a most injured woman. She has her enemies. Who has not? Her life is her answer to them. She busies herself in works of piety. She goes to church, and never without a footman. Her name is in all the Charity Lists. The Destitute Orange-girl, the Neglected Washerwoman, the Distressed Muffin-man find in her a fast and generous friend. She is always having stalls at Fancy Fairs for the benefit of these hapless beings.

Again Thackeray's tone is virtually indecipherable. I would soften it if I could, but that is not a legitimate reaction for a reader. I yield to Thackeray for his final comment, with its deep echoes of Qoheleth or Ecclesiastes, where *vanitas* in the Hebrew is *hevel,* "emptiness":

Ah! *Vanitas Vanitatum!* Which of us is happy in this world? Which of us has his desire? or, having it, is satisfied?—Come children, let us shut up the box and the puppets, for our play is played out.

CHAPTER 14

Moby-Dick (1851)

HERMAN MELVILLE

EXCEPT FOR *Don Quixote, Clarissa,* and *In Search of Lost Time,* my personal favorite among all prose epics or vast novels is *Moby-Dick*. I have loved it since I was a child and have never given up my passionate conviction that Ahab is more a hero than a hero-villain.

I cannot recall how many times I have taught *Moby-Dick*. Though I keep rereading it, I have most of it by heart, and that possession alters my perception of many other books. With Walt Whitman's *Leaves of Grass,* it is for me a kind of American Scripture. One does not want to lose perspective. Whitman and Melville are the two titans of American literature. Neither of them is Isaiah of Jerusalem or Dante. Homer and the Athenian tragic dramatists, Plato and Pindar, Lucretius and Virgil, are also larger on the scale of the Sublime. Very old age plays its tricks upon even a mind passionate for the survival of aesthetic and cognitive values. I read Walt Whitman and he places his hand upon me and says he wants me to be his poem. I go back to the first chapter of *Moby-Dick,* "Loomings," and become Ishmael:

Call me Ishmael. Some years ago—never mind how long precisely—having little or no money in my purse, and nothing particular to interest me on shore, I thought I would sail about a little and see the watery part of the world. It is a way I have of driving off the spleen, and regulating the circulation. Whenever I find myself growing grim about the mouth; whenever it is a damp, drizzly November in my soul; whenever I find myself involuntarily pausing before coffin warehouses, and bringing up the rear of every funeral I meet; and especially whenever my hypos get such an upper hand of me, that it requires a strong moral principle to prevent me from deliberately stepping into the street, and methodically knocking people's hats off—then, I account it high time to get to sea as soon as I can. This is my substitute for pistol and ball. With a philosophical flourish Cato throws himself upon his sword; I quietly take to the ship. There is nothing surprising in this. If they but knew it, almost all men in their degree, some time or other, cherish very nearly the same feelings towards the ocean with me.

Ishmael, whose name means "the Almighty listens," was Abraham's firstborn son by his Egyptian concubine, Hagar. In Islam, Ishmael is the ancestor of Muhammad and founded the shrine at Mecca. After a dispute between Sarah and Hagar, the Egyptian woman fled to the desert and bore Ishmael, archetype of all wanderers.

Melville's Ishmael is a pilgrim and a survivor. Only he will survive the wreck of the *Pequod*, Ahab's whaler. My friend Paul Brodtkorb, Jr., wrote a book called *Ishmael's White World* (1965) founded on J. H. Van Den Berg's *The Changing Nature of Man* (1961). Van Den Berg argued against Freud that psychology had to be historical, that miracles could happen in one age but not in another, and that the self was as mutable and metamorphic as Ovid and Shakespeare took it to be. Brodtkorb's Ahab is a High Romantic in the mode of Milton's Satan, Shelley's Prometheus, Byron's Byron. Ahab belongs to the middle of the nineteenth century. He is an American, a Quaker, and a Jobean rebel. But, then, Walt Whitman is an American, a Hicksite Quaker, and another rebel against Leviathan, the tyranny of nature over women and men as ordained by a Blakean Nobodaddy who calls himself Yahweh.

Shakespeare is the dominant influence on *Moby-Dick*. The poet-seer Charles Olson, with whom I had several conversations during the 1960s, pioneered in studying that influence in his book *Call Me Ishmael* (1947). Olson was a giant of a man, six foot seven or so, but I found his manner gentle and engaging, though we could not agree on the poetry of Ezra Pound, who more than Melville sparked Olson's own "projective verse."

This is the essence of Olson on *Moby-Dick:*

Melville isolates Ahab in "a Grand-Lama-like exclusiveness." He is captain of the *Pequod* because of "that certain sultanism of his brain." He is proud and morbid, willful, vengeful. He wears a "hollow crown," not Richard's. It is the Iron Crown of Lombardy which Napoleon wore. Its jagged edge, formed from a nail of the Crucifixion, galls him. He worships fire and swears to strike the sun.

OVER ALL, hate—huge and fixed upon the imperceptible. Not man but all the hidden forces that terrorize man is assailed by the American Timon. That HATE, extra-human, involves his Crew, and Moby-Dick drags them to their death as well as Ahab to his, a collapse of a hero through solipsism which brings down a world.

At the end of the book, in the heart of the White Whale's destruction, the Crew and Pip and Bulkington and Ahab lie down together.

All scatt'red in the bottom of the sea.

Ishmael is the one survivor. I wonder what Melville made of *The Tempest*. Most of his Shakespearean allusions are to the High Tragedies: *Hamlet, Othello, King Lear, Macbeth, Antony and Cleopatra*. I disagreed with Olson and still do as to Ahab's "solipsism." Captain Ahab is well aware of what Emily Dickinson called "Neighbors and the Sun." He plays upon his crew like a master conductor leading a small orchestra. Little Pip, crazed by a dangerous immersion in the sea, becomes the Fool to Ahab's Lear. Starbuck, the heroic first mate, yields to Ahab's monomania because he cannot resist authentic authority.

Ishmael gives us the first intimation of the eternal Moby-Dick:

By reason of these things, then, the whaling voyage was welcome; the great flood-gates of the wonder-world swung open, and in the wild conceits that swayed me to my purpose, two and two there floated into my inmost soul, endless processions of the whale, and, mid most of them all, one grand hooded phantom, like a snow hill in the air.

Though Melville's sources included several accounts of a White Whale, Moby-Dick has a white forehead and a white hump. The rest of the great Leviathan is striated, yet in Ishmael's imagination the whiteness of the whale is paramount. There are many puzzles to Melville's epic.

No one in this vast volume ever refers to Ishmael by that assumed name or indeed by any other. Ishmael is and is not Herman Melville. Only at times is he the narrator. And yet it is his book as much as it is Ahab's. As the only survivor of the *Pequod,* Ishmael strangely and powerfully speaks "this six-inch chapter" as memorial for Bulkington's stoneless grave.

Before proceeding to Nantucket with Queequeg, Ishmael unaccompanied goes to the whalemen's chapel in New Bedford to hear a sermon by the extraordinary preacher Father Mapple, who closes in an eloquent rhapsody:

He dropped and fell away from himself for a moment; then lifting his face to them again, showed a deep joy in his eyes, as he cried out with a heavenly enthusiasm,—"But oh! shipmates! on the starboard hand of every woe, there is a sure delight; and higher the top of that delight, than the bottom of the woe is deep. Is not the main-truck higher than the kelson is low? Delight is to him—a far, far upward, and inward delight—who against the proud gods and commodores of this earth, ever stands forth his own inexorable self. Delight is to him whose strong arms yet support him, when the ship of this base treacherous world has gone down beneath him. Delight is to him, who gives no quarter in the truth, and kills, burns, and destroys all sin though he pluck it out from under the robes of Senators and Judges. Delight,—top-gallant delight is to him, who acknowledges no law or lord, but the Lord his God, and is only a patriot to heaven. Delight is to him, whom all the waves of the billows of the seas of the boisterous mob can never shake from this sure Keel of the Ages. And eternal delight and deliciousness will be his, who coming to lay him down, can say with his final breath—O Father!—chiefly known to me by Thy rod—mortal or immortal, here I die. I have striven to be Thine, more than to be this world's, or mine own. Yet this is nothing; I leave eternity to Thee; for what is man that he should live out the lifetime of his God?"

Superbly delivered by Orson Welles in John Huston's film, this both exalts me and makes me wonder. It is surely more Melvillean than Christian. Mortal or immortal we die, but what is the lifetime of Father Mapple's God? And which God is this? Is it the spirit of delight, or is it the God of Job, Jonah, Jeremiah?

The spirit of delight certainly attends the marriage of Ishmael and Queequeg:

If there yet lurked any ice of indifference towards me in the Pagan's breast, this pleasant, genial smoke we had, soon thawed it out, and left us cronies. He seemed to take to me quite as naturally and unbiddenly as I to him; and when our smoke was over, he pressed his forehead against mine, clasped me round the waist, and said that henceforth we were married; meaning, in his country's phrase, that we were bosom friends; he would gladly die for me, if need should be. In a countryman, this sudden flame of friendship would have seemed far too premature, a thing to be much distrusted; but in this simple savage those rules would not apply.

After supper, and another social chat and smoke, we went to our room together. He made me a present of his embalmed head; took out his enormous tobacco wallet, and groping under the tobacco, drew out some thirty dollars in silver; then spreading them on the table, and mechanically dividing them into two equal portions, pushed one of them towards me, and said it was mine. I was going to remonstrate; but he silenced me by pouring them into my trowsers' pockets. I let them stay. He then went about his evening prayers, took out his idol, and removed the paper fire-board. By certain signs and symptoms,

I thought he seemed anxious for me to join him; but well know-ing what was to follow, I deliberated a moment whether, in case he invited me, I would comply or otherwise.

Ishmael complies and joins his mates in worshipping the little idol. The happiest moment in *Moby-Dick* follows:

How it is I know not; but there is no place like a bed for con-fidential disclosures between friends. Man and wife, they say, there open the very bottom of their souls to each other; and some old couples often lie and chat over old times till nearly morning. Thus, then, in our hearts' honeymoon, lay I and Queequeg—a cosy, loving pair.

Queequeg gifts Ishmael with the story of his life, dominated by a desire to behold all the horizons of the world:

By hints, I asked him whether he did not propose going back, and having a coronation; since he might not consider his father dead and gone, he being very old and feeble at the last accounts. He answered no, not yet; and added that he was fearful Christi-anity, or rather Christians, had unfitted him for ascending the pure and undefiled throne of thirty pagan Kings before him. But by and by, he said, he would return,—as soon as he felt himself baptized again. For the nonce, however, he proposed to sail about, and sow his wild oats in all four oceans. They had made a harpooner of him, and that barbed iron was in lieu of a sceptre now.

After Ishmael and Queequeg have signed to join the crew of the *Pequod*, Ishmael inquires about the captain:

"And what dost thou want of Captain Ahab? It's all right enough; thou art shipped."

"Yes, but I should like to see him."

"But I don't think thou wilt be able to at present. I don't know exactly what's the matter with him; but he keeps close inside the house; a sort of sick, and yet he don't look so. In fact, he ain't sick; but no, he isn't well either. Any how, young man, he won't always see me, so I don't suppose he will see thee. He's a queer man, Captain Ahab—so some think—but a good one. Oh, thou'lt like him well enough; no fear, no fear. He's a grand, ungodly, god-like man, Captain Ahab; doesn't speak much; but when he does speak, then you may well listen. Mark ye, be fore-warned; Ahab's above the common; Ahab's been in colleges, as well as 'mong the cannibals; been used to deeper wonders than the waves; fixed his fiery lance in mightier, stranger foes than whales. His lance! aye, the keenest and the surest that out of all our isle! Oh! he ain't Captain Bildad; no, and he ain't Captain Peleg; *he's Ahab*, boy; and Ahab of old, thou knowest, was a crowned king!"

"And a very vile one. When that wicked king was slain, the dogs, did they not lick his blood?"

"Come hither to me—hither, hither," said Peleg, with a sig-nificance in his eye that almost startled me. "Look ye, lad; never say that on board the *Pequod*. Never say it anywhere. Captain Ahab did not name himself. 'Twas a foolish, ignorant whim of his crazy, widowed mother, who died when he was only a twelvemonth old. And yet the old squaw Tistig, at Gayhead, said that the name would somehow prove prophetic. And, per-haps, other fools like her may tell thee the same. I wish to warn thee. It's a lie. I know Captain Ahab well; I've sailed with him as mate years ago; I know what he is—a good man—not a pious, good man, like Bildad, but a swearing good man—something like me—only there's a good deal more of him. Aye, aye, I know that he was never very jolly; and I know that on the passage home, he was a little out of his mind for a spell; but it was the sharp shooting pains in his bleeding stump that brought that about, as any one might see. I know, too, that ever since he lost his leg last voyage by that accursed whale, he's been a kind of moody—desperate moody, and savage sometimes; but that will all pass off. And once for all, let me tell thee and assure thee, young man, it's better to sail with a moody good captain than a laughing bad one. So good-bye to thee—and wrong not Captain Ahab, because he happens to have a wicked name. Besides, my boy, he has a wife—not three voyages wedded—a sweet, resigned girl. Think of that; by that sweet girl that old man has a child; hold ye then there can be any utter, hopeless harm in Ahab? No, no, my lad; stricken, blasted, if he be, Ahab has his humanities!"

Melville's skill speaks through Peleg and intimates more than it says. Ahab is in his late fifties, old for a whaler, but he cannot rest until his metaphysical quest to avenge himself upon Moby-Dick is accomplished. "He's a grand, ungodly, god-like man, Captain Ahab." One could say precisely the same of Herman Melville. But Ahab's wife is now a "sweet, resigned girl." She has their child for company, and doubtless still Ahab's love, but his leg and manhood have been lost to Moby-Dick. Before that catastrophe, he had been in every sense a complete man, college-educated, fierce in battle against men as against whales, and a king among men.

An excursus on Ahab's name seems in order. In the stories of Elijah and his disciple Elisha in 1 Kings 17 to 2 Kings, King Ahab and his wife, Queen Jezebel, are the villains, a kind of Macbeth and Lady Macbeth. Elijah is abrupt and semi-divine, as indicated by his name, which fuses "El," "the almighty," and "Yahweh." After Elijah overcomes the priests of Baal, he flees the vengeance of Jezebel. So terrified is King Ahab of Elijah that he will not execute him, but both Ahab and Jezebel fulfill Elijah's prophecy. After Ahab is killed in battle, his blood is licked by dogs, Jezebel is tossed out of the window, and most of her remains are devoured by the dogs. I have no reason to believe that either Ahab or Jezebel was in any way wicked: Kings is religious propaganda. Still, Melville exploits this when a vagabond sailor calling himself Elijah accosts Ishmael and Queequeg:

"Yes," said I, "we have just signed the articles."
   "Anything down there about your souls?"
   "About what?"
   "Oh, perhaps you hav'n't got any," he said quickly. "No matter though, I know many chaps that hav'n't got any,—good luck to 'em; and they are all the better off for it. A soul's a sort of a fifth wheel to a wagon."
   "What are you jabbering about, shipmate?" said I.

"*He's* got enough, though, to make up for all deficiencies of that sort in other chaps," abruptly said the stranger, placing a nervous emphasis upon the word *he*.

"Queequeg," said I, "let's go; this fellow has broken loose from somewhere; he's talking about something and somebody we don't know."

"Stop!" cried the stranger. "Ye said true—ye hav'n't seen Old Thunder yet, have ye?"

"Who's Old Thunder?" said I, again riveted with the insane earnestness of his manner.

"Captain Ahab."

"What! the captain of our ship, the *Pequod*?"

"Aye, among some of us old sailor chaps, he goes by that name. Ye hav'n't seen him yet, have ye?"

"No, we hav'n't. He's sick they say, but is getting better, and will be all right again before long."

"All right again before long!" laughed the stranger, with a solemnly derisive sort of laugh. "Look ye; when Captain Ahab is all right, then this left arm of mine will be all right; not before."

"What do you know about him?"

"What did they *tell* you about him? Say that!"

"They didn't tell much of anything about him; only I've heard that he's a good whale-hunter, and a good captain to his crew."

"That's true, that's true—yes, both true enough. But you must jump when he gives an order. Step and growl; growl and go—that's the word with Captain Ahab. But nothing about that thing that happened to him off Cape Horn, long ago, when he lay like dead for three days and nights; nothing about that deadly skrimmage with the Spaniard afore the altar in Santa?— heard nothing about that, eh? Nothing about the silver calabash he spat into? And nothing about his losing his leg last voyage, according to the prophecy. Didn't ye hear a word about them matters and something more, eh? No, I don't think ye did; how could ye? Who knows it? Not all Nantucket, I guess. But hows'ever, mayhap, ye've heard tell about the leg, and how he lost it; aye, ye have heard of that, I dare say. Oh yes, *that* every one knows a'most—I mean they know he's only one leg; and that a parmacetti took the other off."

Ishmael shrugs off this Elijah, though we do not. But why does Melville give us this foreboding? To answer that, I must turn to Job and to Jonah. The first five *"Extracts,"* supposedly supplied by a Sub-Sub-Librarian, that lead off *Moby-Dick* begin to tell us:

"And God created great whales."   *Genesis.*

"Leviathan maketh a path to shine after him;
One would think the deep to be hoary."   *Job.*

"Now the Lord had prepared a great fish to swallow up Jonah."
                                                                  Jonah.

"There go the ships; there is that Leviathan whom thou hast made to play therein."   *Psalms.*

"In that day, the Lord with his sore, and great, and strong sword, shall punish Leviathan the piercing serpent, even Leviathan that crooked serpent; and he shall slay the dragon that is in the sea."   *Isaiah.*

Job precedes Jonah here. The book of Job, though one of the crowns of ancient Hebrew poetry, remains one of the most curious of sublime performances. Job's name seems to derive from the Arabic *awab,* one who returns to God. His accuser is *ha-satan,* the opponent, who is not at all the Satan of the New Testament. This adversary seems to be a prosecuting attorney welcomed by the heavenly court of Yahweh. After Yahweh starts all the trouble by praising Job's virtues, *ha-satan* sneers that Job has been favored by God. Losing His divine temper, God delivers Job into the accuser's hands, saying that he cannot kill him but may do anything else that pleases him. The results are splendid. All of Job's children and flocks are murdered, and poor Job is afflicted with sore boils all over his body. Job curses his own existence but does not blame God. Job's wife admirably tells her husband: Do you still retain your integrity? Curse God and die! Job's friends or "comforters" assure him that he must be very wicked to deserve all this pain. Despite this immoral idiocy, Job remains stubborn and wants to justify both God and himself, which is simply impossible. Eventually, out of a storm, God speaks and addresses a series of rhetorical questions to His wretched believer.

1 Canst thou draw out leviathan with an hook? or his tongue with a cord *which* thou lettest down?

2 Canst thou put an hook into his nose? or bore his jaw through with a thorn?

3 Will he make many supplications unto thee? will he speak soft *words* unto thee?

4 Will he make a covenant with thee? wilt thou take him for a servant for ever?

5 Wilt thou play with him as *with* a bird? or wilt thou bind him for thy maidens?

6 Shall the companions make a banquet of him? shall they part him among the merchants?

7 Canst thou fill his skin with barbed irons? or his head with fish spears?

8 Lay thine hand upon him, remember the battle, do no more.

9 Behold, the hope of him is in vain: shall not *one* be cast down even at the sight of him?

10 None *is so* fierce that dare stir him up: who then is able to stand before me?

11 Who hath prevented me, that I should repay *him*? *whatsoever is* under the whole of heaven is mine.

12 I will not conceal his parts, nor his power, nor his comely proportion.

13 Who can discover the face of his garment? *or* who can come *to him* with his double bridle?

14 Who can open the doors of his face? his teeth *are* terrible round about.

15 His scales *are his* pride, shut up together *as with* a close seal.

16 One is so near to another, that no air can come between them.

17 They are joined one to another, they stick together, that they cannot be sundered.

18 By his neesings a light doth shine, and his eyes *are* like the eyelids of the morning.

19 Out of his mouth go burning lamps, *and* sparks of fire leap out.

20 Out of his nostrils goeth smoke, as *out* of a seething pot or caldron.

21 His breath kindleth coals, and a flame goeth out of his mouth.

22 In his neck remaineth strength, and sorrow is turned into joy before him.

23 The flakes of his flesh are joined together: they are firm in themselves; they cannot be moved.

24 His heart is as firm as a stone; yea, as hard as a piece of the nether *millstone*.

25 When he raiseth up himself, the mighty are afraid: by reason of breakings they purify themselves.

26 The sword of him that layeth at him cannot hold: the spear, the dart, nor the habergeon.

27 He esteemeth iron as straw, *and* brass as rotten wood.

28 The arrow cannot make him flee: slingstones are turned with him into stubble.

29 Darts are counted as stubble: he laugheth at the shaking of a spear.

30 Sharp stones *are* under him: he spreadeth sharp pointed things upon the mire.

31 He maketh the deep to boil like a pot: he maketh the sea like a pot of ointment.

32 He maketh a path to shine after him; *one* would think the deep *to be* hoary.

33 Upon earth there is not his like, who is made without fear.

34 He beholdeth all high *things:* he *is* a king over all the children of pride.

(Job 41, KJV)

Confronting this rhetorical power, I myself become another Job. Even a decade ago I would have fought back, but, aged and weakened, I lack the resilience. And yet I began as a scholar of William Blake and of Percy Bysshe Shelley, visionary poets who imbued me in childhood with their apocalyptic humanism. No matter that Blake considered himself a Christian and Shelley thought himself an atheist; both believed in what Blake called "the human form divine" and Shelley termed "shapes too bright to see." At eighty-eight, I find that their faithless faith has abandoned me.

I was raised in the Covenant between Yahweh and the Jewish people. Even as a child I winced at this cruel verse: "Will he make a covenant with thee? wilt thou take him for a servant for ever?"

The book of Job is an extraordinary poem, and it is very difficult to interpret. The devastation of "the day of the locust" is counterbalanced by Jonah's vision of survival. It may seem capricious to speak of a favorite book in the Bible, but mine is Jonah, by far. A sly masterpiece of four brief chapters, Jonah reverberates in *Moby-Dick*, where it is the text for Father Mapple's grand sermon. Tucked away in the Book of the Twelve, with such fierce prophets as Amos and Micah, Jonah is out of place. It should be with the Writings—Song of Songs, Job, Qoheleth—because it, too, is a literary sublimity, almost the archetypal parable masking as short story. The irony of the J writer is augmented by the author of Jonah, who may well be composing a parody of the prophet Joel's solemnities. Joel's vision is of nature's divine caprice.

I first was charmed by Jonah as a little boy in synagogue on the afternoon of the Day of Atonement, when it is read aloud in full. It seemed to me so much at variance, in tone and implication, from the rest of the service as to be almost Kafkan in effect. The author of Jonah probably composed it very late in prophetic tradition, sometime during the third century B.C.E. There is a prophetic Jonah in 2 Kings 14:25 who has nothing in common with the feckless Jonah sent to announce to the people of Nineveh that God intends to destroy their city to punish them for their wickedness. The earlier Jonah is a war prophet, whereas our Jonah sensibly runs away from his mission, boarding a ship sailing for Tarshish.

No one emerges honorably from the book of Jonah, whether God, Jonah, the ship captain and his men, or the king of Nineveh and his people. Even the gourd sheltering Jonah from the sun comes to a bad end. There is of course the giant fish (not, alas, a whale) who swallows up Jonah for three days but then disgorges him at God's command. No Moby-Dick, he inspires neither fear nor awe.

Jonah's book is magnificent literature because it is so funny. Irony, even in Jonathan Swift, could not be more brilliant. Jonah himself is a sulking, unwilling prophet, cowardly and petulant. There is no reason why an authentic prophet should be likable: Elijah and Elisha are savage, Jeremiah is a bipolar depressive, Ezekiel a madman. Paranoia and prophecy seem to go together, and the author of Jonah satirizes both his protagonist and Yahweh in a return to the large irony of the J writer, whose voice is aristocratic, skeptical, humorous, deflationary of masculine pretense, believing nothing and rejecting nothing, and particularly aware of the reality of personalities.

The prophet Jonah, awash with the examples and texts of Isaiah, Jeremiah, and Joel, rightly resents his absurd status as a latecomer sufferer of the anxiety of prophetic influence. Either Nineveh will ignore him and be destroyed, making his mission needless, or, if it takes him to heart, he will prove to be a false prophet. Either way, his sufferings are useless, nor does Yahweh show the slightest regard for him. Praying from the fish's belly, he satirizes the situation of all psalmists whosoever.

As for poor Nineveh, where even the beasts are bedecked in sackcloth and ashes, Yahweh merely postpones its destruction. That leaves the Cain-like gourd, whose life is so brief and whose destruction prompts poor Jonah's death-drive. What remains is Yahweh's playfully rhetorical question: And should not I spare Nineveh, that great city, wherein are more than sixscore thousand persons that cannot discern between their right hand and their left hand; and also much cattle?

Presumably the cattle ("beasts" in the Hebrew) are able to tell one direction from another, unlike the citizens of Nineveh, Jerusalem, or New York City. Tucking Jonah away as another minor prophet was a literary error by the makers of the canon. Or perhaps they judged the little book aptly, and were anxious to conceal this Swiftian coda to prophets and prophecy.

Father Mapple, unorthodox as to finalities, is traditional enough in his quirky retelling of Jonah's story. But the White Whale Moby-Dick in my judgment is all but identical with Job's Leviathan, king over all the children of pride. If you read Job as Melville did, you, too, might want to answer No in thunder. Yet it may be that the poet of Job was as fierce an ironist as the God he shows us. My friend and former student Herbert Marks acutely points to the ambiguity of Job's verse in the final chapter:

Wherefore I abhor *myself,* and repent in dust and ashes.

That *myself* is not in the Hebrew. Job does not despise himself. He is, as Marks says, fed up. Job holds his ground and pities all of us for having to survive somehow under so dubious a God. The poet of Job is not a Calvinist. Nor is he an Ahab. Call him a skeptic. Ahab, maimed by Leviathan, fights back.

I think that there will never be general agreement as to Ahab's bad eminence. I write those last two words and I resent them. Yes, he owes much to Milton's Satan and more to Macbeth, Hamlet, Lear, Cleopatra, Antony, not to mention the Prometheus of Shelley and of Byron. And yet he is an Emersonian American despite Melville's acute ambivalence in regard to the Sage of Concord.

Read Emerson's last great book, *The Conduct of Life* (1860), particularly the essays "Fate," "Power," and "Illusions." I do not think Emerson ever read Melville, yet I wish he had read *Moby-Dick* (1851). Melville attended all of Emerson's lectures in New York City, and he owned and annotated the two series of *Essays* and *The Conduct of Life.* He bitterly satirized Emerson as Plotinus Plinlimmon in *Pierre* (1852), a disaster of a novel, and as Mark Winsome in *The Confidence-Man* (1857), which is rather a mixed bag. Probably his most effective rejoinder to Emerson is "Bartleby, the Scrivener," one of the best of *The Piazza Tales* (1856).

Nevertheless, both Ahab and Ishmael are Emersonians, American Adams puzzling out their fates in our Evening Land. And so is Herman Melville, despite his vexed relationship to Emerson. Describing the first mate, Starbuck, Ishmael could as well be Emerson or Walt Whitman exalting the greatness of the common man:

> But were the coming narrative to reveal, in any instance, the complete abasement of poor Starbuck's fortitude, scarce might I have the heart to write it; for it is a thing most sorrowful, nay shocking, to expose the fall of valor in the soul. Men may seem detestable as joint stock-companies and nations; knaves, fools, and murderers there may be; men may have mean and meagre

faces; but man, in the ideal, is so noble and so sparkling, such a grand and glowing creature, that over any ignominious blemish in him all his fellows should run to throw their costliest robes. That immaculate manliness we feel within ourselves, so far within us, that it remains intact though all the outer character seem gone; bleeds with keenest anguish at the undraped spectacle of a valor-ruined man. Nor can piety itself, at such a shameful sight, completely stifle her upbraidings against the permitting stars. But this august dignity I treat of, is not the dignity of kings and robes, but that abounding dignity which has no robed investiture. Thou shalt see it shining in the arm that wields a pick or drives a spike; that democratic dignity which, on all hands, radiates without end from God; Himself! The great God absolute! The centre and circumference of all democracy! His omnipresence, our divine equality!

If, then, to meanest mariners, and renegades and castaways, I shall hereafter ascribe high qualities, though dark; weave round them tragic graces; if even the most mournful, perchance the most abased, among them all, shall at times lift himself to the exalted mounts; if I shall touch that workman's arm with some ethereal light; if I shall spread a rainbow over his disastrous set of sun; then against all mortal critics bear me out in it, thou just Spirit of Equality, which hast spread one royal mantle of humanity over all my kind! Bear me out in it, thou great democratic God! who didst not refuse to the swart convict, Bunyan, the pale, poetic pearl; Thou who didst clothe with doubly hammered leaves of finest gold, the stumped and paupered arm of old Cervantes; Thou who didst pick up Andrew Jackson from the pebbles; who didst hurl him upon a war-horse; who didst thunder from higher than a throne! Thou who, in all Thy mighty, earthly marchings, ever cullest Thy selectest champions from the kingly commons; bear me out in it, O God!

John Bunyan, a tinker and the son of a tinker, served in Cromwell's army, where he absorbed the many currents of nonconformist Protestantism. After the Restoration, he was imprisoned for twelve years, during which he attained spiritual illumination. *The Pilgrim's*

Progress: From This World to That Which Is to Come (1678) resulted from this experience. Cervantes, who lost use of one arm at the naval Battle of Lepanto, survived poverty, imprisonment, and neglect to write *The Ingenious Gentleman Don Quixote of La Mancha* (1605, 1615). Andrew Jackson, known as Old Hickory, served as the seventh president of the United States of America (1829–37). He inaugurated what we still call Jacksonian Democracy, which was celebrated by Walt Whitman and by Melville.

Captain Ahab is anything but a democrat in his absolute rule, not only over the *Pequod* and all its crew, but in kinging his will over all the humanities in his nature. In response to Starbuck's sane protest at vengeance against what he calls "a dumb brute," Ahab proclaims his quest to strike through the mask:

> "Hark ye yet again,—the little lower layer. All visible objects, man, are but as pasteboard masks. But in each event—in the living act, the undoubted deed—there, some unknown but still reasoning thing puts forth the mouldings of its features from behind the unreasoning mask. If man will strike, strike through the mask! How can the prisoner reach outside except by thrusting through the wall? To me, the white whale is that wall, shoved near to me. Sometimes I think there's naught beyond. But 'tis enough. He tasks me; he heaps me; I see in him outrageous strength, with an inscrutable malice sinewing it. That inscrutable thing is chiefly what I hate; and be the white whale agent, or be the white whale principal, I will wreak that hate upon him. Talk not to me of blasphemy, man; I'd strike the sun if it insulted me. For could the sun do that, then could I do the other; since there is ever a sort of fair play herein, jealousy presiding over all creations. But not my master, man, is even that fair play. Who's over me? Truth hath no confines. Take off thine eye! more intolerable than friends' glarings is a doltish stare! So, so; thou reddenest and palest; my heat has melted thee to anger-glow. But look ye, Starbuck, what is said in heat, that thing unsays itself. There are men from whom warm words are small indignity. I meant not to incense thee. Let it go. Look! see yonder Turkish cheeks of spotted tawn—living, breathing pictures painted by the sun. The Pagan leopards—the unreck-

ing and unworshipping things, that live; and seek, and give no reasons for the torrid life they feel! The crew, man, the crew! Are they not one and all with Ahab, in this matter of the whale? See Stubb! he laughs! See yonder Chilian! he snorts to think of it. Stand up amid the general hurricane, thy one tost sapling cannot, Starbuck! And what is it? Reckon it. 'Tis but to help strike a fin; no wondrous feat for Starbuck. What is it more? From this one poor hunt, then, the best lance out of all Nantucket, surely he will not hang back, when every foremost-hand has clutched a whetstone? Ah! constrainings seize thee; I see! the billow lifts thee! Speak, but speak!—Aye, aye! thy silence, then, *that* voices thee. (Aside) Something shot from my dilated nostrils, he has inhaled it in his lungs. Starbuck now is mine; cannot oppose me now, without rebellion."

Who among us has the right to oppose Ahab? High Romantic poetry relies upon the power of the imagination over a universe of death. Moby-Dick, who heaps Ahab, sets a limit beyond which even the most heroic of questers cannot go. The White Whale is a daemonic agent, a Demiurge whose principal is the God imposing nature upon us. Captain Ahab, who indeed would strike the sun if it insulted him, is a rival daemonic agent, a human aspiring to be a counter-Demiurge. Whose book is it anyway? Melville's? Ahab's? Ishmael's? The grand chapter "The Whiteness of the Whale" is Ishmael's meditation:

Thus, then, the muffled rollings of a milky sea; the bleak rustlings of the festooned frosts of mountains; the desolate shiftings of the windrowed snows of prairies; all these, to Ishmael, are as the shaking of that buffalo robe to the frightened colt!

Though neither knows where lie the nameless things of which the mystic sign gives forth such hints; yet with me, as with the colt, somewhere those things must exist. Though in many of its aspects this visible world seems formed in love, the invisible spheres were formed in fright.

But not yet have we solved the incantation of this whiteness, and learned why it appeals with such power to the soul; and more strange and far more portentous—why, as we have seen, it is at once the most meaning symbol of spiritual things, nay, the very veil of the Christian's Deity; and yet should be as it is, the intensifying agent in things the most appalling to mankind.

Is it that by its indefiniteness it shadows forth the heartless voids and immensities of the universe, and thus stabs us from behind with the thought of annihilation, when beholding the white depths of the milky way? Or is it, that as in essence whiteness is not so much a color as the visible absence of color, and at the same time the concrete of all colors; is it for these reasons that there is such a dumb blankness, full of meaning, in a wide landscape of snows—a colorless, all-color of atheism from which we shrink? And when we consider that other theory of the natural philosophers, that all other earthly hues—every stately or lovely emblazoning—the sweet tinges of sunset skies and woods; yea, and the gilded velvets of butterflies, and the butterfly cheeks of young girls; all these are but subtile deceits, not actually inherent in substances, but only laid on from without; so that all deified Nature absolutely paints like the harlot, whose allurements cover nothing but the charnelhouse within; and when we proceed further, and consider that the mystical cosmetic which produces every one of her lures, the great principle of light, for ever remains white or colorless in itself, and if operating without medium upon matter, would touch all objects, even tulips and roses, with its own blank tinge—pondering all this, the palsied universe lies before us a leper; and like wilful travellers in Lapland, who refused to wear colored and coloring glasses upon their eyes, so the wretched infidel gazes himself blind at the monumental white shroud that wraps all the prospect around him. And of all these things the Albino whale was the symbol. Wonder ye then at the fiery hunt?

This is the American blank, derived ultimately from Shakespeare and from Milton, adapted by Emerson and then by Melville, Emily Dickinson, Walt Whitman, Robert Frost, and obsessively by Wallace Stevens. The dumb blank is the colorless, all-color of atheism. When I lie awake at night reciting parts of *Moby-Dick* to myself, I keep returning to Ishmael's crucial maxim: "Though in many of its aspects this visible world seems formed in love, the invisible spheres were formed in fright."

The deepest, darkest element in Captain Ahab expresses itself in the Parsee whaleboat crew he has smuggled aboard the *Pequod,* and in particular his strange double, the harpooner Fedallah:

But at this critical instant a sudden exclamation was heard that took every eye from the whale. With a start all glared at dark Ahab, who was surrounded by five dusky phantoms that seemed fresh formed out of air.

. . . .

The phantoms, for so they seemed, were flitting on the other side of the deck, and, with a noiseless celerity, were casting loose the tackles and bands of the boat which swung there. This boat had always been deemed one of the spare boats, though technically called the captain's, on account of its hanging from the starboard quarter. The figure that now stood by its bows was tall and swart, with one white tooth evilly protruding from its steel-like lips. A rumpled Chinese jacket of black cotton funereally invested him, with wide black trowsers of the same dark stuff. But strangely crowning this ebonness was a glistening white plaited turban, the living hair braided and coiled round and round upon his head. Less swart in aspect, the companions of this figure were of that vivid, tiger-yellow complexion peculiar to some of the aboriginal natives of the Manillas;—a race notorious for a certain diabolism of subtilty, and by some honest white mariners supposed to be paid spies and secret confidential agents on the water of the devil, their lord, whose counting-room they suppose to be elsewhere.

While yet the wondering ship's company were gazing upon these strangers, Ahab cried out to the white-turbaned old man at their head, "All ready there, Fedallah?"

"Ready," was the half-hissed reply.

"Lower away then; d'ye hear?" shouting across the deck. "Lower away there, I say."

Such was the thunder of his voice, that spite of their amazement the men sprang over the rail; the sheaves whirled round in the blocks; with a wallow, the three boats dropped into the sea; while, with a dexterous, off-handed daring, unknown in any other vocation, the sailors, goat-like, leaped down the rolling ship's side into the tossed boats below.

Hardly had they pulled out from under the ship's lee, when a fourth keel, coming from the windward side, pulled round under the stern, and showed the five strangers rowing Ahab, who, standing erect in the stern, loudly hailed Starbuck, Stubb, and Flask, to spread themselves widely, so as to cover a large expanse of water. But with all their eyes again riveted upon the swart Fedallah and his crew, the inmates of the other boats obeyed not the command.

We can share in the astonishment of the *Pequod*'s crew. The narrator more than gratifies our initial response:

Among whale-wise people it has often been argued whether, considering the paramount importance of his life to the success of the voyage, it is right for a whaling captain to jeopardize that life in the active perils of the chase. So Tamerlane's soldiers often argued with tears in their eyes, whether that invaluable life of his ought to be carried into the thickest of the fight.

But with Ahab the question assumed a modified aspect. Considering that with two legs man is but a hobbling wight in all times of danger; considering that the pursuit of whales is always under great and extraordinary difficulties; that every individual moment, indeed, then comprises a peril; under these circumstances is it wise for any maimed man to enter a whaleboat in the hunt? As a general thing, the joint-owners of the *Pequod* must have plainly thought not.

Ahab well knew that although his friends at home would think little of his entering a boat in certain comparatively harmless vicissitudes of the chase, for the sake of being near the scene of action and giving his orders in person, yet for Captain Ahab to have a boat actually apportioned to him as a regular headsman in the hunt—above all for Captain Ahab to be supplied with five extra men, as that same boat's crew, he well knew that such generous conceits never entered the heads of the owners of the *Pequod*. Therefore he had not solicited a boat's crew from them, nor had he in any way hinted his desires on that head. Nevertheless he had taken private measures of his own touching all that matter. Until Cabaco's published discovery, the sailors had little foreseen it, though to be sure when, after being a little while out of port, all hands had concluded the customary business of fitting the whaleboats for service; when some time after this Ahab was now and then found bestirring himself in the matter of making thole-pins with his own hands for what was thought to be one of the spare boats, and even solicitously cutting the small wooden skewers, which when the line is running out are pinned over the groove in the bow: when all this was observed in him, and particularly his solicitude in having an extra coat of sheathing in the bottom of the boat, as if to make it better withstand the pointed pressure of his ivory limb; and also the anxiety he evinced in exactly shaping the thigh board, or clumsy cleat, as it is sometimes called, the horizontal piece in the boat's bow for bracing the knee against in darting or stabbing at the whale; when it was observed how often he stood up in that boat with his solitary knee fixed in the semicircular depression in the cleat, and with the carpenter's chisel gouged out a little here and straightened it a little there; all these things, I say, had awakened much interest and curiosity at the time. But almost everybody supposed that this particular preparative heedfulness in Ahab must only be with a view to the ultimate chase of Moby Dick; for he had already revealed his intention to hunt that mortal monster in person. But such a supposition did by no means involve the remotest suspicion as to any boat's crew being assigned to that boat.

The other outsiders are of little interest compared with Fedallah, who from this point on is crucial to the epic. No reader can respond to Fedallah without considerable unease:

But be all this as it may, certain it is that while the subordinate phantoms soon found their place among the crew, though still as it were somehow distinct from them, yet that hair-turbaned

Fedallah remained a muffled mystery to the last. Whence he came in a mannerly world like this, by what sort of unaccountable tie he soon evinced himself to be linked with Ahab's peculiar fortunes; nay, so far as to have some sort of a half-hinted influence; Heaven knows, but it might have been even authority over him; all this none knew. But one cannot sustain an indifferent air concerning Fedallah. He was such a creature as civilized, domestic people in the temperate zone only see in their dreams, and that but dimly; but the like of whom now and then glide among the unchanging Asiatic communities, especially the Oriental isles to the east of the continent—those insulated, immemorial, unalterable countries, which even in these modern days still preserve much of the ghostly aboriginalness of earth's primal generations, when the memory of the first man was a distinct recollection, and all men his descendants, unknowing whence he came, eyed each other as real phantoms, and asked of the sun and the moon why they were created and to what end; when though, according to Genesis, the angels indeed consorted with the daughters of men, the devils also, add the uncanonical Rabbins, indulged in mundane amours.

Melville invents Fedallah's name, though it could be parsed as a diabolic enemy of Allah. Fedallah is a Parsee, a Zoroastrian from the group that fled Persia for India. Evidently, he and Ahab have a shared past, during which the captain from Nantucket was a Zoroastrian fire-worshipper. The reference to uncanonical Rabbins is to the Book of Enoch, where the giants in the earth copulate with the daughters of men.

In an extraordinary scene, involving the corpusants or Saint Elmo's fire, Ahab repudiates Fedallah's faith and converts himself to Herman Melville's palpable Gnosticism:

Now, as the lightning rod to a spire on shore is intended to carry off the perilous fluid into the soil; so the kindred rod which at sea some ships carry to each mast, is intended to conduct it into the water. But as this conductor must descend to considerable depth, that its end may avoid all contact with the hull; and as moreover, if kept constantly towing there, it would be liable to many mishaps, besides interfering not a little with some of the rigging, and more or less impeding the vessel's way in the water; because of all this, the lower parts of a ship's lightning-rods are not always overboard; but are generally made in long slender links, so as to be the more readily hauled up into the chains outside, or thrown down into the sea, as occasion may require.

"The rods! the rods!" cried Starbuck to the crew, suddenly admonished to vigilance by the vivid lightning that had just been darting flambeaux, to light Ahab to his post. "Are they overboard? drop them over, fore and aft. Quick!"

"Avast!" cried Ahab; "let's have fair play here, though we be the weaker side. Yet I'll contribute to raise rods on the Himmalehs and Andes, that all the world may be secured; but out on privileges! Let them be, sir."

"Look aloft!" cried Starbuck. "The corpusants! the corpusants!"

All the yard-arms were tipped with a pallid fire; and touched at each tri-pointed lightning-rod-end with three tapering white flames, each of the three tall masts was silently burning in that sulphurous air, like three gigantic wax tapers before an altar.

"Blast the boat! let it go!" cried Stubb at this instant, as a swashing sea heaved up under his own little craft, so that its gunwale violently jammed his hand, as he was passing a lashing. "Blast it!"—but slipping backward on the deck, his uplifted eyes caught the flames; and immediately shifting his tone, he cried—"The corpusants have mercy on us all!"

Sensible sailors follow superstition by finding fright in the corpusants, but Captain Ahab welcomes them:

At the base of the mainmast, full beneath the doubloon and the flame, the Parsee was kneeling in Ahab's front, but with his head bowed away from him; while near by, from the arched and overhanging rigging, where they had just been engaged securing a spar, a number of the seamen, arrested by the glare, now cohered together, and hung pendulous, like a knot of numbed wasps from a drooping, orchard twig. In various enchanted attitudes, like the standing, or stepping, or running skeletons in Herculaneum, others remained rooted to the deck; but all their eyes upcast.

"Aye, aye, men!" cried Ahab. "Look up at it; mark it well; the white flame but lights the way to the White Whale! Hand me those mainmast links there; I would fain feel this pulse, and let mine beat against it; blood against fire! So."

Then turning—the last link held fast in his left hand, he put his foot upon the Parsee; and with fixed upward eye, and high-flung right arm, he stood erect before the lofty tri-pointed trinity of flames.

"Oh! thou clear spirit of clear fire, whom on these seas I as Persian once did worship, till in the sacramental act so burned by thee, that to this hour I bear the scar; I now know thee, thou clear spirit, and I now know that thy right worship is defiance. To neither love nor reverence wilt thou be kind; and e'en for hate thou canst but kill; and all are killed. No fearless fool now fronts thee. I own thy speechless, placeless power; but to the last gasp of my earthquake life will dispute its unconditional, unintegral mastery in me. In the midst of the personified impersonal, a personality stands here. Though but a point at best; whencesoe'er I came; wheresoe'er I go; yet while I earthly live, the queenly personality lives in me, and feels her royal rights. But war is pain, and hate is woe. Come in thy lowest form of love, and I will kneel and kiss thee; but at thy highest, come as mere supernal power; and though thou launchest navies of full-freighted worlds, there's that in here that still remains indifferent. Oh, thou clear spirit, of thy fire thou madest me, and like a true child of fire, I breathe it back to thee."

(Sudden, repeated flashes of lightning; the nine flames leap lengthwise to thrice their previous height; Ahab, with the rest, closes his eyes, his right hand pressed hard upon them.)

"I own thy speechless, placeless power; said I not so? Nor was it wrung from me; nor do I now drop these links. Thou canst blind; but I can then grope. Thou canst consume; but I can then be ashes. Take the homage of these poor eyes, and shutter-hands. I would not take it. The lightning flashes through my skull; mine eye-balls ache and ache; my whole beaten brain seems as beheaded, and rolling on some stunning ground. Oh, oh! Yet blindfold, yet will I talk to thee. Light though thou be, thou leapest out of darkness; but I am darkness leaping out of light, leaping out of thee! The javelins cease; open eyes; see, or not? There burn the flames! Oh, thou magnanimous! now I do glory in my genealogy. But thou art but my fiery father; my sweet mother, I know not. Oh, cruel! what hast thou done with her? There lies my puzzle; but thine is greater. Thou knowest not how came ye, hence callest thyself unbegotten; certainly knowest not thy beginning, hence callest thyself unbegun. I know that of me, which thou knowest not of thyself, oh, thou omnipotent. There is some unsuffusing thing beyond thee, thou clear spirit, to whom all thy eternity is but time, all thy creativeness mechanical. Through thee, thy flaming self, my scorched eyes do dimly see it. Oh, thou foundling fire, thou hermit immemorial, thou too hast thy incommunicable riddle, thy unparticipated grief. Here again with haughty agony, I read my sire. Leap! leap up, and lick the sky! I leap with thee; I burn with thee; would fain be welded with thee; defyingly I worship thee!"

The right worship of the fathering flame is defiance. But the puzzle is the absent mother. It is pure Gnosticism when Ahab dimly sees "some unsuffusing thing" beyond the fire, the true breath or inmost soul that is no part of the Creation-Fall. The sweet mother is the Primal Abyss from which the fiery Demiurge stole the very stuff of existence. Here is Melville's "Fragments of a Lost Gnostic Poem of the Twelfth Century" (1866):

Found a family, build a state,
The pledged event is still the same:
Matter in end will never abate
His ancient brutal claim.

Indolence is heaven's ally here,
And energy the child of hell:
The Good Man pouring from his pitcher clear,
But brims the poisoned well.

This homage to the doomed Cathars of southern France, destroyed by the Albigensian Crusade (1209–29) of the Roman Catholic Church and its warriors, has the distinct accent of William Blake, but I know of no evidence that Melville had read him. The Cathars called themselves the Good Men and were slaughtered totally, women, children, men, at the orders of a bishop who is supposed to have cried out, "Kill them all; God will know His own."

I am not suggesting that *Moby-Dick* is a Gnostic epic. When the White Whale swims away with the drowned Ahab tied to him, the *Pequod* sunk, and all its mariners save one destroyed, I find myself dividing my deep respect between mad Ahab, his heroic crew, and the tormented but triumphant Leviathan. There remains Ishmael, somewhat beyond my understanding but strong in my affection. I revere survivors.

Moby-Dick achieves a total poignance in the great Chapter 132, "The Symphony":

Starbuck saw the old man; saw him, how he heavily leaned over the side; and he seemed to hear in his own true heart the measureless sobbing that stole out of the centre of the serenity around. Careful not to touch him, or be noticed by him, he yet drew near to him, and stood there.

Ahab turned.

"Starbuck!"

"Sir."

"Oh, Starbuck! it is a mild, mild wind, and a mild looking sky. On such a day—very much such a sweetness as this—I struck my first whale—a boy-harpooneer of eighteen! Forty—forty—forty years ago!—ago! Forty years of continual whaling! forty years of privation, and peril, and storm-time! forty years on the pitiless sea! for forty years has Ahab forsaken the peaceful land, for forty years to make war on the horrors of the deep! Aye and yes, Starbuck, out of those forty years I have not spent three ashore. When I think of this life I have led; the desolation of solitude it has been; the masoned, walled-town of a Captain's exclusiveness, which admits but small entrance to any sympathy from the green country without—oh, weariness! heaviness! Guinea-coast slavery of solitary command!—when I think of all this; only half-suspected, not so keenly known to me before—and how for forty years I have fed upon dry salted fare—fit emblem of the dry nourishment of my soil!—when the poorest landsman has had fresh fruit to his daily hand, and broken the world's fresh bread to my mouldy crusts—away, whole oceans away, from that young girl-wife I wedded past fifty, and sailed for Cape Horn the next day, leaving but one dent in my marriage pillow—wife? wife?—rather a widow with her husband alive! Aye, I widowed that poor girl when I married her, Starbuck; and then, the madness, the frenzy, the boiling blood and the smoking brow, with which, for a thousand lowerings old Ahab has furiously, foamingly chased his prey—more a demon than a man?—aye, aye! what a forty years' fool—fool—old fool, has old Ahab been! Why this strife of the chase? why weary, and palsy the arms at the oar, and the iron, and the lance? how the richer or better is Ahab now? Behold. Oh, Starbuck! is it not hard, that with this weary load I bear, one poor leg should have been snatched from under me? Here, brush this old hair aside; it blinds me, that I seem to weep. Locks so grey did never grow but from out some ashes! But do I look very old, so very, very old, Starbuck? I feel deadly faint, bowed, and humped, as though I were Adam, staggering beneath the piled centuries since Paradise. God! God! God!—crack my heart!—stave my brain!—mockery! mockery! bitter, biting mockery of grey hairs, have I lived enough joy to wear ye; and seem and feel thus intolerably old? Close! stand close to me, Starbuck; let me look into a human eye; it is better than to gaze into sea or sky; better than to gaze upon God. By the green land; by the bright hearth-stone! this is the magic glass, man; I see my wife and my child in thine eye. No, no; stay on board, on board!—lower not when I do; when branded Ahab gives chase to Moby Dick. That hazard shall not be thine. No, no! not with the far away home I see in that eye!"

"What is it, what nameless, inscrutable, unearthly thing is it; what cozening, hidden lord and master, and cruel, remorseless emperor commands me; that against all natural lovings and longings, I so keep pushing, and crowding, and jamming myself on all the time; recklessly making me ready to do what in my own proper, natural heart, I durst not so much as dare? Is Ahab, Ahab? Is it I, God, or who, that lifts this arm? But if the great sun move not of himself; but is as an errand-boy in heaven; nor one single star can revolve, but by some invisible power; how then can this one small heart beat; this one small brain think thoughts; unless God does that beating, does that thinking, does that living, and not I. By heaven, man, we are turned round and round in this world, like yonder windlass, and Fate is the handspike. And all the time, lo! that smiling sky, and this unsounded sea! Look! see yon Albicore! who put it into him to chase and fang that flying-fish? Where do murderers go, man! Who's to doom, when the judge himself is dragged to the bar? But it is a mild, mild wind, and a mild looking sky; and the air smells now, as if it blew from a far-away meadow; they have been making hay somewhere under the slopes of the Andes, Starbuck, and the mowers are sleeping among the new-mown hay. Sleeping? Aye, toil we how we may, we all sleep at last on the field. Sleep? Aye, and rust amid greenness; as last year's scythes flung down, and left in the half-cut swaths— Starbuck!"

But blanched to a corpse's hue with despair, the Mate had stolen away.

Ahab crossed the deck to gaze over on the other side; but started at two reflected, fixed eyes in the water there. Fedallah was motionlessly leaning over the same rail.

Fedallah may be Ahab's shadow self or he may be more instrument than agency. He performs the function of the Fatal Sisters in *Macbeth*, both holding off and prophesying Ahab's destruction by the White Whale.

The three-day chase of Moby-Dick begins. Ahab's, Stubbs's, Flask's boats pursue, but Ahab orders Starbuck to stay with the *Pequod:*

Soon all the boats but Starbuck's were dropped; all the boat-sails set—all the paddles plying; with rippling swiftness, shooting to leeward; and Ahab heading the onset. A pale, death-glimmer lit up Fedallah's sunken eyes; a hideous motion gnawed his mouth.

Like noiseless nautilus shells, their light prows sped through the sea; but only slowly they neared the foe. As they neared him, the ocean grew still more smooth; seemed drawing a carpet over its waves; seemed a noon-meadow, so serenely it spread. At length the breathless hunter came so nigh his seemingly unsuspecting prey, that his entire dazzling hump was distinctly visible, sliding along the sea as if an isolated thing, and continually set in a revolving ring of finest, fleecy, greenish foam. He saw the vast involved wrinkles of the slightly projecting head beyond. Before it, far out on the soft Turkish-rugged waters, went the glistening white shadow from his broad, milky forehead, a musical rippling playfully accompanying the shade; and behind, the blue waters interchangeably flowed over into the moving valley of his steady wake; and on either hand bright bubbles arose and danced by his side. But these were broken again by the light toes of hundreds of gay fowl softly feathering the sea, alternate with their fitful flight; and like to some flag-staff rising from the painted hull of an argosy, the tall but shattered pole of a recent lance projected from the white whale's back; and at intervals one of the cloud of soft-toed fowls hovering, and to and fro skimming like a canopy over the fish, silently perched and rocked on this pole, the long tail feathers streaming like pennons.

A gentle joyousness—a mighty mildness of repose in swiftness, invested the gliding whale. Not the white bull Jupiter swimming away with ravished Europa clinging to his graceful horns; his lovely, leering eyes sideways intent upon the maid; with smooth bewitching fleetness, rippling straight for the nuptial bower in Crete; not Jove, not that great majesty Supreme! did surpass the glorified White Whale as he so divinely swam.

On each soft side—coincident with the parted swell, that but once leaving him, then flowed so wide away—on each bright side, the whale shed off enticings. No wonder there had been some among the hunters who namelessly transported and allured by all this serenity, had ventured to assail it; but had fatally found that quietude but the vesture of tornadoes. Yet calm, enticing calm, oh, whale! thou glidest on, to all who for the first time eye thee, no matter how many in that same way thou may'st have bejuggled and destroyed before.

And thus, through the serene tranquillities of the tropical sea, among waves whose hand-clappings were suspended by exceeding rapture, Moby Dick moved on, still withholding from sight the full terrors of his submerged trunk, entirely hiding the wrenched hideousness of his jaw. But soon the fore part of him slowly rose from the water; for an instant his whole marbleized body formed a high arch, like Virginia's Natural Bridge, and warningly waving his bannered flukes in the air, the grand god revealed himself, sounded, and went out of sight. Hoveringly halting, and dipping on the wing, the white sea-fowls longingly lingered over the agitated pool that he left.

It is Melville's peculiar daemon that gives us the disturbing identity of the white bull Jupiter ravishing Europa with the White Whale awarding death to his provokers:

But soon resuming his horizontal attitude, Moby Dick swam swiftly round and round the wrecked crew; sideways churning the water in his vengeful wake, as if lashing himself up to still another and more deadly assault. The sight of the splintered boat seemed to madden him, as the blood of grapes and mulberries cast before Antiochus's elephants in the book of Maccabees. Meanwhile Ahab half smothered in the foam of the whale's insolent tail, and too much of a cripple to swim,—though he could still keep afloat, even in the heart of such a whirlpool as that; helpless Ahab's head was seen, like a tossed bubble which the least chance shock might burst. From the boat's fragmentary stern, Fedallah incuriously and mildly eyed him; the clinging crew, at the other drifting end, could not succor him; more than enough was it for them to look to themselves. For so revolvingly appalling was the White Whale's aspect, and so planetarily swift the ever-contracting circles he made, that he seemed horizontally swooping upon them. And though the other boats, unharmed, still hovered hard by; still they dared not pull into the eddy to strike, lest that should be the signal for the instant destruction of the jeopardized castaways, Ahab and all; nor in that case could they themselves hope to escape. With straining eyes, then, they remained on the outer edge of the direful zone, whose centre had now become the old man's head.

Meantime, from the beginning all this had been descried from the ship's mast-heads; and squaring her yards, she had borne down upon the scene; and was now so nigh, that Ahab in the water hailed her;—"Sail on the"—but that moment a breaking sea dashed on him from Moby Dick, and whelmed him for the time. But struggling out of it again, and chancing to rise on a towering crest, he shouted,—"Sail on the Whale!—Drive him off!"

Fedallah seems beyond affect while Ahab is insanely heroic. Rescued by Stubbs's boat, the warlike Ahab has to suspend his quest as the night comes on, and then returns to the chase for a second day:

"Great God! but for one single instant show thyself," cried Starbuck; "never, never wilt thou capture him, old man—In Jesus' name no more of this, that's worse than devil's madness. Two days chased; twice stove to splinters; thy very leg once more snatched from under thee; thy evil shadow gone—all good angels mobbing thee with warnings:—what more wouldst thou have?—Shall we keep chasing this murderous fish till he swamps the last man? Shall we be dragged by him to the bottom of the sea? Shall we be towed by him to the infernal world? Oh, oh,—Impiety and blasphemy to hunt him more!"

"Starbuck, of late I've felt strangely moved to thee; ever since that hour we both saw—thou know'st what, in one another's eyes. But in this matter of the whale, be the front of thy face to me as the palm of this hand—a lipless, unfeatured blank. Ahab is for ever Ahab, man. This whole act's immutably decreed. 'Twas rehearsed by thee and me a billion years before this ocean rolled. Fool! I am the Fates' lieutenant; I act under orders. Look thou, underling! that thou obeyest mine.—Stand round me, men. Ye see an old man cut down to the stump; leaning on a shivered lance; propped up on a lonely foot. 'Tis Ahab—his body's part; but Ahab's soul's a centipede, that moves upon a hundred legs. I feel strained, half stranded, as ropes that tow dismasted frigates in a gale; and I may look so. But ere I break, ye'll hear me crack; and till ye hear *that,* know that Ahab's hawser tows his purpose yet. Believe ye, men, in the things called omens? Then laugh aloud, and cry encore! For ere they drown, drowning things will twice rise to the surface; then rise again, to sink for evermore. So with Moby Dick—two days he's floated—to-morrow will be the third. Aye, men, he'll rise once more,—but only to spout his last! D'ye feel brave, men, brave?"

"As fearless fire," cried Stubb.

"And as mechanical," muttered Ahab. Then as the men went forward, he muttered on:—"The things called omens! And yesterday I talked the same to Starbuck there, concerning my broken boat. Oh! how valiantly I seek to drive out of others' hearts what's clinched so fast in mine!—The Parsee—the Parsee!—gone, gone? and he was to go before:—but still was to be seen again ere I could perish—How's that?—There's a riddle now might baffle all the lawyers backed by the ghosts of the whole line of judges:—like a hawk's beak it pecks my brain. *I'll, I'll* solve it, though!"

When dusk descended, the whale was still in sight to leeward.

Birnam Wood will come to Dunsinane. Dead Fedallah will be seen again. The Fates govern Ahab. And Melville sails us to the catastrophe of the Third Day:

"...What's that he said? he should still go before me, my pilot; and yet to be seen again? But where? Will I have eyes at the bottom of the sea, supposing I descend those endless stairs? and all night I've been sailing from him, wherever he did sink to. Aye, aye, like many more thou told'st direful truth as touching thyself, O Parsee; but, Ahab, there thy shot fell short. Good-bye, mast-head—keep a good eye upon the whale, the while I'm gone. We'll talk to-morrow, nay, to-night, when the white whale lies down there, tied by head and tail."

He gave the word; and still gazing round him, was steadily lowered through the cloven blue air to the deck.

In due time the boats were lowered; but as standing in his shallop's stern, Ahab just hovered upon the point of the descent, he waved to the mate,—who held one of the tackle-ropes on deck—and bade him pause.

"Starbuck!"

"Sir?"

"For the third time my soul's ship starts upon this voyage, Starbuck."

"Aye, sir, thou wilt have it so."

"Some ships sail from their ports, and ever afterwards are missing, Starbuck!"

"Truth, sir: saddest truth."

"Some men die at ebb tide; some at low water; some at the full of the flood;—and I feel now like a billow that's all one crested comb, Starbuck. I am old;—shake hands with me, man."

Their hands met; their eyes fastened; Starbuck's tears the glue.

"Oh, my captain, my captain!—noble heart—go not—go not!—see, it's a brave man that weeps; how great the agony of the persuasion then!"

"Lower away!"—cried Ahab, tossing the mate's arm from him. "Stand by the crew!"

I always wonder, repeating this to myself, how anyone could not admire Ahab. He is more Job than Macbeth, more Hamlet than Iago, more King Lear than Edmund. These are the American fictive heroes: Ahab, Hester Prynne, Huckleberry Finn and Jim, and the persona: "Walt Whitman, an American, one of the roughs, a kosmos." Add to them from reality Abraham Lincoln and Walt Whitman the Wound-Dresser. Is Ahab culpable for destroying his crew? Except for Starbuck, all of them enthusiastically joined in the quest, including Ishmael the survivor. Perhaps the White Whale is the most American of heroes:

Suddenly the waters around them slowly swelled in broad circles; then quickly upheaved, as if sideways sliding from a submerged berg of ice, swiftly rising to the surface. A low rumbling sound was heard; a subterraneous hum; and then all held their breaths; as bedraggled with trailing ropes, and harpoons, and lances, a vast form shot lengthwise, but obliquely from the sea. Shrouded in a thin drooping veil of mist, it hovered for a moment in the rainbowed air; and then fell swamping back into the deep. Crushed thirty feet upwards, the waters flashed for an instant like heaps of fountains, then brokenly sank in a shower of flakes, leaving the circling surface creamed like new milk round the marble trunk of the whale.

"Give way!" cried Ahab to the oarsmen, and the boats darted forward to the attack; but maddened by yesterday's fresh irons that corroded in him, Moby Dick seemed combinedly possessed by all the angels that fell him from heaven. The wide tiers of welded tendons overspreading his broad white forehead, beneath the transparent skin, looked knitted together; as head on, he came churning his tail among the boats; and once more flailed them apart; spilling out the irons and lances from the two mates' boats, and dashing in one side of the upper part of their bows, but leaving Ahab's almost without a scar.

While Daggoo and Tashtego were stopping the strained planks; and as the whale swimming out from them, turned, and showed one entire flank as he shot by them again; at that moment a quick cry went up. Lashed round and round to the fish's back; pinioned in the turns upon turns in which, during the past night, the whale had reeled the involutions of the lines around him, the half torn body of the Parsee was seen; his sable raiment frayed to shreds; his distended eyes turned full upon old Ahab.

The harpoon dropped from his hand.

"Befooled, befooled!"—drawing in a long lean breath—"Aye, Parsee! I see thee again.—Aye, and thou goest before; and this, *this* then is the hearse that thou didst promise. But I hold thee to the last letter of thy word. Where is the second hearse? Away, mates, to the ship! those boats are useless now; repair them if ye can in time, and return to me; if not, Ahab is enough to die—Down, men! the first thing that but offers to jump from this boat I stand in, that thing I harpoon. Ye are not other men, but my arms and my legs; and so obey me.—Where's the whale? gone down again?"

If *Moby-Dick* has a fault, it is too much flooded by Shakespeare. But what fault could be nobler? The second hearse shall be Queequeg's coffin, upon which Ishmael will ride to safety. It is difficult to judge between the two daemons, Ahab and Moby-Dick, matched in desperate resolution but not, alas, in power:

At length as the craft was cast to one side, and ran ranging along with White Whale's flank, he seemed strangely oblivious of its advance—as the whale sometimes will—and Ahab was fairly within the smoky mountain mist, which, thrown off from the whale's spout, curled round his great, Monadnock hump; he was even thus close to him; when, with body arched back, and both arms lengthwise high-lifted to the poise, he darted his fierce iron, and his far fiercer curse into the hated whale. As both steel and curse sank into the socket, as if sucked into a morass, Moby Dick sideways writhed; spasmodically rolled his nigh flank against the bow, and, without staving a hole in it, so suddenly canted the boat over, that had it not been for the elevated part of the gunwale to which he then clung, Ahab would once more have been tossed into the sea. As it was, three of the oarsmen—who foreknew not the precise instant of the dart, and were therefore unprepared for its effects—these were flung out; but so fell, that, in an instant two of them clutched the gunwale again, and rising to its level on a combing wave, hurled themselves bodily inboard again; the third man helplessly dropping astern, but still afloat and swimming.

Almost simultaneously, with a mighty volition of ungraduated, instantaneous swiftness, the White Whale darted through the weltering sea. But when Ahab cried out to the steersman to take new turns with the line, and hold it so; and commanded the crew to turn round on their seats, and tow the boat up to the mark; the moment the treacherous line felt that double strain and tug, it snapped in the empty air!

"What breaks in me? Some sinew cracks!—'tis whole again; oars! oars! Burst in upon him!"

Hearing the tremendous rush of the sea-crashing boat, the whale wheeled round to present his blank forehead at bay; but in that evolution, catching sight of the nearing black hull of the ship; seemingly seeing in it the source of all his persecutions; bethinking it—it may be—a larger and nobler foe; of a sudden, he bore down upon its advancing prow, smiting his jaws amid fiery showers of foam.

It may be that the White Whale is not so much Job's Leviathan, or Yahweh's, as it is the Gnostic Demiurge incarnate. From Moby-

Dick's perspective, the *Pequod* is Satan, source of all his persecutions. I wish William Blake had lived to read *Moby-Dick*. He would have told us even more forcefully that this history has been adopted by both parties:

From the ship's bows, nearly all the seamen now hung inactive; hammers, bits of plank, lances, and harpoons, mechanically retained in their hands, just as they had darted from their various employments; all their enchanted eyes intent upon the whale, which from side to side strangely vibrating his predestinating head, sent a broad band of overspreading semicircular foam before him as he rushed. Retribution, swift vengeance, eternal malice were in his whole aspect, and spite of all that mortal man could do, the solid white buttress of his forehead smote the ship's starboard bow, till men and timbers reeled. Some fell flat upon their faces. Like dislodged trucks, the heads of the harpooners aloft shook on their bull-like necks. Through the breach, they heard the waters pour, as mountain torrents down a flume.

"The ship! The hearse!—the second hearse!" cried Ahab from the boat; "its wood could only be American!"

Diving beneath the settling ship, the whale ran quivering along its keel; but turning under water, swiftly shot to the surface again, far off the other bow, but within a few yards of Ahab's boat, where, for a time, he lay quiescent.

"I turn my body from the sun. What ho, Tashtego! let me hear thy hammer. Oh! ye three unsurrendered spires of mine; thou uncracked keel; and only god-bullied hull; thou firm deck, and haughty helm, and Pole-pointed prow,—death-glorious ship! must ye then perish, and without me? Am I cut off from the last fond pride of meanest shipwrecked captains? Oh, lonely death on lonely life! Oh, now I feel my topmost greatness lies in my topmost grief. Ho, ho! from all your furthest bounds, pour ye now in, ye bold billows of my whole foregone life, and top this one piled comber of my death! Towards thee I roll, thou all-destroying but unconquering whale; to the last I grapple with thee; from hell's heart I stab at thee; for hate's sake I spit my last breath at thee. Sink all coffins and all hearses to one common pool! and since neither can be mine, let me then tow to pieces, while still chasing thee, though tied to thee, thou damned whale! *Thus,* I give up the spear!"

The harpoon was darted; the stricken whale flew forward; with igniting velocity the line ran through the groove;—ran foul. Ahab stooped to clear it; he did clear it; but the flying turn caught him round the neck, and voicelessly as Turkish mutes bowstring their victim, he was shot out of the boat, ere the crew knew he was gone. Next instant, the heavy eye-splice in the rope's final end flew out of the stark-empty tub, knocked down an oarsman, and smiting the sea, disappeared in its depths.

The *Pequod* goes down but to what purposeless purpose?

But as the last whelmings intermixingly poured themselves over the sunken head of the Indian at the mainmast, leaving a few inches of the erect spar yet visible, together with long streaming yards of the flag, which calmly undulated, with ironical coincidings, over the destroying billows they almost touched;—at that instant, a red arm and a hammer hovered backwardly uplifted in the open air, in the act of nailing the flag faster and yet faster to the subsiding spar. A sky-hawk that tauntingly had followed the main-truck downwards from its natural home among the stars, pecking at the flag, and incommoding Tashtego there; this bird now chanced to intercept its broad fluttering wing between the hammer and the wood; and simultaneously feeling that ethereal thrill, the submerged savage beneath, in his death-gasp, kept his hammer frozen there; and so the bird of heaven, with archangelic shrieks, and his imperial beak thrust upwards, and his whole captive form folded in the flag of Ahab, went down with his ship, which, like Satan, would not sink to hell till she had dragged a living part of heaven along with her, and helmeted herself with it.

Now small fowls flew screaming over the yet yawning gulf; a sullen white surf beat against its steep sides; then all collapsed, and the great shroud of the sea rolled on as it rolled five thousand years ago.

Tashtego takes the hawk as an emblem of the freedom of the air down into the great shroud of the sea. I am a little unnerved by the manifestation of Milton's Satan, yet I think we must read hell and heaven here from a Blakean and Shelleyan perspective. The Gnostic Melville always strikes through the mask. We return to Noah's flood but with an ark consisting only of Queequeg's coffin, with an isolated Ishmael surviving to tell his story. What remains is the superb epilogue:

EPILOGUE
"And I only am escaped alone to tell thee."   *Job.*

The drama's done. Why then here does any one step forth?—
Because one did survive the wreck.

It so chanced, that after the Parsee's disappearance, I was he whom the Fates ordained to take the place of Ahab's bowsman, when that bowsman assumed the vacant post; the same, who, when on the last day the three men were tossed from out the rocking boat, was dropped astern. So, floating on the margin of the ensuing scene, and in full sight of it, when the half-spent suction of the sunk ship reached me, I was then, but slowly, drawn towards the closing vortex. When I reached it, it had subsided to a creamy pool. Round and round, then, and ever contracting towards the button-like black bubble at the axis of that slowly wheeling circle, like another Ixion I did revolve. Till, gaining that vital centre, the black bubble upward burst; and now, liberated by reason of its cunning spring, and, owing to its greatest buoyancy, rising with great force, the coffin life-buoy shot lengthwise from the sea, fell over, and floated by my side Buoyed up by that coffin, for almost one whole day and night, I floated on a soft and dirge-like main. The unharming sharks, they glided by as if with padlocks on their mouths; the savage sea-hawks sailed with sheathed beaks. On the second day, a sail drew near, nearer, and picked me up at last. It was the devious cruising Rachel, that in her retracing search after her missing children, only found another orphan.
FINIS

The epic's final epigraph is the culmination of Job 1:19, where four individuals express the same dreadful report, the destruction of Job's children, servants, flocks. I once wondered whether Ishmael now would be Rachel's son Joseph the Redeemer or her younger son, Benjamin, whom the grieving Jacob kept always by his side. Insofar as Ishmael is a persistent interpreter, he might seem to be Joseph, skilled in the art of clarifying dreams. Yet Ishmael, though very likable, is unreliable, and so has not the eminence of a Joseph. He is a Benjamin, another lost child.

CHAPTER 15

Bleak House (1853)

CHARLES DICKENS

THREE-QUARTERS OF A CENTURY AGO, my favorite Dickens was *The Pickwick Papers* (1836–37), his first novel. I was thirteen and enchanted by it. Five years after, I became obsessed with *Bleak House,* a choice that lasted until I had read all of Dickens and was drawn in by the dank and frightening *Our Mutual Friend,* his last completed novel. *The Mystery of Edwin Drood,* left a bit more than half done when he died on June 9, 1870, is even darker, but we will never know how it was to end. Dickens died at fifty-eight, worn out by his incessant and exhausting public reading of his works to large and enthusiastic audiences. Had he not become one of the greatest novelists, he could have had a remarkable career on the stage. Five years before the stroke that killed him, he and his young actress protégée Ellen Ternan had been in a train wreck that killed ten passengers and injured many, including Dickens, who did his heroic best to attend to the other victims. He had separated from his wife, Catherine, in 1858, after twenty-two years of a rather difficult marriage in which she had endured ten pregnancies.

The liveliest biography of Dickens is by Peter Ackroyd (1991). I have learned a great deal from a study by Alexander Welsh, *The City of Dickens* (1971). Anyone who reads Dickens frequently and deeply will be impressed by the personal quality of his attachment to the figure of Jesus. For Dickens, Christianity *was* Jesus and consisted in compassion, sincerity, charity on an individual basis. Dickens felt contempt for all who professed to be Christian but loathed, exploited, or ignored the sufferings of the poor, the homeless, child laborers, outcast women, all the injured and insulted of London and the world.

The Dickens of *Our Mutual Friend* (1865) has affinities with the Victor Hugo of *Les Misérables* (1862). Both titans defend the wretched of the earth, and both descend into the underbelly of their cities and rivers. Death and resurrection alike come out of the muck, dust piles, and human waste of the Thames and the Seine. And money in all its corruption is identified by both with feces. Hugo is more optimistic ultimately than Dickens, because Victor Hugo confused himself with God. Dickens, to his sorrow, knew better.

Bleak House, which appeared as installments from 1852 to 1853, was judged by the irascible yet brilliant curmudgeon G. K. Chesterton to be Dickens's best novel, though not necessarily his best book. As a formal judgment, this seems right to me. With enormous skill Dickens juggles a remarkably diverse cast of characters and resolves an intricate plot by making precisely appropriate employment of them all.

The most important is Esther Summerson, who, if I remember properly, is the only woman to narrate a substantial part of a Dickens novel. When I was very young, I so loved Esther that I wept when she wept. I have ceased from that but am very moved by her to this day. Raised by a Miss Barbary (her undisclosed aunt), poor Esther was made to feel by that dreadful lady that she was somehow guilty for her birth as the bastard of supposedly unknown parents. In consequence, the sweet-natured Esther has no expectations of joy, lacks all self-esteem, and is heartbreakingly cheered by any good fortune or incident. I sometimes feel Dickens rather piles it on when Esther catches smallpox from a stricken child she is nursing, and loses much of her beauty.

Later in the novel we learn that Lady Honoria Dedlock was Esther's mother and that one Nemo ("nobody" in Latin) was her father in a love affair that could not endure. Nemo was actually Captain James Hawdon, once an army officer and the commander of the admirable trooper Mr. George. Hawdon has been reduced to a scrivener copying law documents for the good-natured Mr. Snagsby, who befriends the street urchin Jo, a pathetic sweeper, as does Nemo until he dies of an opium overdose. Inspector Bucket, who otherwise is very likable indeed, in his one bad act accepts payment from the malign lawyer Mr. Tulkinghorn to harry Jo so as to force him out of London. Tulkinghorn is Sir Leicester Dedlock's attorney and fears needlessly that Nemo might have told Jo the secret of Esther's birth. There are other savage lawyers in Dickens, but I particularly loathe Tulkinghorn and am delighted when he is murdered by Hortense, the French maid to Lady Dedlock, who vies with Madame Thérèse Defarge of *The Tale of Two Cities* as one of Dickens's sexiest avengers.

Esther's guardian is John Jarndyce, a generous and amiable man who is an unwilling principal in the endless Chancery lawsuit of *Jarndyce v. Jarndyce.* He is benignly in love with Esther and in a fatherly way wishes to marry her but readily gives her up when she falls in love with Allan Woodcourt, a young surgeon in every way estimable. After her customary struggle with her sense of personal unworthiness, Esther accepts Woodcourt.

Dickens ingeniously fashions *Bleak House* by intermingling two narratives, Esther's and a voice describing things as they occur. That narrator occupies thirty-four chapters, whereas Esther has thirty-three, but the impression I receive is that the novel is essentially Esther's story. Whose else could it be? There are the vivid characters who carry much of the life of *Bleak House:* Mr. George the trooper, Harold Skimpole the sponger (Leigh Hunt), Lawrence Boythorn (Walter Savage Landor), and Honoria, Lady Dedlock, Esther's mother. Leigh Hunt, a minor poet and radical journalist, is remembered now as the close friend of both Keats and Shelley, while Landor, a very good poet and the author also of the engaging *Imaginary Conversations* (1824–29), was famously irascible, endlessly involved in lawsuits, and quarreling with almost everyone. Dickens skewers Skimpole-Hunt and enjoys Boythorn-Landor as much as we do. Mr. George is a pillar of honor, but the unfortunate Honoria dies a suicidal death, unaware that her bereaved husband forgives her everything.

Yet it remains Esther's book. Flaubert said that he was Madame Bovary. Esther Summerson is neither David Copperfield nor Pip. They are Dickens. Still, I wonder if she also is not the abandoned child in Dickens himself, cast off by his parents into a blacking factory when his father went to prison for debt. Charles Dickens all his life was haunted by that humiliation at the age of just twelve. I find it astonishing that he was kept at the factory by his callous mother. Long after his release from that bondage, he continued to resent his mother. Presumably, his conviction that women should stay home as wives and mothers emerged from this experience.

I love Dickens most fiercely when he is totally outrageous, which is why I now set *Our Mutual Friend* over even *Bleak House*. My favorite character in *Bleak House* could also adorn *Our Mutual Friend*. This is Krook, who lives entirely on gin and runs a shop overflowing with papers, rags, and bottles. The dwellers in his house include Nemo, who dies there, and the mad Miss Flite, an aged crone who is another victim of Chancery and who keeps a horde of little birds, which she says will be released only at the Last Judgment. Krook ignites in spontaneous combustion, a splendid event in whose probability Dickens actually believed.

Richard Carstone, the ultimate victim of Chancery, has secretly married Ada Clare, another ward of Chancery. When the case is resolved and there is no money left, as everything has gone to the lawyers, Carstone collapses and dies rather virtuously, forgiving himself everything and urging his wife to do the same:

'I have done you many wrongs, my own. I have fallen like a poor stray shadow on your way, I have married you to poverty and trouble, I have scattered your means to the winds. You will forgive me all this, my Ada, before I begin the world?'

A smile irradiated his face, as she bent to kiss him. He slowly laid his face down upon her bosom, drew his arms closer round her neck, and with one parting sob began the world. Not this world, O not this! The world that sets this right.

When all was still, at a late hour, poor crazed Miss Flite came weeping to me, and told me she had given her birds their liberty.

This ending of *Bleak House*, whatever one thinks of it, is as close to an apocalypse as Dickens gets until he writes *Our Mutual Friend* and the final fragment, *The Mystery of Edwin Drood*. I think that the last sentence partly redeems the conclusion.

CHAPTER 16

Our Mutual Friend (1865)

CHARLES DICKENS

T HE BEST REMARKS I have seen on *Our Mutual Friend* are made by Adrian Poole in his introduction to the Penguin Classics volume (1997):

Our Mutual Friend boasts less confidence than earlier works in its own last judgements. It finds a truer sense of its deepest attention in the moments of suspense. As if the writer and his readers were poised, like a doctor and his attendants, over the body of a world, the soul of which seems to hover and flicker, between renewal and extinction. The doctor who seeks to revive the dank corpse is only one of the writer's possible guises. There is another doctor who gently eases the passage of a dying child out of this world. And there is plenty of other work to be done over corpses, for coroners and pathologists, for ministers of religion and articulators of bones.

In Poole's view, the title could be read: *Death Is Our Mutual Friend.* A palpable hit. And yet, to quote Robert Browning, "A common greyness silvers everything." Poole once amiably disputed my notion that, except for Macbeth and his Lady, Shakespeare subdued the tragedy's characters to a common grayness. With appropriate amiability, I might venture that death and resurrection fuse in *Our Mutual Friend* in a cosmos so fetid and so fecund that all demarcations are rendered ghostlier even as the sounds of Dickens's diction achieve a new keenness.

Our Mutual Friend is a vast eight-hundred-page prose poem unlike anything else that I have ever read. I can think only of Victor Hugo's *Les Misérables* as a rough analogue. In his postscript, Dickens concluded with a terrible memory of the railway accident of June 9, 1865, in which he was injured but heroically labored to help and comfort the maimed and the dying. He survived to finish *Our Mutual Friend* and ended the postscript with a poignant sentence:

> I remember with devout thankfulness that I can never be much nearer parting company with my readers for ever, than I was then, until there shall be written against my life, the two words with which I have this day closed this book:—The END.
>
> September 2nd, 1865.

Five years to the day after the train wreck, Charles Dickens died, on June 9, 1870, at the age of fifty-eight. There is a gap between *Great Expectations* (1860–61) and *Our Mutual Friend* (1864–65). It was unlike Dickens to lie fallow for almost three years. Trauma may be a part of the explanation. The separation from his wife, Catherine, in 1858 took place a year after he fell in love with the eighteen-year-old actress Ellen Ternan. Peter Ackroyd persuasively argues that the relationship with Ternan, which lasted the rest of Dickens's life, was never sexually consummated. Six years after the novelist's death, she married, then had two children, and died at seventy-five in 1914. Most biographers disagree with Ackroyd's judgment. It seems sound to me, because Dickens at forty-five started to yield again to his childhood traumas and found in Ellen Ternan an idealized object.

The energies that would have given us other novels to read, as we now read and reread *Bleak House* and *Our Mutual Friend,* were absorbed by endless public readings in which Dickens performed to huge audiences his own characters and their stories. If only the art of the film had existed that early, we would have these unrivaled enactments, but since we cannot, and all their auditors are deceased, it has to be regarded as a waste and a loss.

Dickens is almost always magnificent at openings and curiously weak when ending a novel. *Our Mutual Friend* begins on the Thames with grotesque power:

In these times of ours, though concerning the exact year there is no need to be precise, a boat of dirty and disreputable appearance, with two figures in it, floated on the Thames, between Southwark Bridge which is of iron, and London Bridge which is of stone, as an autumn evening was closing in.

The figures in this boat were those of a strong man with ragged grizzled hair and a sun-browned face, and a dark girl of nineteen or twenty, sufficiently like him to be recognizable as his daughter. The girl rowed, pulling a pair of sculls very easily; the man, with the rudder-lines slack in his hands, and his hands loose in his waistband, kept an eager look out. He had no net, hook, or line, and he could not be a fisherman; his boat had no cushion for a sitter, no paint, no inscription, no appliance beyond a rusty boathook and a coil of rope, and he could not be a waterman; his boat was too crazy and too small to take in cargo for delivery, and he could not be a lighterman or river-carrier; there was no clue to what he looked for, but he looked for something, with a most intent and searching gaze. The tide, which had turned an hour before, was running down, and his eyes watched every little race and eddy in its broad sweep, as the boat made slight head-way against it, or drove stern foremost before it, according as he directed his daughter by a movement of his head. She watched his face as earnestly as he watched the river. But, in the intensity of her look there was a touch of dread or horror.

Allied to the bottom of the river rather than the surface, by reason of the slime and ooze with which it was covered, and its sodden state, this boat and the two figures in it obviously were doing something that they often did, and were seeking what they often sought. Half savage as the man showed, with no covering on his matted head, with his brown arms bare to between the elbow and the shoulder, with the loose knot of a looser kerchief lying low on his bare breast in a wilderness of beard and whisker, with such dress as he wore seeming to be made out of the mud that begrimed his boat, still there was a business-like usage in his steady gaze. So with every lithe action of the girl, with every turn of her wrist, perhaps most of all with her look of dread or horror; they were things of usage.

The Thames itself is the protagonist of *Our Mutual Friend*. Lizzie Hexam, Mortimer Lightwood, Eugene Wrayburn, Jenny Wren, Mr. Riah, Bradley Headstone, Fascination Fledgeby, Rogue Riderhood, and the man with three names—John Harmon, John Rokesmith, Julius Handford—are nine vital figures in the book, but without the Thames they might not sustain our full interest. Lizzie Hexam's father, Gaffer; Bradley Headstone; and Rogue Riderhood all suffer death by water. John Harmon supposedly does, but that is his rather peculiar subterfuge. Eugene Wrayburn, after a brutal attack from behind by Headstone, is rescued from the river by Lizzie, who helps nurse him slowly back to health. Rogue Riderhood, before being wrestled into drowning by the suicidal Headstone, himself undergoes a resurrection from near drowning earlier in the book. The abominable Fascination Fledgeby receives a much-deserved beating but unfortunately survives. Mortimer Lightwood, Jenny Wren, and the tiresomely good Jew, Mr. Riah, are the only major figures left unstained by the turgid water (to call it that) of what William Blake in an earlier draft of his poem "London" termed "the dirty Thames."

Riah was Dickens's apology for the wonderful Fagin in *Oliver Twist*, an apology inevitably lame. After Shylock, Fagin is the most persuasive of all anti-Semitic caricatures.

"He Do the Police in Different Voices" was T. S. Eliot's original title for what became *The Waste Land* (1922). Ezra Pound brilliantly hacked away at Eliot's manuscript, thus producing the poem we have all read. Eliot was precise when he invoked *Our Mutual Friend*, which is the London apocalypse that preluded *The Waste Land*.

Who survives in *Our Mutual Friend*? Aside from John Harmon and Bella Wilfer, who achieve harmonious marriage but are pale figures, there are Eugene Wrayburn and Lizzie Hexam, whose saving marriage charms the reader. Wrayburn matures into a resurrected consciousness, and the wonderful Lizzie, whom first we saw rowing her father on his scavenging expedition, becomes even more angelic and comforting. Then there is Mortmer Lightwood, once insouciant and ironic, who is exalted by the relationship between Eugene and Lizzie. With a finer edge of irony, he concludes the novel by returning to Society, and is rightly appalled by it. Best of all are Jenny Wren and Sloppy, who seems to fall in love with her, and Dickens perhaps intimates that they may yet make a match.

Jenny Wren is one of the most underpraised figures in Dickens. A lame teenager, afflicted by her care of an alcoholic father, whom she calls her child and who finally yields to a drunken death, she has a strange wit of her own. At one moment when the abominable Fascination Fledgeby calls to her and Riah in their little roof garden, she cries out: "Come up and be dead! Come up and be dead!"

As a doll maker Jenny Wren is a consummate artist, and maintains herself by it. She calls Riah her fairy godfather and tells him and the rest of us that she awaits her prince to take her away. Sloppy, a foundling, is sweeter and kinder than any prince could be, and if indeed they wind up together, that would be another blessing Dickens confers upon us.

There remains the riding Thames, and nothing mitigates Dickens's vision of the dark waters. Memorable and unforgiving, the river destroys and rarely nourishes.

CHAPTER 17

Madame Bovary (1857)

GUSTAVE FLAUBERT

I FIRST READ *Madame Bovary* in the wooden translation by Eleanor Marx Aveling, with some revisions supposedly by my late friend Paul de Man. Eleanor Marx was a daughter of Karl Marx and became a socialist activist. She committed suicide at the age of forty-three, when she discovered that her partner, Edward, was a bigamist.

Fortunately, in 1987 I finally read it in French and began the long process of being haunted by it. I have just read the marvelous version by Lydia Davis, which seems to me a touchstone for literary translation. Her *Madame Bovary* is a kind of miracle, as is her *Swann's Way* (2004). I am still absorbing her startling short fictions, as they are sui generis.

In 1832, at the age of eleven, Flaubert read *Don Quixote*, which, together with Goethe and, to a smaller extent, Balzac, constituted his prime literary influences, though he read so widely and deeply that he rivals Montaigne in his ambience. Flaubert seems to have had a form of epilepsy, but the major hazards to his health came from his promiscuity with female and male prostitutes in his Middle Eastern tours. He contracted syphilis early in his life, and died at fifty-eight, but probably from a heart attack brought on by epilepsy.

Flaubert did not marry and had no children. In a letter to his sometime mistress, the poet Louise Colet, he denounced childbearing, saying he did not wish to "transmit...the aggravations and the disgrace of existence."

It seems wrong to call Flaubert a misogynist. For many years he had a deep love, scarcely sexual, for Elisa Schlesinger, who was married and a decade older. He famously identifies with Emma Bovary. The critic Albert Thibaudet in his *Gustave Flaubert* (1922) splendidly compares Flaubert's stance toward Emma to Milton's in regard to Eve: "Whenever Emma is seen in purely sensuous terms, he speaks of her with a delicate, almost religious feeling, the way Milton speaks of Eve."

Like so many readers, I feel that Milton desires Eve. Flaubert's love for Emma necessarily is narcissistic. It is a useful truism to call Emma Bovary a female Quixote, since, like the Knight, she is murdered by reality. Emma, who has no Sancho, discovers her enchanted Dulcinea in the absurd Rodolphe. Flaubert punishes her, himself, and us by fusing the poison of provincial social reality with the poison of Emma's hallucinated fantasies of a sublime passion. I find this very cruel, but with Baudelaire one has to grant its unmatched aesthetic dignity. Flaubert so inverts Victor Hugo's Romanticism as to persuade us that his own pure style can represent even ennui with a power that enhances life.

Tomorrow I turn eighty-eight and am, more than ever, a sorrowful Romantic. These last few days, I have been reading and rereading Lydia Davis's *Madame Bovary*. It exalts me yet also makes me very sad. I think John Keats would have loved Emma Bovary, because he was one of those questers who seek no wonder but the human face.

Here is Flaubert at work murdering Emma Bovary:

> At six o'clock tonight, as I was writing the word "hysterics," I was so swept away, was bellowing so loudly and feeling so deeply what my little Bovary was going through, that I was afraid of having hysterics myself. I got up from my table and opened the window to calm myself. My head was spinning. Now I have great pains in my knees, in my back, and in my head. I feel like a man who has been fucking too much (forgive me for the expression)—a kind of rapturous lassitude.
>
> —Flaubert to Louise Colet, letter, December 23, 1853

Charles Baudelaire, reviewing *Madame Bovary* in 1857, regarded Flaubert as a fellow poet and indulged his own catastrophic vision of human life:

> I will not echo the Lycanthrope [Petrus Borel], remembered for a subversiveness which no longer prevails, when he said: "Confronted with all that is vulgar and inept in the present time, can we not take refuge in cigarettes and adultery?" But I assert that our world, even when it is weighed on precision scales, turns out to be exceedingly harsh considering it was engendered by Christ; it could hardly be entitled to throw the first stone at adultery. A few cuckolds more or less are not likely to increase the rotating speed of the spheres and to hasten by a second the final destruction of the universe.

The societal scandal of *Madame Bovary* is as remote now as the asceticism of the spirit practiced by Flaubert and Baudelaire, who seem almost self-indulgent in the era of Samuel Beckett and Thomas Pynchon. Rereading *Madame Bovary* side by side with, say, *Malone Dies,* is a sadly instructive experience. Emma seems as boisterous as Hogarth or Rabelais in the company of Malone and Macmann. And yet she is their grandmother, even as the personages of Proust, Joyce, and Kafka are among her children. With her the novel enters the realm of inactivity, where the protagonists are bored, but the reader is not. Poor Emma, destroyed by usury rather than love, is so vital that her stupidities do not matter. She is a much more than averagely sensual woman, and her capacity for life and love is what moves us to admire her, and even to love her.

Why is Emma so unlucky? If it can go wrong, it will go wrong for her. Freud, like some of the ancients, believed there were no accidents. Ethos is the daemon, your character is your fate, and everything that happens to you starts by being you. Rereading, we suffer the anguish of beholding the phases that lead to Emma's self-destruction. That anguish multiplies despite Flaubert's celebrated detachment, partly because of his uncanny skill at suggesting how many different consciousnesses invade and impinge upon any single consciousness, even one as commonplace as Emma's. Emma's I is an other, and so much the worse for the sensual apprehensiveness that finds it has become Emma.

"Hysterics suffer mainly from reminscences" is a famous and eloquent formula that Freud outgrew. Like Flaubert before him, he came to see that the Emmas—meaning nearly all among us—were suffering from repressed drives. Still later, in his final phase, Freud arrived at a vision that achieves an ultimate clarity in the last section of *Inhibitions, Symptoms and Anxiety*, which reads to me as a crucial commentary on Emma Bovary. It is not repressed desire that issues in anxiety, but a primal anxiety that issues in repression. As for the variety of neurosis involved, Freud speculated that hysteria results from fear of the loss of love. Emma kills herself in a hysteria brought on by a fairly trivial financial mess, but underlying the hysteria is the terrible fear that there will be no more lovers for her.

That *sounds* right enough, yet rereading the novel does not make us desire a larger or brighter Emma. Until she yields to total hysteria, she incarnates the universal wish for sensual life, for a more sensual life. A remarkable Emma might have developed the hardness and resourcefulness that would have made her a French Becky Sharp, and fitted her for survival even in mid-nineteenth-century Paris. But James sublimely chose to miss the point, which Albert Thibaudet got permanently right:

> She is more ardent than passionate. She loves life, pleasure, love itself much more than she loves a man; she is made to have lovers rather than a lover. It is true that she loves Rodolphe with all the fervor of her body, and with him she experiences the moment of her complete, perfect and brief fulfillment; her illness, however, after Rodolphe's desertion, is sufficient to cure her of this love. She does not die from love, but from weakness and a total inability to look ahead, a naivete which makes her an easy prey to deceit in love as well as in business. She lives in the present and is unable to resist the slightest impulse.

Here is the dying moment of Emma Bovary:

> The priest rose to take up the crucifix; at that, she strained her neck forward like someone who is thirsty, and, pressing her lips to the body of the Man-God, she laid upon it with all her expiring strength the most passionate kiss of love she had ever given.

Then he recited the *Misereatur* and the *Indulgentiam,* dipped his right thumb in the oil, and began the unctions: first on the eyes, which had so coveted all earthly splendors; then on the nostrils, greedy for mild breezes and the smells of love; then on the mouth, which had opened to utter lies, which had moaned with pride and cried out in lust; then on the hands, which had delighted in the touch of smooth material; and lastly on the soles of the feet, once so quick when she hastened to satiate her desires and which now would never walk again.

Lydia Davis has found precisely the accurate tone for this fastidious litany. I confess that it ravages me and renders me a touch ungrateful to Gustave Flaubert. This is an irony cutting so many ways that little is spared. The martyr of style is so persuaded of "the disgrace of existence" that he could be an ascetic of the second century of the Common Era, or, like Baudelaire, Nerval, and Rimbaud, a nineteenth-century version of the Valentinian Gnosis.

I myself am sympathetic to Valentinus, since I also believe that the Creation and the Fall were the same event. Flaubert, except for Proust, is the true artist of the novel. Nothing is got for nothing, and there is a cost when existence seems a disgrace.

CHAPTER 18

Les Misérables (1862)

Victor Hugo

Victor Hugo is scarcely the only great poet to have indulged himself in the composition of novels. One thinks of Alessandro Manzoni, Emily Brontë, Herman Melville, Thomas Hardy, and D. H. Lawrence. George Eliot, Willa Cather, James Joyce, and Ursula Le Guin, particularly the latter, wrote some admirable poems, but it is their novels that we reread.

I am content with Paul Valéry's judgment that Victor Hugo was the titan among all French poets. Though I am obsessed with *Les Misérables,* it is not of the company of Stendhal, Balzac, and Flaubert at their best. Is it actually a novel? A vast extravaganza that never knows where to stop, it sprawls over a mass of materials that are irrelevant to the story that supposedly it tells. I have read it straight through only once in the original, and was both exalted and baffled. There is an admirable translation by Norman Denny (1976), now available in Penguin Classics, which performs the necessary task of relegating to appendices Victor Hugo's extraordinary excursions into the idea of the convent and into the Parisian argot of the mid-nineteenth century, particularly in the criminal class. Denny chooses to print all of the detailed account of the Battle of Waterloo that constitutes the initial section of Part Two: Cosette. Only Chapter XIX is in any way crucial to the story, since it recounts the involuntary rescue of Colonel Pontmercy from the battlefield by the scavenger Thénardier. Colonel Pontmercy is the father of Marius, who is intended by Victor Hugo to be the hero of *Les Misérables*. Unfortunately, the two least persuasive characters in this vast book are Marius and his beloved Cosette, the child of the unfortunate Fantine, who has supported her by a miserable life as a prostitute and dies very early. Cosette is then rescued from the Thénardier family that starves her by the heroic protagonist Jean Valjean, who in most regards *is* the book.

Having said that, I wonder if it can be true. When I think back to *Les Misérables*, what first comes to mind are the remarkable band of young revolutionaries gathered together in what they call the ABC Society. They all go down to needless deaths, since their barricade cannot withstand the cannons and overwhelming numbers of the troops sent against them. I list them in Victor Hugo's own order: Enjolras, Combeferre, Jean Prouvaire, Feuilly, Courfeyrac, Bahorel, Lesgle or Laigle, Joly, Grantaire.

The fascinating figure is Enjolras:

We have named Enjolras first, and the reason for this will be seen later. He was the only son of wealthy parents, a charming young man who was capable of being a terror. He was angelically good-looking, an untamed Antinous. From the thoughtfulness of his gaze one might have supposed that in some previous existence he had lived through all the turmoil of the Revolution. He was familiar with every detail of that great event; he had it in his blood as though he had been there. His was a nature at once scholarly and warlike, and this is rare in an adolescent. He was both thinker and man of action, a soldier of democracy in the short term and at the same time a priest of the ideal rising above the contemporary movement. He had deep eyes, their lids slightly reddened, a thick lower lip which readily curled in disdain, and a high forehead—a large expanse of forehead in a face like a wide stretch of sky on the horizon. In common with certain young men of the beginning of this century and the end of the last who achieved distinction early in life, he had the glow of over-vibrant youth, with a skin like a girl's but with moments of pallor. Grown to manhood, he still appeared a youth, his twenty-two years seeming no more than seventeen. He was austere, seeming not to be aware of the existence on earth of a creature called woman. His sole passion was for justice, his sole thought to overcome obstacles. On the Aventine hill he would have been Gracchus, in the Convention he would have been Saint-Just. He scarcely noticed a rose, was unconscious of the springtime and paid no heed to the singing of birds. The bared bosom of the nymph Evadne would have left him unmoved, and like Harmodius he had no use for flowers except to conceal a sword. He was austere in all his pleasures, chastely averting his eyes from everything that did not concern the republic, a marble lover of Liberty. His speech was harsh and intense, with a lyrical undertone, and given to unexpected flights of eloquence. It would have gone hard with any love-affair that sought to lead him astray. Had a grisette from the Place Cambrai or the Rue Saint-Jean-de-Beauvais, seeing that schoolboy face, the pageboy figure, the long, fair lashes over blue eyes, the hair ruffled in the breeze, the fresh lips and perfect teeth, been so taken with his beauty as to seek to thrust herself upon him, she would have encountered a cold, dismissive stare, like the opening of an abyss, which would have taught her not to confuse the Cherubini of Beaumarchais with the cherubim of Ezekiel.

Enjolras is the leader of the small group of revolutionaries who rise up in Paris on June 5, 1832, and who hope to lead a national insurrection against the bourgeois regime of King Louis-Philippe. Their hope is vain. All of them die, and with them dies the most charming person in *Les Misérables*, the street urchin Gavroche. Enjolras, after executing a murderous police spy, Le Cabuc, delivers a prophetic oracle marked by the infinite sadness of idealistic self-sacrifice:

'Citizens,' said Enjolras, 'what that man did was abominable and what I have done is horrible. He killed, and that is why I killed. I was obliged to do it, for this rebellion must be disciplined. Murder is an even greater crime here than elsewhere. We are under the eyes of the revolution, priests of the republic, the tokens of a cause, and our actions must not be subject to calumny. Therefore I judged this man and condemned him to death. But at the same time, compelled to do what I did but also abhorring it, I have passed judgement on myself, and you will learn in due course what my sentence is.'

A quiver ran through his audience.

'We will share your fate,' cried Combeferre.

'It may be,' said Enjolras. 'I have more to say. In executing that man I bowed to necessity. But the necessity was a monster conceived in the old world, and its name is fatality. By the law of progress, this fatality must give way to fraternity. This is a bad moment for speaking the word "love"; nevertheless I do speak it, and glory in it. Love is the future. I have had resort to death, but I hate it. In the future, citizens, there will be no darkness or lightnings, no savage ignorance or blood-feuds. Since there will be no Satan there will be no Michael. No man will kill his fellow, the earth will be radiant, mankind will be moved by love. That time will come, citizens, the time of peace, light, and harmony, of joy and life. It will come. And the purpose of our death is to hasten its coming.'

This high rhetoric is justified by its occasion and by the character of its speaker. Victor Hugo above all was a poet, and *Les Misérables* is a vast prose poem. Enjolras cries out from the top of the barricade:

'Yes, education! Light!—light—all things are born of light and all things return to it! Citizens, our nineteenth century is great, but the twentieth century will be *happy*. Nothing in it will resemble ancient history. Today's fears will all have been abolished—war and conquest, the clash of armed nations, the course of civilization dependent on royal marriages, the birth of hereditary tyrannies, nations partitioned by a congress or the collapse of a dynasty, religions beating their heads together like rams in the wilderness of the infinite. Men will no longer fear famine or exploitation, prostitution from want, destitution born of unemployment—or the scaffold, or the sword, or any other malic of chance in the tangle of events. One might almost say, indeed, that there will be no more events. Men will be happy. Mankind will fulfill its own laws as does the terrestrial globe, and harmony will be restored between the human souls and the heavens. The souls will circle about the Truth as the planets circle round the sun. I am speaking to you, friends, in a dark hour; but this is the hard price that must be paid for the future. A revolution is a toll-gate. But mankind will be liberated, uplifted and consoled. We here affirm it, on this barricade. Whence should the cry of love proceed, if not from the sacrificial altar? Brothers, this is the meeting place of those who reflect and those who suffer. This barricade is not a matter of rubble and paving-stone; it is built of two components, of ideas and of suffering. Here wretchedness and idealism come together. Day embraces night and says to her, "I shall die with you and you will be reborn with me." It is of the embraces of despair that faith is born. Suffering brings death, but the idea brings immortality. That agony and immortality will be mingled and merged in one death. Brothers, we who die here will die in the radiance of the future. We go to a tomb flooded with the light of dawn.'

On March 7, 2018, this prophecy is a sorrow. Victor Hugo, who thought he was a god, speaks through Enjolras, who knows he is only a man about to die. Yet Enjolras in his rapture moves us. Is it possible to die in the radiance of the future? I have known men and women who at the end thought so. When my time comes, in only a few years, doubtless I will think about those I have loved, yet the idea will bring no intimation of immortality. Without Enjolras, *Les Misérables* might not hold me. Jean Valjean is more myth than man. Javert is a man who goes to suicide by knowing only the law. Victor Hugo projected himself as Marius and thus marred his masterwork by sentimentality. I am not sure this matters. *Les Misérables* is more a tidal wave than a book. Baudelaire, a great poet unable to evade Victor Hugo's influence, joked that the Ocean and Hugo deserved one another. Fighting the waves is an idle pastime.

And yet, and yet, *Les Misérables* will live forever. Why? Is it the urchin Gavroche singing even as the bullets strike him? Is it Jean Valjean growing into a reluctant Prometheus? It has to be Victor Hugo, who was his own poem. This is how he concludes his cavalcade of watching and hoping:

Nevertheless, those who study the health of society must now and then shake their heads. Even the strongest-minded and most clear-thinking must have their moments of misgiving. Will the future ever arrive? The question seems almost justified when one considers the shadows looming ahead, the somber confrontation of egoists and outcasts. On the side of the egoists, prejudice—that darkness of a rich education—appetite that grows with intoxication, the bemusement of prosperity which blunts the sense, the fear of suffering which in some cases goes so far as to hate all sufferers, and unshakeable complacency, the ego so inflated that it stifles the soul; and on the side of the outcasts, greed and envy, resentment at the happiness of others, the turmoil of the human animal in search of personal fulfilment, hearts filled with fog, misery, needs, and fatalism, and simple, impure ignorance.

Should we continue to look upwards? Is the light we can see in the sky one of those which will presently be extinguished? The ideal is terrifying to behold, lost as it is in the depths, small, isolated, a pin-point, brilliant but threatened on all sides by the dark forces that surround it: nevertheless, no more in danger than a star in the jaws of the clouds.

CHAPTER 19

A Sportsman's Notebook (1852)

Ivan Turgenev

E RNEST RENAN was the celebrated author of the absurd *Life of Jesus* (1863), a work that asserted Yeshua was not a Jew but an Aryan. Sometimes I have the impression that Renan read only the Gospel of John. Nevertheless, Renan was eloquent and spoke at Turgenev's funeral in Paris in 1883. Henry James later quoted and approved Renan's remarks:

> "Turgenev," said M. Renan, "received by the mysterious decree which marks out human vocations the gift which is noble beyond all others: he was born essentially impersonal." The passage is so eloquent that one must repeat the whole of it. "His conscience was not that of an individual to whom nature had been more or less generous: it was in some sort the conscience of a people. Before he was born he had lived for thousands of years; infinite successions of reveries had amassed themselves in the depths of his heart. No man has been as much as he the incarnation of a whole race: generations of ancestors, lost in the sleep of centuries, speechless, came through him to life and utterance."
>
> (James, "Ivan Turgenev")

The late Randall Jarrell, whom I met only a few times but admired, published *The Anchor Book of Stories* in 1958, where I first encountered Turgenev's *A Sportsman's Notebook*. After sixty years I remember my pleasure in Turgenev's stories. They were indeed "essentially impersonal." "Bezhin Meadow" stayed in my mind, particularly its conclusion:

'D'you remember Vasily?' added Kostya suddenly.
'What Vasily?' asked Fedya.
'The one who was drowned,' answered Kostya. 'In this very same river. What a fine chap he was! Oh, what a fine chap! His mother, Feklista, how she loved him! It was as if she felt, Feklista did, that his death would come by water. Vasily used to come with us in summer to bathe in the river—and she'd get all in a fluster. The other mothers didn't care a bit, they'd walk past with their washpails, they'd waddle by, but Feklista would put her pail down and start calling him. "Come back, come back," she'd say, "come back, light of my eyes! Oh, come back, my little eagle!" And how he came to drown, Lord alone knows. He was playing on the bank, and his mother was there too, raking hay, and suddenly she heard what sounded like someone blowing bubbles under water—she looked, and there was only Vasily's cap floating in the water. Well, since then, Feklista, too, hasn't been right in the head. She comes and lies at the place where he drowned; there she lies, boys, and starts to sing—d'you remember, Vasily always used to sing a song—well that's the one she sings, too, and cries and cries, and complains bitterly to God.
'Here comes Pavel' said Fedya.
Pavel came up to the fire with a full pot in his hand.
'Well, boys,' he began after a silence, 'there's something bad.'
'What?' asked Kostya hurriedly.
'I heard Vasily's voice.'
Everyone shuddered.
'What's that you say?' whispered Kostya.
'So help me God. I'd just begun to bend down to the water, and suddenly I heard my name being called, in Vasily's voice, like it was from under the water: "Pavel, Pavel, come here!" I went away. I got the water, though.'
'Good Lord!' said the boys, crossing themselves.
'That was a water-goblin calling you, Pavel,' added Fedya. 'And we were just talking about Vasily.'

'Oh, that's an evil sign,' said Ilyusha, with deliberation.

'Well, never mind, forget about it!' said Pavel resolutely, and sat down again. 'You can't escape your fate.' The boys became quieter. It was clear that Pavel's story had made a deep impression on them. They began to settle down in front of the fire, as if preparing for sleep.

'What's that?' asked Kostya suddenly, lifting his head.

Pavel listened intently.

'That's curlews flying past and whistling.'

'Where are they flying to?'

'To the country where there's supposed to be no winter.'

'Is there really such a country?'

'Yes, there is.'

'Far away?'

'Far, far away, beyond the warm seas.'

Kostya sighed and closed his eyes.

(trans. Charles and Natasha Hepburn)

Here Turgenev the hunter and narrator has vanished. He and the boys fall asleep. The narrator's waking is rendered exquisitely, almost without affect:

A flood of freshness coursed over my face. I opened my eyes— the day was breaking. There was still no flush of dawn, but a growing pallor in the East. I could vaguely make out my surroundings. The pale-grey sky was growing light, and cold, and blue; the stars twinkled feebly or went out; the earth had grown damp, the leaves dripped, from somewhere came sounds of life, and voices, and the damp breath of dawn was already abroad, hovering above the earth. My body answered it with a faint thrill of exhilaration. I rose quickly and went across to the boys. They were all sleeping like the dead around the dying fire; only Pavel half-raised himself and stared fixedly at me. I nodded to him and went my way along the steaming river. I had not gone two versts when, around me in the broad water-meadow and ahead on the deepening green of the hills, from wood to wood, and behind me over the long dusty track, over the flushed sparkling bushes, and along the river, which was of a timid blue below the thinning mist—flowed scarlet, then red, then golden torrents of youthful, blazing light... The world began to rustle, awoke, began to sing, to murmur, to speak. On all sides the heavy dewdrops flashed into blazing diamonds; to meet me, pure and clear, as if they too had been washed in the coolness of morning, came the sounds of a church bell, and suddenly, driven by my friends the boys, the herd of horses, fresh from sleep, galloped past me...

With sorrow I must add that Pavel died before the year was out. He was not drowned, but killed by a fall from a horse. A pity, he was a splendid lad!

The flight of the curlews to a faraway land with no winter is prologue to obsequies performed for Vasily and Pavel, both of them splendid lads. And that is all.

Men more frequently require to be reminded than informed.
(Samuel Johnson, March 22, 1750, *The Rambler*, Number 2)

That famous apothegm might have been Turgenev's. I read Turgenev with deep sympathy, but I do not know what to make of Turgenev the person. Dostoevsky loathed Turgenev and ridiculed him as Karmazinov in *Demons*. Since Dostoevsky is one of those major writers whom I abominate, and *Demons* is hysterical, I would prefer to think better of Turgenev the man. As his bitterly nostalgic novella *First Love* traces, his parental background was difficult. His father, Sergei Nikolaevich Turgenev, who was to die at only forty-one, was a cavalry colonel who served in the war against Napoleon. His mother, Varvara Petrovna Turgeneva, married Sergei in 1816. Older than her husband, who had married her for her wealth, Varvara was increasingly embittered by his philandering, and became harsh and tyrannical toward their three sons, one of whom died early.

Ivan Turgenev never married, unless you can count his endless relationship with Pauline Viardot, a famous French mezzo-soprano—a *ménage à trois* in which he shared her with her husband Louis, a journalist twenty-one years older than Pauline. Turgenev and Louis Viardot always remained friends, and Turgenev's illegitimate daughter, fathered upon a serf seamstress, was absorbed into the Viardot household.

There seems to have been only one discreditable incident in Turgenev's life. In 1838, the nineteen-year-old writer, bound for Berlin to study, was on a steamer that caught fire and was incinerated. According to his translator and biographer Leonard Schapiro:

> On the third day out the steamer, then about a mile away from Travemünde, caught fire, and was completely destroyed. The great majority of the passengers escaped without injury. Turgenev's behaviour during the fire excited a great deal of talk. According to stories that circulated in Moscow and St Petersburg he had completely lost his head, loudly lamented his approaching end, tried to push his way into the lifeboat, brutally shoving aside women and children, and finally, in full sight of the entire company, seized a sailor by the arm and offered him ten thousand roubles in his mother's name if he would save him, saying that he was the only son of a rich widow and could not bear to die so young.

Leonard Schapiro, a jovial historian of Russia, may have been a fan of the Marx Brothers, as I am, since there is a flavor of Groucho in this paragraph. Varvara castigated her unfortunate son for cowardice, lamenting its effect upon her rather minimal social life.

Turgenev died a slow, painful, rather heroic death, thinking as always of others. He wrote a letter to Tolstoy, with whom he had a tempestuous relationship, urging the great writer of the Russian land to come back to composing fiction rather than moral tracts.

Granted that his childhood had been difficult, with an uncaring father and a sadistic mother who flogged her serfs, Turgenev is a miracle of human goodness and of aesthetic sensibility, somewhat limited in its range. His sketches, stories, fragments, novellas are stronger than his more ambitious novels. Perhaps an impersonal stance cannot sustain a long fiction, unless you are Gustave Flaubert.

I return to *A Sportsman's Notebook* and the lovely vision of the dwarf Kasyan from Fair Springs. Kasyan condemns all letting of blood: bird, beast, human. In the midst of his exchange with the sportsman, there is a visitation of what William Blake called "the human form divine":

Suddenly he started and fell silent, looking fixedly into the undergrowth of the forest. I turned and saw a little peasant-girl of about eight, in a blue dress, with a check handkerchief over her head and a wicker basket over her bare sunburnt arm. She had probably never expected to meet us; she had stumbled on top of us and stood motionless in a green hazel-thicket on a shady patch of grass, looking timorously at me with her black eyes. I had hardly caught sight of her when she darted behind a tree.

'Annushka, come here, don't be afraid,' called the old man tenderly.

'I *am* afraid,' came her thin little voice.

'Don't be afraid, don't be afraid, come to me.'

Annushka slowly abandoned her hiding-place, walked quietly round, her little feet hardly rustling in the thick grass, and came out of the bushes beside the old man. This was no girl of eight, as I had thought at first, judging by her small size, but one of thirteen or fourteen. Her whole body was small and thin, but trim and graceful, and her pretty little face was strikingly like Kasyan's own, although Kasyan himself was no beauty. She had the same sharp features, the same strange expression, at once cunning and trustful, reflective and penetrating, and the same movements... Kasyan looked her over; she was standing beside him.

'Well, have you got some mushrooms?' he asked.

'Yes, some mushrooms,' she answered, with a timid smile.

'Have you found plenty of them?'

'Yes, plenty.' She looked quickly at me and smiled again.

'Some white ones, too?'

'Yes, white ones, too.'

'Show me, do...'

She lowered the basket from her arm and half-lifted a broad burdock leaf which covered the mushrooms.

'Oh,' said Kasyan, stooping over the basket, 'what fine ones! Well done, Annushka!'

'Is she your daughter, Kasyan, eh?' I asked. Annushka's face showed a slight blush.

'She's a sort of relation,' said Kasyan, with assumed carelessness.

'Well, Annushka, off you go,' he added at once; 'off you go, and good luck to you. And be careful...'

'But why should she walk?' I interrupted him. 'We could give her a lift...'

Annushka flushed the colour of a poppy, clutched with both hands at the string handle of her basket and looked anxiously at the old man.

'No, she'll get there all right,' he rejoined in the same indifferent, casual voice. 'Why should we?...She'll get there all right... Be off with you.'

Annushka went nimbly off into the forest. Kasyan looked after her, then lowered his gaze and smiled. In this long smile, in the few words which he had said to Annushka, in the very tone of his voice when he spoke of her, there was more passionate love and tenderness than language can express. He looked again in the direction in which she had vanished, smiled again, wiped his face, and nodded his head several times.

'Why did you send her off so quickly?' I asked him. 'I should like to have bought some of her mushrooms...'

'Why, it does not matter to you, you can buy them at home whenever you like,' he answered me, using the formal 'you' for the first time.

'Well, you've got a pretty one there.'

'No...well...there it is...' he answered, as if reluctantly, and from that moment he relapsed into his earlier mood of silence. Seeing that all my efforts to engage him again in conversation were proving vain, I went off to the clearing. Meanwhile it had grown slightly less hot; but my ill-success continued, and I returned to the hamlet with only one corncrake besides my new axle. As we were driving up to his yard, Kasyan suddenly turned to me: 'Master, I say, Master,' he began. 'I'm sorry for what I did to you; you see, it was I who called all the birds away from you.'

'What do you mean?'

'It's my trick. That's a clever dog you have, and a good one, but all the same there was nothing he could do ... When you come to think of it, what are men? Here's an animal, too, and what have they made of him?'

Annushka clearly is Kasyan's daughter, and the charm of her being offsets the tint of the uncanny in Kasyan. Turgenev refreshingly refused all transcendent argumentations and believed only in the possibility of human goodness. For a nineteenth-century Russian writer, that clear atheism had to cause some scandal, but Turgenev somehow reconciled in himself Western and Eastern modes of sensibility, thought, feeling. He was admired by Henry James, Gustave Flaubert, Edith Wharton, Ernest Hemingway, and Willa Cather: they found in him a Russian crafter of fictions who shared their spirit. Cather rewrote *First Love* in her exquisite *A Lost Lady* (1923), but it now reads to me as Turgenev in a minor key.

The most memorable sketch in *A Sportsman's Notebook* is "The Live Relic," in which poor Lukerya has been dying slowly for a long time, or living—if you can call it that—for too long:

> 'O, I can't!' she said suddenly. 'I haven't the strength...I've been so pleased to see you.'
>
> She closed her eyes.
>
> I put my hand on her tiny, cold fingers . . . She looked up at me—and her dark eyelids, trimmed with golden lashes, like those of an ancient statue, closed again. After a moment, they glittered in the twilight...A tear had moistened them.
>
> I sat there motionless as before.
>
> 'Just look at me!' said Lukerya suddenly, with unexpected force, and, opening her eyes wide, tried to wipe the tears from them. 'Oughtn't I to be ashamed? What do I want? This hasn't happened to me for a long time...not since the day when Vasily Polyakov was here last spring. As long as he was sitting talking to me—I didn't mind—but when he went away—I fairly cried away to myself! Where did it all come from?... But tears cost nothing to girls like us. Master,' added Lukerya, 'I expect you've got a handkerchief...Don't be put off, wipe my eyes.'

I hardly know how one reacts to that unbearable poignance. Yet it is only prelude to what hurts far more:

> 'I need nothing; I'm absolutely content, praise be to God,' she pronounced, with extreme effort, but also with emotion 'May

God grant health to everyone! And you, master, please speak to your mother—the peasants here are poor—if she would only bring down their rent, just a little! They haven't enough land, they make nothing out of it! . . . They would pray to God for you . . . but I need nothing, I'm absolutely content.'

I gave Lukerya my word to carry out her request, and was already making for the door when she called me back.

'D'you remember, master,' she said, with a wonderful brightening of her eyes and lips, 'what hair I had? D'you remember—right down to my knees! For a long time I couldn't make up my mind . . . Such hair it was! . . . But how could I comb it! In my condition! So I cut it off . . . yes . . . Well, good-bye, master! I can't say more . . .'

The same day, before setting out to shoot, I had a talk about Lukerya with the local constable. I learnt from him that in the valley she was called 'the Live Relic', also that she caused no trouble; there was not a grumble to be heard from her, not a complaint. 'She asks nothing for herself, on the contrary she's grateful for everything; she's as quiet as quiet can be, that I must say. She's been smitten by God,' so the constable concluded, 'for her sins, no doubt; but we don't go into that. As for condemning her, for example, no, we certainly don't condemn her. Let her be!'

A few weeks later I heard that Lukerya was dead. Death had come for her after all . . . and 'after St. Peter's'. The story went that on the day of her death she kept hearing the sound of bells, although it is more than five versts from Alexeyevka to the church, and it was on a weekday. Besides, Lukerya said that the sound came, not from church, but 'from above'. Probably she did not venture to say—from heaven.

Turgenev could not believe in miracles, yet what else is this: the bells of madness and of deprivation, or of a jubilee celebrating Lukerya as a sad saint meriting an "above" that is not there.

CHAPTER 20

First Love (1860)

IVAN TURGENEV

I T IS REASONABLE TO SAY that the novella *First Love* is Turgenev's most autobiographical work, unless that be the charmingly crazy *Spring Torrents* (1872). In *First Love*, the narrator, Vladimir, returns to his experience of an initial sorrow when he was sixteen. The princess Zinaida, then twenty-one, is a capricious and mocking beauty who is ingenious at tormenting her phalanx of frustrated suitors. Vladimir's father, Pyotr, a skilled horseman and philanderer, is younger than his hysterical and savage wife, whom he married for her money. Pyotr is cold and reserved in manner, and only rarely shows affection for his son. It is revealed to us slowly that Pyotr and Zinaida are immersed in a covert and sadistic erotic affair, and that Zinaida, a kind of moral masochist, is in love with Pyotr.

Vladimir's narrative is Turgenev at his best: apparently impersonal, withdrawn in affect, yet always intimating that love and life itself are tenuous and on the verge of vanishing:

> Zinaida guessed at once that I had fallen in love with her, but then I wouldn't have thought of concealing it. My passion amused her. She made fun of me, played with me, and tormented me. It is sweet to be the sole source, the arbitrary and irresponsible source of the greatest joys and profoundest miseries to someone else. I was like soft wax in the hands of

Zinaida; not that I alone had fallen in love with her. All the men who visited the house were hopelessly infatuated, and she kept them all on leading-strings at her feet. She found it amusing to excite alternate hopes and fears in them; to twist them according to her whim. She called this 'knocking people against each other'; they did not even think of resistance, but gladly submitted to her. In her whole being, vital and beautiful, there was a peculiarly fascinating mixture of cunning and insouciance, artifice and simplicity, gentleness and gaiety. Over everything she did and said, over every movement there hovered a subtle, exquisite enchantment. Everything expressed the unique, peculiar force of the life which played within her. Her face, too, was constantly changing. It, too, was always in play. It seemed at almost the same instant mocking, pensive and passionate. An infinite variety of feelings, light and swift, succeeded each other like shadows of clouds on a windy summer day, in her eyes and on her lips. Every one of her admirers was necessary to her. Byelovzorov, whom she sometimes called 'my wild beast', or sometimes simply 'mine', would gladly have leapt into the fire for her. With no confidence in his own brains or other qualities, he was constantly proposing marriage to her, implying that the others only talked. Maidanov was responsive to the poetic strain in her soul; somewhat cold by nature, like nearly all writers, he assured her fervently, and perhaps himself too, that he adored her. He composed endless verses in her honour, and recited them with an ardour at once affected and sincere. She sympathized with him and, at the same time, faintly mocked him. She did not really trust him, and after listening to his effusions for a while, used to make him read Pushkin, in order, as she used to say, to clear the air.

Between the lines you can read a certain Turgenevian reserve in regard to the delightful Zinaida. Is it only the joy of flirtation that requires "knocking people against each other"? Zinaida trusts no one, herself included.

'Yes!' she said, looking at me as before, 'it is so. The same eyes—' she added; then became thoughtful and covered her face with her hands. 'Everything has become horrible to me,' she whispered, 'why don't I go to the other end of the world! I can't bear it, I can't make it come right...and what is there before me?... God, I am so wretched!'

'Why?' I asked timidly.

Zinaida did not reply, but only shrugged her shoulders. I went on kneeling and looking at her with infinite distress. Every one of her words pierced my heart like a knife. At that moment I would, I think, gladly have given up my life if only that could end in grief. I looked at her, and still not understanding why she was so unhappy, conjured a vivid image of how, suddenly, in a paroxysm of ungovernable grief, she had walked into the garden and fallen to the ground as though mown down. All round us it was bright and green. The wind murmured in the leaves of the trees, now and then bending the raspberry canes above Zinaida's head. Somewhere doves were cooing and bees were buzzing, flying low from blade to blade over the sparse grass. Overhead, the sky was blue and tender, but I felt terribly sad.

'Read me some poetry,' said Zinaida in a low voice, and raised herself on one elbow. 'I like your reading poetry. You speak it in a sing-song, but I do not mind it, that's youth. Read me *On Georgia's Hills*, only first sit down.'

I sat down, and recited *On Georgia's Hills*.

'"Which it cannot help but love",' Zinaida repeated after me. 'That is what poetry can do. It speaks to us of what does not exist, which is not only better than what exists, but even more like the truth. "Which it cannot help but love"—it would like not to, but cannot help itself!' She was silent again and suddenly started and stood up. 'Let's go. Maidanov is with Mama. He has brought me his poem, but I left him. He is hurt too, now, but what can one do? One day you will discover...only don't be too angry with me.'

She pressed my hand hastily and moved quickly forward. We went back to the lodge.

Turgenev was a sharp psychologist. Vladimir represses a crucial aspect of his new realization: he both knows and does not know that her lover is his father.

I returned home to find a disagreeable state of affairs. My mother was trying to 'have things out' with my father. She was reproaching him for something, and he, as was his habit, answered with polite and frigid sentences, and soon went away. I could not hear what my mother was saying, nor was I in a mood to listen. I remember only that when the scene was over, she sent for me to the study, and spoke with great disapproval about my frequent visits to the old princess, who, in her words, was *une femme capable de tout.* I bowed to kiss her hand (I always did this when I wanted to end a conversation) and went up to my room.

Zinaida's tears were altogether too much for me. I simply didn't know what to think, and was on the point of tears myself. I was after all still a child, in spite of my sixteen years.

Turgenev as a narrator prefers the shallows to the depths, but here he seems to know, at the age of forty-two, that a center of his being will never be older than sixteen.

But there was something which I now fancied I dimly perceived in Zinaida, something to which I could not reconcile myself . . . An adventuress my mother had once called her. An adventuress—she, my idol, my goddess! The word seared me like a flame, I tried to escape from it into my pillow. I burned with indignation, yet at the same time what would I not have done, what would I not have given, to be that darling of fortune, the man by the fountain!

Turgenev had fallen in love at first sight with Pauline Viardot in 1843 and followed her to Paris in 1845. Fifteen years after his Parisian bondage commenced, he composes *First Love* and recalls his mother terming Pauline a Gypsy and an adventuress.

I did not dare to question them, but one of the pantry boys, called Philip, who was passionately fond of poetry and a beautiful guitar player, was a particular friend of mine, and to him I turned. From him I discovered that a terrible scene had taken place between my parents. (Every word of it could be heard in the maids' room; much of it was in French, but Masha, the lady's maid, had lived for five years with a seamstress from Paris and understood every word.) Apparently my mother had accused my father of being unfaithful to her and of having relations with the young lady next door; my father had at first defended himself but then flared up and said something brutal—'something to do with Madame's age'—which had made my mother cry; my mother also alluded to a loan supposed to have been made to the old princess, and then made disagreeable remarks about her and about her daughter too, whereupon my father began to threaten her....

I sent Philip away and flung myself on the bed. I did not sob; I did not give myself up to despair; I did not ask myself where and how all this had happened; I did not wonder how it was that I had not guessed it earlier—guessed it long ago. I did not even harbour bitter thoughts about my father ... what I had learned was too much for me to manage. The sudden revelation crushed me; all was ended. In one swoop all my flowers were torn up by the roots and lay about me—scattered, broken, trampled underfoot.

Turgenev, like Vladimir, was incapable of not revering his father. His hysterical and possessive mother, clearly a martinet, a *koshmar* (Russian for "night hag"), gave him a fear of women from the start.

'I?' I repeated painfully, and my heart began to quiver, as it always did under the spell of her irresistible, inexpressible fascination. 'I? Believe me, Zinaida Alexandrovna, that whatever you did, however much you make me suffer, I shall love you and adore you to the end of my days.'

She quickly turned towards me, and opening her arms wide, put them round my head, and gave me a strong, warm kiss. God only knows for whom that long farewell kiss was seeking, but I tasted its sweetness avidly. I knew that it would never come again.

Sappho famously has a fragment:

Again limb-loosening Eros shakes me;
A helpless crawling thing I am, sweet-bitter.

(trans. Peter Saint-Andre)

In the street, about forty paces from me, before the open window of a small wooden house, with his back to me, stood my father. He was leaning with his chest over the window sill; inside the house, half concealed by a curtain, sat a woman in a dark dress, talking with my father; it was Zinaida.

I was utterly stunned. This, I admit, I did not expect. My first impulse was to run away. 'My father will look round,' I thought—'I shall be lost.' But an odd feeling, a feeling stronger than curiosity, stronger even than jealousy, stronger than fear, gripped me. I stood still and looked. I strained my ears to hear. My father seemed to be insisting on something. Zinaida would not consent. Her face is before my eyes now, sad and serious and beautiful, and upon it the imprint—impossible to convey—of grief, devotion, love, and a kind of despair—I can find no other word for it. She spoke in monosyllables, without lifting her eyes, and only smiled, submissively and stubbornly. By this smile alone I recognized my Zinaida, as she once was. My father gave a shrug of his shoulders, and set his hat straight on his head, which with him was always a sign of impatience... then I could hear the words *'Vous devez vous séparer de cette...'* Zinaida straightened herself and held out her hand. Then something unbelievable took place before my eyes. My father suddenly lifted his riding-crop, with which he had been flicking the dust off the folds of his coat, and I heard the sound of a sharp blow struck across her arm which was bared to the elbow. It was all I could do to prevent myself from crying out. Zinaida quivered—looked silently to my father—and raising her arm slowly to her lips, kissed the scar which glowed crimson upon it.

Turgenev's mother was notorious for severely whipping female serfs, and males also. One can only speculate how Turgenev behaved in his own erotic encounters with *his* female serfs, one of whom bore him a daughter. Yet there is clearly sexual sadism in Turgenev's makeup. Freud would have wondered at the boy Vladimir's transposition of his mother's nature to his father.

Unseeingly I stared at the river, unconscious of the tears which were streaming from my eyes. They are beating her, I thought, beating, beating....

That night I dreamt a strange and frightening dream. I fancied that I entered a low, dark room. My father was standing there, holding a riding-crop in his hand, and stamping with his feet. Zinaida was cowering in the corner, and there was a crimson mark, not upon her arm, but upon her forehead...

The traditional mark upon the forehead seems to make poor Zinaida into a female Cain. Is young Vladimir the brother she has somehow murdered? The actual victim, soon enough, is the father:

Two months later, I entered the University, and six months after that my father died (as the result of a stroke) in St Petersburg, where he had only just moved with my mother and me. Several days before his death he had received a letter from Moscow which upset him greatly. He went to beg some sort of favour of my mother and, so they told me, actually broke down and wept—he, my father! On the morning of the very day on which he had the stroke, he had begun a letter to me, written in French. 'My son,' he wrote, 'beware of the love of women; beware of that ecstasy—that slow poison.'

My mother, after his death, sent a considerable sum of money to Moscow.

That letter, whether fictive or real, prophesies the ecstasy and slow poison that Pauline Viardot brought to Turgenev.

Maidanov gave me Zinaida's address. She was staying in the Hotel Demuth. Old memories began to stir within me ... I promised myself to pay a visit to my 'flame' on the very next day. But various things turned up. A week passed, and then another, and when I made my way to the Demuth, and asked for Madame Dolsky, I was told that she had died four days before, quite suddenly, in childbirth.

I remember how several days after that on which I had learnt of Zinaida's death, I myself, obeying an irresistible impulse, was present at the death of a poor old woman who lived in the same house with us. Covered with rags, lying on bare boards, with a sack for a pillow, her end was hard and painful. Her whole life was spent in a bitter struggle with daily want, she had had no joy, had never tasted the sweets of happiness—surely she would welcome death with gladness—its deliverance—its peace? Yet so long as her frail body resisted obstinately, her breast rose and fell in agony under the icy hand that was laid upon it, so long as any strength was left within her, the little old woman kept crossing herself, kept whispering 'Lord forgive me my sins...' and not until the last spark of consciousness had gone, did the look of fear, of the terror of death, vanish from her eyes...and I remember that there, by the death-bed of that poor old woman, I grew afraid, afraid for Zinaida, and I wanted to say a prayer for her, for my father—and for myself.

Pyotr suffers a fatal stroke, quite possibly augmented by his extraordinary outburst into tears on receipt of a letter from Zinaida. Their relationship, with its sadomasochistic aura and undoubted ecstasy, has slowly poisoned Pyotr, while Zinaida, however battered, survives long enough to make a financially favorable marriage that unfortunately soon slays her in childbirth. Turgenev, too subtle to be explicit, allows his readers to decide what has destroyed Pyotr. My surmise is that the fiercely repressed father and husband, confronted by his own collapse into weeping, could not sustain this loss of an assumed identity, and underwent a psychic fragmentation so intense that it ended him.

Yet that seems inadequate to Vladimir's consuming study of the nostalgias. One wants to begin in the spirit of W. B. Yeats:

But is there any comfort to be found?
Man is in love and loves what vanishes,
What more is there to say?

That is one of the verse passages that I over-quote to myself as I move around my house on a walker or laboriously chug up the stairs to my third-floor study. Thinking about Turgenev's *First Love*, I become rather sad, since most of us have some such memories.

There is a tradition that the dying Turgenev, in great pain, threw an inkwell at Pauline Viardot, who was attempting to comfort him. Scholars sometimes regard this as a metalepsis, a trope in which a word is substituted metonymically for a word in a previous trope, so that a metalepsis can be called, maddeningly but accurately, a metonymy of a metonymy. The precedent trope is a notorious heave of an inkwell by the horribly great Martin Luther at some poor devil or other. Turgenev's sadistic mother always termed Pauline a Gypsy. Permanent infatuation necessarily has its ambivalences, and as he aged, the increasingly desperate Turgenev began to believe that Pauline was partly Jewish. We cannot know what dominated his consciousness in the act of dying. It may well have been a resentment of the passion he could never forsake.

CHAPTER 21

The Cossacks (1863)

Leo Tolstoy

Tolstoy originally wished to call this short novel *Young Manhood* but revised both the book and the title after rereading the *Iliad*. The ostensible protagonist is Olenin, a young nobleman who had been wasting his life in drinking, gambling, love affairs, and aristocratic society. The young Tolstoy went considerably beyond that and was wildly promiscuous, frequently with whores and peasant women, gambled ruinously, struggled with gonorrhea, and I suspect married Sophia Behrs in September 1862 not because he fell in love with her but in the hope of changing his life. He was thirty-four; Sophia was eighteen. In *Anna Karenina*, Levin, Tolstoy's surrogate, is also thirty-four when he marries Kitty, who is eighteen, but he loves her profoundly.

It is a paradox that Tolstoy, almost Shakespearean in his creation of women, was viciously misogynistic. With his permission, I quote from a letter sent to me by David Bethea, clearly the outstanding scholar of Pushkin:

> With regard to Tolstoy and women, yes, he portrayed them as accurately as anyone ever has but at the same time they could enrage him with their power over him, especially their sexual power. He never came to terms with this: even in later years he'd

see a comely peasant woman on a ladder and he'd want to drag her into the bushes and this brought his anger and resentment to a boil. Why should she, with no reasoning power to speak of, possess this animal attraction to make him want to couple with her? Somehow that must be her or "their" fault. Hélène Kuragin's bare shoulders and bust. That's why the anger played out to an extreme logical conclusion (*The Kreutzer Sonata*): rejection of biology through abstinence.

I wrote about *The Kreutzer Sonata* in a book called *The Western Canon* (1994), essentially saying that I was appalled and yet sentenced to read it over and over again. Sometimes I think that the authors I most admire are the ones who can badly hurt me. I teach *The Merchant of Venice* every year, have written essays on it, cannot ever give it up, yet it depresses and infuriates me. My friend and former student Kenneth Gross wrote a strong brief book, *Shylock Is Shakespeare* (2006), arguing that Shylock was Shakespeare's breakthrough, a revelation of his own powers and a reach toward surer control of his audience. That may be. If I were a director, I would have *The Merchant of Venice* played as a farce, akin to Christopher Marlowe's *The Jew of Malta*. Shylock would have a red wig and a false nose and would be played by a great comedian. And yet I myself would not be able to bear watching it.

Olenin is good-natured, generous, kind—"clay with aspirations," as my late friend Philip Roth would say—but he is also colorless and hopelessly absurd in his desire to become a Cossack, marry the beautiful Maryánka, and live a life of hunting, horsemanship, military raiding, absorbing mountain and river scenery, staying close to the natural in every way:

'But what though the grass does grow?' he continued thinking. 'Still I must live and be happy, because happiness is all I desire. Never mind what I am—an animal like all the rest, above whom the grass will grow and nothing more; or a frame in which a bit of the one God has been set,—still I must live in the very best way. How then must I live to be happy, and why was I not happy before?' And he began to recall his former life and he felt disgusted with himself. He appeared to himself to have been terribly exacting and selfish, though he now saw that all the while he really needed nothing for himself. And he looked round at the foliage with the light shining through it, at the setting sun and the clear sky, and he felt just as happy as before. 'Why am I happy, and what used I to live for?' thought he. 'How much I exacted for myself; how I schemed and did not manage to gain anything but shame and sorrow! and, there now, I require nothing to be happy;' and suddenly, a new light seemed to reveal itself to him. 'Happiness is this!' he said to himself. 'Happiness lies in living for others. That is evident. The desire for happiness is innate in every man; therefore it is legitimate. When trying to satisfy it selfishly—that is, by seeking for oneself riches, fame, comforts, or love—it may happen that circumstances arise which make it impossible to satisfy those desires. It follows that it is these desires that are illegitimate, but not the need for happiness. But what desires can always be satisfied despite external circumstances? What are they? Love, self-sacrifice.' He was so glad and excited when he had discovered this, as it seemed to him, new truth, that he jumped up and began impatiently seeking some one to sacrifice himself for, to do good to and to love. 'Since one wants nothing for oneself,' he kept thinking, 'why not live for others?' He took up his gun with the intention of returning home quickly to think this out and to find an opportunity of doing good. He made his way out of the thicket. When he had come out into the glade he looked around him; the sun was no longer visible above the tree-tops. It had grown cooler and the place seemed to him quite strange and not like the country round the village. Everything seemed changed—the weather and the character of the forest; the sky was wrapped in clouds, the wind was rustling in the tree-tops, and all around nothing was visible but reeds and dying broken-down trees. He called to his dog who had run away to follow some animal, and his voice came back as in a desert. And suddenly he was seized with a terrible sense of weirdness. He grew frightened. He remembered the *abreks* and the murders he had been told about, and he expected every moment that an *abrek* would spring from behind every bush and he would have to defend his life and die, or be a coward. He thought of God and of the future life as for long he had not thought about them. And all around was that same gloomy stern wild nature. 'And is it worth while living for oneself,' thought he, 'when at any moment you may die, and die without having done any good, and so that no one will know of it?' He went in the direction where he fancied the village lay. Of his shooting he had no further thought; but he felt tired to death and peered round at every bush and tree with particular attention and almost with terror, expecting every moment to be called to account for his life. After having wandered about for a considerable time he came upon a ditch down which was flowing cold sandy water from the Térek, and, not to go astray any longer, he decided to follow it. He went on without knowing where the ditch would lead him. Suddenly the reeds behind him crackled. He shuddered and seized his gun, and then felt ashamed of himself: the over-excited dog, panting hard, had thrown itself into the cold water of the ditch and was lapping it!

That is the authentic Tolstoyan weather of the mind. It surpasses almost every other writer in its grasp of the tang of the actual. I mean "tang" not as flavor but the secondary meaning of a knife blade so shaped that it can be held securely by the handle. I do not often hear Tolstoy being humorous, and the delight I take in the following may be what I owe to the translators: "He took up his gun with the intention of returning home quickly to think this out and to find an opportunity of doing good."

It is a little difficult to see what good Olenin can do for the Cossacks Daddy Eroshka, Lukáshka, and Maryánka. He hunts and drinks with Eroshka, deceives himself into believing he is in love with Maryánka, and makes her an offer of marriage. She is betrothed to Lukáshka, the most daring "brave" among the Cossacks, and waits only for her father's permission to marry. Olenin, with excessive generosity, gives Lukáshka a horse, resulting in the young Cossack's trading it for an even better horse, and rightly becoming suspicious of Olenin's interest in Maryánka.

Probably no writer can match Tolstoy in depicting violent action. There is an amazing clarity, unmarked by pathos, when Lukáshka is severely, perhaps mortally wounded:

Another moment passed and the Cossacks with a whoop rushed out on both sides from behind the cart—Lukáshka in front of them. Olenin heard only a few shots, then shouting and moans. He thought he saw smoke and blood, and abandoning his horse and quite beside himself he ran towards the Cossacks. Horror seemed to blind him. He could not make out anything, but understood that all was over. Lukáshka, pale as death, was holding a wounded Chéchen by the arms and shouting, 'Don't kill him. I'll take him alive!' The Chéchen was the red-haired man who had fetched his brother's body away after Lukáshka had killed him. Lukáshka was twisting his arms. Suddenly the Chéchen wrenched himself free and fired his pistol. Lukáshka fell, and blood began to flow from his stomach. He jumped up, but fell again, swearing in Russian and in Tartar. More and more blood appeared on his clothes and under him. Some Cossacks approached him and began loosening his girdle. One of them, Nazárka, before beginning to help, fumbled for some time, unable to put his sword in its sheath: it would not go the right way. The blade of the sword was blood-stained.

The Chéchens with their red hair and clipped moustaches lay dead and hacked about. Only the one we know of, who had fired at Lukáshka, though wounded in many places was still alive. Like a wounded hawk all covered with blood (blood was flowing from a wound under his right eye), pale and gloomy, he looked about him with wide-open excited eyes and clenched teeth as he crouched, dagger in hand, still prepared to defend himself. The cornet went up to him as if intending to pass by, and with a quick movement shot him in the ear. The Chéchen started up, but it was too late, and he fell.

We are never told whether Lukáshka survives, though it seems unlikely. Tolstoy employs the wounding to awaken Olenin from his reveries of transformation into a Cossack.

'Maryánka,' said he, 'I say, Maryánka! May I come in?' She suddenly turned. There was a scarcely perceptible trace of tears in her eyes and her face was beautiful in its sadness. She looked at him in silent dignity.

Olenin again said:

'Maryánka, I have come —'

'Leave me alone!' she said. Her face did not change but the tears ran down her cheeks.

'What are you crying for? What is it?'

'What?' she repeated with a rough voice. 'Cossacks have been killed, that's what for.'

'Lukáshka?' said Olenin.

'Go away! What do you want?'

'Maryánka!' said Olenin, approaching her.

'You will never get anything from me!'

'Maryánka, don't speak like that,' Olenin entreated.

'Get away. I'm sick of you!' shouted the girl, stamping her foot, and moved threateningly towards him. And her face expressed such abhorrence, such contempt, and such anger that Olenin suddenly understood that there was no hope for him, and that his first impression of this woman's inaccessibility had been perfectly correct.

Olenin said nothing more, but ran out of the hut.

We are to suppose that Maryánka, a true Cossack, would have given Olenin quite a severe blow. It would have been an instruction in reality. Tolstoy is too great an artist to go beyond implication when more seems unnecessary.

On the scale of *War and Peace* the reader will find only a miniature in *The Cossacks*. Keen as it is, *The Cossacks* lacks the ebullience of *Hadji Murat*. Tolstoyan perfection demands the earth's own exuberance, a vitalism matching Tolstoy's own. Not yet fallen into the abyss of prophetic pretensions, Tolstoy can say farewell to his own youth with calibrated stateliness. It does not much matter that poor Olenin is only a shadow of his godlike creator. Lukáshka remains vivid as an image. Maryánka is another ultimate image of Tolstoy's desires. I complete a rereading of *The Cossacks* and I think of Yeats's "Nineteen Hundred and Nineteen," a meditation on the time of the Irish Revolutionary War between the IRA and the British:

He who can read the signs nor sink unmanned
Into the half-deceit of some intoxicant

From shallow wits; who knows no work can stand,
Whether health, wealth or peace of mind were spent
On master-work of intellect or hand,
No honour leave its mighty monument,
Has but one comfort left: all triumph would
But break upon his ghostly solitude.

But is there any comfort to be found?
Man is in love and loves what vanishes,
What more is there to say? That country round
None dared admit, if Such a thought were his,
Incendiary or bigot could be found
To burn that stump on the Acropolis,
Or break in bits the famous ivories
Or traffic in the grasshoppers or bees.

I hear a final sadness akin to *The Cossacks* in Yeats at his most
memorable:

Man is in love and loves what vanishes,
What more is there to say?

CHAPTER 22

War and Peace (1869)

LEO TOLSTOY

I T SEEMS JUST TO ASSERT that the two most powerful narrative ancient writers in Western tradition are the Homer of the *Iliad*, and the Yahwist, who first told the tales of Abraham, Jacob, Joseph, Moses, in what we now call Genesis and Exodus.

I find little in common between the *Iliad* and the J writer. They are morally and cognitively incompatible. Achilles is the son of the sea nymph Thetis and of Peleus, a warrior king who accompanies Heracles and Jason in the quest for the Golden Fleece. Thetis dips the infant Achilles in the Styx so as to make him immortal, but since she holds him by one heel, that becomes his vulnerability. He survives the *Iliad* but in later poetic legends is slain by a poisoned arrow in that heel.

Jacob wrestles with the Angel of Death and wins the new name Israel, which appears to mean "El (God) struggles." But since the stubborn Jacob, wily even in the womb, held on tight to his twin brother's (Esau's) heel, the Hebrew name might mean "overreach" or "heel" or "to follow."

Except for this curious interplay on "heel," no two literary characters share less than Achilles and Jacob/Israel. Achilles is the best of the Achaeans in courage, appearance, strength, skill in battle. Jacob is cunning, endlessly resourceful, patient, wise, and knows that he bears the blessing of Yahweh.

Tolstoy, as befits the writer since Shakespeare who most has the art of the actual, combines in his representational praxis the incompatible powers of Homer and the Yahwist. Notoriously, Tolstoy loathed William Shakespeare. Surely no other reader of Shakespeare ever has found *Hamlet, Macbeth,* and *King Lear* tedious and offensive. Why Tolstoy could accept the *Iliad's* morality, and not *Hamlet's,* is a profound puzzle, since Hamlet has more in common with Joseph or with the David of 2 Samuel than he does with Achilles or Hector. I surmise that Tolstoy, despite himself, owed too much to Shakespearean representation, and could not bear to acknowledge the inevitable debt. Prince Andrei has more of Hotspur than of Lord Byron in him, and even Pierre, in his comic aspects, reflects the Shakespearean rather than Homeric or Biblical naturalism. If your characters change less because of experience than by listening to themselves reflect upon their relation to experience, then you are another heir of Shakespeare's innovations in mimesis, even if you insist passionately that your sense of reality is morally centered whereas Shakespeare's was not.

Shakespeare and Tolstoy had the Bible rather than the *Iliad* in common, and the Shakespearean drama that should have offended Tolstoy most was *Troilus and Cressida.* Alas, *King Lear* achieved that bad eminence, and only Falstaff, rather surprisingly, convinced Tolstoy. But, then, the effect of the greatest writers upon one another can be very odd. Writing in 1908, Henry James associated *War and Peace* with Thackeray's *The Newcomes* and Dumas's *The Three Musketeers,* since all these were "large loose baggy monsters, with . . . queer elements of the accidental and the arbitrary." Twenty years earlier, James had a vision of Tolstoy as "a monster harnessed to his great subject—all human life!—as an elephant might be harnessed, for purposes of traction, not to a carriage, but to a coach-house."

James's demand for "an absolutely premeditated art" might seem to collide with Tolstoy's notorious polemic, *What Is Art?* (1897), but that is an illusion. Tolstoy is clearly a writer who transcends James as an artist, even as Homer overgoes Virgil and Shakespeare dwarfs Ben Jonson. The representation of persons in *War and Peace* has the authority and the mastery of what we are compelled to call the real that Tolstoy shares with only a few: Homer, the Bible, Dante, Chaucer, Shakespeare, Cervantes, perhaps Proust. Philip Rahv remarked memorably upon "the critic's euphoria in the Tolstoyan weather." The best word there is "weather." *War and Peace,* like our cosmos, has weather, but no one would want to say that Tolstoy, like the High Romantics or Dostoevsky, had created a heterocosm. You suffer and die, or joy and live, on our earth in Tolstoy, and not in a visionary realm.

The Marxist critic Lukács reluctantly conceded that in certain moments Tolstoy broke through to "a clearly differentiated, concrete and existent world, which, if it could spread out into a totality, would be completely inaccessible to the categories of the novel and would require a new form of artistic creation: the form of the renewed epic." Lukács denied that Tolstoy could accomplish this as a totality, but his ideology made him less than generous toward Tolstoy. A short novel like *Hadji Murad* certainly is such a totality, but the more than twelve hundred pages of *War and Peace,* granted the impossibility of an absolute totality at such a length, also gives us "a clearly differentiated, concrete and existent world." Tolstoy does what a nineteenth-century novelist ought not to be able to do: he reveals aspects of our ordinary reality that we could never see if he had not seen them first. Dickens and Balzac render an extraordinary phantasmagoria that we are eager to absorb into reality, but Tolstoy, more like Shakespeare than he could bear to know, persuades us that the imitation of what seems to be essential nature is more than enough.

Shakespeare is inexhaustible to analysis, partly because his rhetorical art is nearly infinite. Tolstoy scarcely yields to analysis at all, because his rhetoric evidently also gives the effect of the natural. You have to brood on the balance of determinism and free will in Tolstoy's personages because he insists that this is your proper work, but you are too carried along by the force of his narrative and the inevitability of his characters' modes of speaking and thinking to question either the structure of plot or the individual images of voice that inhabit the story. If James and Flaubert and Joyce, the three together, are to be considered archetypes of the novelist, then Tolstoy seems something else, larger and more vital, for which we may lack a name, since Lukács was doubtless correct when he insisted that "the great epic is a form bound to the historical moment," and that moment was neither Tolstoy's nor ours.

W. Gareth Jones emphasizes that *War and Peace* is not so much a single narrative related by Tolstoy as a network of many narratives, addressed to us as though each of us were Prince Andrei, receptive and dispassionate. Perhaps that is Andrei's prime function in the novel, to serve as an ideal model for the Tolstoyan reader, even as Pierre perhaps becomes at last the ideal Tolstoyan storyteller. Isaiah Berlin and Martin Price both have illuminated the way that Tolstoy's heroes win through to serenity by coming to accept "the permanent relationships of things and the universal texture of human life," as Berlin phrases it. How can a critic convey either the cognitive wisdom or the restrained yet overwhelming pathos that is manifested in Tolstoy's account of the meeting between Pierre and Natasha at Princess Marya's when Pierre returns to Moscow after his liberation and imprisonment, and subsequent illness and recovery? It is difficult to conceive of an art that is subtler than the one Tolstoy exercises in Pierre's realization that Princess Marya's mourning companion is Natasha, and that he *is* in love with Natasha:

> In a room with a low ceiling, lit by one candle, sat the princess and with her someone else in a black dress. Pierre recalled that the princess always had lady companions, but who and what sort these companions were, Pierre did not know and did not recall. "It's one of her companions," he thought, glancing at the lady in the black dress.
>
> The princess rose quickly to meet him and gave him her hand.
>
> "Yes," she said, looking intently into his changed face after he had kissed her hand, "so this is how you and I meet. During the last days, he often spoke of you," she said, shifting her gaze from Pierre to the companion with a shyness that struck him for a moment.
>
> "I was so glad to learn that you had been saved. It was the only joyful news we had received for a long time." Again, still more uneasily, the princess glanced at her companion and was about to say something, but Pierre interrupted her.
>
> "Can you imagine, I knew nothing about him," he said. "I counted him as killed. All I knew, I knew from other people, at third hand. I know only that he ended up with the Rostovs... What a fate!"

Pierre was speaking quickly, animatedly. He glanced once at the face of the companion, saw an attentively tender, curious gaze directed at him, and, as often happens during a conversation, felt for some reason that this companion in the black dress was a sweet, kind, nice being, who would not hinder his heart-to-heart talk with Princess Marya.

But when he said the last words about the Rostovs, the perplexity on Princess Marya's face showed still more strongly. She again shifted her gaze from Pierre's face to the face of the lady in the black dress and said:

"Don't you recognize her?"

Pierre glanced once more at the pale, fine face of the companion, with its dark eyes and strange mouth. Something dear, long forgotten, and more than sweet looked at him from those attentive eyes.

"But no, it can't be," he thought. "This stern, thin, pale, aged face? It can't be her. It's only a reminiscence of that one." But just then Princess Marya said: "Natasha." And the face, with its attentive eyes, with difficulty, with effort, like a rusty door opening—smiled, and from that open door there suddenly breathed and poured out upon Pierre that long-forgotten happiness of which, especially now, he was not even thinking. It breathed out, enveloped, and swallowed him whole. When she smiled, there could no longer be any doubt: it was Natasha, and he loved her.

(trans. Richard Pevear and Larissa Volokhonsky)

Massively simple, direct, realistic, as this is, it is also, in its full context, with the strength of the vast novel behind it, an absolutely premeditated art. Henry James is not one of the great literary critics, despite the idolatry of his admirers. Tolstoy, Dickens, and Walt Whitman bear not the slightest resemblance to what James saw them as being, though the old James repented on the question of Whitman. If the highest art after all catches us unaware, even as we and Pierre together learn the secret and meaning of his life in this central moment, then no novelistic art, not even that of Proust, can surpass Tolstoy's. "Great works of art are only great because they are accessible and comprehensible to everyone." That rugged Tolstoyan principle is certainly supported by this moment, but we cannot forget that Lear and Gloucester's conversing, one mad and the other blind, is not accessible and comprehensible to everyone, and touches the limits of art as even Tolstoy does not. It is a sadness that Tolstoy could not or would not accommodate the transcendental and extraordinary in *King Lear, Macbeth,* and *Hamlet,* and yet did not resist the Biblical story of Joseph and his brothers, or the strife of Achilles and Hector. The Tolstoyan rejection of Shakespeare may be, however twisted askew, the most formidable tribute that Shakespeare's powers of representation have ever received.

Tolstoy was furious at Shakespeare's pragmatic freedom from Christianity. I am not at all clear as to just what even Tolstoy's rationalized Christianity has to do with *War and Peace,* or with *Anna Karenina.* What matters most in Tolstoy is his altogether Shakespearean gift for individualizing even his minor characters. Shakespeare remains, after four centuries, the greatest of all psychologists, and where else but in Shakespeare could Tolstoy learn his own depth as a psychologist? It is weirdly appropriate that the first sketches of *War and Peace* were entitled *All's Well That Ends Well.* Rereading *War and Peace,* with its effective, almost theatrical alternation of scenes, I also begin to ask: where, but from Shakespeare, did Tolstoy acquire his sense of scene-shifting as a further index to the clash of personalities?

Thomas Mann got it right when he ascribed Tolstoy's hatred of Shakespeare to "antagonism against that universal and all-accepting nature: in the jealousy which a man enduring moral torment was bound to feel in face of the blithe irony of an absolutely creative genius." I wonder if Mann does not give us another clue as to why the philosopher Wittgenstein, who was so fiercely devoted to Tolstoy, was also distrustful of Shakespeare. Wittgenstein insisted, "There are, indeed, things that cannot be put into words." Incessantly rereading Shakespeare, I doubt Wittgenstein, as there is nothing that Shakespeare cannot get into his more than thirty-five thousand words, seventeen hundred of which he had coined for himself.

Viktor Shklovsky famously called attention to Tolstoy's art of "making it strange," of "refusing to recognize an object, of describing it as if it were seen for the first time." Tolstoy sought and achieved originality in object representation, but his modes of portraying personality and character at their best recall Shakespeare's, an observation that would have infuriated Tolstoy. The extraordinary changes in Pierre, in *War and Peace,* follow the Shakespearean paradigm of surprise through involuntary self-overhearing. Tolstoy, who feared his own nihilism, and who secretly had identified God with death, accurately saw that Shakespeare was free of dogmatic shadows, and that Lear's tragedy, and Macbeth's, reflected Shakespeare's pragmatic nihilism. Shakespeare was perhaps the least solipsistic of all great writers; Tolstoy, the most. Tolstoy's resentment of Shakespeare was genius recognizing its antagonist in an opposed genius.

Of all Shakespearean roles, Tolstoy most resented Lear's, as he accurately perceived that *King Lear* was a pagan play directed to a Christian audience. In 1910, at eighty-two, Tolstoy fled his wife and family, to die at a railway station. The image of Lear's death was not in Tolstoy's mind, but it is difficult to keep it away from ours as we contemplate Tolstoy's desperate end.

I have read several of the biographies of Tolstoy: Aylmer Maude, A. N. Wilson, Anthony Briggs, Rosamund Bartlett. In different ways, they are all of considerable use. But I am left puzzled about why and how someone who was both a great writer and a towering moralist failed to love a marvelous wife, Sophia Behrs, who became Countess Sophia Tolstaya, and who gave him thirteen children, eight of whom survived childhood, and devoted her life to him, and to his work as a writer. Except for his daughter Alexandra, Tolstoy quarreled with all of his children, and would have disinherited them if he could.

There was authentic sexual passion between Tolstoy and Sophia, who was sixteen years younger, yet he manifested only the slightest interest in her welfare, and compelled her to break off an innocent friendship with a benign musician. The publication of her diaries in English (2010) was reviewed by my old acquaintance Michael Dirda with a pungency that rendered her belated justice:

> On one page of her husband's diaries, devoted copyist Sofia comes across this sentence: "There is no such thing as love, *only the physical need for intercourse and the practical need for a life companion."* She acidly comments: "I only wish I had read that 29 years ago, then I would never have married him."...
>
> In 1910, just a month before the 82-year-old Tolstoy fled Yasnaya Polyana on the trip that would lead to his death in

a railway station far from his home, Sofia—now in her late 60s—celebrates her "name day," which is also the day that Tolstoy proposed to her. She asks herself: "What did he do to that eighteen-year-old Sonechka Behrs, who gave him her whole life, her love and her trust?" She sums up the 48 years of their life together: "He has tortured me with his coldness, his cruelty and his extreme egotism."

Devoted women readers of Tolstoy can be grateful for his astonishing achievement, but, women and men alike, we owe something also to Sonechka Behrs, and we have to be convinced by her testimony as to his human flaws. Some of the greatest writers have been monsters of egoism. In addition to Tolstoy we can think of Dante, Milton, Goethe, Wordsworth, Victor Hugo, Ibsen, Yeats, Thomas Mann, and in a gentler way Proust and Joyce. From what we know of Cervantes, Montaigne, Molière, Shakespeare, Dr. Samuel Johnson, Jane Austen, George Eliot, and in our time Franz Kafka and Samuel Beckett, literary greatness and humane splendor can coexist.

Recently, I have taken to reading Lydia Ginzburg's *On Psychological Prose* (1971; translated by Judson Rosengrant, 1991) for her insights into personality in Tolstoy's novels. I do not know much of her other work, but I'm surprised that she discusses Montaigne yet does not mention Shakespeare and Cervantes, who with Montaigne invented the literary representation of personality as we know it. Still, her thoughts on Tolstoy stimulate me:

The two types of interior monologue reflect one of the most basic and productive contradictions in Tolstoi's point of view. The zealous analyst in him required "ratiocination" [*rassuditel'stvo*] as a reliable tool of analysis. Connected with this were his "archaistic" enthusiasms, especially his taste for the literature of eighteenth-century rationalism. Tolstoi's world-view, however, was antirationalistic. Using rational, analytical means, including a pointedly logical and sometimes even pedantic syntax, Tolstoi broke through the rational veneer of life, delving into what he regarded as its innate, natural essence. Tolstoi was, in the unique quality of this combination, quite close to his favorite thinker, Rousseau.

To be sure, depiction of the internal discourse of literary characters was widely practiced before Tolstoi (one need only recall the fevered interior monologues of Julien Sorel while in prison). Nonetheless, it is in fact with Tolstoi that the interior monologue is associated, as if he were its inventor. External discourse in pre-Tolstoian literature merged imperceptibly with internal discourse, remaining quite undifferentiated from it. Tolstoi turned internal discourse into something highly distinctive, functionally setting it off from authorial discourse and from the colloquial speech of his characters. And this is true of both the logical and the non-logical varieties of the Tolstoian interior monologue. Tolstoi really was the first to convey the uninterrupted yet disjointed stream of consciousness, and he transformed logical internal discourses into a special, unprecedentedly powerful means of analysis possessing a sort of unmediated authenticity: the individual analyzes himself, resorting for the sake of greater clarity to articulated formulations.

If you substituted "Shakespeare" for "Tolstoi," this would retain much of its force. Infuriated by Shakespeare, Tolstoy nevertheless was contaminated by him, as were all except the French, until the advent of Romanticism. Lydia Ginzburg extends her argument to Anna Karenina:

The brilliant interior monologue of Anna Karenina before her suicide anticipates (as many others have written) the stream of consciousness of twentieth-century novelists. But the remarkable thing about Anna's monologue is that both kinds of internal discourse—both purposes—are in conflict in it. On the one hand there is the famous 'Tiut'kin Coiffeur'... *je me fais coiffer par* Tiut'kin"—an alternation of disjointed but linked thoughts emerging as a result of the intermittent intrusion of accidental impressions from the street and the pressure of the character's obsessive inner awareness of her misfortune. And then in the midst of all this, the persistent and familiar sounds of Tolstoian "rationality" is suddenly audible: "'Well, I shall obtain a divorce and become Vronskii's wife. Will Kitty then stop looking at me the way she did today? No. Will Serezha stop asking and wondering about my two husbands? And what new feeling can I invent between Vronskii and me? Is any kind of feeling, not happiness even, but merely freedom from torment, even possible? No, it is not,' she answered herself without the slightest hesitation" (pt. 7, chap. 30). This clearly articulated discourse is necessary because Anna has come to see everything "in that piercing light that now revealed to her the meaning of life and human relations" (Levin made the acquaintance of that piercing light during his own crisis). But the stream of tortuous, alogical associations is also necessary to give expression to the increasing spiritual confusion that threatens Anna and that draws her toward her death. Tolstoi, boldly combining the alogical interior monologue with the logical variety, understood the conventional nature of what he was doing. But what he was doing was concerned more with artistic cognition of the principles of internal discourses than with an attempt to reproduce it—something that in any case would have been impossible by means of external language intended for intercourse among people. Tolstoi had no wish to undertake naturalistic tasks that were incapable of solution.

This is adroit and useful, yet is exemplified more fully by Shakespeare's tragic protagonists. Brutus, Othello, Cleopatra move to their suicides in different ways, but all of them manifest solutions to naturalistic labors that go beyond the external language of dialogue into the verge of transcendence. Hamlet, more than anyone else in all of literature, calls into question the limits that Lydia Ginzburg believes to be unassailable.

It will always be one of the mysteries of imaginative literature that Leo Tolstoy was outraged by William Shakespeare. His dreadful pamphlet of 1906 begins by quoting Shelley, among others:

"'King Lear' may be recognized as the perfect model of the dramatic art of the whole world," says Shelley.

Anyone who has read Shelley deeply knows that this great lyric poet was also a profound skeptical intellect, and, like Milton, possessed immense learning. I have been teaching *King Lear* for almost two-thirds of a century to many gifted students, and they, like me, agree with Shelley. Tolstoy, a powerful mind determined to narrow its own consciousness, approaches a kind of lunacy in writing about Shakespeare. He warns that the reader will be demoralized and all but ruined by Shakespeare:

> But, above all, having assimilated the immoral view of life which penetrates all Shakespeare's writings, he loses the capacity of distinguishing good from evil. And the error of extolling an insignificant, inartistic writer—not only not moral, but directly immoral—executes its destructive work.
>
> This is why I think that the sooner people free themselves from the false glorification of Shakespeare, the better it will be.
>
> First, having freed themselves from this deceit, men will come to understand that the drama which has no religious element at its foundation is not only not an important and good thing, as it is now supposed to be, but the most trivial and despicable of things. Having understood this, they will have to search for, and work out, a new form of modern drama, a drama which will serve as the development and confirmation of the highest stage of religious consciousness in men.
>
> Secondly, having freed themselves from this hypnotic state, men will understand that the trivial and immoral works of Shakespeare and his imitators, aiming merely at the recreation and amusement of the spectators, can not possibly represent the teaching of life, and that, while there is no true religious drama, the teaching of life should be sought for in other sources.

Confronting Dostoevsky's hatred of Jews is a moral shock. Tolstoy, one of the double handful of Western writers who matter most, is a very different matter. He insisted that he had read Shakespeare in the original, in Schlegel's German translation, in Russian, and in French, and one wonders what he means by "reading." If you begin reading *King Lear* with a moral and spiritual virulence all your own, can you read it at all? And yet this was the author of *The Cossacks, War and Peace, Anna Karenina,* and much the best story I have ever read or could read, *Hadji Murat.*

The critic John Bayley, in some introductory remarks to *The Cossacks,* indicates what he calls "the anxiety of influence" as manifested by the young Tolstoy in regard to Pushkin and Lermontov. Pushkin remained a lifelong inspiration for Tolstoy, though he incessantly denied it. I would suggest that Tolstoy never could get rid of having internalized both Shakespeare and Pushkin. Necessarily, there were other influences: *David Copperfield* by Charles Dickens, *Les Misérables* by Victor Hugo, the philosophy of Arthur Schopenhauer, and, later, Far Eastern scriptures. More than anything else, the Bible and Homer are always present in Tolstoy.

War and Peace is of no genre. It does not help to describe it as a novel. Nor does national epic nor Russian *Iliad* catch its idiosyncratic flight from Western literary convention. If you can say that so vast a panorama has a central protagonist, aside from Tolstoy in the mask of his serenity Field Marshal Mikhail Kutuzov, that would not be Napoleon but Pierre Bezukhov, who in some strange sense emerges from the inward recesses of Tolstoy's own moral character. Pierre is a quixotic quester, an immensely wealthy bastard, and thus initially an outsider, who goes through freemasonry in search of the ethical life and encounters its curious use, probably by way of Rosicrucianism, of the Kabbalistic *gematria:*

> If the words "Le Empereur Napoléon" were constructed by the cipher, the sum total of the figures added together would be 666. Hence Napoleon was the Beast spoken of in the Apocalypse. Moreover, by adding the figures corresponding in the same cipher to the French words quarante-deux, the period of years set for his power, the sum of 666 is again brought out, which indicated that the year 1812, as being the forty-second year of his age, would be the last of his rule.
>
> He then discovers, of course, that the calculation for his own name rendered very awkwardly as L'Russe Bestuhof also made 666, so determining that he would be the one who would put an end to Napoleon!

Thomas De Quincey's "Origin of the Rosicrucians and the Free-Masons" was first published in January 1824. I doubt that De Quincey was a Freemason, but he had read Emanuel Swedenborg, whose visions were appropriated by some Masons who established the Swedenborg Rite. Setting aside Pierre's self-indulgence in mystical speculation, good readers agree that he is a person we are obliged to love. Indeed, all the protagonists of *War and Peace* bring us into a world of love, despite the Napoleonic onslaught. Natasha, Prince Andrei, Princess Marya, Count Nikolai Rostov, Platon Karataev join Pierre, Kutuzov, and Tolstoy himself, narrator and close observer, as benign presences, sometimes erring, but always surging back to a normative consciousness that envelops the reader.

Tolstoy would have been provoked to anger by my necessary conviction that the Bible, the *Iliad*, and Pushkin could not have sufficed to liberate the author of *War and Peace* into his new freedom to form so many separate yet intertwined personalities. Olenin, for all his amiability, is not vivid enough to sustain his role in *The Cossacks*. The book is saved by Lukáshka, Maryánka, and Daddy Eroshka, persuasively rendered Cossacks.

The unforgivable and unforgived precursor was William Shakespeare, who with Cervantes and Montaigne invented what we now call personality. Tolstoy was devoted both to Cervantes and to Montaigne, and he absorbed their influence with gusto. Neither of them could have taught him how to portray women. It is one of the glories of *War and Peace* that its women, not just Natasha and Princess Marya, but also Princess Hélène, Pierre's brazenly unfaithful first wife, and Sonya are totally realized personalities. Their Shakespearean lineage is a complex meander; I would be glad to track it, but this is not the place.

My friend Martin Price deftly employed Wittgenstein in his depiction of the forms of life in Tolstoy. Wittgenstein loved Tolstoy and Dostoevsky, Beethoven and Michelangelo, but went askew when he read Shakespeare, who to him was "a creator of language." I met Wittgenstein once, in the summer of 1948, if I remember accurately, when I lived with Stuart MacDonald Brown, Jr., his wife, Catherine, and their four children. Brown had been my philosophy teacher, and we did a semester of independent study on the works of Saint John of the Cross. Wittgenstein was living with his friends Norman and Lee Malcolm quite close by. I had no idea at that time who Wittgenstein was, but I recall being fascinated by his face and his gentle manner. Once, when both the Browns and Malcolms were shopping at a supermarket, I sat outside with Wittgenstein and we talked about Saint John of the Cross, who clearly interested him. That was seventy years ago, and I do not remember much more. I did not read Wittgenstein until my senior year at Cornell, when I took a course taught by Professor Max Black, who later became a good friend. In

1964, Max published *A Companion to Wittgenstein's "Tractatus,"* which I still find useful, because it employs Wittgenstein's later writings and sayings to illuminate the *Tractatus.*

At my advanced old age, I still find Wittgenstein difficult, though some of his aphorisms never abandon me. Somewhere in the *Tractatus* is the adage: What the solipsist *says* is wrong, but what the solipsist *means* is right. I remember that Max Black traced that to Schopenhauer's presumably early influence upon Wittgenstein. There is a late maxim by Wittgenstein: Love is not a feeling. Love, unlike pain, is put to the test. We do not say that was not a true pain, because it passed away so quickly.

Schopenhauer, whom Tolstoy admired, may be another link between Tolstoy and Wittgenstein. For me the prime connection is their more or less mutual stance toward Shakespeare. It is not that Wittgenstein participated in Tolstoy's extravagant moral outrage. There is a tone of puzzlement in Wittgenstein on Shakespeare. He mentions *King Lear* and evidently had read it, either in English or in what is usually called the Schlegel-Tieck German version. I reflect that Wittgenstein had the instinctive aesthetic capability of recognizing Georg Trakl's subtle and heartbreaking poetry. It seems not possible to me that Ludwig Wittgenstein, confronted by *King Lear,* the ultimate Western tragedy, was not affected by it. Perhaps he was testing himself for what he believed he lacked, and did not like Shakespeare because he did not like himself. I still believe much the best story I have ever read is Tolstoy's *Hadji Murat.* Wittgenstein gave Norman Malcolm a copy of the short novel, urging him to read it. Going into battle as an Austrian officer in World War I, Wittgenstein carried with him Tolstoy's brief version of the Gospels. There can be no question as to Wittgenstein's aesthetic sensibility, yet the capaciousness of Shakespeare offended him. I think Tolstoy and Wittgenstein were quite accurate in seeing that Shakespeare was free of any concern with the Incarnation and had gone beyond limits in empathic portrayals of Iago, Edmund, and Macbeth.

You cannot diminish Shakespeare, even if you are the author of *War and Peace.* The ever-expanding inward self possibly passed from Martin Luther through William Tyndale to Shakespeare, but Hamlet's incredibly capacious consciousness is something radically new, and is attended by a new kind of charismatic personality, prefigured in the Court Historian's King David and then in the Yeshua of the Gospel of Mark.

Maxim Gorky, now remembered not so much for his own fictions but for his complex relations with both Lenin and Stalin, composed the most revealing pages about Tolstoy the man that I have ever read. His Tolstoy worships Tolstoy and truly does not believe in God. Tolstoy the writer is indispensable and always will be. Tolstoy the man disturbs me. He hated women because they gave birth to men but could not give their sons literal immortality. That is madness. What else can we call it? Gorky thought that Tolstoy, the great natural force, wistfully fancied that nature would make an exception for him, so that he could live in the body forever. Goethe and Ibsen sometimes diverted themselves with the same pathetic folly. Tolstoy and Goethe died at eighty-two, Ibsen at seventy-eight. It is alas accurate to assert that none of the three ever deeply loved anyone except himself, be it wives, children, mistresses, friends. Nothing is got for nothing, and I am perpetually grateful for *Hadji Murat, War and Peace, Anna Karenina,* Goethe's poetry and his outrageous *Faust: Part Two,* Ibsen's *Brand, Peer Gynt, Emperor and Galilean, Hedda Gabler, When We Dead Awaken.* Perhaps only sublime solipsists could have managed precisely those breakthroughs. Infants appear to be solipsists, but only at the start.

But, then, one can oppose to Dante, Milton, Goethe, Wordsworth, and Tolstoy the imaginative titans who were anything but solipsists: Chaucer, Cervantes, Montaigne, Shakespeare, Molière, Keats. It is not a choice between, but of. In the literary heaven of heavens, Shakespeare is God. He would have been the last person to think so. That Tolstoy attempted to be not just the Russian prophet and Homer, but also the Russian God, with whatever fervor he would have disavowed that, is simply the cost of his confirmation as the inescapable writer of his language, supplanting even Pushkin.

I return to *War and Peace,* which means to Pierre, who continues to surprise me. Throughout his life and work, Tolstoy trusted to an unmediated will. Pierre has never fired a gun, yet in his duel with the nasty Dolokhov, who supposedly never misses, he seriously wounds Dolokhov, who has been cuckolding him with Hélène, and who misses *his* shot. Rightly discarding his unfaithful wife, who has also had an incestuous affair with her brother Anatole, Pierre tries to begin again, dimly aware that he is in love with Natasha. Eventually, he allows Hélène to return, but in time she destroys herself with an overdose intended to abort her pregnancy.

Pierre's is the most complex personality in all of Tolstoy, more difficult to apprehend fully than his nearest rival, Levin, in *Anna Karenina*. Dostoevsky's protagonists are rarely coherent. The most fascinating—Svidrigailov, Stavrogin, Prince Myshkin, Mitya and Ivan Karamazov—are not so much polyphonic voices as they are vortices of ambivalences.

One problem with both Pierre and Levin is that, unlike Hamlet, they cannot think so well that they think themselves into the truth, but are endlessly frustrated. Hamlet thinks beyond all limits and attains truths that he incarnates, yet lacks time to tell us. Those unspoken truths set inwardness against outwardness, as in the prophetic modes of Amos, Micah, 1 Isaiah, and the tormented Jeremiah, who tells us that Yahweh has written the Law upon our inward parts. It is not that Pierre and Levin are prophets but that Tolstoy victimized himself through becoming one. Prophetic poets, be they Biblical or classical, English or Russian, French or German, or American in the wake of Walt Whitman, more easily contain the double burden of truth telling and imaginings. A prophetic novelist, like Victor Hugo in *Les Misérables* or Tolstoy in *War and Peace*, navigates more perilous tides.

Martin Price accurately sees that Tolstoy was always a vitalist, particularly in his moral and spiritual concerns. For Pierre, life is God and God is metamorphic. For Tolstoy, life is God and God is Tolstoy. Aesthetically, this is justifiable, because Tolstoy, unlike Dostoevsky, knew how to represent fundamental changes in the personality of his protagonists. I find no change in Raskolnikov, Svidrigailov, Prince Myshkin, Stavrogin, and all the others who torment and fascinate me in Dostoevsky's *Schwärmerei*.

I can think of few fictive personalities, outside of Shakespeare's, that change so fully as that of Pierre Bezukhov. As a prisoner of the French, profoundly moved by the Russian serf Platon Karataev, his fellow captive (executed by the French when he is too sick to march farther), Pierre casts away all his doubts about human existence. He achieves a Tolstoyan natural transcendence, which ought to be an oxymoron, and yet Tolstoy's art makes it work:

The sun had set long ago. Bright stars lit up here and there; red as fire, the glow of the rising full moon spread on the edge of the horizon, and the enormous red ball wavered astonishingly in the grayish haze. It was growing light. The evening was already over, but night had not yet begun. Pierre got up and walked away from his new comrades, between the campfires, to the other side of the road, where he was told the captive soldiers were camped. He wanted to talk with them. On the road a French sentry stopped him and told him to go back.

Pierre went back, but not to the campfire, to his comrades, but to an unhitched cart, where there was no one. Crossing his legs and lowering his head, he sat on the cold ground by the wheel of the cart and stayed there motionless for a long time, thinking. More than an hour went by. No one disturbed Pierre. Suddenly he burst into his fat, good-natured laugh, so loudly that people from different sides turned in astonishment towards this strange, evidently solitary laughter.

"Ha, ha, ha," laughed Pierre. And he said aloud to himself: "The soldier wouldn't let me go. They caught me, they locked me up. They're holding me prisoner. Who, me? Me—my immortal soul! Ha, ha, ha!...Ha, ha, ha!..." he laughed, with tears brimming in his eyes.

Some man got up and came to see what the strange, big man was laughing about by himself. Pierre stopped laughing, got up, went further away from the curious fellow, and looked around.

The enormous, endless bivouac, noisy earlier with the crackling of campfires and the talking of men, was growing still; the red flames of the campfires were dying out and turning pale. The full moon stood high in the bright sky. Forests and fields, invisible earlier beyond the territory of the camp, now opened out in the distance. And further beyond these forests and fields could be seen the bright, wavering endless distance calling one to itself. Pierre looked into the sky, into the depths of the retreating, twinkling stars. "And all this is mine, and all this is in me, and all this is me!" thought Pierre. "And all this they've caught and put in a shed and boarded it up!" He smiled and went to his comrades to lie down and sleep.

By any reckoning this is marvelous. Did Tolstoy, somewhere in the abyss of himself, recall Hamlet confronting his treacherous schoolmates Rosencrantz and Guildenstern, and telling them that Denmark is a prison?

> HAMLET: Why, then, 'tis none to you; for there is nothing either good or bad, but thinking makes it so: to me it is a prison.
> ROSENCRANTZ: Why then, your ambition makes it one; 'tis too narrow for your mind.
> HAMLET: O God, I could be bounded in a nutshell and count myself a king of infinite space, were it not that I have bad dreams.
>
> (Act 2, Scene 2, lines 244–48)

The nutshell has become a boarded-up shed; a king of infinite space becomes "And all this is mine, and all this is in me, and all this is me!" Pierre Bezukhov doubtless doubles for the inward Tolstoy, and yet his Hamlet aspect prevails until he comes to know Platon Karataev and absorbs an earthly wisdom.

War and Peace is infinite. As an æsthetic artifact it rivals the masterworks of what once we regarded as literary culture: Tanakh, *Iliad*, Athenian tragedy, Plato, Pindar, Lucretius, Virgil, Dante, Petrarch, Chaucer, Rabelais, Cervantes, Montaigne, Shakespeare, Milton, Molière, Racine, Swift, Pope, Goethe, Rousseau, Blake, Wordsworth, Pushkin, Leopardi, Dickens, Melville, Walt Whitman, Hugo, Balzac, Flaubert, Baudelaire, Chekhov, Ibsen, Yeats, Proust, and Joyce.

Tanakh, or the Hebrew Bible, which the old Tolstoy taught himself to read in the original; Homer; Dante; Chaucer; Cervantes; above all Shakespeare: these stand with *War and Peace*. I myself would add Milton, Goethe, *Moby-Dick*, Whitman. After that it is a question of individual taste and judgment.

To have written *War and Peace*, the profoundly troubling *Anna Karenina*, and the perfect story *Hadji Murat* is to have given such vitalism to readers that, whatever his moralizings, my primary reactions to Tolstoy are awe and gratitude.

CHAPTER 23

Anna Karenina (1877)

Leo Tolstoy

I cannot reread *Anna Karenina,* particularly in the eloquent translation by Richard Pevear and Larissa Volokhonsky, without becoming unnerved. It is upsetting because Tolstoy's vitalism drives me to ask questions I cannot answer. *Anna Karenina* can be called the novel of the drives, since no other narrative centers so fully upon its protagonist's being so swept away by her will to live that almost nothing else matters to her. Anna's love for Vronsky has its rivals in Western literature, but I can recall no similar representation of erotic passion quite so intense. Tolstoy explains nothing about Anna's object-choice to us, whether in idealizing or in reductive terms. What he does show us, with overwhelming persuasiveness, is that there is no choice involved. Anna, vital and attractive in every way, is someone with whom most male readers of the novel fall in love, and Tolstoy clearly loves her almost obsessively. He would not have said that he was Anna, but she resembles something in him, a pulsation more intimate than Levin, his ostensible surrogate, can share.

Why does Anna kill herself? Would we find it as plausible if a contemporary Anna emulated her? Could there be a contemporary Anna? The questions may reduce to: Why did Tolstoy kill her? Did he mean to punish her? I think not. Anna's suicide saddens us, but it also relieves us from shared suffering. Doubtless it relieved Tolstoy also, who was suffering with her. Other legitimate questions would be: How would Schopenhauer have received Anna's death? Is it a heroic release, or a failure in endurance?

Tolstoy read Schopenhauer in the interval between *War and Peace* and *Anna Karenina,* an uneasy interregnum in which he was defeated by his attempt to write a novel about the era of Peter the Great. His enthusiasm for Schopenhauer was essentially a reaffirmation of his own darkest convictions, since he had always been both an apocalyptic vitalist and a dark moralist appalled by some of the consequences of his own vitalism. Schopenhauer's Will to Live, with its metaphysical status as the true thing-in-itself, is simply the Tolstoyan natural ethos turned into pathos. The Will to Live is unitary, active, rapacious, indifferent, universal desire, one of the most extraordinary of nineteenth-century hyperboles:

Let us now add the consideration of the human race. The matter indeed becomes more complicated, and assumes a certain seriousness of aspect; but the fundamental character remains unaltered. Here also life presents itself by no means as a gift for enjoyment, but as a task, a drudgery to be performed; and in accordance with this we see, in great and small, universal need, ceaseless cares, constant pressure, endless strife, compulsory activity, with extreme exertion of all the powers of body and mind. Many millions, united into nations, strive for the common good, each individual on account of his own; but many thousands fall as a sacrifice for it. Now senseless delusions, now intriguing politics, incite them to wars with each other; then the sweat and the blood of the great multitude must flow, to carry out the ideas of individuals, or to expiate their faults. In peace industry and trade are active, inventions work miracles, seas are navigated, delicacies are collected from all ends of the world, the waves engulf thousands. All strive, some planning, others acting; the tumult is indescribable. But the ultimate aim of it all, what is it? To sustain ephemeral and tormented individuals through a short span of time in the most fortunate case with endurable want and comparative freedom from pain, which, however, is at once attended with ennui; then the

reproduction of this race and its striving. In this evident disproportion between the trouble and the reward, the will to live
appears to us from this point of view, if taken objectively, as a
fool, or subjectively, as a delusion, seized by which everything
living works with the utmost exertion of its strength for something that is of no value. But when we consider it more closely,
we shall find here also that it is rather a blind pressure, a tendency entirely without ground or motive.

If this is the characterization of the Will to Live, then the metaphysics of the love of the sexes will reduce to a kind of treason:

In between, however, in the midst of the tumult, we see the
glances of two lovers meet longingly: yet why so secretly, fear-
fully, and stealthily? Because these lovers are the traitors who
seek to perpetuate the whole want and drudgery, which would
otherwise speedily reach an end; this they wish to frustrate, as
others like them have frustrated it before.

Schopenhauer presumably would have found this exemplified as
much by Levin and Kitty as by Vronsky and Anna, but there he and
Tolstoy part, as even Tolstoy is a touch saner upon the metaphysics
of sexual love. What matters most about Anna, at least to the reader,
is her intensity, her will to live (I deliberately remove the Schopen-
hauerian capitalization). Anna's aura renders her first meeting with
Vronsky unforgettable for us:

Vronsky followed the conductor to the carriage and at the door
to the compartment stopped to allow a lady to leave. With the
habitual flair of a worldly man, Vronsky determined from one
glance at this lady's appearance that she belonged to high society. He excused himself and was about to enter the carriage,
but felt a need to glance at her once more—not because she
was very beautiful, not because of the elegance and modest
grace that could be seen in her whole figure, but because there
was something especially gentle and tender in the expression
of her sweet-looking face as she stepped past him. As he looked
back, she also turned her head. Her shining grey eyes, which

seemed dark because of their thick lashes, rested amiably and attentively on his face, as if she recognized him, and at once wandered over the approaching crowd as though looking for someone. In that brief glance Vronsky had time to notice the restrained animation that played over her face and fluttered between her shining eyes and the barely noticeable smile that curved her red lips. It was as if a surplus of something so over-flowed her being that it expressed itself beyond her will, now in the brightness of her glance, now in her smile. She deliberately extinguished the light in her eyes, but it shone against her will in a barely noticeable smile.

A benign vitality, however excessive, is what Tolstoy recognized in himself. What he teaches himself in this novel is that a vitality so exuberant transcends benignity as it does every other quality. The brief but overwhelming Chapter XI of Part Two is not only the novel in embryo, and the essence of Anna, but it is also, to me, the most revelatory scene that Tolstoy ever wrote:

That which for almost a year had constituted the one exclusive desire of Vronsky's life, replacing all former desires; that which for Anna had been an impossible, horrible, but all the more enchanting dream of happiness—this desire had been satisfied. Pale, his lower jaw trembling, he stood over her and pleaded with her to be calm, himself not knowing why or how.

'Anna! Anna!' he kept saying in a trembling voice. 'Anna, for God's sake!...'

But the louder he spoke, the lower she bent her once proud, gay, but now shame-stricken head, and she became all limp, falling from the divan where she had been sitting to the floor at his feet; she would have fallen on the carpet if he had not held her.

'My God! Forgive me!' she said, sobbing, pressing his hands to her breast.

She felt herself so criminal and guilty that the only thing left for her was to humble herself and beg forgiveness; but as she had no one else in her life now except him, it was also to him that she addressed her plea for forgiveness. Looking at him, she physically felt her humiliation and could say nothing more. And he felt what a murderer must feel when he looks at the body he has deprived of life. This body deprived of life was their love, the first period of their love. There was something horrible and loathsome in his recollections of what had been paid for with this terrible price of shame. Shame at her spiritual nakedness weighed on her and communicated itself to him. But, despite all the murderer's horror before the murdered body, he had to cut this body into pieces and hide it, he had to make use of what the murderer had gained by his murder.

And as the murderer falls upon this body with animosity, as if with passion, drags it off and cuts it up, so he covered her face and shoulders with kisses. She held his hand and did not move. Yes, these kisses were what had been bought by this shame. Yes, and this one hand, which will always be mine, is the hand of my accomplice. She raised this hand and kissed it. He knelt down and tried to look at her face; but she hid it and said nothing. Finally, as if forcing herself, she sat up and pushed him away. Her face was still as beautiful, but the more pitiful for that.

'Everything is finished,' she said. 'I have nothing but you. Remember that.'

'How can I not remember what is my very life? For one minute of this happiness...'

'What happiness?' she said with loathing and horror, and her horror involuntarily communicated itself to him. 'For God's sake, not a word, not a word more.'

She quickly stood up and moved away from him.

'Not a word more,' she repeated, and with an expression of cold despair on her face, which he found strange, she left him. She felt that at that moment she could not put into words her feeling of shame, joy, and horror before this entry into a new life, and she did not want to speak of it, to trivialize this feeling with imprecise words. But later, too, the next day and the day after that, she not only found no words in which she could express all the complexity of these feelings, but was unable even to find thoughts in which she could reflect with herself on all that was in her soul.

She kept telling herself: 'No, I can't think about it now; later, when I'm more calm.' But this calm for reflection never came; each time the thought occurred to her of what she had done, of what would become of her and what she ought to do, horror came over her, and she drove these thoughts away.

'Later, later,' she kept saying, 'when I'm more calm.'

But in sleep, when she had no power over her thoughts, her situation presented itself to her in all its ugly nakedness. One dream visited her almost every night. She dreamed that they were both her husbands, that they both lavished their caresses on her. Alexei Alexandrovich wept, kissing her hands and saying: 'It's so good now!' And Alexei Vronsky was right there, and he, too, was her husband. And, marvelling that it had once seemed impossible to her, she laughingly explained to them that this was much simpler and that now they were both content and happy. But this dream weighed on her like a nightmare, and she would wake up in horror.

Abruptly, without even an overt hint of the nature of the con-summation, Tolstoy places us after the event. Anna's tragedy, and in some sense Tolstoy's own, is implicit in this majestic scene. Poor Vronsky, at once victim and executioner, is hopelessly inadequate to Anna's intensity. There is of course nothing he can say and nothing he can do, because he is the wrong man, and always will be. But who could have been the right man? Levin? Perhaps, but Tolstoy and life (the two are one) would not have it so. The serenity, necessary for reflection, might have come to Anna with Levin, yet that is highly doubtful. Tolstoy himself, her double and brother, her psychic twin, would have been inadequate to Anna, and she to him. Anna's dream, with both Alexeis happy as her joint husbands, is a peculiar horror to her, because it so horrified Tolstoy. The outrage expressed by D. H. Lawrence at what he judged to be Tolstoy's murder of Anna might have been mitigated had Lawrence allowed himself to remember that Tolstoy, nearly thirty-five years after Anna, also died in a rail-road station.

"Characters like Anna are tragic figures because, for reasons that are admirable, they cannot live divided lives or survive through repression." That sentence of Martin Price's is the best I have read about Anna, but I wonder if Anna can be called a tragic figure, any more than she can be what Schopenhauer grimly would have called her, a traitor. Tragedy depends upon division and repression, and Anna is betrayed by nature itself, which does not create men as vital as herself, or, if it does, creates them as savage moralists, like Tolstoy. Anna is too integral for tragedy, and too imbued with reality to survive in any social malforming of reality whatsoever. She dies because Tolstoy could not sustain the suffering it would have cost him to imagine a life she could have borne to go on living.

With a sinuous gesture, Tolstoy centers the opening of *Anna Karenina* on Anna's brother, who has been exposed having an affair with the family governess, to the rightful fury of his wife, Dolly:

Stepan Arkadyich was a truthful man concerning his own self. He could not deceive himself into believing that he repented of his behaviour. He could not now be repentant that he, a thirty-four-year-old, handsome, amorous man, did not feel amorous with his wife, the mother of five living and two dead children, who was only a year younger than he. He repented only that he had not managed to conceal things better from her. But he felt all the gravity of his situation, and pitied his wife, his children and himself. Perhaps he would have managed to hide his sins better from his wife had he anticipated that the news would have such an effect on her. He had never thought the question over clearly, but vaguely imagined that his wife had long suspected him of being unfaithful to her and was looking the other way. It even seemed to him that she, a worn-out, aged, no longer beautiful woman, not remarkable for anything, simple, merely a kind mother of a family, ought in all fairness to be indulgent. It turned out to be quite the opposite.

'Ah, terrible! Ay, ay, ay! terrible!' Stepan Arkadyich repeated to himself and could come up with nothing. 'And how nice it all was before that, what a nice life we had! She was content, happy with the children, I didn't hinder her in anything, left her to fuss over them and the household however she liked. True, it's not nice that *she* used to be a governess in our house. Not nice! There's something trivial, banal, in courting one's own governess. But what a governess!' (He vividly recalled Mlle Roland's dark, roguish eyes and her smile.) 'But while she was in our house, I never allowed myself anything. And the worst of it is that she's already... It all had to happen at once! Ay, ay, ay! But what to do, what to do?'

There was no answer, except the general answer life gives to all the most complex and insoluble questions. That answer is: one must live for the needs of the day, in other words, become oblivious. To become oblivious in dreams was impossible now, at least till night-time; it was impossible to return to that music sung by carafe-women; and so one had to become oblivious in the dream of life.

Lacking Russian, I rely upon Pevear and Volokhonsky for the irony and charm of this amiable passage, in which we might be hearing the young Tolstoy of *Childhood, Boyhood, Youth,* and *The Cossacks.* Knowing all the turmoil and destructiveness to come makes it pardonable for the rereader to share Stepan Arkadyich's bliss:

"... But what a governess!" (He vividly recalled Mlle Roland's dark, roguish eyes and her smile.)

Tolstoy, wondrously to the end of his long life, was on fire with lust for women, doubtless engendering his misogyny. At eighty-eight, long beyond the pragmatics of unruly behavior, I marvel at his almost Shakespearean powers of representing women, though he could not cease resenting their sexual potential. Martin Price, interested primarily in a kind of Wittgensteinian conviction that meaning in novels, as in life, is made possible only by "forms of life," relies upon what I find almost mystical in the Austrian Jewish sage:

It is what human beings say that is false and true; and they agree in the language they use. That is not agreement in opinions but in form of life.

(*Philosophical Investigations*)

The results in my late friend Price's insights are both positive and, to me, negative. I think he gets Tolstoy absolutely right on the delayed meeting between Levin and Anna:

When Levin finally meets Anna in Moscow, he is altogether charmed by her seriousness, her beauty, and her intelligence. After a day of largely senseless talk, he is moved by her naturalness and lack of self-consciousness. Levin is moved to make a witticism about French art, which has had so far to go in its return to realism: "They saw poetry in the very fact that they did not lie." Anna's face lights up with pleasure. What gives the episode its sadness is not Kitty's jealousy afterwards, but the disclosure that Anna has "done all she could . . . to arouse in Levin a feeling of love." Seductiveness is perhaps the only behavior she allows herself any more with Vronsky, and with other men as a matter of course.

The truth of that saddens me, but I have to yield to it. I rebel when Price gives us what I suppose might be called a Wittgenstein-ian vision of Anna's suicide:

At the end we see Anna surrendering to powers of destruction, in her savage torture of herself and Vronsky, in her sad effort to stir the pitying Kitty to jealousy. Her world fills with hatred and disgust; everyone she sees is vicious or filthy. The breakdown of mind creates a stream of consciousness, and the rage of her last hours is the form her vitality takes. Unlike her husband, who finds consolation in fashionable superstition, she finds herself outside all forms of life.

It does not seem to me that Anna's vitality forms at the end only into rage. I want to return to the scene of Anna's attempt to seduce Levin, but under the guidance of the Russian Jewish critic Lydia Ginzburg, who, in her 1991 book, *On Psychological Prose,* breaks her discussion into two columns, the right-hand side leaning to analysis:

"It is exceptionally good, is it not?" Stepan Arkad'evich said, upon noticing that Levin was looking at the portrait.

The excerpt begins with a phrase elicited by an external impression—of the portrait and of Levin looking at it. There is also hidden exultation in Oblonskii's question. He wants Anna to conquer Levin (Levin's family principles secretly irritate the wicked Stepan Arkad'evich).

"I have never seen a better portrait."

Levin answers Oblonskii's question.

"It is an exceptional likeness, is it not?" said Vorkuev.

Vorkuev interferes in the conversation in order to say something pleasant to his hostess.

Levin glanced from the portrait to the original. A special brilliance lit up Anna's face when she felt his gaze upon her; Levin blushed, and in order to hide his confusion was about to ask her if it was a long time since she had seen Dar'ia Aleksandrovna, but Anna started talking just as he did:

Levin, confused by the impression Anna has made on him, looks for another topic in order to change the subject. Dolly surfaces logically, both because he is reminded of her by the presence of her husband, and because she is closely related to him and to Anna.

"Ivan Petrovich and I were just now talking about Vashchenkov's latest pictures. Have you seen them?"

Anna continues a conversational line associatively linked to her portrait.

"Yes, I have," replied Levin.

An answer to her remark.

"But excuse me, I interrupted you. You were going to say…"

A phrase prompted by the requirements of courtesy.

Levin asked her if she had seen Dolly lately.

Now that the discussion no longer concerns Anna's portrait but Vashchenkov's pictures, Levin no longer needs Dolly as a topic, but he is forced to return to her anyway.

"She visited me yesterday. She is very angry with the gymnasium because of Grisha.

Anna picks up the topic suggested by Levin.

The Latin master has apparently
been unfair to him."
   "Yes I have seen the pictures.
I did not really care for them,"
Levin said, returning to the
subject she had started.

Levin prefers the topic of Vashchenkov with its ensuing discussion of the "new direction in art" to that of Dolly and her children, and he prefers it because he now wants to say "intelligent
things" so that Anna will hear them. "This time Levin did not
speak in anything like the mechanical way he had spoken that
morning. Every word of his conversation with her took on a
special meaning."

What Lydia Ginzburg captures, however tenuously, is that Levin
rather inexplicably *wants* to be seduced, though only visually and
verbally. The suggestion is that Levin and Anna are both Tolstoy,

divided between two identifications that cannot endure any longer.
Let us look closely at Anna's final moment:

"There!" she said to herself, staring into the shadow of the carriage at the sand mixed with coal poured between the sleepers,
"there, right in the middle, and I'll punish him and be rid of
everybody and of myself."
   She wanted to fall under the first carriage, the midpoint of
which had drawn even with her. But the red bag, which she
started taking off her arm, delayed her, and it was too late: the
midpoint went by. She had to wait for the next carriage. A feeling seized her, similar to what she experienced when preparing
to go into the water for a swim, and she crossed herself. The
habitual gesture of making the sign of the cross called up in
her soul a whole series of memories from childhood and girl-
hood, and suddenly the darkness that covered everything for
her broke and life rose up before her momentarily with all its
bright past joys. Yet she did not take her eyes from the wheels
of the approaching second carriage. And just at the moment

when the midpoint between the two wheels came even with her, she threw the red bag aside and, drawing her head down between her shoulders, fell on her hands under the carriage, and with a light movement, as if preparing to get up again at once, sank to her knees. And in that same instant she was horrified at what she was doing. 'Where am I? What am I doing? Why?' She wanted to rise, to throw herself back, but something huge and implacable pushed at her head and dragged her over. 'Lord, forgive me for everything!' she said, feeling the impossibility of any struggle. A little muzhik, muttering to himself, was working over some iron. And the candle by the light of which she had been reading that book filled with anxieties, deceptions, grief and evil, flared up brighter than ever, lit up for her all that had once been in darkness, sputtered, grew dim, and went out for ever.

"I'll punish him and be rid of everybody and of myself": him is in the first place Vronsky, in the second Karenin, but the third most deserving of punishment is Tolstoy himself. Doubtless he went to his final railway station thinking, "I'll punish her"—Sophia Behrs Tolstoy—"and be rid of everybody"—eight of my nine surviving children, "and of everything in myself that is not peasant, prophet, godlike."

Hugh McLean, in his 2008 book *In Quest of Tolstoy*, has an admirably succinct paragraph on the suicide:

Tolstoy begins with the horrendous image of the terrible, inexorable crushing wheels of the train, advancing and colliding with Anna's body. She has time for one last prayer and then surrenders to the inevitable. The next sentence is ambiguous: there may be a real workman whose presence Anna dimly perceives, linking him with an ominous figure that has appeared in her life several times before, both in reality and in dreams, going back to the workman crushed by a train at the very beginning of the novel (and the beginning of her acquaintance with Vronsky); or this may be only a fantasy, a creature of Anna's soon-to-be-extinguished brain. Finally, Tolstoy invokes an entirely metaphorical candle by whose light Anna can now read, in her last moments of consciousness, the entire "book" of her life, before the candle goes out forever.

Janet Malcolm in 2015 pungently intimated that Tolstoy was the culprit:

> Anna is the special case of poetical sexual awakening turning into terrifying erotomania that reflects Tolstoy's own famous craziness about sex, which in some sense is what the novel is "about." The transformation of the wonderful Anna we first meet at the railway station—"the suppressed eagerness which played over her face . . . as though her nature was so brimming over with something that against her will it showed itself now in the flash of her eyes, and now in her smile"—into the psychotic who throws herself in front of a train is chronicled over the book's length, and doesn't add up.
>
> Standard readings of the novel attribute Anna's descent into madness to the loss of her son and to her ostracism by society. But in fact, as Tolstoy unambiguously tells us, the situation is of her own making. She did not lose her son—she abandoned him when she left for Italy with Vronsky after her recovery from the puerperal fever that propelled Karenin into his "blissful spirituality." Under its influence, he was willing to give up his son and give Anna a divorce that would permit her to marry Vronsky and rejoin respectable society as, even in those days, divorced women were able to do. But as the novel goes on and Anna's life unravels, it is as if this opportunity had never arisen. We experience the novel, as we experience our dreams, undisturbed by its illogic. We accept Anna's disintegration without questioning it. Only later, when we analyze the work, does its illogic become apparent. But by then it is too late to reverse Tolstoy's spell.

As Malcolm notes, the transformation of the vitalizing Anna from a brimming fount of life to a psychotic "doesn't add up." Nor does the breaking apart of her unitive place in aristocratic society make historical sense. We have only Tolstoy to blame and to praise. Does he sacrifice Anna so cruelly to give more life to fresh images that he might hope to beget by breaking her? He lived on for another third of a century. Near the close, he finished but did not publish the heroic *Hadji Murat.* Considering his gifts, too much of his final decades were thrown away on moralistic nonsense.

And yet he was a great wink of eternity. He fled death, desired literal immortality, at the very end seemed to repudiate everything he had given deep readers who sought power over a figurative universe of death.

CHAPTER 24

Hadji Murat (1896–1904; published posthumously, 1912)

LEO TOLSTOY

T OLSTOY RETURNED to his full splendor in the novella *Hadji Murat,* which he worked on for some eight years, and chose not to publish.

I have written about *Hadji Murat* at some length once before in my book *The Western Canon* (1994). Probably I read it first, in the Maude translation, in about 1953. I have been thinking about it for almost two-thirds of a century, and it still seems to me the best story in the world. Fortunately, I have just reread it in the translation by Richard Pevear and Larissa Volokhonsky (2009), and, against all expectation, it seems even better than I remember.

The historical Hadji Murat was born just before the turn into the nineteenth century and died in battle in April 1852, making a desperate last stand with just four devoted followers against a large group of Cossack horsemen augmented by Tartar militiamen paid by the Russians. In his celebrated yet now faded novel *For Whom the Bell Tolls* (1940), Ernest Hemingway clearly founds his descriptions of battle on *War and Peace.* I do not know whether or not Hemingway had read *Hadji Murat,* but he echoes it in the only episode of *For Whom the Bell Tolls* that stays in my mind: El Sordo's last stand. The heroic partisan

El Sordo with only four men holds off a large and heavily armed Fascist contingent until he and his followers are destroyed by airplanes.

I admire Hemingway's short stories, but all his novels are failures. In dismissing *For Whom the Bell Tolls* as a period piece, I am at variance with the judgments of such distinguished personages as former president Barack Obama, Senator John McCain, and the late Fidel Castro. McCain seems to me particularly admirable in expressing admiration for the communist hero Robert Jordan; Obama ranks Hemingway and Toni Morrison with William Shakespeare.

I voted twice for Obama and wish he were still presiding over us, but I am happy I don't have to grade him as a literary critic. Instead, I turn to Tolstoy's beautiful rendition of Hadji Murat's last stand:

> The shaggy Hanefi, his sleeves rolled up, performed the duties of a servant here, too. He loaded the guns that Hadji Murat and Kurban passed to him, taking bullets wrapped in oiled rags and carefully ramming them home with an iron ramrod, and pouring dry powder into the pans from a flask. Khan Mahoma did not sit in the ditch like the others, but kept running between the ditch and the horses, driving them to a safer place, and constantly shrieked and fired freehand without a prop. He was the first to be wounded. A bullet hit him in the neck, and he sat down, spitting blood and cursing. Then Hadji Murat was wounded. A bullet pierced his shoulder. Hadji Murat pulled some cotton wool from his beshmet, stopped the wound with it, and went on firing.
>
> "Let's rush them with our sabers," Eldar said for the third time.
>
> He thrust himself up from behind the mound, ready to rush at his enemies, but just then a bullet hit him, and he reeled and fell backwards onto Hadji Murat's leg. Hadji Murat glanced at him. The beautiful sheep's eyes looked at Hadji Murat intently and gravely. The mouth, its upper lip pouting like a child's, twitched without opening. Hadji Murat freed his leg from under him and went on aiming. Hanefi bent over the slain Eldar and quickly began taking the unused cartridges from his cherkeska. Kurban, singing all the while, slowly loaded and took aim.

The enemy, running from bush to bush with whoops and shrieks, was moving closer and closer. Another bullet hit Hadji Murat in the left side. He lay back in the ditch and, tearing another wad of cotton wool from his beshmet, stopped the wound. This wound in the side was fatal, and he felt that he was dying. Memories and images replaced one another with extraordinary swiftness in his imagination. Now he saw before him the mighty Abununtsal Khan, holding in place his severed, hanging cheek as he rushed at the enemy with a dagger in his hand; now he saw the weak, bloodless old Vorontsov, with his sly, white face, and heard his soft voice; now he saw his son Yusuf, now his wife Sofiat, now the pale face, red beard, and narrowed eyes of his enemy Shamil.

And all these memories ran through his imagination without calling up any feeling in him: no pity, no anger, no desire of any sort. It all seemed so insignificant compared with what was beginning and had already begun for him. But meanwhile his strong body went on doing what had been started. He gathered his last strength, rose up from behind the mound, and fired his pistol at a man running towards him and hit him. The man fell. Then he got out of the hole altogether and, limping badly, walked straight ahead with his dagger to meet his enemies. Several shots rang out, he staggered and fell. Several militiamen, with a triumphant shriek, rushed to the fallen body. But what had seemed to them a dead body suddenly stirred. First the bloodied, shaven head, without a papakha, rose, then the body rose, and then, catching hold of a tree, he rose up entirely. He looked so terrible that the men running at him stopped. But he suddenly shuddered, staggered away from the tree, and, like a mowed-down thistle, fell full length on his face and no longer moved.

He no longer moved, but he still felt. When Ghadji Aga, who was the first to run up to him, struck him on the head with his big dagger, it seemed to him that he had been hit with a hammer, and he could not understand who was doing it and why. That was his last conscious connection with his body. After that he no longer felt anything, and his enemies trampled and hacked at what no longer had anything in common with him. Ghadji Aga, placing his foot on the back of the body, cut the head off with two strokes, and carefully, so as not to stain his chuviaki with blood, rolled it aside with his foot. Bright red blood gushed from the neck arteries and black blood from the head, flowing over the grass.

Karganov, and Ghadji Aga, and Akhmet Khan, and all the militiamen, like hunters over a slain animal, gathered over the bodies of Hadji Murat and his men (Hanefi, Kurban, and Gamzalo had been bound) and, standing there in the bushes amid the powder smoke, talked merrily, exulting in their victory.

The nightingales, who had fallen silent during the shooting, again started trilling, first one close by and then others further off.

This was the death I was reminded of by the crushed thistle in the midst of the plowed field.

Perhaps I am mistaken by starting with this conclusion. It is one of the many strengths of *Hadji Murat* that you can begin anywhere and go around the circle again of the hero's life and death. Tolstoy himself disrupts sequence by showing you the severed head of Hadji Murat before he gives you his hero's last stand:

"Ah, that's good. I'll still have time. I only need to see him for a minute."

"What, on business?" asked Butler.

"Minor business."

"Good or bad?"

"That depends! For us it's good, but for somebody else it's rather nasty." And Kamenev laughed.

Just then the walkers and Kamenev reached Ivan Matveevich's house.

"Chikhirev!" Kamenev called to a Cossack. "Come here."

A Don Cossack moved away from the others and rode up to them. He was wearing an ordinary Don Cossack uniform, boots, a greatcoat, and had saddlebags behind his saddle.

"Well, take the thing out," said Kamenev, getting off his horse.

The Cossack also got off his horse and took a sack with something in it from his saddlebag. Kamenev took the sack from the Cossack's hands and put his hand into it.

"So, shall I show you our news? You won't be frightened?" he turned to Marya Dmitrievna.

"What's there to be afraid of?" said Marya Dmitrievna.

"Here it is," said Kamenev, taking out a human head and holding it up in the moonlight. "Recognize him?"

It was a head, shaved, with large projections of the skull over the eyes and a trimmed black beard and clipped mustache, with one eye open and the other half closed, the shaved skull split but not all the way through, the bloody nose clotted with black blood. The neck was wrapped in a bloody towel. Despite all the wounds to the head, the blue lips were formed into a kindly, childlike expression.

Marya Dmitrievna looked and, without saying a word, turned and went quickly into the house.

Butler could not take his eyes from the terrible head. It was the head of the same Hadji Murat with whom he had so recently spent evenings in such friendly conversation.

"How can it be? Who killed him? Where?" he asked.

"He tried to bolt and got caught," said Kamenev, and he handed the head back to the Cossack and went into the house with Butler.

"And he died a brave man," said Kamenev.

Butler, a gallant officer and fierce gambler, and Hadji Murat had spent many hours with one another, talking, listening to singing, and reminiscing. In their conversations we learn the heroic story of the Avar chieftain's triumphs and sorrows. Tolstoy, with consummate art, stations his hero between two monstrous tyrants, Tsar Nicholas I and the Imam Shamil. Both men are vain, lustful, sadistic, in love only with power and their own selves. The tsar all but destroys Russia with the debacle of the Crimean War, and absurd economic policies. The Imam, after many victories against the Russians, sustained total defeat in 1859 and was sent into exile. He lived on until 1871, dying in Medina.

Nicholas I died in 1855, during the Crimean War. He may have caught pneumonia, or it may have been suicide. Either way, his death was a blessing for his ruined country. Tolstoy wrote many versions of the longest chapter in his book, the one on Nicholas, attempting to get it right. He left it, in his judgment, incomplete, but it is difficult to see how it could be more devastating. Nicholas was very fond of sentencing relatively minor offenders to running the gauntlet, thus receiving thousands of lashes, inevitably a very painful death, though he continued to exult that Russia had no death penalty. Shamil traveled around with an executioner armed with an ax, and freely administered Sharia justice by whim, hands or heads sliced off for the glory of Allah. At least Shamil was personally courageous, whereas Nicholas was a coward pretending to be a warrior.

Hadji Murat achieves perfection as personality, most heroic of warriors, wise and wary negotiator, loving son of his mother, devoted husband to his wives, and profoundly caring father of his eldest son, Yusuf, in particular. His mother, wives, and children are held captive by Shamil, who threatens either to execute or to blind Yusuf.

Tolstoy creates Hadji Murat as the ultimate hero of epic, transcending Achilles, Hector, Odysseus, Aeneas. The Avar warrior kills only when he has to; he does not rejoice in violence for its own sake. Achilles partly remains a child. He kills indiscriminately, as if to protest his own mortality. Hector, in his final battle against Achilles, is strangely passive. Odysseus is endlessly resourceful and sly and decidedly is not a truth teller. Hadji Murat surpasses him. Both long for their wife and son, but Odysseus dallies by the way, whereas Tolstoy's hero remains faithful. Aeneas betrays Dido, decidedly is a prig, and butchers Turnus in an unequal contest, since Turnus has been driven desperate by the Dirae sent against him by Jupiter, after the high god's reconciliation with Juno.

Hadji Murat is the pure warrior, who inspires loyalty in his little knot of followers, and himself is loyal unto the death. His entire career has been a battle against dreadful odds:

Hadji Murat paused and took a deep breath.

"That was all very well," he went on, "then it all went bad. Shamil stood in place of Hamzat. He sent envoys to me to tell me to go with him against the Russians; if I refused, he threatened to lay waste to Khunzakh and kill me. I said I wouldn't go with him and wouldn't let him come to me."

"Why didn't you go to him?" asked Loris-Melikov.

Hadji Murat frowned and did not answer at once.

"It was impossible. There was the blood of my brother

Osman and of Abununtsal Khan upon Shamil. I didn't go to him. Rosen, the general, sent me an officer's rank and told me to be the commander of Avaria. All would have been well, but earlier Rosen had appointed over Avaria, first, the khan of Kazikumykh, Mahomet Mirza, and then Akhmet Khan. That one hated me. He wanted to marry his son to the khansha's daughter Saltanet. She was not given to him, and he thought it was my fault. He hated me and sent his nukers to kill me, but I escaped from them. Then he spoke against me to General Klugenau, said that I wouldn't let the Avars give firewood to the soldiers. He also told him that I had put on the turban—this one," said Hadji Murat, pointing to the turban over his papakha, "and that it meant I had gone over to Shamil. The general did not believe him and ordered him not to touch me. But when the general left for Tiflis, Akhmet Khan did it his way: he had me seized by a company of soldiers, put me in chains, and tied me to a cannon. They kept me like that for six days. On the seventh day they untied me and led me to Temir Khan Shura. I was led by forty soldiers with loaded muskets. My hands were bound, and they had orders to kill me if I tried to escape. I knew that. When we began to approach a place near Moksokh where the path was narrow and to the right there was a steep drop of about a hundred yards, I moved to the right of the soldier, to the edge of the cliff. The soldier wanted to stop me, but I jumped from the cliff and dragged the soldier with me. The soldier was battered to death, but I stayed alive. Ribs, head, arms, legs—everything was broken. I tried to crawl but couldn't. My head whirled around and I fell asleep. I woke up soaked in blood. A shepherd saw me. He called people, they took me to the aoul. Ribs and head healed, the leg healed, too, only it came out short."

And Hadji Murat stretched out his crooked leg.

"It serves me, and that's good enough," he said. "People found out and started coming to me. I recovered, moved to Tselmes. The Avars again invited me to rule over them," Hadji Murat said with a calm, assured pride. "And I agreed."

It is almost as though Tolstoy is telling us that what can be broken should be broken if the hero is to achieve himself. Hadji Murat, fully achieved, goes on until he is stopped, and even then keeps going:

> Then he got out of the hole altogether and, limping badly, walked straight ahead with his dagger to meet his enemies. Several shots rang out, he staggered and fell. Several militiamen, with a triumphant shriek, rushed to the fallen body. But what had seemed to them a dead body suddenly stirred. First the bloodied, shaven head, without a papakha, rose, then the body rose, and then, catching hold of a tree, he rose up entirely. He looked so terrible that the men running at him stopped. But he suddenly shuddered, staggered away from the tree, and, like a mowed-down thistle, fell full length on his face and no longer moved.

This more than merits repeating. I think of Cuchulain, the Gaelic Achilles or Hadji Murat, in Yeats's inevitably phrased death poem "Cuchulain Comforted":

> A MAN that had six mortal wounds, a man
> Violent and famous, strode among the dead;
> Eyes stared out of the branches and were gone.
>
> Then certain Shrouds that muttered head to head
> Came and were gone. He leant upon a tree
> As though to meditate on wounds and blood.

The hero who had been with Yeats throughout his career begins his meditation but, like Hadji Murat, needs the tree. Cuchulain is placed by his poet in the afterlife, not with his peers, but with the cowards:

> "Now must we sing and sing the best we can,
> But first you must be told our character:
> Convicted cowards all, by kindred slain
>
> "Or driven from home and left to die in fear."
> They sang, but had nor human tunes nor words,
> Though all was done in common as before;
>
> They had changed their throats and had the throats of birds.

Yeats regarded this as a sequel to his late play *The Death of Cuchulain,* where the dying hero has a vision:

There floats out there
The shape that I shall take when I am dead,
My soul's first shape, a soft feathery shape,
And is not that a strange shape for the soul
Of a great fighting-man?

And, to the Blind Man who is groping at his neck and asking if he is ready, he affirms:

I say it is about to sing.

Both poem and play deftly allude to Dante's vision of his teacher Brunetto Latini in the *Inferno,* Canto XV, lines 118–24:

"...A people comes with whom I may not be;
Commended unto thee be my Tesoro,
In which I still live, and no more I ask."

Then he turned round, and seemed to be of those
Who at Verona run for the Green Mantle
Across the plain; and seemed to be among them

The one who wins, and not the one who loses.

(trans. Longfellow)

Why Dante places his revered teacher among the sodomites is an enigma. What matters, here as with Cuchulain and with Hadji Murat, is that the defeated transmute into the victorious. Tolstoy, who begins and ends with the crushed but still-resistant thistle (called "the Tartar"), does not mutate his hero into a supernatural bird but gives him the threnody of the nightingales:

The nightingales, who had fallen silent during the shooting, again started trilling, first one close by and then others further off.

CHAPTER 25

The Return of the Native (1878)

THOMAS HARDY

I HAVE BEEN READING Thomas Hardy since I was about fifteen. The first two of his novels I sank into were *The Return of the Native* (1878) and *The Woodlanders* (1887). They are far from being the best of his fictions: those would have to include *Far from the Madding Crowd* (1874), *The Mayor of Casterbridge* (1886), *Tess of the d'Urbervilles* (1891), and *Jude the Obscure* (1895), which was so viciously received that Hardy, in revulsion, turned back from writing novels to composing poetry, which had started his career. Hardy died in 1928, at the age of eighty-seven. There are not many English poets of the twentieth century who are Hardy's equals: setting aside Yeats and Seamus Heaney as Irish, and Eliot as American, they might include D. H. Lawrence, Edward Thomas, Wilfred Owen, the early W. H. Auden, Keith Douglas, and Geoffrey Hill.

As a novelist Hardy was influenced by George Eliot, but his authentic precursor was the High Romantic lyric poet Percy Bysshe Shelley, who had a tragic vision of Eros. This prevails throughout Hardy and is felt particularly in his most vivid heroines: Bathsheba Everdene, Eustacia Vye, Marty South, Tess Durbeyfield, Sue Bridehead. In Shelley the shadow of selfhood always falls between desire and its fulfillment. For him love and the means of love, good and the means of good, were irreconcilable.

Henry James dismissed Hardy as a tedious imitator of George Eliot, and in his *After Strange Gods: A Primer of Modern Heresy* (1934) called Thomas Hardy "a powerful personality uncurbed by any institutional attachment or by submission to any objective beliefs."

D. H. Lawrence, in his *Study of Thomas Hardy* (composed 1914–15, published posthumously, 1932–33), essentially wrote a *Study of D. H. Lawrence* since the book implicitly records his struggle to revise *The Rainbow*. However, it does manifest remarkable acuity in regard to Hardy.

[*The Return of the Native*] is the first tragic and important novel. Eustacia, dark, wild, passionate, quite conscious of her desires and inheriting no tradition which would make her ashamed of them, since she is of a novelistic Italian birth, loves, first, the unstable Wildeve, who does not satisfy her, then casts him aside for the newly returned Clym, whom she marries. What does she want? She does not know, but it is evidently some form of self-realization; she wants to be herself, to attain herself. But she does not know how, by what means, so romantic imagination says, Paris and the beau monde. As if that would have stayed her unsatisfaction.

What is the real stuff of tragedy in the book? It is the heath. It is the primitive, primal earth, where the instinctive life heaves up. There, in the deep, rude stirring of the instincts, there was the reality that worked the tragedy. Close to the body of things, there can be heard the stir that makes us and destroys us. The heath heaved with raw instinct. Egdon, whose dark soil was strong and crude and organic as the body of a beast. Out of the body of this crude earth are born Eustacia, Wildeve, Mistress Yeobright, Clym, and all the others. They are one year's accidental crop. What matters if some are downed or dead, and others preaching or married: what matter, any more than the withering heath, the reddening berries, the seedy furze, and the dead fern of one autumn of Egdon? The heath persists. Its body is strong and fecund, it will bear many more crops besides this. Here is the somber, latent power that will go on producing no matter what happens to the product. Here is the deep, black source whence all these little contents of lives are drawn. And the contents of the small lives are spilled and wasted. There is savage satisfaction in it: for so much more remains to come, such black, powerful fecundity is working there, that what does it matter?

· · ·

That is a constant revelation in Hardy's novels: that there exists a great background, vital and vivid, which matters more than the people who move upon it. Against the background of dark, passionate Egdon, of the leafy, sappy passion and sentiment of the woodlands, of the unfathomed stars, is drawn the lesser scheme of lives: *The Return of the Native, The Woodlanders,* or *Two on a Tower.* Upon the vast, incomprehensible pattern of some primal mortality greater than ever the human mind can grasp, is drawn the little, pathetic pattern of man's moral life and struggle, pathetic, almost ridiculous. The little fold of law and order, the little walled city within which man has to defend himself from the waste enormity of nature, becomes always too small, and the pioneers venturing out with the code of the walled city upon them die in the bonds of that code, free and yet unfree, preaching the walled city and looking to the waste.

You can say that Lawrence is rather too ecstatic about Egdon Heath. He seems to mix it up with Hardy's Immanent Will, which stems from Schopenhauer's Will to Live, just as Lawrence's "leafy, sappy passion" derives from Nietzsche's "Think of the Earth." What Lawrence truly raises is the dark question of *The Return of the Native:* why cannot Eustacia Vye be fulfilled?

When I have stayed away too long from Hardy, all I can remember about *The Return of the Native* are Eustacia, the red man Venn, and Egdon Heath. Clym is one of Hardy's failures in characterization and comes close to ruining the novel. The great glory of the book is the sexually enchanting Eustacia Vye, who finally kills herself. I found and still find this dreadful, but Hardy suffered quite as much as any reader could. Here is the description of her that Hardy gives in the early chapter "Queen of Night":

She was in person full-limbed and somewhat heavy; without ruddiness, as without pallor; and soft to the touch as a cloud.

To see her hair was to fancy that a whole winter did not contain darkness enough to form its shadow. It closed over her forehead like nightfall extinguishing the western glow.

Her nerves extended into those tresses, and her temper could always be softened by stroking them down. When her hair was brushed she would instantly sink into stillness and look like the Sphinx. If, in passing under one of the Egdon banks, any of its thick skeins were caught, as they sometimes were, by a prickly tuft of the large Ulex Europæus—which will act as a sort of hairbrush—she would go back a few steps, and pass against it a second time.

She had pagan eyes, full of nocturnal mysteries. Their light, as it came and went, and came again, was partially hampered by their oppressive lids and lashes; and of these the under lid was much fuller than it usually is with English women. This enabled her to indulge in reverie without seeming to do so: she might have been believed capable of sleeping without closing them up. Assuming that the souls of men and women were visible essences, you could fancy the colour of Eustacia's soul to be flame-like. The sparks from it that rose into her dark pupils gave the same impression.

Hardy's Eustacia may owe something to Walter Pater's *The Renaissance,* published five years before *The Return of the Native,* since in some ways she makes a third with Pater's evocations of the Botticelli Venus and Leonardo's Mona Lisa, visions of antithetical female sexuality. Eustacia's flame-like quality precisely recalls Pater's ecstasy of passion in the "Conclusion" to *The Renaissance,* and the epigraph to *The Return of the Native* could well have been: "This at least of flame-like our life has, that it is but the concurrence, renewed from moment to moment, of forces parting sooner or later on their ways."

This at least of flame-like Eustacia's life has, that the concurrence of forces parts sooner rather than later. But, then, this most beautiful of Hardy's women is also the most doom-eager, the color of her soul being flame-like. The heath brings her only Wildeve and Clym, but Paris doubtless would have brought her scarce better, since as Queen of Night she attracts the constancy and the kindness of sorrow.

At fifteen I fell in love with Eustacia Vye, and at eighty-eight the passion returns. Both of Thomas Hardy's marriages had equivocal elements, including childlessness. And yet, for a while, he was fiercely in love with his first wife. When he writes of Eustacia he catches fire. Across more than seventy years, I remember my first wonder at Hardy's description of Eustacia's conduct when her wild hair was stroked down, even when common gorse performed the caress:

> Her nerves extended into those tresses, and her temper could always be softened by stroking them down. When her hair was brushed she would instantly sink into stillness and look like the Sphinx. If, in passing under one of the Egdon banks, any of its thick skeins were caught, as they sometimes were, by a prickly tuft of the large Ulex Europæus—which will act as a sort of hairbrush—she would go back a few steps, and pass against it a second time.

Who can resist a woman who lives at so high a frequency that she backtracks to have the gorse stroke her again? Hardy's women enlarge and attune his imagination. His men, except for Michael Henchard in *The Mayor of Casterbridge,* never quite come alive. Yet so marvelous are his women that the reader scarcely cares. I find no flaws in Eustacia Vye; her tragedy stems from context and circumstance. Her husband and her lover, Clym and Wildeve, are hopelessly inadequate to her sexual intensity and splendor. In a preface to *The Return of the Native,* Hardy takes care to tell us that Shakespeare's King Lear suffered his agonies on Egdon Heath. Eustacia suffers less expressively, Hardy not being Shakespeare, but she is hated by most of the natives of the heath, who regard her as a witch. She had an Italian father from Corfu, yet much more than her exotic beauty stimulates the hatred. In a minimized world, she is as isolated in her sexual strength as Hester Prynne is in the seventeenth-century Massachusetts Bay Colony of Hawthorne's *The Scarlet Letter.* Alas, she lacks Hester Prynne's stubborn strength of endurance, enhanced by Hester's need to nurture her natural daughter, Pearl. Hester and Pearl survive. Eustacia suffers death by water, probably with deliberation. Wildeve also drowns, vainly attempting to save her. Clym, wifeless and motherless, becomes a lay preacher speaking to whoever will listen.

Sometimes I wish that Hardy had titled the novel *Queen of Night*, since it is Eustacia's book and not Clym's. It may be that Hardy loved her as Flaubert loved Emma Bovary or Tolstoy invested so heavily in Anna Karenina. Flaubert wept as he murdered Emma through her suicide. Tolstoy must have grieved for his wonderful Anna. All three women were great losses. Hardy, despite his primeval power, is not of course the artist that Flaubert was, and only Tolstoy can give us the sense that through him the earth cries out.

CHAPTER 26

The Brothers Karamazov (1880)

FYODOR DOSTOEVSKY

I HAVE WRITTEN about Dostoevsky's final and greatest work before, but I no longer agree with my earlier critique. My father refused to speak Russian after he left Odessa, and I grew up speaking only Yiddish. I studied other languages at Cornell and Yale, and since then, during my teaching years, I have mastered others. It is one of my regrets that I never learned Russian. That means my reading of Pushkin, Gogol, Tolstoy, Chekhov, Turgenev, Goncharov, Lermontov, Dostoevsky, and the other classic authors of nineteenth-century Russia has been enslaved to translations. The earlier ones by Constance Garnett that I read in my youth were a heroic enterprise yet stilted in diction and, I gather, inaccurate and particularly poor in conveying tone.

However, since 1990, the remarkable married team of Richard Pevear and Larissa Volokhonsky have translated many of the Russian classics into persuasive English versions, and I am among their thousands of grateful debtors. Several rereadings of their *The Brothers Karamazov* have not made me love that overpowering novel, but I begin to understand it better, and to clarify my ambivalences concerning Dostoevsky.

Sainte-Beuve, to me the most interesting of French critics except for Paul Valéry, taught us to ask a crucial question of any writer whom we read deeply: what would the author think of us? Dosto-evsky's reaction to me would intensify my lifelong gratitude to my late father for getting out of Odessa and thus giving me a chance to live a good life. Though Dostoevsky sometimes denied he was an anti-Semite, let him testify for himself:

> It is not for nothing that over there [in Europe] the Jews rule all the stock-exchanges; it is not for nothing that they con-trol capital, that they are the masters of credit, and it is not for nothing—I repeat—that they are also the masters of inter-national politics, and what is going to happen in the future is known to the Jews themselves: their reign, their complete reign is approaching! What is coming is the complete triumph of ideas before which sentiments of humanity, the thirst for truth, Christian feelings, the national and popular pride of European peoples, must bow.
>
> I sometimes imagine: what if there were not three million Jews, but three million Russians in Russia, and there were eighty million Jews? Well, how would they treat Russians, and how would they lord it over them? What rights would Jews give Russians?... Wouldn't they slaughter them to the last man, to the point of complete extermination, as they used to do with alien peoples in ancient times?
>
> I repeat: it is impossible to conceive of a Jew without God. Moreover, I do not believe in the existence of atheists even among educated Jews: they are all of the same essence.... They are all...undeviatingly awaiting the Messiah, all of them, from the very lowest Kike to the highest and most learned phi-losopher and rabbi-Kabalist: they all believe that the Messiah will again unite them in Jerusalem and bring by his sword all nations to their feet.
>
> *(Diary of a Writer)*

When I read this, my initial response is to remember the Tal-mudic adage: If someone seeks to take your life, rise up and slay him first. Still, I am now a very old man, and not the involuntary Bronx street-fighter of my early youth. Dostoevsky has a coven of stalwart defenders who brush his hatreds aside. Some of them, now departed, were my good friends. Nothing diminishes the aesthetic power of *The Brothers Karamazov*, but I am uneasy when the novel is praised for its insights into morality and religion. One can be pardoned for preferring Leo Tolstoy:

> The Jew is that sacred being who has brought down from heaven the everlasting fire, and has illuminated with it the entire world. He is the religious source, spring, and fountain out of which all the rest of the peoples have drawn their beliefs and their religions. The Jew is the pioneer of liberty.... The Jew is the pioneer of civilization.... The Jew is the emblem of eternity.

Lacking Russian, I myself cannot give Tolstoy the aesthetic preference over Dostoevsky. But the greatest Russian critics speak of Tolstoy as being of the eminence of Homer, Dante, Shakespeare. Reading Tolstoy rendered by Pevear and Volokhonsky, I am persuaded. Dostoevsky, even in *The Demons* and *The Brothers Karamazov*, is of another order.

There are many strengths in Dostoevsky's culminating novel, but I find Dostoevsky's almost Shakespearean invention of characters most appealing: the three Karamazov brothers, Alyosha, Mitya, Ivan. Alyosha, who is just nineteen, and Ivan are full brothers; the oldest, Mitya, is their half-brother. Their father is the rancid, lustful, gluttonous drunkard Fyodor, who is fifty-five. Smerdyakov, the bastard son of Fyodor, is a surly and resentful cook.

Alyosha is a kind of saint: cheerful, loving, deeply religious. For Dostoevsky, Alyosha is the book's hero. Actually, it is Mitya's novel: he is passionate, spendthrift, an impulsive man of action, yet capable of compassion, restraint, generosity of spirit, and a potential believer in the Russian earth. Doubtless because of my own peculiarities, I prefer Ivan: enormously intelligent, skeptical, tragically caught between a Western regard for cognition and his own Russian soul, whatever that is. Smerdyakov is a beast, but an interesting one.

Grushenka and Katerina are the principal women characters. Unlike Tolstoy, Dostoevsky seems to me uneasy in representing women. Grushenka is beautiful, proud, flirtatious, in no way promiscuous, and is pursued with equal ferocity by old Karamazov and

Mitya. She is gentled by a friendship with Alyosha. Katerina is even prouder, essentially withdrawn, and, though betrothed to Mitya, is abandoned by him for Grushenka. What Freud once called moral masochism is her weakness, and she remains loyal to Mitya even after the reader begins to surmise that she and Ivan have fallen in love.

Zosima, a senior monk, is Alyosha's moral and religious guide, and, like Alyosha, represents the Dostoevskian ideal. He preaches forgiveness, and reverence for the earth, which he kisses and waters with his tears, and is endowed with a clairvoyant understanding of every soul he encounters.

The admirers of *The Brothers Karamazov* include Einstein, Freud, Wittgenstein, Heidegger, Joyce, Kafka, and Cormac McCarthy. They also include Vladimir Putin and Joseph Stalin. Sigmund Freud considered it the greatest novel ever written, but, after all, he wrote an essay on Dostoevsky and parricide. His own fantasy *Totem and Taboo* (1913) is a lurid version of Dostoevsky's phantasmagoria. In Freud, the tribal father insists on possessing all women for himself, and then is murdered by the horde of enemy brothers, who devour the totem father. Stalin and Putin join Tsar Alexander II, who was assassinated the year after *The Brothers Karamazov* was published. Some historians believe Stalin was poisoned at the order of Lavrentiy Beria, Stalin's Himmler, himself executed in 1953. Putin, alas, is still very much with us.

After this uneasy excursus, I return to the Karamazov family and their entanglements with women who are very different from one another, yet each difficult to love or to avoid loving.

One has to begin with old Karamazov, and remember that he is just fifty-five:

> "Don't be angry with my brother! Stop hurting him," Alyosha all of a sudden said insistently.
>
> "Well, well, maybe I will. Oof, what a headache! Take away the cognac, Ivan, it's the third time I'm telling you." He lapsed into thought and suddenly smiled a long and cunning smile: "Don't be angry with an old runt like me, Ivan. I know you don't

love me, but still don't be angry. There's nothing to love me for. You go to Chermashnya, and I'll visit you there, I'll bring presents. I'll show you a young wench there, I've had my eye on her for a long time. She's still barefoot. Don't be afraid of the barefoot ones, don't despise them, they're pearls...!"

And he kissed his hand with a smack.

"For me," he suddenly became all animated, as if sobering up for a moment, once he hit on his favorite subject, "for me...Ah, you children! My babes, my little piglets, for me...even in the whole of my life there has never been an ugly woman, that's my rule! Can you understand that? But how could you understand it? You've still got milk in your veins instead of blood, you're not hatched yet! According to my rule, one can damn well find something extremely interesting in every woman, something that's not to be found in any other—one just has to know how to find it, that's the trick!..."

Old Karamazov loves no one except himself. He and Mitya despise one another. He needs Alyosha's love, which he has, but understands neither the need nor Alyosha. At bottom he fears Ivan and desperately wants Alyosha not to love his full brother, which is impossible. A miser and a shrewd speculator in land, he will leave behind him an estate of a hundred thousand rubles when he is murdered. His vitalism, unlike that of Falstaff, is mindless, without wit, and blind. He might as well be an eating, drinking, sleeping, and whoring machine, which doubtless artificial intelligence will yet bring to us.

For many reasons, some of them quite personal, I have many reservations about Nabokov, both as person and as author. I find it odd that I should cite him on Dostoevsky, whom he regarded as a bad imitator of Gogol. Here, from the lectures I once walked out upon, are his reflections on Dostoevsky:

In the light of the historical development of artistic vision, Dostoevski is a very fascinating phenomenon. If you examine closely any of his works, say *The Brothers Karamazov*, you will note that the natural background and all things relevant to the perception of the senses hardly exist. What landscape there is is a landscape of ideas, a moral landscape. The weather does not exist in his world, so it does not much matter how people dress. Dostoevski characterizes his people through situation, through ethical matters, their psychological reactions, their inside ripples. After describing the looks of a character, he uses the old-fashioned device of not referring to his specific physical appearance any more in the scenes with him. This is not the way of an artist, say Tolstoy, who sees his character in his mind all the time and knows exactly the specific gesture he will employ at this or that moment. But there is something more striking still about Dostoevski. He seems to have been chosen by the destiny of Russian letters to become Russia's greatest playwright, but he took the wrong turning and wrote novels. The novel *The Brothers Karamazov* has always seemed to me a straggling play, with just that amount of furniture and other implements needed for the various actors: a round table with the wet, round trace of a glass, a window painted yellow to make it look as if there were sunlight outside, or a shrub hastily brought in and plumped down by a stagehand....

Let us always remember that basically Dostoevski is a writer of mystery stories where every character, once introduced to us, remains the same to the bitter end, complete with his special features and personal habits, and that they all are treated throughout the book they happen to be in like chessmen in a complicated chess problem. Being an intricate plotter, Dostoevski succeeds in holding the reader's attention; he builds up his climaxes and keeps up his suspenses with consummate mastery. But if you re-read a book of his you have already read once so that you are familiar with the surprises and complications of the plot, you will at once realize that the suspense you experienced during the first reading is simply not there any more....

The misadventures of human dignity which form Dostoevski's favorite theme are as much allied to the farce as to the drama. In indulging this farcical side and being at the same time deprived of any real sense of humor, Dostoevski is sometimes dangerously near to sinking into garrulous and vulgar nonsense....

It is, as in all Dostoevski's novels, a rush and tumble of words with endless repetitions, mutterings aside, a verbal overflow which shocks the reader after, say, Lermontov's transparent and beautifully poised prose. Dostoevski as we know is a great seeker after truth, a genius of spiritual morbidity, but as we also know he is not a great writer in the sense Tolstoy, Pushkin, and Chekhov are. And, I repeat, not because the world he creates is unreal—all the worlds of writers are unreal—but because it is created too hastily without any sense of that harmony and economy which the most irrational masterpiece is bound to comply with (in order to be a masterpiece). Indeed, in a sense Dostoevski is much too rational in his crude methods, and though his facts are but spiritual facts and his characters mere ideas in the likeness of people, their interplay and development are actuated by the mechanical methods of the earthbound and conventional novels of the late eighteenth and early nineteenth centuries.

If all this were to be accepted, *The Brothers Karamazov* would vaporize upon rereading. Nabokov, despite his preciosity, could be a great literary artist, as in *Pale Fire*. And most certainly he knew and loved the Russian language. Yet this is caricature, not criticism. Mitya, Ivan, and Alyosha undergo authentic change as the novel proceeds. Old Karamazov, Grushenka, Katerina do not. Perhaps Smerdyakov changes for the worse, though he had not far to go. Grushenka and Katerina keep changing their minds and then changing back again, but, then, I do not think that anyone extols Dostoevsky as a psychologist in regard to women, or indeed even to men. Nabokov may have been acute in suggesting that Dostoevsky should have been a playwright.

Dostoevsky's youngest son, Alyosha, had died at the age of three in 1878. Had Dostoevsky lived, there would have been a second volume of the novel, centering almost wholly upon the fully mature Alyosha. I am by no means certain that I would have wanted to read it, as I weary of Alyosha from time to time. He can also be disconcerting, as in this exchange between the saintly hero and his beloved Liza:

"I'll always come to see you, all my life," Alyosha answered firmly.

"I tell this to you alone," Liza began again. "Only to myself, and also to you. You alone in the whole world. And rather to you than to myself. And I'm not at all ashamed with you. Alyosha, why am I not at all ashamed with you, not at all? Alyosha, is it true that Jews steal children on Passover and kill them?"

"I don't know."

"I have a book here. I read in it about some trial somewhere, and that a Jew first cut off all the fingers of a four-year-old boy, and then crucified him on the wall, nailed him with nails and crucified him, and then said at his trial that the boy died quickly, in four hours. Quickly! He said the boy was moaning, that he kept moaning, and he stood and admired it. That's good!"

"Good?"

"Good. Sometimes I imagine that it was I who crucified him. He hangs there moaning, and I sit down facing him, eating pineapple compote. I like pineapple compote very much. Do you?"

It is not often that I am so discombobulated as I read that I am just stopped. What is the reader to do with Alyosha's "I don't know"? What are you, whoever you are, to do with Liza's taste for pineapple compote and crucified boys? Consulting the going and accepted scholarly criticism of Dostoevsky does not make me happy. They dodge and they duck, they dance in and out of the question, and finally fall back on the greatness of *The Brothers Karamazov*.

They do sometimes invoke Vladimir Solovyov, a mystical exponent of Russian Orthodox Christianity who died at forty-seven of kidney failure, brought on by destitution. Solovyov was a friend of Dostoevsky, and some find in him a model for Alyosha. Though in his final years Solovyov became obsessed with the Yellow Peril, or Asiatic encroachment upon Russia, at his apex he preached a love authentically universal. In particular, he defended Jewish civil rights in Russia, worked hard to refute the blood libel, and hoped for an eventual reconciliation between Judaism and Christianity. Solovyov was a great man. Dostoevsky, depending upon your aesthetic judgments, may or may not have been a great writer, but to my mind he was a dreadful human being.

To invoke the genre of the novel does not help much in reading

The Brothers Karamazov. We might call it Scripture, though that would be too broad a designation, since Dostoevsky seems to combine the book of Job with the Revelation of Saint John the Divine. Father Zosima's peculiar reading of the book of Job—with the pious padding added to the end, that God gives Job an entirely new set of sons, daughters, and livestock, just as good as those that were destroyed—is exalted as Revelation itself.

It is Mitya's novel, but Dostoevsky gave his own first name to old Karamazov, and the sensual exuberance of this worst of fathers makes us feel his absence after he is murdered by Smerdyakov. Dostoevsky, in his Notebooks, declared, "We are all, to the last man, Fyodor Pavloviches," since we are all sensualists and nihilists, however we attempt to be otherwise. Dostoevsky, who compelled himself to religious belief, was anything but a mystic, and was the ancestor of Kafka's passionate motto: "No more psychology!" There are almost no normative personalities among Dostoevsky's characters: they are what they will to be, and their wills are inconstant. And so is Dostoevsky's. His unfairness to Ivan is exasperating, but Dostoevsky intends to exasperate us.

He was a vehement parodist of Westernization, and firmly believed that Russians were the Chosen People and that Christ was the Russian Christ. It is one thing to be passionate and provocative, and quite another to preach hatred of non-Russians in anticipation of the End of the World. Western literary tradition was not for Dostoevsky the nightmare it constituted for Tolstoy, but I am uncertain that Dostoevsky could see the differences between Shakespeare and the novels of Victor Hugo, whose vision of the wretched of the earth was not far from Dostoevsky's own.

What is left is Ivan's notorious prose poem "The Grand Inquisitor" and the delirium with which Dostoevsky afflicts Ivan in the encounter with the most insipid devil in Western literature. I confess to a sense of indignation that his author so sacrifices Ivan's integrity in order to demonstrate that life without God is impossible. By now the Grand Inquisitor has staled: he is not so much nasty as dreary. Dostoevsky himself deserved the vapid devil he bestows upon Ivan. If you want a devil, go to Iago or to Milton's Satan, or to William Blake's *The Marriage of Heaven and Hell,* or to the agon between Byron and Shelley, or to Hawthorne's Chillingworth, and from there to Nathanael West's Shrike, and on to Cormac McCarthy's Judge Holden.

I am a little dejected in departing from *The Brothers Karamazov* on this note. Richard Pevear gently argues that it is a joyful book, because it ends in the joy of Alyosha and a group of youngsters proclaiming love for one another. I have never been happy with that final scene, as there is an element of cheerleading in it. Still, an exhausted eighty-eight-year-old Gnostic Jew is perhaps the very last person Dostoevsky would have wanted as his reader.

CHAPTER 27

The Princess Casamassima (1886)

HENRY JAMES

I T IS STRIKING that Henry James composed his political novel
The Princess Casamassima, with its vista of London anarchists,
well in advance of Joseph Conrad's *The Secret Agent* and *Under Western Eyes*. At about the same time, he wrote *The Bostonians*, also
political, but there the war is between women and men. I prefer *The
Bostonians* but have considered it at length in a book called *The Daemon Knows* (2015).

The problem of *The Princess Casamassima*, though compelling
as it unfolds, is Hyacinth Robinson, the protagonist. James audaciously compared him to Hamlet and to Lear. I must admit that I
do not understand how James could think that. Poor Hyacinth is a
victim of social, economic, and cultural forces far beyond his ken.
Hamlet's consciousness is more capacious even than that of Henry
James. The Prince of Denmark is his own worst enemy. King Lear's
range of affect transcends anything in the world of Henry James or
of any other writer, be it Homer or Dante, Cervantes or Montaigne.

Hyacinth is the child of an affair between Florentine Vivier, a
French courtesan, and an unnamed English lord. Florentine deftly
stabs her lover, who expires, and she is sentenced to Millbank prison.
As she dies, Hyacinth's adoptive mother, Pinnie (Miss Pynsent, a
close friend of Vivier), brings him into the prison. Much later, Hya-

cinth will learn that Florentine was his mother and the slain lord his father.

In many ways, *The Princess Casamassima* is a study in victimage. Hyacinth is sensitive, intelligent though held back by insufficient education, and is something of an artist, as he demonstrates by becoming an unusually skilled bookbinder. Bewildered by the inequities of London society, Hyacinth joins the anarchist movement, and volunteers to carry out an assassination. This is so clearly incommensurate with his personality that it seems to me a flaw in the novel. The great success is James's representation of Christina Light, the Princess Casamassima, who has abandoned her boring husband and taken on a leading role in the anarchist conspiracy. This sends the reader back to James's early novel *Roderick Hudson* (1875), where the young Christina enchants us with her beauty, high spirits, capriciousness, and endless capacity for mischief making.

Roderick Hudson, which I have just reread after many years, is a mixed performance. Roderick himself is the trouble. He is a perpetual adolescent, a sculptor of some talent but given to tantrums, selfish, egoistic, inconstant to his betrothed Mary Garland, with whom Rowland Mallet, Roderick's generous patron, is hopelessly in love. Mallet at last reproves Roderick, who has requested a large sum of money (he is a perpetual sponger) merely for the purpose of going off to keep an amorous rendezvous with the Princess Christina. Hurt and dazed by some minimal self-recognition, Roderick Hudson wanders off in an Alpine snowstorm and perishes, in what seems more suicide than an accident.

I do not know whether D. H. Lawrence ever read *Roderick Hudson*. There is a foreshadowing of the icy suicidal death of Gerald Crich of *Women in Love* in Roderick's fate. Henry James and Lawrence shared a mutual disdain, yet there are a number of shorter fictions by Lawrence that betray James's influence.

Henry James, unlike Balzac, did not carry over characters from one novel to another. Christina Light is the large exception. He saw that she had potential that he had not fully realized. The happy consequence was *The Princess Casamassima*.

Christina patronizes Hyacinth but turns away when she meets Paul Muniment, chemist by profession, but high in the anarchist hierarchy. Muniment and Christina become lovers, followed from house to house by the wretched Prince Casamassima, still infatuated with his faithless wife. Hyacinth, gentle and caring, attempts to comfort the Prince but he is inconsolable.

When Amanda Pynsent, Hyacinth's foster mother, is dying, she has the comfort of Hyacinth's care and grief for her. On the moderate legacy she has provided, Hyacinth goes to France and Italy and begins to find his authentic self. He falls in love with scenic and atmospheric beauty, and his anarchist zeal vanishes. On his return to London, he cannot evade his pledge to assassinate a duke, and yet it is not possible for him to carry it out. He shoots himself through the heart.

The Princess and a German anarchist, Schinkel, break down Hyacinth's door:

> The light was that of a single candle on the mantel; it was so poor that for a moment she made out nothing definite. Before that moment was over, however, her eyes had attached themselves to the small bed. There was something on it—something black, something ambiguous, something out-stretched. Schinkel held her back, but only for an instant; she saw everything, and with the very act she flung herself beside the bed, upon her knees. Hyacinth lay there as if he were asleep, but there was a horrible thing, a mess of blood, on the bed, in his side, in his heart. His arm hung limp beside him, downwards, off the narrow couch; his face was white and his eyes were closed.

One grants Christina shock but wonders if there is any true grief. Hyacinth would have committed a kind of patricide had he assassinated the Duke. He would also have identified with his murderous mother, an impossibility. It may be that Hamlet held back from slaughtering Claudius because he could not know when the adultery between Gertrude and Claudius had begun. Could he be the son of Claudius? If Shakespeare knows, he will not tell us.

Hyacinth is too good, too rare a growth, for the Dickensian London of *The Princess Casamassima*. Henry James is so subtle that he obliges us to surmise why Hyacinth simply did not walk away from his dilemma. As a skilled bookbinder, he could have survived in Italy or France. The fatality is within him. He knows too much and also too little to work out of entrapment. He may after all be the most Shakespearean figure in all of Henry James.

CHAPTER 28

The Ambassadors (1903)

HENRY JAMES

HENRY JAMES considered *The Ambassadors* the crown of his work. The book has divided qualified critics, the problem being the protagonist, Lewis Lambert Strether. Once, I wondered if Strether deserved to be compared to Isabel Archer, Milly Theale, and Maggie Verver. I thought that, though he is profoundly sympathetic and admirable, he does not give us enough grief to be truly memorable, since his saga is not painful to us. Nietzsche insisted that memory depends upon pain.

At fifty-five, Strether considers himself elderly. He is evidently betrothed to the fearsome and widowed Mrs. Newsome, who wishes her son, Chad, to break off his sojourn in Paris, where he has been greatly improved by his affair with Marie de Vionnet, a beautiful woman alive with tact and sensibility, who has separated from her unpleasant husband. On its surface *The Ambassadors* manifests the progressive re-education of Strether, largely by his conversations with Marie de Vionnet and with an American, Maria Gostrey, who falls in love with Strether and is in every way winsome and open.

I knew nothing about the homoeroticism of Henry James until I read and endorsed Sheldon M. Novick's biographies *Henry James: The Young Master* (1996) and *Henry James: The Mature Master* (2007). Later, I read the letters of James to the sculptor Hendrik Andersen, to Dudley Jocelyn Persse, and to Howard Overing Sturgis and Hugh Walpole, both writers whose reputations have vanished. Clearly all four were James's catamites, and there were others. Since Lambert Strether is a kind of self-portrait of Henry James, this may or may not illuminate his renunciation of the love offered to him by Maria Gostrey and implicitly suggested by Marie de Vionnet.

This is hardly to imply that Strether is homoerotic, since he all but falls in love with both Maria and Marie. Still, he is a widower in late middle age, and James never suggests that Strether has had any sexual experience since the death of his wife and then of his son. It is grotesque to think that so fine a sensibility as Strether's could ever have united itself with the dreadful Mrs. Newsome. Yet James does not adequately explain, at least to me, why Strether (who has independent means) does not stay in Paris and shuttle between his two adoring and marvelous women. I do not mean sexually, since it is not at all clear that Strether now lusts for anyone, though he does admire how handsome Chad has become under the influence of Marie de Vionnet.

It comes down to whether we can detach Lewis Lambert Strether from the Master Henry James. I can do so only with difficulty. I wondered once why James, who loved Balzac, seems to have alluded to *Louis Lambert* (1832), a kind of Swedenborgian fantasy in which the young man of the title has preternatural gifts, and expires all too soon in the arms of his beloved Pauline, so that his true angel-self can rise up to heaven. This remains a Jamesian mystery, but, then, Henry, like his father and his gifted brother, William, entertained curious ideas about extrasensory perception and the ghostliness of our condition. They did and did not believe in life after death.

I return to Strether. The best critics of *The Ambassadors* include Sallie Sears and Tony Tanner. Their Strether is a detached impressionist, an all but Paterian paragon of perception. His genius is to *see*. Unlike Louis Lambert, he is not a seer. Sights, sounds, odors, tastes, touches: these are his world. And all this is raised to a kind of secular ecstasy by the greatness of Paris.

Henry James and his surrogate Strether have a complex relation to such Victorian sages as Carlyle, Ruskin, and Newman, with their emphasis upon *seeing* as the road to the palace of wisdom. James and Strether do not seek for wisdom or for complete knowledge. They want to raise perception itself to the status of an art.

I suppose that I really cannot fully distinguish between Henry

James and Lambert Strether. That may be all to the good. As I reread yet once more, I have to resist becoming more like Strether, though I do not resemble him in the least. I wish that James had allowed himself to end the book with Strether staying on in Paris indefinitely, allowing himself to enjoy the chaste delights of loving and being loved by Maria and Marie. But James is too great the artist for that. Strether insists that he must gain nothing for himself from his Parisian experience.

Back to Woollett, Massachusetts, he goes, but not to the dubious embrace of Mrs. Newsome. What will he do there? I like to believe that his conscience will relent and allow him to return to Paris, and so to Maria Gostrey and Marie de Vionnet. In mere life, it would be probable, but not in the comedic vision of the Master Henry James.

CHAPTER 29

Nostromo (1904)

Joseph Conrad

Joseph Conrad was born Józef Teodor Konrad Korzeniowski in the Ukraine, then part of the Russian Empire, and before that of Poland. He grew up speaking Polish, learned French, and turned to English as a third language.

Conrad's early life was outrageous enough even for a young Polish person of letters, let alone for an English writer. At twenty-seven, he helped run a munitions-smuggling operation for the Carlist rebels in Spain. Before it was over, he came close to being killed, attempted suicide, fell in love with a fatal beauty, and gambled on a grand scale. Four years later, he began a more conventional career in the British merchant marine, which continued until 1894, during which time he commanded his own vessel, and was granted English citizenship. For his remaining thirty years, he was a superb and successful novelist, bringing forth such masterworks as *Lord Jim, Nostromo, The Secret Agent, Under Western Eyes,* and *Victory.*

His early stories and novels reflect the influence of Flaubert and of Maupassant. Henry James, who became a close friend, changed Conrad's literary mode to what we now think of as James's middle style: *The Spoils of Poynton, What Maisie Knew, The Awkward Age.*

It is a truism to see Conrad's swerve away from James in the figure of Marlow, who allowed Conrad an effectively sinuous narrative perspective. Henry James dismissed Marlow as "that preposterous magic mariner," which was good fun, but rather beside the point. Marlow makes the difference, for a while, between the impressionism of Henry James and Joseph Conrad. To judge that Conrad was much less a metaphysical idealist than James is not to suggest that Conrad was the greater novelist. But it helps explain why Conrad, and not Henry James, was the major influence upon the American generation of Ernest Hemingway, F. Scott Fitzgerald, and William Faulkner. The milieu of *The Sun Also Rises, The Great Gatsby,* and *As I Lay Dying* evidences the saliences of *Heart of Darkness* and *Nostromo,* and not of *The Princess Casamassima* and *The Ambassadors.*

I first read *Nostromo* in 1948, for a seminar on the novel conducted by a remarkable teacher, William Merritt Sale, Jr., who, together with M. H. Abrams, guided my undergraduate studies at Cornell University. Sale also introduced me to Samuel Richardson's *Clarissa,* which, with *Don Quixote* and *In Search of Lost Time,* is still one of my favorite novels.

In my later years, teaching at Yale, I learned most about the novel from Martin Price, who died at the age of ninety in 2010. In 1983, Price published a remarkable book: *Forms of Life: Character and Moral Imagination in the Novel.* In the chapter on Conrad, Price subtly traced what he called "the limits of irony" in the novelist's work.

And yet where are the limits of Conrad's irony in *Nostromo*? The magnificent Nostromo is in love with his own magnificence, and though he is a hero of the people, he is essentially hollow. With few exceptions, all of Conrad's protagonists are hollow men. One of the many paradoxes of Conrad is that the mirror of the sea allows us to perceive a heroic ideal, one that is not available in Conrad's great fictions.

What are the limits of irony in Conrad? For Martin Price, a profoundly Conradian ironist, there are no limits. Price sees both the skepticism and the irony of *Lord Jim* and yet also perceives its unrelenting romanticism. Both are allowed their full eloquence, and neither can balance or negate the other. Price ranks *Nostromo* lower, because he sees the irony as triumphant there. Conrad, an astonishing artist, allows the reader to decide. As I age, I abandon my ironies and join Nostromo in his Garibaldi-like romanticism. In

Nostromo, it is flawed and corrupt, but what matter? What matters in Conrad is not *whether* you betray yourself: of course you must and will. Either you betray others or yourself. Those are the Conradian options. Of course, others betray you, but that is of minor interest, another mere irony. Nostromo sells himself for silver and yet betrays nothing except his own authentic splendor.

In Conrad, you submit to the destructive element, the sea of death: no character in all of Conrad has a Hamlet-like power of mind, unless it be Kurtz, in *Heart of Darkness,* and he is self-obliterated, pragmatically speaking. Edward Said shrewdly noted Conrad's persuasive insistence that we can survive, as persons and as writers, only through the agency of our eccentricities. What matters most in Conrad's view of the human is that each of us is unpredictable.

An admirer of Conrad is happiest with his five great novels: *Lord Jim* (1900), *Nostromo* (1904), *The Secret Agent* (1907), *Under Western Eyes* (1911), and *Victory* (1915). Subtle and tormented narratives, they form an extraordinarily varied achievement, and despite their common features they can make a reader wonder that they all have been composed by the same artist. Endlessly enigmatic as a personality and as a formidable moral character, Conrad pervades his own books, a presence not to be put by, an elusive storyteller who yet seems to write a continuous spiritual autobiography. For me, Conrad's masterwork is *Nostromo,* where his perspectives are largest and where his essential originality in the representation of human blindnesses and consequent human affections is at its strongest. Like all overwhelming originalities, Conrad's ensues in an authentic difficulty, which can be assimilated only very slowly, if at all. Repeated rereadings gradually convince me that *Nostromo* is anything but a Conradian litany to the virtue he liked to call "fidelity." The book is tragedy, of a post-Nietzschean sort, despite Conrad's strong contempt for Nietzsche. Martin Decoud, emptied of all illusions, is self-destroyed because he cannot sustain solitude. Nostromo, perhaps the only persuasive instance of the natural sublime in a twentieth-century hero of fiction, dies "betrayed he hardly knows by what or by whom," as Conrad says. But this is Conrad at his most knowing, and the novel shows us precisely how Nostromo is betrayed, by himself, and by what is in himself.

His creator's description of this central figure as "the Magnificent

Capataz, the Man of the People," breathes a writer's love for his most surprising act of the imagination. So does a crucial paragraph from the same source, the "Author's Note" that Conrad added as a preface thirteen years after the initial publication:

> In his firm grip on the earth he inherits, in his improvidence and generosity, in his lavishness with his gifts, in his manly vanity, in the obscure sense of his greatness, and in his faithful devotion with something despairing as well as desperate in its impulses, he is a Man of the People, their very own unenvious force, disdaining to lead but ruling from within. Years afterwards, grown older as the famous Captain Fidanza, with a stake in the country, going about his many affairs followed by respectful glances in the modernized streets of Sulaco, calling on the widow of the cargador, attending the Lodge, listening in unmoved silence to anarchist speeches at the meeting, the enigmatical patron of the new revolutionary agitation, the trusted, the wealthy comrade Fidanza with the knowledge of his moral ruin locked up in his breast, he remains essentially a Man of the People. In his mingled love and scorn of life and in the bewildered conviction of having been betrayed, of dying betrayed he hardly knows by what or by whom, he is still of the People, their undoubted Great Man—with a private history of his own.

Nostromo is only himself when he can say, with perfect truth: "My name is known from one end of Sulaco to the other. What more can you do for me?"

Conrad invents a South American country, Costaguana, whose richest province is called Occidental and which has a port city, Sulaco. We can surmise that Conrad had Colombia in mind. Charles Gould, born in Costaguana though of English descent, is the owner of the silver mine near Sulaco. Weary of the country's turmoil, he backs the dictator Ribiera, but the silver provokes a series of rebellions, including one led by a General Montero, who closes in on Sulaco. Gould, anxious to save his silver, orders the "Capataz de Cargadores" (chief longshoreman) Nostromo to rescue the ingots by taking them upon the water for eventual sale abroad.

Giovanni Battista Fidanza, Nostromo's actual name (in Italian "Nostromo" signifies a boatswain, yet some think it is a play upon the Italian *nostro uomo* or "our man"), is trusted by everyone in Sulaco. Accompanied by Martin Decoud, journalist and *flâneur,* Nostromo sails a lighter out of the harbor, but that night it collides with a vessel carrying rebel forces. The silver is salvaged by grounding the lighter on the island of Great Isabel, which is uninhabited. The magnificent Capataz swims back to shore, abandoning Decoud to guard the silver. Surpassing himself, Nostromo rides over mountains to bring in the army that will save the newly independent state of Sulaco. Poor Decoud, unable to bear solitude, rides a lifeboat to sea, weighs his body down with four ingots, shoots himself, and goes down into the water.

Nostromo is left alone with his guilty secret as to the fate of the treasure. He begins to believe that his heroic exploits have been for nothing, and he is baffled by the disappearance of Decoud and the four ingots of silver. When a lighthouse is constructed on Great Isabel, Nostromo employs his influence to have his friend, the widowed Garibaldino Giorgio Viola, made the lighthouse keeper. In love with Giselle, Viola's younger daughter, the magnificent Capataz in turn is loved by the older daughter, Linda, to whom he is betrothed. Unfortunately, one dark night, as Nostromo attempts to nab more ingots, he is shot and killed by old Viola, under the impression that the interloper is a stranger.

Nostromo's triumph, though he cannot know it, is that an image of his authenticity survives, an image so powerful as to persuade both Conrad and the perceptive reader that even the self-betrayed hero retains an aesthetic dignity that renders his death partly tragic rather than sordid. Poor Decoud, for all his brilliance, dies a nihilistic death, disappearing "without a trace, swallowed up in the immense indifference of things." Nostromo, after his death, receives an aesthetic tribute beyond all irony, in the superb close of the novel:

> Linda's black figure detached itself upright on the light of the lantern with her arms raised above her head as though she were going to throw herself over.
>
> "It is I who loved you," she whispered, with a face as set and white as marble in the moonlight. "I! Only I! She will forget

thee, killed miserably for her pretty face. I cannot understand. I cannot understand. But I shall never forget thee. Never!"

She stood silent and still, collecting her strength to throw all her fidelity, her pain, bewilderment, and despair into one great cry.

"Never! Gian' Battista!"

Dr. Monygham, pulling round in the police-galley, heard the name pass over his head. It was another of Nostromo's triumphs, the greatest, the most enviable, the most sinister of all. In that true cry of undying passion that seemed to ring aloud from Punta Mala to Azuera and away to the bright line of the horizon, overhung by a big white cloud shining like a mass of solid silver, the genius of the magnificent Capataz de Cargadores dominated the dark gulf containing his conquests of treasure and love.

The limits of Joseph Conrad's irony, as Martin Price indicated, cannot be known. Is that "magnificent" ironic or romantic? What are we to make of the progression: the greatest, the most enviable, the most *sinister* of all? Does "sinister" mean "disturbing," or is it heraldic, what Ursula K. Le Guin called "the left hand of darkness"? Conrad abandons the question to the reader's share. I am troubled when I reread *Heart of Darkness* and cannot decipher Marlow's or Conrad's obscurantism. There seems a vacuum in that heart, a misty mid-region I rebel against inheriting. I remember a paragraph at the close of the chapter on *Nostromo* in the poet Aaron Fogel's book *Coercion to Speak: Conrad's Poetics of Dialogue* (1985):

This idea of ownership as forced possession, something inherited against one's will, like existence itself, both resembles and diverges from Harold Bloom's concept of poetic "influence." In *The Prelude* Wordsworth uses the term *inquisition* to describe his examination of himself for possible themes. As in Borges' reference to literature as "other inquisitions," the irony is infinite. Conrad, as his own work progressed, seems however to have turned, or to have tried to turn, partly away from the infinite ironic romance of self-inquisition (represented by the romantically compelled speaker Marlow) toward the representation, during the period of the political novels, of limited, external, crude forced dialogues in the world. There is the hint of a suspicion that it might be a bad defense, a bad infinity, to always internalize the format of coercion to speak as poetic will. Poetics, in Bloomian romanticism, may be the denial, by internalization, of the Oedipal order of forced dialogue in the outside world—the translation of inquisition into an inner feeling of compulsion to quarrel with a forebear or with oneself. In any case, Conrad turned from infinite self-inquisition to emphasize "objective" political scenes in which the enslaved, colonized, or dependent individual is made to speak, to own, to respond. In Bloom's signally moving personal terms, Gould's inheritance of the silver mine from his defeated father symbolizes Conrad's inheritance, from his own father and his "fathers," of Polish poetic dependency, Polish tragic "silence," Polish poetic minority in the greater world. And this is, to say the least, a viable reading. But Conrad's description of historical struggles for independence via dependent means is certainly also meant as a representation of actual political struggle by colonials against outside influences. This is one of the self-critical questions Conrad's later political novels direct, not always successfully, against his early work. He becomes convinced that the compulsion to speak does not always come from within, and that the political aspect of coercion to speak is at times disguised by inner agony.

Quarreling with a precursor or with oneself to me seems a prelude to the greater inquisition: the influence of a writer's mind upon itself. In his political novels—*Nostromo, The Secret Agent, Under Western Eyes*—Conrad increasingly will not allow his characters any freedom except their own eccentricities. They are overdetermined not only by their place in the economic and social order, but by their personalities that become fatalities. Giovanni Battista Fidanza, perpetually insecure despite his renown, dies as a sacrifice to his own sense of glory. Martin Decoud slays himself because solitude is made unbearable by his inward vacuity.

CHAPTER 30

The Secret Agent (1907)

JOSEPH CONRAD

THREE YEARS LATER, in *The Secret Agent,* something like a new Conrad came into being, an almost invisible narrator of a London recalling the dark agonies of Charles Dickens's *Our Mutual Friend* (1865). A generation had greatly altered London. Conrad deeply admired Dickens. On the surface they have little in common, but they dream some of the same metropolitan nightmares. London crime, for Dickens, was violent and sometimes familial. Conrad lived in an age of anarchist outrage against repressive and exploiting regimes.

As with so many political terms, anarchism tended to have a negative aura, as used by its enemies. The Greek *anarchos* means the absence of authority, which in itself was initially a Roman concept with the meaning, as interpreted by Hannah Arendt, of augmenting the foundations of civil society.

Anarchist assassinations became frequent and sensational around the turn of the century. President Carnot of France was slain in 1894; in 1901, President William McKinley of the United States was shot to death. There were other such events, but Joseph Conrad's inspiration for *The Secret Agent* came from the weird attempt to bomb the Royal Observatory at Greenwich in 1894. The would-be bomber, a French anarchist, merely blew himself up.

Conrad had a lifelong aversion to most things Russian, highly understandable in a Polish exile. Like Henry James, he made an exception for Turgenev, and, again like James, enormously undervalued Tolstoy. Though hostile to the tormented Dostoevsky, he could not quite escape the effect of *Crime and Punishment* and *Demons*.

The Secret Agent has the subtitle *A Simple Tale.* That may or may not be ironic. Winnie Verloc's life and death are hardly simple. An attractive working-class young woman whose father kept a pub, she married the older and grossly obese Adolf Verloc for the sake of her old mother and for her younger brother, Stevie, who appears to be autistic. He is immensely sensitive to the suffering of animals and, except for the love of his sister, is totally isolated.

Verloc is a secret agent for the Russians and is ordered by Mr. Vladimir of their embassy to carry out a bombing of the Greenwich Observatory, in order to shock the English government and people into a more severe crackdown upon anarchists. The London group headed by Verloc includes Michaelis; Comrade Alexander Ossipon, who lives by seducing lower-class women; the veteran terrorist Karl Yundt; and, most remarkably, the quite scary creature known as "the Professor," who is gifted at explosives. The Professor walks around London, fierce with hatred, and invulnerable, because the police realize that he is a walking bomb and can at any time explode himself and take with him a number of passing citizens.

Verloc receives a bomb from the Professor, gives it to Stevie, and points him toward the Observatory. After the explosion, the remnants of Stevie have to be gathered by shovels. When Winnie realizes Verloc's enormity, she takes action without reflection:

> She started forward at once, as if she were still a loyal woman bound to that man by an unbroken contract. Her right hand skimmed slightly the end of the table, and when she had passed on towards the sofa the carving knife had vanished without the slightest sound from the side of the dish. Mr. Verloc heard the creaky plank in the floor, and was content. He waited. Mrs. Verloc was coming. As if the homeless soul of Stevie had flown for shelter straight to the breast of his sister, guardian and protector, the resemblance of her face with that of her brother grew at every step, even to the droop of the lower lip, even to the slight

divergence of the eyes. But Mr. Verloc did not see that. He was lying on his back and staring upwards. He saw partly on the ceiling and partly on the wall the moving shadow of an arm with a clenched hand holding a carving knife. It flickered up and down. Its movements were leisurely. They were leisurely enough for Mr. Verloc to recognise the limb and the weapon.

They were leisurely enough for him to take in the full meaning of the portent, and to taste the flavour of death rising in his gorge. His wife had gone raving mad—murdering mad. They were leisurely enough for the first paralysing effect of this discovery to pass away before a resolute determination to come out victorious from the ghastly struggle with that armed lunatic. They were leisurely enough for Mr. Verloc to elaborate a plan of defence involving a dash behind the table, and the felling of the woman to the ground with a heavy wooden chair. But they were not leisurely enough to allow Mr. Verloc the time to move either hand or foot. The knife was already planted in his breast. It met no resistance on its way. Hazard has such accuracies. Into that plunging blow, delivered over the side of the couch, Mrs. Verloc had put all the inheritance of her immemorial and obscure descent, the simple ferocity of the age of caverns, and the unbalanced nervous fury of the age of bar-rooms. Mr. Verloc, the Secret Agent, turning slightly on his side with the force of the blow, expired without stirring a limb, in the muttered sound of the word 'Don't' by way of protest.

Mrs. Verloc had let go the knife, and her extraordinary resemblance to her late brother had faded, had become very ordinary now. She drew a deep breath, the first easy breath since Chief Inspector Heat had exhibited to her the labelled piece of Stevie's overcoat. She leaned forward on her folded arms over the side of the sofa. She adopted that easy attitude not in order to watch or gloat over the body of Mr. Verloc, but because of the undulatory and swinging movements of the parlour, which for some time behaved as though it were at sea in a tempest. She was giddy but calm. She had become a free woman with a perfection of freedom which left her nothing to desire and absolutely nothing to do, since Stevie's urgent claim on her devotion no longer existed. Mrs. Verloc, who thought in images, was not troubled now by visions, because she did not think at all. And she did not move. She was a woman enjoying her complete irresponsibility and endless leisure, almost in the manner of a corpse. She did not move, she did not think. Neither did the mortal envelope of the late Mr. Verloc reposing on the sofa. Except for the fact that Mrs. Verloc breathed these two would have been perfectly in accord: that accord of prudent reserve without superfluous words, and sparing of signs, which had been the foundation of their respectable home life. For it had been respectable, covering by a decent reticence the problems that may arise in the practice of a secret profession and the commerce of shady wares. To the last its decorum had remained undisturbed by unseemly shrieks and other misplaced sincerities of conduct. And after the striking of the blow, this respectability was continued in immobility and silence.

Even for Conrad, this is remarkable writing. Winnie transmutes into Atropos, oldest and most inevitable of the Three Fates. Style becomes implacable: "Hazard has such accuracies." If this is the voice of Joseph Conrad, it has undergone a Shakespearean withdrawal into an enigmatic reserve.

Comrade Ossipon arrives, tries for his customary seduction, hoping to secure Verloc's bank account on the promise of fleeing to France with Winnie. Taking the cash, he takes fright at Winnie's deed and demeanor, and abandons her on the channel ferry. Evidently fearing the gallows, Winnie takes off her wedding ring, and drowns herself in the channel.

What was it in Conrad's daemon or genius that impelled him to compose this "simple tale"? In our Age of Terror, *The Secret Agent* for many readers has an urgent relevancy. Conrad's wife, Jessie George, a working-class Englishwoman, in her memoir mentions how depressed her husband was as he labored on *The Secret Agent*. Anarchism both obsessed and dismayed Conrad. All of his fiction drives toward an idea of order that is hardly to be identified with the morality of the English nation in the early twentieth century. Though he lived in an atmosphere of correctness, there was in him always an agon between irony and romance, in the sense of romanticism.

Rereading *The Secret Agent*, I frequently have the uncanny sense that Conrad holds his ongoing narrative as far away from himself as he can. He does not altogether like what he finds himself doing. I cannot think of any other novel or story by him in which he relies so much upon adjectives. It is as though he wants to modify many substantives so as to make them less unpleasant to him.

When I put down my copy of *The Secret Agent,* I am more relieved than depressed. But then I realize that tomorrow morning's *New York Times* will bring me only depression. Terror and tyranny abroad and at home is the way things are. A time will come in my remaining four or five years when I will reread *The Secret Agent* with admiration and some ingratitude.

CHAPTER 31

Under Western Eyes (1911)

JOSEPH CONRAD

I T IS SOBERING to learn how tense and unhappy Conrad was as
he worked at *Under Western Eyes,* for him the most excruciating
of his novels. Mental and physical breakdown in January 1910 may
have been provoked by a quarrel with his faithful agent, J. B. Pinker,
who had been financing the Conrad family.

It was not until the publication of the novel *Chance* in 1913 that
Conrad's financial problems began to be solved. The book sold
heavily throughout 1914 and finally made the novelist both prosperous and famous. I cannot say that I find *Chance* very readable, but it
is gratifying that he at last found his public.

The final flickering of Conrad's greatness came in the novel *Victory* (1915), which sold well but baffled much of the public. I myself
find it rewarding, though hopelessly sad. At its close the stage is
bare, since all the protagonists have died, whether by murder, suicide, or accident.

Eight years after the publication of *Under Western Eyes,* Conrad
added an author's note that is reflective, a little pugnacious, and consistent with his dark vista of all things Russian:

My greatest anxiety was in being able to strike and sustain the
note of scrupulous impartiality. The obligation of absolute

fairness was imposed on me historically and hereditarily, by the peculiar experience of race and family, in addition to my primary conviction that truth alone is the justification of any fiction which makes the least claim to the quality of art or may hope to take its place in the culture of men and women of its time. I had never been called before to a greater effort of detachment....

"Race" here means being Polish. We can credit Conrad for an astonishing detachment throughout *Under Western Eyes,* though there is always an undercurrent of repressed outrage. "Family" refers to Conrad's father, Apollo Korzeniowski (1820–69), a distinguished poet and dramatist, as well as a translator, and a consistent, frequently underground revolutionary for the Polish cause. Arrested in 1861, he was sent into exile, which destroyed his health. Like his only child, the novelist, Apollo Korzeniowski greatly admired Shakespeare and translated him. From Conrad's author's note:

Razumov is treated sympathetically. Why should he not be? He is an ordinary young man, with a healthy capacity for work and sane ambitions. He has an average conscience. If he is slightly abnormal it is only in his sensitiveness to his position. Being nobody's child he feels rather more keenly than another would that he is a Russian—or he is nothing. He is perfectly right in looking on all Russia as his heritage. The sanguinary futility of the crimes and the sacrifices seething in that amorphous mass envelops and crushes him. But I don't think that in his distraction he is ever monstrous. Nobody is exhibited as a monster here—neither the simple-minded Tekla nor the wrong-headed Sophia Antonovna. Peter Ivanovitch and Madame de S. are fair game. They are the apes of a sinister jungle and are treated as their grimaces deserve. As to Nikita—nicknamed Necator—he is the perfect flower of the terroristic wilderness. What troubled me most in dealing with him was not his monstrosity but his banality.

Conrad's tone here hesitates before going back to detachment. I do not like Razumov and cannot believe Conrad did, either. It is true that Razumov is the bastard son of a nobleman who only barely acknowledges him. Granted also that Razumov is never monstrous. Madame de S. is the wealthy patroness of Peter Ivanovitch, who clearly is based upon Mikhail Bakunin, a notorious firebrand, anti-Semitic and violent, who was the major anarcho-syndicalist theorist. Nikita is brutal, a tsarist double agent who destroys Razumov's eardrums, rendering him deaf. Subsequently, Razumov is run over by a tram and severely crippled. He survives only because Tekla devotes her life to taking care of him. Several critics have noted Conrad's prolepsis of Hannah Arendt's idea of the banality of evil.

> The most terrifying reflection (I am speaking now for myself) is that all these people are not the product of the exceptional but of the general—of the normality of their place, and time, and race. The ferocity and imbecility of an autocratic rule rejecting all legality and in fact basing itself upon complete moral anarchism provokes the no less imbecile and atrocious answer of a purely Utopian revolutionism encompassing destruction by the first means to hand, in the strange conviction that a fundamental change of hearts must follow the downfall of any given human institutions. These people are unable to see that all they can effect is merely a change of names. The oppressors and the oppressed are all Russians together; and the world is brought once more face to face with the truth of the saying that the tiger cannot change his stripes nor the leopard his spots.

The surge of this is in some ways stronger in 2018 than it was in 1920. Conrad wants us to remember Jeremiah 13:23, which in the King James Version reads: "Can the Ethiopian change his skin, or the leopard his spots? then may ye also do good, that are accustomed to do evil." In the age of Putin, what can we do except agree with Conrad's skepticism as to all things Russian? And yet, despite his loathing for Dostoevsky, clearly *Crime and Punishment* serves as a model for Razumov's situation. Raskolnikov comes to realize that by butchering the two old women he has murdered himself; Razumov sees that in betraying Haldin he has sold himself to the state.

There are other traces of Dostoevsky and also of Tolstoy in *Under Western Eyes*. Why are they there? They seem deliberate. Conrad was as civilized as Turgenev or Henry James. Polish at the core, he could not forgive Russia but had learned from Shakespeare, as his father had, that the creation of character transcended moral judgment. It may be that in Conrad allusiveness becomes a form of atonement.

I wonder if *Under Western Eyes* would not have been an even stronger work if, like *The Secret Agent*, it had had an omniscient narrator. Marlow could not fit in the Geneva of Russian revolutionary exiles, but the unnamed, elderly teacher of languages does not persuade me that *his* Western eyes are reliable. He seems to be all but in love with Natalia Victorovna Haldin yet lacks the confidence to guide her wisely. Marlow emerges from the matrix of Conrad; the language teacher is drearily adrift.

But then I am chastened by thinking back to Conrad's torment as he wrote *Under Western Eyes*. W. B. Yeats called upon sages standing in God's holy fire to be the singing masters of his soul. An eclectic occultist, Yeats equated God and death. Joseph Conrad remained a skeptic, famously writing to Edward Garnett in 1902: "I always, from the age of fourteen, disliked the Christian religion, its doctrines, ceremonies and festivals." That questioning spirit saw Conrad through to the end.

CHAPTER 32

The Reef (1912)

EDITH WHARTON

I F YOU SUFFER from the rage for reading and rereading, you are rewarded by lucky surprises. I intended to write this brief commentary upon one of three indubitable masterpieces by Edith Wharton: *The House of Mirth, The Custom of the Country, The Age of Innocence.* I had reread them several times and written about all of them, as well as about *Ethan Frome.* My friend R. W. B. Lewis (1917–2002), who wrote a large biography of Wharton, and edited several volumes of her work, in the year 2000 urged me to read *The Reef.* I have taken eighteen years to follow Dick's advice and have just completed two readings of *The Reef.*

It is a sinuous and disturbing novel, with a complex relation to Wharton's erotic life. She met Morton Fullerton in 1907, when she was forty-five and he was forty-two. Fullerton, an American journalist, was a fabled seducer, androgynous, whose major distinction was that he gave both Edith Wharton and Henry James their first full sexual experience. Part of his charm was an ability to insinuate incest, a repressed and powerful element in the psychosexuality of both Wharton and Henry James. Wharton when very young had an incestuous relationship to her father and perhaps to her brother. Some have speculated that the basis for Henry James's homoeroticism might be found in his early love for his brother, the philosopher and psychologist William James. What is clear is that Fullerton liberated Henry James into many subsequent homosexual relationships, and gave to Edith Wharton the sensual culmination she had not found in her sexless marriage to Edward Wharton.

In her highly Whitmanian erotic poem "Terminus," written in 1909, at the apex of her affair with Fullerton, Wharton achieves a power unmatched elsewhere in her verse. She and Henry James shared an ecstatic appreciation of Walt Whitman. Both accurately regarded him as the greatest of American poets. There is a moving description by Wharton of Henry James crooning Whitman aloud on an evening at the Mount, her estate near Tanglewood. She remarked that we all "sat rapt" as James chanted on "in a mood of subdued ecstasy." One could wish for a recording of that.

For Wharton, Walt Whitman was as much a prophet as a poet, and a great liberator of the passional life, as he was for D. H. Lawrence, Hart Crane, Lorca, Luis Cernuda, Pessoa, Octavio Paz, Neruda, Borges and so many more. There is a weird charm in juxtaposing Walt Whitman, one of the roughs, an American, and the literary mandarins Wharton and James. Whitman and Thoreau met to their mutual delight, and the American Bard left us accounts of his visits to Ralph Waldo Emerson, including a final one during which the poet stationed his chair so that he could look on the benignly amiable countenance of the Seer in his senility.

The Reef is an intricate, surging narrative that shows Wharton to be a master of dialogue and something close to a wisdom writer in matters of the heart. It is not surprising that Henry James preferred it to all her other work. Though Wharton professed mixed reactions to the Master's late phase, the influence of *The Golden Bowl* (1904) pervades *The Reef.*

The central consciousness of *The Reef* is that of Anna Leath, an American woman in her late thirties, widowed and living in Givré, a rural estate in France, with her twenty-three-year-old stepson, Owen Leath, and her nine-year-old daughter, Effie. Fraser Leath, her late husband, was a wealthy dilettante who devoted himself to collecting antique snuffboxes and possibly to the usual philandering.

The two other consequential characters are George Darrow, an American diplomat stationed in London, who may be a year or two younger than Anna, and Sophy Viner, a poignant and rather luckless

American young woman, who hopes to become an actress in Paris. Darrow and Sophy have a brief affair in Paris; it meant little enough to him, but Sophy never gets beyond it. Circumstances make Sophy a live-in tutor for Effie, and Owen Leath falls in love with her.

George Darrow is the aesthetic enigma of the novel. He is admirable enough but a touch shallow, though his authentic love for Anna, which goes back to before her marriage, is enduring. Edith Wharton invests herself in Anna's perplexed awareness of other people, including her stepson, Sophy Viner, and most of all Darrow, whom she loves but distrusts. The revelation of the brief affair of Sophy and Darrow becomes the reef that virtually wrecks her possibility of long-delayed fulfillment in a second marriage.

It is extraordinary how Wharton is able to play out the vicissitudes of Anna's heart. One wonders to what extent Anna is a surrogate for the novelist. The gods gave Edith Newbold Jones every gift—daemonic drive, intellect, imaginative capaciousness—except beauty. She called Walter Van Rensselaer Berry "the love of my life," but that international lawyer and diplomat gave her only friendship, as he did to Henry James and Marcel Proust. Her only lover, after her childhood, seems to have been Fullerton.

All of the women protagonists in Wharton's major phase are beautiful. One thinks of Lily Bart in *The House of Mirth,* whose ill luck and bad timing compel her, at twenty-nine, to kill herself by an overdose of chloral. Imprisoned by the social world of Old New York, and with inadequate means, she desperately needs a marriage into money and good social standing. Despite her charm, goodness, and desirability, she remains unmarried with many debts, some by losing large sums at bridge games. Her true love is a young lawyer, Lawrence Selden, who moves easily through Old New York but lacks money. The only culmination of the love between Lily and Selden is when he grieves for her over her deathbed.

I am a fierce admirer of Janet Malcolm, as writer and as person, but it puzzles me when she says of Wharton, "Her books are pervaded by a deep pessimism and an equally profound misogyny." The pessimism is an abyss, but why term Wharton a misogynist? Undine Spragg, sexual magnet and devourer of husbands, the monstrous protagonist of *The Custom of the Country,* vindicates Malcolm, yet Undine is a vacuous fiend unique in Wharton. The anti-heroine

Undine manifests Wharton's savage genius as a parodist, unlikely ancestor of Nathanael West and Thomas Pynchon.

In *The Age of Innocence,* Ellen Olenska and May Welland are in their different ways admirable, even if neither is truly a match for Newland Archer, who, like George Darrow in *The Reef,* may be modeled on Walter Berry. And yet Malcolm, as always, is on to something vital and dark in the recesses of Wharton's consciousness. Edith Jones Wharton wants to be loved by men and at most respected by women of sufficient eminence. It is absurdly unnecessary to term Wharton a snob; she would fit more than one category of Thackeray's *Book of Snobs.* She has overt debts to Thackeray: Undine Spragg parodies the marvelous Becky Sharp of *Vanity Fair,* though the effect on me makes me miss Becky Sharp more and more.

Wharton's tedious anti-Semitism is everywhere in her work. Still, she is hardly unique in that blot on the American novel: Willa Cather, F. Scott Fitzgerald, Ernest Hemingway, and the Jewish anti-Semite Nathanael West are among many other offenders. Cather had lost one of her lesbian lovers to a Jewish violinist and revenged herself throughout her writings. With Wharton, it is merely the heritage of Old New York.

The friendship between Edith Wharton and Henry James was prolonged, deeply felt, yet vexing because of literary anxieties. Wharton was weary of being termed a female Henry James, while James, almost twenty years older than Wharton, was at times terrified and exhausted by her energy, to the point where he once referred to her as his "Angel of Devastation." Wharton, always in overdrive, was rather more than a natural force. A comparison between their ghostly tales demonstrates that James is gentle at the borders between natural and preternatural, whereas Wharton is wild and daemonic even when she emphasizes silence. For many years she kept an annual vigil on All Souls' Night, recalling her beloved dead and musing on her loneliness. The last story she wrote, concluded in February 1937—six months before her death at the age of seventy-five—has as its protagonist Sara Clayburn, a wealthy old lady living alone except for a houseful of servants. On a chilly late-October evening, she meets an unknown woman walking toward her house who says she wishes to see one of the girls. Sara Clayburn injures her ankle and takes to her bed, with food left nearby by a servant. In the morning, she wakes to find the house deserted and has to limp around to take care of herself. One year later, all this is repeated, with the strange woman reappearing, and Sara understands what is happening. Whether this is a parable of the lonely old Edith Wharton fearing death is unclear, yet the story is brilliantly narrated.

It would be unfair to contrast Wharton's *The Reef* with James's *The Golden Bowl*. Every time I go back to *The Golden Bowl*, I change my mind—or, rather, James changes it. My view both of Maggie Verver and of Charlotte Stant ebbs and flows. Maggie's patience and marital love wear down Charlotte's relentless passion for Prince Amerigo. Adam Verver, widower with only the single child, Maggie, yields to his daughter's shrewd suggestion that he propose marriage to Charlotte, who accepts him. The daughter-father alliance abides too strenuously, so that Charlotte and Amerigo resume their affair. Henry James severs both knots by a tense accord between Maggie and Charlotte that sends Adam, his art collection, and Charlotte, his major acquisition, back to the United States.

Edith Wharton stated that she found *The Golden Bowl* "unreadable." Perhaps, though, she absorbed enough of it to help engender *The Reef*, which floats under the shadow of James's daedal dance of marriages. Henry James, in a letter to Wharton, implicitly recognizes his parentage while complimenting the novel and its author:

There remains with me so strongly the impression of [*The Reef's*] quality and of the unspeakably *fouillée* nature of the situation between the two principals...that I can't but babble of it a little to you even with these weak lips.... Each of these two figures is admirable for truth and *justesse;* the woman an exquisite thing, and with her characteristic finest, scarce differentiated notes...sounded with a wonder of delicacy. I'm not sure her oscillations are not beyond our notation; yet they are so held in your hand, so felt and known and shown, and everything seems so to come of itself. I suffer or worry a little from the fact that in the Prologue, as it were, we are admitted so much into the consciousness of the man, and that after the introduction of Anna (Anna so perfectly named) we see him almost only as she sees him—which gives our attention a different sort of work to do; yet this is really, I think, but a triumph of your method, for he remains of an absolute consistent verity, showing himself in that way better perhaps than in any other, and without a false note imputable, not a shadow of one, to his manner of so projecting himself. The beauty of it is that it is, for all it is worth, a Drama, and almost, as it seems to me, of the psychologic Racinian unity, intensity and gracility. Anna is really of Racine...which is why the whole thing, unrelated and unreferred save in the most superficial way to its *milieu* and background, and to any determining or qualifying *entourage*, takes place *comme cela*, and in a specified, localised way, in France—these non-French people "electing," as it were, to have their story out there....Your Racinian inspiration...absolutely prescribed a vague and elegant French colonnade or gallery, with a French river dimly gleaming through, as the harmonious *fond* you required. In the key of this, with all your reality, you have yet kept the whole thing: and, to deepen the harmony and accentuate the literary pitch, have never surpassed yourself for certain exquisite *moments*, certain images, analogies, metaphors, certain silver correspondences in your *façon de dire....* There used to be little notes in you that were like fine benevolent finger-marks of the good George Eliot—the echo of much reading of that excellent woman, here and there, that is, sounding through. But now you are like a lost and recovered "ancient" whom *she* might have got a reading of (especially were he a Greek) and of whom in *her* texture some weaker reflection were to show. For, dearest Edith, you are stronger and firmer and finer than all of them put together; you go further and you say *mieux*, and your only drawback is not having the homeliness and the inevitability and the happy limitation and the affluent poverty, of a Country of your Own (*comme moi, par exemple!*) It makes you, this does, as you exquisitely say of somebody or something at some moment, elegiac (what penetration, what delicacy in your use there of the term!)—makes you so, that is, for the Racinian-sérieux—but leaves you more in the desert (for everything else) that surrounds Apex City

(*The Letters of Henry James, Vol. II*, ed. Percy Lubbock [1920])

Apex City is the origin of Undine Spragg, her parents, and of her both first and final spouse, Elmer Moffatt, pride both of Kansas and of Wall Street. I suggest that Henry James here is the most useful critic that *The Reef* has attracted. He acutely notes of Anna, "I'm not sure her oscillations are not beyond our notation." *That* is the center of Anna's vacillating consciousness, at once drawing her to George Darrow and spinning her away from him. James also helps us to appreciate Wharton's movement from her initial depiction of Darrow in his affair with Sophy Viner to: "we see him almost only as she sees him—which gives our attention a different sort of work to do; yet this is really, I think, but a triumph of your method." In a sense, we lose Darrow's verity to Anna's internalization of him, yet James is again accurate in judging this "a triumph of your method."

That the method, despite antecedents in George Eliot and in James himself, indeed is newly born in Wharton prompts a subtle and persuasive instance of that return of the precursors as if they were descendants that I once termed *apophrades,* the Athenian unlucky day of the dead, in which they returned to inhabit their former houses:

> There used to be little notes in you that were like fine benevolent finger-marks of the good George Eliot—the echo of much reading of that excellent woman, here and there, that is, sounding through. But now you are like a lost and recovered "ancient" whom *she* might have got a reading of (especially were he a Greek) and of whom in *her* texture some weaker reflection were to show.

In this charming compliment, Wharton has mothered (if that is the right word) George Eliot and Henry James. Aesthetic judgment, however, must admit that the moral splendor of George Eliot and the vibrant indirectness of Henry James far surpass anything in Wharton. If you mass all of Wharton's fictions together, you get a larger impression than any single work provides. I may be moved by my own belatedness in coming upon *The Reef,* though it lingers in my speculations more even than *The House of Mirth* or *The Age of Innocence.* I cannot fully grasp Anna's interminable hesitations, rejections, joyous reacceptances of George Darrow's love and desire to marry her. Something more has to be involved than her conventional shock at the brief affair between Darrow and Sophy Viner, and her subsequent flarings of sexual jealousy. Both Sophy and Darrow have told her the full truth, that for Sophy it was indeed love, and for Darrow a mixed act of kindness and self-indulgence.

I cannot pretend to puzzle Anna out. She is somehow both true gold and a labyrinth. Is she as close to a self-portrait as Wharton would permit herself in a narrative fiction? The shadow of Walter Berry, whose love for Wharton declined sexual expression, falls over Darrow as it does over Newland Archer and Lawrence Selden.

It would be grotesque to find a feminist in Edith Wharton. And yet few other novelists so dramatize the double standard that patriarchy so long maintained against the sexual fulfillment of women. It does not occur to Darrow to think how he would react if Anna had gone through an affair after the death of her husband. Doubtless he would flee. Anna, though tempted, does not take flight. After much agony, she seems to accept marrying George Darrow, but Wharton gives us no certainty. In the weird final scene of *The Reef*, Anna goes in search of Sophy, who has departed for India, and finds instead the blowsy sister of Sophy, Laura, who has a steady succession of husbands and lovers. In some shock, Anna departs, presumably to go back to Darrow and her impending marriage.

It is unclear, after this depressing episode, what we are to assume will happen. Most likely, the emotionally exhausted Anna will be content with Darrow and live a better life. Yet there are too many shadows. Wharton declines to tell us what lies beyond; perhaps she does not know. This is the last exchange between them that Wharton gives us:

"Anna—Anna!"

"Yes; I want to know now: to know everything. Perhaps that will make me forget. I ought to have made you tell me before. Wherever we go, I imagine you've been there with her...I see you together. I want to know how it began, where you went, why you left her...I can't go on in this darkness any longer!"

She did not know what had prompted her passionate outburst, but already she felt lighter, freer, as if at last the evil spell were broken. "I want to know everything," she repeated. "It's the only way to make me forget."

After she had ceased speaking Darrow remained where he was, his arms folded, his eyes lowered, immovable. She waited, her gaze on his face.

"Aren't you going to tell me?"

"No."

The blood rushed to her temples. "You won't? Why not?"

"If I did, do you suppose you'd forget that?"

"Oh—" she moaned, and turned away from him.

"You see it's impossible," he went on. "I've done a thing I loathe, and to atone for it you ask me to do another. What sort of satisfaction would that give you? It would put something irremediable between us."

She leaned her elbow against the mantel-shelf and hid her face in her hands. She had the sense that she was vainly throwing away her last hope of happiness, yet she could do nothing, think of nothing, to save it. The conjecture flashed through her: "Should I be at peace if I gave him up?" and she remembered the desolation of the days after she had sent him away, and understood that that hope was vain. The tears welled through her lids and ran slowly down between her fingers.

"Good-bye," she heard him say, and his footsteps turned to the door.

She tried to raise her head, but the weight of her despair bowed it down. She said to herself: "This is the end...he won't try to appeal to me again ..." and she remained in a sort of tranced rigidity, perceiving without feeling the fateful lapse of the seconds. Then the cords that bound her seemed to snap, and she lifted her head and saw him going.

"Why, he's mine—he's mine! He's no one else's!" His face was turned to her and the look in his eyes swept away all her terrors. She no longer understood what had prompted her senseless outcry; and the mortal sweetness of loving him became again the one real fact in the world.

This is so powerfully wrought that it ought to be definitive. And yet the consciousness of Anna is a vortex. Terrors of the mind will return. Henry James was accurate: there *is* something of Racine's Phèdre in Anna. Lily Bart's fate was too pathetic to be tragic. Anna cannot shed a tragic aura. That may have been the threshold Wharton crossed into a touch of greatness.

CHAPTER 33

The Rainbow (1915)

D. H. LAWRENCE

DAVID HERBERT LAWRENCE died of tuberculosis at the age of forty-four. He was amazingly prolific: a dozen novels, another dozen volumes of shorter fiction, many volumes of increasingly strong poetry that moved from the influence of Thomas Hardy to that of Walt Whitman. But that only begins to catalogue Lawrence's fecundity. He was an incisive literary critic, an intensely vivid travel writer, a polemicist who argued against Freud while getting Freud quite wrong, a dramatist, an incessant letter writer, and a painter. After reading him for more than seventy years, I value him most for two great novels: *The Rainbow* and *Women in Love,* which he had intended to be one long saga to be called *The Sisters.* Of equal importance are his shorter fictions, many of them novellas, and his poetry. Now, in 2018, Lawrence is no longer esteemed as a prophet or a spiritual guide. When I was young, many women and men of my generation were Lawrentians, but that vogue expired when fiercer feminisms arrived.

Lawrence invoked a living God:

then I must know that still
I am in the hands of the unknown God,
he is breaking me down to his own oblivion
to send me forth on a new morning, a new man.

Heightened prose takes on the intensity of sublime poetry in Herman Melville, James Joyce, William Faulkner, and others, but achieves an apex in Lawrence's novel *The Rainbow* (1915). In its first chapter, the rhythms of the King James Bible inform Lawrence's vision of the Brangwens:

> It was enough for the men, that the earth heaved and opened its furrow to them, that the wind blew to dry the wet wheat, and set the young ears of corn wheeling freshly round about; it was enough that they helped the cow in labour, or ferreted the rats from under the barn, or broke the back of a rabbit with a sharp knock of the hand. So much warmth and generating and pain and death did they know in their blood, earth and sky and beast and green plants, so much exchange and interchange they had with these, that they lived full and surcharged, their senses full fed, their faces always turned to the heat of the blood, staring into the sun, dazed with looking towards the source of generation, unable to turn round.

These cadences return in the final paragraph of *The Rainbow*, where Ursula has a vision:

> And the rainbow stood on the earth. She knew that the sordid people who crept hard-scaled and separate on the face of the world's corruption were living still, that the rainbow was arched in their blood and would quiver to life in their spirit, that they would cast off their horny covering of disintegration, that new, clean, naked bodies would issue to a new germination, to a new growth, rising to the light and the wind and the clean rain of heaven. She saw in the rainbow the earth's new architecture, the old, brittle corruption of houses and factories swept away, the world built up in a living fabric of Truth, fitting to the over-arching heaven.

This kind of High Romanticism stems from Lawrence's Nonconformist heritage. After *The Rainbow*, his novels dwindle, unlike his poems and shorter fictions of all lengths. Even *Women in Love* (1920) falls away from the remorseless drive of *The Rainbow*. Ursula Brangwen bears the same name in both books yet scarcely is the same woman. The first Ursula is even more passionate and more determined to live a life altogether her own and to seek and find fulfillment in every sense. After an intense lesbian relationship, she undergoes a turbulent relationship with Anton Skrebensky, a remote cousin from Poland who has become an English soldier.

After dining together, Ursula leads her lover down to the sea:

> She stood on the edge of the water, at the edge of the solid, flashing body of the sea, and the wave rushed over her feet.
>
> "I want to go," she cried, in a strong, dominant voice. "I want to go."
>
> He saw the moonlight on her face, so she was like metal, he heard her ringing, metallic voice, like the voice of a harpy to him.

In ancient mythology a harpy is a predatory bird with the head of a woman, scarcely an accurate description of the passionate Ursula, but a revelation of Skrebensky's sense of his own inadequacy:

> She prowled, ranging on the edge of the water like a possessed creature, and he followed her. He saw the froth of the wave followed by the hard, bright water swirl over her feet and her ankles, she swung out her arms, to balance, he expected every moment to see her walk into the sea, dressed as she was, and be carried swimming out.
>
> But she turned, she walked to him.
>
> "I want to go," she cried again, in the high, hard voice, like the scream of gulls.
>
> "Where?" he asked.
>
> "I don't know."

The reader recalls that this next-to-the-last chapter of *The Rainbow* is called "The Bitterness of Ecstasy." Strangely, this Ursula is very close to the younger sister, Gudrun, of *Women in Love,* and very different from that later Ursula. Each longs to break all bounds and fails to find in sexual intercourse her image for longing:

> And she seized hold of his arm, held him fast, as if captive, and walked him a little way by the edge of the dazzling, dazing water.

Then there in the great flare of light, she clinched hold of him, hard, as if suddenly she had the strength of destruction, she fastened her arms round him and tightened him in her grip, whilst her mouth sought his in a hard, rending, ever-increasing kiss, till his body was powerless in her grip, his heart melted in fear from the fierce, beaked, harpy's kiss. The water washed again over their feet, but she took no notice. She seemed unaware, she seemed to be pressing in her beaked mouth till she had the heart of him. Then, at last, she drew away and looked at him— looked at him. He knew what she wanted. He took her by the hand and led her across the foreshore, back to the sandhills. She went silently. He felt as if the ordeal of proof was upon him, for life or death. He led her to a dark hollow.

"No, here," she said, going out to the slope full under the moonshine. She lay motionless, with wide-open eyes looking at the moon. He came direct to her, without preliminaries. She held him pinned down at the chest, awful. The fight, the struggle for consummation was terrible. It lasted till it was agony to his soul, till he succumbed, till he gave way as if dead, lay with his face buried, partly in her hair, partly in the sand, motionless, as if he would be motionless now for ever, hidden away in the dark, buried, only buried, he only wanted to be buried in the goodly darkness, only that, and no more.

He seemed to swoon. It was a long time before he came to himself. He was aware of an unusual motion of her breast. He looked up. Her face lay like an image in the moonlight, the eyes wide open, rigid. But out of the eyes, slowly, there rolled a tear, that glittered in the moonlight as it ran down her cheek.

He felt as if as the knife were being pushed into his already dead body. With head strained back, he watched, drawn tense, for some minutes, watched the unaltering, rigid face like metal in the moonlight, the fixed, unseeing eye, in which slowly the water gathered, shook with glittering moonlight, then surcharged, brimmed over and ran trickling, a tear with its burden of moonlight, into the darkness, to fall in the sand.

He drew gradually away as if afraid, drew away—she did not move. He glanced at her—she lay the same. Could he break away? He turned, saw the open foreshore, clear in front of him, and he plunged away, on and on, ever farther from the horrible figure that lay stretched in the moonlight on the sands with the tears gathering and travelling on the motionless, eternal face.

He felt, if ever he must see her again, his bones must be broken, his body crushed, obliterated for ever. And as yet, he had the love of his own living body. He wandered on a long, long way, till his brain drew dark and he was unconscious with weariness. Then he curled in the deepest darkness he could find, under the sea-grass, and lay there without consciousness.

She broke from her tense cramp of agony gradually, though each movement was a goad of heavy pain. Gradually, she lifted her dead body from the sands, and rose at last. There was now no moon for her, no sea. All had passed away. She trailed her dead body to the house, to her room, where she lay down inert.

When I was much younger, I could read this intently without suffering it. In my High Eighties (as my late friend Ursula Le Guin taught me to call it), I find it exquisitely painful but aesthetically superb. Lawrence prophesied against what he called "sex in the head." William Blake might have called this "Reasoning from the loins in the unreal forms of Beulah's night." A lifelong admirer of Lawrence, I go with Blake. And yet *The Rainbow* permanently illuminates what Shakespeare and Milton and Tolstoy understood too well: women are sexually superior to men. Adam was God's initial molding out of the red clay. Eve, quarried out of the human, was better made.

CHAPTER 34

Women in Love (1920)

D. H. Lawrence

R EREADING *Women in Love* after many years, I discover it to
be strangely distant from what I had recalled. Several decades
ago, I knew the book so fully that I anticipated many paragraphs,
even chapters, but in those days I had a kind of provisional belief in
Lawrence. The book now appears stranger and richer, more original
than I had recalled. Ambivalences of the will, modes of being are
represented by a sharpness that seems uncanny, since the power to
suggest so many complex apprehensions could be judged without
precedent in the novel.

Lawrence on his heights astonishes, almost showing what cannot be shown. *The Rainbow* and *Women in Love* are his triumphs,
equaled only by a number of his poems and by many of his short
stories. In the endless war between men and women, Lawrence
fights on both sides. He is superb at giving us really murderous lovers' quarrels, as in Chapter 23, "Excurse," of *Women in Love*, where
Ursula and Birkin suffer one of their encounters upon what Lawrence calls "this memorable battlefield":

"I jealous! *I*—jealous! You *are* mistaken if you think that. I'm
not jealous in the least of Hermione, she is nothing to me, not
that!" And Ursula snapped her fingers. "No, it's you who are a

liar. It's you who must return, like a dog to his vomit. It is what Hermione *stands* for that I *hate*. I *hate* it. It is lies, it is false, it is death. But you want it, you can't help it, you can't help yourself. You belong to that old, deathly way of living—then go back to it. But don't come to me, for I've nothing to do with it."

And in the stress of her violent emotion, she got down from the car and went to the hedgerow, picking unconsciously some flesh-pink spindleberries, some of which were burst, showing their orange seeds.

"Ah, you are a fool," he cried bitterly, with some contempt.

"Yes, I am. I *am* a fool. And thank God for it. I'm too big a fool to swallow your cleverness. God be praised. You go to your women—go to them—they are your sort—you've always had a string of them trailing after you—and you always will. Go to your spiritual brides—but don't come to me as well, because I'm not having any, thank you. You're not satisfied, are you? Your spiritual brides can't give you what you want, they aren't common and fleshy enough for you, aren't they? So you come to me, and keep them in the background! You will marry me for daily use. But you'll keep yourself well provided with spiritual brides in the background. I know your dirty little game." Suddenly a flame ran over her, and she stamped her foot madly on the road, and he winced, afraid that she would strike him. "And, *I, I'm* not spiritual enough, *I'm* not as spiritual as that Hermione—!" Her brows knitted, her eyes blazed like a tiger's. "Then *go* to her, that's all I say, *go* to her, *go*. Ha, she spiritual—*spiritual*, she! A dirty materialist as she is. *She* spiritual? What does she care for, what is her spirituality? What *is* it?" Her fury seemed to blaze out and burn his face. He shrank a little. "I tell you it's *dirt, dirt,* and nothing *but* dirt. And it's dirt you want, you crave for it. Spiritual! Is *that* spiritual, her bullying, her conceit, her sordid materialism? She's a fishwife, a fishwife, she is such a materialist. And all so sordid. What does she work out to, in the end, with all her social passion, as you call it. Social passion—what social passion has she?—show it me!—where is it? She wants petty, immediate *power,* she wants the illusion that she is a great woman, that is all. In her soul she's a devilish unbeliever, common as dirt. That's what she is at the bottom. And all the rest is pretence—but you love it. You love the sham spirituality, it's your food. And why? Because of the dirt underneath. Do you think I don't know the foulness of your sex life—and hers?—I do. And it's that foulness you want, you liar. Then have it, have it. You're such a liar."

She turned away, spasmodically tearing the twigs of spindle-berry from the hedge, and fastening them, with vibrating fingers, in the bosom of her coat.

He stood watching in silence. A wonderful tenderness burned in him at the sight of her quivering, so sensitive fingers: and at the same time he was full of rage and callousness.

This passage-at-arms moves between Ursula's unconscious picking of the fleshly, burst spindleberries, open to their seeds, and her turning away, tearing the spindleberry twigs so as to fasten them in her coat. Birkin reads the spindleberries as the exposed flesh of what Freud called one's own bodily ego, suffering here a *sparagmos* by a maenadlike Ursula. It is as though Birkin himself, lashed by her language, becomes a frontier being, caught between psyche and body. Repelled yet simultaneously drawn by a sort of orphic wonder, Birkin yields to her ferocity that is not so much jealousy as it is the woman's protest against Birkin's Lawrentian and male idealization of sexual love. What Ursula most deeply rejects is that the idealization is both flawed and ambivalent, because it is founded upon a displaced Protestantism that both craves total union and cannot abide such annihilation of individuality. Birkin-Lawrence has in him the taint of the Protestant God, and implicitly is always announcing to Ursula, "Be like me, but do not dare to be too like me!," an injunction that infuriates her. As Lawrence is both Birkin and Ursula, he has the curious trait, for a novelist, of perpetually infuriating himself.

The central difficulty of *Women in Love* is Lawrence's split between a Puritan will and a High Romantic sensibility quarried from Shelley, Blake, Thomas Hardy, and Walt Whitman. Division in the self compelled Lawrence to misunderstand totally Sigmund Freud, to the point where the poet-prophet asserted that the founder of psychoanalysis wished to cancel all inhibitions. That is to turn Freud into the Marquis de Sade.

There are five crucial persons in *Women in Love:* Rupert Birkin, who clearly is D. H. Lawrence; Ursula Brangwen, a kind of vision of Frieda von Richthofen, who eloped to the Continent with Lawrence while she was still married to his former teacher, Ernest Weekley, leaving behind their three children. There are the tragic, hopelessly ill-matched Gerald Crich, industrialist and malcontent, and the fascinating Gudrun Brangwen, younger sister of Ursula. Gudrun is a sculptor, a beautiful nihilist who wishes only to *know* others, and loses interest once they are known. Lawrence modeled her on the New Zealand short-story writer Katherine Mansfield, who died of tuberculosis at the age of thirty-four in 1923. Mansfield was married, separated and divorced from, remarried, and separated again from the literary critic John Middleton Murry, whom Lawrence portrayed as Gerald Crich. For a time, Murry was Lawrence's disciple, but betrayed him both by having an affair with Frieda and by writing a rather nasty book: *Son of Woman: The Story of D. H. Lawrence* (1931), in which Lawrence is exhibited as a repressed homosexual, a person so sexually overexcited that he always arrived too soon, as it were, and found release only by anal intercourse with Frieda. All this may well have been true, but Murry's tonality is sometimes offensive. Aside from his appearance as Gerald Crich, there is a delightful travesty of him as one Burlap in Aldous Huxley's *Point Counter Point* (1928). That leaves only Hermione Roddice, Birkin's cast-off mistress, a fierce parody of Lady Ottoline Morrell, an eccentric and wealthy noblewoman who patronized writers and artists. Her husband, a lawyer, threatened to sue Lawrence, and a few changes were made to satisfy him.

It may be that even a brief glance at Lawrence's models is misleading. Ken Russell's wonderful film *Women in Love* (1969) is remarkably true to the novel, partly because the five crucial actors perform superbly, Glenda Jackson as Gudrun in particular. Birkin/Lawrence is played by Alan Bates, who at moments seems to *be* Lawrence. Oliver Reed, dark and saturnine, is threatening as Gerald Crich, while Jennie Linden is a fit lover/antagonist for Bates as Birkin. Not least in any sense is Eleanor Bron as Hermione, always on the verge of hysteria and fury.

When I turn over *Women in Love* in my exhausted moments after the endless exercise I have to perform to keep going in life, I see first the Strindbergian battle to the love-death between Gudrun and Gerald. Lawrence certainly had read Strindberg and could not ward off the influence, though he attempted to do so:

But I don't want to write like Galsworthy nor Ibsen, nor Strindberg nor any of them, *not* even if I could. We have to hate our immediate predecessors, to get free from their authority.

(1913 letter to Edward Garnett)

Strindberg wrote two plays called *The Dance of Death,* both in 1900. Properly directed and performed, they still shock with their dreadful recoil from marriage. Three wives endured Strindberg; his palpable misogyny was hectic and unchecked. Lawrence, whatever his flaws, is in the tradition of male novelists who lovingly and profoundly portrayed women: from Samuel Richardson to James Joyce.

The relationship between Ursula and Birkin, after many vicissitudes, culminates in an authentic marriage between two strong souls who recognize that neither must subsume the other. Joy, in the alert reader, celebrates this union between benign wills, each with its own limitations. Ursula wants a kind of paradise of achieved desire, while Birkin distrusts himself, though not her, and knows that all paradises are lost.

Lawrence attempts to balance the harmonics of this pragmatic wholeness against the discord and mounting danger of the frenetic and finally numbing clash of irreconcilables in the agon of Gerald and Gudrun. When the novel concludes in a Strindbergian dance of death, Gerald wanders off into a landscape of snow and ice and welcomes his death there by freezing. It is just to observe that this is not so much suicide as it is Gudrun's assassination of her lover.

The German sculptor Loerke (the name alludes to the Old Norse god Loki, a mischief maker), homoerotic and deathly, has become friendly with Gudrun and infuriates Gerald by this apparent intimacy. Loerke asks her to join him in Dresden in an aesthetic relationship:

"You won't tell me where you will go?" he asked.

"Really and truly," she said, "I don't know. It depends which way the wind blows."

He looked at her quizzically, then he pursed up his lips, like Zephyrus, blowing across the snow.

"It goes towards Germany," he said.

"I believe so," she laughed.

Suddenly, they were aware of a vague white figure near them.

It was Gerald. Gudrun's heart leapt in sudden terror, profound terror. She rose to her feet.

"They told me where you were," came Gerald's voice, like a judgment in the whitish air of twilight.

"*Maria!* You come like a ghost," exclaimed Loerke.

Gerald did not answer. His presence was unnatural and ghostly to them.

Loerke shook the flask—then he held it inverted over the snow. Only a few brown drops trickled out.

"All gone!" he said.

To Gerald, the smallish, odd figure of the German was distinct and objective, as if seen through field glasses. And he disliked the small figure exceedingly, he wanted it removed.

Then Loerke rattled the box which held the biscuits.

"Biscuits there are still," he said.

And reaching from his seated posture in the sledge, he handed them to Gudrun. She fumbled, and took one. He would have held them to Gerald, but Gerald so definitely did not want to be offered a biscuit, that Loerke, rather vaguely, put the box aside. Then he took up the small bottle, and held it to the light.

"Also there is some Schnapps," he said to himself.

Then suddenly, he elevated the bottle gallantly in the air, a strange, grotesque figure leaning towards Gudrun, and said:

"Gnädiges Fräulein," he said, "wohl—"

There was a crack, the bottle was flying, Loerke had started back, the three stood quivering in violent emotion.

Loerke turned to Gerald, a devilish leer on his bright-skinned face.

"Well done!" he said, in a satirical demoniac frenzy. "C'est le sport, sans doute."

The next instant he was sitting ludicrously in the snow, Gerald's fist having rung against the side of his head. But Loerke pulled himself together, rose, quivering, looking full at Gerald, his body weak and furtive, but his eyes demoniacal with satire.

"Vive le héros, vive—"

But he flinched, as, in a black flash, Gerald's fist came upon him, banged into the other side of his head, and sent him aside like a broken straw.

But Gudrun moved forward. She raised her clenched hand

high, and brought it down, with a great downward stroke on to the face and on to the breast of Gerald.

A great astonishment burst upon him, as if the air had broken. Wide, wide his soul opened, in wonder, feeling the pain. Then it laughed, turning, with strong hands outstretched, at last to take the apple of his desire. At last he could finish his desire.

He took the throat of Gudrun between his hands, that were hard and indomitably powerful. And her throat was beautifully, so beautifully soft, save that, within, he could feel the slippery chords of her life. And this he crushed, this he could crush. What bliss! Oh what bliss, at last, what satisfaction, at last! The pure zest of satisfaction filled his soul. He was watching the unconsciousness come unto her swollen face, watching the eyes roll back. How ugly she was! What a fulfilment, what a satisfaction! How good this was, oh how good it was, what a God-given gratification, at last! He was unconscious of her fighting and struggling. The struggling was her reciprocal lustful passion in this embrace, the more violent it became, the greater the frenzy of delight, till the zenith was reached, the crisis, the struggle was overborne, her movement became softer, appeased.

Loerke roused himself on the snow, too dazed and hurt to get up. Only his eyes were conscious.

"Monsieur!" he said, in his thin, roused voice: "Quand vous aurez fini—"

A revulsion of contempt and disgust came over Gerald's soul. The disgust went to the very bottom of him, a nausea. Ah, what was he doing, to what depths was he letting himself go! As if he cared about her enough to kill her, to have her life on his hands!

A weakness ran over his body, a terrible relaxing, a thaw, a decay of strength. Without knowing, he had let go his grip, and Gudrun had fallen to her knees. Must he see, must he know?

A fearful weakness possessed him, his joints were turned to water. He drifted, as on a wind, veered, and went drifting away.

"I didn't want it, really," was the last confession of disgust in his soul, as he drifted up the slope, weak, finished, only sheering off unconsciously from any further contact. "I've had enough—I want to go to sleep. I've had enough." He was sunk under a sense of nausea.

He was weak, but he did not want to rest, he wanted to go on and on, to the end. Never again to stay, till he came to the end, that was all the desire that remained to him. So he drifted on and on, unconscious and weak, not thinking of anything, so long as he could keep in action.

The twilight spread a weird, unearthly light overhead, bluish-rose in colour, the cold blue night sank on the snow. In the valley below, behind, in the great bed of snow, were two small figures; Gudrun dropped on her knees, like one executed, and Loerke sitting propped up near her. That was all.

Gerald stumbled on up the slope of snow, in the bluish darkness, always climbing, always unconsciously climbing, weary though he was. On his left was a steep slope with black rocks and fallen masses of rock and veins of snow slashing in and about the blackness of rock, veins of snow slashing vaguely in and about the blackness of rock. Yet there was no sound, all this made no noise.

Earlier in the novel, having slapped Gerald after a kiss, Gudrun had vowed that she would give the last blow. Here she uses all her strength:

She raised her clenched hand high, and brought it down, with a great downward stroke on to the face and on to the breast of Gerald.

Perhaps she has saved the wretched Loerke, but she has accomplished her deepest desire: to murder Gerald. And he wants to be murdered, since he bears the mark of Cain, having killed his own brother in a gun accident in their youth. After nearly strangling Gudrun, Gerald chooses what for him is the only alternative:

He had come to the hollow basin of snow, surrounded by sheer slopes and precipices, out of which rose a track that brought one to the top of the mountain. But he wandered unconsciously, till he slipped and fell down, and as he fell something broke in his soul, and immediately he went to sleep.

Sometimes I think that this is the dark glory of *Women in Love*. Whatever Lawrence's intentions, Gerald remains unsympathetic, almost from start to finish. Gudrun frightens me, but it seems not possible to reject her. Her vitalism is negative yet remains suggestive of lost human possibilities, whereas Gerald's vacuity is prolonged and irreversible. Perhaps Lawrence was too severe at the close in denying Gudrun any affect except a poor irony and a contempt she delays turning upon herself. Birkin has come to see Gerald's body and asks Gudrun what he can say to the authorities, if they require explanation:

Gudrun looked up at him, white, childlike, mute with trouble.

"There weren't even any words," she said. "He knocked Loerke down and stunned him, he half strangled me, then he went away."

To herself she was saying:

"A pretty little sample of the eternal triangle!" And she turned ironically away, because she knew that the fight had been between Gerald and herself and that the presence of the third party was a mere contingency—an inevitable contingency perhaps, but a contingency none the less. But let them have it as an example of the eternal triangle, the trinity of hate. It would be simpler for them.

Birkin went away, his manner cold and abstracted. But she knew he would do things for her, nevertheless, he would see her through. She smiled slightly to herself, with contempt. Let him do the work, since he was so extremely *good* at looking after other people.

Something in me rebels at this debasement of Gudrun. I prefer to remember her dancing like a maenad in front of the horned cattle and frightening them away.

CHAPTER 35

Ulysses (1922)

JAMES JOYCE

THE MAJOR NOVELS of the twentieth century are Marcel
Proust's *In Search of Lost Time,* which was published in sec-
tions from 1913 to 1927, Proust himself dying in 1922 at the age of
fifty-one, and the *Ulysses* of James Joyce, composed between 1917
and 1922. Joyce died in 1941, not quite fifty-nine. I do not believe
that Proust ever read Joyce, though they met at one Parisian dinner,
and complained to each other about their mutual bad health. Joyce
read *Swann's Way* (1913) and thought it was quite ordinary, but nevertheless attended Proust's funeral.

I can think of only one peer of Proust and *Ulysses,* and that has
to be *Finnegans Wake,* published by Joyce in 1939 after seventeen
years of extraordinary labor. If forced to choose between Proust,
Ulysses, and the *Wake,* I would be very unhappy. Emotionally, I am
more turned inside out by *In Search of Lost Time,* but the *Wake* is
hilarious, once you have read it a few times, and *Ulysses* has a richness that all but rivals Dante and Shakespeare. Readers are likelier
to absorb Proust and *Ulysses* than to accommodate the *Wake.* I hope
to reread all of *Finnegans Wake* at least once more ere I depart, but
I reread Proust and *Ulysses* several times a year.

There are many ways to read through Joyce's *Ulysses.* It depicts
the day of June 16, 1904, with Leopold Bloom, aged thirty-eight,

as its protagonist. In the world's literary calendar this is known as Bloomsday, and was also the day of the first date between Nora Barnacle and James Joyce, who left Dublin together for the Continent, remained partners, and had two children, Giorgio and Lucia. Giorgio attempted a career as a professional singer but wisely fell in love with an American heiress and was able to treat singing as an avocation. Lucia was schizophrenic and had to be permanently institutionalized. Rather reluctantly, Nora and Joyce were formally married in 1931.

Leopold Bloom had a Hungarian Jewish father, Rudolf Virag, who changed his name to Rudolph Bloom and converted to Protestantism when he married Ellen Higgins. Leopold or Poldy, as we will join Joyce in calling him, was raised a Protestant and therefore was uncircumcised. Poldy converted to Roman Catholicism to marry Molly Tweedy, the astonishing Molly Bloom of the novel. Rudolph Bloom died by his own hand. Molly and Poldy have a daughter, Milly, but their son, Rudy, died only eleven days old.

Poldy, since both his mother and grandmother were Christian, would not be considered Jewish by the Talmud. This becomes a rather complex matter. Though he has been both an unbelieving Protestant and a faithless Catholic, Poldy considers himself to be Jewish, and all of Dublin regards him as such. Why did James Joyce want some kind of Jewish identity for his Ulysses?

The possible answer, as most critics agree, is that James Joyce left Ireland for the European continent in 1904 with Nora Barnacle, and lived abroad until his death in 1941. Most of his life was spent in voluntary exile from Dublin. Yet all of his writing centers on Dublin and its citizens. Joyce frequently thought of himself as the new Dante, and the bitterness of Dante's forced exile from Florence became the model for his life and work, except that James Joyce refused to yield to bitterness. Poldy Bloom feels at home in Dublin, yet his fellow citizens consider him alien, a Wandering Jew.

By abandoning Dublin, Joyce also renounced the Roman Catholicism into which he had been born and baptized. He had even less use for Protestantism and in no way can be regarded as religious, either in temperament or in conviction. Joyce emulated William Blake in casting out both priest and king, but Blake always regarded himself as a Christian even if he was in a sect of one. Poldy knows almost nothing about his ancestral Jewish tradition. He is as secular as James Joyce and William Shakespeare. At the deepest level of *Ulysses*, Poldy *is* Shakespeare and Joyce. This is Joyce's design. Though he admired writers as diverse as Daniel Defoe and Gustave Flaubert, William Wordsworth and Percy Bysshe Shelley, Joyce consciously staged an agon with Dante and with Shakespeare. His aspirations were indeed Homeric; he desired to make a third with Dante and Shakespeare or even to surpass them.

I cannot think of another writer that ambitious, with the likely exceptions of Milton and of Tolstoy. Figures as grand as Goethe, Pushkin, Victor Hugo, Balzac, Manzoni, Jane Austen, Dickens, Melville, George Eliot, Proust, Kafka, and Yeats judiciously held back from too direct an emulation of Dante or of Shakespeare.

To rival Dante and Shakespeare, you have to remake language and change modes of representation. I am hardly competent to judge whether James Joyce so fulfilled his own project as to join Dante and Shakespeare on the final heights. But if not Joyce, then who? Once you have fully enjoyed the reading of *Dubliners, A Portrait of the Artist as a Young Man, Exiles, Ulysses,* even *Finnegans Wake,* you can begin to consider the larger contexts of Joyce's literary desires.

There are three very good discussions of Joyce's relation to Dante. The first is *Joyce and Dante: The Shaping Imagination* by Mary T. Reynolds (1981). I have the happiest memories of many teas shared with Mary Reynolds and Mary Ellmann during the years they were at Yale. Both were witty, kind, brilliant women considerably older than I, and I was glad to sit in their company and learn. Mary Reynolds's study of Joyce and Dante meditates upon the paternal figures of the *Commedia* and their resurrection in the panoply of Joycean works. Joyce found precedent for his own rebellion against Catholicism in Dante's own independence of thought and of figuration. Another vivid treatise is Lucia Boldrini's *Joyce, Dante, and the Poetics of Literary Relations* (2001), which studies Dante's influence on *Finnegans Wake.* More recently, there is James Robinson's *Joyce's Dante* (2016), which traces the unorthodox Dante bequeathed to Joyce by the nineteenth-century tradition that moves from Shelley and Byron to Dante Gabriel Rossetti.

Anglo-American Dante scholarship of the last few generations tends to give us a theological Dante, a poet more intent on Aquinas and Augustine than on his own literary agon with Brunetto Latini, Guido Cavalcanti, and Guido Guinizelli. The latter was the inventor of the lyrical "sweet new style" that Dante acknowledged as one starting point. Cavalcanti was Dante's best friend and a strong influence upon him; Brunetto Latini was his teacher and the author of the *Tesoretto* or *Tesoro,* which served Dante as an example for the *Commedia.*

Ernst Robert Curtius in his *European Literature and the Latin Middle Ages,* translated into English in 1953, was my own starting point in reading Dante as a poet and not as a theologian. Beatrice is granted by Dante a high place in the Catholic scheme of salvation. She will ultimately inspire not only Dante but all Roman Catholic believers to take the true path. So great was Dante's achievement that in time the Church was glad to subsume him. Still, as Curtius insists, the glorification of Beatrice is either heresy or myth. The question is: of what kind? Curtius answers that this glorification is clearly related to Gnosticism, perhaps not in origin but certainly as a scheme or construction.

James Joyce, whose rebellion against the Church was permanent, evidently found in Dante a difference from orthodoxy that could aid the young Irish writer in his quest toward identity with the culminating poet of the Latin tradition.

Dante had a necessarily distorted sense of Virgil's place in that tradition. The poet of the *Commedia* had never heard of Lucretius, whose Epicurean masterpiece, *De rerum natura,* is an overwhelming influence upon Virgil's *Aeneid.* It was not until 1417 that a complete Lucretius was rediscovered in a German monastery. As a lover of both poems, I cannot reread the *Aeneid* without the sensation that Virgil had a copy of Lucretius in front of him, confirming his Epicurean stance toward human suffering. Dante's Virgil is Christianized into a seeker after grace, but in Dante's scheme the historical Virgil belongs in the *Inferno,* side by side with the great Farinata, who stands upright in his flaming tomb, as if of hell he had a great disdain.

Lucretius has a way of contaminating later writers, from Marlowe and Shakespeare on through Shelley and Tennyson and culminating in *Ulysses* and *Finnegans Wake.* Poldy has not read Lucretius, but his stance toward suffering and death is Epicurean and seems to be consonant with that of James Joyce. No labels will work, for either *Ulysses* or the *Wake*. You cannot even describe Poldy's epic as Homeric despite its scaffolding. Perhaps the only word that will work is "completeness." Leopold Bloom, like Odysseus, is the complete man and, like his Dublin, he is comic rather than tragic, except that he appears to be the most humane individual in his world.

When I was very young, I read and was impressed by Aldous Huxley's essay "Tragedy and the Whole Truth" (1931). I have not reread it for more than half a century, but I remember the essential point: in the *Odyssey*, after losing a number of their shipmates to various hazards, Odysseus and the other survivors mourn briefly, and then turn to their meat and wine and subsequent sleep. In Athenian and Shakespearean tragedy, this wholeness would not work. James Joyce in *Ulysses* desires to give us common truths for uncommon readers. He remarked to Frank Budgen that, however rich the language of *Ulysses* and the *Wake* became, what he meant to convey was quite simple. There is some truth in that, particularly in *Ulysses*, but in the *Wake* the disproportion between the extraordinary language and the simple actions may be a permanent impediment to a wider readership.

I intend to say something that may be helpful about the *Wake* later in this chapter, but here I return to *Ulysses*. Many who love the novel set highest the "Circe," the midnight hallucinatory vision of the Nighttown whorehouse, or the "Penelope," the internal monologue of Molly Bloom in the small hours. I would not quarrel with such judgments, but I care most for the opening "Telemachus," set at 8:00 a.m. in the Martello Tower, for which Stephen Dedalus has paid the rent, while the egregious Malachi (Buck) Mulligan secures the key and so dispossesses Stephen. Buck Mulligan has given a dubious immortality to Oliver St. John Gogarty, who is now remembered only for Joyce's exuberant portrait of his former friend and drinking companion. Gogarty died in New York City in 1957, aged seventy-nine. When he abandoned Ireland, embittered by lost lawsuits and the burning of his house by the IRA, he went to London, but then on to the United States, leaving his family behind him.

Until his various debacles, Gogarty enjoyed a remarkable career in Ireland, as a literary figure, a politician, a surgeon, and an athlete. He was close to W. B. Yeats and George Moore, as well as to Arthur Griffith and Michael Collins, important figures in the Irish struggle against England. When civil war ignited Ireland, Gogarty became an Irish Free State senator and had to endure the death of Griffith and the assassination of Michael Collins. In 1922, the year *Ulysses* was published, the IRA kidnapped Gogarty with the intent of murdering him. By wit and stamina, he escaped, leaped into the River Liffey, and, being a champion swimmer, had no trouble getting to safety. Famously, he promised the Liffey two swans and kept his word.

I met Gogarty only once, in about 1955, at the White Horse Tavern in Greenwich Village, where I enjoyed his somewhat intoxicated eloquence and recitations. And yet I could see in him, even in his seventies, the traits of the immortal Buck Mulligan. He was fierce, ribald, unctuous, yet somehow disquieting. I had read some of his poems, none of them impressive, and the rollicking *As I Was Going Down Sackville Street*, a fictionalized memoir in which Yeats, Joyce, and other Irish literary and political notables are caricatured. The book eventually ruined Gogarty financially, as he was sued by one of the Sinclair brothers, Dublin art dealers who were Jewish. The case was decided against him, since clearly he had slandered them in some rather bad anti-Semitic verses, not worth quoting here. A charming element in the trial was the testimony of the young Samuel Beckett, one of whose aunts had been married to a Sinclair brother. A lawyer for Gogarty referred to Beckett as "the bawd and blasphemer from Paris." As someone privileged to have met Beckett, just twice and briefly, in Paris and in New York City, I have to be charmed by the description. Beckett was gentle, kind, sadly noble, and had been a hero of the French Resistance against the Nazis.

I come at last to the beautiful opening of *Ulysses*, leading off the "Telemachus" section:

> Stately, plump Buck Mulligan came from the stairhead, bearing a bowl of lather on which a mirror and a razor lay crossed. A yellow dressinggown, ungirdled, was sustained gently behind him by the mild morning air. He held the bowl aloft and intoned:
> —*Introibo ad altare Dei.*
> Halted, he peered down the dark winding stairs and called up coarsely:
> —Come up, Kinch! Come up, you fearful jesuit.
> Solemnly he came forward and mounted the round gunrest. He faced about and blessed gravely thrice the tower, the sur-

rounding country and the awaking mountains. Then, catching sight of Stephen Dedalus, he bent towards him and made rapid crosses in the air, gurgling in his throat and shaking his head. Stephen Dedalus, displeased and sleepy, leaned his arms on the top of the staircase and looked coldly at the shaking gurgling face that blessed him, equine in its length, and at the light untonsured hair, grained and hued like pale oak.

Buck Mulligan peeped an instant under the mirror and then covered the bowl smartly.

—Back to barracks! he said sternly.

He added in a preacher's tone:

—For this, O dearly beloved, is the genuine Christine: body and soul and blood and ouns. Slow music, please. Shut your eyes, gents. One moment. A little trouble about those white corpuscles. Silence, all.

He peered sideways up and gave a long slow whistle of call, then paused awhile in rapt attention, his even white teeth glistening here and there with gold points. Chrysostomos. Two strong shrill whistles answered through the calm.

—Thanks, old chap, he cried briskly. That will do nicely. Switch off the current, will you?

He skipped off the gunrest and looked gravely at his watcher, gathering about his legs the loose folds of his gown. The plump shadowed face and sullen oval jowl recalled a prelate, patron of arts in the middle ages. A pleasant smile broke quietly over his lips.

—The mockery of it, he said gaily. Your absurd name, an ancient Greek!

He pointed his finger in friendly jest and went over to the parapet, laughing to himself. Stephen Dedalus stepped up, followed him wearily halfway and sat down on the edge of the gunrest, watching him still as he propped his mirror on the parapet, dipped the brush in the bowl and lathered cheeks and neck.   (*Ulysses*, Everyman's Library Edition)

To describe the splendor of "Telemachus" is for me a difficult critical task. I purchased my first copy of *Ulysses* in the Cornell bookstore in September 1947. At once I fell in love with the words "Stately, plump Buck Mulligan," rolling them over and over on my tongue. They felt and still feel delicious. Even in this opening passage, Joyce conveys an amiable distaste for the Buck. The tone, however, flows smoothly as the contrast between Stephen and Mulligan is vividly etched. One hears in the Buck a condescending affection mixed with a wary respect for Dedalus. In Stephen's silence we hear the exile and cunning he will come to embrace.

—Tell me, Mulligan, Stephen said quietly.

—Yes, my love?

—How long is Haines going to stay in this tower?

Buck Mulligan showed a shaven cheek over his right shoulder.

—God, isn't he dreadful? he said frankly. A ponderous Saxon. He thinks you're not a gentleman. God, these bloody English! Bursting with money and indigestion. Because he comes from Oxford. You know, Dedalus, you have the real Oxford manner. He can't make you out. O, my name for you is the best: Kinch, the knife-blade.

He shaved warily over his chin.

—He was raving all night about a black panther, Stephen said. Where is his guncase?

—A woful lunatic! Mulligan said. Were you in a funk?

—I was, Stephen said with energy and growing fear. Out here in the dark with a man I don't know raving and moaning to himself about shooting a black panther. You saved men from drowning. I'm not a hero, however. If he stays on here I am off.

"Kinch" is a Scottish word for a loop or noose of a rope. Presumably, Mulligan associates "noose" and "knife-blade," again intimating a certain fear of Stephen's capacities. Gogarty had saved four men from drowning, but Joyce was as peaceful as his Poldy and avoided violence. Stephen has nowhere to go but chooses departure anyway, distrustful of Mulligan's professed friendship:

—Look at yourself, he said, you dreadful bard!

Stephen bent forward and peered at the mirror held out to him, cleft by a crooked crack, hair on end. As he and others see me. Who chose this face for me? This dogsbody to rid of vermin. It asks me too.

—I pinched it out of the skivvy's room, Buck Mulligan said. It does her all right. The aunt always keeps plain-looking servants for Malachi. Lead him not into temptation. And her name is Ursula.

Laughing again, he brought the mirror away from Stephen's peering eyes.

—The rage of Caliban at not seeing his face in a mirror, he said. If Wilde were only alive to see you.

Drawing back and pointing, Stephen said with bitterness:

—It is a symbol of Irish art. The cracked lookingglass of a servant.

Oscar Wilde, in the preface to his *The Picture of Dorian Gray* (1891), had remarked: "The nineteenth century dislike of Realism is the rage of Caliban seeing his own face in a glass. The nineteenth century dislike of Romanticism is the rage of Caliban not seeing his own face in a glass." Joyce and Wilde both admired Walter Pater, who gave Joyce the idea of "epiphanies," sudden moments in which the commonplace flamed into visionary perception. Proust took his epiphanies from the example of John Ruskin, whom Pater, in an agonistic spirit, resented. Joyce surmounts even Oscar in his splendidly bitter: "It is a symbol of Irish art. The cracked lookingglass of a servant." But, then, James Joyce was the master agonist, daring to contend even against Dante and Shakespeare for the foremost place.

The "Nestor" section begins with Stephen as gentle and reluctant schoolmaster and then, more memorably, passes to his colloquy with Mr. Deasy, the Scottish headmaster of this Dalkey school, not far from Dublin. Mr. Deasy is a dreadful old man who loathes women, Jews, and all those who do not pay their way:

—Mark my words, Mr Dedalus, he said. England is in the hands of the jews. In all the highest places: her finance, her press. And they are the signs of a nation's decay. Wherever they gather they eat up the nation's vital strength. I have seen it coming these years. As sure as we are standing here the jew merchants are already at their work of destruction. Old England is dying.

He stepped swiftly off, his eyes coming to blue life as they passed a broad sunbeam. He faced about and back again.

—Dying, he said again, if not dead by now.

The harlot's cry from street to street
Shall weave old England's winding sheet.

His eyes open wide in vision stared sternly across the sunbeam in which he halted.

—A merchant, Stephen said, is one who buys cheap and sells dear, jew or gentile, is he not?

—They sinned against the light, Mr Deasy said gravely. And you can see the darkness in their eyes. And that is why they are wanderers on the earth to this day.

On the steps of the Paris Stock Exchange the gold-skinned men quoting prices on their gemmed fingers. Gabbles of geese. They swarmed loud, uncouth about the temple, their heads thickplotting under maladroit silk hats. Not theirs: these clothes, this speech, these gestures. Their full slow eyes belied the words, the gestures eager and unoffending, but knew the rancours massed about them and knew their zeal was vain. Vain patience to heap and hoard. Time surely would scatter all. A hoard heaped by the roadside: plundered and passing on. Their eyes knew the years of wandering and, patient, knew the dishonours of their flesh.

—Who has not? Stephen said.

—What do you mean? Mr Deasy asked.

He came forward a pace and stood by the table. His underjaw fell sideways open uncertainly. Is this old wisdom? He waits to hear from me.

—History, Stephen said, is a nightmare from which I am trying to awake.

From the playfield the boys raised a shout. A whirring whistle: goal. What if that nightmare gave you a back kick?

—The ways of the Creator are not our ways, Mr Deasy said. All history moves towards one great goal, the manifestation of God.

Stephen jerked his thumb towards the window, saying:

—That is God.

Hooray! Ay! Whrrwhee!

—What? Mr Deasy asked.

—A shout in the street, Stephen answered, shrugging his shoulders.

Mr Deasy looked down and held for a while the wings of his nose tweaked between his fingers. Looking up again he set them free.

—I am happier than you are, he said. We have committed many errors and many sins. A woman brought sin into the world. For a woman who was no better than she should be, Helen, the runaway wife of Menelaus, ten years the Greeks made war on Troy. A faithless wife first brought the strangers to our shore here, MacMurrough's wife and her leman O'Rourke, prince of Breffni. A woman too brought Parnell low. Many errors, many failures but not the one sin. I am a struggler now at the end of my days. But I will fight for the right till the end.

For Ulster will fight
And Ulster will be right.

Stephen raised the sheets in his hand.

—Well, sir, he began.

—I foresee, Mr Deasy said, that you will not remain here very long at this work. You were not born to be a teacher, I think. Perhaps I am wrong.

—A learner rather, Stephen said.

It is admirable how calmly and evenly Joyce paces this. Though he is dreadful, Deasy is accepted as what he is, however little. This is certainly not the Stephen of *A Portrait of the Artist as a Young Man*, who experienced the temptation of becoming a Jesuit priest and rejected it for the hazardous aesthetic flight of a new Icarus, as though the father could be his own son. William Blake haunts Stephen, and Joyce echoes him throughout *Ulysses* and the *Wake*. Painfully wincing at Deasy's anti-Semitism, Stephen remembers a couplet from William Blake's Notebook poem "Auguries of Innocence":

The harlot's cry from street to street
Shall weave old England's winding sheet

To Mr. Deasy's "They sinned against the light," Stephen replies, "Who has not?" A vision, a kind of negative epiphany, suddenly possesses Stephen:

On the steps of the Paris Stock Exchange the gold-skinned men quoting prices on their gemmed fingers. Gabbles of geese. They swarmed loud, uncouth about the temple, their heads thick-plotting under maladroit silk hats. Not theirs: these clothes, this speech, these gestures. Their full slow eyes belied the words, the gestures eager and unoffending, but knew the rancours massed about them and knew their zeal was vain. Vain patience to heap and hoard. Time surely would scatter all. A hoard heaped by the roadside: plundered and passing on. Their eyes knew their years of wandering and, patient, knew the dishonours of their flesh.

It is not just exile that informs this vista; even in 2018, this retains relevance. My mind wanders to the tragic story of Paul Léon, Joyce's unpaid secretary and adviser, a learned lawyer who had mastered seven languages, and who risked his life by returning to Nazi-occupied Paris so as to save and bring away Joyce's papers. Eventually, Léon was seized by the Nazis and sent off to perish in a death camp. Samuel Beckett, who was close to Léon, intimated that he joined the French Resistance because of this atrocity.

With ironic courtesy, Stephen attempts to rid himself of Deasy, but not without being afflicted by a final nastiness:

—Good morning, sir, Stephen said again, bowing to his bent back.

He went out by the open porch and down the gravel path under the trees, hearing the cries of voices and crack of sticks from the playfield. The lions couchant on the pillars as he passed out through the gate; toothless terrors. Still I will help him in his fight. Mulligan will dub me a new name: the bullock-befriending bard.

—Mr Dedalus!

Running after me. No more letters, I hope.

—Just one moment.

—Yes, sir, Stephen said, turning back at the gate.

Mr Deasy halted, breathing hard and swallowing his breath.

—I just wanted to say, he said. Ireland, they say, has the honour of being the only country which never persecuted the jews. Do you know that? No. And do you know why?

He frowned sternly on the bright air.

—Why, sir? Stephen asked, beginning to smile.

—Because she never let them in, Mr Deasy said solemnly.

A coughball of laughter leaped from his throat dragging after it a rattling chain of phlegm. He turned back quickly, coughing, laughing, his lifted arms waving to the air.

—She never let them in, he cried again through his laughter as he stamped on gaitered feet over the gravel of the path. That's why.

On his wise shoulders through the checkerwork of leaves the sun flung spangles, dancing coins.

The dancing coins return us to Stephen's contempt for much-needed money, and Deasy's worship of cash. I remember Christopher Smart's description of coins as "dead matter with the stamp of human vanity" *(Jubilate Agno)*, though I do not believe Joyce ever read Smart's *Jubilate*, since it was first published in 1939. Joyce endows Stephen with a knifelike edge as a maker of apothegms: "—History, Stephen said, is a nightmare from which I am trying to awake."

Justly famous, that is followed by an even deeper slash into credulity:

—The ways of the Creator are not our ways, Mr Deasy said. All history moves towards one great goal, the manifestation of God.

Stephen jerked his thumb towards the window, saying:

—That is God.

Hooray! Ay! Whrrwhee!

—What? Mr Deasy asked.

—A shout in the street, Stephen answered, shrugging his shoulders.

The "Proteus" episode follows, in which Stephen walks on the beach at 11:00 a.m., brooding on the tides and on his predicament. In the fourth book of the *Odyssey*, Menelaus tells the story of his capture of Proteus, the old man of the sea, on the island of Pharos. Menelaus and his men rush upon Proteus and hold him fast, despite his willed transformations into a lion, a snake, a panther, a boar, running water, a flowering tree. The wily Proteus yields and prophesies that Menelaus will not die but will be taken to the Elysian Fields, reserved for those descended from the gods.

Stephen's meditation on the strand begins with a clear summoning of the great mystic Jacob Boehme (1575–1624), who composed *The Signature of All Things* (1621), which William Blake read and partly absorbed, partly rejected, and which James Joyce evidently read and admired. In Stephen's beach reverie it is Boehme, more than Bishop Berkeley, who is prevalent:

> Ineluctable modality of the visible: at least that if no more, thought through my eyes. Signatures of all things I am here to read, seaspawn and seawrack, the nearing tide, that rusty boot. Snotgreen, bluesilver, rust: coloured signs. Limits of the diaphane. But he adds: in bodies. Then he was aware of them bodies before of them coloured. How? By knocking his sconce against them, sure. Go easy. Bald he was and a millionaire, *maestro di color che sanno.* Limit of the diaphane in. Why in? Diaphane, adiaphane. If you can put your five fingers through it it is a gate, if not a door. Shut your eyes and see.

This rich passage is an epitome of Stephen's and of Joyce's minds. Intricately it mixes Jacob Boehme's idea of correspondences between the physical and the spiritual with a good dose of Aristotle, adding a dash of Dr. Samuel Johnson's kicking a stone to cast aside Bishop Berkeley's Idealism: "I refute it thus." Later legend attributed baldness and enormous wealth to Aristotle, described by Dante as the "master of those who know": *maestro di color che sanno.* Dr. Johnson's dictionary is parodied in the pragmatic difference between gate and door. And yet what matters most here is transparency and its limits, an Aristotelian testing of transcendence against objects.

> Stephen closed his eyes to hear his boots crush crackling wrack and shells. You are walking through it howsomever. I am, a stride at a time. A very short space of time through very short times of space. Five, six: the *nacheinander.* Exactly: and that is the ineluctable modality of the audible. Open your eyes. No.

Jesus! If I fell over a cliff that beetles o'er his base, fell through the *nebeneinander* ineluctably. I am getting on nicely in the dark. My ash sword hangs at my side. Tap with it: they do. My two feet in his boots are at the ends of his legs, *nebeneinander*. Sounds solid: made by the mallet of *Los Demiurgos*. Am I walking into eternity along Sandymount strand? Crush, crack, crick, crick. Wild sea money. Dominie Deasy kens them a'.

> *Won't you come to Sandymount,*
> *Madeline the mare?*

Rhythm begins, you see. I hear. A catalectic tetrameter of iambs marching. No, agallop: *deline the mare*.

Open your eyes now. I will. One moment. Has all vanished since? If I open and am for ever in the black adiaphane. *Basta!* I will see if I can see.

See now. There all the time without you: and ever shall be, world without end.

"The black adiaphane" is the opaque. Lessing's *Laocoön* (1766) provides Stephen with his *nacheinander,* or one thing after another, the audible being temporal and the visible spatial. Eyes tight shut, the Irish magister-to-be thinks of Hamlet being warned not to follow the Ghost lest he be led to a sudden cliff. Wearing Buck Mulligan's shoes and trousers, Stephen plays with the *nebeneinander* or side-by-side aesthetic idea of space. The old Blakean in me always thrills to the invocation of Los the artificer, but Blake might not have been happy with Stephen's identification of his Real Man the Imagination with the Gnostic Demiurge, who at once makes and deforms the world. Still, Blake's spirit is with Stephen as he walks into eternity along the strand:

Spouse and helpmate of Adam Kadmon: Heva, naked Eve. She had no navel. Gaze. Belly without blemish, bulging big, a buckler of taut vellum, no, whiteheaped corn, orient and immortal, standing from everlasting to everlasting. Womb of sin.

Wombed in sin darkness I was too, made not begotten. By them, the man with my voice and my eyes and a ghostwoman with ashes on her breath. They clasped and sundered, did the coupler's will. From before the ages He willed me and now may not will me away or ever. A *lex eterna* stays about him. Is that then the divine substance wherein Father and Son are consubstantial? Where is poor dear Arius to try conclusions? Warring his life long on the contransmagnificandjewbangtantiality. Illstarred heresiarch. In a Greek watercloset he breathed his last: *euthanasia*. With beaded mitre and with crozier, stalled upon his throne, widower of a widowed see, with upstiffed *omophorion*, with clotted hinderparts.

Airs romped round him, nipping and eager airs. They are coming, waves. The whitemaned seahorses, champing, brightwindbridled, the steeds of Mananaan.

Joyce's knowledge of Kabbalah remains a puzzle to me. Both in *Ulysses* and the *Wake* he intimates more detailed and accurate notions of Jewish mysticism than were available to him in the various esotericists of the late nineteenth and early twentieth centuries. Perhaps his genius intuited what it needed to know. In the first paragraph quoted above, the Adam Kadmon is the Divine Man of Kabbalah, androgynous and containing all things in heaven and on earth in himself, as William Blake remarked. "Orient and immortal" is a clear reference to the most famous passage in Thomas Traherne's *Centuries of Meditations:*

The corn was orient and immortal wheat, which never should be reaped, nor was ever sown. I thought it had stood from everlasting to everlasting.

Stephen's meditation proceeds to mix profundity with jesting in regard to the unfortunate end of Arius (256–336), who died in Constantinople in a Greek watercloset, his bowels collapsing. Arius argued that the Father preceded and was of a higher substance than the Son, a view eventually ruled heretical by the Church. It fascinates me that God, in whom Joyce did not believe, having made and not begot Stephen, is bound by eternal law never to end him, so that Joyce becomes a Christ or Messiah. Hamlet, always near in Stephen's consciousness, is echoed throughout this passage. The steeds of Mananaan are the waves, since he is the Celtic god of the sea, a Proteus figure.

In the episode "Scylla and Charybdis," set in the Dublin library at two in the afternoon, Stephen expounds his splendidly outrageous theory of Hamlet, in which he himself says he does not believe. Richard Ellmann, in his definitive biography of Joyce, nevertheless insists that Joyce himself never abandoned the theory.

—A deathsman of the soul Robert Greene called him, Stephen said. Not for nothing was he a butcher's son, wielding the sledded poleaxe and spitting in his palms. Nine lives are taken off for his father's one. Our Father who art in purgatory. Khaki Hamlets don't hesitate to shoot. The bloodboltered shambles in act five is a forecast of the concentration camp sung by Mr Swinburne.

Cranly, I his mute orderly, following battles from afar.

Whelps and dams of murderous foes whom none
But we had spared...

Between the Saxon smile and yankee yawp. The devil and the deep sea.

—He will have it that *Hamlet* is a ghoststory, John Eglinton said for Mr Best's behoof. Like the fat boy in Pickwick he wants to make our flesh creep.

List! List! O List!

My flesh hears him: creeping, hears.

If thou didst ever...

—What is a ghost? Stephen said with tingling energy. One who has faded into impalpability through death, through absence, through change of manners. Elizabethan London lay as far from Stratford as corrupt Paris lies from virgin Dublin. Who is the ghost from *limbo patrum*, returning to the world that has forgotten him? Who is King Hamlet?

John Eglinton shifted his spare body, leaning back to judge. Lifted.

—It is this hour of a day in mid June, Stephen said, begging with a swift glance their hearing. The flag is up on the playhouse by the bankside. The bear Sackerson growls in the pit near it, Paris garden. Canvasclimbers who sailed with Drake chew their sausages among the groundlings.

Local colour. Work in all you know. Make them accomplices.

—Shakespeare has left the huguenot's house in Silver street and walks by the swanmews along the riverbank. But he does not stay to feed the pen chivying her game of cygnets towards the rushes. The swan of Avon has other thoughts.

Composition of place. Ignatius Loyola, make haste to help me!

—The play begins. A player comes on under the shadow, made up in the castoff mail of a court buck, a wellset man with a bass voice. It is the ghost, the king, a king and no king, and the player is Shakespeare who has studied *Hamlet* all the years of his life which were not vanity in order to play the part of the spectre. He speaks the words to Burbage, the young player who stands before him beyond the rack of cerecloth, calling him by a name:

Hamlet, I am thy father's spirit,

bidding him list. To a son he speaks, the son of his soul, the prince, young Hamlet and to the son of his body, Hamnet Shakespeare, who has died in Stratford that his namesake may live for ever.

Is it possible that that player Shakespeare, a ghost by absence, and in the vesture of buried Denmark, a ghost by death, speaking his own words to his own son's name (had Hamnet Shakespeare lived he would have been prince Hamlet's twin), is it possible, I want to know, or probable that he did not draw or foresee the logical conclusion of those premises: you are the dispossessed son: I am the murdered father: your mother is the guilty queen, Ann Shakespeare, born Hathaway?

A detailed exegesis of all the allusions here can be found in the endlessly useful *Notes for Joyce* by Don Gifford and Robert J. Seidman (1974), but I wish to emphasize only a few points. Joyce may have deliberately lost count or may have preferred the number nine. Hamlet is responsible for eight deaths, including his own: he stabs Polonius through a curtain; viciously rejects Ophelia, thus driving her to suicide; insouciantly sends Rosencrantz and Guildenstern to certain execution in England; and in the final poisoned sword and poisoned cup scene stabs Laertes, forces Claudius to drink of the cup that has just slain Gertrude, and with a flourish stabs Claudius also.

.   .   .

Everybody has his own Hamlet. Shakespeare created the only literary character who can compete with the J writer's Yahweh, the Gospel of Mark's Jesus, Dante's Pilgrim, and Don Quixote. Stephen's Hamlet, always affirmed by Joyce himself, is a study in the mystery of the fiction of fatherhood. Who is Hamlet's father? Since we do not know when the sexual relationship between Gertrude and Claudius commenced, is it King Hamlet, now a Ghost, or is it the usurper and murderer Claudius? Hamlet does not know, and though he says nothing about this question, he rarely says exactly what he thinks, and he does not often speak without intentional irony. Why does he not slay Claudius deliberately, long before the end of this enormous play? Patricide might render anyone recalcitrant and inhibit action. And yet I scarcely believe that is the principal cause of Hamlet's delay. He does not want to be the protagonist of one more revenger's tragedy. Anyone can stab a usurper; the most capacious consciousness in all of Western literature is too large for the bloodiness that mars and trivializes the early *Titus Andronicus,* a drama that I can interpret only as a deliberate parody of Thomas Kyd, John Marston, and others.

Stephen's fiction that Shakespeare was cuckolded by all three of his brothers with Anne Hathaway is extravagant and rather silly. But the identification of Shakespeare with the Ghost, a part we know he played, and of Prince Hamlet with Hamnet Shakespeare, who died at the age of eleven, is more troublesome. *Hamlet* may have been composed as early as 1599, three years after the death of young Hamnet. There was an earlier *Hamlet,* staged in 1587, of which we have the text. I have always agreed with Peter Alexander that this first *Hamlet* was by William Shakespeare and not Thomas Kyd. It makes a difference, because the 1587 *Hamlet* failed and was mocked by its audience. In writing his second *Hamlet,* Shakespeare sought vindication and earned it by what in time became his longest and most famous drama.

The uncut *Hamlet,* if you combine the Second Quarto (1604) with the First Folio (1623), runs to about four thousand lines. I have never seen it performed at that length, though such performances have taken place. Played without intermission, it might take up to five hours, depending upon the pacing of the director.

One way of describing James Joyce's audacity is to ask: who else has had the authority and ambition to subvert *Hamlet* and all, indeed, of William Shakespeare's creation? The essayist and poet Robert Atwan, in a generous review of my sprawling *Shakespeare: The Invention of the Human* (1998), gently chided me as forsaking my customary reliance on Milton's Satan and Blake's *The Marriage of Heaven and Hell*: "In Shakespeare has he found a master who finally makes subversion unthinkable?" I suppose my answer has to be "Yes." But I am a teacher by profession and not a poet or a novelist. Of all post-Shakespearean writers, James Joyce alone was able to remake language as Homer, Dante, Cervantes, and Shakespeare had done before him. Proust, master of endless sentences, nevertheless does not attempt the impossible task of purifying the language of Flaubert.

Joyce did not so much seek to subvert Shakespeare as totally to absorb him and transmute that process into something rich and strange, yet cognitively far simpler than Shakespeare. There is a Joycean ambivalence toward Shakespeare that sometimes risks absurdity. Joyce considered Ibsen a much better dramatist than Shakespeare and said this could be proved by comparing *When We Dead Awaken* to anything by the English Bard. There is also the question of creative envy. As he composed the *Wake,* Joyce brooded and compared that book's lack of a ready audience to Shakespeare's situation at the Globe Theatre.

In 1912, Joyce gave a series of a dozen lectures on *Hamlet* to a paying audience in Trieste. As far as I know, we do not have the texts of what he said. But evidently his concern was almost entirely with language, a kind of word-by-word explication of etymologies, puns, and turns of phrase. By then Joyce described Shakespeare as an Italianate Englishman, taking his protagonists from continental sources. That is a partial truth only. Yet Stephen in the library scene of *Ulysses* gives us a series of fascinating speculations:

—There is, I feel in the words, some goad of the flesh driving him into a new passion, a darker shadow of the first, darkening even his own understanding of himself. A like fate awaits him and the two rages commingle in a whirlpool.

They list. And in the porches of their ears I pour.

—The soul has been before stricken mortally, a poison poured in the porch of a sleeping ear. But those who are done to death in sleep cannot know the manner of their quell unless their Creator endow their souls with that knowledge in the life to come. The poisoning and the beast with two backs that urged it King Hamlet's ghost could not know of were he not endowed with knowledge by his creator. That is why the speech (his lean unlovely English) is always turned elsewhere, backward. Ravisher and ravished, what he would but would not, go with him from Lucrece's bluecircled ivory globes to Imogen's breast, bare, with its mole cinquespotted. He goes back, weary of the creation he has piled up to hide him from himself, an old dog licking an old sore. But, because loss is his gain, he passes on towards eternity in undiminished personality, untaught by the wisdom he has written or by the laws he has revealed. His beaver is up. He is a ghost, a shadow now, the wind by Elsinore's rocks or what you will, the sea's voice, a voice heard only in the heart of him who is the substance of his shadow, the son consubstantial with the father.

One could hardly have thought that even James Joyce might give us so persuasive a vision of the inward Shakespeare. Since the poet-dramatist composed the part of the Ghost of King Hamlet for himself to perform, Stephen's scholasticism entertains and disarms. Shakespeare, man and playwright, though a mortal God, suffers the cost of his confirmation. Sexual fury drives the High Tragedies to one apotheosis in *Othello* and then transmutes into the total fury of the human in *King Lear, Macbeth, Antony and Cleopatra*. After that, Shakespeare ebbs with an ebb of the ocean of life: *Coriolanus, Timon of Athens,* and his share of *The Two Noble Kinsmen* show the same revulsions and ambivalences as do the troublesome *Measure for Measure, All's Well That Ends Well, Troilus and Cressida*. Shadow and substance, father and son, Shakespeare alone carries in his heart the inland ocean of desolation, and since he is the son consubstantial with the father, he is both Jesus and Yahweh.

Challenged by his skeptical auditors to prove that William Shakespeare was a Jew, Stephen anticipates Kenneth Gross's *Shylock Is Shakespeare* (2006):

And the sense of property, Stephen said. He drew Shylock out of his own long pocket. The son of a maltjobber and moneylender he was himself a cornjobber and moneylender, with ten tods of corn hoarded in the famine riots. His borrowers are no doubt those divers of worship mentioned by Chettle Falstaff who reported his uprightness of dealing. He sued a fellowplayer for the price of a few bags of malt and exacted his pound of flesh in interest for every money lent. How else could Aubrey's ostler and callboy get rich quick? All events brought grist to his mill. Shylock chimes with the jewbaiting that followed the hanging and quartering of the queen's leech Lopez, his jew's heart being plucked forth while the sheeny was yet alive: *Hamlet* and *Macbeth* with the coming to the throne of a Scotch philosophaster with a turn for witchroasting. The lost armada is his jeer in *Love's Labour Lost*. His pageants, the histories, sail fullbellied on a tide of Mafeking enthusiasm. Warwickshire jesuits are tried and we have a porter's theory of equivocation. The *Sea Venture* comes home from Bermudas and the play Renan admired is written with Patsy Caliban, our American cousin. The sugared sonnets follow Sidney's. As for fay Elizabeth, otherwise carrotty Bess, the gross virgin who inspired the *Merry Wives of Windsor,* let some meinherr from Almany grope his life long for deephid meanings in the depths of the buckbasket.

This is too high-spirited to be refutable. Let it stand. Again Joyce dazzles, lord of wit and of language like his divine precursor.

Saint Thomas, Stephen smiling said, whose gorbellied works I enjoy reading in the original, writing of incest from a standpoint different from that of the new Viennese school Mr Magee spoke of, likens it in his wise and curious way to an avarice of the emotions. He means that the love so given to one near in blood is covetously withheld from some stranger who, it may be, hungers for it. Jews, whom christians tax with avarice, are of all races the most given to intermarriage. Accusations are made in anger. The christian laws which built up the hoards of the jews (for whom, as for the lollards, storm was shelter) bound their affections too with hoops of steel.

Whether these be sins or virtues old Nobodaddy will tell us at doomsday leet. But a man who holds so tightly to what he calls his rights over what he calls his debts will hold tightly also to what he calls his rights over her whom he calls his wife. No sir smile neighbour shall covet his ox or his wife or his manservant or his maidservant or his jackass.

Anthony Burgess called this "keeping love in the family," though he meant Earwicker's lust for his daughter, Isobel. William Blake's name for Yahweh, "old Nobodaddy," delighted Joyce, who called the God of the Christians the "hangman god." Sins and virtues meld.

—A father, Stephen said, battling against hopelessness, is a necessary evil. He wrote the play in the months that followed his father's death. If you hold that he, a greying man with two marriageable daughters, with thirtyfive years of life, *nel mezzo del cammin di nostra vita*, with fifty of experience, is the beardless undergraduate from Wittenberg then you must hold that his seventyyear old mother is the lustful queen. No. The corpse of John Shakespeare does not walk the night. From hour to hour it rots and rots. He rests, disarmed of fatherhood, having devised that mystical estate upon his son. Boccaccio's Calandrino was the first and last man who felt himself with child. Fatherhood, in the sense of conscious begetting, is unknown to man. It is a mystical estate, an apostolic succession, from only begetter to only begotten. On that mystery and not on the madonna which the cunning Italian intellect flung to the mob of Europe the church is founded and founded irremovably because founded, like the world, macro and microcosm, upon the void. Upon incertitude, upon unlikelihood. *Amor matris*, subjective and objective genitive, may be the only true thing in life. Paternity may be a legal fiction. Who is the father of any son that any son should love him or he any son?

If paternity is a legal fiction, then one can go further, as Hamlet does when the image of the ghostly father fades away in Act 5 and appears only in a reference to Claudius as he who killed my king and whored my mother, or in a single mention of my father's signet ring. Confronting Laertes at the grave of Ophelia, Hamlet cries out, "It is I, Hamlet the Dane." Here, then, I go with Stephen's theory, which is a splendid artifact once you divest it of the supposed cuckolding of Shakespeare by Anne Hathaway with his brothers.

James Joyce had a warm relationship with his father, John Stanislaus Joyce, and something of a guilty one with his mother, Mary Jane Murray, since he would not embrace Roman Catholicism again even to comfort her on her deathbed. Educated by the Jesuits, Joyce remained obdurate against priestcraft: "I will not serve."

A deep reader of Thomas Aquinas, Joyce found a precursor in the third-century theologian Sabellius, none of whose writings survived:

> Sabellius, the African, subtlest heresiarch of all the beasts of the field, held that the Father was Himself His Own Son. The bulldog of Aquin, with whom no word shall be impossible, refutes him. Well: if the father who has not a son be not a father can the son who has not a father be a son? When Rutlandbaconsouthamptonshakespeare or another poet of the same name in the comedy of errors wrote *Hamlet* he was not the father of his own son merely but, being no more a son, he was and felt himself the father of all his race, the father of his own grandfather, the father of his unborn grandson who, by the same token, never was born, for nature, as Mr Magee understands her, abhors perfection.

Mr. Magee (John Eglinton in *Ulysses*) was William Kirkpatrick Magee, a contemporary Irish essayist. Sabellius becomes Stephen becomes Shakespeare, who becomes a pre-existent being, a perfection alien to nature. Shakespeare thus goes back before the Creation-Fall, like the Stranger God of the Gnostics. Since Joyce works toward a three-in-one of Shakespeare, Leopold Bloom, and James Joyce, he, too, would achieve aesthetic perfection on this account:

> Man delights him not nor woman neither, Stephen said. He returns after a life of absence to that spot of earth where he was born, where he has always been, man and boy, a silent witness and there, his journey of life ended, he plants his mulberry-tree in the earth. Then dies. The motion is ended. Gravediggers bury Hamlet *père* and Hamlet *fils*. A king and a prince at last in death, with incidental music. And, what though murdered and betrayed, bewept by all frail tender hearts for, Dane or Dubliner, sorrow for the dead is the only husband from whom they refuse to be divorced. If you like the epilogue look long on it:

prosperous Prospero, the good man rewarded, Lizzie, grand-
pa's lump of love, and nuncle Richie, the bad man taken off
by poetic justice to the place where the bad niggers go. Strong
curtain. He found in the world without as actual what was in
his world within as possible. Maeterlinck says: *If Socrates leave
his house today he will find the sage seated on his doorstep. If
Judas go forth tonight it is to Judas his steps will tend.* Every
life is many days, day after day. We walk through ourselves,
meeting robbers, ghosts, giants, old men, young men, wives,
widows, brothers-in-love, but always meeting ourselves. The
playwright who wrote the folio of this world and wrote it badly
(He gave us light first and the sun two days later), the lord of
things as they are whom the most Roman of catholics call *dio
boia,* hangman god, is doubtless all in all in all of us, ostler
and butcher, and would be bawd and cuckold too but that in
the economy of heaven, foretold by Hamlet, there are no more
marriages, glorified man, an androgynous angel, being a wife
unto himself.

Setting aside the splendor of this language (from Joyce we expect
it), I am overwhelmed by what could be called the High Aesthetic
Theosophy of the passage. Like the Hermetic divine man or Blake's
Albion or Kabbalah's Adam Kadmon, Hamlet's dream glorifies man.
There are many accounts of androgynous angels, from John Milton to Ursula K. Le Guin, yet Joyce gives us a new Biblical cadence:
"being a wife unto himself."

Prince Hamlet is a vortex that draws everything in. I tear myself
away and finally move from Stephen and Shakespeare to Leopold
Bloom and Shakespeare. It is much more Poldy's book than it is Stephen's. Mr. Bloom's only rival is Dublin itself, alive with sound, a contentious citizenry, and ancient shadows. When I've been away from
Ulysses for too long, I am liable to believe that Poldy is larger than
his book, as Falstaff is not to be contained by the *Henry IV* plays.
Immersing myself again in *Ulysses* dispels that illusion. Every page,
every sentence, every phrase of Joyce's epic overflows the measure.

And yet Poldy (I have to keep to that name, since I am a lesser
Bloom) is endlessly rammed with life. I return to my bafflement as
to his Jewishness, upon which Joyce insists. You could argue that,

according to Talmud, Molly Bloom is more Jewish than Poldy, because she had a Spanish Jewish mother. That will not work. There is nothing Jewish about her. She is universal. Poldy is the mystery. Since he identifies with his dead father, he thinks of himself as a Jew. All Dublin considers him such. Joyce *is* Poldy *is* Shakespeare: that is the argument of *Ulysses,* finally more central than Homer and Dante. Leopold Bloom is in search of a son, and this quest is Messianic. He finds Stephen Dedalus, who is never quite there since he is both alcoholic and given to authentic visions.

I am not writing a book about *Ulysses;* I cannot pretend to be a Joyce scholar. And I still intend to say something about the *Wake* before I am done. Therefore, I will leap ahead to Episode 12: the "Cyclops," set at 5:00 p.m. in a Dublin pub where Poldy courageously confronts a gigantic, nasty Dublin citizen, who is unnamed, brutal, and abusive. Joyce uses a narrator of little personality, who tells the story of Poldy's agon in the Dublin vernacular. The citizen drinks heavily and predicts a return to Ireland of its émigrés to join in rebellion against the English.

"—Perfectly true, says Bloom. But my point was..."

. . . .

—Persecution, says he, all the history of the world is full of it. Perpetuating national hatred among nations.

   —But do you know what a nation means? says John Wyse.
   —Yes, says Bloom.
   —What is it? says John Wyse.
   —A nation? says Bloom. A nation is the same people living in the same place.
   —By God, then, says Ned, laughing, if that's so I'm a nation for I'm living in the same place for the past five years.
   So of course everyone had the laugh at Bloom and says he, trying to muck out of it:
   —Or also living in different places.
   —That covers my case, says Joe.
   —What is your nation if I may ask? says the citizen.
   —Ireland, says Bloom. I was born here. Ireland.

The citizen said nothing only cleared the spit out of his gullet and, gob, he spat a Red bank oyster out of him right in the corner.

.   .   .

—Are you talking about the new Jerusalem? says the citizen.

—I'm talking about injustice, says Bloom.

—Right, says John Wyse. Stand up to it then with force like men.

That's an almanac picture for you. Mark for a softnosed bullet. Old lardyface standing up to the business end of a gun. Gob, he'd adorn a sweepingbrush, so he would, if he only had a nurse's apron on him. And then he collapses all of a sudden, twisting around all the opposite, as limp as a wet rag.

—But it's no use, says he. Force, hatred, history, all that. That's not life for men and women, insult and hatred. And everybody knows that it's the very opposite of that that is really life.

James Joyce, great artist as he is, nevertheless is beset at this point. Poldy speaks for him, yet the artist should be disengaged, on the model of Homer and Shakespeare rather than that of Dante. When Mr. Bloom returns to the tavern, the citizen Cyclops heightens the contest:

But begob I was just lowering the heel of the pint when I saw the citizen getting up to waddle to the door, puffing and blowing with the dropsy, and he cursing the curse of Cromwell on him, bell, book and candle in Irish, spitting and spatting out of him and Joe and little Alf round him like a leprechaun trying to peacify him.

—Let me alone, says he.

And begob he got as far as the door and they holding him and he bawls out of him:

—Three cheers for Israel!

Arrah, sit down on the parliamentary side of your arse for Christ' sake and don't be making a public exhibition of yourself.

Jesus, there's always some bloody clown or other kicking up a bloody murder about bloody nothing. Gob, it'd turn the porter sour in your guts, so it would.

And all the ragamuffins and sluts of the nation round the door and Martin telling the jarvey to drive ahead and the citizen bawling and Alf and Joe at him to whisht and he on his high horse about the jews and the loafers calling for a speech and Jack Power trying to get him to sit down on the car and hold his bloody jaw and a loafer with a patch over his eye starts singing *If the man in the moon was a jew, jew, jew* and a slut shouts out of her:

—Eh, mister! Your fly is open, mister!

And says he:

—Mendelssohn was a jew and Karl Marx and Mercadante and Spinoza. And the Saviour was a jew and his father was a jew. Your God.

—He had no father, says Martin. That'll do now. Drive ahead.

—Whose God? says the citizen.

—Well, his uncle was a jew, says he. Your God was a jew. Christ was a jew like me.

Gob, the citizen made a plunge back into the shop.

—By Jesus, says he, I'll brain that bloody jewman for using the holy name.

By Jesus, I'll crucify him so I will. Give us that biscuitbox here.

Joyce is subtle and Poldy is not totally accurate. If by Mendelssohn he means the composer Felix, as probably he does, rather than Felix's grandfather Moses Mendelssohn, the eighteenth-century pioneer of Jewish Enlightenment, then he forgets or does not know that the composer was brought up without religion until he was baptized a Protestant at the age of seven. Karl Marx, himself anti-Semitic, was baptized a Lutheran at the age of eight. Saverio Mercadante was an Italian Gentile once famous for his operas. Perhaps Poldy is confusing him with Giacomo Meyerbeer, an operatic composer who was Jewish. As for the great Baruch Spinoza, he was excommunicated by the Jewish community of Amsterdam. It is generally agreed that Jesus Christ was Jewish and that his father, Yahweh, was the God of the Jews. Mr. Bloom's interesting notion that, if Jesus had no father, nevertheless his uncle was Jewish, has its own charm.

The furious citizen flings his biscuit tin in vain, since Poldy and the lawyer J. J. O'Molloy make their escape by motor vehicle. Joyce is as many-minded as Homer or indeed Shakespeare as he seeks to extricate himself from too close an identification with Mr. Bloom:

> When, lo, there came about them all a great brightness and they beheld the chariot wherein He stood ascend to heaven. And they beheld Him in the chariot, clothed upon in the glory of the brightness, having raiment as of the sun, fair as the moon and terrible that for awe they durst not look upon Him. And there came a voice out of heaven, calling: *Elijah! Elijah!* And He answered with a main cry: *Abba! Adonai!* And they beheld Him even Him, ben Bloom Elijah, amid clouds of angels ascend to the glory of the brightness at an angle of fortyfive degrees over Donohoe's in Little Green street like a shot off a shovel.

This explosion of a paragraph undergoes utter change with the transition from "brightness" to the rather Beckett-like remainder of the sentence. I am thinking of the Samuel Beckett of the marvelous *Murphy* (1938), a novel at once an homage to Joyce and an annunciation for Beckett. As far as I know, it was the only work by Beckett that Joyce admired, but, then, their relations were soured when Beckett wisely did not encourage the passion for him of Joyce's daughter, Lucia, who was supposed to be mentally ill, though the nature of her illness remains in dispute.

So vast and deep is *Ulysses* that I am constrained to a somewhat desperate economy, which is contrary to the spirit of the book. I choose to follow Bloom and Stephen into their descent into Nighttown in the "Circe" episode, and only then go on to the "Penelope" episode, spoken by Molly Bloom. That should allow me a brief entry into the night of the *Wake*.

I begin with a wonderful but mixed memory from the autumn of 1959, when, with my wife, I attended in London a performance of *Ulysses in Nighttown*, adapted by Marjorie Barkentin and directed by Burgess Meredith. Zero Mostel was Leopold Bloom, dancing his way through the part on his toes, sometimes seeming airborne. I would have been gloriously happy, identifying myself with Zero, whom I had met, and thus with Poldy, except that I had an impacted wisdom tooth, which was exquisitely painful. It was drawn the next day, but I distinctly recall that when most of the cast pointed to Zero and cried out, "When in doubt persecute Bloom," a shocking pain suddenly shot up. I was caught between ecstasy and suffering and consoled myself by remembering how many ailments James Joyce had to suffer, particularly with his eyes.

Because of a lunatic diet, Mostel died at sixty-two, giving him just three more years than James Joyce. He remains for me a clear image of Poldy, even though he was wholly Jewish and in no way Irish. Milo O'Shea and Stephen Rea have both acted Mr. Bloom on the screen. O'Shea was quite good, but Rea was delightful. Still, too much is lost when you transfer *Ulysses* either to stage or to screen. It is polyphonic and transgresses the limits of the visible in favor of an audibility unmatched since Shakespeare.

Let us break into "Circe" with Poldy trudging along in search of the intoxicated Stephen. Phantasmagoria suddenly overwhelms him:

(The retriever approaches sniffing, nose to the ground. A sprawled form sneezes. A stooped bearded figure appears garbed in the long caftan of an elder in Zion and a smokingcap with magenta tassels. Horned spectacles hang down at the wings of the nose. Yellow poison streaks are on the drawn face.)

RUDOLPH: Second halfcrown waste money today. I told you not go with drunken goy ever. So you catch no money.

BLOOM: *(Hides the crubeen and trotter behind his back and, crestfallen, feels warm and cold feetmeat)* Ja, ich weiss, papachi.

RUDOLPH: What you making down this place? Have you no soul? *(With feeble vulture talons he feels the silent face of Bloom.)* Are you not my son Leopold, the grandson of Leopold? Are you not my dear son Leopold who left the house of his father and left the god of his fathers Abraham and Jacob?

BLOOM: *(With precaution)* I suppose so, father. Mosenthal. All that's left of him.

RUDOLPH: *(Severely)* One night they bring you home drunk as dog after spend your good money. What you call them running chaps?

BLOOM: *(In youth's smart blue Oxford suit with white vestslips, narrowshouldered, in brown Alpine hat, wearing gent's sterling silver waterbury keyless watch and double curb Albert with seal attached, one side of him coated with stiffening mud)* Harriers, father. Only that once.

RUDOLPH: Once! Mud head to foot. Cut your hand open. Lockjaw. They make you kaputt, Leopoldleben. You watch them chaps.

BLOOM: *(Weakly)* They challenged me to a sprint. It was muddy. I slipped.

RUDOLPH: *(With contempt)* Goim nachez! Nice spectacles for your poor mother!

BLOOM: Mamma!

ELLEN BLOOM: *(In pantomime dame's stringed mobcap, widow Twankey's crinoline and bustle, blouse with muttonleg sleeves buttoned behind, grey mittens and cameo brooch, her plaited hair in a crispine net, appears over the staircase banisters, a slanted candlestick in her hand, and cries out in shrill alarm.)* O blessed Redeemer, what have they done to him! My smelling salts! *(She hauls up a reef of skirt and ransacks the pouch of her striped blay petticoat. A phial, an Agnus Dei, a shrivelled potato and a celluloid doll fall out.)* Sacred Heart of Mary, where were you at all at all?

Poldy's "Mosenthal. All that's left of him" refers to Salomon Mosenthal, a nineteenth-century dramatist, and to his play *Leah: The Forsaken* (1886). Joyce does remarkably well at rendering the Yiddish-English of Poldy Bloom's prudential father, Rudolph Virag-Bloom, and of his mother, Ellen's, more Irish-inflected lament.

In a mounting crescendo, Bloom is put on public trial, accused of nuisances, provocations, and invitations to women of all stations to misbehave with him either sexually or more explicitly sadomasochistically. The grand climax is the denunciations by very well-upholstered ladies of society:

MRS BELLINGHAM: He addressed me in several handwritings with fulsome compliments as a Venus in furs and alleged profound pity for my frostbound coachman Palmer while in the same breath he expressed himself as envious of his earflaps and fleecy sheepskins and of his fortunate proximity to my person, when standing behind my chair wearing my livery and the armorial bearings of the Bellingham escutcheon garnished sable, a buck's head couped or. He lauded almost extravagantly my nether extremities, my swelling calves in silk hose drawn up to the limit, and eulogised glowingly my other hidden treasures in priceless lace which, he said, he could conjure up. He urged me (Stating that he felt it his mission in life to urge me.) to defile the marriage bed, to commit adultery at the earliest possible opportunity.

THE HONOURABLE MRS MERVYN TALBOYS: *(In amazon costume, hard hat, jackboots cockspurred, vermilion waistcoat, fawn musketeer gauntlets with braided drums, long train held up and hunting crop with which she strikes her welt constantly)* Also me. Because he saw me on the polo ground of the Phoenix park at the match All Ireland versus the Rest of Ireland. My eyes, I know, shone divinely as I watched Captain Slogger Dennehy of the Inniskillings win the final chukkar on his darling cob *Centaur.* This plebeian Don Juan observed me from behind a hackney car and sent me in double envelopes an obscene photograph, such as are sold after dark on Paris boulevards, insulting to any lady. I have it still. It represents a partially nude señorita, frail and lovely (his wife, as he solemnly assured me, taken by him from nature), practising illicit intercourse with a muscular torero, evidently a blackguard. He urged me to do likewise, to misbehave, to sin with officers of the garrison. He implored me to soil his letter in an unspeakable manner, to chastise him as he richly deserves, to bestride and ride him, to give him a most vicious horsewhipping.

MRS YELVERTON BARRY: Me too.

(Several highly respectable Dublin ladies hold up improper letters received from Bloom.)

THE HONOURABLE MRS MERVYN TALBOYS: *(Stamps her jingling spurs in a sudden paroxysm of fury)* I will, by the God above me. I'll scourge the pigeonlivered cur as long as I can stand over him. I'll flay him alive.

BLOOM: *(His eyes closing, quails expectantly)* Here? *(He squirms.)* Again! *(He pants cringing.)* I love the danger.

THE HONOURABLE MRS MERVYN TALBOYS: Very much so! I'll make it hot for you. I'll make you dance Jack Latten for that.

MRS BELLINGHAM: Tan his breech well, the upstart! Write the stars and stripes on it!

MRS YELVERTON BARRY: Disgraceful! There's no excuse for him! A married man!

BLOOM: All these people. I meant only the spanking idea. A warm tingling glow without effusion. Refined birching to stimulate the circulation.

THE HONOURABLE MRS MERVYN TALBOYS: *(Laughs derisively)* O, did you, my fine fellow? Well, by the living God, you'll get the surprise of your life now, believe me, the most unmerciful hiding a man ever bargained for. You have lashed the dormant tigress in my nature into fury.

MRS BELLINGHAM: *(Shakes her muff and quizzing-glasses vindictively)* Make him smart, Hanna dear. Give him ginger. Thrash the mongrel within an inch of his life. The cat-o'-nine-tails. Geld him. Vivisect him.

BLOOM: *(Shuddering, shrinking, joins his hands: with hangdog mien)* O cold! O shivery! It was your ambrosial beauty. Forget, forgive. Kismet. Let me off this once. *(He offers the other cheek.)*

MRS YELVERTON BARRY: *(Severely)* Don't do so on any account, Mrs Talboys! He should be soundly trounced!

THE HONOURABLE MRS MERVYN TALBOYS: *(Unbuttoning her gauntlet violently)* I'll do no such thing. Pigdog and always was ever since he was pupped! To dare address me! I'll flog him black and blue in the public streets. I'll dig my spurs in him up to the rowel. He is a wellknown cuckold. *(She swishes her huntingcrop savagely in the air.)* Take down his trousers without loss of time. Come here, sir! Quick! Ready?

BLOOM: *(Trembling, beginning to obey)* The weather has been so warm.

This robust chorus becomes a rather specialized variety of our contemporary "MeToo" pastime. Leopold von Sacher-Masoch, who died at fifty-nine in 1895, was a Galician nobleman remembered now for his rather inadequate novel *Venus in Furs* (1870), that gives him the dubious immortality of the word "masochism," or experiencing sexual pleasure through pain. It is reasonable to assume that Joyce gave Leopold Bloom his first name from Sacher-Masoch, who, aside from his sexual vagaries, was a benign social thinker and active philo-Semite.

Though some of Poldy's amiable sins derive from Joyce, I can find no evidence of sadomasochism in the long and happy relationship between Nora Barnacle and James Joyce. Why did Joyce desire so deeply ingrained an element of masochism in Poldy's psychosexuality? It manifests itself in the acquiescence to Molly Bloom's infidelities, particularly with the egregious Blazes Boylan. Ultimately, it achieves a horrifying splendor in Poldy's submission to the whore mistress Bella/Bello Cohen.

That grand phalanx of Mrs. Bellingham, the Honourable Mrs. Mervin Talboys, and Mrs. Yelverton Barry is properly headed by the Honourable Mrs. Mervin Talboys, who proclaims that our poor Poldy has "lashed the dormant tigress in my nature into fury." He is saved by the delirious movement of "Circe": a pageant and a parade. All of Dublin whirls by in a mad procession until, at last, Poldy is crowned as ruler of Ireland:

THE BISHOP OF DOWN AND CONNOR: I here present your undoubted emperor president and king chairman, the most serene and potent and very puissant ruler of this realm. God save Leopold the First!

ALL: God save Leopold the First!

BLOOM: *(In dalmatic and purple mantle, to the bishop of Down and Connor, with dignity)* Thanks, somewhat eminent sir.

WILLIAM, ARCHBISHOP OF ARMAGH: *(In purple stock and shovel hat.)* Will you to your power cause law and mercy to be executed in all your judgments in Ireland and territories thereunto belonging?

BLOOM: *(Placing his right hand on his testicles, swears)* So may the Creator deal with me. All this I promise to do.

MICHAEL, ARCHBISHOP OF ARMAGH: *(Pours a cruse of hairoil over Bloom's head)* Gaudium magnum annuntio vobis. Habemus carneficem. Leopold, Patrick, Andrew, David, George, be thou anointed!

(Bloom assumes a mantle of cloth of gold and puts on a ruby ring. He ascends and stands on the stone of destiny. The representative peers put on at the same time their twentyeight crowns. Joybells ring in Christ church, Saint Patrick's, George's and gay Malahide. Mirus bazaar fireworks go up from all sides with symbolical phallopyrotechnic designs. The peers do homage, one by one, approaching and genuflecting.)

THE PEERS: I do become your liege man of life and limb to earthly worship.

(Bloom holds up his right hand on which sparkles the Koh-i-Noor diamond. His palfrey neighs. Immediate silence. Wireless intercontinental and interplanetary transmitters are set for reception of message.)

BLOOM: My subjects! We hereby nominate our faithful charger Copula Felix hereditary Grand Vizier and announce that we have this day repudiated our former spouse and have bestowed our royal hand upon the princess Selene, the splendour of night.

(The former morganatic spouse of Bloom is hastily removed in the Black Maria. The princess Selene, in moonblue robes, a silver crescent on her head, descends from a Sedan chair, borne by two giants. An outburst of cheering.)

JOHN HOWARD PARNELL: *(Raises the royal standard.)* Illustrious Bloom! Successor to my famous brother!

BLOOM: *(Embraces John Howard Parnell)* We thank you from our heart, John, for this right royal welcome to green Erin, the promised land of our common ancestors.

(The freedom of the city is presented to him embodied in a charter. The keys of Dublin, crossed on a crimson cushion, are given to him. He shows all that he is wearing green socks.)

TOM KERNAN: You deserve it, your honour.

BLOOM: On this day twenty years ago we overcame the hereditary enemy at Ladysmith. Our howitzers and camel swivel guns played on his lines with telling effect. Half a league onward! They charge! All is lost now! Do we yield? No! We drive them headlong! Lo! We charge! Deploying to the left our light horse swept across the heights of Plevna and, uttering their warcry Bonafide Sabaoth, sabred the Saracen gunners to a man.

THE CHAPEL OF FREEMAN TYPESETTERS: Hear! Hear!

JOHN WYSE NOLAN: There's the man that got away James Stephens.

A BLUECOAT SCHOOLBOY: Bravo!

AN OLD RESIDENT: You're a credit to your country, sir, that's what you are.

AN APPLEWOMAN: He's a man like Ireland wants.

BLOOM: My beloved subjects, a new era is about to dawn. I, Bloom, tell you verily it is even now at hand. Yea, on the word of a Bloom, ye shall ere long enter into the golden city which is to be, the new Bloomusalem in the Nova Hibernia of the future.

(*Thirtytwo workmen, wearing rosettes, from all the counties of Ireland, under the guidance of Derwan the builder, construct the new Bloomusalem. It is a colossal edifice with crystal roof, built in the shape of a huge pork kidney, containing forty thousand rooms. In the course of its extension several buildings and monuments are demolished. Government offices are temporarily transferred to railway sheds. Numerous houses are razed to the ground. The inhabitants are lodged in barrels and boxes, all marked in red with the letters: L.B. Several paupers fall from a ladder. A part of the walls of Dublin, crowded with loyal sightseers, collapses.*)

THE SIGHTSEERS: (*Dying*) Morituri te salutant. (*They die.*)

(*A man in a brown macintosh springs up through a trapdoor. He points an elongated finger at Bloom.*)

THE MAN IN THE MACINTOSH: Don't you believe a word he says. That man is Leopold M'Intosh, the notorious fireraiser. His real name is Higgins.

BLOOM: Shoot him! Dog of a christian! So much for M'Intosh!

(*A cannonshot. The man in the macintosh disappears. Bloom with his sceptre strikes down poppies. The instantaneous deaths of many powerful enemies, graziers, members of parliament, members of standing committees, are reported. Bloom's*

bodyguard distribute Maundy money, commemoration med-
als, loaves and fishes, temperance badges, expensive Henry Clay
cigars, free cowbones for soup, rubber preservatives in sealed
envelopes tied with gold thread, butter scotch, pineapple rock,
billets doux *in the form of cocked hats, readymade suits, porrin-*
gers of toad in the hole, bottles of Jeyes' Fluid, purchase stamps,
40 days' indulgences, spurious coins, dairyfed pork sausages,
theatre passes, season tickets available for all tramlines, cou-
pons of the royal and privileged Hungarian lottery, penny din-
ner counters, cheap reprints of the World's Twelve Worst Books:
Froggy And Fritz (politic), Care of the Baby (infantilic), 50
Meals for 7/6 (culinic), Was Jesus a Sun Myth? (historic), Expel
that Pain (medic), Infant's Compendium of the Universe (cos-
mic), Let's All Chortle (hilaric), Canvasser's Vade Mecum (jour-
nalic), Loveletters of Mother Assistant (erotic), Who's Who in
Space (astric), Songs that Reached Our Heart (melodic), Penny-
wise's Way to Wealth (parsimonic). A general rush and scram-
ble. Women press forward to touch the hem of Bloom's robe. The
lady Gwendolen Dubedat bursts through the throng, leaps on
his horse and kisses him on both cheeks amid great acclama-
tion. A magnesium flashlight photograph is taken. Babes and
sucklings are held up.)
THE WOMEN: Little father! Little father!
THE BABES AND SUCKLINGS:
    Clap clap hands till Poldy comes home,
    Cakes in his pocket for Leo alone.

The glorious center of this bravura celebration is Poldy's vision of
the new Bloomusalem. The only sentence that baffles me remains,
"There's the man that got away James Stephens." Joyce and James
Stephens had a curious and long-enduring friendship, partly founded
on the mistaken notion that they had been born on the same day. I
do not think that anyone who has read James Stephens's poetry and
his best-known novel, *The Crock of Gold* (1912), could think that Stephens might have finished the *Wake* had Joyce not lived to do so. Yet
that became an obsession of Joyce as his eye troubles increased the
painful labors of composition. Still, that is a minor detail compared
with this marvelous proclamation:

BLOOM: My beloved subjects, a new era is about to dawn. I, Bloom, tell you verily it is even now at hand. Yea, on the word of a Bloom, ye shall ere long enter into the golden city which is to be, the new Bloomusalem in the Nova Hibernia of the future.

These days readers might well prefer to live in the new Bloomusalem rather than the new Jerusalem. I have not been in Dublin since the mid-1980s but was dismayed, during my final visit, not to find so many Georgian houses and squares that had been part of the Dublin of Yeats and Joyce. Since then there has been a movement to preserve what still was there. But, then, I have not been in Jerusalem since 1985, and from my friends there I gather I would not recognize most of it.

The new Bloomusalem vaporizes with startling rapidity:

LENEHAN: Plagiarist! Down with Bloom!

THE VEILED SIBYL: *(Enthusiastically)* I'm a Bloomite and I glory in it. I believe in him in spite of all. I'd give my life for him, the funniest man on earth.

BLOOM: *(Winks at the bystanders)* I bet she's a bonny lassie.

THEODORE PUREFOY: *(In fishingcap and oilskin jacket)* He employs a mechanical device to frustrate the sacred ends of nature.

THE VEILED SIBYL: *(Stabs herself)* My hero god! *(She dies.)*
   (Many most attractive and enthusiastic women also commit suicide by stabbing, drowning, drinking prussic acid, aconite, arsenic, opening their veins, refusing food, casting themselves under steamrollers, from the top of Nelson's Pillar, into the great vat of Guinness's brewery, asphyxiating themselves by placing their heads in gasovens, hanging themselves in stylish garters, leaping from windows of different storeys.)

ALEXANDER J. DOWIE: *(Violently)* Fellowchristians and antiBloomites, the man called Bloom is from the roots of hell, a disgrace to christian men. A fiendish libertine from his earliest years this stinking goat of Mendes gave precocious signs of infantile debauchery, recalling the cities of the plain, with a dissolute granddam. This vile hypocrite,

bronzed with infamy, is the white bull mentioned in the
Apocalypse. A worshipper of the Scarlet Woman, intrigue
is the very breath of his nostrils. The stake faggots and the
caldron of boiling oil are for him. Caliban!

Alexander J. Dowie, delightful American evangelist, cannot get
much right. There is no white bull mentioned in the Revelation of
Saint John the Divine. There is of course that splendid damozel the
Whore of Babylon, but why drag in the much-tried Caliban? Joyce's
proclivity for esoterica doubtless prompts Dowie's "stinking goat of
Mendes," derived from Éliphas Lévi Zahed, a professional mystifier
whose name was Alphonse Louis Constant and who was a friend
of Nerval and the young Gautier. Éliphas Lévi concocted the goat
of Mendes, who supposedly copulated with the priestesses in that
ancient Egyptian hovel.

THE MOB: Lynch him! Roast him! He's as bad as Parnell was.
　Mr Fox!
　(*Mother Grogan throws her boot at Bloom. Several shopkeep-
　ers from upper and lower Dorset street throw objects of little or
　no commercial value, hambones, condensed milk tins, unsale-
　able cabbage, stale bread, sheep's tails, odd pieces of fat.*)
BLOOM: (*Excitedly*) This is midsummer madness, some
　ghastly joke again. By heaven, I am guiltless as the
　unsunned snow! It was my brother Henry. He is my
　double. He lives in number 2 Dolphin's Barn. Slander, the
　viper, has wrongfully accused me. Fellowcountrymen, *sgenl
　inn ban bata coisde gan capall.* I call on my old friend, Dr
　Malachi Mulligan, sex specialist, to give medical testimony
　on my behalf.
DR MULLIGAN: (*In motor jerkin, green motorgoggles on his
　brow*) Dr Bloom is bisexually abnormal. He has recently
　escaped from Dr Eustace's private asylum for demented
　gentlemen. Born out of bedlock hereditary epilepsy is
　present, the consequence of unbridled lust. Traces of
　elephantiasis have been discovered among his ascendants.
　There are marked symptoms of chronic exhibitionism.
　Ambidexterity is also latent. He is prematurely bald from

selfabuse, perversely idealistic in consequence, a reformed
rake, and has metal teeth. In consequence of a family
complex he has temporarily lost his memory and I believe
him to be more sinned against than sinning. I have made a
pervaginal examination and, after application of the
acid test to 5427 anal, axillary, pectoral and pubic hairs,
I declare him to be *virgo intacta.*

Having found in Gogarty his true black beast, Joyce exploits him
to the limit. The Dublin mob seeking to lynch Poldy associates him
with the fallen Charles Stewart Parnell, who died at forty-five in the
arms of Katharine O'Shea, with whom he had enjoyed a long adulterous relationship. During the romance, he had used "Mr. Fox" as one
pseudonym in his correspondence with her. Cast out by the Roman
Catholic Church, Parnell died in disgrace, though he had long been
the leader in the Irish struggle for emancipation from England.

Gogarty, that is to say Buck Mulligan, is as funny as ever. Joyce,
who had suffered much from Gogarty, nevertheless was artist enough
to endow Mulligan with eternal life. Buck's rhetoric, though pomp-
ous, is orotund: it has the rolling gusto of the great Falstaff, though
Buck is no Sir John. Closer perhaps is Panurge, though that great
Daemon in Books Three and Four of Rabelais, while shrewd and
licentious, is a coward, whereas Gogarty—to grant him that much—
was courageous in action.

The pageant swirls on, and Poldy again manifests Messianic gestures towards oblation:

A VOICE: Bloom, are you the Messiah ben Joseph or ben
David?
BLOOM: *(Darkly)* You have said it.
BROTHER BUZZ: Then perform a miracle like Father Charles.
BANTAM LYONS: Prophesy who will win the Saint Leger.
*(Bloom walks on a net, covers his left eye with his left ear,
passes through several walls, climbs Nelson's Pillar, hangs from
the top ledge by his eyelids, eats twelve dozen oysters (shells
included), heals several sufferers from king's evil, contracts his
face so as to resemble many historical personages, Lord Bea-
consfield, Lord Byron, Wat Tyler, Moses of Egypt, Moses Mai-*

monides, Moses Mendelssohn, Henry Irving, Rip van Winkle, Kossuth, Jean Jacques Rousseau, Baron Leopold Rothschild, Robinson Crusoe, Sherlock Holmes, Pasteur, turns each foot simultaneously in different directions, bids the tide turn back, eclipses the sun by extending his little finger.)

BRINI, PAPAL NUNCIO: *(In papal zouave's uniform, steel cuirasses as breastplate, armplates, thighplates, legplates, large profane moustaches and brown paper mitre.) Leopoldi autem generatio.* Moses begat Noah and Noah begat Eunuch and Eunuch begat O'Halloran and O'Halloran begat Guggenheim and Guggenheim begat Agendath and Agendath begat Netaim and Netaim begat Le Hirsch and Le Hirsch begat Jesurum and Jesurum begat MacKay and MacKay begat Ostrolopsky and Ostrolopsky begat Smerdoz and Smerdoz begat Weiss and Weiss begat Schwarz and Schwarz begat Adrianopoli and Adrianopoli begat Aranjuez and Aranjuez begat Lewy Lawson and Lewy Lawson begat Ichabudonosor and Ichabudonosor begat O'Donnell Magnus and O'Donnell Magnus begat Christbaum and Christbaum begat ben Maimun and ben Maimun begat Dusty Rhodes and Dusty Rhodes begat Benamor and Benamor begat Jones-Smith and Jones-Smith begat Savorgnanovich and Savorgnanovich begat Jasperstone and Jasperstone begat Vingtetunieme and Vingtetunieme begat Szombathely and Szombathely begat Virag and Virag begat Bloom *et vocabitur nomen eius Emmanuel.*

A DEADHAND: *(Writes on the wall)* Bloom is a cod.

CRAB: *(In bushranger's kit)* What did you do in the cattlecreep behind Kilbarrack?

A FEMALE INFANT: *(Shakes a rattle)* And under Ballybough bridge?

A HOLLYBUSH: And in the devil's glen?

BLOOM: *(Blushes furiously all over from frons to nates, three tears falling from his left eye)* Spare my past.

THE IRISH EVICTED TENANTS: *(In bodycoats, kneebreeches, with Donnybrook fair shillelaghs)* Sjambok him!

(Bloom with asses' ears seats himself in the pillory with crossed arms, his feet protruding. He whistles Don Giovanni,

a cenar teco. *Artane orphans, joining hands, caper round him. Girls of the Prison Gate Mission, joining hands, caper round in the opposite direction.)*

THE ARTANE ORPHANS:

> You hig, you hog, you dirty dog!
> You think the ladies love you!

THE PRISON GATE GIRLS:

> If you see Kay
> Tell him he may
> See you in tea
> Tell him from me.

HORNBLOWER: *(In ephod and huntingcap, announces)* And he shall carry the sins of the people to Azazel, the spirit which is in the wilderness, and to Lilith, the nighthag. And they shall stone him and defile him, yea, all from Agendath Netaim and from Mizraim, the land of Ham.

(All the people cast soft pantomime stones at Bloom. Many bonafide travellers and ownerless dogs come near him and defile him. Mastiansky and Citron approach in gaberdines, wearing long earlocks. They wag their beards at Bloom.)

MASTIANSKY AND CITRON: Belial! Laemlein of Istria, the false Messiah! Abulafia! Recant!

Ancient Jewish apocalyptic theology features two Messiahs. The first is the Messiah ben Joseph whose function is to prelude the coming of the true Messiah of the House of David. Whereas the first Messiah, after ingathering the exiles and retaking Jerusalem, is destined to be slain in battle, the second will bring about a new heaven and earth. When Poldy darkly says, "You have said it," Joyce implies Luke 23:3, where Jesus avoids the indictment of the priests that he calls himself Christ a King or the Messiah of the House of David, by subtly answering, "Thou sayest it."

There is always more to Leopold Bloom than I can hope to understand. Ulysses or Odysseus is more than comprehensive but finally less complete than Poldy. Dante's Ulysses, who becomes Tennyson's, is like Dante the Poet rather than Dante the Pilgrim. When Ulysses speaks to the Pilgrim out of the double flame he shares with Diomed in Canto 26 of *Inferno*, he tells the story of his last voyage beyond the limits set by the gods. Dante's reaction is silence. The implication is that he recognizes the affinity between the audacity of Ulysses and his own ambitious voyage from *Inferno* to *Purgatorio* to *Paradiso*.

Though Dante may fuse the allegory of the theologians with the allegory of the poets, he thinks of himself as the supreme poet, transcending even his beloved father Virgil. He places Joachim of Flora in Paradise even though Thomas Aquinas refuted *The Everlasting Gospel*, which Joachim bequeathed to the Franciscans. Dante thought of his *Commedia* as a Third Testament, completing the Old and the New, and confirming Joachim's prophecy of the Third Age of the Spirit, replacing the Ages of the Father and the Son.

Joachim's Age of the Spirit contaminated the radical sectaries of the English Revolution who fought on the side of Cromwell but then protested any restrictions on their access to the Inner Light. These revolutionaries—Ranters, Diggers, Muggletonians, Levellers—were the matrix from which John Milton evolved his highly intricate and personal final religious stance. The line goes from Milton to William Blake, who wrote another "Everlasting Gospel" and who criticized both Dante and Milton in his illustrations to them.

James Joyce, who somehow seems to have known everything, like Shakespeare before him, transmuted Dante and Blake into the anti-Messianic vortices of *Ulysses* and the *Wake*. It is blasphemous fun to behold Poldy accused of Messianic imposture. Is it not more than that? Since Joyce, Poldy, Shakespeare form a new Trinity or three-in-one, and Shakespeare is God the Father, James Joyce the Son, then Poldy may indeed be an omen of Advent for the approach of the Age of the Spirit.

After the insanely jubilant and inventive chant of "begats," various insults and enunciations are hurled at Poldy. Most significantly, Mastiansky and Citron denounce Bloom as the false Messiah Abraham Abulafia. In the most colorful moment of his bizarre career, the prophetic Kabbalist Abulafia arrived in Rome in 1280 and announced that he had come to convert Pope Nicholas III to the true faith of Judaism the day before the Jewish New Year. At that time Pope Nicholas was in Suriano and cheerfully ordered the burning of the Jewish fanatic as soon as he reached that town. Nevertheless, Abulafia marched on Suriano, where a stake had been prepared for him at the inner gate. Miracle! As the unshrinking Abulafia went through the outer gate, he was told that the Pope had died suddenly the night before, of a stroke. After weathering a month's imprisonment in Rome, the prophetic poet Abraham Abulafia went on to Sicily, where he proclaimed himself to be the Messiah.

I return to Poldy the cuckold and by way of him to Shakespeare:

MARION: Let him look, the pishogue! Pimp! And scourge himself! I'll write to a powerful prostitute or Bartholomona, the bearded woman, to raise weals out on him an inch thick and make him bring me back a signed and stamped receipt.

BOYLAN: (Clasps himself.) Here, I can't hold this little lot much longer. (He strides off on stiff cavalry legs.)

BELLA: (Laughing) Ho ho ho ho.

BOYLAN: (To Bloom, over his shoulder) You can apply your eye to the keyhole and play with yourself while I just go through her a few times.

BLOOM: Thank you, sir. I will, sir. May I bring two men chums to witness the deed and take a snapshot? (He holds an ointment jar) Vaseline, sir? Orangeflower...? Lukewarm water...?

KITTY: (From the sofa) Tell us, Florry. Tell us. What. (Florry whispers to her. Whispering lovewords murmur liplapping loudly, poppysmic plopslop.)

MINA KENNEDY: (Her eyes upturned) O, it must be like the scent of geraniums and lovely peaches! O, he simply idolises every bit of her! Stuck together! Covered with kisses!

LYDIA DOUCE: (Her mouth opening) Yumyum. O, he's carrying her round the room doing it! Ride a cock horse. You could hear them in Paris and New York. Like mouthfuls of strawberries and cream.

KITTY: (Laughing) Hee hee hee.

BOYLAN'S VOICE: (Sweetly, hoarsely, in the pit of his stomach) Ah! Gooblazeqruk brukarchkrasht!

MARION'S VOICE: (Hoarsely, sweetly, rising to her throat) O! Weeshwashtkissimapooisthnapoohuck!

BLOOM: (His eyes wildly dilated, clasps himself) Show! Hide! Show! Plough her! More! Shoot!

BELLA, ZOE, FLORRY, KITTY: Ho ho! Ha ha! Hee hee!

LYNCH: *(Points)* The mirror up to nature. *(He laughs.)* Hu hu hu hu hu!

(Stephen and Bloom gaze in the mirror. The face of William Shakespeare, beardless, appears there, rigid in facial paralysis, crowned by the reflection of the reindeer antlered hatrack in the hall.)

SHAKESPEARE: *(In dignified ventriloquy)* 'Tis the loud laugh bespeaks the vacant mind. *(To Bloom)* Thou thoughtest as how thou wastest invisible. Gaze. *(He crows with a black capon's laugh.)* Iagogo! How my Oldfellow chokit his Thursdaymornun. Iagogogo!

BLOOM: *(Smiles yellowly at the three whores)* When will I hear the joke?

ZOE: Before you're twice married and once a widower.

BLOOM: Lapses are condoned. Even the great Napoleon when measurements were taken next the skin after his death...

(Mrs Dignam, widow woman, her snubnose and cheeks flushed with deathtalk, tears and Tunney's tawny sherry, hurries by in her weeds, her bonnet awry, rouging and powdering her cheeks, lips and nose, a pen chivvying her brood of cygnets. Beneath her skirt appear her late husband's everyday trousers and turnedup boots, large eights. She holds a Scottish widow's insurance policy and a large marquee umbrella under which her brood run with her, Patsy hopping on one shod foot, his collar loose, a hank of porksteaks dangling, Freddy whimpering, Susy with a crying cod's mouth, Alice struggling with the baby. She cuffs them on, her streamers flaunting aloft.)

FREDDY: Ah, ma, you're dragging me along!

SUSY: Mamma, the beeftea is fizzing over!

SHAKESPEARE: *(With paralytic rage)* Weda seca whokilla farst.

(The face of Martin Cunningham, bearded, refeatures Shakespeare's beardless face. The marquee umbrella sways drunkenly, the children run aside. Under the umbrella appears Mrs Cunningham in Merry Widow hat and kimono gown. She glides sidling and bowing, twirling japanesily.)

MRS CUNNINGHAM: *(Sings)*

And they call me the jewel of Asia!

MARTIN CUNNINGHAM: *(Gazes on her, impassive)*
Immense! Most bloody awful demirep!
STEPHEN: *Et exaltabuntur cornua iusti.* Queens lay with
prize bulls. Remember Pasiphae for whose lust my
grandoldgrossfather made the first confessionbox. Forget
not Madam Grissel Steevens nor the suine scions of the
house of Lambert. And Noah was drunk with wine. And his
ark was open.
BELLA: None of that here. Come to the wrong shop.

In what ought to be a moment of total degradation, Poldy pleasures himself by watching through a keyhole the plowing of Molly
by Blazes Boylan. To a chorus of laughing whores, Stephen's intoxicated companion Lynch points to a mirror and laughingly quotes
Hamlet: "The mirror up to nature." Then mystery intervenes. Stephen and Bloom, components of James Joyce, gaze in the mirror and
their reflection is the face of Shakespeare, beardless, rigid in facial
paralysis, with the image of the cuckold formed by the reindeer ant-
lers of a hat rack. With amiable dignity, the Bard reproves the mindless Lynch by misquoting Oliver Goldsmith's poem "The Deserted
Village": "'Tis the loud laugh bespeaks the vacant mind." To Poldy
he says, "Thou thoughtest as how thou wastest invisible," a mild
reproof to a Peeping Tom. But then Shakespeare emphasizes to
Poldy: *"Gaze."* With the dark laughter of the tragedian of supposed
cuckoldry, he warns Poldy, "Iagogo! How my Oldfellow chokit his
Thursdaymornun. Iagogo!" Poldy is hardly likely to treat Molly as
Desdemona, but that is not Shakespeare's point. Stephen was born
on a Thursday; he and Poldy fuse, Shakespeare is the ghost of Hamlet's father warning the composite figure not to meld Hamlet with
Othello, which would make Molly into a complex mix of Gertrude,
Desdemona, and Stephen's dead mother.

But why is the image of Shakespeare so transmuted that he is
beardless, a frozen face, and a capon? I think that Shakespeare as
precursor mocks his disciple Bloom/Joyce/Stephen so as to say, "You
are trying to see yourself in me, but, staring in the mirror, you behold
what you are; being beardless, you lack my potency, and, being rigid
in facial paralysis, you are void of my gentle countenance." Shakespeare then adds, in a prophecy of the *Wake,* "Weda seca whokilla
farst," which reworks "None wed the second but who kill'd the first,"

taken from *The Murder of Gonzago,* as revised by Prince Hamlet. Stephen quotes from Psalm 75:10 in the Vulgate: "And the horns of the righteous shall be exalted." He goes on to the copulation of Pasiphaë with a prize bull, and to a wordplay on Noah's Ark and the Ark of the Covenant of Moses. Bella's response to "his Ark was open" is a brusque and strangely virtuous "None of that here. Come to the wrong shop."

The crisis of "Circe" comes with the apparition of Stephen's mother:

STEPHEN: Ho!
  (*Stephen's mother, emaciated, rises stark through the floor in leper grey with a wreath of faded orange blossoms and a torn bridal veil, her face worn and noseless, green with grave mould. Her hair is scant and lank. She fixes her bluecircled hollow eyesockets on Stephen and opens her toothless mouth uttering a silent word. A choir of virgins and confessors sing voicelessly.*)
THE CHOIR:
  Liliata rutilantium te confessorum...
  Iubilantium te virginum...
  (*From the top of a tower Buck Mulligan, in particoloured jester's dress of puce and yellow and clown's cap with curling bell, stands gaping at her, a smoking buttered split scone in his hand*)
BUCK MULLIGAN: She's beastly dead. The pity of it!
  Mulligan meets the afflicted mother. (*He upturns his eyes*)
  Mercurial Malachi!
THE MOTHER: (*With the subtle smile of death's madness*)
  I was once the beautiful May Goulding. I am dead.
STEPHEN: (*Horrorstruck*) Lemur, who are you? What bogeyman's trick is this?
BUCK MULLIGAN: (*Shakes his curling capbel*) The mockery of it! Kinch killed her dogsbody bitchbody. She kicked the bucket. (*Tears of molten butter fall from his eyes into the scone.*) Our great sweet mother! *Epi oinopa ponton.*
THE MOTHER: (*Comes nearer, breathing upon him softly her breath of wetted ashes*) All must go through it, Stephen. More women than men in the world. You too. Time will come.

STEPHEN: *(Choking with fright, remorse and horror)* They said I killed you, mother. He offended your memory. Cancer did it, not I. Destiny.

THE MOTHER: *(A green rill of bile trickling from a side of her mouth)* You sang that song to me. *Love's bitter mystery.*

STEPHEN: *(Eagerly)* Tell me the word, mother, if you know now. The word known to all men.

THE MOTHER: Who saved you the night you jumped into the train at Dalkey with Paddy Lee? Who had pity for you when you were sad among the strangers? Prayer is all powerful. Prayer for the suffering souls in the Ursuline manual, and forty days' indulgence. Repent, Stephen.

STEPHEN: The ghoul! Hyena!

THE MOTHER: I pray for you in my other world. Get Dilly to make you that boiled rice every night after your brain work. Years and years I loved you, O, my son, my firstborn, when you lay in my womb.

ZOE: *(Fanning herself with the grate fan)* I'm melting!

FLORRY: *(Points to Stephen)* Look! He's white.

BLOOM: *(Goes to the window to open it more)* Giddy.

THE MOTHER: *(With smouldering eyes)* Repent! O, the fire of hell!

STEPHEN: *(Panting)* The corpsechewer! Raw head and bloody bones!

THE MOTHER: *(Her face drawing near and nearer, sending out an ashen breath)* Beware! *(She raises her blackened, withered right arm slowly towards Stephen's breast with outstretched finger)* Beware God's hand! *(A green crab with malignant red eyes sticks deep its grinning claws in Stephen's heart)*

STEPHEN: *(Strangled with rage)* Shite! *(His features grow drawn and grey and old)*

BLOOM: *(At the window)* What?

STEPHEN: *Ah non, par exemple!* The intellectual imagination! With me all or not at all. *Non serviam!*

FLORRY: Give him some cold water. Wait. *(She rushes out)*

THE MOTHER: *(Wrings her hands slowly, moaning desperately)* O Sacred Heart of Jesus, have mercy on him! Save him from hell, O Divine Sacred Heart!

STEPHEN: No! No! No! Break my spirit, all of you, if you
can! I'll bring you all to heel!

THE MOTHER: *(In the agony of her deathrattle)* Have mercy
on Stephen, Lord, for my sake! Inexpressible was my
anguish when expiring with love, grief and agony on Mount
Calvary.

STEPHEN: *Nothung!*

*(He lifts his ashplant high with both hands and smashes the
chandelier. Time's livid final flame leaps and, in the following darkness, ruin of all space, shattered glass and toppling
masonry)*

THE GASJET: Pwfungg!

The interplay between the deathly mother, the stricken Stephen,
and the flamboyant Buck Mulligan in his final manifestation is mas-
terly. I have never understood why this passage hurts me. It is so
remote from my memories of my long-ago departed mother that I
have to reflect on the limits of my emotional understanding of an
author who had a Jesuit education, against which he reacted so for-
midably. Perhaps it should be read as a mock apocalypse, since Stephen's ashplant merely tears the paper off the cheap chandelier, for
which Poldy gives Bella one shilling, and yet the stage directions are
almost Blakean: "Time's livid final flame leaps and, in the following
darkness, ruin of all space, shattered glass and toppling masonry."
We could be in Night the Ninth of *The Four Zoas*, except that the
gasjet punctures illusion with a limp "Pwfungg!"

STEPHEN: *(Turns)* Eh? *(He disengages himself)* Why should I
not speak to him or to any human being who walks upright
upon this oblate orange? *(He points his finger)* I'm not
afraid of what I can talk to if I see his eye. Retaining the
perpendicular.

(He staggers a pace back)

BLOOM: *(Propping him)* Retain your own.

STEPHEN: *(Laughs emptily)* My centre of gravity is
displaced. I have forgotten the trick. Let us sit down
somewhere and discuss. Struggle for life is the law of
existence but but human philirenists, notably the tsar and

the king of England, have invented arbitration. (*He taps his brow*) But in here it is I must kill the priest and the king.

BIDDY THE CLAP: Did you hear what the professor said? He's a professor out of the college.

CUNTY KATE: I did. I heard that.

BIDDY THE CLAP: He expresses himself with such marked refinement of phraseology.

CUNTY KATE: Indeed, yes. And at the same time with such apposite trenchancy.

PRIVATE CARR: (*Pulls himself free and comes forward*) What's that you're saying about my king?

It is again very Blakean that Stephen taps his forehead and announces: "But in here it is I must kill the priest and the king." That cheers us, but the soldiers are as drunk as Stephen is, and the young poet is felled by a blow:

BLOOM: (*Over Stephen's shoulder*) Yes, go. You see he's incapable.

PRIVATE CARR: (*Breaks loose*) I'll insult him.

(*He rushes towards Stephen, fists outstretched, and strikes him in the face. Stephen totters, collapses, falls, stunned. He lies prone, his face to the sky, his hat rolling to the wall. Bloom follows and picks it up.*)

No matter how often I reread *Ulysses*, I am always startled when the recumbent Stephen provokes Bloom's vision of his lost son, Rudy:

(*He stretches out his arms, sighs again and curls his body. Bloom holding his hat and ashplant stands erect. A dog barks in the distance. Bloom tightens and loosens his grip on the ashplant. He looks down on Stephen's face and form.*)

BLOOM: (*Communes with the night*) Face reminds me of his poor mother. In the shady wood. The deep white breast. Ferguson, I think I caught. A girl. Some girl. Best thing could happen him... (*He murmurs.*)...swear that I will always hail, ever conceal, never reveal, any part or parts, art

or arts... *(He murmurs.)* in the rough sands of the sea...
a cabletow's length from the shore...where the tide ebbs...
and flows...

(Silent, thoughtful, alert, he stands on guard, his fingers at his lips in the attitude of secret master. Against the dark wall a figure appears slowly, a fairy boy of eleven, a changeling, kidnapped, dressed in an Eton suit with glass shoes and a little bronze helmet, holding a book in his hand. He reads from right to left inaudibly, smiling, kissing the page.)

BLOOM: *(Wonderstruck, calls inaudibly)* Rudy!

RUDY: *(Gazes unseeing into Bloom's eyes and goes on reading, kissing, smiling. He has a delicate mauve face. On his suit he has diamond and ruby buttons. In his free left hand he holds a slim ivory cane with a violet bowknot. A white lambkin peeps out of his waistcoat pocket.)*

Uncomprehending that Stephen is murmuring a Yeatsian lyric, Poldy is prompted to repeat part of his Masonic oath of silence and then beholds a changeling Rudy, now eleven years though he died at eleven days, in fairy garb and evidently reading Torah or Talmud, since he goes from right to left, "inaudibly, smiling, kissing the page." He does not recognize his father, who remembers heartbreakingly that the infant had been buried in a white lambkin.

Though *Ulysses* goes on for three more episodes, culminating in Molly's rapturous monologue, for me the vision of Rudy, which counters the apparition of Stephen's mother, is a destination attained. Poldy wants a son in Stephen but will not find one. Stephen goes forth unaltered, so that jewgreek does not become greekjew. Leopold Bloom returns to his unfaithful Penelope and falls asleep cheerfully enough, resting upon her. Molly's long soliloquy deserves all the admiration it has been accorded and ends quite gloriously with its repeated chorus of "yes," one after another.

I have not read all the critical studies of *Finnegans Wake*, but I have learned most from *Joyce's Book of the Dark: Finnegans Wake* by John Bishop (1986). I recall purchasing it in London and reading it straight through and back again for several days. During the last thirty years, I have made a number of returns to it and have found it perpetually fresh.

John Bishop teaches us to accept that the obscurities of the *Wake* are deliberate and inevitable. Joyce sets himself to write the epic of Night and Dream. The daylight of *Ulysses* is gone. Like Sigmund Freud, Joyce writes his Dream Book. I have studied the *Wake* formally only once, throughout an academic year when I took part in Thornton Wilder's seminar on the *Wake,* conducted in his house at 50 Deepwood Drive in Hamden, overlooking New Haven. I was a graduate student at Yale, but Wilder's seminar was independent of Yale, and you joined by invitation. Mostly we listened, as the dramatist's immersion in Joyce was impressive. Later, at Pembroke College, Cambridge, my tutor and friend was Matthew J. C. Hodgart, who wrote both on song and on Shakespeare's endless presence in the *Wake.*

Shem the Penman, in Book 1, Chapter 7, of the *Wake,* is the author James Joyce at work. But he is the author working under the shadow of Shakespeare:

But would anyone, short of a madhouse, believe it? Neither of those clean little cherubum, Nero or Nobookisonester himself, ever nursed such a spoiled opinion of his monstrous marvellosity as did this mental and moral defective (here perhaps at the vanessance of his lownest) who was known to grognt rather than gunnard upon one occasion, while drinking heavily of spirits to that interlocutor *a latere* and private privysuckatary he used to pal around with, in the kavehazs, one Davy Browne-Nowlan, his heavenlaid twin, (this hambone dog-poet pseudoed himself under the hangname he gave himself of Bethgelert) in the porchway of a gipsy's bar (Shem always blaspheming, so holy writ, Billy, he would try, old Belly, and pay this one manjack congregant of his four soups every lass of nexmouth, Bolly, so sure as thair's a tail on a commet, as a taste for storik's fortytooth, that is to stay, to listen out, ony twenny minnies moe, Bully, his Ballade Imaginaire which was to be dubbed *Wine, Woman and Waterclocks,* or *How a Guy Finks and Fawkes When He Is Going Batty,* by Maistre Sheames de la Plume, some most dreadful stuff in a murderous mirrorhand) that he was avoopf (parn me!) aware of no other shaggspick, other Shakhisbeard, either prexactly unlike his polar andthi-

sishis or procisely the seem as woops (parn!) as what he fancied or guessed the sames as he was himself and that, greet
scoot, duckings and thuggery, though he was foxed fux to fux
like a bunnyboy rodger with all the teashop lionses of Lum-
drum hivanhoesed up gagainst him, being a lapsis linquo with
a ruvidubb shortartempa, bad cad dad fad sad mad nad van-
haty bear, the consciquenchers of casuality prepestered cruss-
words in postposition, scruff, scruffer, scrufferumurraimost
andallthatsortofthing, if reams stood to reason and his lanka-
livline lasted he would wipe alley english spooker, multapho-
niaksically spuking, off the face of the erse.

I do not want to try to decipher this phrase by phrase, word by
word, as there are a plenitude of such translators. Go with the drift,
chanting this aloud, and what matters most will reveal itself to you.
Shaggspick and Shakhisbeard return us to the mirror up to nature
in which Stephen and Bloom beheld a beardless Shakespeare staring out at them and thus proclaiming his priority and his continu-
ance. Shem's pretentions nevertheless prevail. Joyce will not rewrite
Shakespeare, though he cannot stop utilizing him.

What rises above all this are the strongest pages Joyce ever wrote,
where Anna Livia Plurabelle—great mother, river-of-rivers, wife to
Everyone—flows home as the Liffey empties into the Irish Sea:

And it's old and old it's sad and old it's sad and weary I go back
to you, my cold father, my cold mad father, my cold mad feary
father, till the near sight of the mere size of him, the moyles
and moyles of it, moananoaning, makes me seasilt saltsick
and I rush, my only, into your arms. I see them rising! Save
me from those therrble prongs! Two more. Onetwo moremens
more. So. Avelaval. My leaves have drifted from me. All. But
one clings still. I'll bear it on me. To remind me of. Lff! So soft
this morning, ours. Yes. Carry me along, taddy, like you done
through the toy fair! If I seen him bearing down on me now
under whitespread wings like he'd come from Arkangels, I sink
I'd die down over his feet, humbly dumbly, only to washup.
Yes, tid. There's where. First. We pass through grass behush
the bush to. Whish! A gull. Gulls. Far calls. Coming, far! End

here. Us then. Finn, again! Take. Bussoftlhee, mememormee!
Till thous-endsthee. Lps. The keys to. Given! A way a lone a last
a loved a long the

It could be a resurrected Cordelia returning to the arms of King
Lear (Leary). Famously, this returns to the opening of the *Wake:*

riverrun, past Eve and Adam's, from swerve of shore to bend
of bay, brings us by a commodius vicus of recirculation back to
Howth Castle and Environs.

CHAPTER 36

The Magic Mountain (1924)

THOMAS MANN

A s I AGE, I feel increasingly under the influence of the great philologist Ernst Robert Curtius (1886–1956). I had hoped to meet him in Rome in 1955, but the timing did not work. We talked on the phone and may have exchanged letters. His extraordinary book, *European Literature and the Latin Middle Ages* (1948, translated 1953 by Willard Trask), has been reread by me so often that I have worn out three copies.

Curtius demonstrates that European literature is a continuous tradition from Homer to Goethe, and then becomes something else. For Curtius, the true touchstones are Dante and Shakespeare. One could argue that Wordsworth ended a tradition and inaugurated another, which is still very much with us. Thomas Mann (1875–1955), despite his endless (and sometimes wearisome) ironies, attempted to get back to Goethe. His agon with Goethe was loving though ambivalent. From his essay "Goethe and Tolstoy" (1922) through his remarkable triad of Goethe essays in the 1930s (on the man of letters, the "representative of the Bourgeois Age," and Faust) on to the "Fantasy on Goethe" of the 1950s, Mann never wearied of reimagining his great original. The finest of these reimaginings, the novel *Lotte in Weimar,* was published in Stockholm in 1939. We know it in English as *The Beloved Returns,* and it is surely the most neglected of Mann's major fictions. Mann is renowned as the author of *The Magic Mountain,* the tetralogy *Joseph and His Brothers, Doctor Faustus, Death in Venice,* and *Felix Krull,* while even the early *Buddenbrooks* remains widely read. But *Lotte in Weimar,* after some initial success, seems to have become a story for specialists, at least in English-speaking countries. Perhaps this is because Goethe, who exported splendidly to Britain and America in the time of Carlyle and Emerson, now seems an untranslatable author. Or it may be that Goethe's spirit has not survived what happened in and through Germany from 1933 until 1945.

In his essay on *Faust,* Mann remarks that the poem depicts love as a devil's holiday. The meditation upon Goethe's career as a man of letters centers itself in a remarkable paragraph that is as much a commentary upon Mann as upon Goethe:

But this business of reproducing the outer world through the inner, which it re-creates after its own form and in its own way, never does, however much charm and fascination may emanate from it, quite satisfy or please the outer world. The reason is that the author's real attitude always has something of opposition in it, which is quite inseparable from his character. It is the attitude of the man of intellect towards the ponderous, stubborn, evil-minded human race, which always places the poet and writer in this particular position, moulding his character and temperament and so conditioning his destiny. "Viewed from the heights of reason," Goethe wrote, "all life looks like some malignant disease and the world like a madhouse." This is a characteristic utterance of the kind of man who writes: the expression of his smarting impatience with mankind. More of the same thing than one would suppose is to be found in Goethe's works: phrases about the "human pack" in general and his "dear Germans" in particular, typical of the specific irritability and aloofness I mean. For what are the factors that condition the life of the writer? They are twofold: perception and a feeling for form; both of these simultaneously. The strange thing is that for the poet they are one organic unity, in which the one implies, challenges, and draws out the other. This unity is, for him, mind, beauty, freedom—everything. Where it is not, there is vulgar human stupidity, expressing itself in lack of perception and imperviousness to beauty of form—nor can he tell you which of the two he finds the more irritating.

We would hardly know that this aesthetic stance is that of Goethe rather than Flaubert, of Mann rather than T. S. Eliot. That is the subject of the grand essay by Mann on "Goethe as Representative of the Bourgeois Age," which nevertheless makes clear how heroically Goethe (and Mann) had to struggle in order to achieve and maintain such health:

As for Goethe, I may make an observation here having to do with certain human and personal effects and symptoms of the anti-ideal constitution; an observation which, indeed, leads me so far into intimate and individual psychology that only indications are possible. There can be no doubt that ideal faith, although it must be prepared for martyrdom, makes one happier in spirit than belief in a lofty and completely ironic sense of poetic achievement without values and opinions, entirely objective, mirroring everything with the same love and the same indifference. There are in Goethe, on closer examination, as soon as the innocence of the youthful period is past, signs of profound maladjustment and ill humour, a hampering depression, which must certainly have a deep-lying uncanny connection with his mistrust of ideas, his child-of-nature dilettantism. There is a peculiar coldness, ill will, médisance, a devil-may-care mood, an inhuman, elfish irresponsibility— which one cannot indulge enough, but must love along with him if one loves him. If one peers into this region of his character one understands that happiness and harmony are much more the affair of the children of spirit than of the children of nature. Clarity, harmony within oneself, strength of purpose, a positive believing and decided aim—in short, peace in the soul—all this is much more easily achieved by these than by the children of nature. Nature does not confer peace of mind, simplicity, single-mindedness; she is a questionable element, she is a contradiction, denial, thorough-going doubt. She endows with no benevolence, not being benevolent herself. She permits no decided judgments, for she is neutral. She endows her children with indifference; with a complex of problems, which have more to do with torment and ill will than with joy and mirth.

Goethe, Mann, and nature are everywhere the same; their happiness and harmony are aesthetic constructs, and never part of the given. Contradictory, skeptical, and full of the spirit that denies, Goethe and Mann triumph by transferring "liberal economic principles to the intellectual life"; they practice what Goethe called a "free trade of conceptions and feelings." The late "Fantasy on Goethe" has a delicious paragraph on the matter of Goethe's free trade in feelings:

> Goethe's love life is a strange chapter. The list of his love affairs has become a requirement of education; in respectable German society one has to be able to rattle off the ladies like the loves of Zeus. Those Friederikes, Lottes, Minnas, and Mariannes have become statues installed in niches in the cathedral of humanity; and perhaps this makes amends to them for their disappointments. For the fickle genius who for short whiles lay at their feet was never prepared to take the consequences, to bear the restriction upon his life and liberty that these charming adventures might have involved. Perhaps the fame of the ladies is compensation to them for his recurrent flights, for the aimlessness of his wooing, the faithlessness of his sincerity, and the fact that his loving was a means to an end, a means to further his work. Where work and life are one, as was the case with him, those who know only how to take life seriously are left with all the sorrows in their laps. But he always reproved them for taking life seriously. "Werther must—must be?" he wrote to Lotte Buff and her fiancé. "You two do not feel him, you feel only me and yourselves. . . . If only you could feel the thousandth part of what Werther means to a thousand hearts, you would not reckon the cost to you." All his women bore the cost, whether they liked it or not.

It is to this aspect of Goethe as "fickle genius" that Mann returned in *The Beloved Returns*, which can serve here as representative both of the strength and the limitation of Mann's art of irony.

After forty-four years, the model for the heroine of Goethe's notorious *The Sorrows of Young Werther* goes to Weimar on pilgrimage, not to be reunited with her lover, now sixty-seven to her sixty-one, but, rather, in the hopeless quest to be made one both with their mutual past, and with his immortal idea of what she once had been, or could have been. For four hundred pages, Mann plays out the all-but-endless ironies of poor Lotte's fame, as the widowed and respectable lady, who has her limitations but is nobody's fool, both enjoys and endures her status and function as a living mythology. Mann's supreme irony, grotesque in its excruciating banalities, is the account of the dinner that the stiff, old Goethe gives in honor of the object of his passion, some forty-four years after the event. Poor Lotte, after being treated as a kind of amalgam of cultural relic and youthful indiscretion shriven by temporal decay, is dismissed by the great man with a palpably insincere: "Life has held us sundered far too long a time for me not to ask of it that we may meet often during your sojourn."

But Mann was too cunning to conclude his book there. A marvelous final meeting is arranged by Goethe himself, who hears Lotte's gentle question, "So meeting again is a short chapter, a fragment?" and replies in the same high aesthetic mode:

"Dear soul, let me answer you from my heart, in expiation and farewell. You speak of sacrifice. But it is a mystery, indivisible, like all else in the world and one's person, one's life, and one's work. Conversion, transformation, is all. They sacrificed to the god, and in the end the sacrifice was God. You used a figure dear and familiar to me; long since, it took possession of my soul. I mean the parable of the moth and the fatal, luring flame. Say, if you will, that I am the flame, and into me the poor moth flings itself. Yet in the chance and change of things I am the candle too, giving my body that the light may burn. And finally, I am the drunken butterfly that falls to the flame—figure of the eternal sacrifice, body transmuted into soul, and life to spirit. Dear soul, dear child, dear childlike old soul, I, first and last, am the sacrifice, and he that offers it. Once I burned you, ever I burn you, into spirit and light. Know that metamorphosis is the dearest and most inward of thy friend, his great hope, his deepest craving: the play of transformation, changing face,

greybeard to youth, to youth the boy, yet ever the human countenance with traits of its proper stage, youth like a miracle shining out in age, age out of youth. Thus mayst thou rest content,
beloved, as I am, with having thought it out and come to me,
decking thine ancient form with signs of youth. Unity in change
and flux, conversion constant out of and into oneself, trans-
mutation of all things, life showing now its natural, now its
cultural face, past turning to present, present pointing back to
past, both preluding future and with her dim foreshadowings
already full. Past feeling, future feeling—feeling is all. Let us
open wide eyes upon the unity of the world—eyes wide, serene,
and wise. Wouldst thou ask of me repentance? Only wait. I see
her ride towards me, in a mantle grey. Then once more the hour
of Werther and Tasso will strike, as at midnight already midday
strikes, and God give me to say what I suffer—only this first and
last will then remain to me. Then forsaking will be only leave-
taking, leave-taking for ever, death-struggle of feeling and the
hour full of frightful pangs, pangs such as probably for some
time precede the hour of death, pangs which are dying if not yet
death. Death, final flight into the flame—the All-in-One—why
should it too be aught but transformation? In my quiet heart,
dear visions, may you rest—and what a pleasant moment that
will be, when we anon awake together!"

In some complex sense, part of the irony here is Mann's revenge
upon his precursor, since it is Mann who burns Goethe into spirit
and light, into the metamorphosis of hope and craving that is *The
Beloved Returns*. Mann and Goethe die each other's lives, live each
other's deaths, in the pre-Socratic formulation that so obsessed W. B.
Yeats. But for Mann, unlike the occult Yeats, the movement through
death into transformation is a complex metaphor for the influence
relationship between Goethe and his twentieth-century descendant.
What Mann, in his "Fantasy on Goethe," delineated in his precursor
is charmingly accurate when applied to Mann himself:

We have here a kind of splendid narcissism, a contentment
with self far too serious and far too concerned to the very end
with self-perfection, heightening, and distillation of personal

endowment, for a petty-minded word like "vanity" to be applicable. Here is that profound delight in that self and its growth to which we owe *Poetry and Truth,* the best, at any rate the most charming autobiography the world has seen—essentially a novel in the first person which informs us, in the most wonderfully winning tone, how a genius is formed, how luck and merit are indissolubly linked by an unknown decree of grace and how a personality grows and flourishes under the sun of a higher dispensation. Personality! Goethe called it "the supreme bliss of mortal man"—but what it really is, in what its inner nature consists, wherein its mystery lies—for there is a mystery about it—not even he ever explained. For that matter, for all his love for the telling word, for the word that strikes to the heart of life, he never thought that everything must be explained. Certainly this phenomenon known as "personality" takes us beyond the sphere of purely intellectual, rational, analyzable matters into the realm of nature, where dwell those elemental and daemonic things which "astound the world" without being amenable to further elucidation.

The splendid narcissism of Mann, at his strongest, is precisely daemonic, is that profound delight in the self without which works as various as *The Magic Mountain* and *Doctor Faustus* would collapse into the weariness of the irony of irony.

In his remarkable essay "Freud and the Future" (1936), Mann wrote the pattern for his own imitation of Goethe:

The ego of antiquity and its consciousness of itself were different from our own, less exclusive, less sharply defined. It was, as it were, open behind; it received much from the past and by repeating it gave it presentness again. The Spanish scholar Ortega y Gasset puts it that the man of antiquity, before he did anything, took a step backwards, like the bull-fighter who leaps back to deliver the mortal thrust. He searched the past for a pattern into which he might slip as into a diving-bell, and being thus at once disguised and protected might rush upon his present problem. Thus his life was in a sense a reanimation, an archaizing attitude. But it is just this life as reanimation that is the life as myth. Alexander walked in the footsteps of

Miltiades; the ancient biographers of Caesar were convinced, rightly or wrongly, that he took Alexander as his prototype. But such "imitation" meant far more than we mean by the word today. It was mythical identification, peculiarly familiar to antiquity; but it is operative far into modern times, and at all times is psychically possible. How often have we not been told that the figure of Napoleon was cast in the antique mould! He regretted that the mentality of the time forbade him to give himself out for the son of Jupiter Ammon, in imitation of Alexander. But we need not doubt that—at least at the period of his Eastern exploits—he mythically confounded himself with Alexander; while after he turned his face westwards he is said to have declared: "I am Charlemagne." Note that: not "I am like Charlemagne" or "My situation is like Charlemagne's," but quite simply "I am he." That is the formulation of the myth. Life, then—at any rate, significant life—was in ancient times the reconstitution of the myth in flesh and blood; it referred to and appealed to the myth; only through it, through reference to the past, could it approve itself as genuine and significant. The myth is the legitimization of life; only through and in it does life find self-awareness, sanction, consecration. Cleopatra fulfilled her Aphrodite character even unto death—and can one live and die more significantly or worthily than in the celebration of the myth? We have only to think of Jesus and His life, which was lived in order that that which was written might be fulfilled. It is not easy to distinguish between his own consciousness and the conventionizations of the Evangelists. But His word on the Cross, about the ninth hour, that "Eli, Eli, lama sabachthani?" was evidently not in the least an outburst of despair and disillusionment; but on the contrary a lofty messianic sense of self. For the phrase is not original, not a spontaneous outcry. It stands at the beginning of the Twenty-second Psalm, which from one end to the other is an announcement of the Messiah. Jesus was quoting, and the quotation meant: "Yes, it is I!" Precisely thus did Cleopatra quote when she took the asp to her breast to die; and again the quotation meant: "Yes, it is I!"

In effect, Mann quotes Goethe, and thus proclaims, "Yes, it is I." The ego of antiquity is simply the artist's ego, appropriating the precursor in order to overcome the belatedness of the influence process. Mann reveals the true subject of his essay on Freud just two paragraphs farther on:

> Infantilism—in other words, regression to childhood—what a role this genuinely psychoanalytic element plays in all our lives! What a large share it has in shaping the life of a human being; operating, indeed, in just the way I have described: as mythical identification, as survival, as a treading in footprints already made! The bond with the father, and the transference to father-substitute pictures of a higher and more developed type—how these infantile traits work upon the life of the individual to mark and shape it! I use the word "shape," for to me in all seriousness the happiest, most pleasurable element of what we call education (Bildung), the shaping of the human being, is just this powerful influence of admiration and love, this childish identification with a father-image elected out of profound affinity. The artist in particular, a passionately childlike and play-possessed being, can tell us of the mysterious yet after all obvious effect of such infantile imitation upon his own life, his productive conduct of a career which after all is often nothing but a reanimation of the hero under very different temporal and personal conditions and with very different, shall we say childish means. The *imitatio* Goethe, with its Werther and Wilhelm Meister stages, its old-age period of Faust and Diwan, can still shape and mythically mould the life of an artist—rising out of his unconscious, yet playing over—as is the artist way— into a smiling, childlike, and profound awareness.

The profound awareness is Mann's own, and concerns his own enactment of the *imitatio* Goethe. Subtly echoed and reversed here is Goethe's observation in his *Theory of Colours* to the effect that "even perfect models have a disturbing effect in that they lead us to skip necessary stages in our Bildung, with the result, for the most part, that we are carried wide of the mark into limitless error." This is also the Goethe who celebrated his own originality as well as his power of appropriating from others. Thus he could say, "Only by making the riches of the others our own do we bring anything great into being," but also insist, "What can we in fact call our own except the energy, the force, the will!" Mann, acutely sensing his own belatedness, liked to quote the old Goethe's question: "Does a man live when others also live?"

The Goethe of *The Beloved Returns* is not Goethe, but Mann himself, the world parodist prophesied and celebrated by Nietzsche as the artist of the future. E. R. Curtius doubtless was accurate in seeing Goethe as an ending and not as a fresh beginning of the cultural tradition. Mann, too, now seems archaic, not a modernist or post-Romantic, but a belated Goethe, a humanist triumphing through the mystery of his own personality and the ironic playfulness of his art. Like his vision of Goethe, Mann now seems a child of nature rather than of the spirit, but laboring eloquently to burn through nature into the transformation that converts deathliness into a dialectical art.

Defending himself from many characterizations as an incessant ironist, Mann belatedly asked us to think of him as a humorist:

> I always feel a bit bored when critics assign my own work so definitely and completely to the realm of irony and consider me an ironist through and through, without also taking account of the concept of humor.
>
> (Thomas Mann)

The author of *The Magic Mountain* insisted that he wished to draw laughter from his reader's heart, rather than an intellectual smile. He has provoked so many intellectual smiles in his exegetes that they have bored us all more than a bit. The irony of irony is that finally it defeats not meaning (as deconstructionist critics insist) but interest, without which we cannot go on reading. Thomas Mann doubtless was what Erich Heller called him, "the ironic German," but rereading *The Magic Mountain* is much more than an experience in irony. Not that the book ever provokes me to laughter. Mann is hardly S. J. Perelman or Philip Roth. Yet it is now more than ninety years since the novel first was published, and the book clearly has mellowed. The irony of one age is never the irony of another, and *The Magic Mountain* seems now a work of gentle high seriousness—as earnest, affectionate, and solid as its admirable hero, Hans Castorp.

That *The Magic Mountain* parodies a host of literary genres and conventions is finely obvious. The effect of Nietzsche upon Mann was very strong, and parody was Nietzsche's answer to the anxieties of influence. Mann evidently did believe that what remained to be done was for art to become its own parody. Presumably, that would have redeemed an irony that at bottom may have been mere indecisiveness. Reading the novel now, the common reader scarcely will recognize the parody of Romantic convention, and can afford to bypass the endless ambiguities of Mann's late version of romantic irony.

This is not to agree with Erich Heller's ironic conclusion: "Such is our world that sense and meaning have to be disguised—as irony, or as literature, or as both come together: for instance in *The Magic Mountain*." Mann's story now primarily offers neither "meaning" nor irony but, rather, a loving representation of past realities, of a European culture forever gone, the culture of Goethe and Freud. A reader in 2018 must experience the book as a historical novel, the cairn of a humanism forever lost, forever longed for. Mann's superb workmanship fashioned the most vivid version we have of a Europe before the catastrophe of the Nazi horror. Where Mann intended parody, the counter-ironies of time and change have produced instead a transformation that today makes *The Magic Mountain* into an immensely poignant study of the nostalgias.

Hans Castorp himself now seems to me both a subtler and a more likable representation than he did when I first read the novel, nearly three-quarters of a century ago. Despite Mann's endorsement of the notion, Castorp is no quester, and pursues no grail or ideal. He is a character of considerable detachment, who will listen with almost equal contentment to the enlightened Settembrini, the terroristic Naphta, or the heroically vitalistic Peeperkorn. His erotic detachment is extraordinary; after seven months, he makes love to Clavdia just once, and then avoids any other sexual experience for the rest of his seven-year stay at the sanatorium. If he has a high passion for Clavdia, it nevertheless carries few of the traditional signs of love's torments. Whether his detachment has some root in his having been an orphan since the age of seven is unclear, but essentially he is content to see, to be taught, to absorb. It may also be that Clavdia renews his schoolboy relationship with Pribislav Hippe, a homoeroticism never fulfilled with someone whose name is a kind of scythe or sickle in German, an attraction with deathly overtones.

We do not think of Castorp as weak, and yet his nature seems almost totally free of aggressivity. It is as though the death drive in him does not take its origin in a wounded narcissism. Castorp bears no psychic scars, and probably never will acquire any. Whatever his maker's intentions, he is not in himself ironic, nor does he seem anymore to be a parody of anything or anyone whatsoever. The common reader becomes very fond of Castorp, and even begins to regard him as a kind of Everyman, which he most certainly is not. His true drive is toward self-education, education sought for its own sake alone. Castorp is that ideal student the universities always proclaim yet never find. He is intensely interested in everything, in all possible knowledge, and yet that knowledge is an end in itself. Knowledge is not power for him, whether over himself or over others; it is in no way Faustian.

Despite his passion for hermeticism, Castorp is not striving to become an esoteric adept, whether rationalist like Settembrini or antirationalist like Naphta. And though he is fascinated by Peeperkorn as a grand personality and an apostle of vitalism, Castorp is more than content with his own apparent colorlessness, and with his own evasions of his only once fulfilled desire for Clavdia, representative as she is of the dark eros that mingles sexual love and death. Castorp is a survivor, and I do not believe that we are to foresee him as dying upon the battlefields of World War I. Naphta kills himself, in frustration at lacking the courage to kill Settembrini; Settembrini is broken by his contemplation of Naphta's desperate act; Peeperkorn, too, is a suicide, unable to bear the onset of impotence. Only Castorp will go on, strengthened and resolute, and possibly will complete his self-transformation from engineer to artist, so as to write a novel not unlike *The Magic Mountain*.

What kind of magic is it—what enchantment does the mountain sanatorium possess? At one extreme limit, the book admits the occult, when Castorp's dead cousin, Joachim, appears at the séance:

> There was one more person in the room than before. There in the background, where the red rays lost themselves in gloom, so that the eye scarcely reached thither, between writing-desk

and screen, in the doctor's consulting-chair, where in the intermission Elly had been sitting, Joachim sat. It was the Joachim
of the last days, with hollow, shadowy cheeks, warrior's beard
and full, curling lips. He sat leaning back, one leg crossed over
the other. On his wasted face, shaded though it was by his head-
covering, was plainly seen the stamp of suffering, the expression of gravity and austerity which had beautified it. Two folds
stood on his brow, between the eyes, that lay deep in their bony
cavities; but there was no change in the mildness of the great
dark orbs, whose quiet friendly gaze sought out Hans Castorp,
and him alone. That ancient grievance of the outstanding ears
was still to be seen under the head-covering, his extraordinary
head-covering, which they could not make out. Cousin Joachim
was not in mufti. His sabre seemed to be leaning against his
leg, he held the handle, one thought to distinguish something
like a pistol-case in his belt. But that was no proper uniform he
wore. No colour, no decorations; it had a collar like a litewka
jacket, and side pockets. Somewhere low down on the breast
was a cross. His feet looked large, his legs very thin, they
seemed to be bound or wound as for the business of sport more
than war. And what was it, this headgear? It seemed as though
Joachim had turned an army cook-pot upside-down on his
head, and fastened it under his chin with a band. Yet it looked
quite properly warlike, like an old-fashioned foot-soldier,
perhaps.

By thus making the occult prophetic of what was to come—the
uniform and helmet are of World War I—Mann essentially chose, all
ironies aside, a mystical theory of time. Many exegetes have noted
the book's obsession with the number seven, in all its variants. Others have noted that after Joachim dies all temporal references disap-
pear from the novel. Castorp forgets his own age, and the length of
his own stay on the Magic Mountain. He passes into timelessness.

How long Joachim had lived here with his cousin, up to the
time of his fateful departure, or taken all in all; what had been
the date of his going, how long he had been gone, when he
had come back; how long Hans Castorp himself had been up

here when his cousin returned and then bade time farewell; how long—dismissing Joachim from our calculations—Frau Chauchat had been absent; how long, since what date, she had been back again (for she did come back); how much mortal time Hans Castorp himself had spent in House Berghof by the time she returned; no one asked him all these questions, and he probably shrank from asking himself. If they had been put to him, he would have tapped his forehead with the tips of his fingers, and most certainly not have known—a phenomenon as disquieting as his incapacity to answer Herr Settembrini, that long-ago first evening, when the latter had asked him his age.

The opening words of the novel describe Castorp as "an unassuming young man," but this fellow who seems the apotheosis of the average is of course hermetic and daemonic, marked from birth for singular visions of eternity. Bildung, the supposed thematic pattern that the book inherits from Goethe, Stifter, Keller, and others, hardly is possible for Castorp, who does not require the endless cultural instruction nearly everyone else wishes to inflict upon him. He need not develop; he simply unfolds. For he is Primal Man, the Ur-Adam of the Gnostic myth that Mann lovingly expounds in the "Prelude" of his Joseph tetralogy. Indeed, he already is Mann's Joseph, the favored of heaven.

Much of what Mann intended as memorable value in *The Magic Mountain* has, paradoxically, been lost to time. The social satire, intellectual irony, and sense of cultural crisis are all now quite archaic. Settembrini, Naphta, Peeperkorn, Clavdia, and Joachim all possess an antique charm, a kind of faded aesthetic dignity, parodies of parodies, period pieces, old photographs uncannily right and yet altogether odd. Hans Castorp, as colorless now as he was in 1924, retains his immediacy, his relevance, his disturbing claim upon us. He is not the Nietzschean new man, without a superego, but the Nietzschean will to interpretation: receptive rather than rapacious, plural rather than unitary, affective rather than indifferent, distanced from rather than abandoned to desire. In some sense, Castorp knows that he himself is an interpretation, knows that he represents neither Schopenhauer's will to live, nor Freud's mingled drives of love and death, but Nietzsche's will to power over the text of life. The implicit questions Castorp is always putting to everyone else in the book are: who exactly are you, the interpreter, and what power do you seek to gain over my life? Because he puts these questions to us also, with cumulative force, Castorp becomes a representation we cannot evade. Mann, taking leave of his hero, said that Castorp mattered because of his "dream of love," presumably the vision of the chapter "Snow." It was fortunate that Mann, a miraculous artisan, had wrought better than even he himself knew. Castorp is one of those rare fictions who acquire the authority to call our versions of reality into some doubt. The reader, interpreting Castorp, must come to ask herself or himself: what is my dream of love, my erotic illusion, and how does that dream or illusion qualify my own possibilities of unfolding?

Thomas Mann, in this sense only like Tolstoy, was a dreadful husband and a catastrophic father. He had six children with his wife, Katia Pringsheim, who came from a secularized Jewish family. His deepest desires were homosexual, which became a kind of open secret, and his bisexuality was repeated in his children Erika, Klaus, and Golo. Katia Pringsheim, who had obliged Mann by converting to Lutheranism, was perpetually overworked, not only in caring for him and the six children, but by having to make all the daily decisions that kept the household going. She collapsed from exhaustion, and was sent to a Davos sanatorium to rest and recover. Visiting her there, Mann evidently first conceived of *The Magic Mountain.*

Mann's children slowly learned to weather his egoism and to make their way on their own, but two of them, Klaus and Michael, eventually committed suicide. Erika, surely the most remarkable, in time became the true head of the household and presided over her parents and her siblings, insofar as she could.

When I was very young, I greatly enjoyed reading two historical novels by Mann's older brother, Heinrich, both on Henry of Navarre, who was to become King Henry IV of France, first of the Bourbon monarchs. Heinrich Mann seems to me a much more impressive human being than his more gifted brother. Unlike Thomas Mann, he opposed the Nazis from the start and had to go into exile in France, and eventually fled first to Spain, then to Portugal, and finally to the

United States, where he did not prosper. His second wife killed herself, and he died in solitude and poor circumstances in California.

I return to Hans Castorp, whom Thomas Mann ironically deprecated as a perfectly ordinary young man. Castorp is anything but that. Thomas Mann tried to make him superficially drab, but a good reader of the novel learns to shrug that off. Everything and nothing happens to Hans Castorp during his seven-year sojourn on the Enchanted Mountain. He falls in love with the enigmatic Clavdia Chauchat, who grants him only a single tryst. Stubbornly, he retains the passion, if that is the accurate word for a bizarre relationship that is never renewed. Instead, Clavdia returns after a long absence with her new lover, the boisterously Dionysiac Mynheer Peeperkorn, a large Dutch owner of a plantation in Java. Peeperkorn is a manifest parody of Gerhart Hauptmann (1862–1946), a German dramatist and novelist who was rather tainted by Nazi associations, and who preceded Thomas Mann by seventeen years as a winner of the Nobel Prize in Literature.

I think every reader of *The Magic Mountain* enjoys Peeperkorn, since the polemical humanist Ludovico Settembrini and his antagonist, the Jewish-Jesuit-Nietzschean Leo Naphta, who battle for Hans Castorp's soul, begin to weary us until their ghastly duel, in which Settembrini deliberately fires in the air, and the infuriated Naphta then shoots himself in the head. Thomas Mann largely based Naphta on György Lukács (1885–1971), Hungarian Jewish literary critic and philosopher who propounded a kind of Romantic Marxism.

As I have indicated, Hans Castorp seems to me an extraordinary young man and a profoundly realized personality. For all his exquisite diffidence, he is a seeker after otherness, and seems to know that at last he will find it in himself. Moved as he is by Settembrini, and in another mode by Naphta, he finds a culminating figure not in Clavdia but in the burly Dionysiac who so palpably is approaching a terrible end:

At the mention of the word "knife," Mynheer Peeperkorn had changed his sitting position in bed somewhat, suddenly edging away and turning his face to search his guest's eyes. Now he sat up more comfortably, propping himself on his elbows, and said, "Young man, I have heard, and I have the picture. And on the basis of what you have just said, permit me to make an honorable declaration of my own. Were my hair not white and were I not so debilitated by this malign fever, you would see me prepared to give you satisfaction, man to man, weapon in hand, for the injury I have unwittingly inflicted upon you, and for the additional injury caused by my traveling companion, for which I likewise must take responsibility. Agreed, my good sir. You would see me prepared. But as things stand, you will permit me to make another suggestion in lieu of that. It is as follows: I recall a sublime moment, at the very beginning of our acquaintance—I recall it, though I had copiously partaken of wine—a moment when, touched by your pleasant tempera- ment, I was about to offer you the brotherhood of informal pronouns, but could not avoid the realization that such a step would have been overhasty. Fine, I refer today to that moment, I return to it now, I declare the postponement we agreed upon then to be at an end. Young man, we are brothers, I declare us to be such. You spoke of the use of informal pronouns in their full meaning—and our use of them shall also be in the full meaning of a brotherhood of feeling. The satisfaction that old age and infirmity prevent me from offering you by means of weapons, I now offer you in this form; I offer it in the form of a bond of brotherhood, of the sort that is usually established against a third part, against the world, against someone else, but which we shall establish in our feelings for someone. Take up your wineglass, young man, while I reach yet again for my water tumbler—it will do this modest vintage no further harm—"

His captain's hand trembling slightly, he filled the glasses, with the assistance, offered in respectful bewilderment, of Hans Castorp.

"Take it," Peeperkorn repeated. "Link arms with me! And drink now thus. Drink it down!—Agreed, young man. Settled. Here, my hand on it. Are you satisfied, Hans Castorp?"

"That is, of course, no word for it, Mynheer Peeperkorn," said Hans Castorp, who had some difficulty downing the whole glass in one draft, and now took out his handkerchief to wipe the wine he had spilled on his knee. "What I mean is, I am terribly happy and still cannot grasp how this has so suddenly been bestowed on me—it is, I must admit, like a dream. It is an overwhelming honor for me—I don't know how I have earned it, at best in some passive way, certainly not in any other. And one should not be surprised if at first I shall find it rather daring to utter this new form of address and stumble in the attempt—particularly in the presence of Clavdia, who, being but a woman, may not be quite so pleased with this new arrangement."

What is it in Peeperkorn that has found Hans Castorp? The link with Clavdia is secondary, since she was just a later form of Pribislaw Hippe. Peeperkorn's vitalism is ebbing: impotence beckons. Confronted with that inescapable contingency, he has already planned a painless suicide, with a hypodermic needle of his own invention, and a fatal poison from Java carried with him. By embracing Hans Castorp, is he asserting a final allegiance to life?

The best essay I have ever read on *The Magic Mountain* is by Oskar Seidlin, born Salo Oskar Koplowitz (1911–84), a Jewish scholar who left Nazi Germany to spend his remaining lifetime teaching and writing in the United States. His essay "Mynheer Peeperkorn and the Lofty Game of Numbers" (1971) was reprinted by me in a volume I edited, *Thomas Mann's The Magic Mountain: Modern Critical Interpretations* (1986). His game of numbers is Kabbalistic, turning upon Mann's obsession with the number seven. Peeperkorn is both Dionysos and Christ, and his appeal to Hans Castorp is androgynous, hermetic, calling upon a bisexual vision central both to Oskar Seidlin and to Mann:

We have not reached the deepest layer yet. With all the noumenal "Mysterium" and incarnation which we tried to elucidate, Peeperkorn is "only" a human being, and thus the task to embody the divine is bound to be unfulfillable. No matter how strong and enthusiastic the spirit, the flesh plays it a nasty trick. It cannot live up to the exuberance and overflow of life which Peeperkorn feels to be his and whose emanation he considers his mission. In short, he is impotent, impotent in the crassest physical sense of the word: the flesh refuses to accept the challenge with which he knows himself entrusted. This explains the terror and anguish that overcome him; this is the deepest abyss of his Passion. He cannot be God, but at best God's deputy on earth—i.e., not Christ but Peter—and we are not surprised that this is his first name. We now understand, too, why the biblical passage relating to Christ's desolation in the Garden of Gethsemane is so firmly imbedded in Mynheer Peeperkorn's mind that he can recite it verbatim. It is his own story: Christ chiding Peter (and it is Peter whom Christ mainly addresses), who is no one else but he himself, the one who in shame and despair must recognize his insufficiency, because the flesh is weak no matter how willing the spirit.

The anguish of the Garden of Gethsemane has, of course, its pagan counterpart. It is the event that takes place on the last afternoon before Mynheer Peeperkorn's suicide, and is, in fact, the cause of his suicide: nothing more than an excursion to a waterfall near Davos, in which seven persons participate, driving out in two carriages, three in the one, four in the other. We notice, in passing, that the forest through which the seven travel on their way to their destination is sick: afflicted by a cancerous fungus, which overgrows the branches of the conifers and threatens to choke the trees. Upon Peeperkorn's insistence, the picnic (with plenty of bread and wine) is being held not only in full view of the waterfall, but actually so close to the roaring cataract that any conversation becomes impossible. After the collation, something strange happens. Peeperkorn rises, faces the thundering waterfall (which bursts down from a height of approximately seven or eight meters), and starts talking to it as if trying to conjure the wild unleashed energy of nature, whose tumultuous uproar blots out every word the old man utters. Clearly, he tries to measure himself against the riotously unchained force of the elemental, tries to transfix it, but in vain. His voice is drowned in the cosmic noise, and his companions can read from the motions of his lips only the two last words of the strange invocation *perfekt und erledigt* [settled and finished]—*erledigt*, done with, finished. It is the last word that we hear Peeperkorn utter in the novel. On the way back to the sanatorium, hardly a word is spoken in Peeperkorn's carriage. Shortly after two o'clock in the morning, the night nurse, at Madame Chauchat's request, calls Hans Castorp to the Dutchman's room. He is dead. He has killed himself by injecting into his veins some of the violent, exotic poison, the "spice" that he brought with him from India.

Convinced that in the work of every great writer even the minutest detail is significant, we are, with the Dutchman's death, not yet at the end of the Peeperkorn episode. After Hofrat Behrens has diagnosed the suicide, he beckons Hans into a corner of the drawing room and demonstrates to him in a long technical explanation the workings of the instrument with which Peeperkorn ended his life. It is not a simple syringe, but a highly complicated, outlandish mechanism, made up of teeth, honed to pinpoint sharpness, in which are embedded hair-thin cannulae leading to a "rubber-gland" that contains the poison. Upon pressure, the teeth, mounted on tiny springs, squeeze the rubber container, which then squirts the deadly fluid through the tubulae outward. Teeth—gland: we would hardly need Dr. Behrens's explicit statement that this instrument is an exact mechanical replica of the *Beißzeugs der Brillenschlange* [mechanism of the cobra's bite]. What caused Peeperkorn's death was the work of the snake. In the last analysis, he is not the new Adam, but Adam plain and simple, flesh in its weakness and sinfulness, which is man, because this is what the Hebrew word "Adam" actually means.

Yet—and this is his greatness and dignity—he wanted to be and walked through the pages of the book as more than Adam. Just as Hans Castorp, immediately after Peeperkorn's appearance on the Magic Mountain, took a good look at the new guest and assessed his strange individuality, so now, standing at the old man's deathbed, he speaks the epitaph which compresses into a few words the Dutchman's substance and serves as a last verification of the argument we have presented: "*er betrachtete sich als Gottes Hochzeitsorgan, müssen Sie wissen* [For you must know, he regarded himself as the instrument of God's marriage]." Again the images of Dionysos and Christ appear united. The sexual implication, evoking the phallus, signal of carnal fertility and triumphant ruler over the Dionysian mysteries, is obvious. But equally obvious is Christ's role as the heavenly bridegroom, through whom man's soul is wedded to God. There could be no more fitting word than the one Thomas Mann has chosen. It points to the act of consummation, in its physical aspect by the anatomical part of the body, in its spiritual aspect by the *organon,* the medium through which the union of man and God is achieved. As we have tried to show, this was what Mynheer Peeperkorn wanted to live: the sum of three and four.

I find this extremely persuasive. Oskar Seidlin penetrates the matrix of what makes the mountain enchanting. And then he goes beyond that:

> But Hans Castorp gives us more than just the pinpointing of the *"Eigenart* [particularity]*"* of the eleventh-hour visitor on the magic mountain. He pronounces judgment, and much confusion could have been avoided had the readers of the book taken the trouble to listen to him. This divine mission which Mynheer Peeperkorn considered his and which he could not fulfill because he was only Peter and not Christ, was, so we now hear, *"eine königliche Narretei* [a piece of majestic tomfoolery]*."* Foolishness it may have been, but all the detractors of Peeperkorn, inside and outside the book, should take notice that it was a regal foolishness. And Hans Castorp continues, making crystal clear that the word "foolishness" is not to be taken in a deprecatory sense, but as an expression of the deepest emotion and the most solemn respect: *"Wenn man ergriffen ist, hat man den Mut zu Ausdrücken, die kraß und pietätlos klingen, aber feierlicher sind als konzessionierte Andachtsworte* [when one is moved one can say things that sound crass and irreverent, but are after all more solemn than the conventional religious formulas]*."* Peeperkorn's is the rarest and noblest sort of foolishness—perhaps even the wisest—with which man can be afflicted: the self-identification with the living presence of the creatively divine.

William Blake said that if the fool would persist in his folly, he would become wise. Dr. Samuel Johnson, treated by Blake with jocular contempt, nevertheless preceded him by saying that love was the wisdom of fools and the folly of the wise. Hans Castorp ultimately is in love with the mystery of personality. As Seidlin notes, Castorp casts aside both jealousy and passion, so as to enter into a covenant with Clavdia to help preserve the waning Peeperkorn. For Clavdia, sexuality is death. Hans Castorp affirms life, and will not yield to death and its attractions.

In the perhaps too deliberated chapter "Snow," Thomas Mann
sketches an overwrought affirmation:

> Love stands opposed to death—it alone, and not enough, is
> stronger than death. Only love, and not reason, yields kind
> thoughts. And form, too, comes only from love and goodness:
> form and the cultivated manners of man's fair state, of a rea-
> sonable, genial community—out of silent regard for the bloody
> banquet. Oh, what a clear dream I've dreamed, how well I've
> 'played king'! I will remember it. I will keep faith with death
> in my heart, but I will clearly remember that if faithfulness to
> death and to what is past rules our thoughts and deeds, that
> leads only to wickedness, dark lust, and hatred of humankind.
> *For the sake of goodness and love, man shall grant death no*
> *dominion over his thoughts.* And with that I shall awaken.
> For with that I have dreamed my dream to its end, to its goal.
> I've long been searching for that truth: in the meadow where
> Hippe appeared to me, on my balcony, everywhere. The search
> for it drove me into these snowy mountains. And now I have
> it. My dream has granted it to me so clearly that I will always
> remember. Yes, I am overjoyed and filled with its warmth. My
> heart is beating strong and knows why. It beats not for purely
> physical reasons, the way fingernails grow on a corpse. It beats
> for human reasons and because my spirit is truly happy. The
> truth of my dream has refreshed me—better than port or ale, it
> courses through my veins like love and life, so that I may tear
> myself out of my dreaming sleep, which I know only too well
> can be fatal to my young life. Awake, awake! Open your eyes.
> Those are your limbs, your legs there in the snow. Pull yourself
> together and stand up. Look—good weather!

I regret that aesthetically this just does not work. The best thing
in it is the recollection of Hippe, who more than Clavdia was the
portent of love and death. The prologue to Thomas Mann's tetralogy *Joseph and His Brothers* (1943) retells the Hermetic myth of
a divine Man/God who beholds her/his reflection in the Waters of
Night, falls in love with that image, and descends from the Holy
Light into the Darkness of our world. That Darkness is named "Love
and Death." It is also called "Sleep."

It seems to me that all of Thomas Mann is in that prologue. That includes *The Magic Mountain*. On the mountain; sleep, death, desire, close around Hans Castorp like a floating flower.

As Mann ends by saying, "It was a hermetic story." I myself doubt that irony after irony is consistent with Hermetic myth. The author's avuncular tone distresses me, particularly at the close of *The Magic Mountain*. But I am being ungrateful. Thomas Mann is not of the order of Marcel Proust and James Joyce, of Franz Kafka and Samuel Beckett. But who now is? *Buddenbrooks, Death in Venice, The Magic Mountain, Joseph and His Brothers, Doctor Faustus, Confessions of Felix Krull:* all these are still alive.

CHAPTER 37

To the Lighthouse (1927)

VIRGINIA WOOLF

T HE LIFE OF Virginia Woolf was an extended and desperate
agon with psychosis. When she was thirteen, her mother died
and Virginia Stephen collapsed. At twenty-two, she lost her father,
Leslie Stephen, philosopher and historian, and again broke down.
Eight years later, she married Leonard Woolf. The union lasted until
her suicide and undoubtedly sustained her, but it is unlikely the
marriage was ever consummated. Her lesbian relationship with the
bad poet but great gardener Vita Sackville-West continued on and
off for a decade, but then ended because of Vita's frequent escapades
with both female and male lovers. Another cause of the rift was Vita's
fascist sympathies.

A third crisis lasted for three years, from age thirty to thirty-three.
Finally, under the terrible stress of German air bombardment, Woolf
drowned herself at the age of fifty-nine.

Woolf's major novels, by common consent, are *Mrs. Dalloway*
(1925) and *To the Lighthouse* (1927). *Orlando* (1928) remains popular, but is a secondary work. Her later novels are all extraordinary
work, and clearly will survive: *The Waves* (1931), *The Years* (1937),
and a final masterpiece, *Between the Acts* (1941). Formally speaking,
Woolf's finest novel is *To the Lighthouse,* which is a miraculous concentration of her varied gifts.

Woolf insists that the creative power of women "differs greatly from the creative power of men." Iris Murdoch refreshingly disagreed: "I think there's human experience; and I don't think a woman's mind differs essentially from a man's." There are major male novelists—Samuel Richardson, Tolstoy, Henry James—who have explored female consciousness perhaps more fully than did Jane Austen and Virginia Woolf. One can add Marcel Proust and James Joyce, whose depictions of inwardness are equally strong, whether women or men are being portrayed.

Except for her aestheticism, the author of *To the Lighthouse* would be wholly nihilistic, which is true also of Pater, Ruskin, and Proust. Woolf teaches perception, and not politics. Her "androgyny" is not a pragmatic program, but a fusion of perception and sensation with her acceptance of death and meaninglessness, apart from the flow of momentary meanings that art can suggest.

In May 1940, less than a year before she drowned herself, Virginia Woolf read a paper to the Workers' Educational Association in Brighton. We know it as the essay entitled "The Leaning Tower," in which the Shelleyan emblem of the lonely tower takes on more of a social than an imaginative meaning. It is no longer the point of survey from which the poet Athanase gazes down in pity at the dark estate of mankind, and so is not an image of contemplative wisdom isolated from the mundane. Instead, it is "the tower of middle-class birth and expensive education." It would be accurate to suggest that Woolf preferred Shelley to W. H. Auden, though she knew she herself dwelt in the leaning tower, unlike Yeats, to whom the lonely tower remained an inevitable metaphor for poetic stance.

It is proper that "The Leaning Tower," as a speculation upon the decline of a Romantic image into belatedness, should concern itself also with the peculiarities of poetic influence:

> Theories then are dangerous things. All the same we must risk making one this afternoon since we are going to discuss modern tendencies. Directly we speak of tendencies or movements we commit ourselves to the belief that there is some force, influence, outer pressure which is strong enough to stamp itself upon a whole group of different writers so that all their writing has a certain common likeness. We must then have a theory as to

what this influence is. But let us always remember—influences are infinitely numerous; writers are infinitely sensitive; each writer has a different sensibility. That is why literature is always changing, like the weather, like clouds in the sky. Read a page of Scott; then of Henry James; try to work out the influences that have transformed the one page into the other. It is beyond our skill. We can only hope therefore to single out the most obvious influences that have formed writers into groups. Yet there are groups. Books descend from books as families descend from families. Some descend from Jane Austen; others from Dickens. They resemble their parents, as human children resemble their parents; yet they differ as children differ, and revolt as children revolt. Perhaps it will be easier to understand living writers as we take a quick look at some of their forebears.

"A sudden light transfigures a trivial thing, a weather-vane, a windmill, a winnowing flail, the dust in the barn door; a moment— and the thing has vanished, because it was pure effect." That is Walter Pater, and also Virginia Woolf. Woolf, like Pater, sets herself "to realize this situation, to define, in a chill and empty atmosphere, the focus where rays, in themselves pale and impotent, unite and begin to burn. . . ." Against this can be set Lily Briscoe's vision, which concludes the novel:

> Quickly, as if she were recalled by something over there, she turned to her canvas. There it was—her picture. Yes, with all its greens and blues, its lines running up and across, its attempt at something. It would be hung in the attics, she thought; it would be destroyed. But what did that matter? she asked herself, taking up her brush again. She looked at the steps; they were empty; she looked at her canvas; it was blurred. With a sudden intensity, as if she saw it clear for a second, she drew a line there, in the centre. It was done; it was finished. Yes, she thought, laying down her brush in extreme fatigue, I have had my vision.

An "attempt at something" is, for Woolf, a center, however wavering. The apotheosis of perceptive principle here is Woolf's beautifully poised approach to an affirmation of the difficult possibility of meaning. *The Waves* (1931) is a large-scale equivalent of Lily Briscoe's painting. Bernard, the most comprehensive of the novel's six first-person narrators, ends the book with a restrained exultation:

> "Again I see before me the usual street. The canopy of civilisation is burnt out. The sky is dark as polished whale-bone. But there is a kindling in the sky whether of lamplight or of dawn. There is a stir of some sort—sparrows on plane trees somewhere chirping. There is a sense of the break of day. I will not call it dawn. What is dawn in the city to an elderly man standing in the street looking up rather dizzily at the sky? Dawn is some sort of whitening of the sky; some sort of renewal. Another day; another Friday; another twentieth of March, January, or September. Another general awakening. The stars draw back and are extinguished. The bars deepen themselves between the waves. The film of mist thickens on the fields. A redness gathers on the roses, even on the pale rose that hangs by the bedroom window. A bird chirps. Cottagers light their early candles. Yes, this is the eternal renewal, the incessant rise and fall and fall and rise again.
>
> "And in me too the wave rises. It swells; it arches its back. I am aware once more of a new desire, something rising beneath me like the proud horse whose rider first spurs and then pulls him back. What enemy do we now perceive advancing against us, you whom I ride now, as we stand pawing this stretch of pavement? It is death. Death is the enemy. It is death against whom I ride with my spear couched and my hair flying back like a young man's, like Percival's, when he galloped in India. I strike spurs into my horse. Against you I will fling myself, unvanquished and unyielding, O Death!"
>
> *The waves broke on the shore.*

"Incessant rise and fall and fall and rise again," though ascribed to Bernard, has in it the fine pathos of a recognition of natural harshness that does not come often to a male consciousness. And, for all the warlike imagery, the ride against death transcends aggressivity, whether against the self or against others. Pater had insisted that our one choice lies in packing as many pulsations of the artery, or Blakean visions of the poet's work, into our interval as possible. Woolf subtly hints that even Pater succumbs to a male illusion of experiential quantity, rather than to a female recognition of gradations in the quality of possible experience. A male critic might want to murmur, in defense of Pater, that male blindness of the void within experience is very difficult to overcome, and that Pater's exquisite sensibility is hardly male, whatever the accident of his gender.

Parodying Shakespeare is a dangerous mode; the flat-out farce of Max Beerbohm and Nigel Dennis works more easily than Woolf's allusive deftness, but Woolf is not interested in the crudities of farce. *Between the Acts* is her deferred fulfillment of the polemical program set forth in her marvelous polemic *A Room of One's Own* (1929). To me the most powerful and unnerving stroke in that book is in its trope for the enclosure that men have forced upon women:

> For women have sat indoors all these millions of years, so that by this time the very walls are permeated by their creative force, which has, indeed, so overcharged the capacity of bricks and mortar that it must needs harness itself to pens and brushes and business and politics. But this creative power differs greatly from the creative power of men...

Hermione Lee, a superb literary biographer and critic, gave an intense, rather Woolfian reverie on the moral stance of *To the Lighthouse* in her *The Novels of Virginia Woolf* (1977):

> In a novel which criticizes and mocks but finally finds admirable Mr. Ramsay's bleak drama of endurance, the consolations offered for death are based on the real Mr. Ramsay's principles. Completed forms, whether made from a social and family group, an abstract painting, or the journey to the lighthouse, create the only lasting victory over death and chaos.

This deftly recalls Walter Pater's exaltation of sensation and perception as the only chance in our brief interval before the dark. But

Hermione Lee, closer to Virginia Woolf, extends the Paterian vision to a family group or passage to a lighthouse. But can any novel, even the finest and subtlest in mode, approximate a completed form? Shakespeare, at his most astonishing, in *Hamlet* and *King Lear* and *The Tempest*, achieves configurations transcending flaws and touching "the undiscovered country from whose bourn / No traveler returns." Dante conceived a *Commedia* so articulated that form is at once strange beyond all measure and yet so complete that it overcomes my spiritual opposition (but I go on sympathizing with Farinata, who stands upright in his tomb, as if of hell he had a great disdain). It is uncertain whether even Tolstoy or Proust or Joyce (barring the *Wake*) gave us completed forms.

But is Woolf at her keenest—in *To the Lighthouse, The Waves, Between the Acts*—composing novels or prose poems rather like Pater's *Imaginary Portraits*? Here is my favorite passage in *To the Lighthouse*, centering on the beauty of Mrs. Ramsay:

> But which was it to be? They had all the trays of her jewel-case open. The gold necklace, which was Italian, or the opal necklace, which Uncle James had brought her from India; or should she wear her amethysts?
>
> "Choose, dearests, choose," she said, hoping that they would make haste.
>
> But she let them take their time to choose: she let Rose, particularly, take up this and then that, and hold her jewels against the black dress, for this little ceremony of choosing jewels, which was gone through every night, was what Rose liked best, she knew. She had some hidden reason of her own for attaching great importance to this choosing what her mother was to wear. What was the reason, Mrs. Ramsay wondered, standing still to let her clasp the necklace she had chosen, divining, through her own past, some deep, some buried, some quite speechless feeling that one had for one's mother at Rose's age. Like all feelings felt for oneself, Mrs. Ramsay thought, it made one sad. It was so inadequate, what one could give in return; and what Rose felt was quite out of proportion to anything she actually was. And Rose would grow up; and Rose would suffer, she supposed, with these deep feelings, and she said she was ready now, and

they would go down, and Jasper, because he was the gentleman, should give her his arm, and Rose, as she was the lady,
should carry her handkerchief (she gave her the handkerchief),
and what else? oh, yes, it might be cold: a shawl. Choose me a
shawl, she said, for that would please Rose, who was bound
to suffer so. "There," she said, stopping by the window on the
landing, "there they are again." Joseph had settled on another
tree-top. "Don't you think they mind," she said to Jasper, "having their wings broken?" Why did he want to shoot poor old
Joseph and Mary? He shuffled a little on the stairs, and felt
rebuked, but not seriously, for she did not understand the fun
of shooting birds; and they did not feel; and being his mother
she lived away in another division of the world, but he rather
liked her stories about Mary and Joseph. She made him laugh.
But how did she know that those were Mary and Joseph? Did
she think the same birds came to the same trees every night? he
asked. But here, suddenly, like all grown-up people, she ceased
to pay him the least attention. She was listening to a clatter in
the hall.

"They've come back!" she exclaimed, and at once she felt
much more annoyed with them than relieved. Then she wondered, had it happened? She would go down and they would
tell her—but no. They could not tell her anything, with all these
people about. So she must go down and begin dinner and wait.
And, like some queen who, finding her people gathered in the
hall, looks down upon them, and descends among them, and
acknowledges their tributes silently, and accepts their devotion
and their prostration before her (Paul did not move a muscle
but looked straight before him as she passed) she went down,
and crossed the hall and bowed her head very slightly, as if she
accepted what they could not say: their tribute to her beauty.

Virginia Woolf's mother, Julia Duckworth, was widowed before
she married Virginia's father, Leslie Stephen. The beauty of Julia
Duckworth passed to her daughters Vanessa Bell and Virginia Woolf.
Julia (then Julia Stephen) died at just forty-nine and Vanessa Bell
at eighty-one, and Virginia Woolf killed herself at fifty-nine. Julia's
beauty, immortalized in Mrs. Ramsay, is more than visual: it gath-

ers up moments of being in one regnant image. There is a mournful undersong; Virginia was only thirteen when Julia died. I think on this, and Edmund Spenser's "Epithalamion," made for his own marriage, peals in me:

> Now al is done; bring home the bride againe,
> Bring home the triumph of our victory,
> Bring home with you the glory of her gaine,
> With joyance bring her and with jollity.
> Never had man more joyfull day then this,
> Whom heaven would heape with blis.

Leslie Stephen, the least poetical of men, bereaved of Julia when he was sixty-two, has a claim on sympathy in losing so rare a wife. It is not simple to surmise Virginia Woolf's deeper motivations in creating Mr. Ramsay. Shortly before she died, she jotted down a note describing Leslie Stephen as a tripartite father: writer, social being, tyrant. Does one hear a tyrant in the self-pitying, forlorn widower who becomes obsessed with William Cowper's "The Castaway"?

"But I beneath a rougher sea," Mr. Ramsay murmured. He had found the house and so seeing it, he had also seen himself there; he had seen himself walking on the terrace, alone. He was walking up and down between the urns; and he seemed to himself very old and bowed. Sitting in the boat, he bowed, he crouched himself, acting instantly his part—the part of a desolate man, widowed, bereft; and so called up before him in hosts people sympathising with him; staged for himself as he sat in the boat, a little drama; which required of him decrepitude and exhaustion and sorrow (he raised his hands and looked at the thinness of them, to confirm his dream) and then there was given him in abundance women's sympathy, and he imagined how they would soothe him and sympathise with him, and so getting in his dream some reflection of the exquisite pleasure women's sympathy was to him, he sighed and said gently and mournfully,
But I beneath a rougher sea
Was whelmed in deeper gulfs than he,

so that the mournful words were heard quite clearly by them all. Cam half started on her seat. It shocked her—it outraged her.

"The Castaway," perhaps William Cowper's most severe lyric and his last published poem, laments his melancholia and compares it to a crewman washed overboard who cannot be helped by his shipmates because of a violent storm:

No voice divine the storm allay'd,
No light propitious shone;
When, snatch'd from all effectual aid,
We perish'd, each alone:
But I beneath a rougher sea,
And whelm'd in deeper gulfs than he.

If you were Leslie Stephen's daughter, his self-indulgence had to outrage you. But we are readers. We love Mrs. Ramsay and shrug at her uneasy husband. Like another precursor, Samuel Johnson, Virginia Woolf made her appeal to the common reader. There is a paradox here. Most common readers, however devoted, find *To the Lighthouse* and *The Waves* difficult. James Joyce and Virginia Woolf were born about eight days apart in 1882, and he died only two months before her in 1941. Though Leonard Woolf wished to publish *Ulysses* with his Hogarth Press, Virginia demurred. Her diary entries on this are hardly salubrious:

An illiterate, underbred book it seems to me; the book of a self taught working man, and we all know how distressing they are, how egotistic, insistent, raw, striking, and ultimately nauseating.

. . . .

I finished "Ulysses" and think it is a mis-fire. Genius it has, I think; but of the inferior water. The book is diffuse. It is brackish. It is pretentious. It is underbred, not only in the obvious sense, but in the literary sense. A first-rate writer, I mean, respects writing too much to be tricky; startling; doing stunts.

In writing about the many books she loved, Virginia Woolf could be a good Johnsonian critic. On Joyce's *Ulysses,* she is at her rare worst: snobbish, resentful, a touch frightened. And wrong, absolutely wrong. The Jesuit-trained James Joyce was erudite beyond measure and so gifted as to be almost the fusion of Dante and Shakespeare. That was his vaunting ambition. It was beyond reach. You would need an amalgam of Proust, Joyce, Kafka, Beckett to approximate either Dante or Shakespeare.

Virginia Woolf loved Proust, never read Kafka, and was gone before Beckett began to be known. I have been reading her since I was a teenager, and believe I know all of her work, fictional and personal. Before the final parting, I would like to read again *To the Lighthouse, The Waves, Between the Acts,* and the posthumously published *Moments of Being,* a collection of five autobiographical essays, the most intense centering upon the death of her mother.

That panoply is not Joyce or Proust, but is not minor. Her sensibility was so tenuously attuned to the aesthetic ideal that I am reminded of Thomas De Quincey's wonderful remark about Samuel Taylor Coleridge: "He wanted better bread than can be made with wheat."

CHAPTER 38

In Search of Lost Time (1927)

MARCEL PROUST

M ARCEL PROUST died in 1922, the year in which James Joyce published *Ulysses,* and T. S. Eliot, *The Waste Land. Harmonium,* the first book of poems by Wallace Stevens, appeared in 1923, to be followed by Hart Crane's *White Buildings* in 1926. The seer of *In Search of Lost Time* was just fifty-one when he died, having published *Swann's Way* in 1913. During the war years, publication being impossible, Proust vastly expanded his encyclopedic novel. When peace came, individual volumes appeared, with the last, *The Past Recaptured,* published posthumously.

I have written a great deal about Proust, particularly in my last book, *Possessed by Memory.* Since I endlessly reread him, he has to be here, but I do not wish to repeat myself and will confine my relatively brief discussion to his epiphanies, as James Joyce called them, or privileged moments of vision, in Walter Pater's idiom. When I think about them, they change. I cannot hold them steady. That is as it should be. Samuel Beckett deftly called them "fetishes." Roger Shattuck restored them as *moments bienheureux.* The greatest, Beckett suggests, is "The Intermittencies of the Heart," which comes between Chapters 1 and 2 in *Sodom and Gomorrah, Part Two.* Exhausted and ill, the narrator arrives on his second visit to Balbec, and goes to his hotel room:

Disruption of my entire being. On the first night, as I was suffering from cardiac fatigue, I bent down slowly and cautiously to take off my boots, trying to master my pain. But scarcely had I touched the topmost button than my chest swelled, filled with an unknown, a divine presence, I was shaken with sobs, tears streamed from my eyes. The being who had come to my rescue, saving me from bareness of spirit, was the same who, years before, in a moment of identical distress and loneliness, in a moment when I had nothing left of myself, had come in and had restored me to myself, for that being was myself and something more than me (the container that is greater than the contained and was bringing it to me). I had just perceived, in my memory, stooping over my fatigue, the tender, preoccupied, disappointed face of my grandmother, as she had been on that first evening of our arrival, the face not of that grandmother whom I had been astonished and remorseful at having so little missed, and who had nothing in common with her save her name, but of my real grandmother, of whom, for the first time since the afternoon of her stroke in the Champs-Elysées, I now recaptured the living reality in a complete and involuntary recollection. This reality does not exist for us so long as it has not been re-created by our thought (otherwise men who have been engaged in a titanic struggle would all of them be great epic poets); and thus, in my wild desire to fling myself into her arms, it was only at that moment—more than a year after her burial, because of the anachronism which so often prevents the calendar of facts from corresponding to the calendar of feelings—that I became conscious that she was dead. I had often spoken about her since then, and thought of her also, but behind my words and thoughts, those of an ungrateful, selfish, cruel young man, there had never been anything that resembled my grandmother, because, in my frivolity, my love of pleasure, my familiarity with the spectacle of her ill health, I retained within me only in a potential state the memory of what she had been.

·　·　·

I remembered how, an hour before the moment when my grandmother had stooped in her dressing-gown to unfasten my boots, as I wandered along the stiflingly hot street, past the pastry-cook's, I had felt that I could never, in my need to feel her arms round me, live through the hour that I had still to spend without her. And now that this same need had reawakened, I knew that I might wait hour after hour, that she would never again be by my side. I had only just discovered this because I had only just, on feeling her for the first time alive, real, making my heart swell to breaking-point, on finding her at last, learned that I had lost her for ever. Lost for ever; I could not understand, and I struggled to endure the anguish of this contradiction: on the one hand an existence, a tenderness, surviving in me as I had known them, that is to say created for me, a love which found in me so totally its complement, its goal, its constant lodestar, that the genius of great men, all the genius that might have existed from the beginning of the world, would have been less precious to my grandmother than a single one of my defects; and on the other hand, as soon as I had relived that bliss, as though it were present, feeling it shot through by the certainty, throbbing like a recurrent pain, of an annihilation that had effaced my image of that tenderness, had destroyed that existence, retrospectively abolished our mutual predestination, made of my grandmother, at the moment when I had found her again as in a mirror, a mere stranger whom chance had allowed to spend a few years with me, as she might have done with anyone else, but to whom, before and after those years, I was and would be nothing.

Rereading this again on June 12, 2018, a month away from my eighty-eighth birthday, I pause to remember the beloved dead. There are so many of them. My mother and father, my four older siblings, former students who died far too young, friends of my youth who died in battle, and almost all of my peers in my own generation: poets, novelists, scholars now gone forever. Teaching, reading, and writing have become ghost-haunted. Proust helps to heal me. Partly because of my friend Roger Shattuck's influence upon me, I tend to associate *In Search of Lost Time* with Eastern speculations. I read Proust and turn to the *Bhagavad Gita*, which offers me three states of being: *dark inertia, passion, lucidity.* What Proust does is to lead me from dark inertia through passion to his lucidity, which I can only barely share. However good a reader, how shall she surmount all the obstacles on the winding path to lucidity?

Freud warned that mourning, too long prolonged, transmutes into melancholia. What he called "the work of mourning" has to be performed but then to some degree relinquished. Proust does not warn us of anything. He *shows* us how his narrator recaptured the past and achieved lucidity. I wonder if any other novelist has accomplished that.

CHAPTER 39

The Master and Margarita (1928–40)

MIKHAIL BULGAKOV

MIKHAIL BULGAKOV'S APOCALYPSE was not published until 1966; he was still working on it when he died in 1940 at the age of forty-eight. There are a number of useful translations into English. I will rely here mostly on the one by Michael Glenny (1967) but will sometimes contrast it with Richard Pevear and Larissa Volokhonsky's (2001).

That Bulgakov survived at all was because of a vagary of the monstrous Joseph Stalin, who had attended the writer's play *The Days of the Turbins,* perhaps fifteen times, and who appointed Bulgakov to direct the Moscow Art Theater. When Bulgakov encountered political difficulties again, he wrote a letter to Stalin requesting that he be allowed to leave the Soviet Union. Stalin phoned and asked if he really wanted to leave. Bulgakov replied that a Russian writer had to stay in Russia, and thus received further patronage from the dictator.

The Master and Margarita is certainly great fun, but it is very uncanny and mystifying fun. I reread it and cannot keep the kaleidoscope from rotating away. That is as it should be: it is the way of a kaleidoscope. One does not expect a novel to be primarily a magic show. Here is an early encounter between Mikhail Alexandrovich Berlioz, head of the Soviet "literary" bureaucracy MASSOLIT, and the mysterious stranger Professor Woland (Satan) who has arrived in Moscow with an incredible entourage. His band consists first of Koroviev or Fagotto, a fallen angel once master of the heavenly choir, a great illusionist whose name means "bassoon" in Russian and who can translate all languages. Fagotto has forsworn violence and has no sense of humor. Next is a giant cat, Behemoth, who together with Leviathan, was employed by God's voice out of the whirlwind in order to frighten Job into submission. In Hebrew, "Behemoth" means "beasts"; in Russian, a hippopotamus. Aside from his nasty sneering, he is as large as a hog, walks on two feet, can assume human shape, guzzles vodka and food incessantly, likes to wave a pistol and play chess. My favorite is Hella, a gorgeous redhead vampire and succubus who delights in going about naked. Last comes Azazello, the most repellent, whose name recalls Azazel, who, in the Book of Enoch, teaches seductive women to wear jewelry and makeup and men to make weapons. Azazello is cross-eyed, possesses fangs, and is Woland's hitman.

We can begin listening to Bulgakov's voice in the exchange between Berlioz and Satan:

"A brick is neither here nor there," the stranger interrupted persuasively. "A brick never falls on anyone's head. You in particular, I assure you, are in no danger from that. Your death will be different."

"Perhaps you know exactly how I am going to die?" inquired Berlioz with understandable sarcasm at the ridiculous turn that the conversation seemed to be taking. "Would you like to tell me?"

"Certainly," rejoined the stranger. He looked Berlioz up and down as though he were measuring him for a suit and muttered through his teeth something that sounded like: "One, two . . . Mercury in the second house . . . the moon waning . . . six—accident . . . evening—seven," then announced loudly and cheerfully, "Your head will be cut off!"

Bezdomny turned to the stranger with a wild, furious stare, and Berlioz asked with a sardonic grin, "By whom? Enemies? Foreign spies?"

"No," replied their companion, "by a Russian woman, a member of the Komsomol."

"Hm," grunted Berlioz, upset by the foreigner's little joke. "That, if you don't mind my saying so, is most improbable."

"I beg your pardon," replied the foreigner, "but it is so. Oh yes, I was going to ask you—what are you doing this evening, if it's not a secret?"

"It's no secret. From here I'm going home, and then at ten o'clock this evening there's a meeting at the MASSOLIT and I shall be in the chair."

"No, that is absolutely impossible," said the stranger firmly.

"Why?"

"Because," replied the foreigner and frowned up at the sky where, sensing the oncoming cool of the evening, the birds were flying to roost, "Anna has already bought the sunflower oil; in fact, she has not only bought it but has already spilled it. So that meeting will not take place."

With this, as one might imagine, there was silence beneath the lime trees.

"Excuse me," said Berlioz after a pause, with a glance at the stranger's jaunty beret, "but what on earth has sunflower-seed oil got to do with it...and who is Anna?"

"I'll tell you what sunflower oil's got to do with it," said Bezdomny suddenly, having obviously decided to declare war on their uninvited companion. "Have you, comrade, ever had to spend any time in a mental hospital?"

"Ivan!" hissed Mikhail Alexandrovich.

But the stranger was not in the least offended and gave a cheerful laugh. "Yes, I have, I have, and more than once!" he exclaimed laughing, though the stare that he gave the poet was mirthless. "Where haven't I been! My only regret is that I didn't stay long enough to ask the professor what schizophrenia was. But you are going to find that out from him yourself, Ivan Nikolayich!"

"How do you know my name?"

"My dear fellow, who doesn't know you?" With this the foreigner pulled the previous day's issue of *The Literary Gazette* out of his pocket, and Ivan Nikolayich saw his own picture on the front page above some of his own verse. Suddenly what had delighted him yesterday as proof of his fame and popularity no longer gave the poet any pleasure at all.

The youthful, doubtless bad poet Ivan Nikolayich, who employs "Bezdomny" ("homeless" in Russian) as a pen name, performs a hapless role until the very end of the novel, when he transforms himself into a historian who yet sees visions at the full moon. His vicissitudes include shock, fright, near drowning, confinement in a mental hospital, and an encounter there with the Master, Bulgakov's surrogate. He, Berlioz, and an editor share bafflement in confronting Satan/ Professor Woland:

> The two men were embarrassed. "Hell, he overheard us," thought Berlioz, indicating with a polite gesture that there was no need for this show of documents. While the stranger was offering them to the editor, the poet managed to catch a glimpse of the visiting card. On it in foreign lettering was the word "Professor" and the initial letter of a surname which began with a "W."
>
> "Delighted," muttered the editor awkwardly as the foreigner put his papers back into his pocket.
>
> Good relations having been re-established, all three sat down again on the bench.
>
> "So you've been invited here as a consultant, have you, Professor?" asked Berlioz.
>
> "Yes, I have."
>
> "Are you German?" inquired Bezdomny.
>
> "I?" rejoined the professor and thought for a moment. "Yes, I suppose I am German," he said.
>
> "You speak excellent Russian," remarked Bezdomny.
>
> "Oh, I'm something of a polyglot. I know a great number of languages," replied the professor.
>
> "And what is your particular field of work?" asked Berlioz.
>
> "I specialize in black magic."
>
> "Like hell you do!" thought Mikhail Alexandrovich. "And... and you've been invited here to give advice on *that*?" he asked with a gulp.
>
> "Yes," the professor assured him, and went on: "Apparently your National Library has unearthed some original manuscripts of the ninth-century necromancer Herbert Aurilachs. I have been asked to decipher them. I am the only specialist in the world."

Woland is German because of Goethe's *Faust,* where he is called Mephistopheles. The Master appears there as Faust, and Margarita as Gretchen. Herbert Aurilachs was Herbert Aurochs, a necromancer of the ninth century. Necromancy is the art of resurrecting the dead in order to hold converse with them. It has always been widespread throughout the world in every era. Prospero in *The Tempest* is the major literary representation of such a magus.

Poor Ivan Nikolayich will be cured of composing verse by observing the decapitation of Berlioz:

> Without stopping to listen to the choirmaster's begging and whining, Berlioz ran to the turnstile and pushed it. Having passed through, he was just about to step off the pavement and cross the trolley tracks when a white and red light flashed in his face and the pedestrian signal lit up with the words "Stop! Trolley!" A streetcar rolled into view, rocking slightly along the newly laid track that ran down Yermolayevsky Street and into Bronnaya. As it turned to join the main line, it suddenly switched its inside lights on, hooted and accelerated.
>
> Although he was standing in safety, the cautious Berlioz decided to retreat behind the railing. He put his hand on the turnstile and took a step backward. He missed his grip and his foot slipped on the cobbles as inexorably as though on ice. As it slid toward the tramlines his other leg gave way and Berlioz was thrown across the track. Grabbing wildly, Berlioz fell prone. He struck his head violently on the cobblestones and the gilded moon flashed hazily across his vision. He had just time to turn on his back, drawing his legs up to his stomach with a frenzied movement, and as he turned over he saw the woman trolley driver's face, white with horror above her red necktie, as she bore down on him with irresistible force and speed. Berlioz made no sound, but all around him the street rang with the desperate shrieks of women's voices. The driver grabbed the electric brake, the car pitched forward, jumping the rails, and with a tinkling crash the glass broke in all its windows. At this moment Berlioz heard a despairing voice: "Oh, no . . . !' Once more and for the last time the moon flashed before his eyes, but it split into fragments and then went black.
>
> Berlioz vanished from sight under the streetcar, and a round,

dark object rolled across the cobbles, over the curbstone and bounced along the sidewalk.

It was a severed head.

Decapitation is almost routine in *The Master and Margarita*. For readers who have no Russian, the problem of Mikhail Bulgakov's tone is virtually insoluble. Pevear and Volokhonsky are supposedly closer to the original, but I get more sense—however illusory—of tonality from Glenny than I do from that devoted duo. What is to be done? Against a sea of troubles, I have to assert the power of the reader's mind over a universe of death. The ironies of Soviet Russia (1928–40) may or may not be those of Russia after December 25, 1991, when Gorbachev resigned and Yeltsin took over. Now, in 2018, we have Putin, who has been tsar since 1999. If Mikhail Bulgakov were alive now, seventy-eight years after his departure, doubtless he would shrug and emulate Giuseppe Tomasi di Lampedusa in *The Leopard*, saying that if we want things to stay as they are, things will have to change. His hilarity endures and guarantees the continued life of his masterwork. Where I am puzzled is the question of what to make of his religiosity.

I call upon my personal authority in regard to Russian high literature, David M. Bethea, who has also become a friend. I admire his commentary and find it helpful, except that the antinomy between romping and spirituality remains, to me, inexplicable:

> Yeshua's concern is ethical—human perfectibility—and that is why, comforting Pilate, he continues up the path. But if Homeless is a victim of the past and Yeshua and Pilate have their sights on a vision of the distant future, where does this leave the Master and Margarita? They are left in a timeless present, a benign limbo that is both free from the pain of the past and the promise of the future, but from which, with the gift of imaginative empathy, the past can be recaptured and the future anticipated. Such a promised land for the artist cannot of course be imagined in this world, especially in the Soviet Union, but were it to exist, it would look like the little home, with its Venetian window and climbing vine, given to the Master and Margarita. Until God, the final author hovering beyond the

final text, brings history and religious mystery together in this world, we must rely on Bulgakov's version of a *poet ex machina* to make things right. With the New Jerusalem still distant, only art can free Pilate, write history from actuality back into possibility.

I will postpone Pontius Pilate for now. How anyone could be happy with the Master's rehabilitation of the Roman strongman escapes me. The final author is Shakespeare or Homer or Dante or Cervantes or Montaigne or Tolstoy: man, not God. My namesake Poldy rejoices in the New Bloomusalem in the Nova Hibernia of the future. Having lived, taught, and returned to lecture in Jerusalem, I prefer ordinary evenings in New Haven.

Venerating David Bethea, I return to him here:

What Bulgakov is suggesting, in this ending that *continues* what has already ended, is that Homeless, the faithful disciple, must undergo his own spiritual death each Easter season in order to be reborn, if only for an oneiric instant, into that state beyond history where the Master and Margarita now reside. Only at this point in the text, and *not* in the preceding chapter, does Yeshua swear to Pilate that the execution never happened. Suddenly we have returned to the vicious circle of history to discover how, through Homeless's experience of periodic death-in-life, the circle is to be opened. Homeless perceives that endings can be happy after all. As he asks the Master—

"So that is how it [the story of Pilate] *ended* [*kon*chilos']?"

"That's how it *ended* [*kon*chilos'], my disciple…"

and as Margarita concludes—

"Yes, of course [*kon*echo], that's how it did. Everything has *ended* [*kon*chilos'], and everything *ends* [*kon*chaestia]…And I shall kiss you on the forehead and all will be with you as it should…"

With many other readers, it would delight me to be kissed on the forehead by the charming Margarita. She and the devil redeem the book together. They are capricious, wry, humorous, well intentioned (bar a couple of beheadings at the devil's instigation).

> Little wonder, then, that Homeless wakes after his dream feeling calm and healthy. Together with the Master and Margarita, the author, the reader, and perhaps even Pilate himself, he can adjust, knowing that he is free of "the cruel fifth Procurator of Judea, the horseman Pontius Pilate," to this ending.

Bethea is an immensely learned disciple of the great Yuri Lotman (1922–93), who cheered me up at the Turin Book Fair in 1987, where we spent some hours dining together and conversing only in Yiddish. Lotman shrewdly noted that Moscow in *The Master and Margarita* turns into magic, whereas Jerusalem is transformed into the grime of reductive realism. Bethea follows Lotman in crediting Bulgakov with reconciling the two modes in the conclusion. Yes and no. No and yes. I see the attempt at reconciliation, or at least retrievement, but nothing is retrieved. Magical realism is an imposture, even when practiced by Bulgakov or Juan Rulfo or García Márquez.

During the last few weeks, I have been rereading and absorbing David Bentley Hart's marvelous literal translation, *The New Testament* (2017). Hart is a scholar immersed in the study of Eastern Orthodoxy. It could be wished that all who now call themselves Christian might ponder Hart's version and his observations:

> What perhaps did impress itself upon me with an entirely unexpected force was a new sense of the utter strangeness of the Christian vision of life in its first dawning—by which I mean, precisely, its strangeness in respect to the Christianity of later centuries. When one truly ventures into the world of the first Christians, one enters a company of "radicals" (for want of a better word), an association of men and women guided by faith in a world-altering revelation, and hence in values almost absolutely inverse to the recognized social, political, economic, and religious truths not only of their own age, but of almost every age of human culture. The first Christians certainly bore very little resemblance to the faithful of our day, or to any generation of Christians that has felt quite at home in the world, securely

sheltered within the available social stations of its time, com-
placently comfortable with material possessions and national
loyalties and civic conventions. In truth, I suspect that very few
of us, in even our wildest imaginings, could ever desire to be
the kind of persons that the New Testament describes as fitting the pattern of life in Christ. And I do not mean merely
that most of us would find the moral requirements laid out in
Christian scripture a little onerous—though of course we do.
Therein lies the perennial appeal of the venerable early modern theological fantasy that the Apostle Paul inveighed against
something called "works-righteousness" in favor of a purely
extrinsic "justification" by grace—which, alas, he did not. He
rejected only the notion that one might be "shown righteous"
by "works" of the Mosaic Law—that is, ritual *"observances"*
like circumcision or keeping kosher—but he also quite clearly
insisted, as did Christ, that all will be judged in the end according to their deeds (Romans 2:1–16 and 4:10–12; 1 Corinthians 3:12–15; 2 Corinthians 5:10; Philippians 2:16; and so on).
Rather, I mean that most of us would find Christians truly cast
in the New Testament mold fairly obnoxious: civically repro-
bate, ideologically unsound, economically destructive, politi-
cally irresponsible, socially discreditable, and really just a bit
indecent. Or, if not that, we would at least be bemused by the
sheer, unembellished, unremitting otherworldliness of their
understanding of the gospel.

Having written a somewhat contentious little book called *Jesus
and Yahweh: The Names Divine* (2005), I wish now I could revise
the part on the New Testament, because David Bentley Hart has
changed my mind on some things, particularly on Paul. To be
absurdly anachronistic, I wish Mikhail Bulgakov had read Hart's *The
New Testament*. Still, that might not have much affected the Master in his leisurely gavotte with Yeshua and Pilate. Since the Master
is and is not Bulgakov, we can accept that Yeshua is not Yeshua or
Pilate, Pilate. David Bethea, as always, is prompt on such parody:

Yet its essence remains indeterminate. Reflective of both a
nineteenth-century tradition of realism and fierce ethical com-

mitment and a twentieth-century tradition of post-symbolism and destabilizing irony, the novel seems a kind of marvelous stone that with each stroke of the critic's blade reveals a new facet but that for this very reason can never be apprehended in the totality of its lapidary brilliance. That Bulgakov managed to encode elaborate parodies of the Bible story and Goethe's *Faust* in his novel is by now critical commonplace; that the fate of his hero and of his hero's manuscript is in many ways a fictionalization—even up to the point of that manuscript's secret vitality after its author's death—of Bulgakov's life with and through his novel has been corroborated by Marietta Chudakova's seminal research and commented on elsewhere as well. Thus, with its deep interest in questions of good and evil (à la Tolstoy and Dostoevsky) meshed with an exceedingly complex structure (the baldly "realistic" inner text ramifying into a diabolically playful outer text suggests parallels not only with *Hamlet*'s play-within-a-play but also with Gide's *Les Faux-Monnayeurs* and several of Nabokov's novels), *The Master and Margarita* might legitimately be called the Soviet-Russian "modern" novel *par excellence,* an artistic first among a large group of artistically lackluster equals.

I find Bethea's comparison with Prince Hamlet's play-within-a-play more stimulating than Gide or even Nabokov in this context. Nabokov's master Gogol fits better. Bulgakov adapted *Dead Souls* for production by Stanislavski in 1932. Hamlet revises *The Murder of Gonzago* into *The Mousetrap* to catch Claudius, incestuous usurper and murderer. But, being Hamlet, keenest of Western consciousnesses, he himself usurps the entire play from Shakespeare and makes it into a series of plays-within-plays-within-plays. Bulgakov is appetizingly crazy, but Hamlet is crazier than you are, whoever you are. As I read and teach the play again and again, increasingly I confound the Prince of Denmark with David, King of Jerusalem, and with the original Yeshua of the weird Gospel of Mark. That Yeshua does not know who he is or what he is going to be, and only the demons are able to recognize him for whatever it is he will become.

Bulgakov's Ophelia is the much livelier and more fortunate Margarita:

Follow me, reader! Who told you that there is no such thing as real, true, eternal love? Cut out his lying tongue!

Follow me, reader, and only me and I will show you that love!

The master was wrong when he told Ivan with such bitterness, in the hospital that hour before midnight, that she had forgotten him. It was impossible. Of course she had not forgotten him.

First let us reveal the secret that the master refused to tell Ivan. His beloved mistress was called Margarita Nikolayevna. Everything the master said about her to the wretched poet was the strict truth. She was beautiful and clever. It is also true that many women would have given anything to change places with Margarita Nikolayevna. Thirty years old and childless, Margarita was married to a brilliant scientist, whose work was of national importance. Her husband was young, handsome, kind, honest and he adored his wife. Margarita Nikolayevna and her husband lived alone in the whole of the top floor of a delightful house in a garden on one of the side streets near the Arbat. It was a charming place. You can see for yourself whenever you feel like having a look. Just ask me and I'll tell you the address and how to get there; the house is standing to this day.

Margarita Nikolayevna was never short of money. She could buy whatever she liked. Her husband had plenty of interesting friends. Margarita never had to cook. Margarita knew nothing of the horrors of living in a shared apartment. In short...was she happy? Not for a moment. Since the age of nineteen, when she had married and moved into her house, she had never been happy. Good God! What more did the woman need? Why did her eyes always glow with a strange fire? What else did she want, that witch with a very slight squint in one eye, who always decked herself with mimosa every spring? I don't know. Obviously she was right when she said she needed him, the master, instead of a Gothic house, instead of a private garden, instead of money. She was right—she loved him.

Even I, the truthful narrator, yet a mere onlooker, feel a pang when I think what Margarita went through when she came back to the master's basement the next day (fortunately she had not been able to talk to her husband, who failed to come home at the time arranged) and found that the master was not there. She did everything she could to discover where he might be, but in vain. Then she returned home and took up her old life.

In the new life, again the Master's mistress, the ebullient Margarita becomes a witch flying through the air on a broomstick, a guise also adopted by her former maid Natasha. By a pact with the devil, she becomes the hostess of his annual grand ball, greeting a splendid array of poisoners and similar malefactors:

By now people were advancing from below like a phalanx bent on assaulting the landing where Margarita stood. The naked women mounting the staircase between the tail-coated and white-tied men floated up in a spectrum of colored bodies that ranged from white through olive, copper and coffee to quite black. In hair that was red, black, chestnut or flaxen, sparks flashed from precious stones. Diamond-studded orders glittered on the jackets and shirt fronts of the men. Incessantly Margarita felt the touch of lips to her knee, incessantly she offered her hand to be kissed, her face stretched into a rigid mask of welcome.

"Charmed," Koroviev would monotonously intone, "we are charmed...her majesty is charmed."

"Her majesty is charmed," came a nasal echo from Azazello, standing behind her.

"I am charmed!" squeaked the cat.

"Madame la marquise," murmured Koroviev, "poisoned her father, her two brothers and two sisters for the sake of an inheritance...Her majesty is delighted, Madame Minkin!... Ah, how pretty she is! A trifle nervous, though. Why *did* she have to burn her maid with a pair of curling irons? Of course, in the way she used them it was bound to be fatal.... Her majesty is charmed! ... Look, your majesty—the Emperor Rudolf—magician and alchemist ... Another alchemist—he was hanged....Ah, there she is! What a magnificent brothel she used to keep in Strasbourg!... We are delighted, madame!... That woman over there was a Moscow dressmaker who had the brilliantly funny idea of boring two peepholes in the wall of her fitting-room…"

"And didn't her lady clients know?" inquired Margarita.

"Of course, they all knew, your majesty," replied Koroviev. "Charmed!…That young man over there was a dreamer and an eccentric from childhood. A girl fell in love with him and he sold her to a brothel keeper.…"

On and on poured the stream from below. Its source—the huge fireplace—showed no sign of drying up. An hour passed, then another. Margarita felt her chain weighing more and more. Something odd was happening to her hand: she found she could not lift it without wincing. Koroviev's remarks ceased to interest her. She could no longer distinguish between slant-eyed Mongol faces, white faces and black faces. They all merged into a blur, and the air between them seemed to be quivering. A sudden sharp pain like a needle stabbed at Margarita's right hand, and clenching her teeth she leaned her elbow on the little pedestal. A sound like the rustling of wings came from the rooms behind her as the horde of guests danced, and Margarita could feel the massive floors of marble, crystal and mosaic pulsating rhythmically.

Margarita showed as little interest in the Emperor Caius Caligula and Messalina as she did in the rest of the procession of kings, dukes, knights, suicides, poisoners, gallows birds, procuresses, jailers, card sharpers, hangmen, informers, traitors, madmen, detectives and seducers. Her head swam with their names, their faces merged into a great blur, and only one face remained fixed in her memory—that of Malyuta Skuratov with his fiery beard. Margarita's legs were buckling, and she was afraid that she might burst into tears at any moment. The worst pain came from her right knee, which all the guests had kissed. It was swollen, and the skin had turned blue in spite of Natasha's constant attention to it with a sponge soaked in fragrant ointment. By the end of the third hour Margarita glanced wearily down and saw with a start of joy that the flood of guests was thinning out.

"Every ball is the same, your majesty," whispered Koroviev. "At about this time the arrivals begin to decrease. I promise you that this torture will not last more than a few minutes longer. Here comes a party of witches from the Brocken—they're always the last to arrive. Yes, there they are. And a couple of drunken vampires...is that all? Oh, no, there's one more—no, two more."

The last two guests mounted the staircase. "Now this is someone new," said Koroviev, peering through his monocle. "Oh, yes, now I remember. Azazello called on him once and advised him, over a glass of brandy, how to get rid of a man who was threatening to denounce him. So he made a friend, who was under an obligation to him, spray the other man's office walls with poison."

"What's his name?" asked Margarita.

"I'm afraid I don't know," said Koroviev. "You'd better ask Azazello."

"And who's that with him?"

"That's his friend who did the job. Delighted to welcome you!" cried Koroviev to the last two guests.

The staircase was empty, and although the reception committee waited a little longer to make sure, no one else appeared from the fireplace.

A second later, half-fainting, Margarita found herself beside the pool again, where, bursting into tears from the pain in her arm and leg, she collapsed to the floor. Hella and Natasha comforted her, doused her in blood and massaged her body until she revived again.

"Once more, Queen Margot," whispered Koroviev. "You must make the round of the ballrooms just once more to show our guests that they are not being neglected."

Again Margarita floated away from the pool. In place of Johann Strauss's orchestra the stage behind the wall of tulips had been taken over by a jazz band of frenetic apes. An enormous gorilla with shaggy sideburns and holding a trumpet was leaping clumsily up and down as he conducted. Orangutan trumpeters sat in the front row, each with a chimpanzee accordionist on his shoulders. Two baboons with manes like lions' were playing the piano, their efforts completely drowned by the roaring, squeaking and banging of the saxophones, violins and drums played by troops of gibbons, mandrills and marmosets.

Innumerable couples circled round the glassy floor with amazing dexterity, a mass of bodies moving lightly and gracefully as one. Live butterflies fluttered over the dancing horde, flowers drifted down from the ceiling. The electric light had been turned out, the capitals of the pillars were now lit by myriads of glowworms, and will-o'-the-wisps danced through the air.

One wants to appreciate this with a "bravo, bravi!" And certainly Margarita is almost equal to the amiable occasion. Still, it does not captivate me. If someone invites me to dinner and gives me only an enormous bar of chocolate-covered halvah, does that suffice? Fun is fun, and too much fun is not funny. Am I being ungrateful? Possibly in Russian *The Master and Margarita* can sustain endless rereadings. In translation, over-absorption troubles me. Mikhail Bulgakov is not Nikolai Gogol, but I wish he were even more Gogolian, like the finicky Vladimir Nabokov in his final Russian novel, *The Gift* (1952). Except for that parodistic fantasia, and for the immortal *Pale Fire* (1962), I have never been very happy with the lepidopterist and chess master. And yet I admire Nabokov, émigré Russian to the core, for being so free of Slavic piousness. Gogol was literally and sublimely crazy, and so is his fanatic religiosity, but, as by everything else in him, we are swept away. Mikhail Bulgakov cannot do that to me, though doubtless my own mix of Judaism and Gnosticism is the blocking agent.

Essentially, Gnosticism, of whatever variety, begins with the vision that the Creation and the Fall were one event only. Our world is ruled by an Archon, or Demiurge, who disordered the cosmos even more thoroughly. Ancient and modern Gnosticism alike distinguish between *psyche* and *pneuma*, Self and Soul. You might call Gnosticism the ultimate origin of the Romantic tradition in Western literature.

The Master's story of Pilate and Yeshua is hardly Eastern Orthodoxy and might be called Bulgakov's personal gnosis:

Approximately at midnight, sleep finally took pity on the hegemon. With a spasmodic yawn, the procurator unfastened and threw off his cloak, removed the belt girded over his shirt, with a broad steel knife in a sheath, placed it on the chair by his couch, took off his sandals, and stretched out. Banga got on the bed at once and lay down next to him, head to head, and the procurator, placing his hand on the dog's neck, finally closed his eyes. Only then did the dog also fall asleep.

The couch was in semi-darkness, shielded from the moon by a column, but a ribbon of moonlight stretched from the porch steps to the bed. And once the procurator lost connection with what surrounded him in reality, he immediately set out on the shining road and went up it straight towards the moon. He even burst out laughing in his sleep from happiness, so wonderful and inimitable did everything come to be on the transparent, pale blue road. He walked in the company of Banga, and beside him walked the wandering philosopher. They were arguing about something very complex and important, and neither of them could refute the other. They did not agree with each other in anything, and that made their argument especially interesting and endless. It went without saying that today's execution proved to be a sheer misunderstanding: here this philosopher, who had thought up such an incredibly absurd thing as that all men are good, was walking beside him, therefore he was alive. And, of course, it would be terrible even to think that one could execute such a man. There had been no execution! No execution! That was the loveliness of this journey up the stairway of the moon.

There was as much free time as they needed, and the storm would come only towards evening, and cowardice was undoubtedly one of the most terrible vices. Thus spoke Yeshua Ha-Nozri. No, philosopher, I disagree with you: it is the most terrible vice!

(trans. Pevear and Volokhonsky)

For the first time, I quote a version other than the Glenny. I cannot judge which is more reliable. Yet I am astonishingly moved by this passage, and wonder if I have been inattentive to the dark situation that Mikhail Bulgakov and the Master had to confront. As David Bethea observes, all-powerful Woland is akin to all-powerful Stalin, except that Woland is so often benign, particularly in regard to Margarita and the Master. Bulgakov passes severe judgment upon himself by finding the final Limbo of calm and not the Eternity of light. That seems much too severe. He stubbornly resisted becoming a Stalinist mouthpiece and he suffered for it, though not as did the great Jewish poet Osip Mandelstam, who died of privation at forty-seven *en route* to Siberian exile.

Riding out of Moscow back to their presumable Hades, Woland and his three male subordinates become the Four Horsemen of the Apocalypse:

The storm had passed and a rainbow had arched itself across the sky, its foot in the Moscow River. On top of a hill between two clumps of trees could be seen three dark silhouettes. Woland, Koroviev and Behemoth sat mounted on black horses, looking at the city spread out beyond the river with fragments of sun glittering from thousands of west-facing windows, and at the onion domes of the Novodevichy monastery.

There was a rustling in the air and Azazello, followed in a black cavalcade by the master and Margarita, landed by the group of waiting figures.

"I'm afraid we had to frighten you a little, Margarita Niko-layevna, and you, master," said Woland after a pause. "But I don't think you will have cause to complain to me about it or regret it. Now—" he turned to the master—"say good-bye to this city. It's time for us to go." Woland pointed his hand in its black gauntlet toward where countless glass suns glittered beyond the river, where above those suns the city exhaled the haze, smoke and vapor of the day.

The master leaped from his saddle, left his companions and ran to the hillside, black cloak flapping above the ground behind him. He looked at the city. For the first few moments a tremor of sadness crept over his heart, but it soon changed to a delicious excitement, the gypsy's thrill of the open road.

"Forever ... I must think what that means," whispered the master and licked his dry, cracked lips. He began to listen to what was happening in his heart. His excitement, it seemed to him, had given way to a profound and grievous sense of hurt. But it was only momentary and gave place to one of proud indifference and finally to a presentiment of eternal peace.

(trans. Glenny)

Like an echo came a piercing laugh and a whistle from Behemoth. The horses leaped into the air, and the riders rose with them as they galloped upward. Margarita could feel her fierce horse biting and tugging at the bit. Woland's cloak billowed out over the heads of the cavalcade, and as evening drew on, his cloak began to cover the whole vault of the sky. When the black veil blew aside for a moment, Margarita turned round in flight and saw that not only the many-colored towers but the whole city had long vanished from sight, swallowed by the earth, leaving only mist and smoke where it had been.

(trans. Glenny)

These are the impressive accents of authentic apocalypse. Woland is now austerely garbed; soon enough, Behemoth will be a fresh-faced pageboy; Koroviev is a dour dark knight; Azazello is seen in his true form, a demon white-faced with vacant, dark eyes. The Master and Margarita have died and been resurrected and will go to a lissome Limbo, where they will be forever joined in a post-existence of calm and peace, though still far from the light.

Huddling inside *The Master and Margarita* is Goethe's scandalous *Faust: Part Two*, in which Faust has even less personality than the Master. Here, Mephistopheles is more a Christian devil than Woland, who is probably the best Christian in Mikhail Bulgakov, surpassing the problematic Yeshua.

Confronting a classical Walpurgis Night, Mephistopheles is shocked by all sorts of legendary monsters, "offering us both rear and frontal views." Bulgakov cannot compete with the witches' sabbath of Goethe, which goes on for one thousand five hundred lines, my favorite being:

Grau, grämlich, griesgram, greulich, Gräber, grimmig.
(Gray, grieving, grungy, gruesome, graves, and groaning.)

These are the monstrous griffins who hoard treasure yet are so used up that they cannot frighten even Mephistopheles. Goethe is the master of grotesquerie: his Sirens cannot sing, and his Lamiae, who should be rather vicious vampires, are overpainted worn-out whores whose only resource is to render their embraces most unpleasant. In this big league, Woland and Margarita would lose their positions.

I do not know precisely why Margarita and the Master are granted their pliable proxy for paradise. Even less can I surmise why the Master's Pilate is exonerated and finally walks with Yeshua up a ray of light in conversational companionship. Happy endings need never be deprecated:

> "Ye gods!" says the man in the cloak, turning his proud face to his companion. "What a disgusting method of execution! But please, tell me—" here the pride in his face turns to supplication—"it did not take place, did it? I beg you—tell me that it never took place?"
>
> "No, of course it never took place," answers his companion in a husky voice. "It was merely your imagination."
>
> "Can you swear to that?" begged the man in the cloak.
>
> "I swear it!" answers his companion, his eyes smiling.
>
> "That is all I need to know!" gasps the man in the cloak as he strides on toward the moon, beckoning his companion on. Behind them walks a magnificently calm, gigantic dog with pointed ears.
>
> (trans. Glenny)

Had my beloved father remained in Odessa, I might have been born, but I would have been incinerated before my bar mitzvah. He reached Orchard Street on the Lower East Side of Manhattan, by way of London, and gave up speaking Russian for good. I like that calm and gigantic dog with pointed ears.

I intuit that my ambivalences toward Mikhail Bulgakov's enchanted vision are not cognitive or aesthetic but are lodged in my own inward division between Jewish Gnosticism and my mother's Orthodoxy. In my advanced years, she enters my dreams. She never admonishes, since she did not in this life, but still I wake with "The Auroras of Autumn" in my ears:

> That we partake thereof,
> Lie down like children in this holiness,
> As if, awake, we lay in the quiet of sleep,
>
> As if the innocent mother sang in the dark
> Of the room and on an accordion, half-heard,
> Created the time and place in which we breathed...

And of each other thought—in the idiom
Of the work, in the idiom of an innocent earth,
Not of the enigma of the guilty dream.

I come down to breakfast and face my wife at the table's other
end and murmur to her that I am weary "of the enigma of the guilty
dream." Yet tonight a guilty dream will recur. Yesterday afternoon,
too exhausted to write any more, I sat with my research assistant and
watched a Russian television serial of *The Master and Margarita*
and focused upon the satanic ball, where Margarita is hostess. It was
very well done, with many delicious naked damozels emerging from
the fireplace, side by side with various malefactors. That entered
my dreams last night and somehow augmented my guilt. I think I
will end here with this tribute to Mikhail Bulgakov: he pervades my
nightmares, and so indubitably has influenced me.

CHAPTER 40

Absalom, Absalom! (1936)

WILLIAM FAULKNER

FAULKNER IS THE ONLY American novelist of my lifetime who has joined our national tradition of Hawthorne, Melville, Mark Twain, and Henry James. The influence of his work upon his life was that it became his life. That is true also of his forerunners Hawthorne, Melville, Mark Twain, and of Henry James, who meant little to Faulkner. In his late parable "Carcassonne," chosen to end his collected stories, Faulkner's surrogate prophesies a grand fate:

> I want to perform something bold and tragical and austere he repeated, shaping the soundless words in the pattering silence me on a buckskin pony with eyes like blue electricity and a mane like tangled fire, galloping up the hill and right off into the high heaven of the world. Still galloping, the horse soars outward; still galloping, it thunders up the long blue hill of heaven, its tossing mane in golden swirls like fire.
>
> Steed and rider thunder on, thunder punily diminishing: a dying star upon the immensity of darkness and of silence within which, steadfast, fading, deepbreasted and grave of flank, muses the dark and tragic figure of the Earth, his mother.

Here his work triumphs over his outer life, and his fiction, the inward life, prevails. There were American poets contemporary to

Faulkner who may be called great—Frost, Eliot, Wallace Stevens, Hart Crane—and in one aspect of his art Faulkner was their peer: he was an extraordinary prose poet, akin to the Hemingway of the short stories or to Sherwood Anderson at Anderson's rare best. The prose lyricism of Willa Cather and of F. Scott Fitzgerald is also worthy of this comparison, as are the best works of Faulkner's disciples Robert Penn Warren and Cormac McCarthy.

The prose poetry is one aspect of Faulkner's achievement, his romance side, which projects a world like Sir Walter Scott's, chivalric and defeated. Equally large was his power of characterization, which owed much to Shakespeare and Cervantes, Dickens and Balzac. This power belongs to Faulkner the novelist, who emerged in *As I Lay Dying*. The earlier *Flags in the Dust*, published as the revised *Sartoris*, has Faulkner's verbal splendor but not his extraordinary novelistic, almost Shakespearean ability to create separate selves.

Speaking to a class at the University of Virginia on April 13, 1957, Faulkner rather hazily reflected on *Absalom, Absalom!:*

> The central character is Sutpen, yes. The story of a man who wanted a son and got too many, got so many that they destroyed him. It's incidentally the story of—of Quentin Compson's hatred of the—the bad qualities in the country he loves. But the central character is Sutpen, the story of a man who wanted sons.

It puzzles me why Faulkner burdened himself with the power of King David's lament for his rebel son Absalom:

> Then said Absalom to Ahithophel, Give counsel among you what we shall do. And Ahithophel said unto Absalom, Go in unto thy father's concubines, which he hath left to keep the house; and all Israel shall hear that thou art abhorred of thy father: then shall the hands of all that are with thee be strong. So they spread Absalom a tent upon the top of the house; and Absalom went in unto his father's concubines in the sight of all Israel. And the counsel of Ahithophel, which he counselled in those days, was as if a man had enquired at the oracle of God: so was all the counsel of Ahithophel both with David and with Absalom. Moreover, Ahithophel said unto Absalom, Let

me now choose out twelve thousand men, and I will arise and pursue after David this night: And I will come upon him while he is weary and weak handed, and will make him afraid: and all the people that are with him shall flee; and I will smite the king only: And I will bring back all the people unto thee: the man whom thou seekest is as if all returned: so all the people shall be in peace.

(2 Samuel 16:20–17:3, KJV)

And the king commanded Joab and Abishai and Ittai, saying, Deal gently for my sake with the young man, even with Absalom. And all the people heard when the king gave all the captains charge concerning Absalom. So the people went out into the field against Israel: and the battle was in the wood of Ephraim; Where the people of Israel were slain before the servants of David, and there was there a great slaughter that day of twenty thousand men. For the battle was there scattered over the face of all the country: and the wood devoured more people that day than the sword devoured. And Absalom met the servants of David. And Absalom rode upon a mule, and the mule went under the thick boughs of a great oak, and his head caught hold of the oak, and he was taken up between the heaven and the earth; and the mule that was under him went away. And a certain man saw it, and told Joab, and said, Behold, I saw Absalom hanged in an oak. And Joab said unto the man that told him, And, behold, thou sawest him, and why didst thou not smite him there to the ground? and I would have given thee ten shekels of silver, and a girdle. And the man said unto Joab, Though I should receive a thousand shekels of silver in mine hand, yet would I not put forth mine hand against the king's son: for in our hearing the king charged thee and Abishai and Ittai, saying, Beware that none touch the young man Absalom. Otherwise I should have wrought falsehood against mine own life: for there is no matter hid from the king, and thou thyself wouldest have set thyself against me. Then said Joab, I may not tarry thus with thee. And he took three darts in his hand, and thrust them through the heart of Absalom, while he was yet alive in the midst of the oak. And ten young men that bare Joab's armour compassed about and smote Absalom, and slew him. And Joab blew the trumpet, and the people returned from pursuing after Israel: for Joab held back the people. And they took Absalom, and cast him into a great pit in the wood, and laid a very great heap of stones upon him: and all Israel fled every one to his tent.

(2 Samuel 18:5–17, KJV)

And Ahimaaz called, and said unto the king, All is well. And he fell down to the earth upon his face before the king, and said, Blessed be the Lord thy God, which hath delivered up the men that lifted up their hand against my lord the king. And the king said, Is the young man Absalom safe? And Ahimaaz answered, When Joab sent the king's servant, and me thy servant, I saw a great tumult, but I knew not what it was. And the king said unto him, Turn aside, and stand here. And he turned aside, and stood still. And, behold, Cushi came; and Cushi said, Tidings, my lord the king: for the Lord hath avenged thee this day of all them that rose up against thee. And the king said unto Cushi, Is the young man Absalom safe? And Cushi answered, The enemies of my lord the king, and all that rise against thee to do thee hurt, be as that young man is. And the king was much moved, and went up to the chamber over the gate, and wept: and as he went, thus he said, O my son Absalom, my son, my son Absalom! would God I had died for thee, O Absalom, my son, my son!

(2 Samuel 18:28–33, KJV)

Thomas Sutpen, the ruthless, obsessive, destructive protagonist of what may well be Faulkner's masterpiece, voices his will with a fervor so archaic that he suggested to his bardic maker the situation, though certainly not the character or personality, of the Biblical King David, whose saga commences in 2 Samuel and concludes in 1 Kings. I have been reading Faulkner since 1948 and writing about him intermittently since 1986. *As I Lay Dying* (1930) will always seem to me his most original and shattering work, but Cormac McCarthy, authentic disciple of Faulkner, prefers *The Sound and the Fury* (1929), and at an earlier time I valued *Light in August* (1932) more highly than anything else by the seer of Yoknapatawpha County, his imagined land. As a very old father of two middle-aged sons, I discover that my reactions to *Absalom, Absalom!* have changed.

Thirty years ago, it bothered me that Sutpen was so empty a personality. I almost agreed with Rosa Coldfield that he was a kind of Gothic demon rather than a man. He seems to have only one will and to possess only a specious morality. His weird desire for sons and grandsons has absolutely nothing to do with affection. I see now that none of this matters. There are three strong personalities in *Absalom, Absalom!:* Quentin Compson; his Canadian friend and roommate at Harvard, Shreve; William Faulkner the narrator. Quentin, Faulkner's Hamlet, studies suicide at Harvard. Shreve, his Horatio— refreshingly, an outsider in Faulkner's world—has a prophetic understanding of Sutpen's saga, which is that in time all of the United States, not just the South, will be populated by a majority ensuing from miscegenation. Faulkner, who would like to get the entire novel into one long sentence, has nothing of Sutpen in him, and shares Quentin's dark interest in incest. My former student Thomas Frosch illuminates Shelley's defense of brother-sister incest:

> The theme of incest, frequent in Romanticism, found a particularly strong "correspondent breeze" in Shelley. He calls incest "like many other *incorrect* things a very poetical circumstance. It may be the excess of love or of hate. It may be... the highest heroism" or "cynical rage" and "selfishness." Incest is a paradigm of the kind of situation that typically compels his fascination, one in which the extremes of the ideal and the morbid meet. And yet in the case of *Athanase,* Shelley claims that something beyond incest lies at the root of his hero's melancholy; he speaks of "Tears bitterer than the blood of agony" of "those who love their kind, and therefore die." What lies beyond incest in Shelley, so unacceptable to him that, unlike incest, it cannot break through into poetic themes and images, at least idealized ones? (Frosch)

Faulkner had read Shelley's *The Cenci* and *Laon and Cythna,* the earlier version of what became *The Revolt of Islam.* In *The Cenci,* the horrible Count rapes his daughter, Beatrice, who retaliates by having him murdered, for which she is executed with the Pope's approval.

Father-daughter incest is seen as part of the heavenly tyranny of the European nation-state. But in *Laon and Cythna,* the martyred lovers are brother and sister, and Shelley's ideal includes the breaking of the taboo against brother-sister incest. In a complex act of creation, Faulkner assimilated Shelley to Balzac's *The Girl with the Golden Eyes,* where an unsympathetic, hedonistic male decides to murder his mistress for having deceived him. But he has been forestalled by her lesbian lover, his half-sister, who has slain her for similar motives.

Thomas Sutpen in his youth had worked as an overseer in a West Indian plantation, where he had helped to subdue a black rebellion. He then married Eulalia Bon, the daughter of the plantation owner, who bore him a son, Charles. Discovering that Eulalia had black ancestry, Sutpen repudiated both wife and son, though leaving them what fortune he had accumulated. Later, he manifests in Mississippi, where he purchases one hundred square miles of land from a Native American tribe so whiskey-soaked that they do not realize they are being bilked. He builds a mansion on Sutpen's Hundred and marries Ellen Coldfield, with whom he fathers Henry Sutpen as his presumed heir, and Henry's sister, Judith.

At the University of Mississippi, Henry befriends Charles Bon, ten years his senior, without knowing that Charles is his half-brother. Thomas, Henry, and Charles go off to fight for the Confederacy, but only after Charles and Judith fall in love. After the war is lost, Thomas tells Henry the truth that Charles is not only his half-brother but also partly black. Though Henry accepts a possible marriage of half-siblings, he cannot accept a "black" as a brother-in-law. He murders Charles in front of the mansion and then flees:

> —*You will have to stop me, Henry.* "And he never slipped away," Shreve said. "He could have, but he never even tried. Jesus, maybe he even went to Henry and said, 'I'm going, Henry' and maybe they left together and rode side by side dodging Yankee patrols all the way back to Mississippi and right up to that gate; side by side and it only then that one of them ever rode ahead or dropped behind and that only then Henry spurred ahead and turned his horse to face Bon and took out the pistol; and Judith and Clytie heard the shot, and maybe Wash Jones was

hanging around somewhere in the back yard and so he was there to help Clytie and Judith carry him into the house and lay him on the bed, and Wash went to town to tell the Aunt Rosa and the Aunt Rosa comes boiling out that afternoon and finds Judith standing without a tear before the closed door, holding the metal case she had given him with her picture in it but that didn't have her picture in it now but that of the octoroon and the kid. And your old man wouldn't know about that too: why the black son of a bitch should have taken her picture out and put the octoroon's picture in, so he invented a reason for it. But I know. And you know too. Don't you? Don't you, huh?" He glared at Quentin, leaning forward over the table now, looking huge and shapeless as a bear in his swaddling of garments. "Don't you know? It was because he said to himself, 'If Henry dont mean what he said, it will be all right; I can take it out and destroy it. But if he does mean what he said, it will be the only way I will have to say to her, *I was no good; do not grieve for me.*' Aint that right? Aint it? By God, aint it?"

"Yes," Quentin said.

"Come on," Shreve said. "Let's get out of this refrigerator and go to bed."

Returning from the lost war, Thomas Sutpen starts over, though his plantation is now reduced to one square mile. He proposes marriage to Rosa Coldfield, Ellen's younger sister, but only on condition that she first bear him a son. Rosa refuses. The desperate Thomas Sutpen then impregnates the fifteen-year-old granddaughter of Wash Jones, a loyal poor white on the plantation. Milly Jones bears a daughter, and the enraged Sutpen says that mother and daughter are not worthy even to enter the stable, since one of Sutpen's mares has just given him a male colt. Wash Jones, properly incensed, murders Sutpen with a scythe. When the furious scene concludes, Milly, the baby girl, and Wash himself are all dead, Wash having resisted arrest:

"...So they waited in front of the dark house, and the next day Father said there were a hundred that remembered about the butcher knife that he kept hidden and razor-sharp—the one thing in his sloven life that he was ever known to take pride in or care of—only by the time they remembered all this it was too late. So they didn't know what he was about. They just heard him moving inside the dark house, then they heard the granddaughter's voice, fretful and querulous: 'Who is it? Light the lamp, Grandpaw' then his voice: 'Hit wont need no light, honey. Hit wont take but a minute' then de Spain drew his pistol and said, 'You, Wash! Come out of there!' and still Wash didn't answer, murmuring still to his granddaughter: 'Wher air you?' and the fretful voice answering, 'Right here. Where else would I be? What is—' then de Spain said, 'Jones!' and he was already fumbling at the broken steps when the granddaughter screamed; and now all the men there claimed that they heard the knife on both the neckbones, though de Spain didn't. He just said he knew that Wash had come out onto the gallery and that he sprang back before he found out that it was not toward him Wash was running but toward the end of the gallery, where the body lay, but that he did not think about the scythe: he just ran backward a few feet when he saw Wash stoop and rise again and now Wash was running toward him. Only he was running toward them all, de Spain said, running into the lanterns so that now they could see the scythe raised above his head; they could see his face, his eyes too, as he ran with the scythe above his head, straight into the lanterns and the gun barrels, making no sound, no outcry while de Spain ran backward before him, saying, 'Jones! Stop! Stop, or I'll kill you! Jones! Jones! Jones!'"

"Wait," Shreve said. "You mean that he got the son he wanted, after all that trouble, and then turned right around and—"

"Yes. Sitting in Grandfather's office that afternoon, with his head kind of flung back a little, explaining to Grandfather like he might have been explaining arithmetic to Henry back in the fourth grade: 'You see, all I wanted was just a son. Which seems to me, when I look about at my contemporary scene, no exorbitant gift from nature or circumstance to demand—'"

"Will you wait?" Shreve said. "—that with the son he went to all that trouble to get lying right there behind him in the cabin, he would have to taunt the grandfather into killing first him and then the child too?"

"—What?" Quentin said. "It wasn't a son. It was a girl."

"Oh," Shreve said. "—Come on. Let's get out of this damn icebox and go to bed."

The tragic farce culminates when Quentin accompanies Rosa to Sutpen's Hundred, where they find an ailing Henry and Clytie, Thomas Sutpen's daughter by a slave woman. Some months later, Rosa returns with a doctor. Clytie, thinking that it is the police, sets fire to the mansion, and burns to death with Henry. Presumably, the final Sutpen will be Jim Bond, a black grandson of Charles Bon.

I hate plot summaries, and this one is bound to be wrong anyway, because Faulkner so designs (if that is the right word) *Absalom, Absalom!* that it is not coherent. Faulkner, like his precursor Joseph Conrad, did not believe that any single perspective could yield the truth. Rosa Coldfield, Quentin's grandfather and father, Quentin, and even Shreve, who is primarily a listener, see different versions of the story. Here is an opening trace of Rosa Coldfield's perspective:

From a little after two oclock until almost sundown of the long still hot weary dead September afternoon they sat in what Miss Coldfield still called the office because her father had called it that—a dim hot airless room with the blinds all closed and fastened for forty-three summers because when she was a girl someone had believed that light and moving air carried heat and that dark was always cooler, and which (as the sun shone fuller and fuller on that side of the house) became latticed with yellow slashes full of dust motes which Quentin thought of as being flecks of the dead old dried paint itself blown inward from the scaling blinds as wind might have blown them. There was a wistaria vine blooming for the second time that summer on a wooden trellis before one window, into which sparrows came now and then in random gusts, making a dry vivid dusty sound before going away: and opposite Quentin, Miss Coldfield in the eternal black which she had worn for forty-three years now, whether for sister, father, or nothusband none knew, sitting so bolt upright in the straight hard chair that was so tall for her that her legs hung straight and rigid as if she had iron shinbones and ankles, clear of the floor with that air of impotent and static rage like children's feet, and talking in that grim haggard amazed voice until at last listening would renege and hearing-sense self-confound and the long-dead object of her impotent yet indomitable frustration would appear, as though by outraged recapitulation evoked, quiet inattentive and harmless, out of the biding and dreamy and victorious dust.

It seems unlikely that Rosa wears mourning for the nothusband, Thomas Sutpen. One is not even certain she wears it for sister and father. Is it for the end of the Old Order? That end was prophesied in the remarkable passage introducing Sutpen's frustrate design:

Out of quiet thunderclap he would abrupt (man-horse-demon) upon a scene peaceful and decorous as a schoolprize water color, faint sulphur-reek still in hair clothes and beard, with grouped behind him his band of wild niggers like beasts half tamed to walk upright like men, in attitudes wild and reposed, and manacled among them the French architect with his air grim, haggard, and tatter-ran. Immobile, bearded and hand palm-lifted the horseman sat; behind him the wild blacks and the captive architect huddled quietly, carrying in bloodless paradox the shovels and picks and axes of peaceful conquest. Then in the long unamaze Quentin seemed to watch them overrun suddenly the hundred square miles of tranquil and astonished earth and drag house and formal gardens violently out of the soundless Nothing and clap them down like cards upon a table beneath the up-palm immobile and pontific, creating the Sutpen's Hundred, the *Be Sutpen's Hundred* like the oldentime *Be Light*. Then hearing would reconcile and he would seem to listen to two separate Quentins now—the Quentin Compson preparing for Harvard in the South, the deep South dead since 1865 and peopled with garrulous outraged baffled ghosts, listening, having to listen, to one of the ghosts which had refused to lie still even longer than most had, telling him about old ghost-times; and the Quentin Compson who was still too young to deserve yet to be a ghost, but nevertheless having to be one for all that, since he was born and bred in the deep South the same as she was—the two separate Quentins now talking to one another in the long silence of notpeople in notlanguage, like this: *It seems that this demon—his name was Sutpen—(Colonel Sutpen)—Colonel Sutpen. Who came out of nowhere and without warning upon the land with a band of strange nig-gers and built a plantation—(Tore violently a plantation, Miss Rosa Coldfield says)—tore violently. And married her sister Ellen and begot a son and a daughter which—(Without gen-tleness begot, Miss Rosa Coldfield says)—without gentleness. Which should have been the jewels of his pride and the shield and comfort of his old age, only—(Only they destroyed him or something or he destroyed them or something. And died)—and died. Without regret, Miss Rosa Coldfield says—(Save by her) Yes, save by her. (And by Quentin Compson) Yes. And by Quen-tin Compson.*

The Compsons, like the Bundrens in *As I Lay Dying*, manifestly constitute another of the most terrifying visions of family romance in literary history. But their extremism is not eccentric in the 1929–39 world of Faulkner's fiction. That world is founded upon a horror of families, a limbo of outcasts, an evasion of all values other than stoic endurance. It is a world in which what is silent in the other Bundrens speaks in Darl, what is veiled in the Compsons is uncov-ered in Quentin. So tangled are these returns of the repressed with what continues to be estranged that phrases like "the violation of the natural" and "the denial of the human" become quite meaning-less when applied to Faulkner's greater fictions. In that world, the natural is itself a violation and the human already a denial. Is the weird quest of the Bundrens a violation of the natural, or is it what Blake would have called a terrible triumph for the selfish virtues of the natural heart? Darl judges it to be the latter, but Darl luminously denies the sufficiency of the human, at the cost of what seems schizo-phrenia. Quentin Compson pragmatically denies it by suicide.

What matters in major Faulkner is that the people have gone back, not to nature but to some abyss before the Creation-Fall. Eliot insisted that Joyce's imagination was eminently orthodox. This can be doubted, but in Faulkner's case there is little sense in baptizing his imagination. One sees why he preferred reading the Old Testa-ment to the New, remarking that the former was stories and the latter, ideas. The remark is inadequate except insofar as it opposes Hebraic to Hellenistic representation of character. There is little that is Homeric about the Bundrens, or Sophoclean about the Compsons. Faulkner's irony is neither classical nor romantic, neither Greek nor German. It does not say one thing while meaning another, or trade in contrasts between expectation and fulfillment. Instead, it juxtaposes incommensurable realities: of self and other, of parent and child, of past and future. When Gide maintained that Faulkner's people lacked souls, he simply failed to observe that Faulkner's ironies were Biblical. To which an amendment must be added. In Faulkner, only the ironies are Biblical. What Faulkner's people lack is the Blessing; they cannot contend for a time without boundaries. Yahweh will make no Covenant with them. Their agon therefore is neither the Greek one for the foremost place nor the Hebrew one for the Blessing, which honors the father and the mother. Their agon is the hopeless one of waiting for their doom to lift:

> "'You see, I had a design in my mind. Whether it was a good or a bad design is beside the point; the question is, Where did I make the mistake in it, what did I do or misdo in it, whom or what injure by it to the extent which this would indicate. I had a design. To accomplish it I should require money, a house, a plantation, slaves, a family—incidentally of course, a wife. I set out to acquire these, asking no favor of any man. I even risked my life at one time, as I told you, though as I also told you I did not undertake this risk purely and simply to gain a wife, though it did have that result. But that is beside the point also: suffice that I had the wife, accepted her in good faith, with no reservations about myself, and I expected as much from them. I did not even demand, mind, as one of my obscure origin might have been expected to do (or at least be condoned in the doing) out of ignorance of gentility in dealing with gentleborn people. I did not demand; I accepted them at their own valuation while insisting on my own part upon explaining fully about myself and my progenitors: yet they deliberately withheld from me the one fact which I have reason to know they were aware would have caused me to decline the entire matter, otherwise they would not have withheld it from me—a fact which I did not

learn until after my son was born. And even then I did not act hastily. I could have reminded them of these wasted years, these years which would now leave me behind with my schedule not only the amount of elapsed time which their number represented, but that compensatory amount of time represented by their number which I should now have to spend to advance myself once more to the point I had reached and lost. But I did not. I merely explained how this new fact rendered it impossible that this woman and child be incorporated in my design, and following which, as I told you, I made no attempt to keep not only that which I might consider myself to have earned at the risk of my life but which had been given to me by signed testimonials, but on the contrary I declined and resigned all right and claim to this in order that I might repair whatever injustice I might be considered to have done by so providing for the two persons whom I might be considered to have deprived of anything I might later possess: and this was agreed to, mind; agreed to between the two parties. And yet, and after more than thirty years, more than thirty years after my conscience had finally assured me that if I had done an injustice, I had done what I could to rectify it—' and Grandfather not saying 'Wait' now but saying, hollering maybe even: 'Conscience? Conscience? Good God, man, what else did you expect? Didn't the very affinity and instinct for misfortune of a man who had spent that much time in a monastery even, let alone one who had lived that many years as you lived them, tell you better than that? didn't the dread and fear of females which you must have drawn in with the primary mammalian milk teach you better? What kind of abysmal and purblind innocence could that have been which someone told you to call virginity? what conscience to trade with which would have warranted you in the belief that you could have bought immunity from her for no other coin but justice?'—"

This is Sutpen, as reported by Quentin's grandfather, and ends with the latter admonishing Sutpen. For the rhetoric here of both men not to seem excessive, Sutpen must be of some eminence and his "design" of some consequence. But nothing in the novel persuades one of Sutpen's stature or of his design's meaningfulness. Like Kurtz in *Heart of Darkness,* Sutpen is a blind will in a cognitive vacuum; both figures seem to represent nothing more than a Nietzschean spirit of mere resentment, rather than the will's deep revenge against time, and time's "It was." Faulkner evidently was persuaded of Sutpen's importance, if only as a vital synecdoche for Southern history. More a process than a man, Sutpen has drive without personality. One can remember a few of his acts, but none of his words, let alone his thoughts—if he has thoughts. He is simply too abrupt a mythic representation, rather than a man who becomes a myth. Only the scope of his failure interests Faulkner, rather than anything he is or means as a person.

But Sutpen is indeed more like Conrad's Kurtz than like Melville's Ahab, in that his obsessions are not sufficiently metaphysical. Sutpen's Hundred is too much Kurtz's Africa, and too little the whiteness of the whale. From *The Sound and the Fury* through the debacle of *A Fable,* Faulkner centers upon the sorrows of fathers and sons, to the disadvantage of mothers and daughters. Faulkner's brooding conviction that female sexuality is closely allied with death seems essential to all of his strongest fictions. It may even be that Faulkner's rhetorical economy, his wounded need to get his cosmos into a single sentence, is related to his fear that origin and end might prove to be one. Nietzsche prophetically had warned that origin and end were separate entities, and for the sake of life had to be kept apart, but Faulkner (strangely like Freud) seems to have known that the only Western trope participating in neither origin nor end is the image of the father.

One can regret the weakness in structure manifested by the novels. Those weaknesses are minor: they scarcely bother us as we read *As I Lay Dying, The Sound and the Fury, Light in August,* and *Absalom, Absalom!* These extraordinary novels are enormous in imaginative and spiritual conception; their flaws are Shakespearean, careless and aesthetically inconsequential. As with Shakespeare, the sweep and richness are Biblical, and, indeed, it seems to me that Faulkner frequently writes in counterpoint to the Bible, largely against it, in a family quarrel akin to Emily Dickinson's and to Herman Melville's. C. Vann Woodward's *American Counterpoint* catches the precise accent of Faulkner's Gnostic undermining of Biblical typology when Woodward discusses the ravages of patriarchal tradition in the realm of miscegenation, in which blood kin frequently were on the other side of the racial divide.

Like Shakespeare, Faulkner learned to achieve apotheosis in tragedy while remaining a comic genius at the core. This helps to account for his ways of handling the influence of the tragic ironist Joseph Conrad and the sublimely comic James Joyce. Conrad's "impressionism" finally was to count for more than Joyce's polyphony: Faulkner's protagonists, rather like Hemingway's and F. Scott Fitzgerald's, almost always are self-ruined idealists, knowingly failed High Romantic questers.

And yet Faulkner is more a Biblical than a Conradian novelist. This has misled critics as astute as Cleanth Brooks, who found a Christian residuum in Faulkner. Faulkner invariably subverts Biblical typology, and has a Gnostic quarrel with God that is closely related to Melville's. His men and women know they are doomed, and they hope only for an interval during which their doom may be lifted. Faulkner's greatness lies in the extension of that interval, crowding into it something close to a heterocosm, a world that is an alternative to nature and to history while powerfully representing both. The voices of Quentin, Shreve, and Faulkner rise and fall in that interval:

"I am older at twenty than a lot of people who have died," Quentin said.

"And more people have died than have been twenty-one," Shreve said. Now he (Quentin) could read it, could finish it— the sloped whimsical ironic hand out of Mississippi attenuated, into the iron snow:

—or perhaps there is. Surely it can harm no one to believe that perhaps she has escaped not at all the privilege of being outraged and amazed and of not forgiving but on the contrary has herself gained that place or bourne where the objects of the outrage and of the commiseration also are no longer ghosts but are actual people to be actual recipients of the hatred and the pity. It will do no harm to hope—You see I have written hope, not think. So let it be hope. —that the one cannot escape the censure which no doubt he deserves, that the other no longer lack the commiseration which let us hope (while we are hoping) that they have longed for, if only for the reason that they are about

to receive it whether they will or no. The weather was beautiful though cold and they had to use picks to break the earth for the grave yet in one of the deeper clods I saw a redworm doubtless alive when the clod was thrown up though by afternoon it was frozen again.

"So it took Charles Bon and his mother to get rid of old Tom, and Charles Bon and the octoroon to get rid of Judith, and Charles Bon and Clytie to get rid of Henry; and Charles Bon's mother and Charles Bon's grandmother got rid of Charles Bon. So it takes two niggers to get rid of one Sutpen, dont it?" Quentin did not answer; evidently Shreve did not want an answer now; he continued almost without a pause: "Which is all right, it's fine; it clears the whole ledger, you can tear all the pages out and burn them, except for one thing. And do you know what that is?" Perhaps he hoped for an answer this time, or perhaps he merely paused for emphasis, since he got no answer. "You've got one nigger left. One nigger Sutpen left. Of course you cant catch him and you dont even always see him and you never will be able to use him. But you've got him there still. You still hear him at night sometimes. Dont you?"

"Yes," Quentin said.

This comes just before the famous conclusion of *Absalom, Absalom!*, when Quentin Compson cries out, in desperate response to Shreve:

"I dont hate it," Quentin said, quickly, at once, immediately; "I dont hate it," he said. *I dont hate it* he thought, panting in the cold air, the iron New England dark: *I dont. I dont! I dont hate it! I dont hate it!*

CHAPTER 41

The Death of the Heart (1938)

ELIZABETH BOWEN

E LIZABETH BOWEN died in 1973 at the age of seventy-three. I recall meeting her once in London and once in the United States. She was intensely civilized, gracious, and emanated an aura of goodwill. I fear that she is not widely read at this time, and I find that to be a great loss. Her best works were the novels *The Death of the Heart* (1938) and *The Heat of the Day* (1949), as well as a marvelous volume of short stories *Ivy Gripped the Steps* (1945). It may be that the shadows of Henry James and of Virginia Woolf, who befriended Bowen, are too heavy upon the novels, but the stories seem to me, after those of Katherine Mansfield, James Joyce, and D. H. Lawrence, as strong as any composed in Great Britain in the twentieth century.

Bowen had a curious twenty-nine-year marriage to Alan Cameron, who worked as an educational administrator and later for the BBC. It seems to have been amiable, but like the marriage of Virginia and Leonard Woolf, never consummated. Instead Bowen had a long relationship to a Canadian diplomat, Charles Ritchie, and briefer ones to other men and women, including the very minor American poet May Sarton.

My friend the gifted American poet Mona Van Duyn, who died at eighty-three in 2004, wrote a pungent essay on *The Death of the*

Heart in 1961, "Pattern and Pilgrimage." It concludes with an acute apprehension of Bowen's complex sensibility in regard to her protagonist, the sixteen-year-old Portia:

> We are not shown in the novel's action whether Portia can "come back" to achieve the womanliness, intelligence and charm of her Shakespearian namesake, for whom traditional wisdom, to which she was bound in choosing a husband, so happily corroborated the heart's spontaneous wish. ("But why was she called Portia?," St. Quentin asks. Anna, surprised, said, "I don't think we ever asked.") Such a wound may turn her into an Anna who is tempted to toss Pidgeon's letters at Portia and tell her, "This is all it comes to, you little fool." First she must come back to Windsor Terrace, dependence, and later make a perhaps more fortunate re-beginning of her adult life. It is clear to the reader that the Quaynes have done the right thing by sending Matchett to fetch her, and that Matchett is the only remaining means of helping her.
>
> Matchett, treated through most of the novel as a looming and awe-inspiring figure, is given, in the final scene of the taxi ride to Karachi, the full weight of humorous and fallible humanity. This "downfall" sets limits on her power, though she opens the hotel door "with an air of authority." Tradition, custom, the personal and communal past, the novel suggests, are supports only, not mystical or magical maps for the course of the grown-up life.
>
> Does innocence lead to the death of this particular, but representative, heart? The title is unequivocal. "Happy that few of us are aware of the world until we are already in league with it," says the author, and Portia's awareness was catastrophically premature.

I have reread *The Death of the Heart* several times with increasing sadness. Poor Portia, the child of a brief affair that led to a catastrophic divorce and exile for her father and mother, has lived abroad, on the Continent, moving from one cheap hotel to another, or one blighted villa to yet another. First her father dies, and then her mother. There is no place for her to go except to her half-brother in

London, whose wife, Anna, is hostile to the young girl from the start. Anna and her husband and their friend, a writer named St. Quentin, are brittle sophisticates and already dead at heart.

Portia, who is puzzled by the strangeness of adults, keeps a diary honestly reflecting her dilemmas. Anna has the bad taste to find it and read it and is enraged at the portrait rendered of herself. Evidently, the portrait is merely accurate, since Portia is so innocent that she does not know how to absorb people's not saying what they mean. Her heart is so pure that irony is beyond her.

Eddie, a would-be novelist and a rather unpleasant young fellow, flirts with Anna to flatter her and becomes a semi-boyfriend of Portia, yet neither falls in love with the other. It is not just that Portia at sixteen is too young for a serious passion, but her cloistered life has given her no background for sorting out and mastering emotion. She may think she loves Eddie, but soon learns that there is no one there to love. Eddie is a blank. His true condition is an inward terror, and he cannot endure any actual exchange of affection.

Bowen is not primarily an ironist. Her prevailing mode is a tentative compassion. And yet *The Death of the Heart* works because of the wise irony by which Portia's innocence destroys the sophisticated pretensions of the Quaynes, of St. Quentin, and of Eddie. Her openness is a pure flame that singes every sleeve. That is certainly not her intention, and I sometimes wonder if it was Bowen's.

Aside from the book's dark title, its three parts are "The World," "The Flesh," and "The Devil." That world is brittle and valueless; there is little sign of any intimation of desire; but the devil is certainly present when Portia discovers that Anna has been reading her diary and divulging it to others. Portia flees the house and offers herself to Eddie for life, which terrifies him into reality:

> "But you used to talk a lot before you got to know me, didn't you? Before you had said you loved me, or anything. I remember hearing you talking in the drawing-room, when I used to go up or down stairs, before I minded at all. Are you her lover?"
>
> "You don't know what you're saying."
>
> "I know it's something you're not with me. I wouldn't mind what you did, but I cannot bear the things I think now that you say."

"Then why keep asking?"

"Because I keep hoping you might tell me you were really saying something not that."

"Well, I am Anna's lover."

"Oh...Are you?"

"Don't you believe me?"

"I've got no way of telling."

"I thought it didn't seem to make much impression. Why make such a fuss if you don't know what you do want? As a matter of fact, I'm not: she's far too cautious and smart, and I don't think she's got any passion at all. She likes to be far more trouble."

"Then why do you—I mean, why—?"

"The trouble with you has been, from the very start, that you've been too anxious to get me taped."

"Have I? But *you* said we loved each other."

"You used to be much gentler, much more sweet. Yes, you used to be, as I once told you, the one person I could naturally love. But you're different, lately, since Seale."

It is a remarkable dialogue, in which Portia's now aggressive innocence is virtually daemonic and comes close to destroying the vapid Eddie. Bowen, like a hound on the scent, closes in upon what has become Portia's quarry:

"You said everything was over," Portia said, looking straight up into his eyes. They stayed locked in this incredulous look till Eddie flinched: he said: "Have I been unkind?"

"I've got no way of telling."

"I wish you had." Frowning, pulling his lip down in the familiar way, that made this the ghost of all their happier talks, he said: "Because I don't know, do you know. I may be some kind of monster; I've really got no idea.... The things I have to say seem never to have had to be said before. Is my life really so ghastly and so extraordinary? I've got no way to check up. I do wish you were older; I wish you knew more."

"You're the only person I ever—"

"That's what's the devil; that's just what I mean. You don't know what to expect."

Not taking her anxious eyes from his face—eyes as desperately concentrated as though she were trying to understand a lesson—she said: "But after all, Eddie, anything that happens has never happened before. What I mean is, you and I are the first people who have ever been us."

Eddie's invocation of the devil is apposite and is massively answered by the strangely wise perplexity of what speaks out of Portia. They part with finality, and Portia runs off to the dilapidated hotel where Major Brutt lives. He is a tired and defeated pensioner who has never lived and relies upon Anna's dubious hospitality:

"There's nothing to mess," she [Portia] said in a very small voice that was implacable. "You are the other person that Anna laughs at," she went on, raising her eyes. "I don't think you understand: Anna's always laughing at you. She says you are quite pathetic. She laughed at your carnations being the wrong colour, then gave them to me. And Thomas always thinks you must be after something. Whatever you do, even send me a puzzle, he thinks that more, and she laughs more. They groan at each other when you have gone away. You and I are the same."

The unfortunate Brutt is middle aged and afraid of women. In her now pragmatically daemonic mode, Portia all but destroys him:

"... I'm not *going* home, Major Brutt."
He said, very reasonably: "Then what do you want to do?"
"Stay here—" She stopped short, as though she felt she had said, too soon, something important enough to need care. Deliberately, with her lips tight shut, she got off the bed to come and stand by him—so that, she standing, he sitting, she could tower up at least a little way. She looked him all over, as though she meant to tug at him, to jerk him awake, and was only not certain where to catch hold of him. Her arms stayed at her sides, but looked rigid, at every moment, with their intention to move in unfeeling desperation. She was not able, or else did not wish, to inform herself with pleading grace; her sexlessness made her deliver a stern summons: he felt her knocking through him like another heart outside his own ribs. "Stay here

with you," she said. "You do like me," she added. "You write to me; you send me puzzles; you say you think about me. Anna says you are sentimental, but that is what she says when people don't feel nothing. I could do things for you: we could have a home; we would not have to live in a hotel. Tell Thomas you want to keep me and he could send you my money. I could cook; my mother cooked when she lived in Nottinghill Gate. Why could you not marry me? I could cheer you up. I would not get in your way, and we should not be half so lonely. Why should you be dumbfounded, Major Brutt?"

"Because I suppose I am," was all he could say.

"I told Eddie you were a person I made happy."

"Good God, yes. But don't you see—"

"Do think it over, please," she said calmly. "I'll wait."

"It's no good beginning to think, my dear."

"I'd like to wait, all the same."

"You're shivering," he said vaguely.

"Yes, I am cold." With a quite new, matter-of-fact air of possessing his room, she made small arrangements for comfort— peeled off his eiderdown, kicked her shoes off, lay down with her head into his pillow and pulled the eiderdown snugly up to her chin. By this series of acts she seemed at once to shelter, to plant here and to obliterate herself—most of all that last. Like a sick person, or someone who has decided by not getting up to take no part in a day, she at once seemed to inhabit a different world. Noncommittal, she sometimes shut her eyes, sometimes looked at the ceiling that took the slope of the roof. "I suppose," she said, after some minutes, "you don't know what to do."

She obliterates Brutt rather more than she does herself. All that he can know to do is to get her back to the only home she has, which she does not want, and which, except for Matchett, the strong-minded servant, does not want her. The book ends with Matchett collecting her and with the implicit hope that Matchett will complete the bringing up of Portia.

After the short stories and *The Death of the Heart,* the Bowen I most care for is her World War II novel *The Heat of the Day* (1949), an intensely vivid portrayal of London under the Blitz. Its protagonist, Stella, is admirable but has to sustain the loss of what William Blake called "organized innocence," which is demonstrated to be only another illusion. Bowen rather famously remarked, "No, it is not only our fate but our business to lose innocence, and once we have lost that it is futile to attempt a picnic in Eden." Blake would not have agreed, and I think I would go with him, despite my admiration for Bowen. Whatever good Matchett will do Portia, it is difficult to see how the young girl can prosper in the world of experience. Bowen was too honest to prophesy. When I asked her, in one of our two brief meetings, what hope we are to have for her Portia, she wisely smiled at me and said nothing.

CHAPTER 42

Invisible Man (1952)

RALPH ELLISON

M Y FRIEND Ralph Waldo Ellison was born in Oklahoma City in 1914. To my grief he died in New York City in 1994 at the age of eighty. We had known each other a long time, having been introduced by R. W. B. Lewis and Kenneth Burke in the middle 1960s. During his final years, we lunched together once a week at the Century Club in New York and talked about literature and jazz. Sometimes Albert Murray made a third. Ellison was fierce on the issue of aesthetic merit. He chided me for having praised Zora Neale Hurston's *Their Eyes Were Watching God,* though there we went on disagreeing. The major African American achievements in the arts certainly include Ellison's *Invisible Man,* the poetry of Jay Wright, born in 1935, and the music essentially inaugurated by Louis Armstrong and then carried on by so many grand figures, including Duke Ellington, Charlie Parker, Bud Powell, Charles Mingus, John Coltrane, Sonny Rollins, Miles Davis, Ornette Coleman, Max Roach, and others.

Though Ellison declined to join my expeditions to the Blue Note in the Village and Minton's in Harlem, he loved Louis Armstrong, Ellington, and Jimmy Rushing, and was captivated almost against his will by Charlie Parker and Charles Mingus. He could not abide John Coltrane, which mystified me. As Ellison aged into the author of a single great book, he sometimes seemed defensive in his vision of jazz as the African American outlaw protest against white America.

Early in the 1980s, I was an overnight guest of Berndt and Jutta Ostendorf in Munich, introduced to them by my friend Miriam Hansen, a film historian who died in 2011 at the age of sixty-one. Berndt Ostendorf is probably the most noted German scholar of African American literature and of jazz. We talked about jazz and about Ellison. For Ostendorf, Louis Armstrong in particular mediated James Joyce, Franz Kafka, T. S. Eliot, and William Faulkner for Ellison, thus allowing him to reconcile aesthetic modernism with black American folklore.

I have just finished another rereading of *Invisible Man*. It is sixty years since I first read it, and I have gone back and forth in it several times since. Perhaps Kenneth Burke overpraised it in saying that it made its own epoch rather than reflecting a particular time. You could say that of Proust or Joyce, Kafka or Beckett, but not of Ellison. His only completed novel is a permanent work, akin say to Flannery O'Connor's *The Violent Bear It Away* (1960) or Philip Roth's *Sabbath's Theater* (1995) and *American Pastoral* (1997). These are all perpetually fresh, but none of them is of the eminence of William Faulkner on his heights: *The Sound and the Fury* (1929), *As I Lay Dying* (1930), *Light in August* (1932), and *Absalom, Absalom!* (1936). However I should mention Thomas Pynchon, whose permanent achievements include *The Crying of Lot 49* (1966), *Gravity's Rainbow* (1973), and *Mason & Dixon* (1997). It seems just to observe that Pynchon is the most considerable American writer of prose fiction since the death of Faulkner in 1962.

Invisible Man is a difficult book to describe. In some ways it is naturalistic, in others symbolic, sometimes surrealistic, and concludes in an irrealism that possibly influenced Pynchon. Named for Ralph Waldo Emerson, Ellison had both pragmatic and transcendental impulses, like the Concord Sage. In flight from both the Brotherhood (the Communist Party) and Ras the Exhorter, a forerunner of the Black Panthers, the nameless narrator, Invisible Man, escapes from a Harlem race riot and goes underground. Down below, he meditates on self-reliance, after judiciously illuminating himself by 1,369 old-fashioned filament lightbulbs. He thus pays nothing to Monopolated Light & Power (Consolidated Edison).

Ellison deliberately absorbs into his style and narrative stance elements of Joseph Conrad, James Joyce, T. S. Eliot, William Faulkner, and André Malraux. But to my ear the crucial influence is Herman Melville's *Moby-Dick,* particularly Father Mapple's wonderful sermon on Jonah. Following Mapple, Invisible Man listens to a recording of Louis Armstrong playing and singing "What Did I Do to Be So Black and Blue," a song composed by the great Fats Waller in collaboration with Harry Brooks and Andy Razaf:

> How will it end? Ain't got a friend
> My only sin is in my skin
> What did I do to be so black and blue?

Suddenly, within Louis Armstrong's jazz, Invisible Man hears a different music, in which a preacher cries out to his congregation: "It'll put you, glory, glory, Oh my Lawd, in the WHALE'S BELLY." The reluctant prophet Jonah survives, and so does Invisible Man, Ellison's version of Melville's Ishmael, who narrates much of *Moby-Dick.*

I feel very somber as I reread *Invisible Man* in June 2018, when the United States is in many ways hopelessly divided between so-called whites and people of black, brown, Hispanic, East Asian, Native American, and other groupings. My friend Ralph Ellison died a quarter-century ago, and we are more split and shattered as a nation than ever before in my long lifetime. We cannot despair; there are millions among us who resist the racist regime that must be ended, before the country itself begins to die. It is not the function of the greatest prose fiction to redeem us or our society. Faulkner, the best we have had since Theodore Dreiser, who died in 1945, knew he could not heal us, and Ellison once told me sadly that Faulkner's powers were beyond him.

Ellison's grandfather had been a slave, and Lewis Ellison, Ralph's father, had to watch a lynching when he was five years old. Ralph's mother, Ida Millsap, belonged to the Socialist Party of Eugene V. Debs and was a radical activist. After studying music at Tuskegee Institute in Alabama, Ellison reached New York City in 1936 and continued his studies. Encouraged by Richard Wright and Langston Hughes, Ellison began writing short stories and essays. He became close to the Communist Party and was hired by the Federal Writers'

Project in 1938 to collect black folklore. In 1943, Ellison joined the merchant marine as a cook.

In 1938, Ellison married Rosa Araminta Poindexter, a stage actress. The marriage ended in 1943. In 1946, he married Fanny McConnell, a strong-minded and brilliant writer and theater organizer. The marriage was very successful, though childless, and Fanny worked hard to support Ellison during the four years in which he wrote *Invisible Man*. Fanny survived Ralph by eleven years, dying in 2005. I remember her as being very beautiful and endlessly gracious.

Invisible Man is structured as a series of picaresque escapades, all of them morally painful to the narrator and to the reader. The first grotesque phantasmagoria is also dreadfully realistic, as a gathering of white bourgeois monsters sets black high-school graduates to fight against one another, while a white female dances lasciviously in front of both groups. Pursued by lustful whites, she manages to escape, but the young boys hurt one another grievously. Invisible Man then has to repeat his high-school commencement address: for social responsibility. Threatened by the audience, he does not quite back down, and then the Board of Education awards him a new briefcase and a scholarship to the state college for Negroes.

That night he suffers a dream:

When I reached home everyone was excited. Next day the neighbors came to congratulate me. I even felt safe from grandfather, whose deathbed curse usually spoiled my triumphs. I stood beneath his photograph with my brief case in hand and smiled triumphantly into his stolid black peasant's face. It was a face that fascinated me. The eyes seemed to follow everywhere I went.

That night I dreamed I was at a circus with him and that he refused to laugh at the clowns no matter what they did. Then later he told me to open my brief case and read what was inside and I did, finding an official envelope stamped with the state seal; and inside the envelope I found another and another, endlessly, and I thought I would fall of weariness. "Them's years," he said. "Now open that one." And I did and in it I found an engraved document containing a short message in letters of gold. "Read it," my grandfather said. "Out loud!"

"To Whom It May Concern," I intoned. "Keep This Nigger-Boy Running."

I awoke with the old man's laughter ringing in my ears.

(It was a dream I was to remember and dream again for many years after. But at that time I had no insight into its meaning. First I had to attend college.)

Like Ralph Ellison and Albert Murray, Invisible Man attends a black college based on Tuskegee University, cofounded by Booker T. Washington in 1881. Its president, Dr. Bledsoe, has the principle: "The only way to please a white man is to tell him a lie!" In the second term of his junior year, Invisible Man is ordered by Dr. Bledsoe to drive an immensely rich white trustee, Mr. Norton, who is visiting the campus, out into the countryside for relaxation between meetings. With his usual picaresque bad luck, feckless Invisible Man delivers the bewildered Norton to a former slave shack, where a black share-cropper tells his tale of incest, with both his wife and daughter, each pregnant, standing nearby. Norton, who has related the early death of his own daughter, "too pure for life," is so shocked that he begs for whiskey. Inevitably, Invisible Man drives to the nearest bar, the Golden Day, which is a bordello frequented by mentally deranged black war veterans. Seeing Norton, they proclaim him the Messiah, and a wild melee commences. Attempting to preserve Norton, Invisible Man takes him upstairs, to be greeted by a bevy of whores and an insane former medical person who revives Norton and denounces Invisible Man for his toadying to the whites. Somehow our unfortunate protagonist gets the wilting Norton back to the dreadful Bledsoe.

I do not know whether Ralph had read Nathanael West's superb parody novel, *A Cool Million: The Dismantling of Lemuel Pitkin* (1934), before he finished *Invisible Man*. He certainly read it later, with much enjoyment, after I had recommended it to him at one of our lunches. Lemuel Pitkin is a white New England version of Invisible Man. Eventually, Lemuel is literally dismantled, whereas Ellison's protagonist suffers endless psychic dismemberment.

Bledsoe expels our hero with a sealed letter of supposed recommendation that urges anyone to regard him as a stray and a pariah. Poor Invisible Man takes a job at a paint factory, only to lose consciousness when a valve fails and covers him with a torrent of white paint. He awakens to find he has suffered an electroshock treatment that causes him to forget his own identity. He takes refuge in Harlem with an amiable landlady, Miss Mary, and rests for some months as her guest.

Walking out on the Harlem streets in cold weather, Invisible Man stumbles upon an ongoing eviction of an old black couple by two brutal whites. An angry crowd has gathered and is on the verge of violence when the old woman is blocked from re-entering the building. Our protagonist takes charge with a rousing oration and restores order, and then oversees the restoration of the aged couple and their furniture to their home. Cops arrive, and Invisible Man departs, but is detained by one Brother Jack, a high personage in the Brotherhood (Communist Party), who offers the narrator a job in that organization. After initially declining, our unfortunate hero joins and is proclaimed the new Booker T. Washington.

The Brotherhood is posh and pays Invisible Man a substantial salary on condition he abandon his past life and take up a new name and dwelling. After speaking with his customary eloquence to a rally of blacks, he becomes the principal spokesman for the Harlem district. He meets Tod Clifton, a charismatic Brother, who bears the scar of a recent tangle with the followers of the remarkable Ras the Exhorter, who sees accurately that the Brotherhood is only another white instrument for exploiting blacks:

> "Mahn," Ras blurted, "I ought to kill you. Godahm, I ought to kill you and the world be better off. But you *black, mahn.* Why you be black, mahn? I swear I ought to kill you. No mahn strike the Exhorter, godahmit, no mahn!"
>
> I saw him raise the knife again and now as he lowered it unused he pushed Clifton into the street and stood over him, sobbing.
>
> "Why you with these white folks? Why? I been watching you a long time. I say to myself, 'Soon he get smart and get tired. He get out of that t'ing.' Why a good boy like you still with them?"
>
> Still moving forward, I saw his face gleam with red angry tears as he stood above Clifton with the still innocent knife and the tears red in the glow of the window sign.
>
> "You *my* brother, mahn. Brothers are the same color; how the

hell you call these white men *brother*? Shit, mahn. That's shit!
Brothers the same color. We sons of Mama Africa, you done
forgot? You black, BLACK! You—*Godahm,* mahn!" he said,
swinging the knife for emphasis. "You got bahd *hair!* You got
thick *lips!* They say you *stink!* They hate you, mahn. You African. AFRICAN! Why you with them? Leave that shit, mahn.
They sell you out. That shit is old-fashioned. They enslave us—
you forget that? How can they mean a black mahn any good?
How they going to be your *brother*?"

The two grand characters in Ellison's novel are Ras the Exhorter
and Rinehart the Runner, a numbers racketeer who is also a pimp
as well as the Rev. B. P. Rinehart, Spiritual Technologist. Even when
Ras becomes Ras the Destroyer, it is difficult not to sympathize with
the deeply emotional black seer:

"Hell, no," Ras cried, wiping his eyes with his fists. "I talk! Bust
me with the pipe but, by God, you listen to the Exhorter! Come
in with us, mahn. We build a glorious movement of black people. *Black People!* What they do, give you money? Who wahnt
the dahm stuff? Their money bleed black blood, mahn. It's
unclean! Taking their money is shit, mahn. Money without
dignity— That's *bahd* shit!"
    Clifton lunged toward him. I held him, shaking my head.
"Come on, the man's crazy," I said, pulling on his arm.
    Ras struck his thighs with his fists. "*Me* crazy, mahn? You
call *me* crazy? Look at you two and look at me—is this *sanity?*
Standing here in three shades of blackness! Three black men
fighting in the street because of the white enslaver? Is that sanity? Is that consciousness, scientific understahnding? Is that
the modern black mahn of the twentieth century? Hell, mahn!
Is it self-respect—black against black? What they give you to
betray—their women? You fall for that?"
    "Let's go," I said, listening and remembering and suddenly
alive in the dark with the horror of the battle royal, but Clifton
looked at Ras with a tight, fascinated expression, pulling away
from me.
    "Let's go," I repeated. He stood there, looking.
    "Sure, you go," Ras said, "but not him. You contahminated

but he the real black mahn. In Africa this mahn be a chief, a black king! Here they say he rape them godahm women with no blood in their veins. I bet this mahn can't beat them off with a baseball bat—shit! What kind of foolishness is it? Kick him ass from cradle to grave then call him *brother*? Does it make mahthematics? Is it logic? Look at him, mahn; open your eyes," he said to me. "I look like that I rock the blahsted world! They know about me in Japan, India—all the colored countries. Youth! Intelligence! The mahn's [a] natural prince! Where is your eyes? Where your self-respect? Working for them dahm people? Their days is numbered, the time is almost here and you fooling 'round like this was the nineteenth century. I don't understahnd you. Am I ignorant? Answer me, mahn!"

"Yes," Clifton burst out. "Hell, yes!"

"You t'ink I'm crazy, is it c'ase I speak bahd English? Hell, it ain't my mama tongue, mahn, I'm African! You really t'ink I'm crazy?"

"Yes, yes!"

"You believe that?" said Ras. "What they do to you, black mahn? Give you them stinking women?"

Clifton lunged again, and again I grabbed him; and again Ras held his ground, his head glowing red.

"Women? *Godahm*, mahn! Is that equality? Is that the black mahn's freedom? A pat on the back and a piece of cunt without no passion? Maggots! They buy you that blahsted cheap, mahn? What they *do* to my people! Where is your brains? These women dregs, mahn! They bilge water! You know the high-class white mahn hates the black mahn, that's simple. So now he use the dregs and wahnt you black young men to do his dirty work. They betray you and you betray the black people. They tricking you, mahn. Let them fight among themselves. Let 'em kill off one another. We organize—organization is good—but we organize black. BLACK! To hell with that son of a bitch! He take one them strumpets and tell the black mahn his freedom lie between her skinny legs—while that son of a gun, *he* take all the power and the capital and don't leave the black mahn not'ing. The good white women he tell the black mahn is a rapist and keep them locked up and ignorant while he makes the black mahn a race of bahstards.

"When the black mahn going to tire of this childish perfidity? He got you so you don't trust your black intelligence? You young, don't play you'self cheap, mahn. Don't deny you'self! It took a billion gallons of black blood to make you. Recognize you'self inside and you wan the kings among men! A mahn knows he's a mahn when he got not'ing, when he's naked—nobody have to tell him that. You six foot tall, mahn. You young and intelligent. You black and beautiful—don't let 'em tell you different! You wasn't them t'ings you be dead, mahn. Dead! I'd have killed you, mahn. Ras the Exhorter raised up his knife and tried to do it, but he could not do it. Why don't you do it? I ask myself. I will do it now, I say; but somet'ing tell me, 'No, no! You might be killing your black king!' And I say, yas, yas! So I accept your humiliating ahction. Ras recognized your black possibilities, mahn. Ras would not sahcrifice his black brother to the white enslaver. Instead he *cry*. Ras is a mahn—no white mahn have to tell him that—and Ras *cry*. So why don't you recognize your black duty, mahn, and come jine us?"

Tod Clifton, who tells Invisible Man that it is on the inside that Ras is dangerous, in some sense yields to this irrefutable eloquence. As a reader I cannot resist. Poor Clifton is demoralized and takes to selling little black puppets on the streets, until he is murdered by a white policeman. Only that, and the later realization that the Brotherhood wishes Harlem to explode in a vast race riot, restores the narrator to himself, whatever that self may be.

Putting on dark glasses and a wide hat, the protagonist plays at being Rinehart the Runner, until he encounters the epiphany of the religion of Rinehart:

Several blocks away I stopped, out of breath. And both pleased and angry. How stupid could people be? Was everyone suddenly nuts? I looked about me. It was a bright street, the walks full of people. I stood at the curb trying to breathe. Up the street a sign with a cross glowed above the walk:

HOLY WAY STATION
BEHOLD THE LIVING GOD

The letters glowed dark green and I wondered if it were from the lenses or the actual color of the neon tubes. A couple of drunks stumbled past. I headed for Hambro's, passing a man sitting on the curb with his head bent over his knees. Cars passed. I went on. Two solemn-faced children came passing out handbills which first I refused, then went back and took. After all, I had to know what was going on in the community. I took the bill and stepped close to the street light, reading.

Behold the Invisible
Thy will be done O Lord!
I See all, Know all. Tell all, Cure all.
You shall see the unknown wonders.
—REV. B. P. RINEHART,
Spiritual Technologist.

The old is ever new
Way Stations in New Orleans, the home of mystery,
Birmingham, New York, Chicago, Detroit and L.A.
No Problem too Hard for God.

Come to the Way Station.
BEHOLD THE INVISIBLE!
Attend our services, prayer meetings Thrice weekly
Join us in the NEW REVELATION of the OLD TIME RELIGION!
BEHOLD THE SEEN UNSEEN
BEHOLD THE INVISIBLE
YE WHO ARE WEARY COME HOME!
I DO WHAT YOU WANT DONE! DON'T WAIT!

I dropped the leaflet into the gutter and moved on. I walked slowly, my breath still coming hard. Could it be? Soon I reached the sign. It hung above a store that had been converted into a church, and I stepped into the shallow lobby and wiped my face with a handkerchief. Behind me I heard the rise and fall of an old-fashioned prayer such as I hadn't heard since leaving the campus; and then only when visiting country preachers were asked to pray. The voice rose and fell in a rhythmical, dreamlike recital—part enumeration of earthly trials undergone by the congregation, part rapt display of vocal virtuosity, part appeal to God. I was still wiping my face and squinting at crude Biblical scenes painted on the windows when two old ladies came up to me.

"Even', Rever'n Rinehart," one of them said. "How's our dear pastor this warm evening?"

Oh, no, I thought, but perhaps agreeing will cause less trouble than denying, and I said, "Good evening, sisters," muffling my voice with my handkerchief and catching the odor of the girl's perfume from my hand.

"This here's Sister Harris, Rever'n. She come to join our little band." "God bless you, Sister Harris," I said, taking her extended hand.

"You know, Rever'n, I once heard you preach years ago. You was just a lil' ole twelve-year-old boy, back in Virginia. And here I come North and find you, praise God, still preaching the gospel, doing the Lord's work. Still preaching the ole time religion here in this wicked city—"

"Er, Sister Harris," the other sister said, "we better get on in and find our seats. Besides, the pastor's kind of got things to do. Though you are here a little early, aren't you, Rever'n?"

"Yes," I said, dabbing my mouth with my handkerchief. They were motherly old women of the southern type and I suddenly felt a nameless despair. I wanted to tell them that Rinehart was a fraud, but now there came a shout from inside the church and I heard a burst of music.

"Just lissen to it, Sister Harris. That's the new kind of guitar music I told you Rever'n Rinehart got for us. Ain't it heavenly?"

"Praise God," Sister Harris said. "Praise God!"

"Excuse us, Rever'n, I have to see Sister Judkins about the money she collected for the building fund. And, Rever'n, last night I sold ten recordings of your inspiring sermon. Even sold one to the white lady I work for."

"Bless you," I found myself saying in a voice heavy with despair, "bless you, bless you."

Then the door opened and I looked past their heads into a small crowded room of men and women sitting in folding chairs, to the front where a slender woman in a rusty black robe played passionate boogie-woogie on an upright piano along with a young man wearing a skull cap who struck righteous riffs from an electric guitar which was connected to an amplifier that hung from the ceiling above a gleaming white and gold pulpit. A man in an elegant red cardinal's robe and a high lace collar stood resting against an enormous Bible and now began to lead a hard-driving hymn which the congregation shouted in the unknown tongue. And back and high on the wall above him there arched the words in letters of gold:

LET THERE BE LIGHT!

Ellison's novel is replete with eloquent climaxes, but this may be my favorite. The heightened prose is worthy of the metamorphic Rinehart, who is as much of an answer as Invisible Man can give us:

It was too much for me. I removed my glasses and tucked the white hat carefully beneath my arm and walked away. Can it be, I thought, can it actually be? And I knew that it was. I had heard of it before but I'd never come so close. Still, could he be all of them: Rine the runner and Rine the gambler and Rine the briber and Rine the lover and Rinehart the Reverend? Could he himself be both rind and heart? What is real anyway? But how could I doubt it? He was a broad man, a man of parts who got around. Rinehart the rounder. It was true as I was true. His world was possibility and he knew it. He was years ahead of me and I was a fool. I must have been crazy and blind. The world in which we lived was without boundaries. A vast seething, hot world of fluidity, and Rine the rascal was at home. Perhaps only Rine the rascal was at home in it. It was unbelievable, but perhaps only the unbelievable could be believed. Perhaps the truth was always a lie.

Are we persuaded by this? My former acquaintance the journalist Michael Anderson, whom I have not seen for many years, once argued with me about Ellison, whom he regarded as an aesthetic failure. Anderson himself is African American, and wrote a brief essay with this severe judgment:

...a man for whom paradox too often has been mistaken for profundity: a writer who did not write, the expositor of "complexity" whose ideas were simple when not simplistic, the delineator of "chaos" whose commentary was a compendium of complacency, the advocate of social fluidity whose vision was frozen in times past, the proponent of aesthetic discipline whose work is marked by formlessness and lack of control, a "race man" who disdained his race, the critic of sociology whose own novel has been distorted into a sociological cliché, the proponent of individualism whose career was propelled at every step by an astonishing array of selfless supporters, an artist all the more honored the less he produced, a public presence as an invisible man...

I am still fond of Michael Anderson, but this is simply not so. Ellison left two thousand manuscript pages which were edited into an unfortunate novel he would never have published: *Juneteenth* (1999). Ralph was a perfectionist, and his sorrow was that he could not again write an *Invisible Man*. It is dreadfully inaccurate to say that Ellison disdained his race. Anderson concluded by saying: "That Ellison was not fitted for the art he professed to admire is his pathos. He sought to be the black T. S. Eliot when he could have been the black Beckett."

It would be truer to say that Ellison sought to be the black Dostoevsky, whose Underground Man he resurrected in his Invisible Man. Why Anderson invokes Samuel Beckett is beyond my surmise. I will end this tribute to a permanent novel with its conclusion, in which we are invited into its universalism:

"Ah," I can hear you say, "so it was all a build-up to bore us with his buggy jiving. He only wanted us to listen to him rave!" But only partially true: Being invisible and without substance, a disembodied voice, as it were, what else could I do? What else but try to tell you what was really happening when your eyes were looking through? And it is this which frightens me:

Who knows but that, on the lower frequencies, I speak for you?

CHAPTER 43

The Left Hand of Darkness (1969)

Ursula K. Le Guin

I NEVER MET Ursula K. Le Guin, who died on January 22, 2018, at the age of eighty-eight in Portland, Oregon, her home for many years. And yet we became good friends during the last two months of her life, entirely by way of e-mail. I inaugurated the correspondence on November 21, 2017, and she replied on November 24. After that we exchanged letters sixteen times, until her final letter of January 16, 2018, which concluded:

> One of the things I like least about being very old is the unreliability of my energy. Up one day, down the next, bleh! Working at poetry or a story is, always has been, the job I want to be doing, the work that keeps me steady and content. But too often there just isn't the wherewithal. I suspect your work is central to your wellbeing in much this way, and hope you aren't suffering such periods of enforced idleness.
>
> > I value our friendship.
> > Ursula

I replied after an interval, during which I was very ill, on January 23, 2018, not yet knowing that Ursula had died the day before. I hope, in tribute to her, that I live to edit her poems for the Library of America, thinking she might have wanted me to do that. For now, I turn to her two strongest novels, *The Left Hand of Darkness* (1969) and *The Dispossessed* (1974).

Though I have written about *The Left Hand of Darkness* before, in 1987 and again in 2000, I have forgotten what I said and do not want to consult it now, but, rather, make a fresh start on this marvelous romance. In one of her letters Ursula remarked that writing *The Dispossessed* was liberating for her, and she seemed to prefer it to *The Left Hand of Darkness*. Rereading both, I find myself torn between the two. The protagonist Shevek in *The Dispossessed* is far more interesting than anyone in the earlier book, and yet he and his story manifest something of the ambivalence of Le Guin's subtitle: *An Ambiguous Utopia*.

In a fierce introduction to *The Left Hand of Darkness,* Le Guin charmingly remarks, "A novelist's business is lying." She adumbrates:

> I talk about the gods; I am an atheist. But I am an artist too, and therefore a liar. Distrust everything I say. I am telling the truth.
>
> The only truth I can understand or express is, logically defined, a lie. Psychologically defined, a symbol. Aesthetically defined, a metaphor.

Always in Le Guin we hear reverberations of Lao Tzu's *Tao Te Ching,* which she translated, with J. P. Seaton, as *A Book About the Way and the Power of the Way* (1997). We corresponded about her understanding of the Tao, yet I had to confess my permanent difficulty in absorbing this way that is not a way. I myself always keep to hand a copy of *The Bhagavad-Gita* as rendered by Barbara Stoler Miller, which I purchased in the autumn of 1986, the year of its publication. After hundreds of readings, I think I know what Krishna means by "dark opacity," "passion," and "lucidity," but a dozen readings of the Le Guin–Seaton *Tao Te Ching* have left me muttering that I do not apprehend the water and stone of the Way. Is it that I am not enough open to my own female component? That seems not right. I am more my late mother than my late father. What moves me most in Ursula is the serenity. I lack it utterly.

. . .

Commenting upon the fascinating vision of sexuality in *Left Hand*, Le Guin continues in gusto:

> This book is not about the future. Yes, it begins by announcing that it's set in the "Ekumenical Year 1490–97," but surely you don't *believe* that?
>
> Yes, indeed the people in it are androgynous, but that doesn't mean that I'm predicting that in a millennium or so we will all be androgynous, or announcing that I think we damned well ought to be androgynous. I'm merely observing, in the peculiar, devious, and thought-experimental manner proper to science fiction, that if you look at us at certain odd times of day in certain weathers, we already are. I am not predicting, or prescribing. I am describing. I am describing certain aspects of psychological reality in the novelist's way, which is by inventing elaborately circumstantial lies.

The burden of *Left Hand* is whether Genly Ai can persuade the king of Karhide on the planet Gethen or Winter to join the Ekumen or union of many planets in exchanges of trade and culture. Genly Ai speaks much of the book, but frequently Le Guin moves into third-person narration. Though Ai is a man of goodwill and adequate intelligence, he can never quite understand the consciousness of the androgynes whom he seeks to win over. Here Le Guin is admirably subtle. She tended to distrust Freud, since her heart and mind were with the Tao, and yet she shows what he meant in observing that for almost all of us thought could not be liberated from its sexual past.

Rather wickedly, Le Guin devotes Chapter 7 to the field notes of one Ong Tot Oppong, a woman investigator on behalf of the Ekumen who lands on Gethen/Winter to study "The Question of Sex." Oppong speculates that whoever colonized this odd planet practiced human genetic manipulation in order to produce Gethenian sexual physiology:

> The sexual cycle averages 26 to 28 days (they tend to speak of it as 26 days, approximating it to the lunar cycle). For 21 or

22 days the individual is *somer*, sexually inactive, latent. On about the 18th day hormonal changes are initiated by the pituitary control and on the 22nd or 23rd day the individual enters *kemmer*, estrus. In this first phase of kemmer (Karh. *secher*) he remains completely androgynous. Gender, and potency, are not attained in isolation. A Gethenian in first-phase kemmer, if kept alone or with others not in kemmer, remains incapable of coitus. Yet the sexual impulse is tremendously strong in this phase, controlling the entire personality, subjecting all other drives to its imperative. When the individual finds a partner in kemmer, hormonal secretion is further stimulated (most importantly by touch—secretion? scent?) until in one partner either a male or female hormonal dominance is established. The genitals engorge or shrink accordingly, foreplay intensifies, and the partner, triggered by the change, takes on the other sexual role (? without exception? If there are exceptions, resulting in kemmer-partners of the same sex, they are so rare as to be ignored). This second phase of kemmer (Karh. *thorharmen*), the mutual process of establishing sexuality and potency, apparently occurs within a timespan of two to twenty hours. If one of the partners is already in full kemmer, the phase for the newer partner is liable to be quite short; if the two are entering kemmer together, it is likely to take longer. Normal individuals have no predisposition to either sexual role in kemmer; they do not know whether they will be the male or the female, and have no choice in the matter. (Otie Nim wrote that in the Orgoreyn region the use of hormone derivatives to establish a preferred sexuality is quite common; I haven't seen this done in rural Karhide.) Once the sex is determined it cannot change during the kemmer-period. The culminant phase of kemmer (Karh. *thokemmer*) lasts from two to five days, during which sexual drive and capacity are at maximum. It ends fairly abruptly, and if conception has not taken place, the individual returns to the somer phase within a few hours (note: Otie Nim thinks this "fourth phase" is the equivalent of the menstrual cycle) and the cycle begins anew. If the individual was in the female role and was impregnated, hormonal activity of course continues, and for the 8.4-month gestation period and the 6- to 8-month lac-

tation period this individual remains female. The male sexual organs remain retracted (as they are in somer), the breasts enlarge somewhat, and the pelvic girdle widens. With the cessation of lactation the female reenters somer and becomes once more a perfect adrogyne. No physiological habit is established, and the mother of several children may be the father of several more.

That last sentence must have delighted Ursula K. Le Guin, whose capacity for amiable irony is almost unsurpassed. It certainly pleases me! Going on eighty-eight, I am beyond all this, but even if I were twenty-eight it might send me to the nearest bar. Since King Argaven of Karhide is both crazy and pregnant, Genly Ai's quest seems foolish yet it is earned by a sacrifice of the book's hero, Harth rem ir Estraven.

Estraven is introduced to us at the close of the first chapter, but we see and hear him only through the misconceptions of Genly Ai. The noble Estraven is a prime minister on the way out—no surprise to him, because he candidly remarks that King Argaven is both crazy and stupid. But he is in some danger from rivals and has concern that Ai may be in danger also. Gethen is an absolute monarchy, itself an entity totally unknown to Genly Ai. No wars are fought on the planet Winter, but assassinations, blood feuds, sudden outbursts of violence are common.

The patriotism of Estraven has modulated into a realization that Karhide is outmoded and needs to join the interplanetary union of worlds. In the eyes of King Argaven and his more duplicitous servitors, Estraven's desire is treasonable, and in time he will suffer death for it. He flees into exile and a ban is proclaimed:

"…Let all countrymen of Karhide know and say that the crime for which Harth rem ir Estraven is exiled is the crime of Treason: he having urged privily and openly in Assembly and Palace, under pretense of loyal service to the king, that the Nation-Dominion of Karhide cast away its sovereignty and surrender up its power in order to become an inferior and subject nation in a certain Union of Peoples, concerning which let all men know and say that no such Union does exist, being a device and baseless fiction of certain conspiring traitors who seek to weaken the Authority of Karhide in the king, to the profit of the real and present enemies of the land. Odguyrny Tuwa, Eighth Hour, in the Palace in Erhenrang: ARGAVEN HARGE."

After a rather frightening meeting with the king, Genly Ai begins to understand Estraven's concern for him and vows to leave Karhide for Orgoreyn, Karhide's rival and neighbor. He goes east to seek information from the Foretellers. My favorite chapter in *Left Hand* is 5, "The Domestication of Hunch," the chapter of the Foretellers. Their leader is Faxe, a benign follower of the Negative Way, who eventually will attain power in Karhide. Faxe is a weaver, a craft associated with the preternatural throughout human history. I always think of the delightful Bottom the Weaver in Shakespeare's *A Midsummer Night's Dream*, who is the only human who can see and apprehend the faerie world of Titania, Puck, Oberon, Mustardseed, Cobweb, Peaseblossom, Moth.

Faxe the Foreteller centers an amazing scene, in a high hall surrounded by eight other proleptic figures, two of them being quite insane and one a curious male pervert. In return for two rubies, Genly Ai asks the question: will Karhide join the Ekumen and when? Suddenly a woman appears merged with Faxe, bathed in silver light, encased in silver armor, and bearing a sword. She screams aloud, in pain and terror, a triple yes! She vanishes. The answer is that five years hence Gethen will be a member of the Ekumen.

The ultimate wisdom of Faxe the Foreteller seems to me Ursula's eloquent evasion of the Freudian maxim that we must make friends with the necessity of dying:

> "The unknown," said Faxe's soft voice in the forest, "the unforetold, the unproven, that is what life is based on. Ignorance is the ground of thought. Unproof is the ground of action. If it were proven that there is no God there would be no religion. No Handdara, no Yomesh, no hearthgods, nothing. But also if it were proven that there is a God, there would be no religion. . . . Tell me, Genry, what is known? What is sure, predictable, inevitable—the one certain thing you know concerning your future, and mine?"
>
> "That we shall die."

"Yes. There's really only one question that can be answered, Genry, and we already know the answer.... The only thing that makes life possible is permanent, intolerable uncertainty: not knowing what comes next."

To me that seems an aesthetic formulation: the only thing that makes it possible to read and reread the best novels is not knowing what comes next, even though we have read them before. In Le Guin, as much the novelist as poet as were Victor Hugo and Emily Brontë, the poetry itself becomes Foretelling. We don't have to pay her two rubies; we need only read and reread. Directly after the foreboding by Faxe of the uncertainty of mortality, Le Guin changes the narrator into Estraven, who has to flee into Orgoreyn, scarcely an easy purpose. He has to steal a boat and row it, though wounded by a sonic gun. Picked up by a patrol ship, he is taken to a safe port in Orgoreyn.

The novel's plot begins with fresh intensity when Estraven seeks out Genly Ai in Orgoreyn and warns him not to be used by any faction in that country. Later, Estraven rescues Genly from a prison farm, and their escape takes them on a tremendous trek across the ice, pulling a sledge together. In that adventure they become overwhelmingly close friends and develop a poignance in their mutual understanding that takes them to the border of sexual love, where they pause. At that moment Le Guin creates a remarkable excursus:

Since we came up out of the volcano-murk our spirit is not all spent in work and worry, and we talk again in the tent after our dinner. As I am in kemmer I would find it easier to ignore Ai's presence, but this is difficult in a two-man tent. The trouble is of course that he is, in his curious fashion, also in kemmer: always in kemmer. A strange lowgrade sort of desire it must be, to be spread out over every day of the year and never to know the choice of sex, but there it is; and here am I. Tonight my extreme physical awareness of him was rather hard to ignore, and I was too tired to divert it into untrance or any other channel of the discipline. Finally he asked, had he offended me? I explained my silence, with some embarrassment. I was afraid he would laugh at me. After all he is no more an oddity, a sexual freak, than I am: up here on the Ice each of us is singular, isolate, I as cut off from those like me, from my society and its rules, as he from his. There is no world full of other Gethenians here to explain and support my existence. We are equals at last, equal, alien, alone. He did not laugh, of course. Rather he spoke with a gentleness that I did not know was in him. After a while he too came to speak of isolation, of loneliness.

"Your race is appallingly alone in its world. No other mammalian species. No other ambisexual species. No animal intelligent enough even to domesticate as pets. It must color your thinking, this uniqueness. I don't mean scientific thinking only, though you are extraordinary hypothesizers—it's extraordinary that you arrived at any concept of evolution, faced with that unbridgeable gap between yourselves and the lower animals. But philosophically, emotionally: to be so solitary, in so hostile a world: it must affect your entire outlook."

"The Yomeshta would say that man's singularity is his divinity."

"Lords of the Earth, yes. Other cults on other worlds have come to the same conclusion. They tend to be the cults of dynamic, aggressive, ecology-breaking cultures. Orgoreyn is in the pattern, in its way; at least they seem bent on pushing things around. What do the Handdarata say?"

"Well, in the Handdara . . . you know, there's no theory, no dogma. . . . Maybe they are less aware of the gap between men and beasts, being more occupied with the likenesses, the links, the whole of which living things are a part." Tormer's Lay had been all day in my mind, and I said the words,

Light is the left hand of darkness
And darkness the right hand of light
Two are one, life and death, lying
together like lovers in kemmer,
like hands joined together,
like the end and the way.

My voice shook as I said the lines, for I remembered as I said them that in the letter my brother wrote me before his death he had quoted the same words.

Ai brooded, and after some time he said, "You're isolated, and undivided. Perhaps you are as obsessed with wholeness as we are with dualism."

"We are dualists too. Duality is an essential, isn't it? So long as there is *myself* and *the other*."

"I and Thou," he said. "Yes, it does, after all, go even wider than sex...."

Le Guin's Taoist poem gives her more than a title. It is the book, the woman, the spirit unappeasable and peregrine that I recall saluting in the last letter I sent to her, unknowingly written the day after her death. She gives Ai his finest moment in expressing an understanding of the love between Estraven and himself:

For it seemed to me, and I think to him, that it was from that sexual tension between us, admitted now and understood but not assuaged, that the great and sudden assurance of friendship between us rose: a friendship so much needed by us both in our exile, and already so well proved in the days and nights of our bitter journey, that it might as well be called, now as later, love. But it was from the difference between us, not from the affinities and likenesses, but from the difference, that that love came: and it was itself the bridge, the only bridge, across what divided us. For us to meet sexually would be for us to meet once more as aliens. We had touched, in the only way we could touch. We left it at that. I do not know if we were right.

This is so precisely phrased that the voice is Le Guin's. She also is unsure if they were right, and as her reader I, too, am uncertain. It would be a very different book if they had become lovers in the complete sense. Somewhere Le Guin remarks that her true subject is marriage, and here she gives us a Shakespearean marriage of true minds. Le Guin being Le Guin, she does not stop there. One of her inventions is mindspeech, by which two empathics can communicate without speech, a praxis that Ai teaches Estraven:

We tried mindspeech again. I had never before sent repeatedly to a total non-receiver. The experience was disagreeable.

I began to feel like an atheist praying. Presently Estraven yawned and said, "I am deaf, deaf as a rock. We'd better sleep." I assented. He turned out the light, murmuring his brief praise of darkness; we burrowed down into our bags, and within a minute or two he was sliding into sleep as a swimmer slides into dark water. I felt his sleep as if it were my own: the empathic bond was there, and once more I bespoke him, sleepily, by his name—"*Therem!*"

He sat bolt upright, for his voice rang out above me in the blackness, loud. "Arek! is that you?"

"No: Genly Ai: I am bespeaking you."

His breath caught. Silence. He fumbled with the Chabe stove, turned up the light, stared at me with his dark eyes full of fear. "I dreamed," he said, "I thought I was at home—"

"You heard me mindspeak."

"You called me—It was my brother. It was his voice I heard. He's dead. You called me—you called me Therem? I . . . This is more terrible than I had thought." He shook his head, as a man will do to shake off nightmare, and then put his face in his hands.

"Harth, I'm very sorry—"

"No, call me by my name. If you can speak inside my skull with a dead man's voice then you can call me by my name! Would *he* have called me 'Harth'? Oh, I see why there's no lying in this mindspeech. It is a terrible thing. . . . All right. All right, speak to me again."

"Wait."

"No. Go on."

With his fierce, frightened gaze on me I bespoke him: *"Therem, my friend, there's nothing to fear between us."*

He kept on staring at me, so that I thought he had not understood; but he had. "Ah, but there is," he said.

After a while, controlling himself, he said calmly, "You spoke in my language."

"Well, you don't know mine."

"You said there would be words, I know. . . . Yet I imagined it as—an understanding—"

"Empathy's another game, though not unconnected. It gave

us the connection tonight. But in mindspeech proper, the speech centers of the brain are activated, as well as—"

"No, no, no. Tell me that later. Why do you speak in my brother's voice?" His voice was strained.

"That I can't answer. I don't know. Tell me about him."

"*Nusuth* ... My full brother, Arek Harth rem ir Estraven. He was a year older than I. He would have been Lord of Estre. We ... I left home, you know, for his sake. He has been dead fourteen years."

The two Estravens had been lovers, incest not being a Gethenian taboo. They had sworn faithfulness to one another and had a son. Therem will join Arek in death when he attempts valiantly to make his escape from Karhide:

But he was off, downhill: a magnificent fast skier, and this time not holding back for me. He shot away on a long quick curving descent through the shadows over the snow. He ran from me, and straight into the guns of the border-guards. I think they shouted warnings or orders to halt, and a light sprang up somewhere, but I am not sure; in any case he did not stop, but flashed on towards the fence, and they shot him down before he reached it. They did not use the sonic stunners but the foray gun, the ancient weapon that fires a set of metal fragments in a burst. They shot to kill him. He was dying when I got to him, sprawled and twisted away from his skis that stuck up out of the snow, his chest half shot away. I took his head in my arms and spoke to him, but he never answered me; only in a way he answered my love for him, crying out through the silent wreck and tumult of his mind as consciousness lapsed, in the unspoken tongue, once, clearly, *"Arek!"* Then no more. I held him, crouching there in the snow, while he died. They let me do that. Then they made me get up, and took me off one way and him another, I going to prison and he into the dark.

It is a tribute to Le Guin's art that every time I reread this I become very sad. In some ways Genly Ai plays Horatio to Therem Estraven's Hamlet, but Shakespeare's Hamlet dies upward in an apotheosis, whereas Therem descends to icy darkness, crying out the name of his long-dead brother as though Genly has fused with Arek.

Genly Ai is soon liberated by royal orders and has another audience with King Argaven, after arranging to bring down the Ekumen spaceship:

> After some silence, he said, "How was it, that pull across the Ice?"
>
> "Not easy."
>
> "Estraven would be a good man to pull with, on a crazy trek like that. He was tough as iron. And never lost his temper. I'm sorry he's dead."
>
> I found no reply.
>
> "I'll receive your…countrymen in audience tomorrow afternoon at Second Hour. Is there more needs saying now?"
>
> "My lord, will you revoke the Order of Exile on Estraven, to clear his name?"
>
> "Not yet, Mr. Ai. Don't rush it. Anything more?"
>
> "No more."
>
> "Go on, then."
>
> Even I betrayed him. I had said I would not bring the ship down till his banishment was ended, his name cleared. I could not throw away what he had died for, by insisting on the condition. It would not bring him out of this exile.

The Left Hand of Darkness concludes with Genly Ai visiting the Hearth of the Lord of Estre, who had borne both Arek and Therem.

> Esvans Harth rem ir Estraven was an old man, past seventy, crippled by an arthritic disease of the hips. He sat erect in a rolling-chair by the fire. His face was broad, much blunted and worn down by time, like a rock in a torrent: a calm face, terribly calm.
>
> "You are the Envoy, Genry Ai?"
>
> "I am."
>
> He looked at me, and I at him. Therem had been the son, child of the flesh, of this old lord. Therem the younger son; Arek the elder, that brother whose voice he had heard in mine

bespeaking him; both dead now. I could not see anything of my friend in that worn, calm, hard old face that met my gaze. I found nothing there but the certainty, the sure fact of Therem's death:

The old lord looked at the boy, then at me.

"This is Sorve Harth," he said, "heir of Estre, my sons' son."

There is no ban on incest there, I knew it well enough. Only the strangeness of it, to me a Terran, and the strangeness of seeing the flash of my friend's spirit in this grim, fierce, provincial boy, made me dumb for a while. When I spoke my voice was unsteady. "The king will recant. Therem was no traitor. What does it matter what fools call him?"

The old lord nodded slowly, smoothly. "It matters," he said.

"You crossed the Gobrin Ice together," Sorve demanded, "you and he?"

"We did."

"I should like to hear that tale, my Lord Envoy," said old Esvans, very calm. But the boy, Therem's son, said stammering, "Will you tell us how he died?—Will you tell us about the other worlds out among the stars—the other kinds of men; the other lives?"

Le Guin had a special genius for endings. In the boy Sorve's voice we hear Therem's spirit speak again, and we realize freshly the ironic necessity of his dying, a sacrifice to open up his closed society to otherness, indicated by the triple repetition of the refrain "other."

CHAPTER 44

The Dispossessed (1974)

Ursula K. Le Guin

I N ONE OF HER LETTERS TO ME, in response to my praise for
The Dispossessed, Le Guin said that the process of writing this
book was particularly important for her, in that she felt it had taught
her how to make her work more capacious. Certainly Shevek, the
novel's protagonist, is by far her most complex character, a physicist of genius, a dedicated anarchist, and a pilgrim who mediates
between antithetical worlds.

The book begins and ends at the launch port of the anarchist
nation of Anarres. Between the port and the rest of the land there is
a forbidding wall, more ominous for looking so commonplace:

> There was a wall. It did not look important. It was built of
> uncut rocks roughly mortared. An adult could look right over
> it, and even a child could climb it. Where it crossed the road-
> way, instead of having a gate it degenerated into mere geom-
> etry, a line, an idea of boundary. But the idea was real. It was
> important. For seven generations there had been nothing in the
> world more important than that wall.
>
> Like all walls it was ambiguous, two-faced. What was inside
> it and what was outside it depended upon which side of it you
> were on.

Looked at from one side, the wall enclosed a barren sixty-acre field called the Port of Anarres. On the field there were a couple of large gantry cranes, a rocket pad, three warehouses, a truck garage, and a dormitory. The dormitory looked durable, grimy, and mournful; it had no gardens, no children; plainly nobody lived there or was even meant to stay there long. It was in fact a quarantine. The wall shut in not only the landing field but also the ships that came down out of space, and the men that came on the ships, and the worlds they came from, and the rest of the universe. It enclosed the universe, leaving Anarres outside, free.

Looked at from the other side, the wall enclosed Anarres: the whole planet was inside it, a great prison camp, cut off from other worlds and other men, in quarantine.

Between Shevek and the spaceship is an angry crowd determined to prevent his departure:

Some of them had come there to kill a traitor. Others had come to prevent him from leaving, or to yell insults at him, or just to look at him; and all these others obstructed the sheer brief path of the assassins. None of them had firearms, though a couple had knives. Assault to them meant bodily assault; they wanted to take the traitor into their own hands. They expected him to come guarded, in a vehicle. While they were trying to inspect a goods truck and arguing with its outraged driver, the man they wanted came walking up the road, alone. When they recognized him he was already halfway across the field, with five Defense syndics following him. Those who had wanted to kill him resorted to pursuit, too late, and to rock throwing, not quite too late. They barely winged the man they wanted, just as he got to the ship, but a two-pound flint caught one of the Defense crew on the side of the head and killed him on the spot.

Once safely on board, Shevek is disoriented as he tries to absorb attitudes and information totally alien to his life experience. The doctor tending to him expresses views on gender that are senseless to the anarchist and physicist never exposed to such societal nonsense:

Shevek turned the conversation, but he went on thinking about it. This matter of superiority and inferiority must be a central one in Urrasti social life. If to respect himself Kimoe had to consider half the human race as inferior to him, how then did women manage to respect themselves—did they consider men inferior? And how did all that affect their sex lives? He knew from Odo's writings that two hundred years ago the main Urrasti sexual institutions had been "marriage," a partnership authorized and enforced by legal and economic sanctions, and "prostitution," which seemed merely to be a wider term, copulation in the economic mode. Odo had condemned them both, and yet Odo had been "married." And anyhow the institutions might have changed greatly in two hundred years. If he was going to live on Urras and with the Urrasti, he had better find out.

Odo was the heroic theoretician of the anarchist idea on which Anarres was founded some seven generations before *The Dispossessed* opens. The novel subtly traces Shevek's career on Urras, alternating it chapter by chapter with his past life on Anarres. A great theoretical physicist, he had had his work inhibited by the relatively primitive resources and institutions of Anarres. His flight to Urras fuses elements of scientific truth seeking, personal restlessness, and at last a revival of his anarchist beliefs.

Initially, Shevek is happy enough with his teaching and research activities at the university on Urras. The creature comforts are new to him, and for a while he is content. When he falls ill, he is visited by his mother, Rulag, a cold and brilliant person who had abandoned him soon after his birth. No relationship can develop between them, and she comes to oppose his mission. When he is strong enough, Shevek abandons the university and finds his way to join the anarcho-syndicalists of Urras in their mass protest against the regime. The uprising is quelled bloodily, and Shevek finds his way to be reunited with his life partner, Takver, and their four-year-old daughter, Sadik, whom he meets for the first time. As he lies awake, with a sleeping Takver in his arms, his consciousness begins to fuse his life experience with his quest as a physicist for a new theory of time as simultaneity:

Fulfillment, Shevek thought, is a function of time. The search for pleasure is circular, repetitive, atemporal. The variety seeking of the spectator, the thrill hunter, the sexually promiscuous, always ends in the same place. It has an end. It comes to the end and has to start over. It is not a journey and return, but a closed cycle, a locked room, a cell.

Outside the locked room is the landscape of time, in which the spirit may, with luck and courage, construct the fragile, makeshift, improbable roads and cities of fidelity: a landscape inhabitable by human beings.

It is not until an act occurs within the landscape of the past and the future that it is a human act. Loyalty, which asserts the continuity of past and future, binding time into a hole, is the root of human strength; there is no good to be done without it.

So, looking back on the last four years, Shevek saw them not as wasted, but as part of the edifice that he and Takver were building with their lives. The thing about working with time, instead of against it, he thought, is that it is not wasted. Even pain counts.

The quiet fervor of this contemplation has elements in it of Le Guin's adherence to Taoism, of her anarchism, which she derives from Shelley, Kropotkin, and Paul Goodman, and most of all her lifelong meditation upon the meaning of marriage. As *The Dispossessed* approaches its end, Takver has a second baby, again a girl, and Shevek, against the opposition of his estranged mother, Rulag, helps organize a Syndicate of Initiative, which will force the free publication of scientific and aesthetic works on all the known worlds.

On returning from Urras, Shevek is joined by a Terran first mate of the spaceship who decides to go through the wall with him:

"It is your own wish, then—your own initiative?"

"Entirely."

"And you understand that it might be dangerous?"

"Yes."

"Things are . . . a little broken loose, on Anarres. That's what my friends on the radio have been telling me about. It was our purpose all along—our Syndicate, this journey of mine—to

shake up things, to stir up, to break some habits, to make people ask questions. To behave like anarchists! All this has been
going on while I was gone. So, you see, nobody is quite sure
what happens next. And if you land with me, even more gets
broken loose. I cannot push too far. I cannot take you as an
official representative of some foreign government. That will
not do, on Anarres."

"I understand that."

"Once you are there, once you walk through the wall with
me, then as I see it you are one of us. We are responsible to you
and you to us; you become an Anarresti, with the same options
as all the others. But they are not safe options. Freedom is never
very safe." He looked around the tranquil, orderly room, with its
simple consoles and delicate instruments, its high ceiling and
windowless walls, and back at Ketho. "You would find yourself
very much alone," he said.

"My race is very old," Ketho said. "We have been civilized for
a thousand millennia. We have histories of hundreds of those
millennia. We have tried everything. Anarchism, with the rest.
But *I* have not tried it. They say there is nothing new under the
sun. But if each life is not new, each single life, then why are
we born?"

"We are the children of time," Shevek said, in Pravic. The
younger man looked at him a moment, and then repeated the
words in Iotic: "We are the children of time."

There is a quality of the luminous in Le Guin's style at its best, as
it is here. As I told her once in our exchange of letters, she is capable
of the lucidity urged upon Arjuna by Krishna in the *Gita*. To be the
children of time is to be Titanic, to descend from Saturn or Cronos.

"You're sure you want to walk through this wall with me, Ketho?
You know, for me, it's easy. Whatever happens, I am coming
home. But you are leaving home. 'True journey is return...'"

"I hope to return," Ketho said in his quiet voice. "In time."

"When are we to enter the landing craft?"

"In about twenty minutes."

"I'm ready. I have nothing to pack." Shevek laughed, a laugh of clear, unmixed happiness. The other man looked at him gravely, as if he was not sure what happiness was, and yet recognized or perhaps remembered it from afar. He stood beside Shevek as if there was something he wanted to ask him. But he did not ask it. "It will be early morning at Anarres Port," he said at last, and took his leave, to get his things and meet Shevek at the launch port.

Alone, Shevek turned back to the observation port, and saw the blinding curve of sunrise over the Temae, just coming into sight.

"I will lie down to sleep on Anarres tonight," he thought. "I will lie down beside Takver. I wish I'd brought the picture, the baby sheep, to give Pilun."

But he had not brought anything. His hands were empty, as they had always been.

"True journey is return" is an adage of Odo, the woman who brought anarcho-syndicalism into Urras and thus ultimately founded Anarres. The perpetual emptiness of Shevek's hands is paradoxically their fullness. Le Guin's Taoism is her foundation, and her work was augmentation of the foundations. What moves me most in her books is the voice of authentic authority, at once aesthetic and moral:

Words are my matter. I have chipped one stone
for thirty years and still it is not done,
that image of the thing I cannot see.
I cannot finish it and set it free,
transformed to energy.

CHAPTER 45

The Loser (1983)

THOMAS BERNHARD

I HAVE READ MOST OF Thomas Bernhard in German. That may have augmented how disconcerting I found him. Now, at the age of eighty-eight, I have started to reread him in translation. That takes less effort but gives me more leisure to be upset by him. It is accurate to observe that Bernhard delighted in rattling even his most sympathetic readers. Jack Dawson's version of *The Loser* seems faithful to me, though I have not compared it to the German text. At my age, climbing up the steps to my third-floor study and library is something I can manage only once a day. I gather that Mark Anderson, an admirable scholar of modern German literature, took the name of Jack Dawson for his own translation of *The Loser*. There is something Bernhardian about that.

There was everything (or almost everything) about the life of the great Canadian pianist Glenn Gould (1932–82) that was Bernhardian, though the two men never met. Probably Bernhard heard Gould play twice in Salzburg, in 1958 and 1959. The least Bernhardian aspect of Glenn Gould's life was his five-year love affair with Cornelia Foss, wife of the conductor and composer Lukas Foss. When Gould began to show signs of paranoia and of weird overdosings with unnecessary medications, Cornelia Foss and her two children returned to Lukas Foss, doubtless to Gould's sorrow.

Bernhard could have known nothing about that, which is just as well, since it would have crippled his novel. He was free to indulge his bizarre inventiveness. Thus, Vladimir Horowitz never taught, and particularly could not have taught Glenn Gould, who loathed Horowitz. In *The Loser,* Horowitz supposedly teaches the narrator, Gould, and Wertheimer, whom Glenn Gould first labels "the loser" in the agon between Gould, the obsessive narrator, and the unfortunate Wertheimer, who commits suicide at the age of fifty-one. Glenn Gould died at fifty, but Bernhard adds a year to Gould's life to abet the fearful symmetry of his novel. Bernhard himself was an assisted suicide at the age of fifty-eight.

Bernhard was born in Holland, the son of an unmarried mother. After living with his grandparents, he was taken to Bavaria, where he was required to serve in the Hitler Youth, not at all congenial to him. His father, whom he never met, was a crooked carpenter who seems to have committed suicide in 1940. Fortunately for Bernhard, one of his grandfathers arranged for him a musical and artistic education, in Austria. Again fortunately, Bernhard became attached to a much older woman, in a filial rather than sexual way. She became an emotional support or true mother to him. After she died, he was essentially alone, and always lived as an ascetic. Because he had tuberculosis, he could not become a singer, turned to journalism, and then to composing novels and plays.

Bernhard tends to write an endless paragraph of his narrator's dialogue with himself. When I try to read him out loud, in German or English, I quickly become breathless. He is a kind of interior orator on the verge of dying. One cannot call him a satirist, a parodist, or an ironist. Ambivalent about everything, Austria most of all, he wants us to believe that the inevitability of dying makes all of us ridiculous. I suppose that is in him an aesthetic stance, but I am unhappy with it. Sigmund Freud, the greatest of all Austrian exiles, urged us to make friends with the necessity of dying. That is somber, mature, and a tonic: it enlarges life. Bernhard's artistry is compelling. His views have their own dignity. But I cannot believe that my own dying, which cannot be far away, makes any of us ridiculous. That of course does not vitiate Bernhard's achievement.

How can one define what is new and valuable in Bernhard? He does give a strangeness allied to Kafka and Canetti, but swerving from them into an actual celebration of ambivalence, as though it were the true form of love:

> And I myself wasn't free of Glenn hatred, I thought, I hated Glenn every moment, loved him at the same time with the utmost consistency. For there's nothing more terrible than to see a person so magnificent that his magnificence destroys us and we must observe this process and put up with it and finally and ultimately also accept it, whereas we actually don't believe such a process is happening, far from it, until it becomes an irrefutable fact, I thought, when it's too late. Wertheimer and I had been necessary for Glenn's development, like everything else in his life, Glenn misused us, I thought in the inn. The arrogance with which Glenn set about everything, Wertheimer's fearful hesitation on the other hand, my reservations about everything and anything, I thought. Suddenly Glenn was *Glenn Gould,* everybody overlooked at the moment of the Glenn Gould transformation, as I have to call it, even Wertheimer and I.

To be destroyed by magnificence is the destiny of weak artists. To accept both magnificence and destruction is to move toward incipient strength. Mark M. Anderson, in his admirable afterword to *The Loser,* suggests that what saves the novel from its own self-mockery is the narrator's love of Glenn Gould and Wertheimer. "Love" is beyond definition: it means everything and nothing. The worship of Johann Sebastian Bach is an all-but-universal form of love. Whenever I become too depressed, I listen to Neville Marriner's recording of *The Musical Offering* (Academy of St Martin in the Fields). To my uneducated ear it is the ultimate music, more than I deserve to hear.

The actual Glenn Gould and Bernhard disdained what they considered to be narcissistic aesthetic forms, like sonatas by Haydn or Mozart, novels by Stendhal, Balzac, and Victor Hugo. These achieved turning points or recognitions leading to resolution. Gould and Bernhard worshipped Bach, admired Webern and Schoenberg, and distilled Bach through the twelve-tone serialism of Schoenberg and his school: Webern, Alban Berg, Ernst Krenek, and others.

I think the best preparation for reading Bernhard's novels is to absorb first *Gathering Evidence: A Memoir* (1973–82), translated by

David McLintock. The five German volumes seem at least as much fiction as autobiography. *Gathering Evidence* concludes with a section on "My Prizes." The accounts of the prizes, three speeches on receiving awards, and Bernhard's resignation from the Darmstadt Academy for Language and Poetry, also mix fierce fiction and truth telling, though Bernhard felt that only lies could be uttered and believed. For him the National Socialism of Hitler and the Roman Catholic Church alike were nothing but lies.

Near the close of *Gathering Evidence,* Bernhard gives us an extraordinary passage:

> All contact with home had ceased. I got no news from my family, and as far as I remember I had no interest whatever in how things were at home. They did not write to me, though there was nothing to stop them; they no longer had any excuse after they had buried their dead. They had their reasons. I got no mail and I expected none. I immersed myself in Verlaine and Trakl, and I also read Dostoyevsky's novel *The Demons.* Never in my whole life have I read a more engrossing and elemental work, and at the time I had never read such a long one. It had the effect of a powerful drug, and for a time I was totally absorbed by it. For some time after my return home I refused to read another book, fearing that I might be plunged headlong into the deepest disappointment. For weeks I refused to read anything at all. The monstrous quality of *The Demons* had made me strong; it had shown me a path that I could follow and told me that I was on the right one, *the one that led out.* I had felt the impact of a work that was both wild and great, and I emerged from the experience like a hero. Seldom has literature produced such an overwhelming effect on me. Using slips of paper which I had bought in the village, I tried to keep a record of certain dates which seemed important to me, certain crucial points in my existence, fearing that what was now so clear might blur and suddenly be lost on me, that it might suddenly vanish, and that I might no longer have the strength to save all these decisive occurrences, enormities, and absurdities from the obscurity of oblivion. On these slips of paper I tried to preserve everything that could be preserved, everything without exception which

seemed to me to be worth preserving. I had now discovered my method of working, my own brand of infamy, my particular form of brutality, my own idiosyncratic taste, which had virtually nothing in common with anyone else's method of working, anyone else's infamy, anyone else's brutality, or anyone else's taste. What is important? What is significant? I believed that I must save everything from oblivion by transferring it from my brain onto these slips of paper, of which in the end there were hundreds, for I did not trust my brain. I had lost faith in my brain—I had lost faith in everything, hence even in my brain. The shame I felt at writing poetry was greater than I expected, and so I did not write a single poem. I tried to read my grandfather's books, but found it impossible: I had experienced too much in the meantime, I had seen too much, and so I put them aside. What I needed I had found in *The Demons*. I searched the sanatorium library for other such elemental works, but there were none. It would be superfluous to enumerate the authors whose books I opened and immediately shut again, repelled by their cheapness and triviality. Apart from *The Demons* I had no time for literature, but I felt sure that there must be other books like it. But there was no point in looking for them in the sanatorium library, which was chock-full of tastelessness and banality, of Catholicism and National Socialism.

Dostoevsky's *The Demons* (1871–72) is his wildest work, and rereading it frightens me. It is an assault on Russian nihilism, incarnated in Nikolai Stavrogin, a figure who exceeds Arkady Svidrigailov of *Crime and Punishment* (1866) in veiled savagery and malevolence. Stavrogin rapes and brings about the suicide of an eleven-year-old girl. He does not bother to save his own incapacitated wife from being murdered. Svidrigailov, in contrast, finally shows some compassion and behaves benignly, and then commits suicide with the splendid remark: "Going to America."

Thomas Bernhard's debt to *The Demons* is extensive, as he says. I find it interesting that, in his greatest extremity, Bernhard could read Paul Verlaine and Georg Trakl, major lyric poets. Verlaine (1844–96) died at fifty-one from alcoholism and drug addiction. Though his notoriety stems from his relationship with Arthur Rimbaud

(1854–91)—a poet comparable in eminence to Victor Hugo, Charles Baudelaire, Stéphane Mallarmé, and Paul Valéry—Verlaine nevertheless was a permanent poet. Georg Trakl (1887–1914) seems to me the major German-language poet of the twentieth century, surpassing even Hugo von Hofmannsthal, Stefan George, Rilke, Gottfried Benn, Paul Celan, Ingeborg Bachmann, Else Lasker-Schüler, Bertolt Brecht, and others. Trakl died at twenty-seven of a cocaine overdose, after having suffered the horrors of being a medical officer on the Austro-Hungarian Eastern Front against Russia. He had been sustained, as had Rilke, by the generosity of the great Austrian philosopher Ludwig Wittgenstein, who was summoned to the hospital but arrived too late to save Trakl.

There is something Dostoevskian about Trakl's tormented consciousness. He has affinities with Rimbaud, though the major passion of his life was an incestuous relationship with his own sister, a remarkable musician. Bernhard must have found in Trakl something of his own fatalism, and reverence for a silence that Trakl could achieve in language but that was beyond Bernhard's gift.

I find it very difficult to clarify my own troubled esteem for Bernhard's novels. They hurt me more than I think they should. I grew up, like so many Yiddish-speaking children, with the inescapable yet unmerited guilt of a survivor. I tend to shun literature of the Shoah. Bernhard and Sebald are ineluctable writers, and I yield to that.

CHAPTER 46

Blood Meridian (1985)

Cormac McCarthy

I T SEEMS STRANGE TO ME to be writing about *Blood Meridian* on July 17, 2018. I speak to Cormac McCarthy on the phone; we have exchanged a few letters and sent each other books. In three days McCarthy will turn eighty-five, just a few days after I touched eighty-eight. I know little about his personal life, except that three marriages ended in divorce and he has two sons, born thirty-six years apart. He does his writing at the Santa Fe Institute, surrounded by scientists, whom he finds more congenial than literary folk.

I last wrote about *Blood Meridian* in 2000, about a decade after I first got to the end of it. Robert Penn Warren and Ralph Ellison had recommended it to me, but my early attempts to read it found me flinching at its incredible and incessant violence. It took a while, but I learned to read it by rereading. McCarthy accurately says, "Books are made out of books," and *Blood Meridian* is quarried from many masterpieces in the Western tradition: the King James Bible, Dante, Shakespeare, Milton, Blake, Wordsworth, Herman Melville, Joseph Conrad, William Faulkner, in particular. There are many others, including the mystics Jacob Boehme and Meister Eckhart.

Blood Meridian still seems to me the authentic American apocalyptic novel, even in 2018, a third of a century since its publication. Cormac McCarthy is the disciple of Melville, Conrad, and Faulkner.

In what follows, I will try to be faithful to him except for my own addiction to semicolons, and in using capital letters for the Kid and Judge Holden.

There are three epigraphs to *Blood Meridian,* a strange medley of Jacob Boehme, Paul Valéry, and *The Yuma Daily Sun* for June 13, 1982:

> Your ideas are terrifying and your hearts are faint. Your acts of pity and cruelty are absurd, committed with no calm, as if they were irresistible. Finally, you fear blood more and more. Blood and time.
>
> Paul Valéry

> It is not to be thought that the life of darkness is sunk in misery and lost as if in sorrowing. There is no sorrowing. For sorrow is a thing that is swallowed up in death, and death and dying are the very life of the darkness.
>
> Jacob Boehme

> Clark, who led last year's expedition to the Afar region of northern Ethiopia, and UC Berkeley colleague Tim D. White, also said that a reexamination of a 300,000-year-old fossil skull found in the same region earlier showed evidence of having been scalped.
>
> *The Yuma Daily Sun,* June 13, 1982

The epigraph from Valéry is taken from "The Yalu," a dialogue between the poet and a Chinese scholar who tells the Westerner:

> You are in love with intelligence, until it frightens you. For your ideas are terrifying and your hearts are faint. Your acts of pity and cruelty are absurd, committed with no calm, as if they were irresistible. Finally, you fear blood more and more. Blood and time.

The Boehme is from *Six Theosophic Points:*

> And yet it is not to be thought that the life of darkness sinks down into misery, that it would forget itself as if it were sorrowful. There is no sorrowing; but what with us on earth is sorrowing according to this property, is in the darkness power and joy

according to the property of the darkness. For sorrowfulness is a thing that is swallowed up in death. But death and dying is the life of the darkness, just as anguish is the life of the poison. The greater the anguish becomes in the poison, the stronger becomes the poison-life, as is to be seen in the external poison.

Boehme, like Zohar, is not easy reading. Late in his career, he seems to have read some Kabbalistic texts. No comment needs to be made on the third epigraph, which would have delighted Judge Holden. *Blood Meridian* begins with a vision of its protagonist, the Kid:

See the child. He is pale and thin, he wears a thin and ragged linen shirt. He stokes the scullery fire. Outside lie dark turned fields with rags of snow and darker woods beyond that harbor yet a few last wolves. His folk are known for hewers of wood and drawers of water but in truth his father has been a schoolmaster. He lies in drink, he quotes from poets whose names are now lost. The boy crouches by the fire and watches him.

Night of your birth. Thirty-three. The Leonids they were called. God how the stars did fall. I looked for blackness, holes in the heavens. The Dipper stove.

The mother dead these fourteen years did incubate in her own bosom the creature who would carry her off. The father never speaks her name, the child does not know it. He has a sister in this world that he will not see again. He watches, pale and unwashed. He can neither read nor write and in him broods already a taste for mindless violence. All history present in that visage, the child the father of the man.

In 1802, William Wordsworth wrote "My Heart Leaps Up":

My heart leaps up when I behold
A rainbow in the sky:
So was it when my life began;
So is it now I am a man;
So be it when I shall grow old,
Or let me die!
The Child is father of the Man;

And I could wish my days to be
Bound each to each by natural piety.

I do not believe that Cormac McCarthy is employing Wordsworth ironically. The brutality of the context contaminates the Kid with "a taste for mindless violence." That violence starts on the next page, when the fifteen-year-old Kid is shot in the back and just below the heart, and continues almost with no respite until the end, twenty-eight years later, when Judge Holden, the most frightening figure in all of American literature, smothers the Kid in an outhouse.

Blood Meridian is a canonical imaginative achievement, an American and a universal tragedy of blood. Judge Holden is a villain worthy of Shakespeare, Iago-like and demoniac, a theoretician of war everlasting. The novel changed radically as McCarthy worked at it, particularly when the Judge began to be, together with the Kid, a central figure. And the book's magnificence—its language, landscape, persons, conceptions—at last transcends the violence, and converts goriness into terrifying art, an art comparable to Melville's and to Faulkner's.

Even as you learn to endure the slaughter McCarthy describes, you become accustomed to the book's high style, again as overtly Shakespearean as it is Faulknerian. There are passages of Melvillean-Faulknerian baroque richness and intensity in *The Crying of Lot 49*, and elsewhere in Pynchon, but we can never be sure that they are not parodistic. The prose of *Blood Meridian* soars, yet with its own economy, and its dialogue is always persuasive, particularly when the uncanny Judge Holden speaks:

> The judge placed his hands on the ground. He looked at his inquisitor. This is my claim, he said. And yet everywhere upon it are pockets of autonomous life. Autonomous. In order for it to be mine nothing must be permitted to occur upon it save by my dispensation.
>
> Toadvine sat with his boots crossed before the fire. No man can acquaint himself with everthing on this earth, he said.
>
> The judge tilted his great head. The man who believes that the secrets of this world are forever hidden lives in mystery and fear. Superstition will drag him down. The rain will erode the deeds of his life. But that man who sets himself the task of

singling out the thread of order from the tapestry will by the decision alone have taken charge of the world and it is only by such taking charge that he will effect a way to dictate the terms of his own fate.

Judge Holden is the spiritual leader of Glanton's filibusters, and McCarthy persuasively gives the self-styled judge a mythic status, appropriate for a deep Machiavelli whose "thread of order" recalls Iago's magic web, in which Othello, Desdemona, and Cassio are caught. Though all of the more colorful and murderous raiders are vividly characterized for us, the killing machine Glanton with the others, the novel turns always upon its two central figures, Judge Holden and the Kid. We first meet the Judge on page 6: "an enormous man, bald as a stone...no trace of a beard," and eyes without either brows or lashes. A seven-foot-tall albino, he almost seems to have come from some other world, and we learn to wonder about the Judge, who never sleeps, dances and fiddles with extraordinary art and energy, rapes and murders little children of both sexes, and who says that he will never die. By the book's close, I have come to believe that the Judge is immortal. And yet the Judge, while both more and less than human, is as individuated as Iago or Macbeth, and is quite at home in the Texan-Mexican borderlands where we watch him operate in 1849–50, and then find him again in 1878, not a day older after twenty-eight years, though the Kid, a sixteen-year-old at the start of Glanton's foray, is forty-four when murdered by the Judge at the end.

Here is the first, wonderfully outrageous, manifestation of the Judge:

The kid nodded. An enormous man dressed in an oilcloth slicker had entered the tent and removed his hat. He was bald as a stone and he had no trace of beard and he had no brows to his eyes nor lashes to them. He was close on to seven feet in height and he stood smoking a cigar even in this nomadic house of God and he seemed to have removed his hat only to chase the rain from it for now he put it on again.

The reverend had stopped his sermon altogether. There was no sound in the tent. All watched the man. He adjusted the hat and then pushed his way forward as far as the crateboard pulpit where the reverend stood and there he turned to address the reverend's congregation. His face was serene and strangely childlike. His hands were small. He held them out.

Ladies and gentlemen I feel it my duty to inform you that the man holding this revival is an imposter. He holds no papers of divinity from any institution recognized or improvised. He is altogether devoid of the least qualification to the office he has usurped and has only committed to memory a few passages from the good book for the purpose of lending to his fraudulent sermons some faint flavor of the piety he despises. In truth, the gentleman standing here before you posing as a minister of the Lord is not only totally illiterate but is also wanted by the law in the states of Tennessee, Kentucky, Mississippi, and Arkansas.

Oh God, cried the reverend. Lies, lies! He began reading feverishly from his opened bible.

On a variety of charges the most recent of which involved a girl of eleven years—I said eleven—who had come to him in trust and whom he was surprised in the act of violating while actually clothed in the livery of his God.

A moan swept through the crowd. A lady sank to her knees.

This is him, cried the reverend, sobbing. This is him. The devil. Here he stands.

The superb talent of the Judge for theatrical improvisation is immediately in play:

These here is on the judge, he said.

They drank. The teamster set his glass down and looked at the kid or he seemed to, you couldnt be sure of his gaze. The kid looked down the bar to where the judge stood. The bar was that tall not every man could even get his elbows up on it but it came just to the judge's waist and he stood with his hands placed flatwise on the wood, leaning slightly, as if about to give another address. By now men were piling through the doorway, bleeding, covered in mud, cursing. They gathered about the judge. A posse was being drawn to pursue the preacher.

Judge, how did you come to have the goods on that no-account?

Goods? said the judge.

When was you in Fort Smith?

Fort Smith?

Where did you know him to know all that stuff on him?

You mean the Reverend Green?

Yessir. I reckon you was in Fort Smith fore ye come out here.

I was never in Fort Smith in my life. Doubt that he was.

They looked from one to the other.

Well where was it you run up on him?

I never laid eyes on the man before today. Never even heard of him.

He raised his glass and drank.

There was a strange silence in the room. The men looked like mud effigies. Finally someone began to laugh. Then another. Soon they were all laughing together. Someone bought the judge a drink.

McCarthy subtly shows us the long, slow development of the Kid from another mindless scalper of Indians to the courageous confronter of the Judge in their final debate in a saloon. But though the Kid's moral maturation is heartening, his personality remains largely a cipher, as anonymous as his lack of a name. The three glories of the book are the Judge, the landscape, and (dreadful to say this) the slaughters, which are aesthetically distanced by McCarthy in a number of complex ways.

Judge Holden was, like John Joel Glanton, an actual freebooter. In the summer of 1849, after the conclusion of the Mexican-American War, Glanton, Judge Holden, and a mercenary group of thugs were commissioned by Mexico to destroy the Apaches. Since the Glanton Gang was paid by the scalp, they proceeded to butcher and scalp Mexicans as well as Indians. By December 1849, the government of Chihuahua denounced them as outlaws and offered a bounty for their destruction. Glanton, Holden, and the others went to Arizona, where they usurped the ferry at Yuma on the Colorado, an essential transit point for anyone going out to or returning from the California Gold Rush. They murdered both Mexican and American prospectors, stole their gold, and then made the mistake of killing some Yuma Native Americans. On April 23, 1850, Glanton and almost all of his gang were slain and scalped by a large band of Yumas. Whether the historical Judge Holden was one of the survivors is unknown.

The rogue Samuel Chamberlain is quoted in John Sepich's *Notes on Blood Meridian* (2008):

The second in command, now left in charge of the camp, was a man of gigantic size called "Judge" Holden of Texas. Who or what he was no one knew but a cooler blooded villain never went unhung; he stood six feet six in his moccasins, had a large fleshy frame, a dull tallow colored face destitute of hair and all expression. His desires was blood and women, and terrible stories were circulated in camp of horrid crimes committed by him when bearing another name, in the Cherokee nation and Texas; and before we left Frontreras a little girl of ten years was found in the chapperal, foully violated and murdered. The mark of a huge hand on her little throat pointed him out as the ravisher as no other man had such a hand, but though all suspected, no one charged him with the crime.

Holden was by far the best educated man in northern Mexico; he conversed with all in their own language, spoke in several Indian lingos, at a fandango would take the Harp or Guitar from the hands of the musicians and charm all with his wonderful performance, and out-waltz any poblana of the ball. He was "plum centre" with rifle or revolver, a daring horseman, acquainted with the nature of all the strange plants and their botanical names, great in Geology and Mineralogy, in short another Admirable Crichton, and with all an arrant coward. Not but that he possessed enough courage to fight Indians and Mexicans or anyone where he had the advantage in strength, skill and weapons, but where the combat would be equal, he would avoid it if possible. I hated him at first sight, and he knew it, yet nothing could be more gentle and kind than his deportment towards me; he would often seek conversation with me and speak of Massachusetts and to my astonishment I found he knew more about Boston than I did.

He also was fluent regarding the ancient races of Indians that at a remote period covered the desert with fields of corn, wheat, barley and melons, and built large cities with canals bringing water from rivers hundreds of miles distant. To my question "how he knew all this," this encyclopaedian Scalp Hunter replied, "Nature, these rocks, this little broken piece of clay (holding up a little fragment of painted pottery such [as] are found all over the desert), the ruins scattered all over the land, tell me the story of the past."

Chamberlain rather strangely refers to Holden as "another Admirable Crichton," a reference to the resourceful butler in J. M. Barrie's 1902 play. Only the resourcefulness is in common. The rape and murder of a ten-year-old girl is very much the mode of Judge Holden.

What are we to make of the Judge? He is immortal as principle, as War Everlasting, but is he a person, or something other? McCarthy will not tell us, which is all the better, since the ambiguity is fecund. Melville's Captain Ahab, though a Promethean demigod, is necessarily mortal, and perishes with the *Pequod* and all its crew, except for Ishmael. After he has killed the Kid, *Blood Meridian*'s Ishmael, Judge Holden is the last survivor of Glanton's scalping crusade. Destroying the Native American nations of the Southwest is hardly analogous to the hunt to slay Moby-Dick, and yet McCarthy gives us some curious parallels between the two quests. The most striking is between Melville's Chapter 19, where a ragged prophet who calls himself Elijah warns Ishmael and Queequeg against sailing on the *Pequod,* and McCarthy's Chapter IV, where "an old disordered Mennonite" warns the Kid and his comrades not to join Captain Worth's filibusters, a disaster that preludes the greater catastrophe of Glanton's campaign.

McCarthy's invocation of *Moby-Dick,* though impressive and suggestive, in itself does not do much to illuminate Judge Holden for us. Ahab has his preternatural aspects, yet these are transparencies compared with the enigmas of Judge Holden, who seems to judge the entire earth, and whose name suggests a holding, presumably of sway over all he encounters. McCarthy tells us as much as he is willing, in the Kid's dream visions of Judge Holden, toward the close of the novel:

In that sleep and in sleeps to follow the judge did visit. Who would come other? A great shambling mutant, silent and serene. Whatever his antecedents he was something wholly other than their sum, nor was there system by which to divide him back into his origins for he would not go. Whoever would seek out his history through what unraveling of loins and ledgerbooks must stand at last darkened and dumb at the shore of a void without terminus or origin and whatever science he might bring to bear upon the dusty primal matter blowing down out of the millennia will discover no trace of ultimate atavistic egg by which to reckon his commencing.

I think that McCarthy is warning his reader that the Judge is Moby-Dick rather than Ahab. As another white enigma, the albino Judge, like the albino whale, cannot be slain. Melville, a professed Gnostic, who believed that some "anarch hand or cosmic blunder" had divided us into two fallen sexes, gives us a Manichean quester in Ahab. McCarthy gives Judge Holden the powers and purposes of the bad angels or Demiurges that the Gnostics called Archons, but he warns us not to make such an identification. No "system," including the Gnostic one, will divide the Judge back into his origins. The "ultimate atavistic egg" will not be found. What can the reader do with the haunting and terrifying Judge?

Let us begin by saying that Judge Holden, though his gladsome prophecy of eternal war is authentically universal, is first and foremost a Western American, no matter how cosmopolitan his background (he speaks all languages, knows all arts and sciences, and can perform magical, shamanistic metamorphoses). The Texan-Mexican border is a superb place for a war god like the Judge to be. He carries a rifle, mounted in silver, with its name inscribed under the checkpiece: *Et In Arcadia Ego*. In the American Arcadia, death is also always there, incarnated in the Judge's weapon, which never misses. I resort, though, as before, to Iago, who transfers war from the camp and the field to every other locale, and is a pyromaniac setting everything and everyone ablaze with the flame of battle. The Judge might be Iago before *Othello* begins, when the war god Othello was still worshipped by his "honest" color officer, his ancient or ensign. The Judge speaks with an authority that chills me even as Iago leaves me terrified:

This is the nature of war, whose stake is at once the game and the authority and the justification. Seen so, war is the truest form of divination. It is the testing of one's will and the will of another within that larger will which because it binds them is therefore forced to select. War is the ultimate game because war is at last a forcing of the unity of existence.

If McCarthy does not want us to regard the Judge as a Gnostic Archon or supernatural being, the reader may still feel that it hardly seems sufficient to designate Holden as a nineteenth-century Western American Iago. The Glanton Gang passes into a sinister aesthetic glory at the close of Chapter XIII, when they progress from murdering and scalping Indians to butchering the Mexicans who have hired them:

> They entered the city haggard and filthy and reeking with the blood of the citizenry for whose protection they had contracted. The scalps of the slain villagers were strung from the windows of the governor's house and the partisans were paid out of the all but exhausted coffers and the Sociedad was disbanded and the bounty rescinded. Within a week of their quitting the city there would be a price of eight thousand pesos posted for Glanton's head.

I break into this passage, partly to observe that from this point on the filibusters pursue the way down and out to an apocalyptic conclusion, but also to urge the reader to hear, and admire, the sublime sentence that follows directly, because we are at the visionary center of *Blood Meridian.*

> They rode out on the north road as would parties bound for El Paso but before they were even quite out of sight of the city they had turned their tragic mounts to the west and they rode infatuate and half fond toward the red demise of that day, toward the evening lands and the distant pandemonium of the sun.

Since Cormac McCarthy's language is deliberately archaic, the *meridian* of the title probably means the zenith or noon position of the sun in the sky. Glanton, the Judge, the Kid, and their fellows are not described as "tragic"—their long-suffering horses are—and they are "infatuate" and half mad ("fond") because they have broken away from any semblance of order. McCarthy knows, as does the reader, that an "order" urging the destruction of the entire Native American population of the Southwest is an obscene idea of order, but he wants the reader to know also that the Glanton Gang is now aware that they are unsponsored and free to run totally amok. The sentence I have just quoted has a morally ambiguous greatness to it, but that is the greatness of *Blood Meridian,* and indeed of Homer and of Shakespeare. McCarthy so contextualizes the sentence that the amazing contrast between its high gestures and the murderous thugs who evoke the splendor is not ironic but tragic. The tragedy is ours, as readers, and not the Glanton Gang's, since we are not going to mourn their demise except for the Kid's, and even there our reaction will be equivocal.

Here is the final encounter between the preternatural Judge Holden and the Kid, who had broken with the insane crusade twenty-eight years before, and now, at middle age, must confront the ageless Judge. Their dialogue may be the most memorable interchange in the book.

The Judge and the Kid drink together, after the avenging Judge tells the Kid that this night his soul will be demanded of him. Knowing he is no match for the Judge, the Kid nevertheless defies Holden, with laconic replies playing against the Judge's rolling grandiloquence. After demanding to know where their slain comrades are, the Judge asks, "And where is the fiddler and where the dance?"

I guess you can tell me.
  I tell you this. As war becomes dishonored and its nobility called into question those honorable men who recognize the sanctity of blood will become excluded from the dance, which is the warrior's right, and thereby will the dance become a false dance and the dancers false dancers. And yet there will be one there always who is a true dancer and can you guess who that might be?
  You aint nothin.

To have known Judge Holden, to have seen him in full operation, and to tell him that he is nothing, is heroic. "You speak truer than you know," the Judge replies, and two pages later murders the Kid, most horribly. *Blood Meridian*, except for a one-paragraph epilogue, ends with the Judge triumphantly dancing and fiddling at once, and proclaiming that he never sleeps and he will never die.

The strangest passage in *Blood Meridian*, the epilogue, is set at dawn, where a nameless man progresses over a plain by means of holes that he makes in the rocky ground. Employing a two-handled implement, the man strikes "the fire out of the rock which God has put there." Around the man are wanderers searching for bones, and he continues to strike fire in the holes, and then they move on. And that is all.

The subtitle of *Blood Meridian* is *The Evening Redness in the West,* which belongs to the Judge, last survivor of the Glanton Gang. My own surmise is that the man striking fire in the rock at dawn is an opposing figure in regard to the evening redness in the West. The Judge never sleeps, and perhaps will never die, but a new Prometheus may be rising to go up against him.

CHAPTER 47

The Rings of Saturn (1995)

W. G. SEBALD

I AM A LATECOMER to Sebald. My close friend the late Geoffrey Hartman, who was born in Frankfurt, Germany, in 1929, and died in 2016 near New Haven, Connecticut, introduced me to Sebald in 2002 by kindly giving me a copy of the novel *Austerlitz* in German. I read *Austerlitz* and was both moved and upset. It had the same effect on me as reading Primo Levi (1919–87), the Italian Jewish scientist and survivor of Auschwitz.

My initial reaction to Sebald and to Primo Levi was both temperamental and historical. I had grown up in a Yiddish-speaking household. My mother, Paula Lev, came from a small Jewish town near Brest-Litovsk. My father, William Bloom, came from Odessa. They met on Orchard Street in Manhattan, married, and had five children, of whom I was the youngest. All four of my grandparents, many aunts and uncles, and a great many cousins were murdered by the Germans and their Slav helpers in the Shoah. My father was stoic and quiet, but I have many memories of my mother and her sister weeping for their lost family throughout the early 1940s.

Geoffrey Hartman himself, like Sebald's Jacques Austerlitz, came to England in 1939 on a *Kindertransport*. Stronger in trust than I was, Geoffrey helped found the Fortunoff Video Archive for Holocaust Testimonies at Yale in 1981. We talked about Sebald, and I expressed an admiration but said it was too much for me to take. Hartman remarked that if I were patient and read the rest of Sebald, the aesthetic and moral reward would be immeasurable. He was right, as I have slowly learned.

I have read Sebald's poetry in German but otherwise have relied upon the exemplary English translations. At their best, the poems are lucid, disciplined, eloquent, and all but major. Sebald's lasting poetry is his prose, always essayistic, learned, contemplative, morally compelling, and almost a new kind of fiction. That "almost" is simply an echo of Sebald himself, who celebrates his many precursors with somber elegance: Rousseau, Goethe, Gottfried Keller, Johann Hebel, Eduard Mörike, Robert Walser, Kafka, Borges, Thomas Bernhard, and others.

One does not ask either Borges or Sebald for this massive music, yet Sebald subdues himself to a quieter harmony:

> The train rolled slowly out of Liverpool Street station, past the soot-stained brick walls the recesses of which have always seemed to me like parts of a vast system of catacombs that comes to the surface there. In the course of time a multitude of buddleias, which thrive in the most inauspicious conditions, had taken root in the gaps and cracks of the nineteenth-century brickwork. The last time I went past those black walls, on my way to Italy in the summer, the sparse shrubs were just flowering. And I could hardly believe my eyes, as the train was waiting at a signal, to see a yellow brimstone butterfly flitting about from one purple flower to the other, first at the top, then at the bottom, now on the left, constantly moving. But that was many months ago, and this butterfly memory was perhaps prompted only by a wishful thought. There was no room for doubt, however, about the reality of my poor fellow travelers, who had all set off early that morning neatly turned out and spruced up, but were now slumped in their seats like a defeated army and, before they turned to their newspapers, were staring out at the desolate forecourts of the metropolis with fixed unseeing eyes. Soon, where the wilderness of buildings thinned out a little, three tall blocks of flats entirely boxed in scaffolding and surrounded by uneven patches of grass became visible at some dis-

tance, while much further off, before the blazing strip of sky on
the western horizon, rain fell like a great funeral pall from the
dark-blue cloud that hung over the entire city. When the train
changed track, I was able to glance back at the great towers of
the City, rising far above everything around them, the topmost
storeys gilded by the rays of the sun slanting in from the west.
The suburbs swept past—Arden, Forest Gate, Maryland—
before we reached the open countryside. The light over the
western horizon was gradually extinguished. The shadows of
evening were already settling on the fields and hedgerows. Idly
I turned the pages of an India paper edition of Samuel Pepys's
diary, Everyman's Library, 1913, which I had purchased that
afternoon, and read passages at random in this 1,500-page
account, until drowsiness overcame me and I found myself
going over the same few lines again and again without any
notion what they meant. And then I dreamed that I was walking through a mountainous terrain. A white roadway of finely
crushed stone stretched far ahead and in endless hairpins went
on and up through the woods and finally, at the top of the pass,
led through a deep cutting across to the other side of the high
range, which I recognised in my dream as the Alps. Everything
I saw from up there was of the same chalky colour, a bright,
glaring grey in which a myriad of quartz fragments glimmered,
as if the rocks, by a force deep inside them, were being dissolved
into radiant light. From my vantage-point the road continued
downward, and in the distance a second range of mountains at
least as lofty as the first one arose, which I feared I would not
be able to cross. To my left there was a drop into truly vertigi-
nous depths. I walked to the edge of the road, and knew that I
had never gazed down into such chasms before. Not a tree was
there to be seen, not a bush, not even a stunted shrub or a tus-
sock of grass: there was nothing but ice-grey shale. The shadows of the clouds scudded across the steep slopes and through
the ravines. The silence was absolute, for even the last traces
of plant life, the last rustling leaf or strip of bark, were long
gone, and only the stones lay unmoved upon the ground. Into
that breathless void, then, words returned to me as an echo
that had almost faded away—fragments from the account of

the Great Fire of London as recorded by Samuel Pepys. We saw the fire grow. It was not bright, it was a gruesome, evil, bloody flame, sweeping, before the wind, through all the City. Pigeons lay destroyed upon the pavements, in hundreds, their feathers singed and burned. A crowd of looters roamed through Lincoln's Inn. The churches, houses, the woodwork and the building stones, ablaze at once. The churchyard yews ignited, each one a lighted torch, a shower of sparks now tumbling to the ground. And Bishop Braybrooke's grave is opened up, his body disinterred. Is this the end of time? A muffled, fearful, thudding sound, moving, like waves, throughout the air. The powder house exploded. We flee into the water. The glare around us everywhere, and yonder, before the darkened skies, in one great arc the jagged wall of fire. And, the day after, a silent rain of ashes, westward, as far as Windsor Park.

(*Vertigo*)

Sebald transmutes a vivid moment in Pepys, when the housemaid Jane informs him of the fire's devastation:

By and by Jane comes and tells me that she hears that above 300 houses have been burned down to-night by the fire we saw, and that it is now burning down all Fish Street, by London Bridge. So I made myself ready presently, and walked to the Tower; and there got up upon one of the high places, Sir J. Robinson's little son going up with me; and there I did see the houses at that end of the bridge all on fire, and an infinite great fire on this and the other side the end of the bridge; which, among other people, did trouble me for poor little Michell and our Sarah on the bridge. So down, with my heart full of trouble, to the Lieutenant of the Tower, who tells me that it began this morning in the King's baker's house in Pudding Lane, and that it hath burned St. Magnus's Church and most part of Fish Street already. So I down to the waterside, and there got a boat, and through bridge, and there saw a lamentable fire. Poor Michell's house, as far as the Old Swan, already burned that way, and the fire running farther, that in a very little time it got as far as the Steelyard, while I was there. Everybody endeavouring to remove their goods, and flinging into the river, or bringing them into lighters that lay off; poor people staying in their houses as long as till the very fire touched them, and then running into boats, or clambering from one pair of stairs, by the waterside, to another. And, among other things, the poor pigeons, I perceive, were loath to leave their houses, but hovered about the windows and balconies till they burned their wings, and fell down. Having stayed, and in an hour's time seen the fire rage every way; and nobody, to my sight, endeavouring to quench it, but to remove their goods, and leave all to the fire; and having seen it get as far as the Steelyard, and the wind mighty high and driving it into the City; and everything, after so long a drought, proving combustible, even the very stones of churches, and, among other things, the poor steeple by which pretty Mrs. —— lives, and whereof my old schoolfellow Elborough is parson, taken fire in the very top, and there burned till it fell down; I to Whitehall, with a gentleman with me who desired to go off from the Tower, to see the fire, in my boat; and there up to the Kings closet in the Chapel, where people came about me, and I did give them an account dismayed them all, and word was carried in to the King. So I was called for, and did tell the King and Duke of York what I saw; and that unless his Majesty did command houses to be pulled down nothing could stop the fire. They seemed much troubled, and the King commanded me to go to my Lord Mayor from him, and command him to spare no houses, but to pull down before the fire every way. The Duke of York bid me tell him that if he would have any more soldiers he shall; and so did my Lord Arlington afterwards, as a great secret.

Vertigo is a lesser work than *The Emigrants* and, even more, *The Rings of Saturn*. What I like best in *Vertigo* are the loving and disconcerting visions of Stendhal and Kafka. There is also that great scamp Giacomo Girolamo Casanova—swindler, devourer of womankind, celebrity chaser—whose ingenious escape from a Venetian prison is a Sebaldian dazzlement.

In the autumn of his second year of imprisonment, Casanova's preparations had reached the stage at which he could contemplate an escape. The moment was propitious, since the inquisitors were to cross to the *terra firma* at that time, and Lorenzo, the warder, always got drunk when his superiors were away. In order to decide on the precise day and hour, Casanova consulted Ariosto's *Orlando Furioso,* using a system comparable to the *Sortes Virgilianae.* First he wrote down his question, then he derived numbers from the words and arranged these in an inverse pyramid, and finally, in a threefold procedure that involved subtracting nine from every pair of figures, he arrived at the first line of the seventh stanza of the ninth canto of *Orlando Furioso,* which runs: *Tra il fin d'ottobre e il capo di novembre.* This instruction, pinpointing the very hour, was the all-decisive sign Casanova had wanted, for he believed that a law was at work in so extraordinary a coincidence, inaccessible to even the most incisive thought, to which he must therefore defer. For my part, Casanova's attempt to plumb the unknown by means of a seemingly random operation of words and numbers later caused me to leaf back through my own diary for that year, whereupon I discovered to my amazement, and indeed to my considerable alarm, that the day in 1980 on which I was reading Grillparzer's journal in a bar on the Riva degli Schiavoni between the Danieli and Santa Maria della Visitazione, in other words near the Doge's Palace, was the very last day of October, and thus the anniversary of the day (or rather, night) on which Casanova, with the words *E quindi uscimmo a rimirar le stelle* on his lips, broke out of the lead-plated crocodile.

An occultist as well as a charlatan, the wily Casanova "broke out of the lead-plated crocodile"—that is, lead-lined cells just under the roof of the Doge's Palace. I myself was accustomed to loiter on that waterfront street, drinking in one bar or another with a young friend who was kindly wandering with me around Italy.

Vertigo opens with a bittersweet essay-fiction: "Beyle, or Love Is a Madness Most Discreet." Its protagonist is Marie-Henri Beyle (1783–1842), known to all of us as the novelist Stendhal. Sebald's Beyle, a wistful would-be Italian, scarcely duplicates Casanova's success with women.

And once fully apparelled in the uniform of a dragoon, this seventeen-and-a-half-year-old went around for days on end with an erection, before he finally dared disburden himself of the virginity he had brought with him from Paris. Afterwards, he could no longer recall the name or face of the *donna cattiva* who had assisted him in this task. The overpowering sensation, he wrote, blotted out the memory entirely. So thoroughly did Beyle serve his apprenticeship in the weeks that followed that in retrospect his entry into the world became a blur of the city's brothels, and before the year was out he was suffering the pains of venereal infection and was being treated with quicksilver and iodide of potassium; although this did not prevent him from working on a passion of a more abstract nature. The object of his craving was Angela Pietragrua, the mistress of his fellow-soldier Louis Joinville. She, however, merely gave the ugly young dragoon the occasional pitying look.

A true obsessive, Beyle after eleven years journeyed to Milan, and overwhelmed Angela with a torrent of language, finally enjoying her just once on her condition that he quit Milan. Sebald dryly chronicles this career of erotic vicissitudes until the death of Beyle/ Stendhal at the age of fifty-nine by a stroke probably brought on by ghastly medication rather than the syphilis itself. There is no mention of *The Charterhouse of Parma, The Red and the Black, Lucien Leuwen.*

Droll as Beyle and Casanova have been, the apotheosis of *Vertigo* is "Dr. K. Takes the Waters at Riva." Sebald's Kafka cannot be *the* Kafka, since he cannot exist. Of the multitude of Kafkas, Sebald selects the hunter Gracchus, who is neither alive nor dead, and sails perpetually on his ship, which has no rudder, and is propelled by a wind that comes from the icy region of death.

Vertigo concludes with a return to Wertach, Bavaria, where Sebald passed his childhood. He beholds another dead hunter, suffers diphtheria, and returns to England and to reading Samuel Pepys on the Great Fire.

Though it does not have the continuous strength of *The Emigrants* (1992), let alone of Sebald's masterpiece, *The Rings of Saturn, Vertigo* fascinates because it inaugurates his highly original mode. As he said, Sebald writes prose and not novels. His voice is uncanny; that is his true strength. I have read more of Thomas Bernhard in German than I have of Sebald, which may account for my tendency to prefer

Bernhard, though that might be a matter of sheer temperament. I first read Bernhard at the suggestion of my close friend the novelist Walter Abish, who, like Sebald, shows the influence of Bernhard's shattering vision. Walter, who is Jewish, was born in Vienna and taken by his family to live in Shanghai (1940–49) to escape Hitler. In 1949, he and his parents went to Israel, where Abish served in the Israeli Defense Force, and began to write fiction. Walter came to the United States in 1957 and has been a citizen since 1960. His novels and stories, rather neglected, are memorable for their Bernhardian humor and for their skill at characterization.

In an illuminating essay, Leland de la Durantaye wrote of what he called "the facts of fiction" in Sebald's *The Emigrants,* which is constituted of four quasi-documentary tales of emigrants from Germany, two of whom commit suicide. The third chooses a series of brutal electric-shock treatments to cancel his memories, while the fourth tells the story of his father and mother in Bavaria awaiting their deportation to the death camps. Strong as the book is, I personally find it frightening and wonder if, after all, it exemplifies Theodor W. Adorno's critique of the possibilities for aesthetic contemplation after the Shoah.

By common consent, *The Rings of Saturn* is Sebald's masterwork. Though I do not know the plays, that judgment seems accurate. The best preparation for *The Rings of Saturn* is to read or reread *Memoirs from Beyond the Grave: 1768–1800* by François-René de Chateaubriand, now best available in translation by Alex Andriesse (2018).

Chateaubriand was a Breton nobleman, the last of ten children, and had an unhappy childhood. He began a military career, interrupted by the French Revolution; he initially supported it, but then was horrified by the Terror and went into exile, all the way to the United States. His memoirs are evidently not very reliable, whether as to meeting George Washington or as to living with Native Americans.

Chateaubriand, after returning to France, joined an army of Royalist exiles and was severely wounded in a battle against revolutionary forces. He was sent to recovery and exile, first in Jersey and then in England, where he suffered poverty. His French wife, imposed upon him by his family, was someone he had never even met, and he left her behind. He describes an idyllic and innocent love with Charlotte Ives, a young Englishwoman, but he had to reveal that he was already married, and that ended his hopes.

He returned to France under the Consulate, won early favor from Napoleon, then courageously denounced Bonaparte, who threatened him with execution but instead exiled him from Paris. In his solitude, Chateaubriand began to write a series of successful books, including fiction. These established him as the forerunner of French Romanticism and influenced Lord Byron, Victor Hugo, and even Stendhal, who despised Chateaubriand's politics.

Here is Sebald in *The Rings of Saturn*, giving us the most charming interlude in Chateaubriand's long and amorous life:

They spent long hours in the afternoon together reading Tasso's *Gerusalemme Liberata* and the *Vita Nuova*, and in all likelihood there were times when the young girl's throat flushed scarlet and the Vicomte felt the thud of his heartbeat right under his Jacob. Their day always ended with a music lesson. When dusk was settling inside the house, but the light streaming in from the west still lit the garden, Charlotte would play some piece or other from her repertoire, and the Vicomte, appuyé au bout du piano, would listen to her in silence. He was aware that their studies brought them closer every day, and, convinced that he was not fit to pick up her glove, sought to conduct himself with the utmost restraint, but nonetheless remained irresistibly drawn to her. With some dismay, as he later wrote in his *Mémoires d'outre-tombe*, I could foresee the moment at which I would be obliged to leave. The farewell dinner was a sad occasion during which no one knew what to say, and when it was over, much to the astonishment of the Vicomte, it was not the mother but the father who withdrew with Charlotte to the drawing room. Although he was on the point of departure, the mother—who, the Vicomte noticed, was herself most seductive in the unusual role which she was now playing in the teeth of convention—asked his hand in marriage for her daughter, whose heart, she said, was entirely his. You no longer have a native country, your property has been disposed of, your parents are no longer alive: what could possibly take you back to France? Stay here with us and be our adopted son and heir. The Vicomte, who could scarcely believe the generosity of this offer made to an impoverished emigrant, was thrown into the greatest conceivable inner turmoil by her proposal, which it seemed the Reverend Ives had approved. For while on the one hand, he wrote, he desired nothing so much as to be able to spend the rest of his life unknown to the world in the bosom of this solitary family, on the other hand the melodramatic moment had now come when he would have to disclose the fact that he was married. While the alliance he had entered into in France had been arranged by his sisters almost without consulting him and had remained a mere formality, this did not in the slightest alter the untenable situation in which he now found himself. Mme Ives had put her offer to him with her eyes half downcast, and when he responded with the despairing cry Arrêtez! Je suis marié! she fell into a swoon, and he was left with no other choice than to leave that hospitable house at once with the resolution never to return. Later, setting down his memories of that ill-omened day, he wondered how it would have been if he had undergone the transformation and led the life of a gentleman chasseur in that remote English county. It is probable that I should never have written a single word. In due course I should have even forgotten my own language. How great would France's loss have been, he asks, if I had vanished into thin air like that? And would it not, in the end, have been a better life? Is it not wrong to squander one's chance of happiness in order to indulge a talent? Will what I have written survive beyond the grave? Will there be anyone able to comprehend it in a world the very foundations of which are changed?

Perhaps Sebald delighted in this as I do, because Chateaubriand is so outrageously egoistic. Twenty-seven years after he gave up Charlotte Ives, Chateaubriand, then the French ambassador to London, was visited by Lady Sutton and her two sons. Three years after their forlorn love, Charlotte had married Admiral Sutton, one of Horatio Nelson's flag captains.

.   .   .

The *Rings of Saturn* begins in August 1992, with Sebald walking the entire county of Suffolk, in the hope of combatting a spell of emptiness. A year later, he has to be taken to a Norwich hospital. When he has recovered, his mind turns to Sir Thomas Browne, long one of Sebald's preoccupations. A train of associations brings him to a remarkable section devoted to Joseph Conrad and Sir Roger Casement, who knew one another in the Congo, when it was a vast den of horrors suffered by the Africans in order to enhance the private wealth of King Leopold II of the Belgians. It is now believed that as many as ten million blacks died because of torture, mutilation, starvation, and illnesses.

Conrad created *Heart of Darkness* out of witnessing some of this. Casement, a heroic humanitarian, exposed the scandal to the Western world, a service he was to repeat in South America. Knighted by the British government, Roger Casement was stripped of all honors and hanged by the British on August 3, 1916. The Easter Rising took place in Dublin and elsewhere in Ireland April 24–29, 1916. Casement had been committed to the Irish cause for many years. In the autumn of 1914, Casement went to Germany to propose a German-Irish alliance, in which Germany would provide arms and trained officers to assist the Irish uprising. But Sebald transcends me, and his account contrives to be at once informative and strangely aesthetic:

> The first news of the nature and extent of the crimes committed against the native peoples in the course of opening up the Congo came to public attention in 1903 through Roger Casement, then British consul at Boma. In a memorandum to Foreign Secretary Lord Lansdowne, Casement—who, so Korzeniowski told a London acquaintance, could tell things that he, Korzeniowski, had long been trying to forget—gave an exact account of the utterly merciless exploitation of the blacks. They were compelled to work unpaid throughout the colony, given a bare minimum to eat, often in chain-gangs, and labouring to a set timetable from dawn to dusk till in the end they literally dropped dead. Anyone who travelled the upper reaches of the Congo and was not blinded by greed for money, wrote Casement, would behold the agony of an entire race in all its heart-rending details, a suffering that eclipsed even the most calamitous tales in the Bible.

Casement made it perfectly clear that hundreds of thousands of slave labourers were being worked to death every year by their white overseers, and that mutilation, by severing hands and feet, and execution by revolver, were among the everyday punitive means of maintaining discipline in the Congo. King Leopold invited Casement to Brussels for a personal talk aimed either at defusing the tension created by Casement's intervention or at assessing the threat his activities posed to the Belgian colonial enterprise. Leopold explained that he considered the work done by the blacks as a perfectly legitimate alternative to the payment of taxes, and if the white supervisory personnel at times went too far, as he did not deny, it was due to the fact that the climate of the Congo triggered a kind of dementia in the brains of some whites, which unfortunately it was not always possible to prevent in time, a fact which was regrettable but could hardly be changed. Since Casement's views could not be altered with arguments of this kind, Leopold availed himself of his royal privilege in London, as a result of which, with a certain duplicity, Casement was on the one hand praised for his exemplary report and awarded the CMG, while on the other hand nothing was done that might have had an adverse effect on Belgian interests. When Casement was transferred to South America some years later, probably with the ulterior motive of getting his troublesome person out of the way for a while, he exposed conditions in the jungle areas of Peru, Colombia and Brazil that resembled those in the Congo in many respects, with the difference that here the controlling agent was not Belgian trading associations but the Amazon Company, the head office of which was in the city of London. In South America too, whole tribes were being wiped out at that time and entire regions burnt to the ground. Casement's report, and his unconditional partisanship for the victims and those who had no rights, undoubtedly earned him a certain respect at the Foreign Office, but at the same time many of the top-ranking officials shook their heads at what seemed to them a quixotic zeal incompatible with the professional advancement of otherwise so promising an envoy. They tried to deal with the matter by knighting Casement, in express recognition of his services to

the oppressed peoples of the earth. But Casement was not prepared to switch to the side of the powerful; quite the contrary,
he was increasingly preoccupied with the nature and origins
of that power and the imperialist mentality that resulted from
it. It was only to be expected that in due course he should hit
upon the Irish question—that is to say, his own. Casement had
grown up in County Antrim, the son of a Protestant father and
a Catholic mother, and by education and upbringing he was
predestined to be one of those whose mission in life was the
upholding [of] English rule in Ireland. In the years leading up
to the First World War, when the Irish question was becoming acute, Casement espoused the cause of "the white Indians
of Ireland". The injustice which had been borne by the Irish
for centuries increasingly filled his consciousness. He could
not rid his thoughts of the fact that almost half the population of Ireland had been murdered by Cromwell's soldiers, that
thousands of men and women were later sent as white slaves
to the West Indies, that in recent times more than a million
Irish had died of starvation, and that the majority of the young
generation were still forced to emigrate from their native land.
The moment of decision for Casement came in 1914 when the
Home Rule programme proposed by the Liberal government to
solve the Irish problem was defeated by the fanatical resistance
of Ulster Protestants with the support, both open and covert,
of various English interest groups. We will not shrink from
Ulster's resistance to Home Rule for Ireland, even if the British
Commonwealth is convulsed declared Frederick Smith, one of
the leading representatives of the Protestant minority whose
so-called loyalism consisted in their willingness to defend their
privileges against government troops by force of arms if necessary. The hundred-thousand-strong Ulster Volunteers were
founded. In the south, too, an army of volunteers was raised.
Casement took part in the recruiting drive and helped equip
the contingents. He returned his decorations to London, and
refused the pension he had been offered. In early 1915 he trav-
elled to Berlin on a secret mission, to urge the government of
the German Reich to supply arms to the Irish army of liberation and persuade Irish prisoners of war in Germany to form

an Irish brigade. In both endeavours Casement was unsuccessful, and he was returned to Ireland by a German submarine. Deadly tired and chilled to the bone by the icy water, he waded ashore in the bay of Banna Strand near Tralee. He was now fifty-one; his arrest was imminent.

All he could do was to send the message *No German help available* through a priest, to stop the Easter rising which was planned for all Ireland and was now condemned to failure. If the idealists, poets, trade unionists and teachers who bore the responsibility in Dublin nonetheless sacrificed themselves and those who obeyed them in seven days of street fighting, that was none of his doing. When the rising was put down, Casement was already in a cell in the Tower of London. He had no legal adviser. Counsel for the prosecution was Frederick Smith, who had risen to become Director of Public Prosecutions, which meant that the outcome of the trial was as good as decided before it began. In order to pre-empt any petitions for pardon that might have been made by persons of influence, excerpts from what was known as the Black Diary, a kind of chronicle of the accused's homosexual relations found when Casement's home was searched, were forwarded to the King of England, the President of the United States, and the Pope. The authenticity of this Black Diary, kept until recently under lock and key at the Public Records Office in Kew, was long considered highly debatable, not least because the executive and judicial organs of the state concerned with furnishing the evidence and drawing up the charge against alleged Irish terrorists have repeatedly been guilty, until very recent times, not only of pursuing doubtful suspicions and insinuations but indeed of deliberate falsification of the facts. For the veterans of the Irish freedom movement it was in any case inconceivable that one of their martyrs should have practised the English vice. But since the release to general scrutiny of the diaries in early 1994 there has no longer been any question that they are in Casement's own hand. We may draw from this the conclusion that it was precisely Casement's homosexuality that sensitized him to the continuing oppression, exploitation, enslavement and destruction, across the borders of social class and race, of those who

were furthest from the centres of power. As expected, Casement was found guilty of high treason at the end of his trial at
the Old Bailey. The presiding judge, Lord Reading, formerly
Rufus Isaacs, pronounced sentence. You will be taken hence, he
told Casement, to a lawful prison and thence to a place of execution and will there be hanged by the neck until you be dead.
Not until 1965 did the British government permit the exhuma-
tion of the remains of Roger Casement, presumably scarcely
identifiable any more, from the lime pit in the courtyard of Pen-
tonville prison into which his body had been thrown.

The *Black Diaries* of Roger Casement still provokes disputes as
to its authenticity. But Casement's homoerotic orientation is certain enough. The Anglo-Irish arch-poet William Butler Yeats was of
another opinion:

I say that Roger Casement
Did what he had to do.
He died upon the gallows,
But that is nothing new.

Afraid they might be beaten
Before the bench of Time,
They turned a trick by forgery
And blackened his good name.

A perjurer stood ready
To prove their forgery true;
They gave it out to all the world,
And that is something new;

For Spring Rice had to whisper it,
Being their Ambassador,
And then the speakers got it
And writers by the score.

Come Tom and Dick, come all the troop
That cried it far and wide,

Come from the forger and his desk,
Desert the perjurer's side;

Come speak your bit in public
That some amends be made
To this most gallant gentleman
That is in quicklime laid.

This is hardly the Yeats of "The Second Coming," the "Byzantium" poems, "Vacillation," "Cuchulain Comforted," and scores of other magnificences, but the angry poet did better in "The Ghost of Roger Casement":

I poked about a village church
And found his family tomb
And copied out what I could read
In that religious gloom;
Found many a famous man there;
But fame and virtue rot.
Draw round, beloved and bitter men,
Draw round and raise a shout;

The ghost of Roger Casement
Is beating on the door.

I find that one of my problems in absorbing Sebald is that in his end is his beginning. Here is the close of *The Rings of Saturn*:

Hence the Reich ministers of food and agriculture, of labour, of forestry and of aviation had launched a sericulture programme, inaugurating a new era of silk cultivation in Germany. The Reich Association of Silkworm Breeders in Berlin, a constituent group within the Reich Federation of German Breeders of Small Animals, which in turn was affiliated to the Reich Agricultural Commission, saw its task as increasing production in every existing workshop, advertising silk cultivation in the press, in the cinema and on radio, establishing model rearing units for educational purposes, organizing advisory bodies at local, district and regional level to support all silk-growers, providing mulberry trees, and planting them by the million on unutilized land, in residential areas and cemeteries, by roadsides, on railway embankments and along the Reich's autobahns. According to Professor Lange, the author of educational pamphlet F213/1939, the significance of silk cultivation in Germany lay not only in obviating the need to buy from abroad, and so easing the pressure on foreign currency reserves, but also in the importance silk would have in the dawning era of aerial warfare and hence in the formation of a self-sufficient economy of national defence. For that reason, it was desirable that schools should interest the youth of Germany in silk cultivation, although not under compulsion, as in the days of Frederick the Great. Rather, the teaching staff and pupils should be motivated to practise sericulture of their own accord. Schools might do pioneering work in this sector, suggested Professor Lange. Schoolyards might have mulberries planted along their perimeters, and silkworms could be reared in the school buildings. After all, the Professor added, quite apart from their indubitable utility value, silkworms afforded an almost ideal object lesson for the classroom. Any number could be had for virtually nothing, they were perfectly docile and needed neither cages nor compounds, and they were suitable for a variety of experiments (weighing, measuring and so forth) at every stage in their evolution. They could be used to illustrate the structure and distinctive features of insect anatomy, insect domestication, retrogressive mutations, and the essential measures which are taken by breeders to monitor productivity and selection, including extermination to preempt racial degeneration.—In the film, we see a silk-worker receiving eggs despatched by the Central Reich Institute of Sericulture in Celle, and depositing them in sterile trays. We see the hatching, the feeding of the ravenous caterpillars, the cleaning out of the frames, the spinning of the silken thread, and finally the killing, accomplished in this case not by putting the cocoons out in the sun or in a hot oven, as was often the practice in the past, but by suspending them over a boiling cauldron. The cocoons, spread out on shallow baskets, have to be kept in the rising steam for upwards of three hours, and when a batch is done, it is the next one's turn, and so on until the entire killing business is completed.

Today, as I bring these notes to a conclusion, is the 13th of April 1995. It is Maundy Thursday, the feast day on which Christ's washing of the disciples' feet is remembered, and also the feast day of Saints Agathon, Carpus, Papylus and Hermengild. On this very day three hundred and ninety-seven years ago, Henry IV promulgated the Edict of Nantes; Handel's *Messiah* was first performed two hundred and fifty-three years ago, in Dublin; Warren Hastings was appointed Governor-General of Bengal two hundred and twenty-three years ago; the Anti-Semitic League was founded in Prussia one hundred and thirteen years ago; and, seventy-four years ago, the Amritsar massacre occurred, when General Dyer ordered his troops to fire on a rebellious crowd of fifteen thousand that had gathered in Jallianwala Bagh square, to set an example. Quite possibly some of the victims were employed in silk cultivation, which was developing at that time, on the simplest of foundations, in the Amritsar region and indeed throughout India.

Fifty years ago to the day, British newspapers reported that the city of Celle had been taken and that German forces were in the headlong retreat from the Red Army, which was advancing up the Danube valley. And finally, Maundy Thursday, the 13th of April 1995, was also the day on which Clara's father, shortly after being taken to hospital in Coburg, departed this life. Now, as I write, and think once more of our history, which is but a long account of calamities, it occurs to me that at one time the only acceptable expression of profound grief, for ladies of the upper classes, was to wear heavy robes of black silk taffeta or black crêpe de chine. Thus at Queen Victoria's funeral, for example, the Duchess of Teck allegedly made her appearance in what contemporary fashion magazines described as a breathtaking gown with billowing veils, all of black Mantua silk of which the Norwich silk weavers Willett & Nephew, just before the firm closed down for good, had created, uniquely for this occasion, and in order to demonstrate their unsurpassed skills in the manufacture of mourning silks, a length of some sixty paces. And Sir Thomas Browne, who was the son of a silk merchant and may well have had an eye for these things, remarks in a passage of the *Pseudodoxia Epidemica* that I can no longer find that in the Holland of his time it was customary, in a home where there had been a death, to drape black mourning ribbons over all the mirrors and all canvasses depicting landscapes or people or the fruits of the field, so that the soul, as it left the body, would not be distracted on its final journey, either by a reflection of itself or by a last glimpse of the land now being lost for ever.

Every sentence, indeed every phrase, in this passage carries a catastrophic burden but one sentence is the matrix of everything that Sebald wrote:

They could be used to illustrate the structure and distinctive features of insect anatomy, insect domestication, retrogressive mutations, and the essential measures which are taken by breeders to monitor productivity and selection, including extermination to preempt racial degeneration.

I never met Sebald, but I recall conversations with his friend Michael Hamburger in both England and the United States at various times from 1955 through the late 1990s. After that we lost touch, and he died in 2007 at his home in Suffolk. I admired Hamburger's own poems as well as his translations, which included Sebald and Paul Celan. We never discussed Sebald, but I remember listening to Hamburger closely as he recited Celan, first in German and then in Hamburger's own arresting versions. Celan drowned himself in the Seine at the age of forty-nine, taking with him a poetic gift almost incommensurable. Like Kafka, Celan writes German as if he is writing in Hebrew. Celan's image haunts me as I conclude *The Rings of Saturn*.

CHAPTER 48

Book of Numbers (2015)

Joshua Cohen

A NOVELIST WHO HAS just turned thirty-eight, Joshua Cohen has a charmed and doomed gift for evoking equivocal emanations from excessively eminent essayists. I cannot exert enthusiasm for these ambivalent echoing reverberations, but, then, I do not possess extensive erudition on the question of our younger American novelists. In addition to Cohen, I admire William Giraldi and Nell Freudenberger, among others.

I agree with William Giraldi's exaltation of American audacity. Joshua Cohen is audacious beyond audacity and doubtless will remain so. In order to become an aesthetic value, audacity must acquire authentic freedom.

My former student Andrew Ford, in his book *Homer: The Poetry of the Past* (1992), mulls over the contest that *Iliad* and *Odyssey* had to conduct with prior epics now lost to us. Agon, the competition for the foremost place, is the center of ancient Greek culture. Pindar strives with Hesiod and with Homer, and the Athenian tragedians challenge one another. Joshua Cohen has a double burden as a novelist. On the one side, he contends with the earlier Thomas Pynchon, the maker of *The Crying of Lot 49*, *Gravity's Rainbow*, *Mason & Dixon*. More darkly, he is the inheritor of the Jewish American novel: Nathanael West's *Miss Lonelyhearts* (1933); Henry Roth's

Call It Sleep (1934); Bernard Malamud's *The Assistant* (1957); Saul Bellow's *Humboldt's Gift* (1975); Cynthia Ozick's *The Messiah of Stockholm* (1987); Philip Roth's *Sabbath's Theater* (1995).

As befits Joshua Cohen, I will take the end of *Book of Numbers* as my beginning:

A body was hauled out of the river Ganges, Varanasi, India, 11/19 or 20, apparently. This was just downstream from the Manikarnika Ghat, the main crematorium ghat, a perpetual stream of burning bodies plunging down the stairs but not plashing at bottom because by the bottom all was ash, a cloud of flies scattering across the waters.

I can only assume that the Indian authorities wouldn't ordinarily bother with a floater, but he was white, or what was left of him was white, apparently. Other or the same Indian authorities, evincing impressive operational prerogative, ordered an autopsy that determined the COD as accidental/suicide, ordered a DNA test and copied both the results and report to the US State Department, which matched the genetic markers as being Principal's. Sari Apt Le Vay petitioned for the body's return, but it was in such a bitten crocodilian or ultimately imaginary condition that it was cremated, not at the Manikarnika but in a facility. No pics or vids of the body exist or have—like a missing pancreas—leaked yet.

It was Moe all over again—but because I switched off the TV after PBS had on Seth without Lisabeth, I can only piece this together from scrap bits of the *Asbury Park Press*, the *NJ Jewish News*, and whatever general interest nonpotting rags Moms still subscribes to, though delivery's been iffy. And the house modem, which has been broken since I got here—Moms doesn't even remember it breaking.

I couldn't go to Wawa and couldn't have Moms go for me, so I quit drinking, quit smoking, I guess. I made myself useful in the attic department, heirloom rearrangements. Suddenly everything heavy in the house had to be moved. The coverage didn't leave the lawn until purdah season's winter storm advisory.

Cal called and left a msg, and I still haven't gotten back to him. Finn called and left a msg saying he'd consider a reprint of my book, be sure to be in touch.

I haven't been. I never made a statement—I wrote.

Consider this: A dozen Moes crashed Principal's "medimorial" (meditation memorial) held at the Tetplex, four of them legally named Vishnu, and one even named Vishnu Fernandes. Cullen de Groeve and Owmar O'Quinn read a selection from the Tibetan Book of the Dead: "Void cannot injure void, the qualityless cannot injure the qualityless."

Kori Dienerowitz did not attend due to a prior commitment in Bermuda, a premature retirement with prosecutorial immunity.

A Pew Research poll, of around this date, queried a responsible sampling of Americans as to whether their government's online surveillance initiatives were justified (62%)? or unjustified (28%)? with only 10% undecided.

Into December, another whitish body washed up in a drainage culvert at the Verna Industrial Estate, Goa, and the boy who found it, shockingly recognizing his find, posted the pics and vids online, which were reasonably convincing, according to the convinced: Principal, already decaying. Anyway, something happened next like the boy's father without contacting anyone, perhaps without even being privy to his son's exploits, tried selling the body. But he was caught. Or the guy who'd bought it from him and contacted Sari Apt Le Vay was caught, the body taken into custody or whatever, but lost before tests, according to the tabloids. Subsequent corpses turned up in Cairo, Lisbon, Kifl Haris outside Nablus (Palestinian Territories). The great wheel turned and memed. Live in the flesh spottings in Brazil were a thing. Principal was a wayfarer in a Finnish disco. The wheel was turning me 40. A child was born in Kanazawa, Ishikawa, whose soul was recognized as his.

Principal is the other Joshua Cohen, founder and high satrap of Tetration, the ultimate startup turned tech titan of the Internet, computers, smartphones, and government surveillance. He has hired *our* Joshua Cohen, familiarly Josh, to ghostwrite his autobiography. Josh, with somewhat justified bitterness but with an inaccurate sense of prophecy, likes to refer to himself as "a failed novelist."

.　　.　　.

If you are to do critical justice to Joshua Cohen, you have to begin with the necessity of difficulty. He is a difficult writer and is likely to become even more difficult. These days readers shun difficulty, because they are so desperately distracted. The Age of the Screen jeopardizes the art of the novel. Joshua Cohen is an immensely ambitious novelist. His innermost desire is to transcend his precursors, Jewish and Gentile. *Book of Numbers* is difficult enough and has to call upon invention to palliate readers having an arduous experience.

When I reread *Book of Numbers* I remember my personal acquaintance with the late William Gaddis and the uncanny experience of first reading *The Recognitions* in 1955. Since Joshua Cohen has read everything, and in the original languages, doubtless he knows *The Recognitions*. I reread *The Recognitions* last year and was again a reader who fought against immersion but gradually yielded to it. It is linked to the Clementine Recognitions, a work dubiously ascribed to the third century of the Common Era. Ostensibly set against the Gnostics, the Clementine Recognitions curiously exalt the marvelous figure of Simon Magus of Samaria, a first-century c.e. grand charlatan and miracle worker who asserted an identity with the divine, and who matched himself with a whore of Tyre. Simon declared her the reincarnation of Helen of Troy, and the fallen element in God's thought. Since the Clementine Recognitions are Christian, Simon Magus is declared the founder of all Gnosticism. In a levitation contest with Saint Peter, Simon plunges to his death.

Joshua Cohen is no Gnostic but something close to a normative Jew. Implicitly he trusts in the Covenant between Yahweh and the Jewish people. He has no illusions, because he knows the full burden of Jewish history. Yet there is a wistful quality whenever he turns to the Sages, whether ancient, Hasidic, or modern. I myself am aware that when I do so, I am studying the nostalgias and little more. Yahweh broke the Covenant, and who am I to gather the shards? A novelist, poet, or dramatist might do it, but not a secular exegete. Both Joshua Cohen and Harold Bloom are addicted to quoting Rabbi Tarfon: "You are not required to complete the work, but neither are you free to desist from it." Joshua Cohen is trying to complete the work. Long ago I desisted from it.

The vessels of Judaic trust and of Jewish identity have broken.

Gershom Scholem (1897–1982), to whom I listened attentively during many hours we spent together in the last year and eight months of his life, would have denied that sentence. And yet Scholem, who masked as a historical scholar of Kabbalah, truly was a *navi*, a throwback to Amos and Micah. Joshua Cohen has no such exalted ambition, yet he also wants to see the broken vessels mended.

One of Joshua Cohen's dazzling ambitions is to conduct an agon with phantoms. He is haunted by all the losses in Jewish tradition—of language, trust, benignity. His lamentation extends also to the transcendence of Emerson and of Walt Whitman, which is lost to us. *Tikkun,* the mending of the broken vessels, is his deepest desire. His exorbitant hope is that his books will *be the mending*. I must not neglect his recent novel, *Moving Kings* (2017), since that attempts *tikkun*. For Joshua Cohen, that is to achieve a perilous balance between mending the Oral Law or being overwhelmed by it. I take the liberty of quoting from a letter he kindly sent me:

> The first section of *Moving Kings* is my homage to Roth/Malamud/Bellow—David King is a creature of their times, not of mine. The second section is my homage to the Israeli novel—written with the impulse to create a new language in a new land, but constantly recalled to the Tanach, and alternately reveling in and wary of that tension. The third section is my attempt to unite the two, but perversely to do it partially in the voice of a black Muslim who mistrusts both.
>
> This, I think, is the best summation of my attitude toward the "unity" of healing: A broken tradition can never be made whole again in and of itself, but rather its pieces can only be combined with the pieces of another broken tradition, into a new and never-before-imagined whole, bound together by someone suspicious of and even ashamed by the very activity but unable—historically unable—to do anything else.
>
> This binding I take to be perpetual, and perpetualizing—as I write in *Moving Kings,* "The thing about following a star is where do you stop? Hard to tell where it's telling you to lay down your burden. Because a star can always seem to be above everything, it can always seem a block beyond. All you can do is follow until you've fooled yourself."

I cannot hope to achieve that urgency but it moves me almost beyond measure. Yet so ingenious is Cohen's account of Tetration that it can be read as mock-heroic frolic. In one way, *Book of Numbers* is a missile launched against the Internet, yet in another, it boldly attempts to appropriate that vacant ocean. Unlike Philip Roth and *his* many precursors, for whom doubling hooked identities, Joshua Cohen seeks his other self in the abyss of the Internet. It may be that Cohen's true forerunner is Herman Melville, who sought out the ambiguities in scriveners' offices and on whalers. A patience willing to accept a bad time can prevail until the good time comes again, if ever it can. That may be why Joshua Cohen can so perilously absorb what bedevils me:

Basically, Kor had called a VC meeting, had not invited us but had invited Moe. This was the first we had been informed about any of this. Apparently, Moe had been under the impression that the purpose of the meeting was to examine his plans for the DCent, which, for him, was culminant. Anyone else would have resented the lack of notice, but he was primed. He had been primed since birth. His first birth. This was why he had endured the quibbly servers and Tetplex delays, this was what he had been mounting and sealing and soldering and suffering for through every karmic deferral, countless reincarnations counted as like retroincarnations until the bodies released their egos. All existence had been just a mobilization for this, the mindful manifestation of his sadhana, his purpose, this slideshow presentation.

After Moe finished presenting Kor applauded and said they were tabling on the absence of table the DCent for later. For now Moe had to focus on this thing called a Sapp.

Rather, he had to turn it into a STrapp. To make it searchcapable. That was the agenda in its entirety. In this, Kor was the decider.

Moe was speechless initially.

The rationale was revenue, Keiner said. An outcampus server could wait, but a tetrating storage device could not. It was y2K sensitive. And y2K was sensitive.

Waiting, Dustin said, is what servers do.

The decision, not as like the commissioned product, made itself.

Moe yelled in Hindi, and if you recall your Mahabharata or Ramayana, how the bowstring is said to snap and the arrow is said to wail through the air as like the god Rama slays the king of the monkeys, that was the yell with which Moe fled the meeting.

Joshua Cohen has taught us how to distinguish between Moe and Kor, yet the fun of this transcends the distinction. The novelist's accumulative ear has absorbed the soul-killing jargon of how we live now. Where are the poems of our climate? Where is Emersonian freedom? Why did Walt Whitman sing and chant the things that are part of him, the worlds that were and will be, death and day? Is this all that is left of the Oral Tradition? Is Silicon Valley the Valley of the Shadow of Death?

The Changeling

I N LAST NIGHT'S DREAM, I sat alone at a long table. There was no one else in the room, but a voice rather harshly kept questioning me.

Do you believe in the resurrection of the dead?

I wondered which part of the "you" ought to reply. As a child I was an Orthodox Ashkenazi Jew raised by an intensely religious mother and a father indifferent to such "foolishness." My four older siblings remained Orthodox, but by the age of fourteen I venerated Elisha ben Abuya, who was regarded as a villain by the men who taught me Talmud:

> The oldest and most striking reference to the views of Elisha is found in the following baraita (Ḥag. 14b; Yer. ii. 1):
>
> "Four [sages] entered paradise—Ben 'Azzai, Ben Zoma, Aḥer, and Akiba. Ben 'Azzai looked and died; Ben Zoma went mad; Aḥer destroyed the plants; Akiba alone came out unhurt."
>
> (The Four Who Entered Paradise)

There can be no doubt that the journey of the "four" to paradise, like the ascension of Enoch (in the pre-Christian books of Enoch) and of so many other pious men, is to be taken literally and not allegorically. This conception of the baraita is supported by the use of the phrase ("entered paradise"), since נכנס לג״ע ("entered the Garden of Eden" = paradise) was a common expression (Derek Erez Zuṭa i.; Ab. R. N. xxv.). It means that Elisha, like Paul, in a moment of ecstasy beheld the interior of heaven—in the former's case, however, with the effect that he destroyed the plants of the heavenly garden.

I have quoted this from *The Jewish Encyclopedia*, which is careful not to endorse any single judgment of Elisha ben Abuya. *Aḥer* means "the Other" or "the Stranger," one of the *minim* or Gnostic heretics. He was slandered by the disciples of Rabbi Akiva, who denounced him, quite falsely, as a Roman collaborator. His true offense was that in a vision he entered the Heavenly Court and found two Gods sitting on thrones, Yahweh and Metatron, an angel who had been Enoch:

> And Enoch walked with God: and he was not; for God took him.   (Genesis 5:24, KJV)

Even as a boy I admired Aḥer for the way in which he had "torn up the young shoots," an endeavor I have followed in my two-thirds of a century as a teacher.

Like Elisha ben Abuya, I believe in what became a Kabbalist version of the resurrection of the dead. Those of us who have failed to realize all of our potential will be reborn in others who will try to do better. Who among us has become everything she or he ought to have been?

When you are dying you will recite Shakespeare and the other poets you have loved best: Milton, Blake, Shelley, Walt Whitman, Wallace Stevens, Hart Crane, and many more. Why at eighty-eight are you writing a book about novels to reread ere you vanish?

As a child, I read novels and short stories incessantly but in a very different spirit from reading poetry or drama. What early sophistication I had went into the apprehension of poetry. I was and remain a naïve reader of prose fiction. At ten or so, I fell in love with Marty South in Thomas Hardy's *The Woodlanders*. When she cuts off her long and beautiful hair, I was moved to tears. When I read *The Return of the Native*, I was captivated by Eustacia Vye, Thomas Hardy's Queen of the Night. In that way, I have scarcely changed in extreme old age.

My closest friends have all died. I desperately need new ones. My students are remarkable people but very young. Ursula Le Guin, to whom this book is dedicated, became a dear friend without our ever meeting, since we exchanged a multitude of e-mails in the last two months of her life. But she, too, is gone. I go back to reread novels to find old friends still living and to make new ones.

Is that not merely another illusion? When Charles Dickens died at fifty-eight, do you think in his final stroke he somehow felt the presence of all the people he had created?

Peter Ackroyd, in his marvelous biography, charms me with that surmise. But, then, Ackroyd is himself a good novelist. I have always believed in Vico's adage: "You only know what you yourself have made." I cannot know Wallace Stevens's "The Course of a Particular" as its creator knew it, and I will never know *Bleak House* or *Our Mutual Friend* as Dickens must have known it, from the inside out. As a teacher of Shakespeare and the poets, I endeavor to get as far inside *King Lear* or *The Auroras of Autumn* as I can, yet I cannot get as far inward as I desire. With prose fiction, my hope is more modest. Never fond of plot or of social history, I attempt to place myself within the characters, a vain drive yet for me inescapable.

When I was a Cornell freshman, I walked out of Vladimir Nabokov's initial lecture in a course on the European novel. At that time, I had read only *The Real Life of Sebastian Knight* (1941) and *Bend Sinister* (1947), which had just come out in English. My adviser M. H. Abrams, a permanent influence on my life and work, was a friend of Nabokov and urged me to take the course. I recall that Nabokov began by unfavorably comparing Gogol and Jane Austen. He added that women just could not write. At seventeen, I was brash enough to walk out. This was observed by Nabokov and by his wife, Vera. That evening, I received a phone call from Mrs. Nabokov, inviting me to tea at their house at 957 East State Street, Ithaca, the next afternoon and gently telling me that her husband was displeased and intended to destroy me in a chess match after tea.

I was only an amateur chess player and knew Nabokov's reputation as a composer of chess problems. In some terror, I went over to the Cornell library and took out José Capablanca's *Chess Fundamentals.* Relying on memory, I ingested five or six sample games. After tea the next afternoon, which was outdoors on a balmy September day, during which Nabokov did not speak at all, Mrs. Nabokov cleared everything away and the novelist led me over to a very ornate and large chessboard, placed in the shade of a tree. I had never seen such beautiful chessmen, and I was awed. Silently, Nabokov graciously indicated I had the first move, and I commenced one of Capablanca's favorite games. I held my host off for about eight moves, during which he looked perplexed. Suddenly his face cleared and he cried out, "You young rascal, you have memorized Capablanca!" With great relish he said, "Now I will destroy you in just four moves." He did exactly that. Without a word, he walked back into his house. I walked home.

In later years, I edited two volumes of essays on Nabokov, which I do not remember at all. I had a mixed reaction to *Lolita* but greatly enjoyed *Pale Fire* and one short story called "The Vane Sisters." Sometimes I still find him unreadable. His preciosity, linguistic exhibitionism, vanity shine through everywhere. Nabokov had a passion for Gogol, which I share, but Gogol's authentic daemonism could only be parodied by the author of *Ada, or Ardor: A Family Chronicle* (1969). One of my closest friends, who had been my tutor at Pembroke College, Cambridge, Matthew J. C. Hodgart (1916–96), wrote a sparkling essay on *Ada* in *The New York Review of Books*. In 1967–68, we and our families spent a year together at the Cornell Society for the Humanities. Matthew gave me his review copy, and I read it with considerable discomfort. We argued the book, but Matthew, while granting excesses, was delighted by its ingenuity and mad allusiveness. Himself an enthusiastic scholar of *Finnegans Wake*, which I tried to be in his wake, Hodgart yielded to Nabokov's disciplined outrageousness.

W. G. Sebald cultivated Nabokov amid his other creative obsessions. All through *The Emigrants,* the figure of Nabokov flits with a butterfly net, endearingly bestowing a touch of cheer to the four dismal narratives. *Speak, Memory* (1951), Nabokov's memoir, fuses with *Ada, or Ardor,* in Sebald's capacious reflections.

Throughout my teaching career, I have suggested to my students that a literary work can be an aesthetic triumph and yet not very likable. Sebald is a writer likable in every way, even when he saddens me. I cannot abide Nabokov. That is a judgment upon me and not on him. I would have thought that no one of sensibility could dislike

Jane Austen, but my hero Ralph Waldo Emerson dismissed her in his journal from 1861:

> I am at a loss to understand why people hold Miss Austen's novels at so high a rate, which seem to me vulgar in tone, sterile in artistic invention, imprisoned in their wretched conventions of English society, without genius, wit, or knowledge of the world. Never was life so pinched and narrow. . . . All that interests in any character [is this]: has he (or she) the money to marry with . . . ? . . . Suicide is more respectable.

Emerson did not much like novels: in his journal from 1842, he dismissed those by his walking companion Nathaniel Hawthorne:

> Nathaniel Hawthorne's reputation as a writer is a very pleasing fact, because his writing is not good for anything, and this is a tribute to the man.

It should never be forgotten that Emerson, in an extraordinary act of immediate critical perception, received in the mail from Walt Whitman the first *Leaves of Grass* (1855) and responded magnificently:

> DEAR SIR—
>
> I am not blind to the worth of the wonderful gift of "LEAVES OF GRASS." I find it the most extraordinary piece of wit and wisdom that America has yet contributed. I am very happy in reading it, as great power makes us happy. It meets the demand I am always making of what seemed the sterile and stingy nature, as if too much handiwork, or too much lymph in the temperament, were making our western wits fat and mean.
>
> I give you joy of your free and brave thought. I have great joy in it. I find incomparable things said incomparably well, as they must be. I find the courage of treatment which so delights us, and which large perception only can inspire.
>
> I greet you at the beginning of a great career, which yet

must have had a long foreground somewhere, for such a start. I rubbed my eyes a little, to see if this sunbeam were no illusion; but the solid sense of the book is a sober certainty. It has the best merits, namely, of fortifying and encouraging.

I did not know until I last night saw the book advertised in a newspaper that I could trust the name as real and available for a post-office. I wish to see my benefactor, and have felt much like striking my tasks and visiting New York to pay you my respects.

R. W. EMERSON.

I love Walt Whitman with a passion beyond bounds, and yet I wonder how I would have reacted to a first reading of *Leaves of Grass*. When I reread, teach, write about Shakespeare or Milton, I build, sometimes involuntarily, on immense traditions of commentary. To read is to encounter ghosts of all the forerunners in literature or life. Almost every night I dream about departed friends, sometimes mixing them up with fictive characters.

A few nights ago, on the eve of my eighty-eighth birthday, I dreamed about changelings. In my friend John Crowley's *Little, Big,* the fairies kidnap Lilac, Sophie's daughter, and carry the child off to Mrs. Underhill, the *grande dame* of the faerie folk. A false Lilac replaces the human child, and in time it explodes. I cannot recall ever dreaming about John Crowley, but I do about some of his characters, like Lilac, Mrs. Underhill, and Grandfather Trout. As I was writing these sentences, a charmingly wild young man burst in, and we discoursed about Jarry's 'Pataphysics, or the science of imaginary solutions. I was introduced to Jarry by my friend Roger Shattuck, who charmed me by uttering Jarry's credo: "'Pataphysics is a science which we have only just invented and for which there is a crying need." The young man had attended classes by me about a decade ago, one on *The Tempest* and the other on Hart Crane. He wanted to talk about my ancient treatise *The Anxiety of Influence* (1973), which I intended as a contribution to 'Pataphysics and, if possible, to the tradition of Jewish antithetical vitalism that goes back to Tanakh and its exegetes. I was glad to listen to him, because I have not looked at the book for some decades and fear I would no longer totally agree with it.

Harold Bloom lived in New Haven and was a Sterling Professor of Humanities at Yale University. Before that, he was Charles Eliot Norton Professor at Harvard. His more than forty books include *Possessed by Memory, The Anxiety of Influence, Shakespeare: The Invention of the Human, The Western Canon, The American Religion,* and *The Daemon Knows: Literary Greatness and the American Sublime.* He was a MacArthur Fellow, a member of the American Academy of Arts and Letters, and the recipient of many awards and honorary degrees, including the American Academy of Arts and Letters' Gold Medal for Belles Lettres and Criticism, the Catalonia International Prize, and Mexico's Alfonso Reyes International Prize. He lived in New Haven until his death on October 14, 2019, at the age of eighty-nine.

A NOTE ON THE TYPE

The text in this book was set in Miller, a transitional-style typeface designed by Matthew Carter (b. 1937) with assistance from Tobias Frere-Jones and Cyrus Highsmith of the Font Bureau. Modeled on the roman family of fonts popularized by Scottish type foundries in the nineteenth century, Miller is named for William Miller, founder of the Miller & Richard foundry of Edinburgh.

The Miller family of fonts has a large number of variants for use as text and display, as well as Greek characters based on the renowned handwriting of British classicist Richard Porson.

Typeset by Scribe, Philadelphia, Pennsylvania

Printed and bound by Berryville Graphics, Berryville, Virginia

Designed by Maggie Hinders